AGRICULTURAL MODERNISATION AND THE GREEN REVOLUTION IN THE TWENTIETH-CENTURY WORLD

Boydell Studies in Rural History

Series Editor
Professor Richard W. Hoyle

This series aims to provide a forum for the best and most influential work in agricultural and rural history, and on the cultural history of the countryside. While it is anchored in the rural history of Britain and Ireland, it also includes within its remit Europe and the colonial empires of European nations (both during and after colonisation). All approaches and methodologies are welcome, including the use of oral history.

Proposals or enquiries are welcomed. They may be sent directly to the editor or the publisher at the email addresses given below.

Richard.Hoyle@reading.ac.uk
editorial@boydellandbrewer.com

Previous titles in the series are listed at the back of the volume.

Agricultural Modernisation and the Green Revolution in the Twentieth-Century World

Edited by Juan Pan-Montojo,
Lourenzo Fernández-Prieto and Miguel Cabo

THE BOYDELL PRESS

First published 2026
The Boydell Press, Woodbridge

ISBN 978 1 83765 331 7

The Boydell Press is an imprint of Boydell & Brewer Ltd
and of Boydell & Brewer Inc.
website: www.boydellandbrewer.com

Our Authorised Representative for product safety in the EU is Easy Access System Europe – Mustamäe tee 50, 10621 Tallinn, Estonia, gpsr.requests@easproject.com

A CIP catalogue record for this book is available from the British Library

CONTENTS

List of illustrations viii
List of contributors xi
List of abbreviations xvii
Preface xxi

1. From rural modernities to agricultural modernisation: a new narrative 1
Miguel Cabo, Lourenzo Fernández-Prieto and Juan Pan-Montojo

PART I: BRIDGES AND TRANSITIONS

2. Flow, stock and epistemic change: using biotic and consuming mineral resources in agricultural production 27
Juri Auderset and Peter Moser

3. Inventing new seeds: genetics research and Iberian connections during the dictatorships 43
Dulce Freire

4. Racial productivism: agrarian change under the Nazi regime in German-annexed Austria, 1938–1945 65
Ernst Langthaler

5. Agrarian parties in the twentieth century: rise and fall of an alternative modernity 85
Miguel Cabo

6. From the International Institute of Agriculture to the Food and Agriculture Organization 101
Federico D'Onofrio

PART II: AGRICULTURAL MODERNITIES AND MODERNISATION IN THEIR POLITICAL CONTEXTS

7. UK agriculture before and after the Second World War: agricultural policies and the adoption of new technologies, 1920–1970 121
Paul Brassley

8. The 'Green Evolution' in Denmark, 1930–1972 140
Thomas Christiansen

9. The 'Green Revolution' in the Red Zone: the case of socialist Hungarian agriculture 162
Zsuzsanna Varga

10. Reordering rural Congo: Agricultural development and the *paysannats indigènes* in the Belgian Congo, 1930s–1950s 182
Yves Segers

11. Back to the future: international agrarian development in Ethiopia and the legacy of Italian colonialism 202
Michele Sollai

12. New models for agriculture in the post-war American Southern Cone 217
Luis Ernesto Blacha

13. 'Taking risks to create value': agricultural modernisation and the making of 'Progressive' Indian farmers, 1947–1967 233
Madhumita Saha

PART III: THE TRIUMPH OF THE MODERNISING LOGIC AFTER 1945

14. Agricultural modernisation from a biophysical point of view: Spain, *c.* 1900–2008 251
Manuel González de Molina

15. The 'modernisation' of agriculture in the Global South after 1945: Green Revolution as 'American revolution' 270
Jonathan Harwood

16. US agricultural cooperation programmes in Latin America since the Second World War 292
Wilson Picado-Umaña and José A. Fernández Molina

17. Gender and agricultural modernisation: agricultural extension in Spain and France in the 1960s and 1970s 310
Sylvain Brunier, Ana Cabana Iglesia and Alba Díaz-Geada

18. Resisting the Green Revolution epic in Brazil and India 323
Poonam Pandey and Lídia Cabral

Index 344

ILLUSTRATIONS

TABLES

3 *FREIRE*, 'INVENTING NEW SEEDS'

3.1 Founding research centres contributing to *Genética Ibérica* 64

7 *BRASSLEY*, 'BRITISH AGRICULTURE'

7.1 Volume of output from UK agriculture, 1914–19 to 1966–70 122
7.2 Quantities produced on UK farms, 1922–68 123
7.3 Yields of principal products on UK farms, 1922–68 127
7.4 UK agricultural output, employment, and labour productivity, 1920–70 128
7.5 Current output and gross fixed capital formation in UK agriculture, 1951–60 to 1966–75 129
7.6 Technologies adopted in UK farming, 1920–70 130

8 *CHRISTIANSEN*, '"GREEN EVOLUTION" IN DENMARK'

8.1 Agricultural land, 1930–4 to 1970–4 147
8.2 Consumption of fertilisers, 1929/30–33/4 to 1969/70–73/4 149

9 *VARGA*, 'GREEN REVOLUTION' IN THE RED ZONE

9.1 The average yield of key crops in Hungary, select years, 1935–89 178

10 *SEGERS*, REORDERING RURAL CONGO: AGRICULTURAL DEVELOPMENT AND THE *PAYSANNATS INDIGÈNES* IN THE BELGIAN CONGO, 1930S–1950S

10.1 Area of crops grown under the *paysannats* system in 1958, hectare per province 183

14 *GONZÁLEZ DE MOLINA*, 'AGRICULTURAL MODERNISATION FROM A BIOPHYSICAL POINT OF VIEW'

14.1 Net primary productivity according to land use types 254

14.2 Net primary productivity according to origin 255
14.3 Crop domestic extraction (without residues) in Spain 259
14.4 Livestock production in tonnes of dry matter, 1900–2008 264

16 *PICADO AND FERNÁNDEZ MOLINA*, 'US AGRICULTURAL COOPERATION PROGRAMMES IN LATIN AMERICA'

16.1 Countries with food production programmes, their duration and financial responsibilities, 1942–7 303

Figures

4 *LANGTHALER*, 'RACIAL PRODUCTIVISM'

4.1 Pathways of agrarian change in Austria, 1938–45 68
4.2 Agricultural productivity in Austria, 1930–60 72
4.3 The range of agrosystems and corresponding farming styles in Niederdonau, 1941 73
4.4 Advertisement for oil seed cultivation, 1940 79

8 *CHRISTIANSEN*, '"GREEN EVOLUTION" IN DENMARK'

8.1 Total crop harvest, 1930–4 to 1970–4 146
8.2 Numbers of main farm animals, 1930–74 150
8.3 Composition of feedstuff usage by main categories, 1929–30 to 1973–4 151
8.4 Number of cows and cows in calf, total milk production, and average milk production per cow, 1930–74 153
8.5 Production, export and domestic consumption of pig meat, 1930–74 153
8.6 Farm machinery and horses, 1944–74 155
8.7 Agricultural labour, 1933–34 to 1973–4 155
8.8 Number of farms according to size, 1929–75 158
8.9 Process of farm production specialisation, 1968–90 160

14 *GONZÁLEZ DE MOLINA*, 'AGRICULTURAL MODERNISATION FROM A BIOPHYSICAL POINT OF VIEW'

14.1 Evolution of types of land use, in thousands of hectares, 1900–2008 253
14.2 Domestic biomass extraction by origin, in millions of tonnes of dry matter, 1900–2008 256

14.3 Destination of biomass domestic extraction in millions of tonnes of dry matter, 1900–2008 258
14.4 Evolution of live livestock weight in thousands of tonnes, 1865–2008 261
14.5 Origin of animal feed, in millions of tonnes of dry matter, 1900–2008 263
14.6 Energy value of inputs used in Spanish agriculture, 1900–2008 268

16 *PICADO-UMAÑA AND FERNÁNDEZ MOLINA*, 'US AGRICULTURAL COOPERATION PROGRAMMES IN LATIN AMERICA'

16.1 Distribution of American allocations for technical cooperation programmes in Latin America, 1943–55 302

The editors, contributors and publisher are grateful to all the institutions and persons listed for permission to reproduce the materials in which they hold copyright. Every effort has been made to trace the copyright holders; apologies are offered for any omission, and the publisher will be pleased to add any necessary acknowledgement in subsequent editions.

CONTRIBUTORS

Juri Auderset is reader in the history of the nineteenth and twentieth centuries at the Institute of History at the University of Bern and research fellow at the Archives of Rural History. Among his research and teaching interests are the history of agriculture and the environment, labour history and the history of capitalism, as well as conceptual and intellectual history. In collaboration with Peter Moser, he wrote *Die Agrarfrage in der Industriegesellschaft: Wissenskulturen, Machtverhältnisse und natürliche Ressourcen in der agrarisch-industriellen Wissensgesellschaft (1850–1950)* (Böhlau, 2018).

Luis Ernesto Blacha is a researcher at the Argentinian National Scientific and Technical Research Council and serves as a lecturer and researcher at the Institute for Studies in Science and Technology at the National University of Quilmes. He is also part of the social studies in science, technology, innovation and development programme. His research focuses on the sociology of food, and the power dynamics shaping the relationship between malnutrition, hunger and social inequalities in the nutrition. He is the author of three books and numerous journal articles.

Paul Brassley is an honorary university fellow in the Centre for Rural Policy Research at the University of Exeter. From 2009 he worked there on a project to investigate the process of technical change in English agriculture after the Second World War. He and his colleagues published the results in *The Real Agricultural Revolution: the transformation of English farming 1939–1985* (Boydell, 2021). Earlier, he had contributed to *The Agrarian History of England and Wales* (Cambridge University Press).

Sylvain Brunier is a research fellow at the CNRS, attached to the Centre de sociologie des organisations (Sciences Po/CNRS). His research focuses on the history and sociology of the agricultural world. He has published a book on the history of agricultural advisors in France titled *Le bonheur dans la modernité* (ENS Éditions, 2018), in which he shows how this professional group implemented modernisation policies after the Second World War. He is currently working on the influence of agribusiness on the technical, economic and political direction of farms.

Ana Cabana Iglesia is an associate professor in the department of history at the University of Santiago de Compostela where she is a member of the research group Agrarian History and Rural World Policy, 19–20th Centuries (HISTAGRA) and is affiliated to the Inter-University Research Centre for Cultural Atlantic Landscapes (CISPAC). Her main research interests are social attitudes during the Franco dictatorship, rural conflict and the history of peasant women in twentieth century. Her latest book is *Mujeres y agricultura en la política española del siglo XX* (co-authored with T. Ortega, L. Cabezas and S. Canalejo: Cátedra, 2024).

Miguel Cabo Villaverde is professor at the University of Santiago de Compostela. His main fields of interest are associations and collective action in the rural world, violence and conflicts, Spanish political history between 1874 and the Franco dictatorship, and nation-building processes in Europe. His latest publications are 'Agrarian movements, the national question, and democracy in Europe, 1880–1945' (with Fernández-Prieto), in Núñez Seixas (ed.), *The First World War and the Nationality Question in Europe* (Brill, 2020); 'Agrarian parties in Europe prior to 1945 and beyond', in Van Molle *et al.*, (eds) *Making Politics in the European Countryside, from the 1780s to the 1930s* (Brepols, 2022) and 'Farming The Nation: Agrarian Parties and the National Question in interwar Europe', *Studies on National Movements* 8 (2021).

Lídia Cabral is a research fellow at the Institute of Development Studies, United Kingdom. She is a social scientist with an interest in the politics of policy and knowledge, and the connections between justice, equity and sustainability in agrifood systems. Her recent research has focused on the enduring effects of Green Revolutions in Brazil, China and India, examining how epic narratives of the past sustain top-down approaches to knowledge production and inhibit alternatives. Currently, she is researching how rewilding in the UK can integrate food justice with nature recovery goals. She is also partnering with research-activist networks in Brazil and the UK to strengthen territorial food equity.

Thomas Christiansen is an independent Danish researcher and economic historian. His main publications are 'Conflictos políticos y administrativis en el sector agrario durante el primer franquismo: El caso de Cuenca', *Historia Agraria* 18 (1999); 'Intervención del Estado y mercado negro en el sector oleícola durante el primer franquismo', *Historia Agraria* 27 (2002); *The reason why: The post-civil war agrarian crisis in Spain* (Prensas Universitarias de Zaragoza, 2012); and 'From food surplus to even more food surplus: agrarian politics and prices in Denmark, 1945–1962', in Martin *et al.* (eds), *Agriculture in Capitalist Europe, 1945–1960* (Routledge, 2016).

ALBA DÍAZ GEADA is currently a Ramón y Cajal researcher (RYC2021-034738-I, funded by MCIN/AEI/10.13039/ 501100011033 and by the European Union 'NextGenerationEU'/PRTR'), at the University of Santiago de Compostela. A member of the HISTAGRA research group, she has been principal researcher of the project 'Community, conflict and revolt in rural Galiza in the 20th century – COREGAL', funded by the Ministry of Science and Innovation (PID2020-117858RA-I00). She has held postdoctoral research fellowships at the Laboratoire d'Etudes Rurales – Universitè Lyon 2 and at the Program in Agrarian Studies – Yale University. Among her research interests are social change, social conflict and the dynamics of class inequalities in contemporary rural communities.

FEDERICO D'ONOFRIO is an associate professor of History of Economics at the Department of Political Science of the University of Bologna. His research focuses on the history of agricultural economists and their role in policy-making during the early twentieth century, with particular emphasis on the use of data in shaping agricultural practices and economic decisions. His book, *Observing Agriculture: Agricultural Economists and Policy-Making in Early Twentieth-Century Italy* (Routledge, 2016), explored the role of agricultural economists in Italy, highlighting their contribution to the modernisation of agriculture through data and economic analysis. He is the principal investigator of the ERC-funded project Datarev ('Leading the first data revolution in European agriculture'), which investigates the centrality of accounting data in agricultural economics and their implications for policy and rural development.

JOSÉ ANTONIO FERNÁNDEZ MOLINA is retired professor of history, Universidad Nacional, Costa Rica. Among his publications are 'Los treinta y un meses. Contextos y procesos en la agregación del Partido de Nicoya a Costa Rica', *Revista del Archivo Nacional (Costa Rica)* 79 (2015); 'Los Ejércitos Expedicionarios costarricenses en la Campaña Nacional: campesinos-milicianos ante la disyuntiva entre la obediencia y el grano de oro', *Mesoamérica* 32 (2011), 74–105; *Mercado, empresarios y trabajadores. La siderurgia en el Reino de Guatemala* (CONCULTURA, 2005); and *Pintando el mundo de azul. El auge añilero y el mercado centroamericano. 1750–1810* (CONCULTURA, 2003).

LOURENZO FERNÁNDEZ PRIETO is professor of modern history at the University of Santiago de Compostela and director of the CISPAC (Galician Research Centre for Atlantic Cultural Landscapes). He has undertaken research into twentieth-century rural society (technological and social change) and the Spanish civil war and politics of memory. Recent publications: with Lanero Taboas, Martiin and Herment (eds), *From Breeding and Feeding to Medicalization* (Turnhout: Brepols, 2023); with

Soto and Esperante, 'How farmers adopt new technologies: connections between farmer and technician knowledges in Galicia (1880–1940)', *Rural History* 35 (2024); and with Pan-Montojo and Cabo, *Agriculture in the Age of Fascism* (Turnhout: Brepols, 2013). He is the current President of the Society for Agrarian History Studies.

Dulce Freire is an associate professor of economic and social history at the Faculty of Economics and a researcher at the Centre for Interdisciplinary Studies, University of Coimbra. Her research focuses on Iberian rural and agrarian history. She has coordinated various scientific projects related to changes in agriculture, food, society and public policies. She has been the principal investigator of the ERC-funded ReSEED project (Rescuing seed's heritage), which has studied the local impact of cultivated seeds that reached Europe from the 15th century onwards. Among her latest publications is the edited book (with Pedro Lains) *An Agrarian History of Portugal, 1000–2000. Economic Development on the European Frontier* (Brill, 2017). She is currently president of the European Rural History Organisation.

Manuel González de Molina is full professor of modern history and coordinator of the agroecosystems history laboratory. His work focuses on the study of the rural world, the biophysical analysis of agroecosystems and food systems and the design of public policies from an agroecological point of view. He served as president of the Spanish Society for Agrarian History from 2016 to 2023. The author of several books, among the most recent: *Energy in Agroecosystems: A Tool for Assessing Sustainability* (CRC Press, 2017); *Political Agroecology: Advancing the Transition to Sustainable Food Systems* (CRC Press, 2021); *The Social Metabolism: A Socio-ecological theory of historical change* (Springer, 2023).

Jonathan Harwood is emeritus professor of the history of science and technology at the University of Manchester. Based on a general interest in the political economy of technical change, his recent work has focused on agricultural 'revolutions' since the nineteenth century. His most recent book is *Europe's Green Revolution and Others Since: the Rise and Fall of Peasant-Friendly Plant Breeding* (Routledge, 2016). Over the past decade he has written primarily as a public historian, publishing in journals of development studies and of sustainable agriculture.

Ernst Langthaler is professor of social and economic history at the Johannes Kepler University, Linz, and head of the Institute of Rural History in St Pölten. He has been a visiting professor at the Universities of Innsbruck and Vienna and visiting fellow at the Rachel Carson Centre for Environment and Society at the University of Munich. His research focuses on agricultural and food history from regional to global scales in the era of globalisation. His current research project, funded by the Austrian Science Fund, deals with agro-food change through the lens of soy since 1870.

Peter Moser is founder and director of the Archives of Rural History in Bern. His current research focuses on female farmers in Ireland and Switzerland and the gender relations in agriculture. Together with Juri Auderset, he has co-authored the book *Die Agrarfrage in der Industriegesellschaft: Wissenskulturen, Machtverhältnisse und natürliche Ressourcen in der agrarisch-industriellen Wissensgesellschaft (1850–1950)* (Böhlau, 2018).

Poonam Pandey is a Maria Zambrano fellow at the University of Vigo, Spain. She is an interdisciplinary researcher working at the interface of STS, development studies and innovation studies. Broadly, her research focuses on understanding knowledge politics, inclusion and justice in socio-technical systems with special focus on agriculture. Her recent work focuses on Zero Budget Natural Farming and politics of transformational agroecology in India. Currently, she is working on the role of the social and solidarity economy in addressing vulnerabilities in agri-rural societies.

Juan Pan-Montojo is professor of modern history at the Universidad Autónoma de Madrid. His main fields of research are related to agrarian history and history of public economics. Among the books that he has edited are: with Martiin and Brassley, *Agriculture in capitalist Europe: from food shortages to food surpluses* (Routledge, 2016); with Brassart, Marache and Van Molle, *Making politics in the European countryside, 1790s–1930s* (Brepols, 2022); and with Martykánová *Misioneros del capitalismo. Aventureros, hombres de negocios y expertos transnacionales en el siglo XIX* (Comares: 2023).

Wilson Picado-Umaña is professor at the Universidad Nacional, Costa Rica. His research focuses on the history of the Green Revolution in Latin America. He is author of 'The Protein Factor: CIAT's Bean Improvement Research in Central America', in Helen Anne Curry and Timothy W. Lorek (eds), *Agricultural Science as International Development: Historical Perspectives on the CGIAR Era* (Cambridge University Press, 2024).

Madhumita Saha is an associate professor of history at Amity University, Uttar Pradesh. Her research focuses on the history of agriculture, environmental history and the history of science and technology in nineteenth and twentieth-century India. She attained her PhD in history of science and technology from Iowa State University and has been a Fulbright Doctoral Fellow and PACHS Dissertation Writing Fellow. She is currently working on the history of agricultural science at the juncture of colonialism and rising nationalism in India. Recent publications include, *The Making of Modern Agriculture in Independent India: Global Knowledge Network, National Planning, and the Green Revolution* (Routledge, 2025).

Yves Segers is professor of rural history at KU Leuven and director of the Interfaculty Centre for Agrarian History. His research interests focus on the history and heritage of agriculture, the countryside and food systems in Belgium and Europe since the eighteenth century. Recent publications include Yves Segers and Leen Van Molle (eds), *Agricultural Knowledge Networks in Rural Europe, 1700–2000* (The Boydell Press, 2022); and Anton Schuurman, Jordi Planas and Yves Segers (eds), *The Formation of Agricultural Governance. The Interplay between State and Civil Society in European Agriculture, 1870–1940* (Brepols, 2025).

Michele Sollai is a postdoctoral researcher at UniDistance Switzerland. Previously he was SNSF postdoctoral researcher at the Chair for the History of the Anthropocene at the University of Zurich and a visiting scholar at the Rachel Carson Centre in Munich and at Sciences Po in Paris. He obtained his PhD in 2021 from the Geneva Graduate Institute, with a thesis on the history of agrarian development in Ethiopia from the Italian occupation to early post-war international aid. His current research focuses on agrarian science and plant breeding in fascist Italy, the Green Revolution and the global history of dryland regions.

Zsuzsanna Varga is currently head of the modern Hungarian history department at Eötvös Loránd University (Budapest). She was a founding member of the European Rural History Organisation and currently serves as its vice president. Her main field of research is the history of socialist agriculture in Hungary: her current work focuses on the place of women in socialist and post-socialist rural transformations. Her most recent monograph was published in the Harvard Cold War Studies Book Series: *The Hungarian Agricultural Miracle? Sovietization and Americanization in a Communist Country* (Lexington Books, 2020).

ABBREVIATIONS

ABA	Associação Brasileira de Agroecologia [Brazilian Agroecology Association]
AES	Agrarian Extension Service [Servicio de Extensión Agraria], Spain
AIA	American International Association
AID	Agency of International Development, USA
AKIS	Agricultural Knowledge and Innovation System
ARC	Agricultural Research Council, UK
BBA	Beej Bachao Andolan [Seed Saving Movement], India
BBSM	Bharat Beej Swaraj Manch [Seed Sovereignty Alliance], India
BNF	Biolocal nitrogen fixation
CAN	Consejo Agrario Nacional [Agricultural National Council], Argentina
CAP	Common Agricultural Policy
CBA	Congresso Brasileiro de Agroecologia [Brazilian Agroecology Conference]
CIMMYT	Centro Internacional de Mejoramiento de Maíz y Trigo [International Centre for the Maize and Wheat Improvement]
CNPA	Centro Nacional de Pesquiza Agrícola [National Centre for Agricultural Research], Brazil
COMECON	Council for Mutual Economic Assistance
CONSEA	Conselho Nacional de Segurança Alimentar e Nutricional [National Council of Food and Nutrition Security], Brazil
CREA	Consorcios Regionales de Experimentación [Regional Consortia for (Agricultural) Experimentation], Argentina

CSIC	Consejo Superior de Investigaciones Científicas [Superior Council for Scientific Research], Spain
DE	Domestic Extraction
EAN	Estação Agronómica Nacional [National Agronomic Station], Portugal
ECLAC	Economic Commission for Latin America and the Caribbean
EEC	European Economic Community
ENA	Encontro Nacional de Agroecologia [National Agroecology Meeting], Brazil
EPRDF	Ethiopian Peoples' Revolutionary Democratic Front
ETH	Eidgenössische Technische Hochschule [Swiss Federal Technical High School], Zürich
FAO	Food and Agriculture Organization
FEA	Foreign Economic Administration, USA
GATT	General Agreement on Tariffs and Trade
GDA	Groupes de Développement Agricole [Groups for Agricultural Development], France
GMO	Genetically modified organism
HCB	Huileries du Congo Belge [Oil mills of the Belgian Congo]
HWP	Hungarian Workers's Party
HYV	High-Yielding Varieties
IAC	Instituto para a Alta Cultura [Institute for High Culture], Portugal
IARI	Indian Agricultural Research Institute
IBEC	International Basic Economy Corporation
IEFC	International Emergency Food Council
IFAD	International Fund for Agricultural Development
IIA	International Institute of Agriculture
IIA	Instituto de Investigaciones Agrícolas [Institute for Agricultural Research], Mexico
IIAA	Institute for Inter-American Affairs
INEAC	Institut National pour l'Étude Agronomique du Congo Belge [National Institute for the Agronomic Study of Belgian Congo]

INIA	Instituto Nacional de Investigación Agropecuaria [National Institute for the Agricultural and Livestock Research], Spain
INTA	Instituto Nacional de Tecnología Agropecuaria [National Institute for the Agricultural and Livestock Technology], Argentina
IPU	International Peasant Union
IRA	Institut de la Recherche Agronomique [Institute for Agronomic Research], France
ISI	Import Substitution Industrialisation
JACF	Jeunesses Agricoles Catholiques Féminines [Catholic Agricultural Female Youth], France
JAE	Junta de Ampliación de Estudios [Council for Further Studies], Spain
JEN	Junta de Educação Nacional [Council for National Education], Portugal
JUNALD	Junta Nacional para Combatir la Desocupación [National Council to Fight Unemployment], Argentina
KRRS	Karnataka Rajya Raitha Sangha [Farmer's movement of Karnataka], India
MAS	Ministry of Agriculture and Food, Hungary
MST	Movimento dos Trabalhadores Rurais Sem Terra [Landless Workers' Movement], Brazil
MTS	Machine and Tractor Stations
NEM	New Economic Mechanism
NPP	Net primary productivity
OAS	Organization of American States
OECD	Organisation for Economic Co-operation and Development
ONC	Opera Nazionale Combattenti [National Association of Combatants], Italy
PC	Political Committee
PIL	Public Interest Litigations
PNȚ	Partidul Național-Țărănesc [National Peasant Party], Romania
SNA	Sociedade Nacional de Agricultura, Brazil

STICA	Servicio Técnico Interamericano de Cooperación Agrícola [Inter-American Technical Service for Agricultural Co-operation
TCA	Technical Cooperation Administration
UNESCO	United Nations Educational, Scientific and Cultural Organization
UNRRA	United Nations Relief and Rehabilitation Administration
USAID	United States Agency for International Development
USDA	US Department of Agriculture
ZBNF	Zero Budget Natural Farming

PREFACE

In 1957, the Swiss author Max Frisch published a novel titled *Homo Faber*. The protagonist, an engineer who approaches reality through a purely rational lens and 'scientific' methods, ends up in unpredictable situations that reveal the limits of such a narrow understanding of the world. Frisch's *Homo Faber* worked for UNESCO. His mentality was shared by some of his peers – not only engineers, but also economists, scientists and lawyers – in other international and national institutions, who in the 1950s were busy planning or fulfilling earlier plans to reshape world agriculture according to a model of modernisation, a model that a few years later would be given the name of the Green Revolution.

Allegedly based upon techno-scientific certainties, this model of agricultural modernisation, heralded by the US and international bodies backed by the US, rested on a Manichean quandary of backwardness or progress and the depreciation, twisting or denial of any other models or ways to imagine the transformation of agriculture. In fact, the only other path of change that was broadly recognised as a real alternative was the communist one, which, despite its clear differences with the Western modernisation of agriculture (especially when it came to its sociopolitical justification and its conception of property rights), did not differ much in its techno-economic foundations, a common ground that enabled dialogue, copying and transfers between countries situated on rival sides of the Cold War divide. Hence, both the capitalist and the communist projects for agriculture coincided in their uncritical acceptance of the superiority of techno-scientific specific solutions (despite their being often fragmentary and short term), their underestimation of the environmental risks and actual impacts on the atmosphere, soils, biodiversity or water wrought by new technologies, their preference for large farms and their supposed economies of scale, or their implicit subordination of agriculture to industry.

This book deals with agricultural modernisation, and therefore with the Green Revolution, after the Second World War, but also with pre-existing and sometimes conflicting projects for a modern agriculture and a modern rural society – two spheres that were not the same but highly connected – that had existed before the war and even since the end of the nineteenth century. What we refer to with 'modernisation' and 'modern' will be one of the main issues of the first chapter of this book. But, before arriving there, we wanted to tell the story of the book itself, since this book, like all books, and almost everything else, did not come out of the blue.

The three editors of this volume belong to the second and third generation of Spanish agrarian historians, understood to include those who committed themselves to the field with the creation of a society for agrarian history (the SEHA, initially the Seminar of Agrarian History, and now Society of Studies in Agrarian History) back in the late 1980s. The SEHA – one of the largest academic communities in the field of agrarian/rural history in the world – has played a very active role in the past three decades in the construction of transnational networks and institutions such as the European Rural History Organisation (EURHO) that aim at renovating the narratives of the rural societies of the past and their agrarian activities. Making historical narratives is not just collecting curious facts and linking them through some kind of pre-theoretical thread, or pressing them into a pre-conceived theory. Historical narratives are the result of writing down the results of our analyses of the past, with all the tools of historiography and relevant social sciences and humanities, in light of present concerns, to understand better not only what we observe in a given chronological period, but also our present time and our future. Moreover, making a convincing analysis of the past to produce a narrative not only enables us to look at the present with different eyes, it also can push direct and indirect readers to act in new ways.

In the new context created by the SEHA, and then by the European and the world networks that came into being after 2000, the editors of this volume led a series of sessions in a succession of conferences over a number of years to think about how to construct a new narrative on the transition from the advanced organic agriculture that could be identified before the Great War and the agriculture shaped by the agents of modernisation and the Green Revolution. The reason to accept that a new narrative was necessary, to replace the one created by modernisers themselves, was unanimous: we are going through a green transition, slow, hesitating and lacking general consensus, that seeks to undo the worst environmental excesses of the Anthropocene. In the green transition, agriculture is not just another activity that needs rethinking. Agriculture, which once was the productive activity that originated a large part of the energy we needed, now consumes it. Agriculture, which used to absorb carbon, now causes large emissions. Agriculture that used to employ and distribute water now pollutes and destroys it. In any environmental transition, the role of agriculture is hence central: no transition can be imagined without altering the way we get the food for the growing number of human beings. Therefore, we must explain how and why agriculture became what it is today. We need to discover what advanced organic agriculture and its management, the limits it imposed that industrial agriculture attempted to overcome, can teach us for the future.

Addressing our topic was and is not easy. It has required many meetings, many conversations and many draft papers. The meetings started in the EURHO conference of Bern in 2013, continued in the EURHO conference of Girona and in the Association of History, Literature, Science and Technology in Coimbra, both in 2015, the EURHO conference of Leuven in 2017, the European Social Science History of Belfast in 2017, the EURHO conference in Paris in 2019, and the EURHO conference at Uppsala in 2022. This has been a long journey that reflects the scale of the problems that we were addressing. Many of those who took part in these sessions have been able to write a chapter for this book. For different reasons, many more, both participants in the sessions and people who wrote papers for them, could not make it. The dialogue with those who are absent from the book has shaped its content: history writing is a collective endeavour that relies on published works but also on fruitful debates. We cannot list all those who have participated in the project, but we would like to mention Deborah Fitzgerald and Daniel Lanero, who, in different ways, have especially contributed to the new narrative that we want to present in the pages that follow. We must thank, too, our series editor, Richard Hoyle, Caroline Palmer and others at our publishing house, Boydell, and Philip Webb, our linguistic revisor; because without them this book would not have seen the light of day.

A very complex topic like ours needs a combination of perspectives, time and spatial scales. That is what we have aimed for in this book. It cannot be comprehensive, but it offers, we believe, a panorama of the various levels of study that we have been able to identify. What were the modern futures designed by peasant and agricultural organisation in the inter-war period? What changed during the Second World War? How can it be that a similar paradigm could be applied in both authoritarian and in democratic regimes? What was the relationship between the Cold War and the modernisation programmes? Who resisted a top-down technological model that endangered the survival of thousands of farms? These are some of the issues the long and varied list of authors who write in this volume attempt to answer. In so doing they aim at a new narrative, one that provides answers but also asks questions. As historians, we consider such an outcome to be the right one.

July 2025

1

From rural modernities to agricultural modernisation: a new narrative

Miguel Cabo, Lourenzo Fernández-Prieto
and Juan Pan-Montojo

In the past two decades, a growing number of agrarian and environmental historians have started to question the conventional narrative of the Green Revolution. By doing so, they are trying to address the persistent tendency to articulate political macro-proposals that nowadays, in response to the growing danger of a global food crisis, continue to guide the construction of a fully industrialised and homogenised primary sector. These projects, which are designed with the same technocratic logic that underlay the Green Revolution, are often legitimised by an imperfect memory of the Green Revolution as a largely successful but incomplete political endeavour, led by the USA in the context of the Cold War, to put an end to world hunger.

Most of the voices that talk about a 'new Green Revolution' belong to one of the three groups that Harwood has identified, each one based on one of the following propositions: the Green Revolution was a success and can be used as a model; the Green Revolution was a success but cannot be replicated; or the Green Revolution was flawed.[1] Obviously, those who maintain that the Green Revolution was flawed and is not the way forward, a position that Harwood terms the radical critique, do not encourage a new green revolution, and in fact regard any proposal for one as dangerous.

Whatever the opinions of the editors and authors of this book on the desirability and possibility of any future wide-ranging programmes of transformation in agriculture to avoid food crises in a world endangered

1 Jonathan Harwood, 'Another Green Revolution? On the Perils of "Extracting Lessons" from History', *Development* 61 (2018), 43–53.

by global warming, trade wars and actual wars, we do not find the existing history of twentieth-century agriculture to be wholly persuasive. An overarching and complete history of the origins, development and application of agricultural innovation in the past, and of the paradigms and institutional frameworks in which innovations were developed in the twentieth century, seems necessary. Such a narrative must include accounts of the intentions of the programmes, how they were diverted from the original plans and intentions, what power relations they embodied, what cultural filters they applied, and the alternatives they ignored. Sustainability must be a substantive trait of any project for environmental transition, and the requirements for it in agriculture can sometimes be found in the pathways that were not followed as well as in those that were adopted and produced good results in the long run. Many of the useful elements of the past are buried, however, under the weight of the stories and global myths of the Green Revolution. Now that millennia of agriculture as practised by smallholders, peasants and small-scale farmers have come to an end in many countries, above all but not only in what we can term the Global North, we – historians – need to recover their knowledge of organic agriculture for the coming environmental transition. This is true especially with regard to what we call advanced organic agriculture, which arose from dialogues with science in a context of complex systems for the management of local territories and communitarian approaches to the environment and technology.

The hegemonic views on the Green Revolution are not the result of historians' workshops. They were shaped by those who coined and spread the term Green Revolution in the 1960s. These people were collectively involved in the diffusion of a specific technological (and politico-economic) package. They included politicians and technicians in 'developing countries' who saw in its adoption an opportunity for the transformation of what they called traditional (and backward) agriculture into a modern sector, as Harwood argues in chapter 15. The texts in which such views were circulated had no analytical aims and created an oversimplified and ahistorical image of the process: it seems that a revolutionary project like theirs did not need any past other than the one implicit in the metanarrative of scientific progress. The articles and books that disseminated the concept of the Green Revolution were mainly propaganda or justifications of on-going policies. For this reason, they ignored any modern elements that were present in pre-existing agricultural practices and knowledge, or the proximity of some of their modernising formulae and their aims to those of the defeated fascist model (as Langthaler, chapter 4, and Sollai, chapter 11, show) or to the rival Soviet one (as Varga argues in chapter 9).

Gradually, throughout the 1980s and 1990s, and especially now in the twenty-first century, a historiography of the Green Revolution has emerged.[2] When it has looked for precedents for the big leap of the 1960s, it has referred to the years of reconstruction of a devastated Europe after the Second World War, or it has selected certain aid programmes managed by American technicians in the 1940s and the 1950s in Latin America or Asia. The resulting stories have certain traits (a disconnect between overarching stories and national analyses, a focus on the Global South, the prominence of specific individual innovations such as high-yielding varieties and so on) that render them useless for overcoming the prevailing narrative and thinking critically about the future of agriculture through the understanding of its past.

The history of the Green Revolution should be located in a much longer story of modern agriculture, extending beyond the Second World War. It necessitates explaining the innovations and technological changes that produced a range of agricultural modernities over time. It cannot be limited to a passive 'Third World', the object of the Green Revolution, and to the USA, its active protagonist. For most 'first-world' historians, especially European ones, the inclusion of the Green Revolution in a much wider process does not aim to downplay the relevance of the mostly bio-technological, arguably neo-colonial, and overtly anti-communist set of US-led agrarian projects that William Gaud called the 'Green Revolution' (in opposition to the 'Red Revolution') in 1968.[3] To place the Green Revolution in a longer context is to understand it as one specific phase within a larger and older family of political programmes designed to transform rural societies through complex policies. Such programmes started in Europe and the Americas after the 1880s. They included the social engineering project unleashed in the USSR at the end of the 1920s, non-governmental programmes like those of the Rockefeller foundation, and even plans for the development of colonial agriculture designed in the 1920s and 1930s. These policies were allegedly driven by or subordinate to a paradigm of technical and productive change, often modelled on that of industry, and were eventually based on the

2 We cannot reference here the whole bibliography of writings on the history of the Green Revolution. Among particularly useful titles, apart from the ones cited throughout the book, are the following: Raj Patel, 'The Long Green Revolution', *J. Peasant Studies* 40 (2013), 1–63; Wilson Picado, 'En busca de la genética guerrera: Segunda Guerra Mundial, cooperación agrícola y Revolución Verde en la agricultura de Costa Rica', *Historia Agraria* 56 (2012), 107–34; Gabriela Soto, 'Beyond Borlaug's Shadow: Octavio Paz, Indian Farmers, and the Challenge of Narrating the Green Revolution', *Agricultural History* 95 (2021), 576–608; Marci Baranski, *The Globalization of Wheat: A Critical History of the Green Revolution* (Pittsburgh, PA: University of Pittsburgh Press, 2022).

3 William S. Gaud, 'The Green Revolution: Accomplishments and Apprehensions', Address, 8 March 1968, www.agbioworld.org/biotech-info/topics/borlaug/borlaug-green.html (accessed 6 January 2025).

commodification and externalisation of farm inputs and, especially after the Second World War, the massive use of fossil fuels.[4] But before the 1940s, projects and policies were quite heterogeneous; there were many modernities. The discourses of the European 'green international', built around the Commission Internationale d'Agriculture in the inter-war period, or those of the agrarian parties that Cabo explores in chapter 5, rejected any agricultural future that did not preserve peasants as the social core of agriculture. Implicit in their projects were the kind of approaches to technology that Schumacher would defend in his *Small is beautiful*, in 1973.[5]

Contextualising the Green Revolution in a long but continuous series of agrarian policies and technological choices, built on a combination of private and public agents, institutions and proposals, can help to underline the internal pluralism of modern agriculture and its innovation systems: a fact before 1945, a possibility in the post-war period. At the same time, this long-term perspective highlights the apparent convergence of all these programmes in the 1950s and 1960s towards a much more uniform package of technologies, these being the ones that American technical aid and international organisations and technicians, as well as other modernisers, exported to Latin America, Asia and Africa, and that were appropriated, in those regions and elsewhere, in different ways. Convergence was heralded by the triumph of a pair of densely loaded concepts: development and modernisation, as opposed to backwardness and traditionalism. Such terms and many other concepts and metaphors, that Fitzgerald as well as Auderset and Moser analyse, show that the Green Revolution should be explored at the most basic level as an issue of the production and circulation of knowledge and cultural artefacts, both technical and social (to the extent that those two spheres can be disentangled).[6] Agrarian modernisation should be seen in that light, always bearing in mind that the circulation of knowledge is not an autonomous and self-propelled process, nor the result of mechanisms analogous to those of competitive markets in the field of ideas, nor necessarily a top-down transfer of technology and economic proposals. Neither is it a one-way road from a hegemonic power to the rest of the world, but

4 Juri Auderset and Peter Moser, *Die Agrarfrage in der Industriegesellschaft: Wissenskulturen, Machtverhältnisse und natürliche Ressourcen in der agrarisch-industriellen Wissensgesellschaft (1850–1950)* (Vienna: Böhlau Verlag, 2018).

5 Fritz Georg Von Graevenitz, *Argument Europa. Internationalisierung in der globalen Agrarkrise der Zwischenkriegzeit (1927–1937)* (Frankfurt am Main: Campus, 2017). Ernst Friedrich Schumacher, *Small is Beautiful: Economics as if People Mattered* (London: Blond and Briggs, 1973).

6 Auderset and Moser, *Die Agrarfrage in der Industriegesellschaft*; Deborah Fitzgerald, *Every Farm a Factory: The Industrial Ideal in American Agriculture* (New Haven, CT, and London: Yale University Press, 2003).

a complex flow of ideas and discourses among multiple (hierarchical) centres and multiple (and unequal) peripheries.[7]

Modernity and modernisation are well-known terms. As often happens with abstract concepts that find their place in daily language, their meaning differs from user to user. If we take Giddens's view, modernity is a historical condition that entails the past being superseded as the only reference for collective and individual behaviours, while the future, and the progress that it promises from the modern point of view (progress being hence an essential ingredient of any modernity), guides and legitimises our present actions and decisions.[8] Modernity means acting with the future in mind at every level, a way of thinking that can include past devices and solutions, but as possibilities among many others. Modernity puts technological change, and in particular that achieved through scientific methods, at the centre of material and social transformations.

When we refer to the rural world and agricultural production, the concept of modernity reveals a specific historicity that needs to be located in chronological terms. Modern rural society and modern agriculture are associated with the second phase of industrialisation that coincided with the high age of imperialism. Before the 1880s, there were experiments, promises and new horizons for a modern agriculture led by agronomists and other techno-scientists, but their effectiveness and their reach, without institutionalised channels, was limited, as Flaubert satirised in his unfinished novel *Bouvard et Pécuchet* (1881). Transformations in rural society were wide and deep, but peasants were still peasants, even as Riehl in his *Land und Leute* of 1867 complained that liberal society was threatening their survival. Rural communities were undergoing slow but profound changes that made plausible the dichotomy of ideal types – declining (rural) community versus rising (urban) society – that Tönnies made in his book *Gemeinschaft und Gesellschaft* in 1887. After the Second World War, 'modernisation' became a widely used term in agrarian discourse, often used in conjunction with 'development'. It was sustained by an elaborate theory of universal social change, the theory of modernisation, and by the expanding discipline of development economics.[9]

Before the time of reflexive modernity and post-modernity, modernity meant – to its numerous spokespersons – an open future that human

7 See chapters 3, 10, 11 and 12 for discussions this multiplicity of agronomic transfers. A regional analysis that confirms this polycentrism in *Engineering Asia: Technology, Colonial Development, and the Cold War Order*, Hiromi Mizuno, Aaron S. Moore and John Di Moia (eds) (London, New York, Sidney and Delhi: Bloomsbury, 2018).

8 Anthony Giddens and Christopher Pierson, *Making Sense of Modernity: Conversation* (Stanford, CA: Stanford University Press, 1998).

9 Nils Gilman, *Mandarins of the Future: Modernization Theory in Cold War America* (Baltimore, MD: John Hopkins University Press, 2003).

beings had to build and shape through their growing knowledge and, hence, through their growing control of the physical and the social worlds; or in other words, through the unbound and continuous flow of techno-scientific solutions. Rural society could also become modern, despite its being on the wrong side of the rural/urban dichotomy. This was especially the case once the second wave of industrialisation opened up new possibilities for agriculture, enabling it to go beyond the organic frame in which most innovations had taken place up until then: new chemical products, the internal combustion engine, the evolution of genetics that set the basis for a new plant and animal biotechnology. New technical horizons and the mobilisation of agricultural groups in the final decades of the nineteenth century and the first half of the twentieth century multiplied the thinkable futures. Many modern rural societies were imagined, many rural modernities were described and prescribed to replace actual rural societies, struck by modern forces but anchored in different ways to a pre-modern past. The horizons differed between societies where democratic pluralism prevailed and those where colonial rule, authoritarian regimes or communist or fascist control of the state apparatus very much limited the range of these alternative futures and put them out of reach of those whose future was at stake.

As we shall describe throughout this book, these plural rural modernities, which always had agricultural modernities at their core, seem to have merged into one after the Second World War: the one to which modernisation was to lead. Modernisation was 'a process that emphasised and even hypostatised modernity as an immanent truth and a value of reference, unleashing a generalised normative process': modernisation was not a possibility, but an obligation of every human group.[10] Modernisation implied the definition of what was modern in every subfield of human life and turning a defined canon into the inescapable goal of human action. The rhythms, the order, the diversions that potential disequilibria in the process of modernisation recommended could be debated; the goals could not.

Agricultural modernisation acquired a rather homogeneous content from the point of view of policy and pointed towards a uniform industrialised agriculture at the end of its transformation. Agricultural modernisation was relatively independent of rural modernisation: modernisation meant, among other things, the differentiation of agricultural production, undertaken by entrepreneurial, professional (and implicitly male) agriculturalists. Rural society had to become a space for decentralised industrial production, services, tourism, leisure, and management of natural resources, among other functions, as well as for agricultural activities, although the latter were no longer conceived to be

10 Pierre Cornu, 'El giro sistémico en los estudios rurales franceses', *Ayer* 120 (2020), 83–112.

the axis of its socio-economic life. A symptom of the social sense of this transformation was the fact that the variegated family of terms used to talk about those who lived in the countryside and practised agriculture, alongside many other activities, tended to be replaced by a single professional term: farmer, in the case of English.

1.1 Rural societies, innovation systems and food regimes in the first half of the twentieth century: mixed farming and mixed knowledge until 1950

The period of 1880–1940 was one of accelerated technological change in agriculture, with important innovations linked to the second wave of industrialisation and powerful scientific advances in agricultural chemistry, mechanics and animal and plant genetics. These novelties included the commercial development of mineral and chemical fertilisers, improvements in agricultural machinery and equipment with new designs and materials, new varieties of seeds, new livestock breeds and improvements in crop rotation, cultivation systems and irrigation. All this occurred in the aftermath of the Long Depression in Europe (1870s–90s) and offered those European farms that survived the competition from overseas (where those technologies multiplied production on the Great Plains, the Pampas, in Oceanian settlements, among others) new possibilities for increasing production and productivity, reducing costs, improving efficiency and expanding the competitive capacity of agriculture.[11]

At the turn of the twentieth century, agriculture still required handling nature in a paradigm that could neither master nor disregard the agricultural environment. Innovations were closely linked to their social and physical context. Before 1945, no technology existed for transporting or using large amounts of energy to re-create homogeneous environmental conditions. The productivity of an agroecosystem was still determined by its own capacity to produce biomass, although the role of fossil energy was growing.[12] On the other hand, farmers were often able to exercise their technological choices in accordance with their productive, reproductive and environmental needs. Given the scientific complexity of applying chemical, genetic or biological technologies produced by technoscientists, it was no longer possible to wait for the usual process of local

11 This period was characterised by the spread of biomass that entailed fossil materials, a tendency accelerated by the growing importance of oil after the Second World War, in the analysis of Niek Koning, *Food Security, Agricultural Policies and Economic Growth: Long-term Dynamics in the Past, Present and Future* (London/New York: Routledge, 2017).

12 Manuel González de Molina and Víctor Manuel Toledo, *The Social Metabolism: A Socio-Ecological Theory of Historical Change* (Cham: Springer, 2014).

imitation and word-of-mouth propaganda. The key words were applicability, adaptation and implementation. Farming innovation required the transfer of technology, and greater public intervention was necessary. In fact, the new role of the state in innovation was an important outcome of the political and agronomic debates regarding agriculture during the decades of depression and specific policy attempts to resolve them.[13]

Until then, the liberal state had left technological change in the hands of innovative landowners, and limited its role to fostering elite associations, providing information and supplying a restricted number of formal institutions for agricultural education, but at this juncture the state took on a more proactive role.[14] Turn-of-the-century European and American societies became a space in which farmers and tenants demanded and often obtained recognition as voters and political subjects. With universal male suffrage and peasant demands for ownership over the land they cultivated, those who ran small and middle-sized farms became the subject and object of public policy. They replaced idealised landowners as the new potential agents of innovation. Accordingly, public institutions, led by agronomists and veterinary surgeons, were envisioned and constructed to facilitate training, experimentation and demonstration. Politicians and public servants sought to develop an apparatus that could expose cultivators to innovations and help them to adopt new technologies. Precedents from Germany and the United States dating from the mid-nineteenth century inspired the European and Latin American creation of state innovation systems for these purposes. The institutional development of input and output markets co-existed with the logic of an organic system in which innovations could be accepted or rejected. At the same time, peasants, farm workers and landowners reinforced or created unions, societies and cooperatives through which they intervened in the market and innovation processes. This period combined the logic of organic agriculture and farmers' knowledge with the potential for science-based intensification without disrupting the organic domain or the farmers' agency. Contrary to the standard assumptions, this stage cannot be considered as an antecedent to or part of an inevitable teleological transition to hyper-intensive agriculture after the Second World War.

13 Jonathan Harwood, *Europe's Green Revolution and Others Since: The Rise and Fall of Peasant-Friendly Plant Breeding* (London: Routledge, 2012); Harro Maat, *Science Cultivating Practice: a History of Agricultural Science in the Netherlands and its Colonies, 1863–1986* (Wageningen: Ponsen and Looijen, 2001); Lourenzo Fernández Prieto, David Soto and Bruno Esperante, 'How Farmers Adopt New Technologies: Connections Between Farmer and Technician Knowledges in Galicia (NW Iberian Peninsula) (1880–1940)', *Rural History* 34 (2023), 1–18.

14 *The State and Rural Societies: Policy and Education in Europe, 1750–2000*, Nadine Vivier (ed.) (Turnhout: Brepols. 2008).

We can identify three key areas for the action of the agents of innovation and the creation of hybrid spaces for dialogue between techno-scientific and local and empirical knowledge: spaces for the linking of interests that did not always coincide and might even be contradictory. Among them we can include technicians and scientists in possession of knowledge that they considered new and superior; the producers and sellers of machinery, seeds or fertilisers; and those cultivators who had the final say about whether a particular innovation was adopted. These three areas functioned as three interconnected networks of knowledge. First, the public innovation system acted to facilitate the adaptation or adoption of scientific and industrial innovation. For innovative agents, the state innovation model was decisive, with its network of research and innovation facilities, regional farms and local demonstration camps. Second, there were the industrial and commercial companies that fulfilled the role of promoting and supplying innovations. Third, there were the local communities and the agrarian associations that took the decisions on the reception, selection and adoption of technology. This complex framework has been called the triple helix innovation system.[15]

The triple helix system expanded and seemed to be working in different countries during the *Belle Époque*, when agrarian prices, rents and incomes tended to rise, even though protectionist policies had been adopted by many countries and state technical policies were not understood as a sufficient and an equally positive scheme by many sectors of organised rural society. Cooperation, combination, active agency and other words we have used do not imply the absence of conflict. On the contrary, the period 1880–1939 was characterised by social mobilisation in the countryside and confrontation between opposed rural projects, which often caused violent turmoil.

Although the Great War entailed meaningful changes for world agriculture and the 1920s were years of instability and conflict in many rural societies, the boldest responses to the transformations of international agrarian markets and rural societies did not take place until after the 1929 crisis. In retrospect, this was the year that was the real turning point for the supply of food both nationally and internationally, for the organisation of food chains across the globe and the institutions that regulated them.[16]

15 Prieto, Soto and Esperante, 'How Farmers Adopt New Technologies' used this concept adapted from the terms employed by Henry Etzkowitz and Loet Leydesdorff, 'The Triple Helix – University-Industry-Government Relations: A Laboratory for Knowledge Based Economic Development', *EASST Review*, 14 (1995), 14–19.

16 Ernst Langthaler, 'The Great Depression as Great Transformation? Global Food Regime Crisis and (Inter-)National Transition Pathways, 1925–39', in *Agriculture and the Great Depression: The Rural Crisis of the 1930s in Europe*

After the powerful shock caused by the 1914–18 war on international agricultural markets, the liberal free-trade food regime dominated by the British Empire could not be totally restored. The formula whereby Britain and, gradually, other European countries imported cheap food, produced extensively in European settlement colonies or ex-colonies, and tropical products from other mostly colonial or semi-colonial lands, and exported industrial products back to them, did not work as smoothly as it had before 1914. Despite the relatively quick recovery of agricultural trade after its abrupt fall during the war, some countries, which were food importers and had practised a selective form of protectionism before the war, started to resort to the general protection of agriculture.[17] However, no alternative food regime came into being in the 1920s.[18] As for the national regulation of agriculture, groundbreaking measures were exceptional. The partial land reforms in the new European states apart, many pathways for new agrarian policies were opened up throughout the world under the pressure of diverse social movements in the countryside. The inter-war period saw the rise of peasant and agricultural parties, as Cabo explains in his chapter, and the expansion and consolidation of what can be called the agrarian movement.[19]

After 1900 and especially after the Great War, the growing mobilisation of rural society fostered a path of technological change without wholly abandoning organic frameworks and using, at least in certain social environments, peasant-friendly techniques. This path was rendered possible by the powerful innovation systems that had already been created. It led to intensification and an increase in yields per cultivated hectare with the support of each state's techno-scientific apparatus or the mediation of professionalised techno-scientists. The techniques were peasant-friendly because very often the empirical knowledge of cultivators and the resources available to peasants and farmers were taken into account by technicians and economists, in an asymmetrical but constant dialogue between both parts. A specific agricultural knowledge

and the Americas, Gérard Béaur and Francesco Chiapparino (eds) (London: Routledge, 2023), 21–38.

17 Gema Aparicio, Vicente Pinilla and Raúl Serrano, 'Europe and the International Trade in Agricultural and Food Products, 1870–2000', in *Agriculture and Economic Development in Europe Since 1870*, Pedro Lains and Vicente Pinilla (eds) (London: Routledge, 2009), 52–75.

18 Vicente Pinilla and Gema Aparicio, 'Navigating in Troubled Waters: South American Exports of Food and Agricultural Products, 1900–1950', *Revista de Historia Económica* 33 (2015), 223–55.

19 On the agrarian movement, see Miguel Cabo and Juan Pan-Montojo, 'Agrarian Organisations and Parties in Europe, 1970–1939', in *The Formation of Agricultural Governance: The Interplay Between State and Civil Society in European Agriculture, 1870–1940*, Jordi Planas and Yves Segers (eds) (Turnhout, Brepols, in press).

and innovation system (AKIS), which did not necessarily focus on peasants and small farmers but was open to their necessities, had been created gradually since the 1880s.[20] It was exemplified in the German, French, Italian or Spanish systems of experimental stations and farms, and even by the USA Land Grant Colleges, but similar institutions and policies could be found or were established in other countries. Almost everywhere, this AKIS experienced a clear growth in the 1920s, preserving the interaction between scientific and cultivators' knowledges.[21] Most peasant and agrarian organisations played a central role but did not explicitly defend this or any other system of technological development. Many of them, though, shared a common aim of reproduction of the peasantry: they favoured, therefore, technology that was accessible to small farms. As Stefania Barca has explained, for most cultivators at the time, production and reproduction could not be separated. In peasant households, those who took decisions were thinking at the same time about domestic goods and commodities, about producing for

20 AKISs are systems of organisation and transmission of knowledge among people, organisations and institutions that use, produce and reproduce know-how and technological solutions in agriculture and related fields. AKIS as a concept emerged in 2008 under the French Presidency of the EU Council and was subsequently developed within the Standing Committee on Agricultural Research, Strategic Working Group on Agricultural Knowledge and Innovation Systems, Fourth Report, https://knowledge4policy.ec.europa.eu/publication/preparing-future-akis-europe_en (2019) (accessed 10 January 2025). This AKIS, the one for which the term was created, maintained that cultivators had to be the centre of innovation systems and proposed to improve knowledge flows through a multi-stakeholder and interactive approach that enhanced innovation. However, we apply the term to circumstances before it was created, and hence we must acknowledge that there have been different AKISs with other features. The EU model AKIS is also linked to a new conception of the capacity of farmer agency and its work, which goes through the recognition of knowledge and the need not to lose decades or even centuries of experience, knowledge and local history. See Rob J. F. Burton, Jérémie Forney, Paul Stock and Lee-Ann Sutherland, *The Good Farmer: Culture and Identity in Food and Agriculture* (London: Routledge, 2020).

21 *Agriculture Knowledge Networks in Rural Europe, 1700–2000,* Yves Segers and Leen Van Molle (eds) (Woodbridge: Boydell Press, 2022); Lourenzo Fernández Prieto *et al.*, 'How Farmers Adopt New Technologies'. A comparative analysis of the construction of the innovation system in Europe can be found in the classic work of W. W. Wade, *Institutional Determinants of Technical Change and Agricultural Productivity Growth. Denmark, France and Great Britain, 1870–1965* (New York: Arno Press, 1981). On the Spanish case: Lourenzo Fernández Prieto, *El apagón tecnológico del franquismo. Estado e innovación en la agricultura española del siglo XX* (Valencia: Tirant Lo Blanc, 2007). About the USA, Joseph Fitzharris, 'Science for the Farmer: The Development of the Minnesota Agricultural Experiment Station, 1868–1910', *Agricultural History* 48 (1974), 202–14.

the market, but without endangering self-production and reproductive necessities, moreover, putting marketable production at the service of the family's needs.[22]

At a time when the metaphor of the nation as a large family was commonplace, economic nationalism made sense for agricultural families who saw themselves as members of larger and looser communities, starting with their local ones, whether hamlets, parishes or municipalities. Wherever peasants and small farmers had a distinct voice, they also demanded, together with the representatives of capitalist agriculture, a tighter regulation of international trade that would protect their market position. If after the Great War, international agricultural organisation was undergoing complex changes in a highly unstable process, it retained many features from the pre-war organisations. The final blow to the food regime inherited from the nineteenth century came with the Great Depression. The downturn of the New York Stock Exchange that began on 29 October 1929, opened the door to an international crisis in the following weeks, months and years, which despite shorter and longer recovery times in different places, would only come to a real end with the Second World War. Whatever the role of agriculture among the causes of the crisis, the international trade in agricultural products underwent a severe reduction and domestic sales of food and other primary resources tended to stagnate.[23]

It is therefore understandable that agriculture became one of the central issues of public policies that attempted to compensate for the depression and that, in that field, policy design was highly innovative. In the United States, the Agricultural Adjustment Act of 1933 aimed at raising the purchasing parity of agricultural products. A large social-planning scheme under the direction of the Tennessee Valley Authority started to work in the following years. The national regulation of the cereal sector was launched in France, in a model that would be copied in other countries; and, at another level, a new emphasis was placed on the nutritional side of all analyses of international trade and agricultural production by a number of voices with a strong international projection. All these and other novel policies and cultural turns were not without precedents, but in their sheer magnitude and ambition would not have taken place without the new context created by the Great Depression.[24]

22 Stefania Barca, *Forces of Reproduction: Notes for A Counter-Hegemonic Anthropocene* (Cambridge: Cambridge University Press, 2022).

23 A recent survey of the conflicting analyses of the role of agriculture in the Great Depression can be found in Gérard Béaur and Francesco Chiapparino, 'Introduction: Agriculture and the Big Crash', in *Agriculture and the Great Depression*, Béaur and Chiapparino (eds), 1–18.

24 On these different political, institutional and cultural innovations, see G. D. Libercap, 'The Great Depression and the Regulating State: Federal

On 7 November 1929 (nine days after the Wall Street Crash, but well before its reach and consequences could be envisaged), Stalin published an article in *Pravda* under the title *Velikii Perelom* [Great turn or Great change] in which he announced the collectivisation of Soviet agriculture. This took place at a considerable pace and with huge human cost during the following year – it would be virtually complete by 1932. This Soviet turning point and the turning point in the international food regime were asymmetrically connected. The 'great turn' in the USSR was both a result of the view of the future of agriculture held by most Bolsheviks (this was not very different from the by then orthodox Marxist view reflected in Kautsky's book, *Die Agrarfrage*) and a specific answer to the issues raised by the supply of agricultural products and raw materials for the industrialisation of the country. It was also an instrument for Stalin in the internal struggle for hegemony within the Communist Party.[25] Alexander Chayanov, a leading agrarian economist who had played a central role in Soviet agrarian governance under the New Economic Policy and belonged to a trans-Atlantic epistemic community of rural/agricultural thinkers that theorised about family agriculture and the ways to preserve it, was dismissed, arrested, put on trial and sent to a labour camp, where he was murdered in 1937.[26] The dismissal of Chayanov and the rejection of his theories reflected the decision to deny peasants any future under communism. However, collectivisation, the destruction of the peasantry and the parallel full subordination of agriculture to industrialisation and economic growth, foreseen in the first five-year plan, became a clear inspiration for the politicians who were facing the crisis

Government Regulation of Agriculture', in *The Defining Moment: The Great Depression and the American Economy in the Twentieth Century*, M. D. Bordo, C. Godlin and E. N. White (eds) (Chicago, IL: University of Chicago Press, 1998), 181–226; Alain Chatriot, *Organiser les marches agricoles. Le temps des fondateurs* (Paris: Armand Colin, 2012); Sarah T. Phillips, *This Land, This Nation: Conservation, Rural America, and the New Deal* (Cambridge: Cambridge University Press, 2007); Frank Trentmann, 'Before Fair Trade: Empire, Free Trade and the Moral Economies of Food in the Modern World', in *Food and Globalization: Consumption, Markets and Politics in the Modern World*, Alexander Nützenadel and Frank Trentmann (eds) (Oxford/New York: Berg, 2008), 253–76.

25 On the chain of political debates and conflicts that eventually led to collectivisation, Moshe Lewin, *Russian Peasants and Soviet Power: A Study of Collectivization* (New York: The Norton Library, 1975) remains a good guide.

26 Lluis Argemí d'Abadal, 'La historia de la economía agraria: una primera aproximación', *Estudios Agrosociales y Pesqueros* 192 (2002), 9–31. See also Katja Bruisch, 'Historicizing Chaianov. Intellectual and scientific roots of the Theory of Peasant Economy', in *Transforming Rural Societies: Agrarian Property and Agrarianism in East Central Europe in the Nineteenth and Twentieth Centuries*, Dietmar Müller and Angela Harre (eds) (Innsbruck: Studienverlag, 2010), 96–113.

in capitalist countries.[27] The role of scientific research in the solution to agricultural technological problems in the USSR, in the framework of its inclusion within the plan, or at least the one perceived by foreigners during their controlled visits, was also praised in other countries: the French agrarian politician, Víctor Boret, in his highly critical book on the Soviet Union, *Le paradis infernal*, published in 1933, complained about the lack of resources for the French public research institute for agriculture, the IRA, in comparison to the research institutes he had visited during his tour in the USSR.[28]

Fascism offered a second reference point in the field of agrarian policy, both for the authoritarian regimes that were established in the 1930s on both sides of the Atlantic, but also for liberal democracies. Italian fascism with its techno-scientific and regulatory programme for agriculture, first put into effect in the *battaglia del grano* after 1925, which aimed at increasing the self-sufficiency of Italy in cereals through a combination of extensive growth and intensification (new seeds, tractors, better use of fertilisers), and that led to a real leap in productivity, at least in the north of the country, was a precedent for the campaign for national self-sufficiency in 1935.[29] Especially after the 1929 crisis, the fascist regime advanced towards a more sweeping regulation of agriculture. The fascist authorities gave significant support to techno-biological innovation, such as high-yielding hybrid seeds developed under the leadership of Strampelli in the public *Stazione esperimentale* in Rieti, and multiplied the number of ambulant advisors in the countryside.[30] The infrastructural policy of the *bonifica* and *colonizzazione* (draining, land consolidation and landscape design, combined with settlement and creation of urban

27 The influence of Soviet cooperatives (kolkhozy), State farms (sovkhozy) and state planning on the USA's agricultural views in Deborah Fitzgerald, 'Collectivization and Industrialization: Learning from the Soviets', in Fitzgerald, *Every Farm a Factory*, 157–83. A more general overview of the relevance of Soviet planning for economic policies in the USA and elsewhere can be found in Kiran Klaus Patel, *The New Deal: A Global History* (Princeton, NJ, and Oxford: Princeton University Press, 2016).

28 Victor Boret, *Le paradis infernal* (Paris: Librairie Aristide Quillet, 1933), 296–7, cited by Gilles Denis, 'De l'Institut de recherches agronomiques au premier Institut national de la recherche agronomique (1916–1946)', in *Sciences, chercheurs et agriculture. Pour une histoire de la recherche agronomique*, Christophe Bonneuil, Gilles Denis and Jean-Luc Mayaud (eds) (Paris: Éditions Quae, 2008), 85–112.

29 Tiago Saraiva, *Fascist Pigs: Technoscientific Organisms and the History of Fascism* (Boston, MA: The MIT Press, 2018).

30 Stefano Grandi and Gianluca Volpi, 'Backwardness, Modernization, Propaganda: Agrarian Policies and Rural Representations in the Italian Fascist Regime', in *Agriculture in the age of fascism: Authoritarian technocracy and rural modernization, 1922–1945*, Lourenzo Fernández Prieto, Juan Pan-Montojo and Miguel Cabo Villaverde (eds) (Turnhout: Brepols, 2014) 43–83.

centres) at the Agro Pontino and other wetlands and marshes, in the first half of the 1930s, did not fulfil their ambitious aims, but it was a successful propaganda operation for fascism.

Portugal also started a wheat campaign in 1929 (*A campanha do trigo*) that multiplied production. The Ministry of Agriculture opened the *Estação agronómica nacional* in 1936 under the direction of the agronomist António da Câmara, after a reorganisation of agricultural services that intended to turn them into useful devices for productive intensification and diversification, as Dulce Freire explains in chapter 3. Neither for Portugal nor for Nazi Germany were Italian policies the only model available to them. The Third Reich inherited a wide range of instruments to regulate technical change and used them to advance its autarkic and imperial aims: in 1936 it passed a four-year economic plan that set agricultural objectives in preparation for war.[31] Agrarian policies aiming at the self-sufficiency of an expansive Nazi empire, which included the generous support of agronomic research, only apparently contradicted pro-peasant legislation and political measures wrapped in a ruralist rhetoric.[32]

The communist and fascist models of agrarian policy entailed a top-down approach to rural society. But where Italian fascism favoured the big estates of the North, national socialism sought to protect the peasantry. Some aspects of both models were attractive to experts and politicians in democratic and liberal societies (planning, research institutes, large infrastructure projects, and so on) but they could not invariably replicate these features. Many of the agrarian intellectuals who led the US Department of Agriculture in the late 1930s envisaged what they called a 'planning democracy', which would have included local farmer committees, local voting on administrative measures, group discussion and cooperative planning, in a project that tried to coordinate government officers, scientists and citizens on tenets that were akin to those of community development in India twenty years later.[33] A similar dialogue between peasants and technicians was expected in the unfulfilled plans of land reform of the Spanish Second Republic, which in

31 Gustavo Corni, 'La politica agraria del fascismo: Un confronto fra Italia e Germania', *Studi Storici* 2 (1987), 385–421. Corni offered a very interesting analysis that recognised for the first time the modernising nature of fascist agricultural policies. We do not agree, though, with his view that German agricultural policies were conservative, for reasons Langthaler outlines in his chapter.

32 Gesine Gerhard, 'The Modernisation Dilemma: Agrarian Policies in Nazi Germany', in *Agriculture in the Age of Fascism, 1922–1945*, Fernández Prieto, Pan-Montojo and Cabo (eds), 139–58.

33 Jess Gilbert, *Planning Democracy: Agrarian Intellectuals and the New Deal* (New Haven, CT: Yale University Press, 2015). On community development, see Daniel Immerwahr, *Thinking Small: The United States and the Lure of Community Development* (Cambridge, MA: Harvard University Press, 2015).

any case foresaw a labour-intensive agriculture.[34] A parallel land reform undertaken by President Cárdenas in Mexico in the 1930s, backed by agronomists, had at its centre the *ejidos* that villages would work collectively. The Mexican project offers a further example of the large menu of modern agricultures or rural modernities that the Great Depression produced in Europe and America.[35]

The decade after the Great Depression was a time of failed far-reaching projects. At the same time, many of the agrarian policies adopted were considered 'as an interim solution', as Brassley, Segers and Van Molle show, especially in relation to price regulations and commercial policies.[36] However, some responses to the crisis of agriculture lived on through the Second World War, becoming permanent, while others were abandoned or reshaped during or after the conflict, which gave birth to a new food regime and a new and uniform horizon for agriculture at different levels. Giovanni Federico sees the war of 1939–45 as a long-run discontinuity for agriculture in terms of production and international trade.[37] Both elements of discontinuity must be connected to institutional, political and cultural changes during the conflict.

1.2 Second World War consolidates discontinuity

The Second World War brought about changes in agriculture that have seldom been analysed. In the first place, it turned the USA into the hegemon of the capitalist world, as the winner of the war, challenged by a rival power, the Soviet Union, the other winner. For this reason, the American combination of agriculture, industry and techno-science, with the market as a driver, became much more than a possible model for the world. In political, cultural and economic terms, the USA was in a strong position after 1945 to impose a new food regime based on high input–high output, mainly non-organic, agricultural production, and the expansion of food processing industries in the USA. It could also spread the institutional and technical solutions of the new agriculture and

34 On land reform in Spain see the very different views of Ricardo Robledo, *La tierra es vuestra. La reforma agraria, un problema no resuelto. España, 1900–1950* (Barcelona: Crítica, 2022); and James Simpson and Juan Carmona, *Why Democracy Failed: The Agrarian Origins of the Spanish Civil War* (Cambridge: Cambridge University Press: 2020).

35 Joseph Eugene Cotter, *Troubled Harvest: Agronomy and Revolution in Mexico, 1880–2002* (Westport, CT, and London: Praeger Publishers, 2003).

36 *War, Agriculture, and Food: Rural life in Europe from the 1930s to the 1950s*, Paul Brassley, Yves Segers and Leen Van Molle (eds) (London, Routledge: 2012), 254.

37 Giovanni Federico, 'Natura Non Fecit Saltus. The 1930s as the Discontinuity in the History of European Agriculture', in *War, Agriculture, and Food*, Brassley, Segers and Van Molle (eds), 15–32.

agribusiness to the rest of the world. Furthermore, European countries were in no position to resist American proposals, even if they had seen any alternative, ravaged and impoverished as they were by the war. What they did was to adapt to the new situation: an adaptation that would prove successful and turn Western Europe into a food exporter too.[38] The American technological and economic proposals were included in an agricultural paradigm born and constructed in the environmental, social, economic and political circumstances of the USA, not European or Latin American ones, let alone those of the colonial world. The hegemony of the USA, exercised directly and indirectly through a large grid of institutions, did not, therefore, remove from the European, Latin American or Asian countries their autonomy. They continued to apply their own agricultural and commercial version of 'modernisation'. They created their own local food regimes integrated into the global one.[39]

The Second World War changed the political priorities of the USA. Roosevelt himself stated in 1943: 'I am not convinced that we can be realists about the war and planners for the future at this critical time.'[40] Winning the war entailed, according to the New Dealers, a close relationship between the American administration and the big corporations that could mobilise resources, and postponing any reforms that could hamper the war effort. Regulatory institutions, including those of the Department of Agriculture, were co-opted by what would later be called agribusiness, and big corporations, with their campaigns against big government and public intervention, defeated the New Dealers.[41] The decision to stop public distribution of hybrids and other seeds and leave it in the hands of private companies was a clear sign of the new relationship between the private sector and the public sphere.[42] The fact

38 *Agriculture in Capitalist Europe, 1945–1960: From Food Shortages to Food Surpluses,* Carin Martin, Juan Pan-Montojo and Paul Brassley (eds) (Abingdon and New York: Routledge, 2016).

39 John Wilkinson and David Goodman, 'Les analyses en termes de "food regime": une relecture', in *Transformations agricoles et agroalimentaires. Entre écologie et capitalisme,* Gilles Allaire and Benoit Daviron (eds) (Versailles: Quae, 2017), 277–90.

40 Quoted in David Brody, 'The New Deal and World War II', in *The New Deal,* John Braeman, Robert H. Bremner and David Brody (eds) (Columbus, OH: Ohio State University Press, 1975), 270.

41 Martin Hart-Landsberg, 'US Economic Planning in the World War II and the Planetary Crisis', *Monthly Review* 74–9 (2023), 25–40. Although it focuses on the military industries, Mark Wilson, *Destructive Creation: American Business and the Winning of World War II* (Philadelphia PA: University of Pennsylvania Press, 2016) explains the long campaign undertaken by industrial leaders to denigrate government action and underline their own contribution to the war effort.

42 Jack Ralph Kloppenburg, *First the Seed: The Political Economy of Plant Biotechnology, 1492–2000* (Madison, WI: University of Wisconsin Press, 2004).

that the candidate of the old New Dealers against Truman in 1948 was Roosevelt's secretary of Agriculture, Henry A. Wallace, is not unconnected with this gradual abandonment of New Deal values.

Third, the war brought about not so much brand-new agricultural and agro-industrial technologies as it did lower prices, a greater availability of inputs and diversification of food products. US, Canadian and British manufacturers of agricultural machinery, who had grown and become more concentrated during the 1930s, in some cases increased the size and reach of their operations in non-agricultural fields during the war, only to renew their production for agricultural markets at its end.[43] Diverse agricultural inputs benefited from the war effort: it is well known that DDT, a chemical product developed as an insecticide by a Swiss company in the 1930s, was promoted by the US Army sanitary authorities to destroy insects that threatened soldiers fighting in tropical areas after 1942. It was produced on a massive scale by the end of the 1940s, enabling its use in agriculture.[44] A slightly different story can be told about nitrates, which had both military and agricultural uses. The large amounts of ammonia that awaited use in explosives factories by the end of the war pushed down the prices of nitrogenated fertilisers in the late 1940s and expanded their use in agriculture.[45] Higher and cheaper production of inputs went hand in hand with the development of a new food industry. American food production, which had had to adapt to intense changes in supply and demand after 1939 caused by the disruption of international trade, became crucial for avoiding hunger in different Allied countries. The growth of the American food industry was not reversed with the end of the war, and neither was the world-wide impact of American processed food.[46]

A fourth effect of the Second World War that would have an impact on agriculture was that the bipolar world born out of the war created a new need for legitimation on the part of the USA. The discourse of

43 See, for instance, Edward Neufeld, *A Global Corporation: A History of the International Development of Massey-Ferguson Limited* (Toronto: University of Toronto, 2020). In relation to the USA, William White, 'Economic History of Tractors in the United States'. *EH.Net Encyclopedia*, Robert Whaples (ed.), 26 March 2008, https://eh.net/encyclopedia/economic-history-of-tractors-in-the-united-states/ (accessed 11 January 2025).

44 Thomas Dunlap, *DDT: Scientists, Citizens, and Public Policy* (Princeton, NJ: Princeton University Press, 2014); and Edmund Russell, *War and Nature: Fighting Humans and Insects with Chemicals from World War I to Silent Spring* (Cambridge: Cambridge University Press, 2001).

45 Edward D. Melillo, 'The First Green Revolution: Debt Peonage and the Making of the Nitrogen Fertilizer Trade, 1840–1930', *American Historical Review* 117 (2012), 1028–60.

46 Lizzie Collingham, *The Taste of War: World War Two and the Battle for Food* (London: Allen Lane, 2011).

modernisation played that role and cast a long shadow over the imagining of alternative futures. The conflicting rural modernities of the inter-war period gave way to a uniform project for agricultural modernisation, with relatively few variations, that aimed at the industrialisation of agriculture. Considering peasants to be a socio-economic remnant of premodern times (at least those in Western Europe, Japan and Latin America), its aim was to bring them out of their backwardness and turn them into farmers embedded in national and international markets. Even in a country like Denmark, where commodification was more advanced before the war and producers were politically well represented, American modernisation succeeded, as Christiansen shows subsequently in his chapter later in this book. The number of Danish farmers fell, farms became larger, and inputs were obtained increasingly through the market. But lacking the transfer of American resources, with less cooperation from the political centre of the Bloc, and more hesitation and contradictions than their capitalist counterparts, many communist countries adopted the collectivist solution already fully developed in the USSR, although some needed to revert to private farms, as Varga underlines.

Finally, changes in the USA or the USSR were not the only ones that mattered. On the one hand, as D'Onofrio explains in chapter 6, the war opened the door to the Food and Agriculture Organization (FAO), a supranational organisation that replaced the International Institute of Agriculture (IIA) and attempted to construct a new international order in the field, taking advantage of the disappearance of the agrarian elites who had been central to the IIA. The project of a world regulation of agricultural trade failed, however, and income support and price regulation continued to be a national problem (with the one exception of Western European countries integrated in the EEC after 1957), while the FAO dedicated its resources to technical aid and famine relief. On the other hand, the policies adopted against the crisis and the mobilisation of rural populations in the 1930s as well as the reforms introduced after the victory over fascism in 1945 brought about diverse reactionary counter-reforms during the war and after 1947. There were many international and national political dynamics that shaped agricultural policies, making the analysis of homogenising trends in the post-war period even more complex.

1.3 The time of agricultural modernisation

For the reasons summarised above, the origins of the Green Revolution, understood as a specific phase of agricultural modernisation, can be traced back to the Second World War, and as the road to a specific modernity, to the 1880s. We might argue (as others have done) that that it was the development and successful use of the atomic bomb that raised expectations:

if mankind could destroy itself, what could it not do? The technocratic projects that emerged in both the USA and the USSR after this time, albeit implemented at different speeds, were united by concepts, ideas and models that had been defined in the nineteenth century and by innovations that had been born out of the second wave of industrialisation. Among the ideas embraced by both camps was the prognosis of a future without peasants; the development of a much-reduced agrarian proletariat to run capitalised farms and the gradual growth of farming units until they reached their technical and economic optimum; that is, until economies of scale were exhausted. Among the innovations were the internal combustion engine to power farm machinery and break the limits that draught livestock had imposed on farm extension; chemical fertilisers and pesticides to control attacks on plants; the new opportunities for seed and livestock selection that genetics opened up; or the massive use of new materials such as plastics. All these technologies seemed to make possible an agriculture gradually liberated from environmental constraints and in which biological cycles could be somehow subject to human necessities, as chapters 2 and 3 reveal. Hence, an agricultural industry looked like a possible future. Proposals to accelerate the industrialisation of agriculture blossomed in the inter-war period. The collectivisation of 1929 onwards reinforced them, as did the autarkic projects of fascism (contradicting their paradoxical defence of the peasant as the key social element of the nation), and even the macro-plans for irrigation under the democratic New Deal in the 1930s, notwithstanding the sincere aspiration of many of its supporters, officers and leaders to achieve a farm democracy.

The proposals and models of an industrial agriculture, despite their growing strength, only left behind their ambiguities and became hegemonic after 1945. Robert Solow, winner of the Nobel Prize for Economics in 1987, had argued thirty years earlier that without a thorough technical change, agricultural production would become static, and famine a permanent reality. Only through inventions and innovations developed outside the sector could such a threat be prevented.[47] A similar ahistorical view was the theme of the book by Theodore W. Schultz of 1964, *Transforming Traditional Agriculture.*[48] 'Traditional agriculture', as the very idea of its use of factors of production 'for generations' implied, was considered static precisely because it was efficient: no change in the allocation of productive factors could improve its results. Despite its efficiency, traditional agriculture in most cases did not generate enough income for the farmers and or sufficient food for consumers; it implied

47 Robert Solow, 'Technical Change and The Aggregate Production Function', *Review of Economic and Statistics* 39 (1957), 312–20.

48 Theodore Schultz, *Transforming Traditional Agriculture* (New Haven, CT: Yale University Press, 1964), 3.

poverty. To overcome its lack of dynamism, traditional agriculture needed to receive modern means of production and other types of labour and entrepreneurship that demanded new inputs and could profitably employ them. Since traditional farmers had no incentives for change, a sort of acculturation – our term – had to take place in the countryside through the action of external agents who at the same time would provide new productive instruments or enable access to them. In 1979, Schultz was awarded the Nobel Prize for Economics, largely because of his 1964 book, even though it had completely overlooked the historical dynamism of organic agriculture. Top-down and external modernisation became economic common sense, and simultaneously biotechnological innovation was turned into the flagship of agricultural modernisation. The agronomist Norman E. Borlaug received the 1970 Nobel Peace Prize for his contribution to the high-yielding varieties of wheat that were allegedly about to bring an end to hunger, although the famines of the early 1970s in the Sahel and in India and Bangladesh showed that technology, even that which multiplied production in the short term, could not solve food problems by itself, and that the increase in production was not always an efficient vaccine against hunger.[49]

The chapters of this book attempt to show from different angles how modernisation and its economic and technological solutions for agriculture managed to prevail. Those in Part II describe the transition to modernisation in two European countries, the United Kingdom and Denmark (chapters 7 and 8), the successive projects to increase production in communist Hungary (chapter 9), policies of development in Belgian Congo and post-fascist Ethiopia (chapters 10 and 11), and the Southern Cone and India (chapters 12 and 13). One of the conclusions of these chapters is that despite the diverse political situations of all these countries and the huge differences among their agricultural sectors, many common traits can be identified in the policies that were applied. Their chronologies are not very different, nor is the top-down approach to technical change, nor the cross-fertilisation of projects between countries. They include fascist developments that were continued by the United Nations Relief and Rehabilitation Administration, the FAO and American technicians in Ethiopia (chapter 11); colonial powers observing and copying their schemes for rural development in Africa (chapter 10); Hungary importing American technology (chapter 9); Argentina importing French institutions or looking at rural development centres elsewhere in Latin America (chapter 12); or even the need to foster a new attitude or mentality among cultivators (chapter 13). There are obviously differences too, some of which are very pertinent, but they concern local contexts more than policy instruments and horizons.

49 Christian Gerlach, 'Die Weltnährungskrise 1972 bis 1975', *Geschichte und Gesellschaft* 31 (1975), 546–85.

Under the title 'The Triumph of the Modernising Logic', Part III groups together some general explanations of agricultural modernisation: environmental consequences (chapter 14); the interrelationship between the Green Revolution and American hegemonic power, both in the Global South (chapter 15) and in the western hemisphere (chapter 16); the role of gender relations in the process of modernisation (chapter 17); and resistance to modernisation in two countries of the Global South (chapter 18). The specific case of Spain, analysed by González de Molina in chapter 14, offers an analysis of the effects of the industrialisation of agriculture. Spain has increased total production in terms of tons of physical production and in monetary production. However, its efficiency from the point of view of energy production has sharply declined. In fact, agriculture that used to turn solar energy into food and other resources and was, hence, a net energy-producing activity, now produces biomass through the use of fossil fuels and is a net consumer of energy. Furthermore, as de Molina demonstrates:

> the fund elements that maintain ecosystem services, such as soil fertility, biodiversity, carbon sequestration, water quality, etc., have all been degraded. In addition, agricultural and livestock activities have become an active source of pollution and cause the depletion of scarce resources such as fossil fuels and mineral nutrient sources.[50]

On the other hand, the number of farmers has shrunk everywhere, endangering not only the continuity of agriculture, but the other functions that rural inhabitants used to fulfil in the countryside.

American 'soft power' and its institutional projection, which actually embodied intense collaboration between the hegemonic USA and the elites of its allied countries, triggered the process that we call the Green Revolution, the attempt to turn a Western – in this context, the equivalent to OECD member states – technological model for agriculture into a world-wide recipe for accelerated modernisation, the adoption (or importation) of which could be therefore legitimately labelled a revolution.

Social change cannot avoid affecting gender relations. Modernisation and its revolutionary phase consciously and explicitly fostered the construction of new rural, non-agricultural women and, hence, of new agricultural and rural men, which is the topic addressed in chapter 17. Because modernisation changed so many things in the countryside and because it was not socially neutral, it was confronted with different forms of resistance. Leaving agriculture or agricultural employment was often the main response (and especially for women). Chapter 18 closes Part III and the book itself with an analysis of the forms taken by resistance to the Green Revolution in India and Brazil.

50 Below, 000.

1.4 Epilogue

The triumph of the industrialisation of agriculture after 1945 was the triumph of modernisation in its American meaning and the triumph of collectivisation in the Soviet understanding. Both blocs shared an old ideal of turning farms into factories that had its roots in the Enlightenment and the first wave of industrialisation. Both had many traits in common: motorisation to replace draught livestock and human labour, chemicalisation to replace biological processes, land and labour-saving techniques that would eventually lead to dispensing with these two productive factors (as some intensive livestock farms almost managed to do at the beginning of the twenty-first century). Agricultural modernisation was successful in its productive expansion: between 1950 and 1985, the world production of cereals multiplied 2.6 times thanks to the increase in the consumption of fertilisers from 17 million tonnes in 1950 to 130 million tonnes at the end of the 1980s, and the multiplication of pesticide use by a factor of 20 in the same period.[51]

Attempts to put an end to organic agriculture and its dependence on natural cycles and environmental conditions in the last decades of the twentieth century faced the obstacle of the lack of sustainability of the new model, as well as the absence of food safety and sufficiency. However, the prevailing model, created in the time of the Cold War, has proven very resilient. Its cultural hegemony, its popularity among cultivators, and the threat of an insufficient food supply if it is not continued, support an agriculture that cannot be sustained for much longer. In many regions of the world, and for many technicians and farmers, the criticism of the industrialising paradigm is tantamount to going back to a past of backwardness that they or their parents were fortunate enough to leave behind. There is room, though, and there is an urgent need to reverse this, by now, antique model that has no future and is incompatible with any green transition.

The first step in that direction is the aim of this book: a new historical narrative that explains that the specific industrialisation of agriculture in the twentieth century was a historical process among many other possible ones. It was not a given nor natural nor inevitable. It was the result of concrete decisions and policies that tended to impose a top-down, technocratic logic – akin to the one that prevailed in fascist attempts to attain self-sufficiency – which tended to be aligned with the interests of agribusiness in the capitalist world and with the aim of industrial supremacy, as interpreted by the *nomenklatura*, in the communist one.

The second one must be to recover the surviving elements of the peasant-friendly techniques of the past, starting at the foundations: political

51 Marcel Mazoyer and Laurence Roudart, *Histoire des agricultures du monde. Du Néolithique à la crise contemporaine* (Paris: Le Seuil, 2002), 506.

decisions must be taken in light of a thorough and constant dialogue between techno-scientists and cultivators. A new organic agriculture cannot feed the world or maintain farmers' incomes, and hence ensure their survival, without science and its resulting technologies. However, it cannot be conceived without the participation of rural dwellers either, but rather it needs the concrete knowledge they hold about soils, seeds, routines, and so forth. Especially important is the knowhow of those rural women who used to tend orchards or maintained a hotbed next to their house and who can offer many tips and material elements (including locally adapted varieties) for this new organic agriculture. It needs also to reconstruct farmers' abilities to innovate collectively in response to signals from markets. It must take their futures into account, making possible the democratic planning that New Dealers, peasant parties, agrarian organisations and cooperative movements dreamed of, and the low modernism it could have paved the way for.

Third, democratic planning and public discussion of the future implies recovering a central role for politics, leaving behind the neoliberal phase of modernisation that has dominated the past fifty or so years, a period outside the range of this book. Market failure in the regulation of food production entails that collective decisions and the corresponding public policies are necessary, although nothing guarantees that democratic choices will be compatible with the sustainability of agriculture and food sufficiency, unless the public takes food production seriously and realises that both goals, sustainability and sufficiency, must be attained simultaneously.

Any historical work that offers a view of the past as retrotropia – an age where things were better managed and organised – peddles a historical myth to the reader. There were, before the modernisation paradigm became dominant, no agrarian or rural paradises, not even where advanced organic agriculture prevailed. Modern projects were plural in the first half of the twentieth century because the rural world was full of social asymmetries between classes and genders, between imperial public servants and politicians and colonised subjects, between state and agribusiness projects and the necessities of peasants and farmers. The triple helix worked but not without confrontation and clashes. In the decades that followed the end of the Great War, let alone in the previous ones, food production did not cover the necessities, in terms of nutrients, of large sections of the world population, and famines were more frequent than today, after the post-war transformations. Our critical approach to modernisation aims at undoing the legends created around the Green Revolution and to recover elements of past futures that were never fulfilled, not at vindicating a time that has passed into history. Thus, it is our aim in this book to establish a new historical narrative that will inform the construction of a new sustainable agriculture in the future.

PART I

BRIDGES AND TRANSITIONS

2

Flow, stock and epistemic change: using biotic and consuming mineral resources in agricultural production

Juri Auderset and Peter Moser

In 1950, John M. Brewster, a philosopher who had worked for much of his career among agricultural economists at the USDA, published an article on the 'Machine Process in Agriculture and Industry'. He argued that 'the "Industrial Revolution" in agriculture' was 'merely a spectacular change in the implements of production whereas in industry it is a further revolution in the sequence (order) in which men use their implements'. Brewster obviously felt the need to elucidate this rather apodictic statement a little further and enlarged upon it in a footnote. Here he explained why motorised technologies had developed in different ways in the factories and in the fields since the invention of the steam engine in the late eighteenth century. To his eyes, these diverging developments stemmed from the 'contrasting nature of materials' used in agriculture and consumed in industrial manufacturing. 'Land' is a 'basic resource' in agricultural production. Farming deals, as Brewster put it, essentially with 'living things, fixed in the soil'. In industrial manufacturing, in contrast, the meaning of the land is usually reduced to being a 'building site' and the materials used are 'lifeless' and, therefore, much more 'mobile' and malleable to the requirements of the spatially fixed, continuously operated manufacturing system that has characterised the modern factory since its emergence in the late eighteenth and early nineteenth century. It was precisely the specific 'nature of materials' in industry that enabled an 'increased scale of production' and the 'concentration of operations required for their simultaneous performance', whereas agriculture remained tied to 'the seasonality of climate, biological cycles of living things, and the "spreadoutness" of the soil'. Therefore, Brewster argued, the 'machine process in agriculture and in industry' was subject to different temporal and spatial logics of production stemming from the respective specific materiality used in the production process.[1]

It is as characteristic as is it is revealing for the transition period of the post-war decades that Brewster was eager to remind the readers of the *Journal of Farm Economics* of these differing material conditions of agricultural production and industrial manufacturing, but that he relegated these fundamental reflections to a footnote. This episode mirrors a broader shift in the history of agriculture as well as in its perception in the age of nineteenth- and twentieth-century industrial capitalism, a shift we call the transition from an *agrarian-industrial* knowledge society to an *industrial-agrarian* knowledge society.[2] The inversion of the two characterising adjectives is much more than a play on words. It indicates a fundamental epistemic shift in the perception and conception of agriculture closely related to the expansion of the material resource base of agricultural production. Whereas the epistemic reflection and practical consideration of the differences between the use of biotic and the consumption of fossil resources belonged to the main features of the agrarian-industrial knowledge society from the last third of the nineteenth century to the mid-twentieth century, this kind of reasoning on the 'contrasting nature of materials' in industry and agriculture was increasingly ignored (or, in Brewster's case, pushed to the footnotes) in the 1950s and 1960s. To integrate agriculture into the patterns of capitalist industrialisation on the verge of its 'great acceleration',[3] it had to be interpreted *as if it were* based on the same resources as industry. Had the representatives of the agrarian-industrial knowledge society struggled to find an adequate terminology to express the differentiation between the use of biotic and the consumption of mineral resources, many agricultural economists now began to identify this body of knowledge as an obstacle for a successful development of the agricultural sector in the post-war period. In Switzerland, for instance, the young agronomist Karl Steiner stated in 1955 that agricultural production had become 'an underdeveloped branch of the Swiss economy' because agricultural economists had for generations ignored 'the methodology and terminology of general business administration'. Instead of modelling the conceptual framework of agricultural economics on the idiosyncrasies

1 John M. Brewster, 'The Machine Process in Agriculture and Industry', *J. Farm Economics* 32 (1950), 69–70. On Brewster see John M. Brewster, *A Philosopher Among Economists*, J. Patrick Malden and David E. Brewster (eds) (Philadelphia, PA: J. T. Murphy, 1970).

2 Juri Auderset and Peter Moser, *Die Agrarfrage in der Industriegesellschaft: Wissenskulturen, Machtverhältnisse und natürliche Ressourcen in der agrarisch-industriellen Wissensgesellschaft (1850–1950)* (Vienna: Böhlau, 2018).

3 Christophe Bonneuil and Jean-Baptiste Fressoz, *The Shock of the Anthropocene: The Earth, History and Us* (London: Verso, 2017), 51.

of agricultural production, Steiner called for an active disregard of these specificities. Only by way of prescinding from agriculture's particularities could the theory of agricultural economics be aligned with 'the existing economic laws', and only when governed by the same allegedly universal principles of neoclassical economic theory could agriculture catch up with the pace of industrial development.[4]

This epistemic shift was tightly interwoven with the newly won access to the lithosphere and the growing use of mineral and fossil resources in agricultural production. The dream of turning farms into factories and of fitting agriculture completely into industrial capitalism reached back to the first half of the nineteenth century, but in the post-war years, this vision met with much more favourable material conditions for being turned into reality. In the 1940s, 1950s and 1960s, the long-term technological development of versatile, multifunctional, oil-fuelled tractors, equipped with power take-offs that transferred power directly to implements under tow, and endowed with rubber tyres that increased mobility between spatially dispersed fields and enabled a relatively flexible adhesion to changing soil conditions, was finally successful and marked a breakthrough in the process of motorisation of agricultural production.[5] Together with the growing use of chemical implements such as artificial fertilisers, pesticides, herbicides and insecticides that were also derived from minerals, agriculture began to participate to a significant degree in the consumption of mineral and fossil resources.[6] The intermeshing processes of motorisation and chemicalisation were not only crucial pre-conditions for the replacement of the innumerable draft animals that had powered the mechanisation of agricultural production since the nineteenth century, but they also made severe cutbacks in the

4 Karl Steiner, *Ein Fünf-Punkte-Plan zur Gesundung der schweizerischen Agrarwirtschaft* (Winterthur: Keller, 1959), 31 and 50. All translations from non-English sources are by the authors. On the influence of neoclassical economic theory see also Shane Hamilton, 'Managing the Farm: Bullshit in Theory and Practice', *Agricultural History* 98 (2024), 1–22.

5 Juri Auderset and Peter Moser, 'Mechanisation and Motorisation. Natural Resources, Knowledge, Politics and Technological Change in 19th and 20th Century Agriculture', in *Agriculture in Capitalist Europe, 1945–1960: From food shortages to food surpluses*, Carin Martiin, Juan Pan-Montojo and Paul Brassley (eds) (London: Routledge, 2016), 145–64. A detailed account of the technological developments of tractorisation is provided by Alan L. Olmstead and Paul W. Rhode, 'Reshaping the Landscape: The Impact and Diffusion of the Tractor in American Agriculture, 1910–1960', *J. Economic History* 61 (2001), 663–98. See also the contribution by Paul Brassley in this volume.

6 Nathalie Jas, *Au carrefour de la chimie et de l'agriculture: Les sciences agronomiques en France et en Allemagne, 1850–1914* (Paris: Édition des archives contemporaines, 2001); Adam M. Romero, *Economic Poisoning: Industrial Waste and the Chemicalization of American Agriculture* (Los Angeles, CA: University of California Press, 2021).

agricultural labour force possible. In conjunction with lithosphere-based inputs, the drastic decrease of men, women and working animals on farms enabled an impressive increase of the agricultural production for the markets in the post-war years.[7] What neoclassical economists conceptualised as a simple process of substituting labour through capital was in material reality an increasing consumption of non-renewable resources by an agriculture that simultaneously remained dependent on the use of living resources like animals, plants and soil.

From a historical perspective that emphasises the entanglements between the changing use of natural resources and the knowledge of agriculture in nineteenth- and twentieth-century industrial capitalism, the transition from an agrarian-industrial to an industrial-agrarian knowledge society is crucial since it marks the beginning of what we might call – following Foucault – a 'history of the present'.[8] In order to better grasp this shift in the interactions between the history of knowledge and the history of material resources in the post-war years, we must look a little further back into the twisting history of agriculture under the conditions of industrialisation in the nineteenth and twentieth centuries. In the following sections of this chapter, therefore, we will first sketch how agricultural production and industrial manufacturing came to rely on different resources in the context of the industrial revolution, which was more precisely a thermo-industrial revolution since it was the energy base and not the machines themselves that underwent revolutionary changes in that period. How did the rise of the steam-powered factory system in the middle of the nineteenth century unleash an indiscriminate belief that the agricultural practices of reproducing plants and animals could and should be modelled on the principles of industrial manufacturing? Second, we will discuss why this industrial paradigm ran up against the idiosyncrasies of agricultural production and explain why the experience of failure turned into an incentive to account for the peculiar features of agricultural reproduction from the 1870s onwards. In our understanding, these learning processes marked the beginning of the agrarian-industrial knowledge society and became one of its defining features until the 1940s. In this period, the appeal of the 'industrial ideal' remained intact,[9] yet the endeavours to modernise agriculture accounted for the specific logics of an agricultural mode of production embedded in

7 Giovanni Federico, 'Natura Non Fecit Saltus. The 1930s as the Discontinuity in the History of European Agriculture', in *War, Agriculture, and Food: Rural Europe from the 1930s to the 1950s*, Paul Brassley, Yves Segers and Leen Van Molle (eds) (London: Routledge, 2012), 15–32.

8 Michael S. Roth, 'Foucault's "History of the Present"', *History and Theory* 20 (1981), 32 –46.

9 Deborah Fitzgerald, *Every Farm a Factory: The Industrial Ideal in American Agriculture* (New Haven, CT: Yale University Press, 2003).

a great variety of ecological systems. In the third section our argument will come full circle and move back once again to the transition period of the post-war years. We will discuss the implications of this shift not only for the history of agriculture from the second half of the twentieth century to our present, but also for the historiographical narratives on agriculture that were – and often still are – deeply shaped by the ideological assumptions rooted in the post-war era.[10] In fact, as Miguel Cabo, Lourenzo Fernández Prieto and Juan Pan-Montojo remind us in the introduction to this volume, many of the dominating narratives about the development of post-war agriculture are enmeshed in the same conceptual schemes that contemporary advocates of a new type of industrialised and 'productivist' agriculture had proposed, continuing in their indifference towards the environmental and economic implications arising out of human activities that use biotic resources and those that consume mineral resources.

2.1 The rise of the industrial paradigm and its disenchantment

From the mid-nineteenth century, agriculture had increasingly become the 'other' in industrialising societies. This perception of agriculture's 'otherness' stemmed first and foremost from its differing resource base in comparison with industrial manufacturing.[11] Since the thermo-industrial revolution and the rise of the steam engine, the stationary, weather-independent system of industrial manufacturing was mainly based on the consumption of fossil and mineral resources stored in the lithosphere of the earth.[12] This technological breakthrough at the core of the thermo-industrial revolution not only made possible, for the first time in history, a decoupling of the production and reproduction processes, but it also enabled the transformation of a (temporary) abundance of coal (and later oil and uranium) into an affluence of kinetic energy. As Wrigley explained, this new 'resource capitalism' enabled industrialising societies to break free from the energy, raw material and food constraints of the previous 'organic economies' by way of consuming the '*stocks*' of mineral resources to complement the 'unvarying *flow* of energy arriving annually at the earth's surface':

10 Jonathan Harwood, 'Another Green Revolution? On the Perils of "Extracting Lessons" from History', *Development* 61 (2018), 43–53; Christophe Bonneuil, Léna Humbert and Margot Lyautey, 'Un renouveau de l'histoire contemporaine des mondes agricoles et des espaces ruraux', in *Histoire des modernisations agricoles au XXe siècle*, Margot Lyautey, Léna Humbert and Christophe Bonneuil (eds) (Rennes: Presses universitaires de Rennes, 2021), 7–20.

11 Nicholas Georgescu-Roegen, *Energy and Economic Myths: Institutional and Analytical Economic Essays* (New York: Pergamon 1976).

12 E. A. Wrigley, *Energy and the English Industrial Revolution* (Cambridge: Cambridge University Press, 2010).

> Within the context of an organically based economy, sustained and substantial growth sufficient to transform the standard of living was a utopian dream, whatever the prevailing economic system. To make the dream come true there had to be an escape to an economy not dependent on the annual product of the earth for all supplies of raw materials and energy. Such a regime involved a shift to mineral sources of supply and meant dependence upon a different kind of capital.[13]

Regardless of whether the 'dream' of an abundant disposability of mineral resources may always have had elements of a nightmare as well,[14] it doubtlessly installed a new economic regime that departed sharply from the 'organic economy' of earlier times. The 'resource capitalism' emanating from this access to the stores of mineral energy contained in the lithosphere and its consumption in the steam engine provided the necessary means for a continuous and linear, and thus accelerated, production that became the leading progressive vision in industrial societies in the nineteenth and twentieth centuries. Steam engines, a disciplined workforce, assembly lines, continuous manufacturing and scientific management with its 'time and motion studies' became the key symbols of this new industrial time- and space-regime.[15]

In the light of this industrial paradigm, the reproduction of plants and animals in agriculture that was heavily reliant on the use of biotic resources and the soil, and, by its very nature, bound to seasonally determined regeneration cycles, was increasingly seen to be in need of major transformation. The embeddedness of agricultural reproduction processes in the flows of the solar-biotic energy system and the bounds imposed on them by the limited surface area of the land encumbered a revolution of both labour and the production process, similar to the one observable in the factories.[16] As the German economist Werner Sombart observed at the beginning of the twentieth century, the use of fossil resources in industry enabled it:

> to break down the production process into its individual components and to order the operation in such a way that the individual sub-processes are carried out side by side or, this being no different,

13 E. A. Wrigley, *Poverty, Progress and Population* (Cambridge: Cambridge University Press, 2004), 76 and 85.

14 Andreas Malm, *Fossil Capital: The Rise of Steam Power and the Roots of Global Warming* (London: Verso, 2016), 223–48.

15 Harry Braverman, *Labor and Monopoly Capital: The Degradation of Work in the 20th Century* (New York: Monthly Review Press, 1974); Stephen Kern, *The Culture of Time and Space 1880–1914* (Cambridge, MA: Harvard University Press, 1983); Joshua B. Freeman, *Behemoth: A History of the Factory and the Making of the Modern World* (New York: W. W. Norton, 2018).

16 Susan A. Mann and James M. Dickinson, 'Obstacles to the Development of a Capitalist Agriculture', *J. Peasant Studies* 5 (1978), 466–81.

> at the same time. This happens, as we know, in every manufactory or factory, where at the same time the cotton bales are opened, the cotton is cleaned, roved, spun and the finished yarn is bleached and packed [...]. On the whole, the process is faster, and its overall duration is shortened [...]. In agriculture all of this is out of the question: both the total production process (from tilling to harvesting) is fixed in its duration, as well as its individual parts, which follow each other in a necessary, because natural, sequence. One cannot plough, sow and harvest at the same time (on the same crop).[17]

The resulting unevenness in the temporal and spatial regimes of agricultural production and industrial manufacturing was soon translated into the pervasive dichotomies and the conceptual teleologies that the nineteenth-century language of economic progress provided.[18] Pitting industrial manufacturing on the side of 'modernity' against agricultural production on the side of 'tradition', this mode of thought constructed farming as the 'other' in industrial societies by what the anthropologist Johannes Fabian calls 'temporal distancing' and a 'denial of coevalness'.[19] However, out of such conceptual dichotomies arose not only the assertion of difference, but also, and probably even more importantly, a new 'horizon of expectation'.[20] For agriculture to march in sync with industrial progress, it had to become industry-like. Integrating agriculture into the realm of an industrial society thus required both its subordination under the hegemonic conceptions of industrial progress and its involvement in the use of the same resource base that had shaped manufacturing industry since the times of the thermo-industrial revolution.[21]

2.2 From an agrarian-industrial knowledge society ...

By the 1870s, however, a growing number of farmers and agricultural observers concluded that the idiosyncrasies of agricultural production must also be taken into account, because many of the industrially

17 Werner Sombart, *Die deutsche Volkswirtschaft im neunzehnten Jahrhundert und im Anfang des 20. Jahrhunderts*, 5th edn (Berlin: Georg Bondi, 1921), 344.

18 Peter Wagner, 'Autonomy in History: Teleology in Nineteenth-Century European Social and Political Thought', in *Historical Teleologies in the Modern World*, Henning Trüper, Dipesh Chakrabarty and Sanjay Subrahmanyam (eds) (London: Bloomsbury, 2015), 323–38.

19 Johannes Fabian, *Time and the Other: How Anthropology Makes its Object* (New York: Columbia University Press, 2002), 30–1.

20 Reinhart Koselleck, *Futures Past: On the Semantics of Historical Time* (New York: Columbia University Press, 2004), 255–75.

21 Peter Moser and Tony Varley, 'The State and Agricultural Modernisation in the Nineteenth and Twentieth Centuries in Europe', in *Integration through Subordination: The Politics of Agricultural Modernisation in Industrial Europe*, Peter Moser and Tony Varley (eds) (Turnhout: Brepols, 2013), 13–39.

inspired schemes for modernising farming ran up against the specific logics of agricultural production. The manifold attempts to introduce the steam engine in agriculture, for instance, were, if not a downright failure, at least only a very partial success. To keep the heavy steam engine going in the fields required nearly as many horses and oxen for transporting coal and water as had been made obsolete in the process of ploughing. The distribution and successful application of steam engines in agriculture were limited to activities in the farmyard like threshing. In other words, the power of the steam engine was not used to facilitate the production process itself, but, just as in industry, for the stationary transformation of a product: in this case, cereals into grain and straw.[22] Thus, the use of the steam engine in agriculture proved to be advantageous only for stationary work. It failed to revolutionise agricultural fieldwork that required a much more mobile, adaptable and flexible source of power. Even Karl Kautsky, who was otherwise convinced that agriculture would henceforward develop in the wake of industrial development, acknowledged in his 1899 classic *The Agrarian Question*, that the introduction of motorised machinery in agriculture faced more hurdles than the motorisation of manufacturing in industry because 'the industrial workplace, the factory, is an artificial creation, adapted to the requirements of the machine' whereas in agriculture 'most machines have to work in and adapt to natural surroundings'.[23]

It was the challenge of adapting to heterogeneous, weather-dependent and rapidly changing natural surroundings that was not met by agricultural machine engineering for a long time. Consequently, neither the steam engine nor early combustion motors replaced draft animals in agriculture to any significant degree. Quite the contrary: at the same time as contemporaries heralded the 'age of steam' and witnessed the rise of a 'machine age', working animals experienced their apotheosis on the farms (and, for a few decades, in the transport systems of cities).[24] Whereas the technological exploitation of fossil resources gradually displaced working animals from factory production and long-distance transportation, they continued to perform a wide variety of tasks in other areas of social life, especially in rural areas. Their numbers on farms rose significantly until the 1930s, and in some regions until the mid-twentieth century. Indeed,

22 David Goodman, Bernardo Sorj and John Wilkinson, *From Farming to Biotechnology: A Theory of Agro-Industrial Development* (Oxford: Basil Blackwell, 1987), 21.

23 Karl Kautsky, *The Agrarian Question: In Two Volumes* (London: Pluto Press edn, 1988), 32.

24 Ann Norton Greene, *Horses at Work: Harnessing Power in Industrial America* (Cambridge: Cambridge University Press, 2008); Peter Moser and Andreas Wigger, *Working Animals: Hidden Modernisers Made Visible*. ARH/ERHFA Video Essay No. 1, Bern, 2022. https://ruralfilms.eu/ruralfilms/video-essays/working-animals (accessed 22 September 2023).

the mechanisation of agriculture in the nineteenth and in the first half of the twentieth century depended much more on the muscular power of animals (and human beings) than on the consumption of coal and petrol.[25] As one keen observer noted in an American newspaper in 1872: 'Our talk has been for so many years of the railroad and steamboat and telegraph, as the great "agents of progress", that we have come almost totally to overlook the fact that our dependence on the horse has grown almost *pari passu* with our dependence on steam'.[26]

Such reasoning was emblematic for the rise of the agrarian-industrial knowledge society that shaped the relations between agriculture and industrial culture from the 1870s to the 1940s. In this period an ensemble of actors, institutions, discourses and practices began to address agrarian questions not solely from a perspective that emphasised farming's alleged deficiencies in comparison to industrial production but tried to accommodate agriculture's specificities with the demands of the industrial age. From this constellation emerged a variety of contested and hybrid forms of knowledge that were highly significant in shaping agriculture's transformation in industrial-capitalist societies. Thus, the knowledge regime emanating in this period was characterised by myriad endeavours to accommodate agricultural production to the expectations of industrial modernity, while simultaneously respecting agriculture's specificities, especially its anchoring in the biosphere. This became the core epistemic feature of the agrarian-industrial knowledge societies on both sides of the Atlantic.[27]

Again, the topic of mechanisation is instructive in this regard as disenchantment with attempts to use steam and combustion engines in agricultural production by no means led to an abandonment of efforts to motorise agriculture. On the contrary, machine engineers and farmers were busy developing agricultural machinery that was suitable for the varying and heterogeneous conditions of agriculture from the last quarter of the nineteenth century onwards.[28] At the very same time, however, the increasing importance of working animals intensified the practical and

25 Juri Auderset and Hans-Ulrich Schiedt, 'Arbeitstiere: Aspekte animalischer Traktion in der Moderne', *Traverse* 2 (2021), 27–42.

26 'The Position of the Horse in Modern Society', in *The Nation*, 31 October 1872.

27 Justus Hillebrand, 'To Know the Land with Hands and Minds: Negotiating Agricultural Knowledge in Late-Nineteenth-Century New England and Westphalia' (PhD diss., University of Maine 2021); Juri Auderset and Peter Moser, 'Exploring Agriculture in the Age of Industrial Capitalism: Swiss Farmers and Agronomists in North America and the Transnational Entanglements of Agricultural Knowledge', *Agricultural History* 96 (2022), 91–127.

28 Deborah Fitzgerald, 'Technology and Agriculture in Twentieth-Century America', in *A Companion to American Technology*, Carroll Pursell (ed.) (Malden: Blackwell, 2008), 69–82.

scientific preoccupation with these 'living motors'. While the endeavours to develop suitable motorised technologies struggled with the diversities of soil, weather and topographies, farmers, agronomists, veterinary surgeons and animal breeders began to conceptualise animals not only as producers of milk and meat for human and animal consumption but, simultaneously, also as 'prime movers' in agricultural production. The body and mind of the multifunctional draft animals became an 'epistemic object', worthy of elaborate and sometimes expensive observations, studies and scientific experimentations.[29] Breeders began to collect data concerning the ancestry of the animals, kept records on their performance, applied information processing procedures, statistics and theories of inheritance for selective breeding and thus increased the average weight, height and pulling power of draft animals along with simultaneously increasing their milk and meat production. Veterinary surgeons and agronomists analysed the physiology, anatomy and motion of their bodies, and tried to improve their versatility and the relationship of energy incorporated in feed and exhausted by work. The farming population sharpened its long-established hermeneutic culture of observation of the behaviour of the animals, often crediting them with qualities reserved in industrial circles for human beings, such as character, memory and capacities to learn. In short, the farm became a crucial site of observation and an important intersection of scientific and tacit knowledge production regarding the animal as an 'intelligent' and variable energy source for increasing and facilitating agricultural production. Working animals were by no means simply a source of power to be replaced by steam engines, locomotives, electric streetcars, automobiles, tractors and combine harvesters. They became polyvalent and versatile agricultural 'working companions'[30] and, as such, factors of agricultural modernisation itself. Animal-powered agriculture 'was a great modernising force', as Edgerton reminds us.[31]

In agricultural production from the 1870s until the middle of the twentieth century, working animals, steam engines, combustion and electric motors were thus 'technologies in tension'.[32] The history of working animals and motors in this period is less a history geared towards

29 Juri Auderset and Hans-Ulrich Schiedt, 'Die Vermessung des animalischen Motors. Körpergrössen, Zugkraft und Metabolismus der Arbeitstiere, 1800–1950', *Body Politics* 10 (2022), 57–87.

30 Peter Moser, 'Working Animals – A Historical Approach', in *Draft Animals in the Past, Present and Future*, Claus Kropp and Lena Zoll (eds) (Heidelberg: Propylaeum, 2022), 129–36.

31 David Edgerton, *The Shock of the Old: Technology and Global History Since 1900* (London: Profile, 2019), 34.

32 Gijs Mom and David A. Kirsch, 'Technologies in Tension: Horses, Electric Trucks, and the Motorization of American Cities', *Technology and Culture* 42 (2001), 489–518.

replacement than one of the plural uses of differently available and differently reliable sources of power. It is thus a history of simultaneity, interaction and complementarity of human, animal and motor energy. It is revealing for the character of the agrarian-industrial knowledge regime that the discourse on the farm power question was by no means structured by an antagonistic pattern that pitted the draft animals against the motor or by one-dimensional future-orientated narratives that heralded the overcoming of the animal's muscular force by fossil fuels. Rather, animals and motors were conceptualised as complementary tools. Farmers and agronomists distinguished between operations more suitable for motorised machinery and others that required the brains and bodies of working animals or humans. In this sense, farmers were – to use Claude Lévi-Strauss' concept – in many ways 'bricoleurs' who pragmatically combined different forms of energy provision because they were aware of the heterogeneous and changing conditions of their work, which in turn required versatile and adaptive strategies.[33] This intellectual culture of distinguishing the properties of different kinds of natural resources and to value a certain source of energy in relation to the tasks to be completed and to the specific conditions under which work had to be done is one of the leitmotifs that permeates the discourse on mechanisation and motorisation in the period of the agrarian-industrial knowledge society.

2.3 … to an industrial-agrarian knowledge society

In the post-war years, however, the relations between agricultural production and the hegemony of industrial culture shifted again, as it had in the period before the 1870s, towards a one-sided orientation on the industrial paradigm. Reflections on the specific material logics of biotic resources, which were crucial in the era of the agrarian-industrial knowledge society, rapidly vanished from agronomic discourses, especially from the textbooks of agricultural economics, giving way to a far-reaching embrace of what came to be called 'industrial' agriculture as part of a general perception of modernity. The voices that insisted on continuing to differentiate between the implications of the use of living and the consumption of mineral resources were pushed to the margins or, in agronomic literature, to the footnotes, as becomes clear from Brewster's article quoted above. Thus, the *agrarian-industrial* knowledge society mutated into an *industrial-agrarian* knowledge society. In sharp contrast to the earlier knowledge regime, the epistemic consensus now rested on the assumption that there were no significant differences in the resource bases of industry and agriculture. In the course of this epistemic transition,

33 Claude Lévi-Strauss, *La pensée sauvage* (Paris: Plon, 1962), 26.

a faith in scientific progress and technological advancement along the lines of industrial manufacturing spread through industrialised societies in Western and Eastern Europe alike.[34] Under the specific geopolitical conditions of the Cold War, moreover, this conception of a universally valid modernisation as the cure to all possible ills soon translated into suggestions for the agricultural and rural development of the so-called Global South.[35] The 'belief – in the face of contrary evidence – in the redemptive power of science and economic growth' permeated what came to be called the Green Revolution,[36] giving rise to a world-wide version of agricultural progress that James C. Scott labelled 'high modernist agriculture'.[37]

To be sure, this vision of agricultural change originated in the middle of the nineteenth century when books with titles like *The ... peasant as he should be, and is not, and how he is and should not be* were first published.[38] This wishful thinking has a long history and has fuelled attempts to integrate agriculture into industrial capitalism for decades, but – as we have seen – in the age of the agrarian-industrial knowledge society from the 1870s to the 1950s it resulted in a complex process of accommodation as the farming population and agronomists reflected on the different ecological implications of the use of biotic and the consumption of mineral resources. In the 1950s and 1960s, however, the unbroken desire to transform farms into industrial enterprises – or peasants into farmers – regained traction. Unlike in the middle of the nineteenth century, it now fell on more fertile ground because broadened access to fossil resources made it possible to replace working animals with motor-driven machines and the relatively cheap, seemingly unlimited availability of fertilisers

34 Arnd Bauerkämper, 'The Industrialization of Agriculture and its Consequences for the Natural Environment: An Inter-German Comparative Perspective', *Historical Social Research* 29 (2004), 124-49.

35 See the contributions in *Staging Growth: Modernization, Development, and the Global Cold War*, David C. Engerman, Nils Gilma and Mark H. Haefele (eds) (Amherst, MA: University of Massachusetts Press, 2003); Corinna R. Unger, 'Developing Rural Regions: Europe in the World', in *Living With the Land: Rural and Agricultural Actors in Twentieth Century Europe*, Liesbeth van de Grift, Dietmar Müller and Corinna R. Unger (eds) (Berlin: de Gruyter, 2022), 61–82.

36 Nick Cullather, 'Miracles of Modernization: The Green Revolution and the Apotheosis of Technology', *Diplomatic History* 28 (2004), 227–54, at 230. See also the contributions by Jonathan Harwood, Luis E. Blach, Madhumita Saha, Michele Sollai, as well as by Wilson Picado-Umaña and José A. Fernández Molina in this volume.

37 James C. Scott, *Seeing Like a State: How Certain Schemes to Improve the Human Condition Have Failed* (New Haven, CT: Yale University Press, 1998), 262.

38 [Zacharias Gysel], *Der Schaffhauser Bauer, wie er sein sollte, und wie er nicht ist, wie er ist, und wie er nicht sein sollte* (Schaffhausen: Brodtmann, 1854).

and pesticides made a level of uniformity and standardisation in farming feasible in a way that was without historical precedent.[39]

But this shift was not only based on the new access to the lithosphere (and accompanied by far-reaching ecological and social consequences): it also stemmed from fundamentally changing epistemic frameworks. As the farmer and author Wendell Berry observed in 1984, 'farmers and consumers alike dance to a tune called by the industrial economy'. The capabilities of farmers as producers of knowledge, based on 'skill, intelligence, experience and imagination' and sensitive to 'many possible solutions' that had to be applied 'with skill in the right place at the right time' were increasingly pushed to the margins as an 'industrial version of agriculture' became hegemonic. Under the conditions of this industrial way of seeing, Berry writes, 'farming brings the farmer annually, over and over again, to the same series of problems, to each one of which there is always the same generalized solution, and, therefore, that industry's solution can be simply and safely substituted for his solution'.[40]

From such a point of view, the farmer's knowledge, derived from the labour process working with living resources, was no longer perceived as an empowering intellectual force, but rather as an obstacle to the shaping of agriculture according to industrial models. Indeed, the post-war years saw a thrust towards conceiving the farm as a site of applied science and neoclassical business economics, reinforcing the belief that the idiosyncrasies of agricultural production could and should be overcome. This in turn opened the farm gates to the intrusion of 'expert' knowledge produced and disseminated by a growing number of agronomists, technicians, veterinary surgeons, inseminators, advisors, accountants and salesmen. But the farm gates opened not only for these experts and the knowledge needed to exploit the new production possibilities, but also for capital. One of the most significant changes in agricultural production after the Second World War was the displacement of production activities from the actual farm to upstream and downstream agribusinesses, a process that the Swiss agronomist Oskar Howald called

39 Christian Pfister, 'The "1950s Syndrome" and the Transition from a Slow-Going to a Rapid Loss of Global Sustainability', in *The Turning Points of Environmental History* (ed.) Frank Uekötter (Pittsburgh, PA: Pittsburgh University Press, 2010), 90–118; Peter Moser, 'Zugriff auf die Lithosphäre: Gestaltungspotenziale unterschiedlicher Energiegrundlagen in der agrarisch-industriellen Wissensgesellschaft', *Traverse* 3 (2013), 37–48; Céline Pessis, Sezin Topçu and Christophe Bonneuil (eds), *Une autre histoire des 'Trente Glorieuses': Modernisation, contestations et pollutions dans la France d'après-guerre* (Paris: La Découverte, 2013).

40 Wendell Berry, 'Whose Head Is the Farmer Using? Whose Head is Using the Farmer?', in *Meeting the Expectations of the Land: Essays in Sustainable Agriculture and Stewardship*, Wes Jackson, Wendell Berry and Bruce Colman (eds) (San Francisco, CA: North Point Press 1984), 23 and 25.

the 'dis-integration' of the farm.[41] Instead of reproducing a substantial part of the means of production on the farm, farmers were now increasingly forced to purchase them as commodities supplied by private enterprises. This not only altered the relative positions of capital and labour in agriculture, but also necessitated the active intervention of the state in backing the farmer's need for capital since agricultural re-production was (still) not attractive enough for private capitalists to invest in.[42] In sum, agriculture in the 1950s and 1960s witnessed parallel to its dramatically increasing dependence on fossil fuels and far-reaching social and economic disruptions, a significant epistemic shift away from an intellectual occupation with the temporal and spatial logics of living resources towards a 'voice of decontextualized rationality'[43] that saw in agricultural practice little more than the management of an 'industrial unit' detached from its embeddedness in specific ecological, social and cultural contexts.

These changes were part of a broader shift towards a 'dematerialization of the economic discipline'.[44] Peter Rieder, professor of agricultural economics at the Swiss Technical University (ETH) in Zürich wrote in hindsight about the 1960s: 'We all learned neoclassical economics and mathematics for economists' and became 'model builders'.[45] The abstracting logic of constructing models serving the allegedly 'rational' decision-making of farmers pushed considerations of the material bases of agricultural production to the margins. Plants, animals or the soil and their differing potentials and limitations disappeared from mainstream economic theory and from agricultural economics alike.[46] Agricultural

41 Oskar Howald, 'Betrachtungen zur Abgrenzung des Geltungsbereiches des Landwirtschaftsgesetzes von 1951', *Agrarpolitische Revue* 20 (1963/4), 460–1. On this process see also Jack R. Kloppenburg Jr, *First the Seed: The Political Economy of Plant Biotechnology, 1492–2000* (Madison, WI: University of Wisconsin Press, 2004), 31.

42 Søren Mau, *Stummer Zwang: Eine marxistische Analyse der ökonomischen Macht im Kapitalismus* (Berlin: Dietz, 2021), 263.

43 Jack R. Kloppenburg Jr, 'Social Theory and the De/Reconstruction of Agricultural Science. Local Knowledge for an Alternative Agriculture', in *Geographic Thought: A Praxis Perspective,* George Henderson and Marvin Waterstone (eds) (London: Routledge, 2009), 248.

44 Jean-Baptiste Fressoz and Christophe Bonneuil, 'Growth unlimited: The idea of infinite growth from fossil capitalism to green capitalism', in *History of the Future of Economic Growth: Historical Roots of Current Debates in Sustainable Degrowth,* Iris Borowy and Matthias Schmelzer (eds) (London: Routledge, 2017), 57.

45 Peter Rieder, 'Bauern und Dörfer im Berggebiet – Realität, Theorien und Modelle', *Yearbook of Socioeconomics in Agriculture* (2012), 11–30.

46 Juri Auderset and Peter Moser, 'Permanenz des Unbehagens: Epistemischer Wandel und agrarpolitische Re-Regulierungen im Zeitalter des Neoliberalismus', in *Zwang zur Freiheit: Krise und Neoliberalismus in der Schweiz,*

economy too was now conceptualised as a totality of exclusively monetary relations linking production, distribution and consumption. Re-conceived as such, economic activities were severed from their embeddedness in material resources and, therefore, from any material limits to economic growth. In this dematerialised conception of the economy, the hegemony of the 'growth paradigm' set in.[47] As Timothy Mitchell puts it:

> Older ways of thinking about wealth were based upon physical processes that suggested limits to growth: the expansion of cities and factories, the colonial enlargement of territory, the accumulation of gold reserves, the growth of population and absorption of migrants, the exploitation of new mineral reserves, increasing volumes of trade in commodities. All these were spatial and material processes that had physical limits [...] [From the 1930s on], the leading contributions to the academic formulation of the economy [...] paid no attention to the depletion of energy. The economics of growth of the 1950s and 1960s could conceive of long-run growth as something unrestrained by the availability of energy.[48]

This scientific 'generation of ignorance'[49] towards the material basis of economic processes in general and agricultural processes in particular had far-reaching implications, not only for environmental degradation, but also for historical narratives of agricultural change in the post-war era. The rise of what Nicholas Georgescu-Roegen termed 'growthmania'[50] coincided with the 'third agricultural revolution', the most critical feature of which was the newly gained access to the vast but finite fuel reserves of the lithosphere. In other words, since the 1950s food production, processing and transport are largely, albeit never fully, based on the consumption of the same fossil fuel reserves that the manufacturing industry has relied on since the early days of the thermo-industrial revolution. The growing use of fossil resources to fuel motorised machinery, combined with the cultivation of high-yielding varieties that depended on massive inputs of fertilisers and pesticides, not only led to a sharp drop in demand for human and animal labour on farms and unprecedented increases in production for the markets, but also to a range of environmental degradations such

Regula Ludi, Matthias Ruoss and Leena Schmitter (eds) (Zurich: Chronos, 2018), 37–60.

47 Matthias Schmelzer, 'The Growth Paradigm: History, Hegemony, and the Contested Making of Economic Growthmanship', *Ecological Economics* 118 (2015), 262–71.

48 Timothy Mitchell, 'Carbon Democracy', *Economy and Society* 38 (2009), 417–18.

49 Jan Douwe van der Ploeg, *The New Peasantries: Struggles for Autonomy and Sustainability in an Era of Empire and Globalization* (London: Earthscan, 2009), 17.

50 Nicholas Georgescu-Roegen, 'Inequality, Limits and Growth from a Bioeconomic Viewpoint', *Review of Social Economy* 35 (1977), 372.

as loss of biodiversity, the nitrification of groundwater, as well as soil erosion and soil compression.[51] However, the environmental consequences of these agricultural modernisation programmes were in general either ignored, exculpated in the name of economic growth, or turned into collateral damages that the imagined scientific and technological progress would take care of sometime in the future.

The post-war knowledge regime had thus unburdened itself of the need to think about the idiosyncrasies of different natural resources and their respective logics. Within this epistemic framework, it became increasingly impossible to think of the modernisation of agriculture in any way other than in terms of its industrialisation. In practice, however, this continually created ecological fault-lines and social dislocations and continues to do so today. They remind us that an agriculture based on the sustainable use of biotic resources inevitably comes into conflict at the material level with industrial capitalist expectations of growth and efficiency fed by a mode of production based on the consumption of fossil and mineral resources. These tensions may be temporarily obscured by the ideology of dominant development narratives and short-term technological fixes, but they keep haunting us in the agricultural realities of our present. Looking back at the agricultural revolutions of past centuries, we might recall Walter Benjamin's words: 'Marx says that revolutions are the locomotive of world history. But perhaps it is quite otherwise. Perhaps revolutions are an attempt by the passengers of the train – namely the human race – to activate the emergency brake'.[52]

51 Frank Uekötter, *Die Wahrheit ist auf dem Feld: Eine Wissensgeschichte der deutschen Landwirtschaft* (Göttingen: Vandenhoeck & Ruprecht, 2010).

52 Walter Benjamin, quoted from Michael Löwy, *Fire Alarm: Reading Walter Benjamin's 'On the Concept of History'*, (London: Verso, 2005), 66–7.

3

Inventing new seeds: genetics research and Iberian connections under the dictatorships

Dulce Freire

Having access to the best seeds for cultivation has always been an ambition of farmers. Superior seeds generated expectations of better harvests, the main objective of agriculture.[1] For millennia, the selection of the best seeds for sowing was almost exclusively done by farmers who developed very specific skills based, above all, on the morphological characteristics of each plant or fruit.[2] From at least the eighteenth century onwards, private companies invested in the crossing, selection and controlled multiplication of seeds, promising to offer the best genes to increase the quantity and quality of harvests. But it was in the twentieth century that the recognition of the relevance of genetics, and in particular plant genetics, boosted the expansion of private and public systems of research and applied science. Since the early years of the twentieth century, developments in genetic research applied to plants have reinforced the

1 The research for this chapter was developed in the framework of the 'ReSEED Project – Rescuing seeds' heritage: engaging in a new framework of agriculture and innovation since the eighteenth century', with Dulce Freire as Principal Investigator. It has received funding from the European Research Council under the European Union's Horizon 2020 research and innovation programme (DOI 10.3030/760090) and is hosted by the University of Coimbra at the Centre of Interdisciplinary Studies (UIDB/00460/2025). This chapter reflects only the author's views. The European Commission and European Research Council Executive Agency are not responsible for any use that may be made of the information it contains.

2 Focused on the Iberian Peninsula, the research carried out by the ReSEED project team has been identifying the dynamics of dissemination of knowledge and practices connected with crops, mainly from the fifteenth century onwards. See https://reseed.uc.pt/ for a full list of the publications arising out the project (accessed 31 December 2024).

promise *to invent* the most productive seeds ever offered to farmers. In fact, attempts to achieve this objective entailed significant changes in the strategies followed up until then, promoting dynamics that continue to determine the seeds that grow each year in fields around the world.[3]

Based on the cases of Portugal and Spain, this chapter discusses how the farmers' ancestral objectives were reformulated through the development of knowledge of genetics and institutional practices during the twentieth century. In the West, public education and science systems began to be built in the nineteenth century and were consolidated during the twentieth century. For genetics, and following Bonneuil and Thomas, three regimes can be established: between the end of the nineteenth century and the Second World War when the expansion of the space of public research was underway; from the end of the Second World War to the 1970s, when public investment in research and its application to agriculture reached its apogee; and since the 1980s, which has seen a reduction in the participation of public science and technology systems in genetics innovation.[4] The studies carried out for Portugal and Spain allow us to understand how the development of national scientific and innovation organisations follows (or does not follow), these international trends.[5] However, the interactions between scientists from these neigh-

3 The bibliography on these issues is abundant, offering different and complementary perspectives. See in particular Jack R. Kloppenburg Jr, *First the Seed: The Political Economy of Plant Biotechnology, 1492–2000* (Madison, WI: University of Wisconsin Press, 2004); Christophe Bonneuil, Staffan Müller-Wille and Hans Jörg Rheinberger, *A Cultural History of Heredity, IV, Heredity in the Century of the Gene* (Berlin: Max Planck Institute for the History of Science, 2008); Jonathan Harwood, *Europe's Green Revolution and Its Successors: The Rise and Fall of Peasant-friendly Plant Breeding* (London: Routledge, 2012); Christophe Bonneuil and Frédéric Thomas, *Semences, une histoire politique: amélioration des plantes, agriculture et alimentation en France depuis la Seconde Guerre mondiale* (Paris: Èditions Charles Léopold Mayer, 2012); Tiago Saraiva, *Fascist Pigs: Technoscientific Organisms and the History of Fascism* (Cambridge, MA: MIT Press, 2018); Helen Anne Curry, *Evolution Made to Order: Plant Breeding and Technological Innovation in Twentieth-Century America* (Chicago, IL: University of Chicago Press 2019).

4 Christophe Bonneuil and Frédéric Thomas, *Gènes, pouvoirs et profits: recherche publique et régimes de production des savoirs de Mendel aux OGM* (Montpellier: IRD Editions, 2009).

5 Historically, the organisations that built these systems in Portugal and Spain combined civil society and state initiatives. The available studies are very diverse, produced mainly within the scope of Economic History, Institutional and Political History and History of Science. They include AAVV, *Estação Agronómica Nacional. 50 anos de atividade 1936–1986* (Oeiras: Estação Agronómica Nacional, 1986); Antonio Bernárdez and Miguel Cabo, 'Ciencia y Dictadura: la investigación agronómica en Galicia durante el primer franquismo (1936–1950)', *Noticiario de Historia Agraria* 12 (1996), 119–39; José Manuel Sánchez Ron, *Cincel, Martillo y Piedra. Historia de la ciencia*

bouring countries are less known. It has also not yet been fully assessed how these Iberian scientific contacts mutually influenced the design of public laboratories and the results of the scientific research carried out in them. For these reasons, this chapter analyses how the Portuguese and Spanish public scientific and pedagogic systems responded to the new challenges posed to plant genetics during the twentieth century. The analysis is mostly focused on the two or three decades after the Second World War, contributing to an evaluation of how in these decades the 'regime of planned genetic progress'[6] took place in Portugal and Spain. In fact, those decades were crucial for the international expansion of plant genetics, particularly through the hegemony of the Green Revolution model that was gaining ground in the context of Western Europe's agricultural and food recovery.[7]

Looking to the Iberian Peninsula allows us to understand how the international dynamics of the consolidation of genetics knowledge and its international epistemic communities intersect with national ones. By studying plants, geneticists form part of the natural sciences, which has been considered one of the most visible scientific fields and deserving of attention from public authorities. Since the fifteenth century, privileged

---

en España (siglos XIX y XX) (Madrid: Taurus, 1999); *Historia del Ministerio de Agricultura, 1900–2008. Política agraria y pesquera de España,* Ricardo Robledo (ed.) (Madrid: Ministerio de Medio Ambiente y Medio Rural y Marino, 2011); *Los orígenes de la Genética en España,* Milagros Candela (ed.) (Madrid: Sociedad Estatal de Conmemoraciones Culturales, 2003); AAVV, *Internacionalização da Ciência: Internacionalismo Científico* (Lisboa: Caleidoscópio, 2015); Maria Fernanda Rollo *et al.*, *Ciência, cultura e língua em Portugal no século XX. Da Junta de Educação Nacional ao Instituto Camões* (Lisboa: Instituto Camões e Imprensa Nacional Casa da Moeda, 2012); Amélia Branco and Ester Gomes da Silva, 'Growth, Institutional Change and Innovation, 1820–1930', in *An Agrarian History of Portugal, 1000–2000: Economic Development on the European Frontier,* Dulce Freire and Pedro Lains (eds) (Leiden: Brill, 2017), 217–44; Tiago Brandão, Maria Fernanda Rollo and Maria Inês Queiroz, 'A Associação Portuguesa para o Progresso das Ciências (1917–1974): um resgate de sua trajetória histórica', *Estudos Ibero-Americanos* 49 (2023): e44539–e44539.

6 Bonneuil and Thomas, *Gènes, pouvoirs et profits,* 26.

7 *Agriculturas e innovación tecnológica en la Península Ibérica (1946–1975),* Daniel Lanero and Dulce Freire (eds) (Madrid: Ministerio Medio Ambiente, Medio Rural y Marino, 2011); *War, Agriculture, and Food: Rural Europe from the 1930s to the 1950s,* Paul Brassley, Yves Segers and Leen Van Molle (eds) (London: Routledge, 2012); *Integration through Subordination: The Politics of Agricultural Modernisation in Industrial Europe,* Peter Moser and Tony Varley (eds) (Turnhout: Brepols, 2013); *Agriculture in the Age of Fascism: Authoritarian Technocracy and Rural Modernization, 1922–1945,* Lourenzo Fernández Prieto, Juan Pan-Montojo and Miguel Cabo (eds) (Turnhout: Brepols Publishers, 2014); *Agriculture in Capitalist Europe, 1945–1960: From Food Shortages to Food Surpluses,* Carin Martiin, Juan Pan-Montojo and Paul Brassley (eds) (London: Routledge, 2016).

connections with the exotic flora of other continents have placed the Iberian Peninsula on the routes of international knowledge regarding nature. From the nineteenth century onwards, those legacies of knowledge and practices were integrated in various ways into disciplines that were being defined, particularly biology and agronomy. Since 1900, with the rediscovery of the so-called Mendel's laws, genetics has become one of the most important challenges for biology and agronomy.

This study argues that Iberian scientists associated with genetics research during the twentieth century, particularly in those twenty or thirty years following the Second World War, found themselves in a framework marked by contradictory trends. On the one hand, the scientific research that they carried out called for integration into international scientific circuits, renewing connections to the epistemic communities in which they had long participated.[8] On the other hand, the consolidation of right-wing nationalist regimes in both Portugal and Spain[9] made it difficult both to establish institutional ties between neighbouring countries and to make connections with peers in these international epistemic communities. However, during the 1940s, a diplomatic rapprochement became strategic for both countries, in which scientists were also called upon to play a role.

Between political strategies and scientific interests, the joint activities carried out by Portuguese and Spanish geneticists during the dictatorships can be considered as a kind of scientific diplomacy.[10] This is because 'ideally, it is attuned by genuine scientific interests, but still, it primarily follows strategic political goals'.[11] From the 1940s, Spain adopted several

8 AAVV, *Internacionalização da Ciência*; Juan Pan-Montojo, 'De los aficionados a los "profesionales" de la agricultura: España, 1793–1940', *Revista Encuentros Latinoamericanos*, segunda época, 3 (2019), 171–93.

9 Between the 1930s and 1970s, Portugal and Spain were governed by a variety of fascist dictatorships, calling themselves Estado Novo/Estado Nuevo (New State). In Portugal, the main leaders were the university law professors Oliveira Salazar (1933–68) and Marcelo Caetano (1968–74). In Spain, after a Civil War (1936–9), General Francisco Franco led the country until his death in 1975. Thus, in the mid-1970s, both countries began the process of democratisation: Portugal due to the Revolution of 25 April 1974; Spain due to the death of the dictator. In 1986, both countries became members of the European Economic Community.

10 More precisely as a scientific proto-diplomacy, following the authors who emphasise the need to use a recent concept with precision; Tim Flink and Nicolas Rüffin, 'The Current State of the Art of Science Diplomacy', in *Handbook on Science and Public Policy*, Dagmar Simon, Stefan Kuhlmann, Julia Stamm and Weert Canzler (eds) (Cheltenham: Edward Elgar, 2019), 104–21, at 105. In 2010, the American Association for the Advance of Science and the Royal Society of London published a joint definition of Diplomacy for Science.

11 Flink and Rüffin, 'The Current State of the Art of Science Diplomacy', 106.

strategies to reposition itself within the international sphere. It is argued in this study that the promotion of an Iberian journal was one of the strategies used by the Spanish government and researchers in the broad field of the natural sciences to advance this international diplomatic and scientific repositioning.

This chapter is divided into two parts. The first one is dedicated to the scientific and political backgrounds to the construction of publicly funded scientific systems in Portugal and Spain. This approach seeks above all to follow the individuals and organisations that stood out in the trajectory of plant genetics within the framework of the dictatorships' public scientific systems in each country. The second one is focused on the journal *Genética Ibérica,* (Iberian Genetics) launched in 1949 and closed in 1989. This publication brought together Portuguese and Spanish scientists from the various disciplines concerned with the study of flora and fauna. Our analysis focuses on the circumstances in which the journal was established and its activity during its early decades of publication, showing, how it worked as an instrument of scientific and political intervention that fulfilled several objectives. Thus, moving from the general to the particular, this chapter allows us to conclude that these epistemic communities managed to reconcile scientific cooperation strategies with the diplomatic interests of each country. In fact, these strategies for collaboration between scientists from Portugal and Spain renewed relationships that had been observed since the beginning of the twentieth century, even at a time when nationalist discourses seemed more hostile to it. Future investigations will help to fully evaluate these strategies' scientific and political impacts.

3.1 Institutional trajectories of Iberian plant genetics

Since the end of the nineteenth century, concepts of food self-sufficiency had been becoming hegemonic, focusing the political decisions of different Iberian governments on increasing internal food supplies. Even though there were those who aimed to value the regional comparative advantages of the Iberian Peninsula and use them to consolidate positions in international trade, these proposals were losing political weight.[12] Throughout the twentieth century, the state expanded its mechanisms of intervention in the economy, promoting protectionist policies until at least the 1980s.

12 Dulce Freire, 'Produzir mais e melhor. Estado, agricultura y consumo alimentario en Portugal (1926–1974)', *Ayer* 83 (2011), 101–26; Juan Pan-Montojo, 'International Institutions and European Agriculture. From the IIA to the FAO', in *Agriculture in Capitalist Europe, 1945–1960,* Martiin, Pan-Montojo and Brassley (eds), 171–93.

The actions of economic protectionism reinforced by the state intersected with the growing belief in science as a way of finding solutions to solve national problems. The creation of public services to promote teaching, research or the transfer of knowledge associated with agricultural and livestock production for human consumption fell within the state's concern with the vital conditions for ensuring the internal supply of essential goods. In the Iberian countries, the creation of these public services began in the mid-nineteenth century, although provision was uneven in terms of both the geographic areas and products covered.[13]

Therefore, the support given by both Iberian states to research into plant genetics must be understood either as a way to explore available resources to increase the national production of food or as a political strategy for the infrastructural consolidation of the modern state. In this context, public services associated with the application of science and technology to agriculture and livestock acquired great relevance in the political disputes that shook both countries in the decades at the end of the nineteenth and beginning of the twentieth century. For right-wing governments, political and economic nationalism was connected with the support of genetics for increasing domestic supply capacity.[14]

In Portugal and Spain the institutional capacity to undertake research in genetics become more evident during the first decades of the twentieth century, with public investment to train and employ scientists and to create and finance laboratories. However, in the 1930s, the consolidation of the dictatorships took place with the removal of many scientists and the destruction of much of this previous infrastructure. In Portugal, the beginning of the rebuilding of scientific institutions took place soon after in the 1930s, but in Spain, the impacts of the Civil War (1936–9) postponed this reconstruction until the 1940s. The public scientific system created by the dictatorships dissatisfied even those who were its scientific and political advocates, but, to a large extent, it was this infrastructure that continued to serve as the basis for the reformulations that took place in the following decades, even under democracy. Focusing on genetics applied to agriculture, the organisational design of these public system bodies and the scientists who led this construction are presented below.

13 Lourenzo Fernández Prieto, *Labregos con ciencia: estado, sociedade e innovación tecnolóxica na agricultura galega, 1850–1939* (Santiago de Compostela: Xerais, 1992); Carmen Fernández Díez, 'Evolución histórica de la investigación agraria en España', *Historia Agraria* 22 (2000), 181–205; Dulce Freire, *Portugal e a terra. Itinerários de modernização da agricultura na segunda metade do seculo XX* (Doctoral dissertation, Lisboa: Faculdade de Ciências Sociais e Humanas/ Universidade Nova de Lisboa, 2007); *Historia del Ministerio de Agricultura, 1900–2008*, Robledo (ed.); Branco and Gomes da Silva, 'Growth, Institutional Change and Innovation, 1820–1930'.

14 Saraiva, *Fascist Pigs*.

Since the end of the nineteenth century, formal practices had been established that promised greater guarantees of productive viability for the seeds sown each year. This formalisation was part of the broader processes of defining standards associated with the dynamics of globalisation, which also extended to nature and agriculture.[15] Among the state's first institutional and scientific concerns was the ability to produce, select, multiply and certify cultivated seeds.

From the beginning of the twentieth century, with the rediscovery of the so-called Mendel's laws of heredity and research into chromosomes, developments in genetics promised to fulfil the ancestral ambition of offering farmers the most productive seeds. Although there may have been other trajectories of genetic research and application, as happened in France,[16] it appears that in Spain and Portugal, state-sponsored research privileged Mendelian genetics.

Public investment in the training of specialised human resources became visible in the first years of the twentieth century. Both countries financed the training of young scientists in agronomy in the most prestigious centres, particularly in Germany and the United States, but also in England, France and Sweden.[17] At the same time, laboratories were created in each country, promoting research at the national level.

In Spain, these periods abroad were coordinated and financed by the Junta de Ampliación de Estudios e Investigación Científicas (JAE; Board for the Expansion of Scientific Studies and Research), the JAE, an organisation dependent on the Ministry of Public Instruction created in 1907. The JAE expressed the spirit of 'regenerationism'; that is, an attempt at modernisation that permeated the intellectual environment of the time. It meant an enormous advance in the sciences in Spain, even though it had a rather centralised approach and paid relatively little attention to regional differences.[18]

With regard to genetics, a biology laboratory was first organised in the Museum of Natural Sciences (Madrid), where Antonio de Zulueta worked. He was the initiator of experimental research in that field in Spain, being interested mainly in basic research related to the mechanisms of inheritance. Later the JAE founded the Misión Biológica de Galicia (Biological Mission of Galicia), in 1921, which from its establishment until 1960, was

15 Jim Bingen and Lawrence Busch, *Agricultural Standards* (Amsterdam: Springer, 2006).

16 Christophe Bonneuil, 'Mendelism, Plant Breeding and Experimental Cultures: Agriculture and the Development of Genetics in France', *J. History of Biology* 39 (2006), 281–308.

17 Maria do Mar Gago, 'The Emergence of Genetics in Portugal: J. A. Serra at the Crossroads of Politics and Biological Communities (1936–1952)' (Masters dissertation, Lisbon: Faculdade de Ciência, Universidade de Lisboa, 2009); Ron, *Cincel, Martillo y Piedra.*

18 Sánchez Ron, *Cincel, Martillo y Piedra*, 171–211.

directed by Cruz Ángel Gallástegui Unamuno, and worked in genetics applied to cultivated plants and livestock.[19] These were the two leading centres for the study of genetics.[20] The JAE was fundamental in the development of genetics in Spain in the first decades of the twentieth century, in part because the discipline had little presence in the universities.

Aware that scientific organisations were being built in the neighbouring country, the establishment of the Portuguese Republic in 1910 opened opportunities for scientists to influence government decisions. During the First World War, a group of Portuguese specialists visited Madrid to learn about the functioning of the JAE.[21] After several attempts, the Portuguese Junta de Educação Nacional (JEN; National Education Board) was established in 1929. Although the character of the country's government changed in 1926, with the beginning of the military dictatorship that was the origin of the Estado Novo, the JEN was still imbued with the regenerating spirit of the liberal republic.

However, even without a body in charge of national coordination, there were Portuguese scientists who spent time abroad during the 1910s and 1920s.[22] Eduardo Lima Basto's contribution appears to have been essential in promoting international training in genetics. As a teacher and manager at the Instituto Superior de Agronomia (Higher Institute of Agronomy) in Lisborn, Lima Basto 'initiated this trend in our university education'.[23] The commitment of this prestigious agronomist and republican politician to genetic research must be understood within the context

19 In Spain, one of the pioneers of genetics was Cruz Gallástegui Unamuno, who, between 1914 and 1916, completed his higher education in France and Germany before moving to the USA in 1917. Miguel Cabo, 'O labor da Misión Biolóxica de Pontevedra ata 1936 e a reforma da agricultura galega en Cruz Gallástegui Unamuno', *Cuadernos de estudios gallegos* 44 (1997), 103–52.

20 Susana Pinar, 'The Emergence of Modern Genetics in Spain and the Effects of the Spanish Civil War (1936–1939) on its Development', *J. History of Biology* 35 (2002),111–48, at 112; Raquel Álvarez Peláez, 'La genética y la Junta para Ampliación de Estudios e Investigaciones Científicas', *Asclepio. Revista de Historia de la Medicina y de la Ciencia*, 59 (2007), 16 –80, at 169.

21 At this stage, the leading Portuguese figures were doctors who admired the Spaniard Santiago Ramón y Cajal, winner of the Nobel Prize in Physiology (1906), as a scientist and promoter of the JAE; Augusto Fitas and Maria de Fátima Nunes, 'Da Junta de Educação Nacional (JEN) ao IAC e à JNICT: organização da ciência e política científica', in *Ciência, tecnologia e medicina na construção de Portugal: Novos horizontes, IV, Século XX*, Ana Simões and Maria Paula Diogo (eds) (Lisboa: Tinta-da-China, 2021), 215–22.

22 For instance, Ruy Mayer (1888–1959). Drawing mainly on the French literature, Mayer had written one of the first dissertations presented in Portugal on Mendelian genetics; 'Biometric Methods and their applications on thrematology' (thesis presented to the Superior Institute of Agronomics of the Technical University of Lisbon, 1914). In 1915, Mayer went to study in the United States.

23 Maria do Mar Gago, 'Emergence of genetics in Portugal', 26.

of the long-standing concern to increase the quantity and quality of national food production.

Both the JAE in Spain and JEN in Portugal had, as a priority, the promotion of the international training of national academics and researchers, providing scholarships that financed stays in the most relevant centres of scientific innovation in each field. Among the hundreds of young people financed by these institutions who had the opportunity to work in Europe and the US,[24] geneticists were a minority, which reflects the marginal nature that genetics still had at this time. These organisations were extinguished by the dictatorships. In Portugal, the Estado Novo replaced the JEN in 1936, and the functions previously carried out by the JEN were handed over to the Instituto para a Alta Cultura (IAC; Institute for High Culture), which was a section of the new Junta Nacional de Educação (JNE; National Education Board). Although the designations were similar, the scientific and pedagogical project was very different.[25] In Spain, the JAE was extinguished by the victorious Francoism and replaced by the Consejo Superior de Investigaciones Científicas (CSIC) a few months after the war ended in 1939.

In the 1930s, the consolidation of dictatorial regimes of a fascist nature in both countries brought about a profound change in the organisations and leading figures in scientific research community. These changes were associated with the removal, for political reasons, of a number of scientists who had held important positions in previous decades, and also implied the reorganisation of institutions or the creation of new research centres. Many of the fellows who had obtained training abroad under the JAE and JEN, were dismissed and the organisation abolished.

In Portugal, the dictatorship's actions became more visible from 1935 onwards, with the enactment of laws that forced dozens of higher education teachers and researchers to leave their positions. They were forced to retire or were expelled from the public system, pushing some into exile. Among the scientists affected by political persecution were those responsible for the genetic research that was being carried out in laboratories and museums at the main Portuguese universities (Coimbra, Lisbon and Porto), which were emptied of important human capital accumulated over several decades.[26] Although this persecution of repub-

24 Among the JEN and JAE scholarship holders are two figures who were later prominent in the *Genética Ibérica* journal programme: the Portuguese scientist António de Sousa Câmara (a specialist in genetics and cytogenetics) and the Spaniard José María Albareda (a soil scientist).

25 Fitas and de Fátima Nunes, 'Da Junta de Educação Nacional (JEN) ao IAC e à JNICT'.

26 Among the thirty-three civil servants, military personnel and university professors dismissed in 1935 were Abel Salazar, Faculty of Medicine, University of Porto; Aurélio Quintanilha, Faculty of Sciences, University of Coimbra and Álvaro Isidro de Faria Lapa, Faculty of Medicine, University of

lican and liberal scientists did not completely remove them from political activities, it ended their contribution to the public science and innovation system that was under construction and that faced new challenges.[27]

The strategy of the Portuguese Estado Novo is also reflected in the reorganisation of the scientific and pedagogical infrastructure effected in 1936, which led to the extinction of several organisations created in previous decades. In addition to what happened with the JEN, specifically in the field of agronomy, in 1936 the Estação Agrária Central (Central Agrarian Station) was closed. This body reflected the republican ambition of combining research and agricultural education, expanding instruction in rural territories.[28] A social and economic research and intervention programme, which involved an integrative vision of agronomy was thus brought to an end.[29] The Central Agrarian Station was replaced by the Estação Agronómica Nacional (EAN; National Agronomic Station). Again, the nomenclature is similar, but not its programme. The EAN had a more centralised vision and focused on science applied to solving

---

Lisbon. Rita M. G. Correia, 'Contribuição para a história social da biotecnologia em Portugal' (Doctoral dissertation, Universidade de Lisboa, 2014), 10. In 1947, nine scientists were forced to leave the public organisations for which they worked for political reasons; Correra, 'Contribuição para a história social da biotecnologia em Portugal', 18.

27 From 1958 onwards, scientists from a number of different areas (including some genetic specialties) found support at the Calouste Gulbenkian Foundation, which created research centres and provided scholarships to study abroad; Dulce Freire, 'Modernising Ambitions: Agronomists in Action Between Dictatorship and Democracy (Portugal, 1957–1986)', in *Associations and Other Groups in Science: An Historical and Contemporary Perspective*, Ana Delicado (ed.) (Newcastle: Cambridge Scholars, 2013), 92–107; *Ciência, cultura e língua em Portugal no século XX*, Rollo *et al.* (eds), 253. Others left the country or moved away from science.

28 Some of the most prominent individuals were at the end of their careers (such as Joaquim Rasteiro, who died in 1933; Eduardo Lima Basto, who died in 1942). Others had a career marked by political persecution, such as Azevedo Gomes (a prestigious republican and last director of the National Agrarian Station, which was closed in 1936) and Henrique de Barros (an outstanding agronomist and opponent of the dictatorship) was removed from teaching at the Higher Institute of Agronomy for a period.

29 More than a discipline merely aimed at solving productivity problems, agronomy was understood as an instrument for improving living conditions in the countryside, being closely connected with Rural Sociology and Agrarian Economics; Dulce Freire, 'Portugal e a terra'; ead., 'Ensayos de Ingeniería Social: reforma agraria y modernización de la agricultura en las últimas décadas del Estado Novo (1954–1974)', in *Agriculturas e innovación tecnológica en la Península Ibérica*, Lanero and Freire (eds), 213–41; Frederico Ágoas, 'Saber e poder. Estado e investigação social agrária nos primórdios da sociologia em Portugal' (Doctoral dissertation, Faculdade de Ciências Sociais e Humanas, Universidade de Lisboa, 2015).

agricultural productivity, physiological and phytosanitary problems. In 1937, António de Sousa Câmara was appointed the first director of the EAN and remained in the position for twenty-three years. At the same time, he became one of the most prominent personalities in genetics and agronomy in Portugal and Spain.

In 1935, António de Sousa Câmara had created a small genetics laboratory at the Instituto Superior de Agronomia, where he was teaching this subject. It was in the experience of this laboratory that 'the idea of an expanded agronomic research centre germinated, later materialising in the National Agronomic Station'.[30] Not by chance, in 1937 a Department of Genetics and Cytology was created at EAN, headed by de Sousa Câmara, which became one of the most important areas of research in this organisation.

In these first years, two more individuals were also present at EAN who would be responsible for research centres that would be linked to collaboration with Spain in the following decades. One was Joaquim Vieira da Natividade, who had research interests in the cork oak and pomology, who headed the research centres focused on these areas located in Alcobaça (about 100 kilometres north of Lisbon). Another was Domingos Vitória Pires, who in 1942 created the Estação de Melhoramento de Plantas (Plant Improvement Station), located in Elvas (Alentejo region, close to the Spanish border in Extremadura). During the 1950s and 1960s, when he held senior positions in the Ministry of Economy, Vitória Pires did not neglect his research interests in genetics.[31]

In 1940 and in the following years, the new IAC reorganised or created around twenty centres dedicated to pure and applied research, mostly linked to universities.[32] As had happened under the JEN, those new infrastructures were necessary to welcome the dozens of scholarship holders who were returning from stays abroad.[33] These centres were not part of any formal national scientific research network and, in many cases, they may have had only limited institutional collaboration.

In Spain, the consolidation of the Francoist Estado Nuevo required a Civil War with catastrophic and prolonged effects. The war destroyed infrastructure, scientific results and collaborative networks, and brought about the political persecution of scientists. Many died in the conflict, others went into exile, contributing to the expansion of scientific systems

30 AAVV, *Estação Agronómica Nacional. 50 anos de atividade 1936–1986, VII*, 3.

31 Vitória Pires was appointed to the highest government positions in agriculture: undersecretary of state (1950–8) and secretary of state (1965–9). After the abolition of the Ministry of Agriculture in 1940, this area was integrated into the Ministry of Economy.

32 Fitas and de Fátima Nunes, "Da Junta de Educação Nacional (JEN) ao IAC e à JNICT', 227.

33 By the start of the Second World War, sixty scholarship holders had already returned to Portugal and more arrived in the following years; ibid., 227.

in other countries (Mexico, for example).[34] The implementation of the dictatorship led to the dismantling of the institutional structures that had supported science in previous decades, either with the closure of organisations (such as the JAE) or the loss of skills and competencies and funding, as was seen at the Natural History Museum (Madrid) and the Biological Mission of Galicia (Pontevedra). These organisations, which had gained recognition in the field of genetic research over previous decades, retained the same leaders and continued to exist formally, but now lacked scientists and the material conditions for research.[35]

Under Francoism, the reconfiguration of the Spanish public system of science and technology involved the creation of a network of state laboratories, which started as early as 1939. This network, which integrated some of the laboratories that had been created earlier (but not the universities), was CSIC. As has been demonstrated, the CSIC was constituted as a tool for political action for Francoism.[36] Despite its constraints and tensions, the CSIC covered different sciences and extended a network of research centres across several regions. As discussed below in the case of plant genetics, during its first decades, CSIC initiatives took on a double dimension: political and scientific.

In the 1930s and 1940s, when Spanish scientists had little opportunity of international scientific exchange and had little funding, contacts with their Portuguese counterparts became even more important. The missions and research stays of geneticists from Spain at the National Agronomic Station and the Plant Improvement Station were part of the collaborations established at that time. As Portugal, unlike Spain, was part of the Marshall Plan, in the early 1950s Portuguese scientists and technicians had the possibility of making extended stays in the USA.[37] In Spain these possibilities and other US contributions to agricultural transformation were opened up by the 1953 agreements.[38]

34 It is estimated that 'a total of 173 professors active in 1936 suffered some kind of sanction after the war, including those who were temporarily removed for a few weeks as well as those who definitively lost a job and the 18 victims of political killings and death sentences'; Antoni Malet, 'José María Albareda (1902–1966) and the Formation of the Spanish Consejo Superior de Investigaciones Científicas', *Annals of Science* 66 (2009), 307–32, at 308.

35 Pinar, 'Emergence of Modern Genetics in Spain', 136–40.

36 Sánchez Ron, *Cincel, Martillo y Piedra; Los orígenes de la Genética en España*, Candela (ed.); Malet, 'José María Albareda (1902–1966)'.

37 Maria Fernanda Rollo, 'Ambiciones frustradas: las vías de modernización y el programa de asistencia técnica americana a la agricultura portuguesa en la posguerra (1948–1956)', in *Agriculturas e innovación tecnológica en la Península Ibérica*, Lanero and Freire (eds), 107–33.

38 Dulce Freire and Daniel Lanero Táboas, 'The Iberian Dictatorships and Agricultural Modernisation after the Second World War', in *Integration through Subordination*, Moser and Varley (eds), 183–201.

During these decades, in Portugal and Spain the combination of political strategies with specific scientific interests inaugurated a new phase of collaboration between technicians and scientists from both countries. In 1969 the President of the Republic of Portugal in recognition of the importance of these collaborations decorated six employees of the Spanish Ministry of Agriculture. The decorations were conferred during an official visit to Spain by the Portuguese Secretary of State for Agriculture, Vasco Leónidas the following year. In a speech, he stressed the importance of the collaborations that had been developed over the previous thirty years between scientists and technicians from the two countries. These collaborations mainly covered activities in scientific research in the fields of soil, technological chemistry, plant physiology, phytosystematics, geobotany, genetics, plant breeding, entomology, phytopathology, seed testing and statistics, agrarian structures and irrigation. He highlighted the contributions of de Sousa Câmara, responsible for the EAN, and Ibañez-Martín as president of the CSIC. As might be expected, Vasco Leónidas overlooked the contacts established before the dictatorships, while at the same time underlining the importance of genetics in all the collaborations developed over the previous three decades.[39]

3.2 Science and politics: the journal *Genética Ibérica*

The scientific journal *Genética Ibérica* emerged as a response to the scientific and international challenges faced by the dictatorships that continued to govern Portugal and Spain after the Second World War. The first issue of the journal came out in 1949 and the last in 1989. For forty years *Genética Ibérica* published the research results produced by scientists from both countries and provided other information useful to these scientific communities. Having the characteristics of a scientific journal, with a graphic sobriety and content comparable to similar international publications, this was also a political project. It is considered that in Portugal and Spain 'the relationships between science and ideology were creatively explored by the ruling elite' during the dictatorships led by Salazar and Franco.[40] In this case, this dual scientific and political ambition is expressed in a number of different ways in the journal.

The publication asserts itself as an Iberian project, although clearly led by Spain. This was despite the fact that, at this time, national diplomacy, especially on the Portuguese side, insisted on the *luso-espanhol*

39 Vasco Leónidas, *Cooperação entre técnicos agrários de Espanha e Portugal. Palavras proferidas na cerimónia de imposição de insígnias da ordem de mérito agrícola a técnicos do ministério da agricultura de Espanha.*

40 Brandão, Rollo and Queiroz, 'A Associação Portuguesa para o Progresso das Ciências (1917–1974)'.

(*Portuguese-Spanish*) designation to refer to initiatives involving the two countries. Historically, the assertion of autonomy from Spain has been part of Portugal's identity and territorial definition. This statement became even more visible during the construction of the nationalism on which was based the fascist-inspired dictatorship that had governed Portugal since the 1930s.[41]

During the first half of the twentieth century, Iberism went through moments of exaltation, with cultural and symbolic expressions that had a strong impact, at least, among some of the elites of both countries.[42] As an ideological project, Iberism supposed an integration between the two countries that the Portuguese Estado Novo sought to avoid. To cite just two examples: economic relations between the two countries were almost non-existent;[43] and diplomatic relations were ones of convenience, highlighting the distinct strategies of each country when this was most appropriate.[44] However, the war situation had forced the signing of an Iberian Pact in 1942. In Portugal, this pact was denied by several members of the elites who supported the Estado Novo.[45] *Genética Ibérica* can be understood as a part of the strategy designed by the Francoist regime to mitigate the isolation resulting from the outcome of the Second World War.

Being part of the elites close to the dictatorships of each country, the promoters of this journal were well aware of the various implications of using the word *Ibérica*. In fact, in the scientific circles that these scientists moved in, the preferred designation seems to have been *luso-espanhol* (*Portuguese-Spanish*), which would ensure the visibility and identity

41 Since the end of the twentieth century, Iberism has freed itself from the stigma of anti-patriotism and has consolidated itself as a scientific and cultural field. Hipólito de la Torre Gómez, 'Historia, identidad nacional y vecindad ibérica', in *Percepciones luso-españolas desde la historia. La mirada del otro*, Hipólito de la Torre Gómez and António José Telo (eds) (Mérida: Editora Regional de Extremadura, 2001), 14; Carlos Reis, 'Nota de abertura', *Revista de Estudos Literários* 11 (2021), 7; Santiago Pérez Isasi, 'Luces y sombras en los estudios ibéricos: un estado de la cuestión diez años después', *Revista de Estudos Literários* 11 (2021), 19–46.

42 José M. Sardica, 'The Cultural Discourse of Contemporary Portuguese Iberianism', *International J. Iberian Studies* 27 (2014), 55–70; Paulo B. R. Ferreira, 'Iberismo, hispanismo e os seus contrários: Portugal e Espanha (1908–1931)', (Doctoral dissertation, Universidade de Lisboa, 2015); Antonio Sáez Delgado, *Literaturas entrelazadas. Portugal y España, del modernismo y la vanguardia al tiempo de las dictaduras* (Bern: Peter Lang, 2020).

43 David Corkill, 'Economia e identidade: as relações luso-espanholas e o mercado ibérico', in *Portugal na Viragem do século. O valor da universalidade*, coord. by Fernando Rosas and Fernanda Rollo (Lisboa: Assírio e Alvim, 1998), 9–47, at 12.

44 Juan Jiménez Redondo, *Franco e Salazar. As relações luso-espanholas durante a guerra fria* (Lisboa: Assírio & Alvim, 1996).

45 Ibid., 89.

of each country. For example, this is the name adopted for the conferences that from 1921 were organised by the Asociación Española para el Progreso de las Ciencias (Spanish Association for the Progress of Sciences) and the Associação Portuguesa para o Progresso das Ciências (Portuguese Association for the Progress of Sciences).[46] These meetings regularly brought together hundreds of scientists from all disciplines in different cities on the Iberian Peninsula. This was also the name adopted at the new conferences that, from 1964 onwards, annually brought together peninsular genetics in different universities: Jornadas de Genética Luso-Espanholas (Luso-Spanish Genetics Conferences).[47]

Scientifically, the new journal covered the fields of genetics and also cytology. In the 1940s, these were research areas undergoing a process of growing autonomy and international expansion led by the USA. In Portugal and Spain, genetic research suffered from the impacts of decisions taken by the dictatorships during the 1930s. However, as a result of the Civil War, these impacts were more severe in Spain. For the recovery of this scientific field in Spain, contacts with Portuguese geneticists and research stays at the new National Agronomic Station (close to Lisbon) and Plant Improvement Station (Elvas, Alentejo) were essential.[48]

The important international scientific developments in genetics since the 1940s and the growing recognition of science as a lever for economic growth,[49] made the reconnection of epistemic communities based in the

46 This Spanish association, created in 1908, influenced the creation of the Portuguese one in 1917. Being liberal in origin, both associations went through several changes during the dictatorships so that they could continue their activities. Ron, *Cincel, Martillo y Piedra*, 171–211; Brandão, Rollo and Queiroz, 'A Associação Portuguesa para o Progresso das Ciências (1917–1974)'. The Spanish association was extinguished in 1979. Although there is no record of the dissolution of the Portuguese one, but it must have disappeared during the 1970s. Ibid., 107.

47 These meetings, which emerged as an initiative of the CSIC, stimulated the creation of the Sociedad Española de Genética (1972) and the Sociedade Portuguesa de Genética (1973). These organisations took over the arrangement of the meetings but they decided in 1994 that the meetings would cease. Milagros Candela and Armando García González, *La Sociedad Española de Genética* (2003). https://segenetica.es/wp-content/uploads/2023/05/Los-Origenes-de-la-genetica-en-Espana-v2.pdf (accessed 16 March 2025).

48 Candela (ed.), Los orígenes de la Genética en España, 84–5.

49 In 1945, the appearance of *Science, the Endless Frontier: A Report to the President*, by Vannevar Bush (director of the Office of Scientific Research and Development), contributed to this recognition. The author, who was Roosevelt's advisor, argued that public financing of science was indispensable for reinforcing the well-being and power of a country; Bonneuil, Müller-Wille and Rheinberger, *A Cultural History of Heredity, IV, Heredity in the Century of the Gene*; Kloppenburg, *First the Seed: The Political Economy of Plant Biotechnology, 1492–2000*.

Iberian Peninsula even more pressing. In this context, the new journal was a way to improve the scientific discussion. In the medium term, this reconnection proved to be a successful strategy in the internationalisation of scientists from both countries.

The new journal was launched in 1949, a date that seems not to have been chosen at random. On the one hand, it marked ten years since the creation of the CSIC, the infrastructure launched by the Francoist Estado Nuevo to replace the JAE. The CSIC expressed the dictatorship's vision for science, and its programme included the creation of more than 100 journals dedicated to different scientific fields by the 1960s,[50] among them the *Genética Ibérica*. On the other hand, this was the year in which Franco made an official visit to Portugal, reciprocating Salazar's visit to Spain in 1942. It was made in acknowledgement of the support he was receiving from the Portuguese government in various spheres of international diplomacy. Franco's visit had great political and symbolic significance, as confirmed by the applause he received in Lisbon and the *honoris causa* doctorate at the University of Coimbra.[51] This academic ceremony has been interpreted as another moment of Iberist exaltation, and can be seen as one in a sequence of other events held since the end of the nineteenth century.[52]

The journal's commitment to the dictatorships of each country is also symbolically expressed in the photographs on the opening pages of the first issue. One is a photograph of Marshal Carmona, the President of Republic of Portugal, 'as a tribute for the collaboration of Portuguese Scientific Institutions with "Iberian Genetics"'. A second is of the head of state Don Francisco Franco, 'under whose patronage the *Genética Ibérica* journal is born'. Portraits of state figures had featured in many publications during the dictatorships in Portugal and Spain, and were therefore one of the signs of the political interpretation to be placed on each initiative.

In the first issue of *Genética Ibérica*, César González Gómez, the Spanish promoter and director of the 'José Celestino Mutis' Institute, highlighted the commitment of the then Spanish minister of national education to strengthening connections with Portuguese geneticists. In 1949, the minister was José Ibáñez Martín, who had been appointed by Franco in 1939 and remained in post until 1951. The political and institutional

50 Malet, 'José María Albareda (1902–1966)', 331.

51 The oration was given by Guilherme Braga da Cruz, distinguished professor at the Faculty of Law of the University of Coimbra. Guilherme Braga da Cruz, 'Discurso de elogio de sua Excelência o chefe do Estado Espanhol Generalíssimo Francisco Franco Bahamonde', *Separata de 'Boletim da Faculdade de Direito'*, 25, fasc. 2 (1950).

52 Miguel Filipe Mochila, 'Eugénio de Castro Ibérico: ideologização da sua receção espanhola', *Revista de Estudos Literários* 11 (2021), 311–42.

weight of the friendship between the minister and José María Albareda has already been noticed.[53] He was a soil specialist, but he left a deeper mark on Spanish science as general secretary of the CSIC, from its establishment in 1939 until his death in 1966. José María Albareda and António de Sousa Câmara were friends. The relationship proved to be crucial for the development of genetics in the two countries. In the 1920s and 1930s, both had received scholarships from their respective countries to study in Europe and the USA. As such, they were known on international scientific circuits.

Editorially, the journal was based on the logistical, financial and organisational resources of the CSIC in Madrid, through the Institute of Genetics and Anthropology. Within the broad CSIC, the journal was formally published by the Laboratorio de Citogenética del Instituto 'José Celestino Mutis' de Farmacognosia (Cytogenetics Laboratory of the 'José Celestino Mutis' Institute of Pharmacognosy). In Portugal, the privileged partner was the National Agronomic Station, through its manager de Sousa Câmara, who was director of the journal between 1949 and 1967.[54] He was one of the most prestigious Portuguese scientists and had been an essential link with Spanish geneticists in previous decades. He also served in international organisations to which Spain had not been admitted.[55]

The journal aimed to prioritise the publication of the results of work carried out in the sixteen collaborating research centres. On the back cover of *Genética Ibérica*, they are presented in alphabetical order (and not country-by-country) as may be seen in Table 3.1. This list underwent some changes in the following decades but maintained its original sense.

These sixteen organisations were the pillars of scientific research in anthropobiology, botany, agronomy and zootechnics in the two countries, even though proportionally they were already very unequal in 1949. Despite having different origins and trajectories, the Spanish institutions were part of the CSIC network. It turned out that universities were not considered as partners, even though scientists circulated between the various organisations.[56] As a scientific infrastructure, the CSIC enunciated a thematic scope and geographic decentralisation,

53 Ron, *Cincel, Martillo y Piedra*, 329–71; Malet, 'José María Albareda (1902–1966)'.

54 From then, until the journal ceased publication in 1989, its director was the Catalan geneticist Antonio Prevosti Pelegrín. António de Sousa Câmara was a member of the Honour Council from 1967 until his death in 1971. Lluis Serra Camo, 'Profesor Doctor Antonio Prevosti Pelegrín: pionero de la genética de poblaciones y estudioso de la evolución', in *Los orígenes de la genética en España*, Candela (ed.), 369–96.

55 At the time, one of his positions was president of the National Committee of the Food and Agriculture Organization (FAO). Portugal became a member of the FAO in 1946, but Spain was only admitted at the end of 1950.

56 *Los orígenes de la Genética en España*, Candela (ed.).

both consolidated in the following decades. On the contrary, Portugal is represented by (old) laboratories and museums within universities or (new) services of the Ministry of Economy (in which agriculture was included). These Portuguese organisations did not include the new laboratories created by the IAC since 1940, in which genetic research does not seem to have been prioritised.

The list of associated institutions shows the concern of the journal's promoters to engage with groups interested in the study of humans, plants and animals, but which had little capacity to keep abreast of research in genetics. At a time when genetics research was becoming more sophisticated and diversified, infrastructures with a different profile were required. The pool of support for this editorial project includes areas of knowledge that at the time already had weak affinities (such as botany, agronomy and pharmacy), and that since the nineteenth century had been trying to consolidate themselves as distinct scientific fields. The names of research centres in Spain symbolically recalled the heritage of scientists who were considered pioneers, associated with the study of nature and ethnicities in the Americas since the sixteenth century. In Portugal this evocation is more indirect, revealing itself through the collections held in herbaria and museums. However, in practice genetics was moving away from a localist conception to focus on the search for seeds and other organisms of interest, that is, those capable of producing in different regions of the world.

Published bi-annually and extending to about 300 pages each year, the journal was a collection of articles that were rarely accompanied by a contextual introduction that located them in ongoing debates. Sometimes, there is information about scientific meetings, decisions with an impact on genetics and an obituary of a renowned scientist linked to the journal's themes. Alongside authors from Iberian research centres, collaborations from other countries also emerged. The articles are published in Iberian or other languages, including English, and reveal the great technical complexity and specificity that genetics was developing. This is a publication produced mainly by the Iberian scientific community, aiming to strengthen connections with peers from other countries and to draw international attention to their research activities.

If a journal with this profile made sense in the 1950s and 1960s, was it still relevant in the 1970s? This was a discussion that underlay the last few years of publication of *Genética Ibérica*. On the one hand, the political context of Portugal and Spain had changed. As a political and ideological project, this journal became increasingly redundant as Spain integrated itself into the international community from the mid-1950s onwards. In the later 1970s, scientific contacts developed in line with the implementation of democratic systems in both countries. By this time, Iberian scientists were already part of very competitive and global research networks. The consolidation of democratic regimes and entry of both countries to the EEC in 1986 improved the conditions for this international academic integration even more.

At the beginning of the 1970s, the Iberian scientific communities concerned with genetic research discussed the utility of having a journal with a specific geographic scope. The discussion emerged among the new scientific organisations that had brought together geneticists from Spain and Portugal since the early 1970s. In fact, there was no consensus. Some scientists saw this kind of publication as necessary. Others understood the opposite: they considered that scientists from the Iberian Peninsula were already qualified to publish among colleagues from other countries in international journals. This was already beginning to happen.

In the 1980s, the CSIC underwent extensive reflection and organisational remodelling.[57] The changes in the scientific communities on genetics in the Iberian Peninsula and the capacity to integrate the research they were carrying out into ongoing international academic debates were not unnoticed. It is likely that it was scientific concerns rather than financial ones that led to the decision to close *Genetica Ibérica* in 1989.[58] *Genetica Ibérica* had become irrelevant to Spanish scientists, who were the authors who published most in this journal.

A more detailed analysis of the content of each of the issues would allow us to understand in greater depth both the impact of this publication on the consolidation of epistemic communities in Portugal and Spain, as well as the way in which the journal followed international research trends during the forty years in which it was published. After the Second World War, genetics aimed to assert itself as the 'last frontier of knowledge', exploring multiple avenues of investigation. In the early 1970s, these pathways included molecular genetics, population genetics, plant genetics and quantitative genetics. At the same time, in some of these areas, growing private and industrial investment deprived the state of its leading role in the research that determined the fate of this scientific field.

3.3 Conclusions

When the First World War worsened the 'subsistence' crisis and, at the same time, important discoveries in the field of genetics were announced, scientists in both Spain and Portugal did not fail to ask the state for more support. At a time when access to basic food supplies was becoming increasingly expensive and difficult, both countries sought to increase agricultural production. As would happen later, during the Green

57 Alfonso Martinez-Arias, 'A Perspective on the Development of Genetics in Spain During the XX Century', *International J. Developmental Biology* 53 (2009), 1179–91; *Los orígenes de la Genética en España*, Candela (ed.).

58 Candela and García González, *La Sociedad Española de Genética*, 135–6.

Revolution, genetics presented itself as a way to achieve the desired increase in domestic food production. In the 1930s, the consolidation of dictatorships in Portugal (1933–4) and in Spain (1936–9) changed perspectives on the functions of science and the political priorities that would underpin public institutions for scientific research and higher education in the future.

In both countries, the 1930s were a decade of changes in the institutions and protagonists associated with genetic research. Even though the strategies were different, it appears that, in science just as in other areas, the consolidation of dictatorships in Portugal and Spain involved the liquidation of the republican and liberal legacies of previous decades. The construction of the public scientific research system in each of the countries had promoted internationalisation and the creation of research centres, capable of accommodating an influx of new scientists. But they were largely dismissed in the restructuring of science imposed by the dictatorships.

The dictatorships in Portugal and Spain sponsored applied science and, as such, instrumental solutions were promoted that promised efficient results. These intentions were combined with some of the dynamics of genetic development after the Second World War, which promised to offer farmers the best seeds to solve one of humanity's most complex problems: ending food shortages. At this time, the success of genetic research applied to agriculture was still largely measured by its contribution to improving cereal cultivation.

It appears that in the two Iberian countries, under the dictatorial regimes in the 1930s and 1940s, there were institutional changes in the public scientific and innovation system, which also corresponded to changing conceptions of the functions of science and scientists. In these processes of change, the advocates of collaboration within the broader community of Iberian geneticists, which became closer after the Second World War, were already present. The consolidation of genetic research in publicly funded laboratories in Portugal and Spain was part of a wider package of institutional changes promoted by the state to keep up with the challenges of scientific and technological innovation that became more pressing from the 1940s onwards. In the 1960s and 1970s, these organisational structures could already seem obsolete to scientists, especially since genetics research was in a state of flux internationally and commercial organisations were increasing in prominence. If internationally the reputation of a scientist was evaluated on the quality of their research, in Portugal and Spain the political profile of each one could continue to be more decisive in the success of their professional career or in obtaining funding for research.

In 1949, the creation of the journal *Genética Ibérica* can be understood as one of the ways the Francoist dictatorship attempted to reestablish lost contacts with the scientific community across borders, at a time when Spain continued to be subjected to international ostracism. The launch of this journal presented multiple scientific, cultural, ideological and political meanings for the dictatorships that governed Portugal and Spain. These meanings would be repositioned in the following years, due to the need to strengthen international commitments within the scope of development programmes and transnational cooperation organisations of which no governments could remain oblivious. In achieving these aims, sciences that were associated with the exploration of natural resources, agriculture and food, such as genetics, became even more relevant.

The analysis of research centres that promoted and collaborated with *Genetica Ibérica* reveals that in Spain, modern genetics only symbolically embraced the legacies associated with the conquest of the Americas and ancient scientific conceptions (Celestino Mutis, pharmacognosy, for example). These references would intersect with the different pathways that were being explored (human, plant, animal, chromosomes) in innovative international genetics. The concerns of the journal's promoters in bringing together all entities even vaguely related to genetics in the 1940s also expressed the weakness of genetic research at the time in the Iberian Peninsula. However, this union of efforts seems to have borne fruit, promoting inter-knowledge and strengthening scientific communities in Portugal and Spain, as indicated by the creation of associations and the holding of specific congresses from the 1960s onwards.

The publication of this journal is part of a vision in which scientific and political networks intersect. In fact, researchers and research centres in Portugal also recognised the strengthening of contacts with Spain as a way of adding value to their work and reinforcing institutional legitimacy. This recognition became even more important given the scarcity of the resources that the Portuguese state made available for science. During this period of approximately thirty years, the scientists of both countries were part of the affirmation of a public scientific and innovation system that relied on applied science to resolve concrete problems that were affecting the economy of each region, from crop pests to production levels and the productivity of each seed, to the adaptation of new animals and plants. It was a system that promoted international exchanges subject to criteria of immediate utility, reducing the experimental and speculative freedom that encourages innovation. However, even if the resources to carry out research in genetics were less than those considered necessary, the conviction that this science was taking fundamental steps towards solving humanity's biggest problems seemed to be very stimulating.

TABLE 3.1: Founding research centres contributing to *Genética Ibérica*.

Centro de Estudios del Tabaco	Seville, Spain
Estação Agronómica Nacional	Sacavém, Portugal
Estación Experimental Aula Dei	Zaragoza, Spain
Estação Experimental Florestal do Sobreiro	Alcobaça, Portugal
Estação de Melhoramento de Plantas	Elvas, Portugal
Instituto de Aclimatación	Almería, Spain
Instituto de Biología Animal	Madrid, Spain
Instituto Botânico da Faculdade de Ciências	Lisbon, Portugal
Instituto Botânico 'Dr Gonçalo Sampaio', Faculdade de Ciências, Universidade do Porto	Porto, Portugal
Instituto Botânico 'Dr Júlio Henriques', Faculdade de Ciências da Universidade de Coimbra	Coimbra, Portugal
Instituto 'José de Acosta', de Ciencias Naturales	Madrid, Spain
Instituto Nacional de Investigaciones Agronómicas (Madrid, Spain)	Madrid, Spain
Misión Biológica de Galicia	Pontevedra, Spain
Museu e Laboratório Antropológico da Faculdade de Ciências, Universidade de Coimbra	Coimbra, Portugal
Museu e Laboratório de Zoologia da Universidade de Coimbra	Coimbra, Portugal
Sección de Antropobiología, Instituto 'Bernardino de Sahagún'	Barcelona, Spain

Source: rear cover of *Genética Ibérica* I pt 1 (1949).

4

Racial productivism: agrarian change under the Nazi regime in German-annexed Austria, 1938–1945

Ernst Langthaler

In April 1938, a few weeks after Austria's annexation by the German Reich (*Anschluss*), a regional newspaper ran a full-page article headed 'Our Homeland in 10 Years'. The author speculated on the improvement of working and living conditions in the region a decade after the *Anschluss*. 'The peasants are no longer doing badly', he concludes.[1] Workload reduction through mechanisation, farm optimisation through specialisation, and income security through profitability – in this way, the article emphasised the contrast between the room of experience, the crisis-ridden years of the past, and the horizon of expectation, the new era within the German 'people's community' in the future.[2] This article shows that blueprints for modernity were taking shape not only in the urban centres of the Third Reich but also in rural peripheries.

This episode draws our attention to the debate about the relationship between National Socialism and modernity since the 1960s. The classical notion of 'modernisation', shaped by the anti-communist spirit of the Cold War, concentrated on industrialisation and democratisation according to the Western model. In consequence, National Socialism appeared as a deviation from the normal path to modernity, as a German *Sonderweg*. Detlev Peukert's pioneering account of National Socialism as

1 *Schwarzataler Zeitung*, 9 Apr. 1938, 5. I would like to thank Ulrich Schwarz-Gräber for bringing this article to my attention and for inspiring discussions about agrarian society under National Socialism.

2 Anders Schinkel, 'Imagination as a Category of History: An Essay Concerning Koselleck's Concepts of *Erfahrungsraum* and *Erwartungshorizont*', *History and Theory* 44 (2005), 42–54.

a 'pathology of modernity' already signalled a shift in perspective.[3] The postmodern critique of classical notions of modernity finally gave way to more reflexive notions of alternative – including fascist – varieties of modernity.[4] Accordingly, Riccardo Bavaj conceives National Socialism as a variety of 'ambivalent modernity'.[5]

Despite this debate's reflexive turn, historians have hesitated to ascribe modernity to agrarian development in the Third Reich. Features such as the failure of the state-led 'battle for production', the ideologically driven introduction of the economically inefficient Reich Hereditary Farm Law, or the 'blood and soil' ideology hailing the peasantry as the backbone of the 'people's community', all seem to demonstrate the anti-modern character of Nazi agrarian policies. Seemingly modern features such as rural-urban migration, technological innovations or professional education are presented as unwanted, feigned or ineffective. In consequence, agrarian modernisation in Nazi Germany is either completely denied or partially affirmed only in combination with anti-modern qualifiers ('destructive', 'reactionary', 'regressive', and so forth).[6] Gesine Gerhard summarises this notion: 'The twelve years of the Third Reich were like an interlude in terms of modernisation, offering a reprieve from the long-term trend of structural change taking place.'[7]

This chapter challenges the conventional wisdom that the Nazi era was an interlude in agrarian development or even represented a backlash by highlighting its modern, albeit ambivalent character. Instead of stressing the over-generalised term 'modernisation', it focuses on productivism as a time-specific and space-specific variety of modernity from the perspective of transition theory.[8] Productivism refers to a capital-

3 Detlev Peukert, *Volksgenossen und Gemeinschaftsfremde. Anpassung, Ausmerze und Aufbegehren unter dem Nationalsozialismus* (Cologne: Bund, 1982).

4 Ernst Langthaler, 'Varieties of Modernity: Fascism and Agricultural Development in Austria, 1934–1945', in *Agriculture in the Age of Fascism: Authoritarian Technocracy and Rural Modernization, 1922–1945*, Miguel Cabo Villaverde, Lourenzo Fernández Prieto and Juan Pan-Montojo (eds) (Turnhout: Brepols, 2014), 159–88.

5 Riccardo Bavaj, *Die Ambivalenz der Moderne im Nationalsozialismus. Eine Bilanz der Forschung* (Munich: Oldenbourg, 2003), 13–56, 199–204.

6 Gustavo Corni and Horst Gies, *Brot, Butter, Kanonen. Die Ernährungswirtschaft in Deutschland unter der Diktatur Hitlers* (Berlin: Akademie-Verlag, 1997); Gustavo Corni, 'Agrarpolitik', in *Handbuch Wirtschaft im Nationalsozialismus*, Marcel Boldorf and Jonas Scherner (eds) (Berlin: De Gruyter, 2023), 395–418.

7 Gesine Gerhard, 'The Modernization Dilemma: Agrarian Policies in Nazi Germany', in *Agriculture in the Age of Fascism*, Cabo Villaverde, Fernández Prieto and Pan-Montojo (eds), 139–58, at 140.

8 John Grin, Jan Rotmans and Johan Schot, *Transitions to Sustainable Development: New Directions in the Study of Long Term Transformative Change* (New York and London: Routledge, 2010); Geoff A. Wilson, *Multifunctional Agriculture: A Transition Theory Perspective* (Wallingford and Cambridge, MA: Cabi, 2007).

intensive, highly specialised and growth-orientated mode of farming, which disconnects agriculture from regional society and nature and links it to downstream and upstream industries via (trans-)national commodity chains. The agro-industrial complex of commodity chains is regulated by market-dominating companies, interventionist nation-states and techno-scientific knowledge, which promote the hegemony of modernisation in the productivist sense.[9] For most European countries, the transition from low to high productivism – the *agrarian transition* – falls in the decades between the world economic crisis of the 1930s and the post-war boom from the 1950s to the 1970s.[10]

To investigate agrarian change under the Nazi regime in general and the agrarian transition in particular, the province of Niederdonau in the north-east of German-annexed Austria is taken as a regional case. What makes Niederdonau a rewarding study case is the diversity of its regional agrosystems, ranging from the Pannonian Plains with their warm and dry climate, to the Alps with their cool and wet climate, from suburban and industrialised to rural and agricultural areas, and from extremely polarised to more equal distributions of landed property. Moreover, the favourable situation regarding sources on the communal, farm, and individual levels makes it possible to explore many specificities and use them as building blocks of the general picture.[11]

4.1 Mainstream farming

The predominant image of the relationship between agrarian society and National Socialism in the older literature is shaped by traditionalism and even anti-modernism: 'The peasantry persisted in its former habits, made use of what appeared to be advantageous, tried to get around any regulations that were a burden to it and was, all things considered, as loyal towards authority as it always had been.'[12] The static nature of the peasantry's behaviour, seen here in relation to the German Reich before the *Anschluss*, only partially applies to Austria, which we now understand

9 Brian Ilbery and Ian Bowler, 'From Agricultural Productivism to Post-Productivism', in *The Geography of Rural Change*, Brian Ilbery (ed.) (London: Longman, 1998), 57–84; Wilson, *Multifunctional Agriculture*, 213–70.

10 Gunther Mai, 'Die Agrarische Transition. Agrarische Gesellschaften in Europa und die Herausforderungen der industriellen Moderne im 19. und 20. Jahrhundert', *Geschichte und Gesellschaft* 33 (2007), 471–514.

11 Ernst Langthaler, *Schlachtfelder. Alltägliches Wirtschaften in der nationalsozialistischen Agrargesellschaft 1938–1945* (Vienna, Cologne and Weimar: Böhlau, 2016), 26–35; id., 'Völkischer Produktivismus. Nationalsozialismus und Agrarmodernisierung im Reichsgau Niederdonau, 1938–1945', *Zeitgeschichte* 45 (2018), 293–318.

12 Friedrich Grundmann, *Agrarpolitik im 'Dritten Reich'. Anspruch und Wirklichkeit des Reichserbhofgesetzes* (Hamburg: Hoffmann und Campe, 1979), 119.

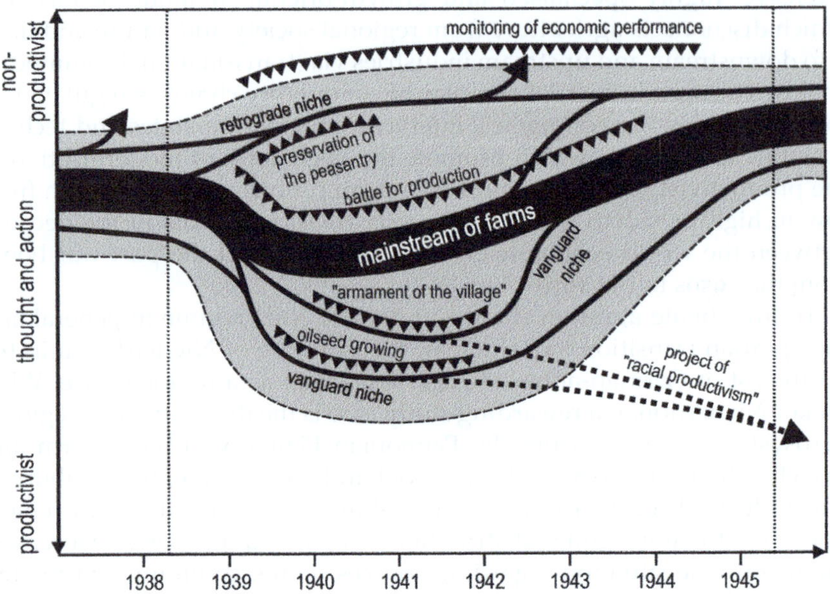

FIGURE 4.1. Pathways of agrarian change in Austria, 1938–45 (Langthaler, *Schlachtfelder*, 744).

to have been much more dynamic in character.[13] To speak of 'the peasantry' is to deny the diversity of everyday practices that were both enabled and limited by the structures of the actors' lifeworlds and of the political-economic system. The room for manoeuvre experienced by people on the farms expanded in both productivist and non-productivist directions – and they manoeuvred within this space between well-trodden and new paths (Figure 4.1).[14]

The state-led preservation of the peasantry, above all the Reich Hereditary Farm Law that sprang from 'blood and soil' ideology,[15] expanded the room for manoeuvre experienced by farming families. It allowed them to distance themselves from the pressing constraints of the land and credit market they had felt during the agrarian crisis of the 1930s. By the end of

13 Langthaler, *Schlachtfelder*; Gerhard Siegl, *Bergbauern im Nationalsozialismus. Die Berglandwirtschaft zwischen Agrarideologie und Kriegswirtschaft* (Innsbruck, Vienna and Bozen: Studienverlag, 2013).

14 Ernst Langthaler, 'Wirtschaften mit Stil. Historisch-anthropologische Perspektiven zum Agrarstrukturwandel als Praxis', *Historische Anthropologie* 20 (2012), 276–96.

15 Grundmann, *Agrarpolitik*; Uwe Mai, *'Rasse und Raum'. Agrarpolitik, Sozial- und Raumplanung im NS-Staat* (Paderborn: Schöningh, 2002).

the war, 20 per cent of farms and 34 per cent of farmland in Niederdonau were subject to regulation, although the ratio varied greatly from region to region.[16] The medium-sized hereditary farm could not be mortgaged, forcibly auctioned off, divided or sold, but was passed down the – primarily male – bloodline within the ethnic German clan. At the same time, farmholders were assessed for their 'peasant capability', above all in terms of respectability and economic capability. Any 'peasant' (*Bauer*) – the owner of a hereditary farm – or 'farmer' (*Landwirt*) – the owner of a farm not registered as a hereditary farm – who did not meet moral or economic criteria could be temporarily or permanently removed from the farm. The rulings in the court districts of Niederdonau show considerable flexibility, with economic measures usually given greater weight than moral ones.[17]

The application of the Reich Hereditary Farm Law was closely interwoven with the programme of 'debt relief and buildup'. This gave indebted farms or those threatened with foreclosure the means to reschedule debt or make investments with the help of state funding – while also attempting to restore their productivity. The agency charged with administering the programme in Vienna and Niederdonau registered 25,000 applications, representing 12 per cent of all farms.[18] In the wake of this support by the German Reich came a bureaucracy that required the keeping of farm records, monitoring and supervision, thus contradicting aspirations for rural autonomy. The programme worked selectively by implementing tailor-made plans for debt management and investment: large, productive farms in favourable locations were given ample investment credit commensurate with their viability, as measured by their economic performance; medium-sized, poor-performing mountain farms, as enterprises deemed 'worthy of existence' in racial terms, predominantly received state subsidies; the rest, usually small farms in need of development, were allocated smaller sums.[19]

According to the logic of the German 'people's community', the preservation of the peasantry by the Reich Hereditary Farm Law and the 'debt relief and buildup' programme went hand in hand with the displacement

16 *Wochenblatt der Landesbauernschaft Niederdonau*, 32 (1944), 342–3.

17 Langthaler, *Schlachtfelder*, 199–230; Ernst Langthaler, 'From Capitalism to "Neo-Feudalism"? Property Relations, Land Markets and the Nazi State in the German Province of Niederdonau, 1938–1945', in *Contexts of Property in Europe: The Social Embeddedness of Property Rights in Land in Historical Perspective*, Rosa Congost and Rui Santos (eds) (Turnhout: Brepols, 2010), 165–86.

18 August Lombar, *Entschuldung und Aufbau der österreichischen Landwirtschaft* (Klagenfurt: Kleinmayr, 1953), 33.

19 Langthaler, *Schlachtfelder*, 386–436; Ernst Langthaler, 'Actor-Networks, Credit Markets and the Nazi State: Monetary Relations in Austrian Rural Societies, 1938–1945', in *Social Networks, Political Institutions and Rural Societies*, Georg Fertig (ed.) (Turnhout: Brepols, 2015), 183–210.

of Jewish landowners through land redistribution by the Nazi state ('aryanisation'). The close connection between the consolidation of medium-sized peasant farms run by Germans and the expropriation of Jewish landowners can be seen in the creation of the Döllersheim military training ground for the army. Some of the relocated peasant families were allocated new settler farms with hereditary farm status on parcels of land confiscated from former Jewish estates. While the buildings on these new farms adhered to the traditional rural aesthetic on the surface, their interiors were designed according to modern farming and householding needs. The connection between exclusion and inclusion, between the 'aryanisation' of Jewish property and the 'regeneration' of the German peasantry, also gained force in other parts of Niederdonau – for example, in the district of Gänserndorf, where large estates under Jewish ownership lay close to the German Reich's administrative and ethnic border to former Czechoslovakia. While in this sensitive zone, the policy of racial cleansing was the driver of state-enforced land transfers from Jewish to German owners, the economic capability of the peasants counted for the decision-makers as well.[20]

The state's protection of the peasantry from unpredictable market forces did not cover all farms but was linked to a certain level of economic performance. The benchmark of 'due and proper farm management' governed not only the application of the Reich Hereditary Farm Law, the 'debt relief and buildup' programmes and the 'aryanisation' of Jewish property but also applied to all other farms. The farming statistics compiled by the Reich Food Estate, the official organisation of all employers and employees in food production, processing and distribution, constituted a pervasive network of control. Using a questionnaire several pages long, the farm files recorded annually a whole range of characteristics about every farm above a certain minimum size – members of the household, employees, land ownership, land use, number of cattle, machinery, income from arable and livestock production and so on. The main purpose of the farm files was to compare performance between farms as well as the performance of each farm over time. Alongside the original copy, which was updated by the Reich Food Estate, farm owners themselves were obliged to keep a regular account of their performance in a notebook titled *My Farm File*.[21] This combination of external and internal control resembled a 'panopticon', a prison whose inmates must always assume that someone is watching – and thus discipline themselves to avoid external disciplinary measures.[22] The farm files and

20 Langthaler, *Schlachtfelder*, 151–99.

21 H. L. Fensch, 'Die bäuerliche Betriebsforschung des Reichsnährstandes', *Gefüge und Ordnung der deutschen Landwirtschaft*, Konrad Meyer (ed.) (Berlin: Reichsnährstand, 1939), 590–4.

22 On 'panopticism' see Michel Foucault, *Discipline and Punish: The Birth of the Prison* (New York: Vintage Books, 1995).

other forms of data collection acted as a hinge between state power and the 'transparent peasant'.[23]

Despite these attempts to raise the intensity of land use through data collection, monitoring and supervision, the increasing shortage of labour and technology after the turning point in the war in 1941–2 pushed mainstream farms towards extensification, the decreasing use of inputs relative to land area – in some cases even to a temporary cessation of activity. With agriculture motorised only to a limited extent, warfare robbed it of its most basic resource – the muscle-power of the men and horses drafted into the military. The overburdened women and young people in these farming families were hardly in a position to offset this loss of labour and power even with the vast numbers of forced labourers deployed in agriculture.[24] As a result, by the end of the Nazi era productivity in Austrian agriculture had fallen considerably below its starting level. Measured against pre-war levels, while the volume of production per worker (labour productivity) remained constant at 103 index points between 1938–41 and 1942–4 – a reflection of families overexploiting their own labour and that of forced labourers – the volume of production per unit of land (land productivity) fell from 93 to 81 index points (Figure 4.2).[25]

While the peasant-friendly regulatory framework expanded the room for manoeuvre in a non-productivist direction, the production campaign known as the 'battle for production' pushed towards market-orientated productivism.[26] Before 1938, the weak demand of the domestic market, which suffered from falling purchasing power due to mass unemployment, had formed a barrier to expansion. After the *Anschluss*, the seemingly insatiable market of 'Greater Germany' was opened up.[27] In terms of inputs to the agrosystem, there was a shift in factor weighting. Where previously rural labour had been abundant and cheap and agricultural technology scarce and expensive, in 1938–9 this price relationship was reversed: rural exodus and military service drove up agricultural wages while tariff reductions and promotional campaigns rendered

23 Ulrich Schwarz-Gräber, 'Gläserne Bauern. Prinzipal-Agent-Probleme nationalsozialistischer Agrarpolitik am Beispiel der Regulierung der landwirtschaftlichen Pacht', *Zeitgeschichte* 45 (2018), 319–42.

24 Ela Hornung, Ernst Langthaler and Sabine Schweitzer, 'Forced Labour in Agriculture', in *German Wartime Society, 1939-1945* (*Germany and the Second World War*, IX (ii)), Jörg Echternkamp (ed.) (Oxford: Oxford University Press, 2014), 581–668.

25 Langthaler, *Schlachtfelder*, 726–42; Ernst Langthaler, 'English and Austrian Wartime Farming, 1939–1945: "Revolution" or Something Else?', in *Integration through Subordination: The Politics of Agricultural Modernisation in Industrial Europe*, Peter Moser and Tony Varley (eds) (Turnhout: Brepols, 2013), 151–81.

26 Corni and Gies, *Brot*, 261–80.

27 Harald Schöhl, *Österreichs Landwirtschaft. Gestalt und Wandlung, 1918–1938* (Berlin: Reichsnährstand, 1938).

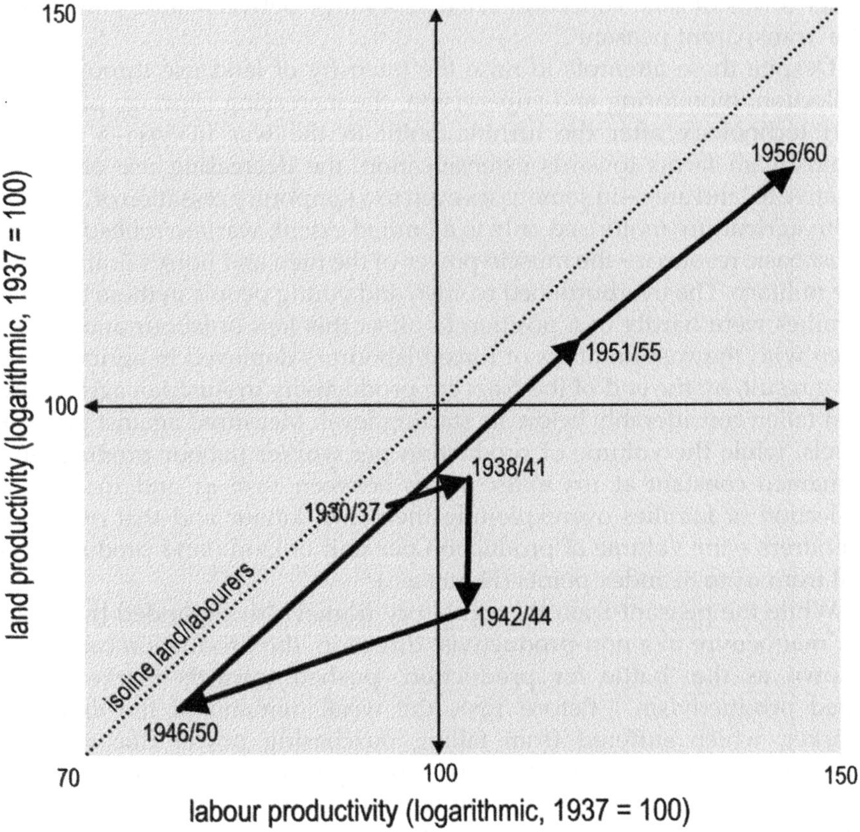

FIGURE 4.2. Agricultural productivity in Austria, 1930–60 (Langthaler, *Schlachtfelder*, 735).

agrochemicals and machinery cheaper. This price shift fuelled a wave of technification, which, while taking hold unevenly across regions and farm types, increased the use of commercial fertilisers and motorised farm equipment. In terms of outputs, institutional innovations – official price-setting, rising black market prices and subsidies for transport costs on the one hand, state production appeals and obligatory delivery of surpluses on the other hand – pushed forward market integration. Until the turning point of the war in 1941–2, the stimulus coming from state-regulated factor and product markets moved the mainstream of farms in the direction of rising land and labour productivity: measured against the 1937 level, the relevant index values rose from 90 and 95 respectively for 1930–7 to 93 and 103 respectively for 1938–41.[28]

28 Langthaler, *Schlachtfelder*, 626–742.

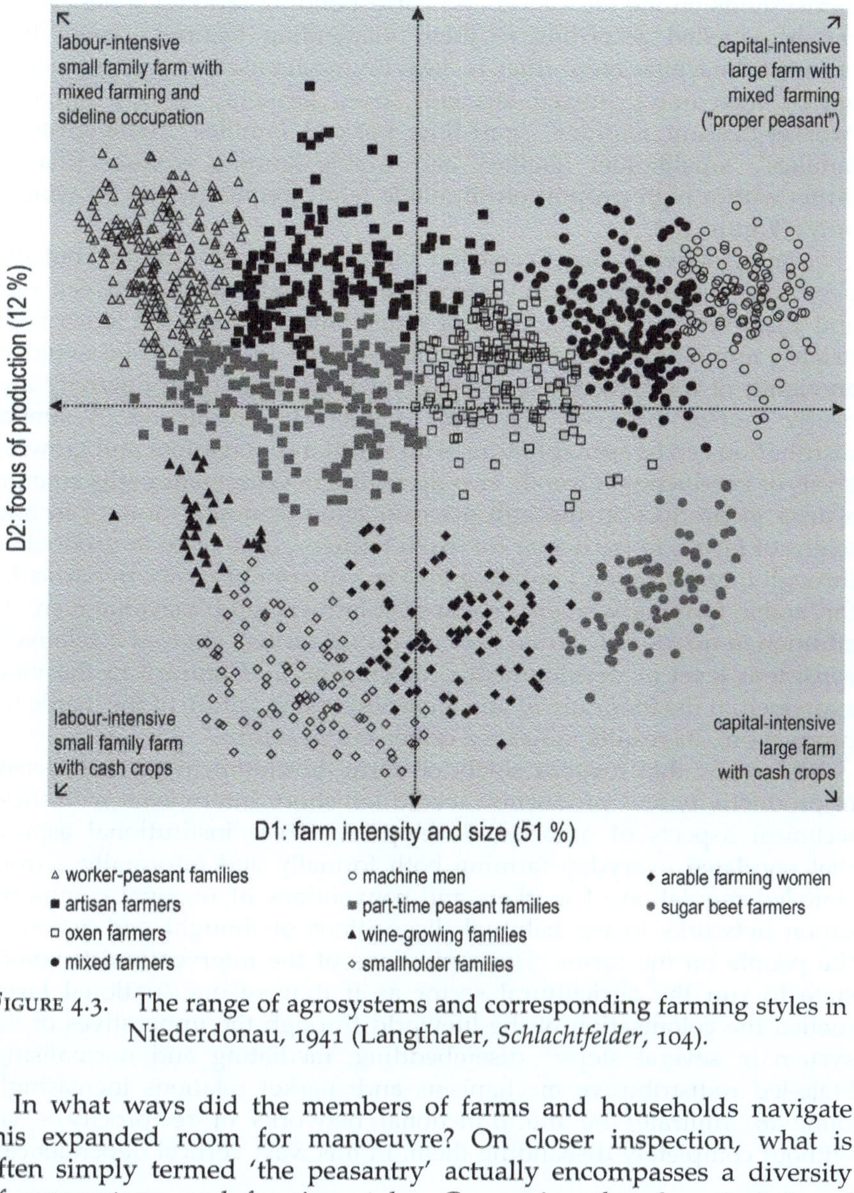

FIGURE 4.3. The range of agrosystems and corresponding farming styles in Niederdonau, 1941 (Langthaler, *Schlachtfelder*, 104).

In what ways did the members of farms and households navigate this expanded room for manoeuvre? On closer inspection, what is often simply termed 'the peasantry' actually encompasses a diversity of agrosystems and farming styles. Comparing the characteristics of a sample of about 1,500 farms, this diversity can be plotted along two axes: the horizontal axis denotes the intensity and size of the farm, with poles running from labour-intensive smallholdings on the left to capital-intensive large estates on the right. The vertical axis indicates the focus of production running from cash crops at the bottom to mixed farming at the top. The dots within this two-dimensional field depict diverse agrosystems on the farm-level and corresponding farming styles, which can be labelled according to their outstanding features: 'sugar beet farmers', 'machine men' (that is, heavily mechanised farms, frequently led by men only), 'mixed farmers', 'oxen farmers', 'artisan farmers', 'worker-peasant families', 'part-time peasant families', 'wine-growing families', 'smallholder families' and 'arable farming women' (that is, farms with a high proportion of arable land, frequently led by women only) (Figure 4.3).[29]

Farming activities are diverse not simply at one point in time, but also over time, as can be seen in three regions of Niederdonau between 1941 and 1944. While just under half of farms failed to meet the Reich Food Estate's stipulation that extensification of land use was to be avoided, an eighth of them recorded a consistent level of land productivity and nearly four-tenths even managed to intensify production. A similar distribution can be seen for farms with shrinking, consistent and growing levels of production. Overall, two diverging development paths emerge: a drop in production through extensification ('running down') in four tenths of farms, in particular for 'oxen farmers', and a rise in production through intensification ('building up') in a quarter of farms, in particular for 'arable farming women', 'sugar beet farmers' and 'machine men'. In addition, a quarter of farms, such as 'mixed farms', showed a relatively consistent level of development ('carrying on').[30] Contrary to the view expressed in the literature of an all-encompassing failure of the 'battle for production', its results indicate a rather mixed return.[31]

Yet a view that focused solely on farm development paths in terms of productivity and production would fall short. Interwoven with these technical aspects of agrarian development were institutional aspects that regulated everyday farming both formally and informally – from state-led regulation of markets and conventions of regional communication networks to the habitual dispositions of thought and action of the people on the farms. The aspirations of the interventionist nation-state to run the agricultural sector as if it were one 'national farm' fuelled the colonisation of the lifeworld through the imperatives of the system in several steps:[32] disembedding, mediating and normalising. State-led redistributive mechanisms and market relations increasingly came to infiltrate the multifunctional networks of reciprocity – yet without completely disbanding them. In this way, vertical dependencies

29 Ibid., 102–16.

30 Ibid., 642–68.

31 Stephanie Degler and Jochen Streb, 'Die verlorene Erzeugungsschlacht. Die nationalsozialistische Landwirtschaft im Systemvergleich', *Jahrbuch für Wirtschaftsgeschichte* 2 (2008), 161–81.

32 On the relation between system and lifeworld, see Jürgen Habermas, *Theorie des kommunikativen Handelns*, II (Frankfurt am Main: Suhrkamp, 1981), 522.

on the state and market came to replace horizontal community relationships within agrarian society when it came to accessing resources such as land, labour, capital, knowledge and products.[33] Running counter to these attempts at colonisation, actors' aspirations towards the autonomous control of their resource base – a core element of peasant farming styles – mobilised various facets of obstinacy: grousing in the pub, ignoring directives, taking a side-step into the shadow economy, and so on. The mediators in these bundles of power relations were functionaries of the Reich Food Estate at district and local levels. Going beyond their formal role as the representatives of state power, they would informally further their interests or those of their village clientele. While this was not enough to stem the alienation of the farming community from the Nazi regime, these low-ranking functionaries were able to dampen any budding dissent to a degree manageable by those in power.[34] Ultimately, the regular interventions necessitated by these regulatory frameworks – providing information to data-collecting agencies, self-monitoring of farm management, reading official farmers' journals, and so on – were so often repeated that they were gradually habituated as part of the normality of everyday life.[35]

This incremental colonisation of day-to-day farming life can be traced through the example of the 'debt relief and buildup' programme. While the office charged with implementing the programme fixed the terms of existing bank loans, private credit given by neighbours and relatives and debts to local traders were redeemed by the German Reich and converted into state loans. As a result, indebtedness to the state as the sole creditor (alongside banking institutions) replaced multifunctional creditor-debtor relationships within rural milieus. However, the accompanying reversal of patron-client relationships among the peasantry and the loss of autonomy in everyday life in favour of financial and bureaucratic dependency came up against the proverbial 'farmer's pride' – a situation that forced the district and local peasant leaders to attempt mediation. As part of these proceedings, official assessors carried out meticulous enquiries in person to assess the applicants' need for, capacity for and worthiness of debt relief. These assessments resulted in plans for 'debt relief and buildup' that not only put figures on farms'

33 On market exchange, redistribution and reciprocity, see Karl Polanyi, *The Great Transformation: The Political and Economic Origins of our Time* (Boston, MA: Beacon Press, 2001), 45–58.

34 Daniela Münkel, *Nationalsozialistische Agrarpolitik und Bauernalltag* (Frankfurt am Main and New York: Campus, 1996); Anette Blaschke, *Zwischen 'Dorfgemeinschaft' und 'Volksgemeinschaft'. Landbevölkerung und ländliche Lebenswelten im Nationalsozialismus* (Paderborn: Schöningh, 2018).

35 On the relation between habitus, field and capital see Pierre Bourdieu, *The Logic of Practice* (Oxford: Polity Press, 1990).

improved performance but also sought to inscribe a new imperative of optimisation onto peasant family farming: the aim would not be to run down or simply maintain the farm, as had hitherto been the case; in future the farm conceived as an enterprise would be built up through investments. For one ambitious young farmer from a mountain village who continued to record farm data years after the collapse of the Third Reich, this entrepreneurial logic had already become the normality of his everyday thoughts and actions.[36]

4.2 Farming in the retrograde niches

Although the benchmark of 'due and proper farm management' set limits on how far the extensification of land and livestock use could safely proceed, after the turning point of the war in 1941–2 more and more farms were forced into the path of declining farming intensity. This retreat from the 'wartime battle for production' emerged in several steps: disconnection, contraction, and shutdown. The driving force behind farmholders' gradual disconnection from state-led market regulation was less a milieu-specific resistance to the Nazi regime; rather, it was driven by strategies of resilience in the face of economic hardship. Crises arose not only internally within farms and households – conflicts between spouses, illness, loss of livestock, damage to machinery, accidental fires, and so on – but were increasingly triggered by external circumstances. Requisitions of plant and animal products as well as members of the family labour force by the civilian and military administration robbed farms and households of important key resources. Quotas for self-supply with food and animal feed as well as official allocations of forced labourers did little to compensate for these losses. Consistent with the logic of the peasant family farm, household members responded to such troubles by increasing their production effort and reducing consumption ('self-exploitation'), thereby relying on their self-controlled resource base.[37] This disconnection from state-controlled markets also manifested itself in greater engagement with the shadow economy, something that sprang not merely from the desire for profit on the lucrative black market. As the records of trials held for violations of wartime economic regulations reveal, giving false information about reserves, engaging in illicit slaughter or using bread grains as animal feed were also ways of securing the resource base controlled by the farm, for example, for provisioning indispensable day labourers.[38]

36 Langthaler, *Schlachtfelder*, 43, 128–49, 385–436.

37 Alexander Chayanov, *The Theory of Peasant Economy* (Homewood: American Economic Association, 1966).

38 Langthaler, *Schlachtfelder*, 570–620.

While the authorities more or less accepted farms' growing disconnection with resignation, in cases of contraction through suspected or obvious neglect in management they found themselves prompted to intervene. The Reich Food Estate, for example, initiated court assessments regarding the 'peasant capability' of the owners of hereditary farms. If the requirements were not fulfilled, the court could order a trustee to administer the hereditary farm on a limited or permanent basis. A closer look at these kinds of hearings reveals that behind the lack of 'peasant capability', there was often a pressing shortage of labour as a result of rural exodus or military service. These troubles mostly concerned farms run by women or smallholdings in adverse locations, which had difficulty replacing missing family labour with prisoners of war or foreign civilian workers. Control, however, came not only from above and outside but also from below and inside. Spouses, family members and relatives could apply to the courts for a review of 'peasant capability' and use this as a public stage for the resolution – to their advantage – of the conflicts brewing in daily life behind the scenes. In this way, actors effected an unintended but no less effective form of self-monitoring in their daily lives, which worked in tandem with the surveillance imposed by the Nazi regime.[39]

With the increasing shortage of labour and resources, disconnection and contraction eventually resulted in the shutdown of farms. From 1941 to 1944, it was most often farms representative of 'worker-peasant families', 'artisan farmers', 'part-time peasant families' and 'wine-growing families' – farms at the lower end of the scale in terms of size – who ceased farming for a year or more. Among 'machine men', 'mixed farmer's and 'sugar beet farmers', who occupied the upper end of the scale, there were no shutdowns of farms. The decision, either forced or voluntary, between carrying on with or shutting down the farm was one faced above all by subaltern groups. For farms that were exposed to the rigid control apparatus of the Reich Food Estate and other authorities, this was hardly feasible. Farming families were able to compensate for the pressing shortage of labour by using one of their most important resources: the flexible mobilisation of (predominantly female) labour reserves via family networks.[40] The feminisation of the basis of agricultural labour according to the logic of the family economy nevertheless conflicted with the ideologically determined ideal of the male 'farm leader'. As more women were forced to take over the management of farms from husbands who had been drafted into the military, the authorities grew more vocal in their criticism. 'Farm adoptions' and 'war farming communities', which involved men taking over the supervision or management of orphaned farms run by women, were intended

39 Ibid., 216–30.
40 Ibid., 230–53.

to restore the patriarchal order.[41] Ultimately, it was left to the women in farming families to get to grips with the contradiction between official relief measures and the day-to-day pressures of running a farm.

4.3 Farming in the vanguard niches

Seen from the commanding heights of the Nazi agricultural administration, the main front in the 'wartime battle for production' was the 'protein and fat gap'. While the self-sufficiency of the German Reich between 1933–4 and 1938–9 increased from 80 per cent to 83 per cent for foodstuffs in general, for fats it rose only from 53 per cent to 57 per cent.[42] Accordingly, the Reich Food Estate focused its production offensive on plant and animal fats. This led some farmholders to carve out vanguard niches of intensification. Launched at the beginning of the war, the campaign to cultivate oilseeds offered a support package consisting of bonus incentives, allocation of resources and expert knowledge. Contrary to the Nazi regime's rhetoric of the community-orientated 'peasant', this campaign addressed the selfish 'farmer' as a male entrepreneur. The textual and visual message was not to settle simply for self-sufficiency, but to strive for maximum output for the farm and for the national economy (Figure 4.4). The material and ideological incentives readily found fertile ground, as can be seen from the expansion in rape cultivation in Niederdonau between 1938 and 1943 from practically nothing to around 6,200 hectares.[43] However, the success of the oilseed campaign varied between regions, agrosystems and farming styles. In addition to large estates in the flat lands of eastern Niederdonau, it was highly mechanised, profit-orientated farms in favourable locations run by staff with specialist training – above all 'machine men' and 'sugar beet farmers' – which made the shift to oil seed cultivation.[44]

This advance on the main front in the 'wartime battle for production' was founded on the interplay between political appeals and economic production incentives, as well as on well-suited agrosystems and entrepreneurial farming styles that interacted with the characteristics of the rape plant. Rape necessitated a series of behaviours from growers

41 Hugo Jury, 'Dorfkameradschaft. Kriegs-Höfegemeinschaften im Dienste der Nachbarschaftshilfe', *Nationalsozialistische Landpost* 42 (1944), 1.

42 Heinrich E. Volkmann, 'Die NS-Wirtschaft in Vorbereitung des Krieges', in *Das Deutsche Reich und der Zweite Weltkrieg, I, Ursachen und Voraussetzungen der deutschen Kriegspolitik*, Militärgeschichtliches Forschungsamt (ed.) (Stuttgart: Deutsche Verlagsanstalt, 1979), 177–368, at 301.

43 *Ergebnisse der landwirtschaftlichen Statistik in den Jahren 1937–1944*, Österreichisches Statistisches Zentralamt (ed.) (Vienna: Österreichisches Statistisches Zentralamt, 1948).

44 Langthaler, *Schlachtfelder*, 642–68.

FIGURE 4.4. Advertisement for oil seed cultivation, 1940 (*Wochenblatt der Landesbauernschaft Donauland*, no. 19, 1940, supplementary flyer).

interested in high yields, as listed in the contemporary agronomic discourse: the plant, sensitive to frost, preferred mild locations; it required the purchase of a proven type of seed; it pushed for the use of sowing machinery; it demanded good grain soil; as a devourer of manure it needed copious quantities of commercial manure; it made it necessary to till the soil several times; it forced the use of mechanical or chemical pesticides against its main pest, the rape pollen beetle; and as a new arable crop, the acquisition of expert knowledge was a prerequisite. A network of mutual dependency thus arose between the rape plant and its cultivators, one whose logic incorporated both human and non-human elements.[45] The corresponding farming style boosted the intensification of land use, through high-yield oilseeds for industrial processing as well as livestock farming, through protein-rich oilcakes from the processing industry as animal feed. In this way, the vanguard of oilseed growers built up an intensified agrosystem that was interlinked with upstream and downstream industries along the supply chain.[46]

The niche in oilseed cultivation was limited to the favourable areas on the plains. But even in mountainous regions that were unfavourable

45 On actor-networks, see Bruno Latour, *Reassembling the Social: An Introduction to Actor-Network-Theory* (Oxford: Oxford University Press, 2005), 54–5.
46 Langthaler, *Schlachtfelder*, 642–68.

in terms of climate and transport, the battle against the 'fat and protein gap' carved out another vanguard niche. While the wide-ranging 'debt relief and buildup' programme sought to increase the productivity of all targeted mountain farms, pilot projects directed towards the technological 'armament of the village' were implemented in a limited number of mountain communes.[47] Although both vanguard niches were intended to close the 'fat and protein gap' using plant fats from oilseeds and animal fats from milk, the performance criteria were differently weighted. While the oilseed cultivation campaign hailed the entrepreneurial farmer as a market-orientated producer, the offensive for dairy farming addressed peasant families on mountain farms. Here, the agricultural apparatus tried to exploit not only the population's productive capacity but also its racial potential – that is, the gene pool of healthy peasant families whose offspring should serve as the 'source of blood' for the German people.

The main thrust of the development scheme for mountainous areas becomes clear in the rural commune of Ybbsitz. According to the plan, the measures – financed overwhelmingly from the public purse – should have fundamentally reshaped mountain farming within five years. The input side envisaged an increase in livestock from sixteen to thirty-three livestock units and machinery from barely 2,000 to over 10,000 Reichsmarks – with hardly any alternation in land and labour availability. On the output side, planners counted on the massive development of milk and livestock marketing, which would raise the farms' profitability, combined with improved connections to transport links. The plans therefore aimed to create a growth- and market-orientated farming style that came with fixed gender roles: development was targeted at capital-intensive, medium-sized farms specialising in grassland farming and dairy cattle run by men; their wives were supposed to take care of the household and offspring. Accordingly, the plans for new farm buildings resulted in an architecture that, behind a traditional façade, took the optimisation of efficient farming and bourgeois family life as its points of reference: larger windows in the house and barns for greater natural daylight; separate working areas for milking and processing feed; a kitchen separated from the living room. Since dairy cows required careful treatment to avoid injury to or diseases of the udder, for instance, when using productivity-raising milking machines, only well-motivated family members were to be employed. This field trial to breed the mountain peasant who would achieve both technical and racial productivity may have collapsed after the turning point in the war in 1941–2 under the pressure of external shortages caused by the war economy and internal contradictions within the local community. Nevertheless, the contours of

47 Siegl, *Bergbauern*.

a development trajectory for mountain farms appeared on the horizon that would, after the war, point the way forward.[48]

Both vanguard niches indicate a developmental project for agrarian society that realigned the pre-existing time-space coordinates of farming. In temporal terms, it marked a break with a past labelled disparagingly as the *System*, referring to the inability of the *Austrian* government before 1938 to resolve the agrarian crisis. At the same time, it set farming's sights on an achievable future after the 'final victory'. In spatial terms, it subordinated regionally embedded modes of work and life to the needs of the national government as the regulator of factor and product markets. This developmental project was hardly anti-modern; rather it envisioned an alternative modernity to that embodied by liberalism and communism:[49] an 'organic revolution'.[50] On the one hand, this project sought to strengthen the biological productivity of the peasantry as the racial backbone of the 'people's body'. On the other hand, it sought to shift the economic performance of the agricultural sector from land to labour productivity to secure national 'food liberty'.[51] The project of 'racial productivism' aimed to create a 'healthy' – that is, biologically and economically efficient – peasantry with medium-sized farms in service of the German 'people's community'.

Racial productivism, like related projects of 'radical restructuring' launched by European dictatorships in the inter-war years,[52] bore traits of high modernism: the planned upheaval – implemented even in the face of resistance – of social relations by the power of a centralised authoritarian state, driven by the utopia of scientific and technological progress.[53] But the planning and decision-making elites applied brute state authority only for exceptional interventions – for example, those relating to transfers of Jewish landholdings or terminations of under-productive 'problem farms'. In most interactions with the peasantry, performance incentives, identification offers, and participation opportunities were the rule. This low-modernist tendency becomes obvious both in the oilseed cultivation campaign and the development scheme

48 Langthaler, *Schlachtfelder*, 436–72.

49 Bavaj, *Amivalenz*, 201.

50 Werner Willikens, 'Organische Revolution', *Nationalsozialistische Landpost* 44 (1939), 3–4.

51 Jochen Streb and Wolfram Pyta, 'Von der Bodenproduktivität zur Arbeitsproduktivität. Der agrarökonomische Paradigmenwechsel im "Dritten Reich"', *Zeitschrift für Agrargeschichte und Agrarsoziologie* 53 (2005), 56–78.

52 Lutz Raphael, *Imperiale Gewalt und mobilisierte Nation. Europa, 1914–1945* (Munich: C. H. Beck, 2011), 186–230.

53 James C. Scott, *Seeing Like a State: How Certain Schemes to Improve the Human Condition Have Failed* (New Haven, CT, and London: Yale University Press, 1998), 87–102.

for mountainous areas. Both actions were underpinned by material and symbolic rewards as well as class- and gender-biased opportunities for engaging in the 'organic community'.[54] Racial productivism shared with high modernism its revolutionary developmental goal, and with low modernism the evolutionary path to achieving that goal.

4.4 Conclusion

The findings outlined above call for a revision of the conventional view of the Nazi regime as an interlude in agrarian development or even a regression; on the contrary, it stands out as a threshold period before the agrarian transition. During the Nazi dictatorship, new agrarian institutions were established in Austria and elsewhere in the German Reich, before the Green Revolution during the post-war boom achieved the breakthrough in new agrarian technologies based on fossil energy. For planning experts, agrarian functionaries and vanguard farmers, the horizon of expectation began to detach itself from the room of experience. The vanishing point of this institutional shift was racial productivism: the creation of a both racially and economically productive peasantry in service of industrial society. Consistent with the idea of the Nazi era as a threshold period, from 1938 onwards institutional change began to outpace technological change, which took off only after 1945. Despite the shift in the use of fossil-energy technologies, the priority given by the Nazi regime to the armaments industry denied agriculture full access to productive resources during the war.

Agrarian change during the Nazi era was made up of two complementary movements: one with qualitative and one with quantitative significance. Of qualitative significance were the connections created between the macro-project of the agricultural apparatus – technology-driven, market-integrated and state-led agriculture – and the micro-projects of the peasant farms. Although most farmholders either failed to respond or turned their backs, some vanguard farmers took advantage of those connections through state-subsidised and market-orientated oilseed and dairy farming. Within their room for manoeuvre, they took steps that solidified into regional development trajectories in the post-war decades – such as the introduction of contract farming for industrial crops in the flatlands, or the transition to dairy farming in the mountainous areas. In this way, the macro-project of racial productivism, combined with

54 Jess Gilbert, *Planning Democracy: Agrarian Intellectuals and the Intended New Deal* (New Haven, CT, and London: Yale University Press, 2015), 79; Thomas Etzemüller, 'Social Engineering als Verhaltenslehre des kühlen Kopfes. Eine einleitende Skizze', in *Die Ordnung der Moderne. Social Engineering im 20. Jahrhundert*, Thomas Etzemüller (ed.) (Bielefeld: Transcript, 2009), 11–39.

the micro-projects of vanguard farms, orientated the region's post-1945 development path towards the agrarian transition.[55]

In quantitative terms, of greater significance than the innovations in the vanguard niches was the gradual colonisation of everyday farming by regulatory mechanisms, which affected farms in the mainstream and those occupying retrograde niches. Thereby, the agrarian apparatus sought to resolve the contradiction between the interventionist state's overarching desire for control and the inadequate information about the dispersed actors whom it sought to control. State-led redistribution and state-regulated market relationships infiltrated multifunctional networks of reciprocity and replaced horizontal with vertical relationships. Festering obstinacy among the peasantry was curbed by low-ranking officials acting as mediators. Consequently, state interventions in farm and household arrangements became a normal feature of everyday life. Surveillance through the Nazi state and its market control went hand in hand with the self-surveillance of those working and living on the farm. To express it in terms of institutional economics, the Reich Food Estate, with its centralised organisation, acted as a 'principal' who was well-informed about the thoughts and actions of the decentralised 'agents' on the farms.[56]

The Nazi regime may have intended the 'total reordering' of agriculture in German-annexed Austria according to racial productivism – and with it the solution to the agrarian question in industrial society.[57] However, this developmental project produced resounding results only at the institutional level of the agrosystem and hardly at all at the technological level. Though agrarian modernisation was intended, it was only partially achieved. The agrarian apparatus failed to launch a Green Revolution in its full, institutional and technological, senses. Nevertheless, the Nazi regime did constitute a pre-revolutionary threshold period that left behind viable institutions that guided the technological take-off of Austrian agriculture in the post-war years. Overall, the Nazi regime fell short of a great leap forward in the agrarian transition. But it took small, irreversible steps in this direction along racial-productivist lines. This conclusion is specific to the case of Austria and must not be generalised

55 Ernst Langthaler, 'Agrarwende in den Bergen. Eine Region in den niederösterreichischen Voralpen (1880–2000)', in *Geschichte der österreichischen Land- und Forstwirtschaft im 20. Jahrhundert, II, Regionen, Betriebe, Menschen*, Ernst Bruckmüller, Ernst Hanisch and Roman Sandgruber (ed.) (Vienna: Ueberreuter, 2003), 563–650, at 588–610; Ernst Langthaler, 'Agrarwende in der Ebene. Eine Region im niederösterreichischen Flach- und Hügelland (1880–2000)', in ibid., 651–70, at 656–83.

56 Schwarz-Gräber, 'Gläserne Bauern'.

57 Juri Auderset and Peter Moser, *Die Agrarfrage in der Industriegesellschaft. Wissenskulturen, Machtverhältnisse und natürliche Ressourcen in der agrarisch-industriellen Wissensgesellschaft (1850–1950)* (Cologne: Böhlau, 2018).

for the whole German Reich; however, recent research has found aspects of agrarian change in other regions as well.[58] As an area that was privileged in Nazi-controlled Europe, but lagging behind more advanced agrarian regions in the German Reich, Austria became an experimental station for the developmental project of racial productivism.[59]

58 As an example, see Blaschke, *'Dorfgemeinschaft'*.

59 Ernst Langthaler, 'Österreichs Wirtschaft im Nationalsozialismus', in *Handbuch Wirtschaft im Nationalsozialismus*, Marcel Boldorf and Jonas Scherner (ed.) (Berlin: De Gruyter, 2023), 667–89.

5

Agrarian parties in the twentieth century: rise and fall of an alternative modernity[1]

Miguel Cabo

The second half of the twentieth century witnessed the triumph of two models of modernisation, which, although opposed in so many aspects and embodied in competing political blocs, shared some basic characteristics. Agriculture was conceived as complementary to the industrial sector. Organic farming was to surrender entirely to synthetic inputs, large mechanised farms were favoured for their efficiency, large numbers of farm workers were considered surplus to the needs of the sector and destined to supply factories with badly needed manpower. Specialisation should have the upper hand over polyculture and the myriad local breeds and plant varieties. It is hardly surprising, therefore, that the overwhelming majority of scholars who have paid attention to agrarian parties have labelled them as archaic, retrograde and nostalgic forces, which fought a hopeless battle against the tide of progress on behalf of a redundant social group.

Marxist-inspired historians, above all those from countries in the Soviet sphere, dismissed these parties as accomplices of fascism, defenders of large landowners and dedicated to opposing an alliance between farmers and their supposedly natural allies, the industrial proletariat. These arguments were for the most part an update of those deployed by communist parties and the Moscow-based Peasant Internationale against agrarian parties and their coordinating body (the International Agrarian Bureau or Prague Internationale) in the 1920s and 1930s. Western historiography has hardly been more generous in its depiction of this political

1 This chapter reports work undertaken as part of the Research Project '*Violencia, delincuencia y conflictividad en tiempos de paz y de guerra en el mundo rural, 1850–1980*' (PID2023-152532NB-I00), financed by the Spanish Ministerio de Ciencia, Innovación y Universidades.

family, downplaying their role in the wider picture of political developments and depicting them along the lines of Seton-Watson, who, just after the war, referred to the agrarian parties in Central-Eastern Europe as ideologically inconsistent, prone to romantic daydreaming and dedicated to promoting the interests of the wealthiest farmers by manipulating the ignorance and narrowmindedness of the bulk of the peasantry.[2] Behind all these views, it is easy to detect the lasting echoes of the prejudices against the peasantry as isolated pre-political beings lagging behind on the road to political citizenship and economic development.

The first serious academic approaches to agrarian parties characterised them as essentially reactive and defensive, doomed to failure because they were simply trying to delay unstoppable changes on behalf of groups that felt threatened by them and unable to adapt. For Lipset and Rokkan, these parties expressed the cleavage between the rural and urban worlds and resistance to capitalist transformations in the countryside.[3] Both Gollwitzer and Urwin studied them along similar lines a few years later and acknowledged some of their contributions to the political education of the masses and their importance as real mass-based parties in countries where democracy still had weak roots.[4]

This chapter is intended to analyse agrarianist ideology in the twentieth century, both before and after the watershed of 1945. Agrarianism permeated to some degree a whole array of organisations, political schools and parties during the inter-war period, but it found its purest expression in agrarian parties, which claimed to represent the peasantry, the countryside and the values supposedly associated with them. Agrarianist ideals were shared by many others who, even so, preferred to articulate their agrarian interests through other means. Ernst Laur, the prominent Swiss agronomist and cooperativist, epitomises this attitude; he encouraged the organisation of farmers but was staunchly opposed, both in his country and across the whole continent, to this organisation being channelled through specific parties.[5] Topics such as the necessity

2 Hugh Seton-Watson, *Eastern Europe between the Wars, 1918–1941* (Cambridge: Cambridge University Press, 1945), 258–60.

3 Seymour M. Lipset and Stein Rokkan (eds), *Party Systems and Voter Alignments: Cross-National Perspectives* (New York: The Free Press, 1967).

4 Heinz Gollwitzer, *Europäische Bauernparteien im 20. Jahrhundert* (Stuttgart: Fischer, 1977); Derek U. Urwin, *From Ploughshare to Ballotbox: The Politics of Agrarian Defence in Europe* (Oslo: Universitetsforlaget, 1980).

5 Werner Baumann and Peter Moser, *Bauern im Industriestaat: Agrarpolitische Konzeptionen und bäuerliche Bewegungen in der Schweiz, 1918–1968* (Zürich: Orell Füssli, 1999). In fact, Laur promoted an organisation during the 1920s, the International Peasant Congress, assembling professional organisations and that tried to build an alternative to the Prague International. 'L'organisation patronale. L'Internationale verte', *Le Peuple. Organe Quotidien du Syndicalisme* (10 September 1921), 4.

of a strong agrarian sector to guarantee both social and economic stability, the appreciation of rural traditions or the glorification of rural dwellers as the purest bearers of national identity were present in fascist, socialist, conservative or social-Catholic discourses, but only within agrarianism did they constitute the core of a coherent worldview and offer priorities for actual policies.

5.1 Agrarian parties and paths to modernity

There are several reasons why it is not easy to analyse the complex relationship between agrarianism and modernity. To begin with, agrarian parties were a heterogenous pack, although the same could be said about any other political family, such as their fascist, social-democratic or liberal counterparts. Even so, it is argued here, as has been done before by other authors and most recently by Alex Toshkov, that above all their differences they shared a core of principles (agrarian reform, parliamentarism, cooperativism) that provided them with enough coherence and commonalities to build up a coordinating body, the *International Agrarian Bureau or Green International*, based in Prague.[6] Another handicap is the scarcity of theoretical approaches beyond booklets, articles and party programmes, although when taken together, they provide enough evidence to draw valid conclusions. Finally, although agrarian parties were in government positions at a given point in most of the countries in Scandinavia and Central-Eastern Europe in the 1920s and 1930s, they were normally coalition partners and were seldom in a position to implement their policies without restrictions. Stamboliyski's Bulgaria between 1919 and 1923, the Romanian agrarian government between 1928 and 1931 and the continuous presence in Czechoslovakia of the Agrarian Republican Party in the ruling coalitions during the First Republic were the main exceptions and will be referred to below.

Agrarianism can be understood as a specific variant of corporatism. The whole corporatist idea has been discredited since 1945, identified with the defeated fascist regimes. Even before them, corporatism without a doubt was a distinct feature of many illiberal thinkers opposed to the transformations put into motion by the French Revolution. The advance of liberal individualism in the nineteenth century provoked the reaction of people across different political fields who held onto conceptions of the human being as inextricably linked to communitarian and collective identities.

6 Alex Toshkov, *Agrarianism as Modernity in Twentieth-Century Europe* (London: Bloomsbury, 2019). For a recent overview see Miguel Cabo, 'Agrarian Parties in Europe Prior to 1945 and Beyond', in *Making Politics in the European Countryside, from the 1780s to the 1930s*, Leen Van Molle, Laurent Brassart, Corine Marache and Juan Pan Montojo (eds) (Turnhout: Brepols, 2022), 313–32.

Corporatist elements were, however, present in perfectly democratic experiments such as the New Deal; the key point is how the speakers for each economic sector were chosen to become interlocutors of the state and how agreements were negotiated.[7] Between both world wars the notion that there existed an essential unity around shared economic activities, and that society and politics had to be organised on the basis of those professional groups instead of atomised individuals fighting each other for their own interests, was a widespread one. The hardships of the Depression only increased its appeal.

Matteo Pasetti identified three theoretical schools for corporatism as a whole (not specifically agrarian), the first being the Catholic one, backed by the *Rerum novarum* in 1891, according to which corporatist bodies were to mediate between individuals and the state. The second one would be the nationalist version, of which the Portuguese *integralismo* or *Action Française* are examples. These were conflated with the third school, the fascist conception according to which each profession and economic sector had to be organised as a tool for societal control and subordinated to a totalitarian project. The class-based reading of history and society on the left precluded any strong corporatist leaning in that field of the political spectrum, although Pasetti identifies a minor branch of the corporatist tree among revolutionary syndicalists in Italy and France, or followers of guild socialism in the UK.[8]

One could add a fourth variety of corporatism: pragmatic, corporatist solutions born out of necessity and practical considerations, which might be given a theoretical basis. In every belligerent country during the Great War, the challenges of industrial warfare were met through corporatist schemes that sought to harmonise the conflicting needs of producers, consumers, the army and the war economy. Boards presided over by public servants and technicians grouped together everyone involved in each particular sector to avoid strikes and labour conflicts, guarantee supplies, regulate prices and so on. Walter Rathenau was not the only one to see this development as more than just a solution forced by the

7 Peter Moser and Tony Varley, 'Corporatism, Agricultural Modernization and War in Ireland and Switzerland, 1935–1955', in *War, Agriculture, and Food. Rural Europe from the 1930s to the 1950s*, Paul Brassley, Yves Seghers and Leen van Molle (eds) (New York and London: Routledge 2012), 137–55.

8 Matteo Pasetti, *L'Europa corporativa* (Bolonia: Bononia University Press, 2016), 45. A comparative approach can be found in *Corporatism and Fascism: The Corporatist Wave in Europe*, Antonio Costa Pinto (ed.) (London: Routledge, 2017). The hostility of the left towards the corporativist notion can also be detected within historiographical debates, such as the one between Pierre Barral and Philippe Gratton and their respective interpretations of the unity (or lack of it) of French *agrarisme* in the twentieth century. Pierre Barral, *Les agrariens français de Méline á Pisani* (Paris: Armand Colin,1968); Philippe Gratton, *Les paysans français contre l'agrarisme* (Paris: François Maspero, 1972).

exceptional circumstances of the conflict, but as a model for the post-war world economy in peacetime.[9] The Great Depression some years later also fostered impromptu solutions that could be defined as corporatist, Roosevelt's New Deal being the most obvious example.

The agrarianist variant was also inspired by practical considerations. Agrarian producers in different contexts in the last decades of the nineteenth century felt overpowered and less cared for than other groups that had taken the initiative to organise before them, such as businesses, workers' trade unions or middlemen. That was the incentive to create cooperatives, agrarian leagues or rural banks in order to speak with one voice to governments, industrialists or traders. Those practical initiatives soon led to the first theorising efforts, imbibed with the corporatist notion of the essential unity of every individual involved in a given productive activity, that being more important than differences such as, in this case, those creating opposition between big and small producers or farmers tilling their own fields as owners or tenants. These corporatist notions were soon to be translated into economic institutions, as will be mentioned below, but sometimes also political ones, such as the French *Parti Agraire et Paysan Français*, which proposed complementing the Parliament with an economic council.[10] Agrarianist corporatism was not conceived as a way of keeping away the state, like in the Catholic version, or to work as a tool of the totalitarian state, as was intended by the Fascists. Its goal was to collaborate with the state while maintaining a sufficient degree of autonomy.

5.2 The agrarianist alternative in the inter-war period

A first step to explore the relationship between agrarian parties and modernity could be simply to examine how they presented themselves in this respect. It is of course possible that a given movement disguised its ideology or portrayed itself in terms that do not reflect its real nature. However, any reactionary force would claim as its main *raison d'être* the rolling-back of recent developments that it considered to be pernicious in order to revive some idealised past that, more often than not, had never existed. Agrarian parties, with the Prague International as their coordinating body, in charge of defining their programme and the requirements for any party to be admitted, never claimed they were simply building a wall to contain the changes that had been taking place in the European countryside since the economic crisis of the last quarter of the nineteenth

9 Rathenau (1867–1922) was a Jewish-German industrialist who played a key role in the organisation of the war economy and was assassinated in 1922 by a radical nationalist while foreign minister.

10 Édouard Lynch, 'Le parti agraire et paysan français, entre politique et manifestation', *Histoire et Sociétés Rurales* 13 (2005), 54–65.

century. What they argued for was for the bulk of agrarian producers to have a voice regarding those changes and a chance to steer the direction of the policies being applied. Their ideal, a prosperous agrarian economy based on farmers owning their own land, organised into cooperatives and fully integrated into markets, both as producers and consumers on an equal footing, was something that never had existed in the past. At that time, it was only in the much-admired Denmark that the dream seemed close to fulfilment.[11]

Through their rhetoric, most of these organisations claimed to represent a third way between capitalism and socialism. They defended private property but with a social function (expropriation and distribution of estates, cooperativism, and so forth). Therefore, they opposed communism and socialism, which they also identified with unions and their promotion of low food prices for urban consumers without taking into consideration if those prices were remunerative for national producers or if such a policy would imply lowering tariffs on foreign grain.[12] There was also no lack of criticism of capitalism. Agrarian parties usually proposed limitations to the free market and financial speculation to safeguard smallholders and rural values. They also distanced themselves from individualism and the pursuit of profit at any cost that clashed with the family and community-based structure of the countryside. However, it was only an apparent equidistance because socialism was rejected fully while capitalism was decried in some of its manifestations, but not as a complete system, a repulsion that on many occasions was tinged with anti-Semitism in places where Jews were overrepresented in activities such as money-lending or livestock-dealing.[13] Wherever they had the chance to implement actual policies, agrarian parties tried to control those characteristics of the capitalist economy that were detrimental to their social base, but not in even a single case (not even in the most radical Bulgarian variety in the early 1920s) to abolish it entirely. Thus, they strived to achieve guaranteed minimum prices for farm products, as in Bulgaria under Stamboliyski through the establishment of a state monopoly on grain, or the regulations agreed upon in 1933 in Sweden between the Social Democrats and the *Bondeförbundet*, which pushed corporativist ideas a step further because cooperatives were allotted public functions in order to control the quantity and quality of dairy production.[14]

11 See chapter 8, this volume.

12 A mutual distrust, given that there exists an inexhaustible bibliography of Marxist theory and practice in relation to the complicated integration of the peasantry. For an overview, *Urban Radicals, Rural Allies: Social Democracy and the Agrarian Issue, 1870–1914*, Aad Blok *et al.* (eds) (Bern: Peter Lang, 2002).

13 Kai Struve, *Bauern und Nation in Galizien. Über Zugehörigkeit und soziale Emanzipation im 19. Jahrhundert* (Göttingen: Vandenhoeck and Ruprecht, 2005).

14 Mats Morell, 'Trade Crisis and Regulation of the Farm Sector: Sweden in the Interwar Years', in *Managing Crises and De-Globalisation: Nordic Foreign Trade*

Cooperativism was considered the key for creating economies of scale and allowing smallholders to survive. Cooperatives were, in addition, invested with meanings and purposes that went beyond the material advantages they could provide, such as revitalising traditional institutions, educating the countryfolk about democratic practices or reinforcing the cohesion of local communities. The promotion of cooperatives was a cornerstone of agrarianist policies and the key to adapting technical novelties and interacting with the markets (both as producers and consumers) in conditions that could make possible what has been termed 'low modernism'.[15] In contrast to 'high modernism',[16] the implementation of technical and scientific advancements had to be negotiated and mediated through civil society in a balancing act between old and new, between the continued predominance of smallholdings and a process of industrialisation that would be complementary to the primary sector and not treat it as a mere provider of resources. This approach also entailed making adaptations in response to local knowledge and traditions, and the participation of farmers through democratic channels, which would be provided by associations and the agrarian parties themselves. Low modernism suited the attitudes of agrarian parties towards the state. Mistrust of schemes and regulations that would be translated into an increasing tax burden, usually to the benefit of the industrial sector, or rearmament, disappeared when public interventions and regulations to safeguard their interests were agreed with agrarian representatives. As usual, pragmatism characterised their vision, so agrarian parties clamoured for the dismantlement of wartime regulations in 1918 but rushed to demand state intervention in the 1930s to lessen the effects of the Great Depression.

Their relationship with agricultural technicians could also offer clues about parties' attitudes towards modernity. In their praise of the virtues of rural society, these parties often indulged in anti-urbanism, anti-individualism, anti-intellectualism and the rejection of excessive bureaucracy.

---

and Exchange, 1919–1939, Sven-Olof Olsson (ed.) (London: Routledge, 2009), 137–57.

15 Jess Gilbert, 'Low Modernism and the Agrarian New Deal: A Different Kind of State', in *Fighting for the Farm: Rural America Transformed*, Jane Adams (ed.) (Philadelphia, PA: University of Pennsylvania Press, 2003), 129–46.

16 Defined by James Scott as 'a supreme self confidence about continued linear progress, the development of scientific and technical knowledge, the expansion of production, the rational design of social order, the growing satisfaction of human needs, and, not least, an increasing control over nature (including human nature) commensurate with the scientific understanding of natural laws. High modernism is thus a particularly sweeping vision of how the benefits of technical and scientific progress might be applied – usually through the State – in every field of human activity'. James C. Scott, *Seeing Like a State: How Certain Schemes to Improve the Human Condition Have Failed* (New Haven, CT: Yale University Press, 1998), 89.

These were not purely rhetorical elements, as is evidenced by the statutes of the Serbian Peasant Party (created in 1920), which prohibited intellectuals from making up more than a quarter of the executive committee, which in any case had to be chaired by a peasant, or certain measures taken by the Stamboliyski government in Bulgaria like the establishment of mandatory work periods in the countryside, designed in particular for youths of urban extraction with the aim of imbuing them with the virtues of rural life. Suspicion towards intellectuals resulted, for example, in a penchant for traditional artistic forms rooted in folklore and popular ways of life. The clash of Stamboliyski with the University of Sofia over the reform of the Cyrillic alphabet is also worth mentioning in that connection.[17] In contrast, the relationship between agrarian parties and technicians was very fluid. Veterinarians and agronomists were overrepresented in leadership positions and in some cases, such as in Czechoslovakia, there even existed formal branches for those kinds of professionals.[18] Furthermore, the Czechoslovakian agrarians were behind the creation in 1931 of an *International Institute for the Cooperation of Agricultural Intellectuals*.[19]

Cooperatives and other forms of rural associations linked formally or informally to agrarian parties collaborated with technicians and served as a bridge with farmers, as well as articulating their respective needs and expectations and overcoming prejudices. In particular, the press published by agrarian organisations made new developments and techniques available to countryfolk, presenting them in a language that made them accessible.[20] In short, the people who more than anyone embodied scientific progress applied to farming and livestock were not viewed with hostility, quite the contrary. Furthermore, in their programmes, and in their policies when they were in a position to implement them, they fostered agricultural education within the school system in rural areas.

The actions of these parties revolved around the defence of agriculture as a sector, but mainly of small and medium holdings, facilitating access

17 Toshkov, *Agrarianism*, 77–93.

18 Just as Czechoslovakia was making its first steps, students of agrarian sciences put themselves at the service of the agrarian leader (then Minister of the Interior and later Prime Minister) Antonín Švehla as representatives of the 'agrarian intelligentsia'. *Národný Archiv* (Prague) 494/1. The small Slovenian peasant party confessed openly that they mistrusted intellectuals and reserved their leadership positions exclusively for agrarian technicians and peasants; *Bulletin du Bureau International Agraire* 3 (1928), 183.

19 *Bulletin du Bureau International Agricole*, 1931–3, 210.

20 Lourenzo Fernández Prieto and Miguel Cabo, 'Bridging Between Rural Culture and Expert Culture: The Agrarian Press in Galicia (Spain), ca. 1900–1950', in *Agricultural Knowledge Networks in Rural Europe, 1700–2000*, Yves Segers and Leen Van Molle (eds) (Martlesham: Boydell Press, 2022), 155–76.

to property and their viability in the framework of the market economy. Therefore, even while waving the flag of agriculture as a whole, it was usual for agrarians to display suspicion or hostility both towards large landowners and agricultural labourers. Even though they were often accused by their leftist critics of representing the interests of the largest landowners, when they had the chance, agrarian parties implemented reforms that meant the expropriation of estates that exceeded a given limit, usually above 250 hectares, proving that this was not merely rhetoric.

Agrarian reforms in Central-Eastern Europe after 1918 provided the perfect testing ground for these ideological tenets. According to Dietmar Müller, such reforms had three potential goals. The first was to provide social stability and curtail the turmoil that rocked the countryside in the immediate post-war period, with wild land occupations and roaming groups of veterans and bandits. The second was to improve the performance of the farming sector to strengthen the economy of the states recognised by the peace treaties, several of them newly created and almost all of them with disputed borders. The third was to bring about nation-building, given that questions of land claims and ethnicity frequently overlapped.[21] An examination of policymakers' actual priorities show that the second goal was by far the most neglected of the three, probably because any measure would take years to bear fruit, while the effects of the other two were almost immediate. As far as agrarian parties are concerned, we could classify land reforms into three categories. Some were carried out without their participation (Yugoslavia) or even aimed to curtail the possibility of an agrarian party consolidating its position, thus cutting the ground from under their feet, as happened in Greece under Venizelos. In some countries the local agrarian party did not initially play a role in agrarian reforms but later gained a chance to modify them and apply them according to its own wishes, as in Romania once the PNȚ won an absolute majority in the 1928 elections. (In 1920 the agrarians had unsuccessfully proposed a more radical reform that would have led to the expropriation of estates over 100 ha.) The agrarian government under Iuliu Maniu supported the building of federations of cooperatives, created a central cooperative bank and doubled the budget of the Ministry of Agriculture, but all of this was negated by the effects of the World Depression.[22]

Only in a few cases were the agrarian parties involved in the design of the reforms and their implementation from the very beginning, Czechoslovakia and Bulgaria being the exceptions, though conditions

21 Dietmar Müller, *Bodeneigentum und Nation. Rumänien, Jugolawien und Polen im europäischen Vergleich, 1918–1948* (Göttingen: Wallstein Verlag, 2020), 8.

22 Dietmar Müller, *Agrarpopulismus in Rumänien: Programmatik und Regierungspraxis der Bauernpartei und der Nationalbäuerlichen Partei Rumäniens in der Zwischenkriegszeit* (St Augustin: Gardez! Verlag, 2001), 122–7.

in the two countries were different in many respects. Czechoslovakia's agrarian party controlled both the Ministry of Agriculture and the Land Reform Office for almost the whole of the First Republic, and the expropriation of large estates was accompanied by effective support measures that are part of the explanation for this being one of the countries where productivity recovered the quickest after the war. In Bulgaria there was almost no need to expropriate land, given the lack of large estates, and Stamboliyski focused on providing credit and maintaining a state monopoly on grain until his assassination in 1923. The Bulgarian leader expressed his corporatist views in several writings, stating that of all professions, that of the peasant was the most noble because peasants were the very foundation of society and state. For him, decision-making and politics in future should rest on the shoulders of organised professional groups instead of political parties.[23]

5.3 Agrarianism in a polarised world: agrarian parties after 1945

The authoritarian tide of the 1930s put an end to the parliamentary regimes of one country after another, depriving agrarian parties of the democratic context they needed to thrive. The dissolution of the Green International in 1938 after the Munich Agreement seemed to signal the end of the agrarianist alternative. During the war, some agrarian thinkers and politicians took part in meetings with British representatives in the UK and published some documents aimed at establishing guidelines for the reconstruction of Europe. An International Agrarian Conference in July 1942 hosted by the Chatham House think-tank published conclusions that had much in common with the principles of the Prague International, although now with the support of a great power that had been absent before: cooperativism, regional economic agreements, public credit schemes, industrialisation based on the primary sector, and so forth.[24]

After the defeat of the Axis, a short-lived transition period led to the establishment of Soviet-style regimes in several of the countries that had been part of the core of the agrarian political family. In Bulgaria, Romania, Hungary and Poland, agrarian parties gained support as the staunchest opponents of communism, not without a touch of

23 Iwan Rankoff, 'Die parteipolitische Entwicklung während der Agrarbewegung in Bulgarien', *Zeitschrift für Agrargeschischte und Soziologie* 21 (1973), 92–105; Roumen Daskalov, 'Agrarian Ideologies and Peasant Movements in the Balkans', in *Entangled Histories of the Balkans* R. Daskalov and D. Mishkova (eds) (Leiden: Brill, 2014), 281–354, at 295.

24 Miguel Cabo, 'El trébol de cuatro hojas. La International Peasant Union y su actuación durante la Guerra fría', *Historia y Política* 40 (2018), 299–329, at 305.

Russophobia in some cases. They embodied the defence of private property, although the leftist parties in power promoted redistributive reforms to dispel fears of a collectivisation following the guidelines of Stalinist policies from a decade earlier. Finally, one after another the reconstituted agrarian parties were attacked, harassed, divided and finally banned.[25] In some countries (Poland, German Democratic Republic, Bulgaria), a tame version of the dissolved agrarian parties was kept by the communists as auxiliaries, appropriating a portion of their cadres and inherited prestige for their own cause.

The agrarianist ideal survived in three redoubts after the dismantling of the agrarian parties of Central-Eastern Europe: in exile, in the remaining parties west of the Iron Curtain, and in agrarian professional organisations. Agarianism in exile was represented by the *International Peasant Union* (IPU), founded in 1947 in the USA by agrarian exiles from countries belonging to the Soviet sphere of influence ('captive nations', in Cold War terminology). Backed and financed by the American administration, the IPU presented itself as the heir of the Prague International. Although it lasted until the early 1980s, it was mainly active during the first decade of the Cold War, acting as a think-tank and provider of inside information to the American government. The IPU was preparing itself for a reversal of the situation that would only take place forty years later, when its founding leaders were long dead and the countries they escaped from had been changed beyond recognition by industrialisation, urbanisation and communist rule. Fiercely critical of the regimes beyond the Iron Curtain, IPU propaganda exacerbated the anti-communism that had already permeated their predecessors, praising the peasantry as the strongest guarantee against the advance of revolutionary ideologies all around the planet. The proclaimed equidistance between the two systems of the inter-war years was now abandoned. The Prague International had never looked to America for inspiration, considering its natural conditions and the lack of a real peasantry in the New World as too alien for Europeans to ever follow an American path. Now they praised the American model, but warned that its imitation outside the USA would create masses of landless workers who would have to migrate to the cities or would fall prey to the deceiving promises of communist agitators.

Forced to choose sides in the bipolar post-1945 world, agrarian leaders could not harbour doubts about the way to go, but in the process they had to leave behind their former criticisms of the industrialist American

25 Nigel Swain, 'The Fate of Peasant Parties during Socialist Transformation', in *Bauerngesellschaften auf dem Weg in die Moderne*, H. Schultz *et al.* (eds) (Wiesbaden: Harrassowitz Verlag), 163–76; Miguel Cabo, 'Fin de trayecto. El desmantelamiento de los partidos agrarios en Europa centro-oriental, 1944–1948', *Historia Social* 102 (2022), 163–83.

model that relied on machinery, huge estates and monoculture. The lack of understanding between Vladko Maček, the president of the Croatian Peasant Party and vice-president of the IPU, and a panel of American economists is very revealing, even symbolic, because he was the only exiled agrarian leader who had also taken part in the Green International during the 1930s, embodying the continuity between both organisations. Maček candidly confessed that he had been unable to reach an understanding with his interlocutors because they:

> considered the peasantry simply a class, fighting like laborers or farmers, for their material prosperity. This concept is entirely incorrect. Peasants of Eastern and Southeastern Europe are not merely a class; they are in themselves *a people*.

For the agrarians, tilling the soil was not a profession but a way of life with deep values attached to it, which made it far more valuable than its purely material contributions to the prosperity of their respective nations.[26]

The IPU group, despite their tireless activities, were more like observers than active actors because they were excluded from the countries where they had once been a force. They witnessed the latest developments in Western Europe with hope and approval, although they worried that the premise of keeping the family farm at all costs would not be sustained in the long run. They praised reforms carried out by Italian Christian Democrat governments that halted the advance of the communist party, the Danish path (as they had before), and the first steps of the Common Agricultural Policy (CAP), although here their praise was nuanced by fears of growing bureaucracy and that a too harsh interpretation of the viability criterion would leave behind a great many small farmers.[27]

Unfortunately for the agrarian political family, Soviet dominance fell precisely over the region from where most of their more outstanding representatives were drawn. Outside that region, their other stronghold were the Nordic countries, where agrarian parties had forged alliances with social democrats in the 1930s and afterwards retained a solid position as minor partners in coalition governments. Even so, as shown for the Danish case in this volume, they were not in a position to oppose the path taken after the war, which implied a drastic reduction in the weight of the primary sector in the economy, the disappearance of small farms and a massive transfer of the agrarian workforce to other economic sectors. The presence of agrarian parties helped assure that this transition took place in favourable economic conditions for those affected and that prices remained remunerative. The benefits of the welfare state were also felt by farmers. But the agrarian parties had no opportunity to alter the

26 International Peasant Union, *Monthly Bulletin*, XI–XII (1954), 3.

27 Cabo, 'El trébol', 317.

direction of travel or offer any viable alternative. This being the case, in the 1960s Nordic agrarian parties successively shed their names, became *Centre* parties (sometimes a party split was the price to pay for this) and, given the reduction of their natural base, turned into catch-all parties just like any other. Even so, they still retained a firmer base in the countryside than the rest and incorporated new ideological tenets to attract the urban electorate, be it environmentalism (Sweden), opposition to the European Union (Norway) or neoliberalism (Denmark).[28]

In Western Europe, agrarian parties had never been political heavyweights, and the circumstances of the post-war economic decades were not the most favourable for a revival. Interestingly, the only significant agrarian parties born in this period were pure protest phenomena, such as the Dutch *Boerenpartij* (Peasant Party, 1958–81). It was simultaneously a reaction against European economic policy (its regulations and its promotion of bigger farm units) that limited the autonomy and initiative of farmers and against the rigid pillarised system in the Netherlands (*verzuiling* or sociopolitical organisation on pillars along confessional and ideological lines). Disrupting the sacred concept of consensus in a 'consociational democracy', it reached a peak of almost 5 per cent of the vote before declining, the victim of internal strife and contradictions but also because it attracted the outsiders *par excellence* of the Dutch political landscape: the former members of the National Socialist Movement (known as the NSB) who had collaborated with the German occupation.[29]

The second agrarian party worth mentioning is the Finnish Rural Smallholders' Party (*Suomen pientalouspoikien puolue*), which emerged in 1959 as a split within the Agrarian Union, which it accused of neglecting poorer farmers.[30] On its part, the Irish *Clann na Talmhan* (1939–65) also found the support of the poorest peasants in the west of the island, as in the former cases by expressing the concerns of those feeling left behind by the state and the course of economic change. Although it reached a peak of 10 per cent of electoral support in 1944 and was included in coalition governments in the 1950s, it failed to consolidate itself as a durable political force.[31]

28 *From Farmyard to City Square? The Electoral Adaptation of the Nordic Agrarian Parties*, David Arter (ed.) (Ann Arbor, MI: Routledge, 2001).

29 Aren Lijphardt, *Democracy in Plural Societies: A Comparative Exploration* (New Haven, CT: Yale University Press, 1977); Koen Vossen, 'Agrarian Parties in the Netherlands: The Plattelandersbond and the Boerenpartij', in *Rural Protest Groups and Populist Political Parties*, D. Strijker (ed.) (Wageningen Academic Publishers, 2015), 291–301; Ismee Tames, *Doorn in het vlees. Foute Nederlanders in de jaren vijftig en zestig* (Amsterdam: Balans, 2013).

30 Ann-Cathrine Jungar, 'Agrarian Populism in Finland: Continuity and Change', in *Rural Protest Groups*, Strijker (ed.), 217–41.

31 Tom Varley, 'On the Road to Extinction: Agrarian Parties in Twentieth-Century Ireland', *Irish Political Studies* 25 (2010), 581–601.

Another location in which agrarianist thought survived was in the influential agrarian federations who were indispensable partners for the implementation of post-war policies. They could no longer advocate for a global alternative to the modernising schemes sponsored by national governments and the EEC, but they retained a substantial level of bargaining power regarding specific policies. In so doing, they evoked themes and arguments that can be traced back to the inter-war period, such as the mystique of the family farm. The *Coldiretti*, for instance, supported the reforms made by Italian governments with American support, but expressed their fears of an Americanisation of people's eating habits (consumption of soda instead of wine, fast food, loss of local varieties and traditions, and so on).[32] Their French counterparts made sure that the transition to a more productivist model was softened by generous subsidies and compensation but at the same time gave voice to critical views on the consequences of the CAP along the same lines, like an early expression of environmentalist ideas or the vindication of local breeds and varieties before the advance of standardisation in both livestock and agricultural products.[33]

5.4 Conclusions

Agrarian parties represented the most extreme expression of an alternative path to modernity whose tenets were shared by a whole array of organisations, thinkers and activists all around Europe, shaping a real transnational movement. Recent writers have tended to emphasise their modernising potential, in spite of their shortcomings, although most have focused on their contribution to the social and political field and not so much on the economic sphere.[34] After 1945 the new status quo stripped them of all viability, because both of the systems imposed on a divided Europe (and also elsewhere) were hostile to and dismissive of their proposals. Agrarian parties were either forbidden in countries ruled under communist regimes or lost ground and decayed in line with deep socio-economic changes that inevitably relegated the agrarian sector to a subordinate role, and led to the deagrarisation of the countryside. After the fall of the Berlin Wall, agrarian parties (re)appeared in countries across

32 Emanuele Bernardi, *La Coldiretti e la storia d'Italia. Rappresentanza e partecipazione dal dopoguerra agli anni ottanta* (Roma: Donzelli, 2020).

33 *Au nom de la terre. Agrarisme et agrariens en France et en Europe du 19e siècle à nos jours*, Pierre Cornu and Jean-Luc Mayaud (eds) (Paris: La Boutique de l'Histoire, 2007).

34 Among the exceptions, Johan Eellend, 'Agrarianism and Modernization in Inter-War Eastern Europe', in *Societal Change and Ideological Formation among the Rural Population of the Baltic Area, 1880–1939*, P. Wawrzeniuk (ed.) (Huddinge: Södertörns högskola, 2008), 35–56.

the former communist bloc, although their electoral clout was reduced.[35] In Poland the Polish People's Party has regained significant political weight, although the recent and surprising breakthrough (in the 2023 provincial elections) of the Dutch *BoerBurgerbeweging* (Farmer-Citizen Movement), just four years after its foundation, hints that agrarianist themes still ring a bell in European public consciousness and can gather significant support, at least as a protest vote.[36]

The agrarianist project was thus swept away mercilessly by the alternative strategies imposed by the victors of the Second World War in their respective spheres of influence. It was dismissed as anachronistic and utopic. What remains of it now that its main standard-bearers have passed into memory? Some themes that were downplayed in the inter-war period by their opponents as mere ruralist mythmaking and unrealistic barriers to economic progress can be seen nowadays in a different light. Food sovereignty is a term coined by *Vía Campesina* in the late 1990s as a reaction against unrestricted productivism, standardisation and the free market as guidelines of economic life, but it sounds familiar to anyone reading the conclusions of the Prague International conferences or of each of their parties. The arguments were different, of course, stressing the need to avoid dependence on imports after the famines experienced during the First World War and the risk this posed for the survival of smallholders. Environmental concerns were not widespread in the first half of the twentieth century, but in the orbit of agrarian parties some exceptions can be noted, as is the case of the Croatian MP and vice-president in charge of education and culture within the Peasant Party, Rudolf Herceg (1887–1954), who published several books advocating causes such as a European federation, pacifism or the need to keep a balance between nature and economic development.[37] The economist Nicholas Georgescu-Roegen (1906–94) was a member of the Romanian peasant party and a high-level official in the late 1930s, although he developed his theories about entropy and bioeconomics decades later as an exile in America (as well as criticising both neoclassical and Marxist economists for their inability to understand the peasantry).[38] Finally, the notion of keeping the population in the countryside has a different ring

35 *Les partis agrariens et paysans en Europe*, Jean Michel De Waele and Daniel-Louis Seiler (eds) (Brussels: Éditions de l'Université de Bruxelles, 2009).

36 For the interesting Polish case, Frédéric Zalewski, 'PSL: un retour aux sources du mouvement paysan?', in Cornu and Mayaud (eds), *Au nom …*, 275–86.

37 Suzana Leček, 'Dream of World Peace: Croatian Peasant Party and Two Concepts of the Community of Nations', in *Historia i tradycje ruchu ludowego, I, Ideologia, polityka i jej kreatorzy*, Janusz Gmitruk and Arkadiusz Indraszczyk (eds) (Warsaw: Muzeum Historii Polskiego Ruchu Ludowego, 2016), 247–63.

38 Mauro Bonaiuti, *From Bioeconomics to Degrowth: Georgescu-Roegen's 'New Economics' in Eight Essays* (Abingdon: Routledge, 2011).

to it nowadays, when rural depopulation has become a worrying reality in most European countries.

The agrarianist discourse has somehow survived with the good image, tinged with a bit of collective remorse, which surrounds any movement or collective action in defence of the countryside and on behalf of farmers. Farmers' mobilisations in France since the twentieth century have enjoyed such a degree of sympathy in public opinion, built on their identification with national identity, that the response has often hindered any harsh repression by the authorities in spite of their disruptive or occasionally violent nature.[39] The subsidies of the CAP have been justified as 'welfare for the farmers' by resorting to clichés and cultural constructions that one could read in the manifests of any agrarian party decades earlier, such as the family farm as a key institution of the sociocultural fabric of rural Europe.[40] In some attempts to redefine the European countryside, once the economic and environmental crisis of the 1970s had exposed the limits and the shortcomings of the modernisation paradigm, it is tempting to hear the echoes of proposals and initiatives from a past when more than one road could have led to modernity.[41]

39 Édouard Lynch, *Insurrections paysannes. De la terre à la rue* (Paris: Vendemiaire, 2019), 305.

40 Ann-Christina Knudsen, *Farmers on Welfare* (Ithaca, NY: Cornell University Press, 2007), 307.

41 Sarah Farmer, *Rural Inventions: The French Countryside After 1945* (Oxford: Oxford University Press, 2020), a case study of France that could be replicated in many other countries.

6

From the International Institute of Agriculture to the Food and Agriculture Organization[1]

Federico D'Onofrio

When the Food and Agriculture Organization (FAO) of the United Nations took over the liquidated International Institute of Agriculture (IIA) in 1948, it signalled a paradigmatic shift in the mission of international organisations devoted to agriculture. While the main focus of the IIA had been, since its foundation, the defence of farmers' income through transparent markets, the new organisation focused instead on food and the ways to increase its production.[2] According to Giuseppe Ugo Papi, then Secretary General of the Italian Committee of the FAO, the Institute, which had been the first instance of international collaboration in agriculture, had concentrated its action on the trade of agricultural commodities and farmers' income. FAO's mission, instead, combined trade with a core concern for 'structure', that is for the productivity of the agricultural sector in developing countries.[3] Indeed, the two organisations had very different purposes.

1 This research has received funding from the European Research Council under the European Union's Horizon 2020 Research and Innovation Programme (Grant Agreement no. 949722).

2 On the Institute's establishment and role, see Niccolò Mignemi, 'Italian Agricultural Experts as Transnational Mediators: The Creation of the International Institute of Agriculture, 1905 to 1908', *Agricultural History Review* 65 (2017), 254–76; id., 'Une Chambre au service des agriculteurs? L'Italie et les origines de l'Institut international d'agriculture' (unpublished memoir of the École française de Rome, Rome, École française de Rome, 2016).

3 Giovanni Ugo Papi, *McDougall Memorial Lecture 1967. Giuseppe Ugo Papi: Meeting the World Food Crisis* (Rome: FAO, 1967).

In this chapter we discuss how such paradigmatic shifts in international agricultural cooperation were brought about by two discontinuities in the international discourse on agriculture. The crises that hit the world economy in the early 1920s and early 1930s caused a first shift, while the primacy assigned to development problems in US policy after 1945 marked a second break that determined the mission and activities of the FAO for most of the post-war period.

The chapter's first section describes the impact of the two economic crises that hit the major world economies before the Second World War; namely, the recession of 1920–1 and the Great Depression, when buffer stocks and restrictions on production were discussed at the IIA and the League of Nations as ways to deal with agricultural surpluses. In fact, during the inter-war years, western Europe, which had traditionally absorbed the agricultural production of many overseas exporters, strived for self-sufficiency, generating a dramatic disequilibrium for certain crucial crops. At the same time, this period – as the second section demonstrates – saw the spreading awareness that global markets for agricultural commodities needed regulation to guarantee nutrition and dispose of excess production. Besides the issue of protecting farmers' income, 'hunger was no longer seen solely as a symptom of regional crises but became an expression of global imbalances; it began to be viewed as a problem that was not going to be solved without some form of international regulation'.[4] As Jachertz and Nutzenadel remarked, the creation of the FAO in the 1940s resulted from these discussions. In its third section, this chapter recalls how the FAO, which was born out of concerns for the food supply, took on, over the years, a mission in development. In the 1950s, the fight against hunger combined with a growing awareness that terms of trade were unfavourable to countries exporting agricultural commodities, and that, therefore, the productivity of their agriculture had to increase while their industry developed. Meanwhile though, the agrarian lobbies of the Atlantic economy that had pushed for the creation of the IIA reorganised themselves at a national level or through regional blocs, such as the EEC, to achieve their policy objectives, such as a disposal of the agricultural surpluses in ways that would not endanger the income levels of producers.

So here we retrace how international organisations were involved in the effort to manage the legacy of the 1920s: tariff protection and structural agricultural surpluses in some countries and widespread famine risk across most of the developing world. During the inter-war years, dramatic drops in prices of agricultural products stimulated international plans for integrating persistent surpluses into the structure of world trade. While historians have already pointed out the continuities between

4 Ruth Jachertz and Alexander Nützenadel, 'Coping with Hunger? Visions of a Global Food System, 1930–1960', *J. Global History* 6 (2011), 102.

development projects of the post-war period and previous colonial experiences as well as Roosevelt's New Deal,[5] this chapter insists specifically on the necessity of multilateral agreements as the main lesson of the inter-war period for international agricultural policies. Finally, it also analyses how the emerging focus on 'plenty' paved the way for the unresolved conflict in the post-war period, between the development policies supported by the FAO and the agricultural policies of developed countries, which ultimately undermined any unitary approach to food and agriculture.

6.1 A tale of two crises

International collaboration in agriculture before the Second World War was dominated by networks of European and North-American farmers' organisations, who put the defence of the interests of agriculturalists at the centre of their action. The IIA, as proven by the investigations carried out by Mignemi, was initially born as an attempt at international collaboration not just between governments but – more importantly – between farmers' organisations from various countries: the US, most European states, the British settler colonies and some South American countries. The group who launched the initiative and gathered international support for the Institute had in mind a sort of international farmers' organisation, an International Chamber of Agriculture, in the words of David Lubin, that should counter the overwhelming power of industrial capital and labour.[6] In the end, governments prevented the direct participation of farmers' organisations in the affairs of the Institute, which developed instead as an inter-governmental international organisation. Its main task was to collect and share information and knowledge, but its original mission – namely, the defence of agricultural interests and, in particular, of farmers' income – remained central to its action and was inscribed in the founding treaty. Its statistics were, indeed, meant to improve the functioning of commodity markets and thus – its promoters hoped – the condition of agricultural producers.[7]

5 Among others, Corinna R. Unger, *International Development: A Postwar History* (London: Bloomsbury Publishing, 2018); David Ekbladh, *The Great American Mission* (Princeton, NJ: Princeton University Press, 2010); Nick Cullather, *The Hungry World: America's Cold War Battle against Poverty in Asia* (Cambridge, MA: Harvard University Press, 2013).

6 Niccolò Mignemi, 'David Lubin and the International Institute of Agriculture', in Food and Agriculture Organization of the United Nations, *The Story of the FAO Library: 65th Anniversary, 1952–2017* (Rome: FAO, 2017), 1–20; Mignemi, 'Une Chambre au service des agriculteurs?'.

7 Federico D'Onofrio and Niccolò Mignemi, 'The International Institute of Agriculture and the Information Infrastructure of World Trade (1905–1946)', *Histoire & Mesure* XXXVIII, (2023), 13–38.

After the First World War the Institute was solicited by the Chinese ambassador in Rome to help relieve the Chinese famine of 1920–1, but it had neither the means nor really the will to coordinate food relief. The Institute was equally uninvolved in the Volga famine of the following year. At the World Economic Conferences of Genoa (1922) and Geneva (1927), instead, the Institute's leadership and its allies in various nations concentrated on issues of international trade and the balance between agricultural and industrial prices. This focus reflected, to a great extent, the interests of (mostly European) farmers' organisations amid the economic turmoil of the post-war period.[8]

Many economists believed that a prolonged period of crisis had lasted from 1920 until 1927, although they acknowledged that the situation had improved a little over time. Economists from the US pointed to the weakness of European demand for foreign foodstuffs, due to failing industrial exports and high indebtedness, as root causes of the enduring agricultural malaise.[9] At the World Economic Conference of 1927, Max Sering, one of Germany's most renowned agricultural experts, arrived with a report on the agricultural depression that stated that the crisis had lasted from 1920 to 1924 and that the subsequent recovery had not been robust. Sering acknowledged that the reduced purchasing power of Europeans, ruined by the war, bore a major responsibility for the crisis, but he insisted on the peculiarly unfortunate situation of agriculturalists: while they had benefitted greatly from price rises during the war, they were subsequently squeezed by industrial prices that rose even faster, a phenomenon known as the 'price scissors'.[10] This narrative obviously underlined the vulnerability of farmers and their weakness vis-à-vis other corporate interests. A similar point of view was confirmed in the report of the Commission Internationale d'Agriculture put together by the French Eugène-Melchior de Vogüé and the Swiss Ernst Laur, the two leaders of a Europe-wide alliance of farmers and landowners.[11] Jules Gauthier,

8 Federico D'Onofrio, 'Agricultural Numbers: The Statistics of the International Institute of Agriculture in the Interwar Period', *Agricultural History Review* 65 (2017), 277–96.

9 Ernest Minor Patterson, *Europe in 1927: An Economic Survey* (American Academy of Political and Social Science, 1927).

10 Max Sering, Axel Schindier and Rudolf Lerch, *Internationale Preisbewegung und Lage der Landwirtschaft in den aussertropischen Ländern* (Berlin: Parey, 1929). Sering denied, nevertheless, that there had been a real problem of overproduction, since Europe had lost one of its main suppliers; namely, the Russian empire. Max Sering, 'Causes of the International Depression of Agriculture', in *Proceedings of the Second International Conference of Agricultural Economists Held at Cornell University, Ithaca; New York, August 18 to August 29, 1930* (Menasha: George Banta Publishing Company, 1930), 19–39.

11 Laur and De Vogüé asked agricultural associations that participated in the Commission Internationale d'Agriculture to request their members to compare 1925/26 prices with pre-war prices, Commission International d'Agriculture to

the Secretary of the Société des Agriculteurs de France and a close collaborator of De Vogüé, the German Andreas Hermes, President of the Association of Farmers' Unions and Harry Lindsay, presented the report to the Preparatory Committee for the International Economic Conference in 1926.[12] The consequence was the conviction that farmers should somehow be protected.

While not all European agrarian leaders shared either the diagnosis or the remedies proposed by the protectionist front – Folckert Posthuma, who represented Dutch milk producers, for instance, heavily criticised Laur and the Commission Internationale in the press[13] – this narrative dominated the discourse of agrarian organisations over the course of the 1920s: farmers had been victims of an imbalance between agricultural and industrial prices (the price scissors) and were therefore entitled to some form of compensation from governments. The IIA came to Geneva with a thick report that insisted on a similar interpretation, though mediating between its diverse membership, which included wheat-exporting Argentina and Yugoslavia, as well as countries, such as Italy, that had embarked on plans for reducing dependency on foreign food imports.[14]

In 1928, Gautier, Hermes and Laur, as the representatives of large agrarian organisations from continental Europe to the League of Nations, repeated that the agricultural distress derived from revenue prices lower than input costs and invoked the creation of agreements between cooperatives of producers and consumers, with the help of the state, in order to increase production without depressing prices.[15] Laur had grandiose

---

Federatieve Nederlandsche Zuivelbond (circular letter), draft questionnaire, Collectie 117 F.E: Posthuma C 22285, 2.21.026.07, omslag 129, Nationaal Archief ten Haag. On the alliance, see Gilbert Noël, 'La solidarité agricole européenne: des congrès d'agriculture à la politique agricole commune', in *Sociétés rurales du 20. siècle: France, Italie et Espagne,* Jordi Canal, Gilles Pecout and Maurizio Ridolfi (eds) (Rome: École Française de Rome, 2004).

12 Jules Gautier, Andreas Hermes and Harry Alexander Fanshawe Lindsay, *L'agriculture et la crise économique internationale: Mémoire* (Genève, Société des Nations, 1927); D'Onofrio, 'Agricultural Numbers'.

13 Laur to Posthuma, 8 July 1927, Collectie 117 F.E: Posthuma C 22285, 2.21.026.07, omslag 130, Nationaal Archief ten Haag.

14 International Institute of Agriculture (ed.), *Agricultural Problems in Their International Aspect* (Monetary and Economic Conference, Rome: Printing Office of the International Institute of Agriculture, 1926).

15 Jules Gautier, Andreas Hermes and Ernst Laur, 'Economic Organisation. Consultative Committee Proposal by MIL Gautier, Hermes and Laur', 25 April 1928. UN Archives Geneva, C-C-E--5_EN, available online at https://archives.ungeneva.org/economic-organisation-consultative-committee-proposal-by-mil-gautier-hermes-and-laur (accessed 25 December 2024). Laur was adamant that tariff protection of agriculture was indispensable: 'he was convinced that it would be impossible to maintain the present area of cultivation in old agricultural countries without a certain measure of protection – and the resolutions adopted in Geneva did not contain a word about that

plans. When the Great Depression broke out in 1929, he restated his analysis of the causes of the agricultural depression, which the industrial depression, according to him, had not sparked but only aggravated.

This narrative was not uncontested. Many economists in the US and the UK blamed the economic downturn of the early 1930s and the persistent weakness of global trade on the growth of agricultural production in Continental Europe and the erection of protectionist barriers in favour of European farmers. Indeed, governments intervened heavily in agriculture in this period. If tariffs did grow compared to the very low level reached at the end of the war (but remained below 1913 levels for most European countries),[16] it was other policies that really incentivised production and reduced European dependence on overseas imports. The famous 'battles of wheat' and other measures in favour of food producers that different European countries engaged in at various moments throughout the 1920s were meant to decrease huge trade deficits, but also to improve the degree of strategic autonomy. They were effective to a great degree. In the wake of the Great Depression, the Australian Frank Lidget McDougall calculated that European imports of wheat had declined from 322 million bushels (113,500,000 hl) in 1929 to 132 million bushels (46,500,000 hl) in 1933. Over the same period, imports of butter had declined from 2,987,000 cwt (151,800 tonnes) to 1,620,000 cwt (82,300 tonnes) and imports of beef and veal from 4,194,000 cwt (213,000 tonnes) to 1,948,000 cwt (99,000 tonnes).[17] At the Conference of the International Association of Agricultural Economists in 1930, Mordecai Ezekiel (who became a central figure in the early FAO) suggested that:

> by 1928, Europe had increased her output to 8 per cent above pre-war, and subsequently to even more; but North American production also increased, exceeding 25 per cent above pre-war in 1928. As a consequence, world production of foodstuffs, which in 1923 and 1924 was but 3 per cent above that of 1913, by 1928 had increased to 16½ per cent above 1913

which was more than the growth in population.[18] While historians have recently disputed the actual occurrence of surpluses before the Great

necessity for protection', as Per Jacobsson recalled in his 'Report on a mission to attend the 13th International Congress on Agriculture May 26th-June 1st 1927', 14 June 1927, UN Archives Geneva, R379/10/59565/21922.

16 Giovanni Federico, *Feeding the World: An Economic History of Agriculture, 1800–2000* (Princeton, NJ: Princeton University Press, 2005), 192.

17 Frank Lidget McDougall, *The McDougall Memoranda* (Rome: Food and Agriculture Organization of the United Nations, 1956), 2.

18 Mordecai Ezekiel, 'The Problem of Agricultural Surpluses in the United States', in *Proceedings of the Second International Conference of Agricultural Economists*, 74.

Depression,[19] it is significant that at the time there was a widespread perception among non-European experts that the growth of European production had undermined global agriculture.

To the League of Nations Economic Committee, the British official Frederick Leith Ross, chief economic advisor to the government in London, presented a report that accused agricultural protectionism of having deepened the crisis. Ross' report was accompanied by a much blander take by the Economic Committee that only condemned 'excessive protectionism'.[20] Laur vehemently rebutted these kinds of argument and responded furiously to Leith Ross and the League, arguing that the increase in European production of wheat had not been substantial and was merely the consequence of European farmers switching from rye to wheat, something only detailed data could reveal. It was up to overseas countries to reduce their production of cereals.[21]

Instead, Laur reiterated that the problems of agriculture originated in the imbalance between the prices of the outputs and inputs of agricultural production. In the case of the surplus production of the Danubian countries, he ruled out the idea that the problems could be solved by increasing the income of city-dwellers in industrial countries because it was a proven law that they would not increase their consumption of foodstuffs in proportion to the increase in income. Moreover, there was a widespread consensus that poor countries in Asia and Africa, which were occasionally stricken by famines, would not be able to support an expanded demand.[22] Neither was it possible to lower input prices significantly. Once cereals had been identified as the price-defining element of agriculture, it became necessary to raise cereal prices by creating national monopolies and international pools that would purchase cereals and sell them at fixed prices, possibly turning excesses into biofuel.[23]

Laur's proposals anticipated the Green Pool project and paved the way for the agricultural policy of western European countries in the

19 Giovanni Federico, 'Not Guilty? Agriculture in the 1920s and the Great Depression', *J. Economic History* 65 (2005), 949–76.

20 Frederick Leith-Ross, *Considerations on the Present Evolution of Agricultural Protectionism* (Geneva: League of Nations, 1935).

21 E. Laur, 'À propos du rapport du Comité économique de la Société des Nations sur le protectionnisme agricole, Brougg, juin 1935', *Archiv fuer Agrargeschichte*, Bern, 161.2.I.11.; E. Laur, 'Comments on Views of the Economic Committee of the League of Nations on Agricultural Protectionism', *J. Farm Economics* 17 (1935), 748–53.

22 A similar point was made in Ezekiel, 'Problem of Agricultural Surpluses', 75.

23 Ernst Laur, 'Note du professeur Laur sur l'organisation d'une société d'achat de céréales des pays de l'Europe orientale', 16 June 1931, R2801/10D/13963/2016, UN Archives Geneva, https://archives.ungeneva.org/questions-agricole-correspondance-avec-lunion-suisse-des-paysans-prof-l-laur (accessed 17 September 2025).

post-war period. As Moser and Baumann have stressed, Laur was acutely aware of the necessity of finding international solutions to price problems.[24] It is clear, though, that his ideas, his politics and contacts were primarily concerned with Europe and limited in ambitions. In a letter dated 8 September 1934, the US American agricultural economist, Henry C. Taylor recalled his meeting with Laur at the International Congress of Agriculture in Budapest: 'He does not have a grasp of the world situation, but a local reaction to it, and I am afraid the world is full of local reactions rather than rational plans.'[25] In 1948, Laur went on to lead the newly-formed Confédération Européenne de l'Agriculture, an umbrella organisation that represented the right wing of European rural interests. It was a testament to the continuity in agrarian interest groups, but the world around him was changing, in Europe and beyond.[26]

6.2 McDougall and Keynes

After the war, the Anglo-American winners decided to dismantle the IIA and transfer its assets to the FAO of the United Nations, which had been created during the war. The mission of the two organisations differed greatly. While the defence of agriculturalists' income had been a major concern for the Institute, the paramount mission of the FAO was:

> raising levels of nutrition and standards of living of the peoples under their respective jurisdictions; securing improvements in the efficiency of the production and distribution of all food and agricultural products; bettering the condition of rural populations; and thus contributing towards an expanding world economy and ensuring humanity's freedom from hunger.[27]

Nutrition, standards of living and hunger were never mentioned in the founding treaty of the International Institute, and this was not merely a consequence of the progress of nutrition studies during the first half of the twentieth century.

The Institute was finally dismantled in 1948, but its enduring legacy was not limited to the decision to move the FAO to Rome. The new organisation inherited the statistical tasks of the Institute, its library and archives, and part of its personnel. For instance, Giuseppe Ugo

24 Werner Baumann and Peter Moser, *Bauern im Industriestaat: agrarpolitische Konzeptionen und bäuerliche Bewegungen in der Schweiz, 1918–1968* (Zürich: Orell Füssli, 1999), 132–3.

25 Taylor to Hobson, 8 September 1934, The State Historical Society of Wisconsin, Henry C. Taylor Papers, 1896–1968, Box 23.

26 Baumann and Moser, *Bauern im Industriestaat*, 358.

27 *FAO constitution in Basic Texts of the Food and Agriculture Organization of the United Nations*, I (Rome: FAO, 2001), 3.

Papi, who had been the Institute's last Secretary General, headed the Italian delegation to the FAO, while Valentino Dore, the chief of the Bureau of Statistics, remained at FAO to lead the transition.[28] When the FAO launched its agricultural census, it counted it as its Second World Agricultural Census, thus continuing the series inaugurated by the IIA in 1929. The new organisation, though, was also inspired by ideas that had been foreshadowed at some of the Institute's meetings in the 1930s. Frank Lidgett McDougall, for instance, had been the permanent delegate of Australia to the IIA, before becoming one of the key personalities behind the creation of the FAO.[29]

McDougall's turn to nutrition science as early as the 1930s is well-known to historians.[30] His reports to the General Assembly of the IIA stand out for the novelty of his approach, although nutrition science had already been making inroads into the realm of policy. The food relief interventions in the wake of the First World War, such as Herbert Hoover's American Relief Administration, had sought collaboration from nutritionists, and by the early 1930s, the League of Nations Health Organisation had begun developing nutrition standards with the help of experts such as W. R. Aykroyd and John B. Orr. The League had already produced internationally agreed dietary requirements in 1935.[31] The studies showed that humans required not merely a certain intake of energy (that was fixed at 3,000 calories a day for a working man), but also 'protective' food and vitamins.[32] In particular, Orr, a medical doctor with broad experience in animal nutrition, had tried to calculate not just the average quantity of food consumed by Britons but the quality of the

28 D'Onofrio and Mignemi, 'The International Institute of Agriculture and the Information Infrastructure of World Trade'.

29 He was member of the permanent committee of the IIA between 1934 and 1940, as is reflected in the proceedings of the various General assemblies of the IIA held during this period. His involvement with the activities of the IIA is apparent in Wendy Way, *A New Idea Each Morning: How Food and Agriculture Came Together In One International Organisation* (Canberra, ACT: ANU E Press, 2013).

30 Way, *A New Idea Each Morning*, 153; Sean Turnell, 'FL McDougall: Eminence Grise of Australian Economic Diplomacy', *Australian Economic History Review* 40 (2000), 51–70; John B. O'Brien, 'FL McDougall and the Origins of the FAO', *Australian J. Politics and History* 46 (2000), 164–74.

31 Paul Weindling, 'The Role of International Organizations in Setting Nutritional Standards in the 1920s and 1930s', in *The Science and Culture of Nutrition, 1840–1940*, Harmke Kamminga and Andrew Cunningham (eds) (Amsterdam: Brill, 1995), 319–32.

32 Frank Lidget McDougall, 'Alimentation et agriculture: rapport présenté au nom du comité permanent à la XIIème assemblée générale', in Institut International d'Agriculture, *Actes de la treizième Assemblée Générale 5–10 Octobre 1936* (Rome: Imprimerie de l'Institute International d'Agriculture, 1937), 500–9.

British diet. With the support of the government, he had surveyed six randomly selected groups of people, showing how the diet changed as income increased. On average, the consumption of fresh milk, butter, meat, fish, eggs, fruit and vegetables correlated positively with income, which suggested that poverty was the main cause of malnutrition. Orr also tried to assess whether the diets within each group were adequate in terms of calories and nutrients and how the health of the poorest was affected by the lack of basic nutrients. His results were published in a widely discussed report in 1936.[33]

McDougall built on this work, and in particular on the enquiries of British consumption carried out by Orr, to argue in favour of a complete reorganisation of markets for agricultural commodities at a world level. According to him, the world needed more rather than less food at affordable prices. His report, addressed to the 1936 General Assembly of the IIA, started from premises that were diametrically opposed to those of Ernst Laur. Instead of underlining the fall in agriculturalists' income and their eroded margins, instead of stressing the gap between prices and costs – as Laur had done – he concentrated on the lack of food to satisfy the consumption needs of the population. Agriculture should be in the service of consumers. Since nutrition science, as it was being developed at the international level, stressed the need to increase the availability of 'protective' foodstuff, including liquid milk, meat, fruit and vegetables, world production should be reorganised accordingly. In particular, agriculturalists in the most densely populated countries (essentially in Western Europe) should concentrate on dairy products, while allowing countries with lower production costs to provide them with cereals and sugar. In this way, international trade would restart and farmers in agricultural countries would improve their living standards. McDougall imagined that, in the near future, Europe should produce only 75 per cent rather than 95 per cent of the wheat that it consumed.[34] For dairy, in particular, he envisaged a complete turnaround of the policies adopted to resist the depression. According to him, subsidies to producers should be turned into subsidies to consumers, and milk could be provided at a lowered cost by governments.

Laur and McDougall shared a concern for structural agricultural surpluses that affected large parts of the world, 'with the exception of Russia and probably most of Asia'.[35] Where they differed was on how to tackle this problem. Laur insisted on the necessity of raising prices through state monopolies on cereals and lowering costs through subsidies (especially for credit) and commercial organisations. He was not ready to

33 J. B. Orr, *Food, Health and Income: A Report on a Survey of Adequacy of Diet in Relation to Income* (London: MacMillan, 1936).

34 McDougall, 'Alimentation et agriculture', 506.

35 McDougall, *McDougall Memoranda*, 2.

accept that European farmers could move away from cereals and did not believe that this could be either a realistic or a desirable outcome, at least in the foreseeable future. McDougall, instead, focused on demand: rather than reduce production, governments should subsidise consumption.

McDougall's idea of subsidising consumption also echoed John Maynard Keynes' emphasis on aggregate demand as paramount for ending the broader economic crisis.[36] Keynes knew commodity markets very well. He had already engaged extensively with stocks of raw materials for his reporting at the London and Cambridge Economic Service since 1923, and a main focus for him and his colleagues at the Economic Service throughout the 1920s had been the (lack of) adjustment of supply and demand. Buffer stocks such as those of the wheat pools created in this period seemed to guarantee price stability and, by June 1924, Keynes had concluded that 'it seems as if relative prices could be kept a good deal steadier if the organisation for carrying stocks at a moderate cost were on a larger scale'.[37] He continued developing his idea of buffer stocks to stabilise international demand even after the Great Depression, when accumulating stocks of raw materials and commodities proved an aggravating rather than alleviating factor for world prices.[38] By 1938, Keynes was openly suggesting a government-sponsored system of storage for foodstuffs and raw materials to stabilise prices.[39] He compared two methods for stabilising prices: a monopoly or restrictions on output. Just like McDougall, Keynes believed that output restrictions were hardly a good idea, given the levels of undernourishment. Instead, governments should step in and, since no government, not even Britain, was big enough to stabilise prices on its own, a world organisation was needed.

While continental Europeans, such as Laur or Hermes, reasoned essentially in terms of the interests of their constituencies and the producers' organisations they represented, McDougall and Keynes reflected a rather technocratic attitude, but also a global perspective. Their proposals originated in their reflection on the relationship between the different parts of Britain's global empire. Way claims that, in the negotiations of the 1930s, McDougall felt he represented the world outside Europe. In fact, he projected onto the world what he experienced in the Empire, with an industrially strong centre, endowed with a small, specialised

36 Way, *A New Idea Each Morning*, 178.
37 John Maynard Keynes, 'Special Memorandum 6', in *The Collected Writings of John Maynard Keynes, XII, Economic Articles and Correspondence: Investment and Editorial*, Donald Moggridge and Elizabeth Johnson (eds) (Cambridge: Royal Economic Society, 1978), 315.
38 Scepticism on the function of stocks was expressed by Ezekiel, 'Problem of Agricultural Surpluses', 80–1.
39 John Maynard Keynes, 'The Policy of Government Storage of Food-Stuffs and Raw Materials', *Economic J.* 48 (1938), 449–60.

agriculture, importing from overseas territories the bulk of its needs in agricultural commodities. These ideas had been relatively minoritarian in the Institute, but were key to the funding of the FAO.

6.3 The FAO, from trade to technical assistance

Food relief was central to the new organisation. In the wake of the Axis' defeat, the European famine made the world food supply a pressing concern, leading to the operations of UNRRA at first and eventually to the creation of an FAO International Emergency Food Council (IEFC).[40] The IEFC relied on extra-European producers, such as Siam and Burma, besides the United States.[41] Nevertheless, the experience of the inter-war period loomed menacingly and surpluses were expected to arise as soon as the food situation in Europe returned to normality.[42] In order to manage world markets, the newly founded FAO of the United Nations, under the leadership of Orr and with McDougall as advisor, immediately began to develop a World Food Board that in many ways was the heir to some of the solutions envisaged in the 1930s to tackle the Depression. While Orr thought in terms of calories and nutrients, he spoke the unavoidable language of commodity boards. Thus, he proposed the creation of an internationally managed and internationally financed operation that would buy and sell agricultural commodities at agreed prices in order to provide buffer stocks against fluctuations but also to sell foodstuffs cheaply to malnourished people.

It was an extremely ramified and ambitious plan to feed the world in an economically sustainable way. It presupposed a reorganisation of global trade flows under a rather centralised management. In the end, though, the British and US American governments came to prefer a scheme based on the International Trade Organisation, which was supposed to deal with all aspects of trade, rather than have a separate organisation for agriculture. In retrospect, such grandiose plans for international cooperation may seem doomed from the start. In fact, the plan of the World Food Board seemed much less utopian in 1946, after more than a decade of discussions on international regulations, the experience of the Imperial Trade Board, and widespread practices of food boards and

40 Amy L. S. Staples, 'To Win the Peace: The Food and Agriculture Organization, Sir John Boyd Orr, and the World Food Board Proposals', *Peace & Change* 28 (2003), 501.

41 Ruth Jachertz, '"To Keep Food Out of Politics": The UN Food and Agriculture Organization, 1945–1965', in *International Organizations and Development, 1945–1990*, Marc Frey, Sönke Kunkel and Corinna R. Unger (eds) (Basingstoke: Palgrave Macmillan, 2014), 80.

42 The Department of State, *Food and Agriculture Organization of the United Nations* (Washington, DC: US Government Printing Office, 1947), 2.

monopolies on foodstuffs in various countries. The scheme, as a booklet printed by the Department of State described it, with characteristically reassuring rhetoric, would reproduce on a global level the kind of 'school lunch or food stamp plans familiar in the United States'.[43]

Indeed, governments initially supported Orr's proposal, which was presented at the Second Annual Conference of the FAO, held in Copenhagen in September 1946, and the two objectives it entailed: 'provide diets on a health standard' and 'stabilizing agricultural prices at levels fair to producers and consumers alike'.[44] The FAO began therefore asking member states to analyse the experience of national offices in each country that managed the distribution of commodities at special prices to protected categories of people, the storage of foodstuffs and the financing of it.

The project in the end was set aside due to the objections of the United States and Great Britain. Before the US Congress decided not to ratify the 1948 Havana Charter of the International Trade Organisation, it seemed preferable to the delegations of the two major Western powers to have the international commodity trade discussed in the framework of overall negotiations on international trade, rather than by a 'forum of likeminded and sympathetic agricultural professionals' such as the FAO.[45] While the opposition of Britain and the United States is well-known and proved fatal to Orr's project, it is interesting to analyse the initial reactions of other countries represented at the Preparatory Committee of the World Food Board in 1946. If these countries had much less weight in the final decision than the US and Britain, their response is revealing in relation to the concerns that emerged in the post-war phase.

Both those countries that were massive exporters, such as Brazil or Siam, and those, such as China or India, that were big importers of foreign foodstuffs but, due to their low income, were not likely to be in a position to pay for their imports in the foreseeable future, manifested a rather lukewarm support for the proposal. The presence of countries from what is (often inappropriately) called 'Global South' at the negotiating table was not a novelty, since they had been largely represented both in the meetings of the League of Nations and within the IIA, but in this context their delegations were confronted with a diminished European representation and their role was therefore much more significant.

43 Ibid., 9.

44 Orr to the Ministers of Foreign Affairs of Australia, Belgium, Brazil, Canada, China, Czechoslovakia, Denmark, Cuba, Egypt, France, India Netherlands, Philippines, Poland, UK, USA, 14 December 1946, FAO Archives, Lord John Boyd Orr's papers, 0_1_1_A_3_01011945-31121948_Outgoing Letters to Governments and Governmental Agencies 1945-1956 before 1951.

45 Ivan D. Trofimov, 'The Failure of the International Trade Organization (ITO): A Policy Entrepreneurship Perspective', *J. Politics and Law* 5 (2012), 61.

The Brazilian delegation underlined that what was needed was not a short-term improvement in nutrition standards brought about by subsidised supplies of foodstuffs. Instead:

> [T]he most rapid and permanent way of raising low standards of living prevalent in underprivileged areas is to increase the productivity of activities in those areas and make available to them the added facilities offered by science and technological progress.[46]

The Siamese delegate, Dr Saras Chuebsaeng, gladly embraced measures for price stabilisation, but he also pointed out the risk that the price of industrial inputs may start recovering more quickly than that of agricultural products – the price scissor of the inter-war period – and demanded investments in transport infrastructures and financial and technical assistance to continue and increase exports from war time levels. Similarly, the delegate of the Philippines also insisted on technical assistance.[47]

Among the structural importers, India and China represented the largest population. The representative of Kuomintang China, Chen Chih-Mai, was clearly too eager to secure food relief from UNRRA and the IEFC to oppose a plan that promised a permanent relief structure, even so he stressed the necessity of expanding domestic production.[48]After recalling the 1943 Bengal famine, the Indian delegate insisted that, while India might indeed accept the supply of basic foodstuffs at a discounted price, the priority was that India increased its production through technical assistance. Agriculture could not be reduced to a commercial issue, and they would willingly take in the agricultural surpluses of the 'chief exporting countries' but would not enable them to 'look for any considerable profits'. '[C]ountries like India' he continued 'should be offered in these few intervening lean years until they are able to stand on their own legs, their share of the marketable surplus almost on the basis of cost of production, and if it must be so, with a trifl[ing] overhead'.[49] The goal though remained self-sufficiency, not a permanent system of regulated exchanges, and the priority was technical assistance to increase production.

This collection of statements by delegates of countries on the periphery, both importing and exporting nations, shows that Orr's project was too radical but also not radical enough. It was not realistic to treat agriculture separately from the overall trade negotiations that were going on at the same time in London. Governments, as underlined by the Dutch delegate, were far from enthusiastic about the accumulation of costly

46 Statement of the Brazilian delegation, 1 Nov. 1946, FAO Archives, Lord John Boyd Orr's papers, 0_1_1_A_3_01011945-31121948_Outgoing Letters to Governments and Governmental Agencies 1945-1956 before 1951.

47 Ibid., Statement of Dr Saras Chuebsaeng.

48 Ibid., Statement of the Chinese delegation.

49 Ibid., Preparatory Committee, 016, 3.

and risky stocks. If developing countries aimed at self-sufficiency and productivity increases that would make competition in international markets even more challenging, European farmers were also organising to reduce foreign imports as soon as the post-war crisis had passed. Already in 1948, Laur activated what was left of his international network (decimated by the loss of Central and Eastern Europe to the Soviets) to create an organisation, the Confédération Européenne des Agriculteurs, to continue his campaign in favour of European farmers against the US-dominated International Federation of Agricultural Producers, at a time when North American grains were still crucial for deficit areas.[50]

After the dismissal of the idea of a World Food Board, the FAO developed, above all, its programmes for direct technical assistance. In so doing, it was orientating its activities according to the new keywords of US-dominated world politics. In his famous re-election speech in 1949, the US president Harry Truman had listed as his fourth point a real pledge for international technical assistance to 'make available to peace-loving peoples the benefits of our store of technical knowledge in order to help them realise their aspirations for a better life'.[51] Assistance to improve agricultural productivity was deemed crucial for the undernourished agricultural countries of the world. This was in part a purely strategic measure, taken to prevent further Communist advances in colonial and post-colonial countries, especially after Mao's victory in the Chinese civil war.[52] In part though, it reflected a growing concern with overpopulation. The reorientation of FAO towards development not only aligned with the Point IV policy of the United States (although Point IV was originally intended to promote industrial development) but, as we stressed above, also met the demands of developing countries, both exporters and importers of foodstuffs. In fact, the UNRRA, which was set up as a relief agency, had, by the end of its mandate in 1947–8, already started engaging in assistance and the FAO took over these activities.[53] For the FAO this became a crucial mission and the agency played a big role in implementing the United Nations Expanded Programme of Technical Assistance, which came into being as a result of Economic and Social Council resolution 222 (IX) approved by resolution 304 (IV) of the UN General Assembly of 1950.[54] Compared to the IIA, which focused on

50 Laur to Dr. F. Porchet, 22 Apr. 1948, Commission Internationale d'agriculture: Statuten und Entwuerfe, 1945-1948, Schweizerisches Bundesarchiv, J2.332-01, 611.0-01, Schachtel 2012/119_115

51 Cited in Ekbladh, *Great American Mission*, 81.

52 Cullather, *Hungry World*, 2–3.

53 Ekbladh, *Great American Mission*, 89.

54 On the Expanded Programme, see *The Structure of United Nations Economic-Aid to Underdeveloped Countries*, Üner Kirdar (ed.), (Dordrecht: Springer Netherlands, 1966), 23 –63.

the collection and dissemination of information and knowledge, the FAO was thus directly involved in developmental work.[55]

The size of FAO operations quickly became correspondingly incomparable to the lean structure of the IIA. Significantly, besides the growing engagement in food relief, this meant a shift of focus away from trade to production. The progressive shrinking of the Economics Division and the rapid growth of the agriculture division between 1951 and 1958 testifies to this change in mission.[56] At the same time, concentrating on production also meant less emphasis was put on nutrition and agricultural welfare. Not only did the global concerns of the post-war era mark a dramatic change from the restricted circles of the IIA, dominated by the concerns of the agrarian elites of Europe, the USA and the British Empire. They also rapidly pushed aside the kind of grand Keynesian plans for economic management that were advocated by former imperial officials and politicians such as McDougall and Stanley Bruce, who was FAO chairman until 1951, in favour of more targeted interventions to raise farmers' output.

Meanwhile, though, the United States began a massive programme of bilateral assistance based on Public Law 480 to dispose of their excess agricultural production and provide subsidised foodstuffs to developing countries. But P.L. 480 caused growing concerns in exporting countries that saw their exports of foodstuffs displaced by US dumping.[57] The World Food Programme was established in 1961 to ease these tensions and deal with the management of world agricultural surpluses on a multilateral basis, but separately from broader issues of international trade and economic conjuncture.[58] Initially, it managed $100 million in contributions, mostly in the form of commodities, from donor countries, thus absorbing but a fraction of the stocks of the EEC, Canada and the United States.[59] For the rest, the Cold War world saw the management of surpluses and deficits in foodstuffs essentially devolved to national or bloc policies (such as the Common Agricultural Policy of the EEC) or to the market, while development efforts concentrated on production

55 Jachertz, 'To Keep Food Out of Politics'.

56 Ralph Wesley Phillips, *FAO: Its Organization and Work and United States Participation* ([Washington, DC] : US Dept of Agriculture, Foreign Agricultural Service, 1964), 8–9.

57 The case of Canada was discussed in Jerome M. Stam, 'The Effects of Public Law 480 on Canadian Wheat Exports', *American J. Agricultural Economics* 46 (1964), 805–19. Nevertheless, others claimed that the effect of P.L. 480 had not been entirely negative for exporting countries, Brady J. Deaton, 'Public Law 480: The Critical Choices', *American J. Agricultural Economics* 62 (1980), 988–92.

58 Aaron D. Rietkerk, '"The Constructive Use of Abundance": The UN World Food Programme and the Evolution of the International Food-Aid System during the Post-War Decades', *International History Review* 38 (2016), 788–813.

59 World Food Programme, General Regulations, FAO Archives 16_WFP_FP1-1_V1_27101960-18121963_General Policy Matters.

increases, especially after the Green Revolution in South Asia during the 1960s. The result was a set of rather uncoordinated and inconsistent initiatives, which pursued contradictory goals of productivity growth, famine relief and surplus disposal.

6.4 Conclusions

This chapter has aimed to show a double shift in the priorities and actors of international collaboration in food and agriculture. As embodied by the League of Nations and the IIA, pre-war international collaboration in agriculture focused on trade in commodities and the protection of the farmers' income on both sides of the Atlantic. International markets of agricultural commodities made for the primary object of diplomatic discussions, since international trade had been an obvious issue of international negotiations. This tendency became even more pronounced when 'managed' trade came to dominate commodity flows in the inter-war period through quotas and bilateral agreements. The Wheat Conferences held during the 1920s and 1930s, for instance, reiterated the need for an international regulation of trade issues.[60] The Great Depression led to a new approach to interdependencies and officials from the British Empire, such as Bruce or McDougall, were extremely innovative and ambitious in their proposals for a new systematic management of world imbalances. Coupling trade policies with the new science of nutrition, they proposed to invert the paradigm of international agricultural collaboration and base it on food needs rather than income protection.

The marginalisation of continental European traditional agrarian elites in the international negotiations held in the USA and Canada during the Second World War opened a (narrow) window of opportunity for plans of systemic regulation led by the USA and the UK. The project of an International Trade Organisation, and the World Food Board plan that Orr failed to push through because of the opposition of several governments, including the USA and the UK, shared an emphasis on the intentional governance of markets, although the International Trade Organisation was meant to encompass all products and the World Food Board introduced a separate organisation for agriculture, based on the exceptional importance of nutrition. Yet, these ideas were never implemented. In fact, the operations of the FAO in the post-war period concentrated primarily on technical assistance and eventually famine relief through the World Food Programme of the United Nations. These activities closely reflected the priorities of the development policy of the US government.

60 Way, *A New Idea Each Morning*.

While trade negotiations continued in the Genevan General Agreement on Tariffs and Trade, the long-term concerns of European agrarian organisations with income support (a goal that had shaped the debates at the League of Nations and the IIA during the inter-war period) led to the proposal of the European Green Pool and eventually to the establishment of the Common Agricultural Policy of the European Economic Community. In most OECD countries, the defence of price stability and farmers' income became the guiding principle of national or regional agricultural policies. Although part of the structural surplus that income subsidies created was absorbed by food relief programmes, part of it was dumped onto developing countries, thus undermining the purpose of technical assistance programmes of UN agencies and other development actors. The wreck of the technocratic hopes of the 1930s and 1940s, in fact, left only regional and national policies to address market regulation and made the world possibly more vulnerable to the crisis of the 1970s.

PART II

AGRICULTURAL MODERNITIES AND MODERNISATION IN THEIR POLITICAL CONTEXTS

7

UK agriculture before and after the Second World War: agricultural policies and the adoption of new technologies, 1920–1970

Paul Brassley

'There is little doubt,' wrote the farmer, journalist and writer A. G. Street in 1951, 'that the present prosperity of British farming is mainly due to one man, who is now dead. His name was Adolf Hitler.' Street was writing an updated epilogue for a new edition of his best-known work, *Farmer's Glory*. Twenty years earlier he had written, in the epilogue to the first edition, 'Probably one of the hardest things for farmers to realize to-day is that they are considered unimportant people by the majority of the community … As a result of this the farmer has no pride in his occupation. The zest has gone out of farming.'[1]

The years between the end of the First World War and the beginning of the Second were not without significant developments in machinery, fertilisers, agricultural science and education, and there were farmers who energetically adopted new methods or practised established ways of farming with enthusiasm and efficiency. But it is generally argued – and it is difficult to disprove – that for most farmers survival was more important than expansion, and adapting to depressed markets was the way to survive. In contrast, by the end of the 1960s, Tristram Beresford, who farmed not far from Street, made the case that farming had recovered 'its spirit, its zest, its vocation … It has dug up its buried talent and put it to work'.[2]

The following chapter attempts to quantify the extent of output and input changes in British agriculture between 1920 and 1970 and to put

1 A. G. Street, *Farmer's Glory* (Harmondsworth: Penguin, 1951), 210, 222, 224.

2 Tristram Beresford, *We Plough the Fields: British Farming Today* (Harmondsworth: Penguin, 1975), 7.

forward some explanations for why the industry changed more after 1939, and especially after 1947, than during the inter-war years.

7.1 Quantifying output changes

Table 7.1 contains estimates of the volume of UK agricultural output, produced by multiplying physical output figures by prices denominated in constant (1986) terms.[3] Although the calculation is relatively complex, the conclusions to be drawn from it are, at first sight, fairly simple: there was little change in the overall volume of UK agricultural output before the Second World War, and a rapid increase from the beginning of the war to 1970. This apparently simple conclusion, however, hides the fact that the composition of the output changed, as Table 7.2 demonstrates, with decreases in some cereals and increases in pigmeat and poultry production between the wars, and increases in cereals, especially barley, and milk production, after the Second World War.[4]

TABLE 7.1. Volume of output from UK agriculture, 1914–19 to 1966–70.

	Volume of output index (1911–13 = 100)
1914–19	99.9
1920–2	97.4
1923–9	99.5
1930–4	109.8
1935–9	123.3
1940–5	129.6
1946–50	138.2
1951–5	168.2
1956–60	201.0
1961–5	240.6
1966–70	268.9

Source: Brassley, 'Output and Technical Change', 84.

3 For more details of the methodology see Paul Brassley, 'Output and Technical Change in Twentieth-Century British Agriculture', *Agricultural History Review* 48 (2000), 60–84.

4 See also Joan Thirsk, *Alternative Agriculture: A History, From the Black Death to the Present Day* (Oxford: Oxford University Press, 1997), chs 6–8.

TABLE 7.2. Quantities produced on UK farms, 1922–68.

	1922	1938	1948	1968
Wheat ('000 tons)	1,742	1,959	2,356	3,469
Barley ('000 tons)	1,096	901	2,021	8,271
Oats ('000 tons)	1,932	1,702	2,571	1,221
Potatoes ('000 tons)	5,203	4,404	10,132	6,872
Sugar Beet ('000 tons)	55	2,191	4,319	7,118
Turnips and Swedes ('000 tons)	17,788	10,605	9,676	5,893*
Beef ('000 tons)	604*	615	584*	906*
Mutton and lamb ('000 tons)	227*	214*	153*	245*
Pigmeat ('000 tons)	294*	423*	135*	829*
Poultrymeat ('000 tons)	n.d.	79*	84*	407*
Milk (million litres)	n.d.	8,065*	8,337*	12,011*
Eggs (million dozen)	189*	545*	451*	1,089*

Notes: Cells marked n.d. = no reliable data available. Cells marked * indicate that the figures are not precisely for 1922, 1938, 1948 or 1968 but for the nearest year or group of years for which data are available.

Source: MAFF [Ministry of Agriculture, Fisheries and Food], *A Century of Agricultural Statistics: Great Britain 1886–1966* (London: HMSO, 1968), 56, 108–119; H. Marks and D. Britton, *A Hundred Years of British Food and Farming: A Statistical Survey* (London: Taylor and Francis, 1989), 164, 204–38.

***

To begin, it is worth noting that the data in Table 7.2 relate to individual years, and of course output could vary considerably from year to year depending on changes in the weather. Higher than normal yields produced a good wheat harvest in 1938, whereas the previous year had produced only 1.5 million tons and the following year produced only 1.6 million. On the other hand, yields and outputs of potatoes, sugar beet, turnips and swedes varied much less. There is therefore a case for averaging outputs over a range of years, although the differences between the pre-Second World War figures and the post-war figures are so great as to be apparent without this refinement.

A second obvious point is that crops are to some degree substitutes for each other. Land that can be used for wheat can also be used for barley or oats and vice versa. Acreages of all three cereal crops had peaked in 1918 as a result of high wartime prices and the introduction of the 1917 Corn Production Act, which guaranteed a reasonable level of prices until 1920. Thereafter the Act was discontinued. C. S. Orwin, Director of the Agricultural Economics Research Institute at Oxford University pointed out that the law of diminishing returns implied that low prices and a falling market called for cost restrictions. If cereals on poor land did not cover the cost of cultivation, the land should be laid to grass.[5] Many farmers followed his advice. The areas of barley and oats fell to half of their peak levels by the 1930s. Initially the wheat area fell too but recovered from 1933 after the introduction of the 1932 Wheat Act, which provided for deficiency payments to be made to wheat growers. There seems little doubt that farmers used land that they might previously have put into barley and oats to grow wheat. The British Sugar (Subsidy) Act of 1925 provided for guaranteed minimum prices to farmers and had a similar impact on the area of turnips and swedes, especially in the arable areas of Eastern England, as Table 7.2 demonstrates.[6] A million acres had been added to the permanent grass area by the early 1930s.[7]

Unfortunately, there are no official figures for the output of milk between the wars, because until the 1930s significant quantities were used for the farm production of butter and cheese, so that liquid milk sales represented only a part of production. Nevertheless, it seems reasonable to infer, from the fact that the number of cows in milk plus heifers in calf increased from less than 3 million in 1920 to 3.6 million in 1940, that milk production was steadily increasing.[8] There were indeed expanding enterprises, sugar beet, pigs, mainly for fresh pork (much of the bacon consumed in the UK was imported) and poultry rearing for egg production in particular, and it was these, together with the increase in liquid milk production, that accounted for the increase in the total volume of output between the wars.[9] Otherwise farmers responded by trying

5 C. S. Orwin, 'Commodity Prices and Farming Policy', *J. Royal Agricultural Society of England* 83 (1922), 3–14.

6 E. H. Whetham, *The Agrarian History of England and Wales, vol. VIII, 1914–1939* (Cambridge: Cambridge University Press, 1978), 166, 243.

7 Ministry of Agriculture, Fisheries and Food [MAFF], *A Century of Agricultural Statistics, 1866–1966* (1968), 96–103.

8 Ibid., 123.

9 P. Brassley, 'Agricultural output, costs and incomes in the United Kingdom, 1919–1940', in J.-M. Chevet and G. Béaur (eds), *Measuring Agricultural Growth: Land and Labour Productivity in Western Europe from the Middle Ages to the Twentieth Century (England, France and Spain)* (Turnhout: Brepols, 2014), 185.

to keep down costs, labour costs in particular. Between 1921 and 1939 the full time employed labour force fell by 183,000, or about a quarter, and the part-time, seasonal and casual labour force was halved.[10] The majority of farmers concentrated on survival. A. G. Street, who farmed in Wiltshire and saved his farm from bankruptcy by changing from a traditional mixed-farming system to one based on low-cost dairying on permanent pasture (and by becoming a successful author and journalist), concluded that English people were not especially keen to see farming flourish, but at the same time they did not wish to see it die. 'Instead they want it kept just alive as a cheap playground during peace, and ready to work hard and save them during war'.[11]

Pigmeat and egg production were both heavily dependent on imported feedingstuffs, so their production was curtailed during the Second World War, whereas the output of cereals, potatoes and sugar beet, which would produce more energy for a given area of land, was encouraged.[12] After the war the continued decline in the area of fodder root crops such as turnips and swedes opened up space for an increased area of cereals, especially barley in the 1950s and 1960s, and, mostly after 1970, for oilseed rape. Liquid milk production continued to increase, and much of the increased cereal output went into livestock feed, especially for pigs and poultry.

As both Tables 7.1 and 7.2 indicate, overall output changed little between 1920 and 1940, although its composition changed in response to changing market forces and government policy. After 1940 market prices and agricultural policy encouraged farmers to increase output, and both tables suggest that they did so. There were only a few exceptions. The replacement of farm horses by tractors, hesitantly pre-1940 and rapidly after 1950, had a big impact on the demand for oats. Only 825,000 acres were sown to oats in 1966, compared with a peak of 3.7 million acres in 1942. Similarly, the potato acreage declined to more normal levels having been increased to meet the emergency demand during the war, and the area of fodder roots declined as they were replaced as winter feed, first by kale, then by hay and silage.[13] How can we explain this marked contrast between the inter-war and post-war years? The remainder of this chapter attempts to do so.

10 MAFF, *Century of Agricultural Statistics*, 62.

11 A. G. Street, *Farming England* (London: Batsford, 1937), 114.

12 J. Martin, 'The Structural Transformation of British Agriculture: The Resurgence of Progressive High-Input Arable Farming', in *The Front Line of Freedom: British Farming in the Second World War*, B. Short, C. Watkins and J. Martin (eds) (Exeter: British Agricultural History Society, 2006), 33.

13 P. Brassle, D. Harvey, M. Lobley and M. Winter, *The Real Agricultural Revolution: The Transformation of English Farming, 1939–1985* (Woodbridge: Boydell Press, 2021), 135–48.

7.2 Changing factor productivities

Street may have been looking back to what he would have called the Great War when he characterised agricultural land as a peacetime playground and a wartime salvation, but within three years of publishing this characterisation of farmers, they had the opportunity to show how they could work hard and respond to war. They were called on to make sure that the country had an adequate and nutritious, if dull and monotonous, diet. They did so, as Tables 7.1 and 7.2 show, not so much by enormous output increases, although the volume of output did increase during the war, as by producing more cereals, potatoes and liquid milk at the expense of meat, eggs, butter and cheese. Land that had been put down to grass in the inter-war years was ploughed up and cropped. More than 100,000 regular workers and nearly as many part-time and seasonal workers came back into the labour force, which, given the extent to which farming still relied on hand labour for all kinds of jobs from milking to weeding to corn carting, was a vital component of the wartime response.[14] And then, in contrast to the years after the First World War, farmers were encouraged to keep on expanding output after the war ended.

One way of producing the increases in the volume of output shown in Table 7.1 is to change from less to more valuable products, and to some extent this did indeed occur after the war. The output of potatoes was restricted, oats were no longer needed for horses, turnips and swedes were replaced by alternative fodder crops or cash crops, whereas the output of meat, milk and eggs increased. But it was more important for farmers to increase the output of whatever they produced from each acre they farmed, or, in other words, by increasing land productivity.

As well as producing human food, UK agriculture needed to make a significant contribution to feeding the country's livestock, which (except for horses) increased in numbers after the war. By the mid-1960s there were 35 per cent more cattle, 12 per cent more sheep, 64 per cent more pigs and 70 per cent more poultry than there had been before the war.[15] Much of the area that had been ploughed up during the war remained in the arable rotation, although some of it was put down to temporary grass, which accounted for nearly one-third of the arable area by the mid-1960s. By then the permanent grassland covered just over 11 million acres, significantly less than the 17 million acres that it had accounted for at the beginning of the war, and the area of rough grazing in England and Wales had decreased by nearly a million acres.[16] The demand for land for purposes other than agriculture, both during the war and after,

14 MAFF, *Century of Agricultural Statistics*, 62.

15 Ibid., 122–8.

16 Ibid., 90–100; Brassley, 'Output and Technical Change', 64.

was considerable. During the war it was mainly for airfields and military training areas; afterwards it was for urban development and forestry. Nearly 1.4 million acres were transferred to these uses between 1950 and 1965. Forestry accounted for more than half of this, but much of it was the more marginal land, often formerly rough grazing. For agriculture, the more serious loss was the land that went to urban development, which was often good land around existing settlements. It was calculated to be equivalent to 3.6 per cent of potential production over the fifteen years between 1950 and 1965, or 0.24 per cent per year. However, this loss was more than offset by increases in yield per acre, which were, overall, about ten times as rapid.[17]

TABLE 7.3. Yields of principal products on UK farms, 1922–68.

	1922	1938	1948	1968
Wheat (hundredweight per acre)	17.1	20.4	20.7	30.6
Barley (hundredweight per acre)	14.0	18.3	19.5	28.2
Oats (hundredweight per acre)	12.3	16.2	17.5	25.1
Potatoes (tons per acre)	7.2	7.2	7.6	9.8
Sugar beet (tons per acre)	n.d.	6.6	10.5	14.6
Turnips/swedes (tons per acre)	14.5	14.2	14.6	19.3
Milk (gallons per cow per year)	540 (pre-war)		517	808*
Eggs per hen per year	149 (pre-war)		120	204

Notes: one hundredweight per acre = 125 kg per hectare. 1 ton per acre = 2,500 kg per hectare. n.d. = no data available. * indicates that this figure is for dairy cows; figures for previous years are for all cows.

Source: MAFF, *A Century of Agricultural Statistics*, 109–19.

Table 7.3 shows that yields of the main products for which it is relatively easy to calculate yields (producing figures for meat yields per acre is a more complex exercise) rose much more in the twenty years after 1948 than in the twenty or thirty years before that date.

17 Brassley *et al.*, *Real Agricultural Revolution*, 166.

***

Yield increases to the extent of those seen in the years after the Second World War can be brought about by increasing inputs, of labour, capital, fertilisers, pesticides, purchased feedingstuffs and so on, or by adopting new technologies. As Table 7.4 indicates, some of the increased output in the war years can be attributed to increases in labour use, which enabled more intensive cultivation and the conversion of previously uncultivated land to profitable agricultural use. The contribution of the Women's Land Army and of prisoners of war has been widely celebrated, but there were also examples of schoolchildren helping with the harvest, and men leaving office jobs to work on the land.[18] But after the Second World War, as after the first, this trend was reversed, and labour left the land in significant numbers, either attracted by higher-paid work in other industries or replaced by machinery. The net effect, as Table 7.4 demonstrates, was an appreciable increase in labour productivity in the inter-war years and an enormous increase after the war.

TABLE 7.4. UK agricultural output, employment and labour productivity, 1920–70.

	Volume of Output (£m 1986)	Employed workers ('000)	Output (£million) per thousand workers	Labour productivity index (1922 = 100)
1920–2	3265	996	3.3	100
1935–9	4134	738	5.6	170
1946–50	4633	865	5.4	164
1966–70	9014	432	20.8	630

Source: output volume from Table 7.1; employed workers from Marks and Britton, *A Hundred Years of British Food and Farming*, 138.

Producing a comparable estimate of capital productivity is a more difficult exercise, because there appear to be no data for fixed capital formation in agriculture before 1955, and those data then ignore changes

18 G. Clarke, 'The Women's Land Army and its Recruits, 1938–50', in *The Front Line of Freedom*, Short, Watkins and Martin (eds), 101–16; J. Custodis, 'Employing the Enemy: The Contribution of German and Italian Prisoners of War to British Agriculture During and After the Second World War', *Agricultural History Review* 60 (2012), 243–65; R. J. Moore-Colyer, 'Kids in the Corn: School Harvest Camps and Farm Labour Supply in England, 1940–1950', *Agricultural History Review* 52 (2004),183-206; R. J. Moore-Colyer, 'The Call to the Land: British and European Adult Voluntary Farm Labour, 1939-49', *Rural History* 17 (2006), 83–101; J. S. Collis, *While Following the Plough* (London: Cape, 1946).

in the value of land, a major component of the capital invested in agriculture, and in the value of working capital invested in important items such as fertiliser stock and breeding livestock. Table 7.5 shows the result of a calculation using the data that are available.

TABLE 7.5. Current output and gross fixed capital formation in UK agriculture, 1951–60 to 1966–75.

Gross Output (£ million, current prices		Gross Fixed Capital Formation (£ million, current prices)		Gross Output per £ GFCF
Average 1951–60	1,400.0	1955	104	13.5
Average 1956–65	1,679.3	1960	141	11.9
Average 1961–70	2,015.2	1965	184	11.0
Average 1966–75	2,974.4	1970	250	11.9

Source: Brassley, 'Output and Technical Change', 80; A. Burrell, B. Hill and J. Medland, 1990, *Agrifacts: A Handbook of UK and EEC Agricultural and Food Statistics* (London: Harvester Wheatsheaf, 1990), 59.

Table 7.5, insofar as it reveals anything, implies diminishing returns to capital invested after the 1950s, but tells us little about the comparison with wartime years or earlier. It does, however, suggest that some of the improvements in labour productivity were brought about at the expense of capital productivity. Previous studies have suggested that farmers provided much of their own capital, so that when profits were high investment increased and vice versa. There were also official grant schemes that encouraged investment, especially in farm buildings and associated technology. A later study concluded that these grants might have been 'more important in determining the extent, pace and nature of technical and structural change in farming than the price support measures'.[19] Overall, total factor productivity (TFP), according to one study, increased in the inter-war period, largely due to the decrease in labour, may have fallen slightly during the war, and increased to a greater extent in the twenty years after the war, possibly by as much as 82 per

19 B. Hill, 'Resources in Agriculture: Capital', in *Agricultural Resources: An Introduction to the Farming Industry of the United Kingdom*, A. Edwards and A. Rogers (eds) (London: Faber, 1974), 145–64; Brassley *et al.*, *Real Agricultural Revolution*, 174–6, 179–81; A. Buckwell, 'Economic Signals, Farmers' Response, and Environmental Change', *J. Rural Studies* 5 (1989), 157.

cent. A more sophisticated study for the period 1949–67 produced a lower but still positive TFP growth rate of 1.87 per cent per annum.[20]

The likelihood that there is a residual, in that increases in land and labour productivity were not balanced by decreases in capital productivity, implies that something other than capital investment contributed to increases in output: technical change and the associated decision to implement it.

7.3 Technical changes in UK agriculture

Numerous technical changes were adopted by UK farmers in the years between 1920 and 1970. The major impact of some was to increase output; others were mostly labour saving without necessarily increasing output. Some were available, if not widely adopted, before 1939; others were only introduced after 1939. This suggests that we can discuss them under the four categories suggested in Table 7.6.

Table 7.6. Technologies adopted in UK farming, 1920–70.

	Available before 1939	Available after 1939
Mostly output increasing	Purchased feedingstuffs Artificial fertilisers Friesian cows Drainage New crop varieties?	New crop varieties Insecticides Fungicides Artificial insemination
Mostly labour saving	Farm machinery and motorisation, including milking machines	Farm machinery and motorisation Herbicides Buildings

Naturally, some significant changes do not fit neatly into one or the other of these four categories. Silage, for example, was undoubtedly an important innovation. It was first introduced to the UK in the late nineteenth century, when it had some impact on increasing output for the few farms that adopted it, but at the expense of considerable labour costs. It was adopted much more widely towards the end of the period under discussion here (and even more widely after 1970), but by then it involved different techniques and considerable use of mechanisation. Silage in its developed form can be seen as both output increasing and

20 Brassley, 'Agricultural Output, Costs and Incomes in the United Kingdom, 1919–1940', 190; C. Thirtle, L. Lin, J. Holding, L. Jenkins and J. Piesse, 'Explaining the Decline in UK Agricultural Productivity Growth', *J. Agricultural Economics* 55 (2004), 343–66.

labour saving.[21] Some farmers changed their farming systems from arable or mixed farming to livestock farming in the inter-war years, mostly with the effect of decreasing labour costs, but post-war system changes often involved specialisation in order to increase output, although some labour-saving might also be involved.[22] Accepting these exceptions, the categorisation adopted in Table 7.6 suggests both a framework for discussion and an important question: if technologies were available before 1939 how widely were they adopted and why were they not more widely adopted?

Purchased feedingstuffs, as Michael Thompson pointed out more than fifty years ago, were an important introduction in the mid-nineteenth century, and the availability of cheap cereal imports after 1870 meant that all farmers would have been aware of them and most would use them to some extent. But whereas the average annual quantity sold, according to one estimate, increased by only 2.7 million tons in the inter-war years, it increased by 4.9 million tons between 1939 and 1969. Moreover, the sophistication of the products involved changed too, with basic ingredients, such as oilcakes and flaked maize that needed to be mixed on the farm, being superseded after the Second World War by compound rations designed for particular purposes and categories of livestock.[23] Similarly, artificial fertiliser use increased little – by less than half a million tons – in the inter-war years, but then rose by 5.5 million tons between 1939 and 1970. Nitrogen fertiliser use especially increased in the post-war years, both on grassland and on cereal crops. Inter-war cereal varieties grew tall, so a little nitrogen often made them 'lodge' or fall to the ground and so become difficult to harvest. The development of shorter-strawed varieties after the war meant that more nitrogen could be used to increase yields without the danger of lodging. One estimate attributed 26 per cent of the increase in wheat yields between 1946 and 1967 to improved varieties and 36 per cent to other factors such as the use of fertilisers and pesticides, reductions in harvest losses, and husbandry improvements. The change from Shorthorn cows to Friesians in the dairy herd increased milk yields, but Friesians remained a less numerous breed until after the war. By the early 1970s they accounted for over 80 per cent of the dairy herd. There was a comparable story with field drainage: a technology introduced in the nineteenth century, employed very little in the inter-war years, but used on an average of 70,000 acres each year in the UK between 1940 and 1968. As a result, some 2 million

21 P. Brassley, 'Silage in Britain 1880–1990: The Delayed Adoption of an Innovation', *Agricultural History Review* 44 (1996), 46–62.

22 Brassley *et al.*, Real *Agricultural Revolution*, ch. 8.

23 F. M. L. Thompson, 'The second agricultural revolution, 1815–80', *Economic History Review*, sec. ser. 21 (1968), 62–77; Brassley, 'Output and Technical Change', 72.

acres were drained, either by pipe drains or less permanent mole drains, out of an arable area of about 18 million acres.[24]

The internal combustion engine-powered tractor was the most notable of the labour-saving technologies to be introduced in the early twentieth century. British manufacturers were making them before the First World War. In 1917–18 some 6,000 Fordson and 2,632 International Harvester tractors were imported from the USA.[25] It is important to remember that these were by no means the first labour-saving machines to be introduced to UK farms, since the nineteenth century had seen numerous horse-drawn machines, from mowers and reaper-binders to hay rakes and seed drills, at work in the fields and replacing the scythe and other hand-operated tools. But, as Auderset and Moser have argued, 'the *motorisation* [my italics] of agricultural production … unleashed an unprecedented potential of production', and that was the process that began in the first two decades of the twentieth century.[26] However, it was a slow beginning, which initially saved little, if any, labour. There were still nearly a million horses working on UK farms in 1920, and only about 20,000 tractors. By 1939, as Felicity McWilliams has demonstrated, tractors, horses and steam power were seen as complementary on farms, and although there were then over 60,000 tractors, there were still ten times as many farm horses. By 1970, however, the horses had disappeared, as had steam power, and there were over 450,000 tractors at work, more than two per farm, and they were more powerful, and had a wider range of associated implements, than pre-war tractors. Especially important was the introduction of the three-point-linkage, which enabled the use of mounted implements and employed the principle of weight transfer, meaning that smaller tractors could compete with larger ones. It was pioneered in the Ferguson TE-20 model, of which more than half a million were sold between 1946 and 1956. Like other post-war tractors it also had a live power-take-off shaft, which meant that it could transmit power to trailed implements such as balers.[27]

It was therefore in this post-war period that the labour-saving potential of the tractor was realised. There was a similar pattern in the adoption of

24 Brassley, 'Output and Technical Change', 67–8; Brassley *et al.*, *Real Agricultural Revolution*, 119; MAFF, *A Century of Agricultural Statistics*, 94.

25 P. Dewey, *Iron Harvests of the Field: The Making f Farm Machinery in Britain Since 1800* (Lancaster: Carnegie, 2008), 126–30, 174.

26 J. Auderset and P. Moser, 'Mechanisation and Motorisation: Natural Resources, Knowledge, Politics and Technology in Nineteenth- and Twentieth-Century Agriculture', in *Agriculture in Capitalist Europe, 1945–1960: From Food Shortages to Food Surpluses*, C. Martiin, J. Pan-Montojo and P. Brassley (eds) (London: Routledge, 2016), 159.

27 Dewey, *Iron Harvests of the Field*, 262; F. McWilliams, 'Equine Machines: Horses and Tractors on British farms, c. 1920–1970' (unpublished PhD thesis, King's College London, 2020); Brassley, 'Output and Technical Change', 74.

milking machines, effective models of which were available by the late 1920s. Nevertheless, the great majority – 90 per cent – of herds were still being milked by hand in cowsheds in 1939. The following twenty-five years saw the position reversed, with over 90 per cent of herds machine-milked in 1964 and the cowshed beginning to give way to various designs of milking parlour.[28]

In short, as with the output-increasing technologies, the most important labour-saving technology was adopted slowly in the inter-war period and much more rapidly in the post-war period. Obviously, this is not strictly to compare like with like, in either output-increasing or labour-saving technologies. Post-war crop varieties were different from those introduced in the inter-war years, and there were considerable post-war changes in farm machinery, most notably in the power of tractors and the replacement of the reaper-binder by the combine harvester for cereal harvesting.[29] Some fungicides, such as Bordeaux mixture, had been available from the late nineteenth century onwards, but the range of herbicides, insecticides and fungicides available increased considerably after the war, although their use increased most rapidly from the 1960s onwards.[30] Farmers were much more likely to invest in specialised, machinery-adapted buildings after the war. But many of the technologies widely adopted after the war were available before it, so clearly something happened from 1939 onwards to change the management decisions made by farmers.

7.4 What changed in 1939?

A. G. Street's explanation, as we saw in the introduction to this chapter, gave the credit to Hitler. Others have agreed. Alan Wilt argues that food and farming became associated with debates about re-armament as early as 1936.[31] The outbreak of war reinforced the need to expand production. Churchill told a meeting of the National Farmers' Union in October 1940 that 'the farms of Britain are the front line of freedom'.[32] Factories producing nitrogen fertilisers also produced the raw material for explosives, so the war saw an expansion in their number and

28 Brassley, 'Output and Technical Change', 74; Brassley *et al.*, *Real Agricultural Revolution*, 149–51.

29 Dewey, *Iron Harvests of the Field*, 254–88.

30 D. Grigg, *English Agriculture: An Historical Perspective* (Oxford: Blackwell, 1989), 75; K. L. Blaxter and N. Robertson, *From Dearth to Plenty: The Modern Revolution in Food Production* (Cambridge: Cambridge University Press, 1995), ch. 6.

31 A. Wilt, *Food for War: Agriculture and Rearmament in Britain Before the Second World War* (Oxford: Oxford University Press, 2001), 1–3.

32 S. Foreman, *Loaves and Fishes: An Illustrated History of the Ministry of Agriculture, Fisheries and Food, 1889–1989* (London: HMSO, 1989), 33.

capacity. British farmers increased their use of fertiliser in the war years in response to the demand for increased output. However, the technical changes that produced more effective and easier-to-use compound fertilisers were a post-war development. Similarly, wartime pressures to avoid losses caused by pests, diseases and weed infestations led to increased research on pesticides, fungicides and herbicides, but again the development of effective products and their widespread adoption by farmers came after the war.[33]

But if Hitler stimulated agricultural research, investment and the subsequent adoption of technical change, why had the Kaiser not had the same impact? It took time, during the First World War, for the government to realise that the food imports on which Britain relied could be affected by war, but by 1916 rising food prices made the problem only too apparent, and the 1917 Corn Production Act guaranteed prices to farmers for four years. The difference was that the encouragement of agricultural production was not continued in the decade after the Kaiser's war in the same way that it was after Hitler's war. Hence Street's pessimism about the way in which farming was perceived by the non-farming majority of the population. And he was not alone. There was a popular inter-war genre of novels and memoirs with rural settings that made, sometimes implicitly, similar arguments.[34]

***

The Labour government that came to power after the Second World War was unlikely to support British agriculture for reasons of sentiment or tradition, but many farmers in the 1960s, all Conservative voters, looked back on Tom Williamson, the Labour Minister of Agriculture in Atlee's government, as one of the best ministers they could remember. He introduced the 1947 Agriculture Act, which ensured that the rapidly falling prices experienced by UK farmers after the First World War were not replicated after the Second. His reasons – the government's reasons – for doing so had little to do with any desire to support farm incomes to ensure the farmers' vote. They were all to do with ensuring food supplies at minimum prices. Before the Second World War, indeed since the late nineteenth century, the UK had imported food raw materials such as cereals, meat and dairy products from the cheapest available sources. Initially these were largely paid for by manufactured exports, and latterly

33 Brassley, 'Output and Technical Change', 69; D. Montague, *Farming, Food and Politics: The Merchant's Tale* (Dublin: IAWS Group plc, 2000), 241–4, 346–56.

34 M. Shaw, 'Cold Comfort Times: Women Writers in the Interwar Period', in *The English Countryside Between the Wars: Regeneration or Decline?*, P. Brassley, J. Burchardt and L. Thompson (eds) (Woodbridge: Boydell Press, 2006), 73–86; P. Brassley, 'Twentieth-Century Georgic and Agricultural Technology', in *A History of English Georgic Writing*, P. Bullard (ed.) (Cambridge: Cambridge University Press, 2023), 99–117.

by the income from overseas investments. By 1945 many UK industries had been redirected to the production of armaments, for which the post-war export markets were limited, and a large proportion of overseas assets had been liquidated to pay for the war. Consequently, there was a shortage of foreign exchange to pay for food imports. British farmers had demonstrated an ability to respond quickly to wartime demands. Therefore, the solution was to continue the expansion of domestic agricultural production while keeping the UK market open to any cheap food imports that the country could afford and maintaining domestic food prices at as low a level as possible for the good of consumers. These potentially conflicting objectives were to be achieved, under the provisions of the 1947 Act, by keeping UK market price levels at world price levels but paying farmers at a higher guaranteed price. The difference between the two prices was paid from central government revenues, or, in other words, by the taxpayer. Thus, when a farmer sold a fat bullock to the meat trade, he received the market price, and a few weeks later also received a payment from the Ministry of Agriculture calculated from the difference between the average market price in the week of the sale and the guaranteed price. It was quite a sophisticated system, because it required a well-established system of recording sales and prices, but it also gave farmers an incentive to produce as high a quality as possible, because if their products sold for more than the average price their total receipts were more than the guaranteed price, and if less than average, correspondingly less.[35]

This system remained in operation under both Labour and Conservative governments until the end of the 1960s, when changes began to be made in preparation for the UK's possible entry into the European Common Agricultural Policy. These forms of support were increasingly supplemented by incentive and capital grant schemes. They were not politically uncontroversial, because they imposed a burden on the taxpayer, but when the immediate post-war food shortages and foreign exchange crises were over the farmers' unions were successful in convincing successive governments that agriculture could help to offset the chronic balance of payments problems that affected the UK in the 1950s and 1960s. Neither was it immediately successful in producing dramatic increases in output, because in the late 1940s and early 1950s farmers often complained of a shortage of both the capital and labour needed to produce more. It also took time for farmers to be convinced that the sudden removal of price guarantees that they had experienced in 1921 would not be repeated. But eventually they began to feel confident, and then they began to acquire

35 For a longer discussion of the history and subsequent development of the 1947 Act, see Brassley *et al.*, *Real Agricultural Revolution*, 94–102.

the capital needed to introduce new technologies and the machinery necessary to replace labour.[36]

As early as 1950 A. G. Street could write that 'Instead of farmers and their employees hoeing their lowly rows, unwept, unhonoured, and unsung, they are now so publicized that they are in danger of suffering from swelled head'.[37] A new kind of high-input/high-output farming was taking over, based on:

> the work of the scientist, the engineer and the plant breeder ... Today the average farmer is able to make much better use of artificial manures; to use machinery to enable him in many ways to overcome climatic handicaps in grain growing; and to adopt ley farming.[38]

Other writers agreed. John Cherrington, who in addition to farming a large acreage in southern England saw a great deal of other people's farming in his roles as a print and broadcast journalist, argued that 'The war did not of itself mend the fortunes of British farming,' he wrote, 'but it did restore its confidence'.[39] Tony Harman, farming an expanding acreage to the north-west of London, felt that although progress might have been slow in the 1950s, 'by the early sixties we had quite a different attitude ... Instead of nurturing strictly limited ambitions about what we could achieve, almost anything seemed possible'.[40] Writing at the end of the 1960s the Donaldsons also credited subsidies, capital grants and the efforts of scientists and advisors with producing a new version of English farming 'with its trim hedges, arable and ley farming, highly capitalized and intensively used buildings' in considerable contrast to the 'broken-backed appearance of yesterday'.[41] A few years later Tristram Beresford, another farmer and journalist, made the same case, that the post-war change had been revolutionary, and attributed it, in the phrase quoted at the beginning of this chapter, to the recovery of spirit and zest.

However, spirit and zest by themselves would have had little effect in the absence of new technologies and the awareness of their existence, so research, technical development and knowledge transfer was a fundamental component of farming change after 1939. It was partly produced by UK government initiatives and partly by private industry. Even before the First World War a few agricultural research establishments

36 Ibid., 102–6.

37 Street, *Farmer's Glory*, 222.

38 Ibid., 224.

39 J. Cherrington, *On the Smell of an Oily Rag* (London: Northwood Publications, 1979), 88–9.

40 T. Harman, *Seventy Summers: The Story of a Farm* (London: BBC Publications, 1986), 216.

41 J. G. S. and Frances Donaldson, in association with Derek Barber, *Farming in Britain Today* (Harmondsworth: Penguin, 1969), xiii–xv.

had been financed by the Development Commission, and more emerged in the inter-war period. In 1931 the Agricultural Research Council (ARC) was set up to fund agricultural research, with a greater emphasis on the production of fundamental scientific knowledge rather than its immediate application on the farm. Its expenditure, and the number of scientists involved, remained small, with fewer than 150 researchers in post in 1939. The Second World War years and the twenty years afterwards saw greater research spending, an increase in the number of agricultural research institutes, an expansion of existing establishments, and at least a tenfold increase in the number of scientists employed. There seems little doubt that this flourishing of the agricultural research community between 1940 and 1960 was a direct result of the bipartisan agricultural policy outlined above.

***

It is difficult to find evidence of much disagreement in policy-making circles over the need for more agricultural research, since it was expected to lead to more and more efficient, agricultural production. Successive Ministers of Agriculture of both major political parties wanted it, and while the National Farmers' Union were not especially active advocates for it, they were certainly not against it.[42] It was simply not controversial. The consensus can be traced back to 1941, when the Hankey Committee gave the ARC the same status as the bodies responsible for medical and industrial research.[43] Wartime government White Papers on research in general and agricultural research in particular only described the organisation of research, with no discussion of whether it was necessary or desirable.[44] The ARC also benefitted from two effective and influential leaders in the post-war period: Lord Rothschild (chair from 1948 to 1958) and Bill (later Sir William) Slater (Secretary from 1949 to 1960).[45] Sir John Russell, a former Director of the Rothamsted research station, writing in 1965 from the perspective of fifty years of experience in agricultural research, noted that requests for more research money had been 'very favourably treated. Never before [had] there been anything approaching this generosity'.[46] This approach to research funding lasted until 1971–2,

42 B. A. Holderness, *British Agriculture Since 1945* (Manchester: Manchester University Press, 1985), 10.

43 Blaxter and Robertson, *From Dearth to Plenty*, 256.

44 Lord President of the [Privy] Council, *Agricultural Research in Great Britain* (Cmd. 6421, HMSO, 1943); id., *Scientific Research and Development* (Cmd. 6514, HMSO, 1944).

45 Sir William Henderson, 'British Agricultural Research and the Agricultural Research Council: A Personal Historical Account', in *Agricultural Research, 1931–1981*, G. W. Cooke (ed.) (London: Agricultural Research Council, 1981), 64–7.

46 Sir E. John Russell, *A History of Agricultural Science in Great Britain* (London: George Allen and Unwin, 1966), 482.

when Rothschild returned to the government research policy world with some rather more critical ideas. Commercial firms in the fertiliser, pesticide, feedingstuffs and seed trades were also prepared to put considerable sums into research as long as agricultural policy encouraged output maximisation, which it did until 1984.[47]

The Second World War also saw the establishment of the Agricultural Improvement Councils, one for England and Wales and another for Scotland. Their job was to ensure that the scientists were aware of the needs of the farming industry and the agricultural policy-makers in government, and that the farming industry and associated civil servants and politicians were kept up to date with scientific developments. They brought together senior figures in the university agriculture departments, the research stations, the agricultural industry and the relevant government ministries, and remained in operation until the 1970s.[48] They were at the heart of the expansion of agricultural knowledge networks in the post-war years. Agricultural education expenditure, and the number of students involved, increased. The National Agricultural Advisory Service was established in 1946; by 1954 the number of advisory visits equated to roughly one per farmer per year in England and Wales. Other organisations, such as the Milk Marketing Board and the British Sugar Corporation, as well as the technical representatives of commercial firms, also provided advice. Most farmers read one or more of the weekly and monthly journals published by the agricultural press, or listened to the regular radio broadcasts on farming. As one farmer put it, they were 'living in a sea of information'.[49]

7.5 Conclusion

The conclusion to be taken from this discussion is fairly simple. Whether or not Adolf Hitler can personally take the credit, there can be little doubt that there were enormous changes in UK farming after 1939, and that they produced a rapid and sustained increase in output. Since many of the technologies adopted after 1939 were in existence earlier, the lack of change before that date must surely be explained in terms of the lack of confidence of the majority of farmers that any investment would produce a sustained return, and their consequent unwillingness to take risks. Conversely, as the references of several writers to immeasurable factors such as attitude, spirit and zest make clear, the post-war

47 Brassley *et al.*, *Real Agricultural Revolution*, 36–42; Montague, *Farming, Food and Politics*, 156.

48 Brassley *et al.*, *Real Agricultural Revolution*, 26–42, 46–9.

49 P. Brassley, 'Technical Change and Knowledge Networks in England, 1945–1980s', in *Agricultural Knowledge Networks in Rural Europe, 1700–2000*, Yves Segers and Leen Van Molle (eds) (Woodbridge: Boydell Press, 2022).

growth in confidence meant that more and more farmers were willing to take risks that they would have hesitated to take before 1939. As Allan Buckwell has argued, much of this changing attitude to risk can be directly attributed to consistent agricultural support policies existing over a long time.[50] To some extent those policies were the result of the Second World War, and to that extent Hitler can take the credit, but after the 1950s their persistence had much more to do with the chronic problems of the British economy and the ability of agricultural pressure groups to convince governments that agriculture could make a contribution to their solution. It was a phase that lasted beyond the period covered by this article and into the first ten years of Britain's membership of the Common Agricultural Policy; it began to change when the introduction of milk quotas in 1984 signalled the end of expansionist (some called them productivist) agricultural policies.

50 Buckwell, 'Economic Signals, Farmers' Response, and Environmental Change', 156; Brassley *et al.*, *Real Agricultural Revolution*, 251–60.

8

The 'Green Evolution' in Denmark, 1930–1972

Thomas Christiansen

Writing about the Green Revolution and Denmark is a bit of a paradox, since the concept of Green Revolution is hardly ever mentioned in relation to Danish agriculture. This is so because 'standard' definitions of the Green Revolution include characteristics that were not present in Denmark. Picado, for example, focuses on the 'Third World' as the geographical space in which the Green Revolution took place, while Cabral, Pandey and Xu define it as a top-down and state-led process.[1] Hence, the modern and market-orientated Danish agriculture that was the outcome of 'the first green revolution', as defined by van Zanden and Melillo,[2] was a precursor or a source of inspiration for the Green Revolution as it is normally understood.[3] Yet, it still makes sense to connect the Danish case with the Green Revolution because Danish

1 Wilson Picado Umaña, 'Revolución verde (Tercer Mundo, 1941–2020)', in *Diccionario del agro iberoamericano*, 3rd edn, Alejandra Salomón and José Muzlera (ed.) (Buenos Aires: TeseoPress, 2021), 917. Lídia Cabral, Poonam Pandey and Xiuli Xu, 'Epic Narratives of the Green Revolution in Brazil, China, and India', *Agriculture and Human Values* 39 (2022), 249.

2 J. L. van Zanden, 'The First Green Revolution: The Growth of Production and Productivity in European Agriculture, 1870–1914', *Economic History Review* 44 (1991), 215–39; Edward D. Melillo, 'The First Green Revolution: Debt Peonage and the Making of the Nitrogen Fertilizer Trade, 1840–1930', *American Historical Review* 117 (2012), 1028–60.

3 As noted recently by agrarian historians, 'Francis Fukuyama has described the issue facing developing countries as the problem of "getting to Denmark", a metaphor for a society characterised by wealth, the rule of law, good governance, and related virtues'. Peter Sandholt Jensen *et al.*, '"Getting to Denmark": The Role of Elites for Development', *Working Paper Series* 362 (Warwick: University of Warwick, 2018), 2.

agriculture adapted many of the Green Revolution's technical aspects when the latter emerged after the Second World War.[4] The interesting point here is that since the Danish agricultural sector was already modern and market-orientated at the start of the Green Revolution, the adoption of its technical aspects was more gradual than revolutionary.

This meant that for some decades farmers were able to utilise some of the general technical aspects of the Green Revolution without fundamentally changing the social and productive model that had evolved in the late nineteenth century. Hence, in Denmark, the Green Revolution did not lead to a revolution in the post-war countryside but instead took the form of a 'Green Evolution' that lasted into the 1960s when the first cracks in the social and productive fabric appeared. Contemporary observers became aware of growing 'structural problems in Danish agriculture', as indicated by the 1964 homonymous report from the Economic Council.[5]

This chapter traces the 'Green Evolution' in Denmark from the 1930s until the early 1970s. The are three main reasons for this demarcation of the analysis. First, it roughly coincides with the Green Revolution elsewhere in the world, making it a useful point of comparison. Second, it is a period where the sector's characteristics inherited from the late nineteenth century remained in place, despite repeated challenges. Third, from the late nineteenth century the main export markets were the United Kingdom and Germany, and there was therefore a significant change when Denmark joined the EEC in 1973. In the end, farmers could not resist the consequences of agrarian modernisation, and this led to a second revolution in Danish agriculture. The first traces of this appeared in the 1960s, but the process was only completed decades later, leading to dramatically changed structures, and Danish agriculture today is very different from that of the 'classical period'. The details of this second revolution, however, are beyond the scope of this chapter.

We start with a short description of Danish agriculture in the 1930s. This is followed by the main sections: Intensification and Output Changes, Mechanisation, Consolidation and Specialisation – Incipient Revolution. The chapter ends with a Conclusion that summarises the findings. The analysis focuses on on-farm developments, while off-farm development is only dealt with briefly.

4 Although William S. Gaud only coined the term in 1968, he referred to a process that was already underway. William S. Gaud, 'The Green Revolution: Accomplishments and Apprehensions'. www.agbioworld.org/biotech-info/topics/borlaug/borlaug-green.html (accessed 6 January 2025).

5 Det Økonomiske Råd, Formandsskabet, *Strukturproblemer i dansk landbrug* (Copenhagen: Statens Trykningskontor, 1964).

8.1 Background

The global changes in agriculture in the late nineteenth century were sweeping, and van Zanden has described them as 'the first green revolution'. The changes in Denmark were indeed profound, leading him to conclude that the 'efficiency frontier' was pushed forward in Denmark, the Netherlands and Belgium between 1870 and 1910.[6]

Developments in Denmark are well-known and can quickly be described.[7] The country had previously been an exporter of cereals, but by the second half of the nineteenth century the Danish agrarian sector had shifted its focus to the products of animals fed partly on cheap imported grains. Consequently, the value of animal exports exceeded that of grain exports by around 1870.[8] The main export products became butter and bacon and the United Kingdom and Germany the major markets.[9]

This change was possible due to a confluence of factors. These included improved domestic and international infrastructure,[10] improved access to

6 van Zanden, 'First Green Revolution', 230.

7 Claus Bjørn, 'Dansk mejeribrug 1882–1914', in *Dansk mejeribrug 1882–2000*, Claus Bjørn (ed.) (Århus: De Danske Mejerier Fællesorganisation, 1982); Ingrid Henriksen, 'The Transformation of Danish Agriculture, 1870–1914', in *The Economic Development of Denmark and Norway since 1870*, Karl Gunnar Persson (ed.) (Aldershot: Edward Elgar Publishing, 1993); Ingrid Henriksen, 'Avoiding Lock-In: Cooperative Creameries in Denmark, 1882–1903', *European Review of Economic History* 3 (1999), 57–78; Ingrid Henriksen,'The Contribution of Agriculture to Economic Growth in Denmark, 1870–1939', in *Agriculture and Economic Development Since 1870*, Pedro Lains and Vicente Pinilla (eds) (London: Routledge, 2008); Ingrid Henriksen and Niels Kærgaard, 'Dansk landbrugs største og mest succesrige omstilling', *Tidsskrift for Landøkonomi* 200 (2014), 169–78; Jensen *et al.*, '"Getting to Denmark"'; Markus Lampe and Paul Sharp, *A Land of Milk and Butter* (Chicago, IL: University of Chicago Press, 2018); Erik Helmer Pedersen *et al.*, *Danske slagterier. De første hundrede år. 1887–1987* (Copenhagen: Danske Slagterier, 1987); Jørgen Dieckermann Rasmussen *et al.*, '1860–1914', in *Det danske landbrugs historie 1810–1914*, Claus Bjørn (ed.) (Odense: Landbohistorisk Selskab, 1988).

8 Henning Otte Hansen, *Andelsbevægelsens evne til forandring og omstilling i landbrugets udvikling fra den lokale til, 'den globale landsby'* (Copenhagen, Handelshøjskolens Forlag, 2011).

9 Statistics available from 1925 onwards show that cattle and pigs contributed over 90 per cent of the gross livestock output. Danmarks Statistik, *Landbrugsregnskaber i 100 år 1916–2015* (Copenhagen: Danmarks Statistik, 2017), 29.

10 After the loss of the Duchies of Schleswig, Holstein, and Lauenburg in 1864, transport infrastructure was orientated towards Copenhagen in the East and the new city and port of Esbjerg in West. The main goals were nation-building and access to the UK market. Steen Bo Frandsen, 'Danmark på langs og på tværs', *Temp. Tidsskrift for historie* 9 (2019), 18–23; Poul Thestrup, *På sporet, 1847–1997. Jernbanerne, DSB og samfundet, I, Dampen binder Danmark sammen, 1847–1914*, Poul Thestrup (ed.) (Odense: Jernbanemuseet, 1997).

cheaper artificial fertilisers and concentrated feedstuffs, seed improvements, technological improvements on and off the farms, the transition from proto-modern creameries to modern dairies usually run on cooperative lines, the emergence of a large farmers' cooperative movement, and ready access to growing markets in the United Kingdom and Germany.[11]

These developments coincided with the fact that – at the existing level of technology – the natural conditions in Denmark were suited for livestock production, but unsuited for crops that were heavy in protein, and better-suited to the cultivation of fodder crops than cereals.[12]

The changes in production logic were a success, as butter production tripled, and pig meat and egg production quadrupled between the late 1870s and the First World War.[13] The symbol of the new paradigm was the establishment of close to 1,200 – mostly cooperative – creameries between 1882 and 1909.[14] Simultaneously, new slaughterhouses emerged in provincial towns. There were some eighty slaughterhouses operating by 1914, of which half were cooperatives. Taken together, the cooperative abattoirs had the larger share of total production.[15] By the First World War, the entire production chain had taken shape.[16]

The typical farm at the beginning of the twentieth century was an integrated enterprise with a diversified production structure,[17] firmly integrated into the market and with animal products as the main commercial outputs. Farms cultivated cereals and root crops, which were mainly used as feedstuffs for pigs and cows. Cows were fed on grass

11 The establishment of cooperatives after 1882 was long seen as the driving force. Yet recent research emphasises the pre-conditions that had been introduced during the previous 100 years, including changed farming practices, secure property rights, a high educational level and technological advances. Lampe and Sharp, *Land of Milk and Butter*; Jensen *et al.*, '"Getting to Denmark"'.

12 P. Døssing, 'Strukturproblemer i dansk landbrug i de sidste 20 år', *Nationaløkonomisk Tidsskrift* 91 (1953), 287.

13 Claus Bjørn, '1810–1860', in *Det danske landbrugs historie, 1810–1914*, Bjørn (ed.), 264. This development was not a given. In 1885–6 a proposal for the introduction of an import tax on cereals was defeated in Parliament by the Liberal Party, which represented the farmers. Karen J. Friedmann, 'Danish Agricultural Policy, 1870–1970: The Flowering and Decline of a Liberal Policy', *Food Research Institute Studies* 13 (1974), 227.

14 There were also 255 private creameries in 1909, down from 468 in 1888.

15 A. Axelsen Drejer, *Andelsslagterierne i Danmark 1887–1937* (Copenhagen: De samvirkende danske Andelsslagteriers Fælleskontor, 1937), 118–19.

16 In the following twenty years, cooperatives also emerged in areas such as grading and marketing of eggs, cattle exports and purchase of feedstuffs, fertilisers and seeds. Friedmann, 'Danish agricultural policy', 228.

17 Integrated farming spread the work effort over the year and was economically robust due to output variety. Moreover, coarse fodder was important in the crop rotation system but was difficult to trade. Det Økonomiske Råd, Formandsskabet, *Strukturproblemer*, 17.

grown on arable fields when they were between crops and on permanent pasture. The cows produced milk, which was transformed into butter at the creameries. The farmers received skimmed milk and buttermilk back from the creameries, and this was fed to the pigs, which were sent for slaughter at the regional slaughterhouse. Butter and bacon were exported, making it possible to buy fertilisers, concentrated feedstuffs, machinery and other inputs, thus facilitating production growth.

Simultaneously, a partially state-sponsored system of breeding of cows and pigs,[18] research into feeding regimes, seed selection, fertiliser tests, disease research, and so forth, improved the quality of the animals, led to higher yields in the fields and produced more robust varieties of both cereals and root crops.[19] Knowledge was disseminated among farmers through consultants, partly paid by the state, but mainly financed directly through the local farmers' organisations. This meant that the consultants were generally very responsive to the farmer's needs.[20]

Within this framework, most farms were small or medium-sized family farms. The smaller farms only employed the farmer and his family, with some of the farmers occasionally working as hired hands for larger farmers, while larger family farms often hired a few hands drawn from outside the family. The main exception to the model was that the largest farms tended to focus on grain production, selling cereals to smaller farms that were not self-reliant in feedstuffs. All in all, the situation was characterised by high productivity and a relatively equal distribution of wealth.

The outcome was that the volume and value of agrarian exports quadrupled between the late 1870s and the early 1910s, and agrarian products came to form 90 per cent of the total value of Danish exports.[21] This export success became a major driver for what has been characterised as the 'balanced development' of the Danish economy.[22]

Because the export trade was heavily reliant on only two products sold into two markets, the sector, and by implication also the entire Danish economy, occasionally faced economic problems. In these cases,

18 The State Experimental Creamery – *Statens Forsøgsmejeri* – was established in 1923 but was very conservative in its approach to product development. Rasmussen *et al.*, '1860–1914', 333.

19 Hans Jørgen Winther Jensen, 'Betydningen af anvendt forskning i omlægningen af dansk landbrug ca 1880–1914 – et eksempel', *Bol og by* 5 (1989), 93–118.

20 Jette Mackintosh, 'Landmanden og hans rådgivere', in *Landboforeninger i 200 år*, II, Erik Helmer Pedersen and Mette Ehlers (eds) (Odense: De danske Landboforeninger, 1993).

21 Some authors have argued that butter and bacon were industrial products, as they were the outputs from creameries and slaughterhouses. Henriksen, 'Contribution of Agriculture', 204.

22 Lampe and Sharp, *Land of Milk and Butter*, 202.

various forms of political intervention were applied depending on the specific circumstances.

The individual farmers adapted to changing circumstances. This was especially the case after the Second World War, when new technologies enabled farmers to maintain the basic social and productive structure well into the 1960s, although with increasing difficulties due to lack of market access prior to Denmark joining the EEC in 1973.

8.2 Intensification and technical change

The first of the farmer's gradual adaptions to be analysed is the intensification of production and output changes. This led to an increase in crop yields and a decline in the relative amount of land used for grazing. The result was more efficient feedstuff utilisation and increased output per production animal. Output changes were mainly found in the fields, where different crops were preferred over time, partly because of changes in production costs. After the first Green Revolution the crop harvest was mainly used for animal feed that the official statistics measured in tons of output and in 'feed units'.[23] This cross-crop output measurement facilitates the analysis of the development of the crop production seen from the perspective of the farmer even though the crop mix changed. Figure 8.1 shows that the total harvest calculated in feed units increased by almost 30 per cent from the early 1930s to the early 1960s,[24] but also that total production then levelled out. The figure also shows that cereals and pulses increased in importance, going from 36 per cent to 54 per cent of total production between the early 1930s and the early 1970s. This development was the consequence of several simultaneous changes. These included a decline in the total agricultural area, an intensification of land usage, a change in the crop mix, and higher-yielding crop varieties.

As for the total agricultural area, Table 8.1 shows that it declined by approximately 10 per cent from the 1930s to the 1970s, with the largest change taking place after 1960. The figure also demonstrates that this coincided with intensified land usage. The area of arable land farmed under a rotation used for both grazing and green fodder in different years

23 One feed unit equals 1 kilo of grain (barley, wheat, rye or pulses), 1.1 kilos of mixed grains, 1.2 kilos of oats, 5 kilos of straw, between 1 kilo and 1.2 kilos of dry matter of root crops, and between 2.3 and 2.5 kilos of hay. Danmarks Statistik, *Statistiske undersøgelser nr. 22. Landbrugsstatistik 1900–1965, I, Landbrugsareal, og høstudbytte samt gødningsforbrug* (Copenhagen: Danmarks Statistik, 1968), 37, 49, 122, 193.

24 During the German occupation total average production only declined by 2 per cent compared to the level of the previous five years, reflecting the special wartime conditions in Denmark.

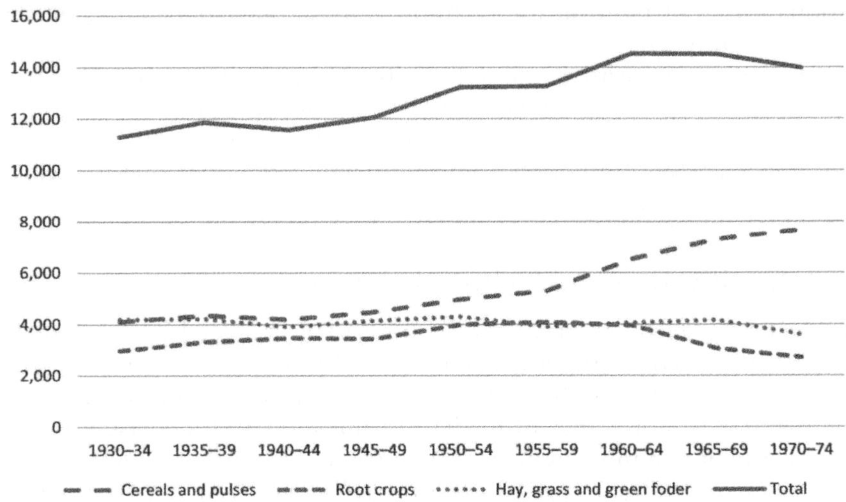

FIGURE 8.1. Total crop harvest, 1930–4 to 1970–4 (million feed units) (five-year averages). Source: Danmarks Statistik, *Statistiske undersøgelser nr. 22*, Danmarks Statistik, *Statistisk tiårsoversigt 1975*.

declined by approximately 35 per cent, and land not in a rotation (that is, permanent grass) declined by approximately 45 per cent in the same years. Fallow was reduced to virtually nothing over the same time.

Table 8.1 also shows a change in the crop mix after the Second World War, when cereals gained in importance at the cost of root crops.[25] This was related to the fact that the cultivation of root crops was labour-intensive well into the 1960s,[26] making cereal cultivation more attractive as farm hands left the sector in the post-war years. Later, root crops also lost ground to grass (which was ensilaged and required less work) and corn.[27] Consequently, the amount of land used for cereals increased in relative and absolute terms despite the 10 per cent reduction in total agricultural land.

25 Root crops in general provided higher yields of feed units per hectare than cereals, meaning that, everything else being equal, the relative increase in land used for cereals reduced the total average yields in feed units per hectare.

26 Thinning of the beets was especially difficult to mechanise. Erik Helmer Pedersen, *Det danske landbrugs historie, IV, 1914–1988* (Odense: Landbohistorisk Selskab, 1988), 276.

27 Ibid., 279.

TABLE 8.1. Agricultural land (hectares) (five-year averages 1930–4 to 1970–4).

	1930–4	1935–9	1940–4	1945–9	1950–4	1955–9	1960–4	1965–9	1970–4
Peas and beans	4,160	3,580	7,760	10,316	9,164	7,397	8,208	10,200	15,763
Root crops	524,460	525,480	534,520	554,119	580,868	578,096	492,975	361,101	280,229
Cereals	1,327,480	1,356,540	1,325,520	1,292,173	1,311,133	1,381,728	1,532,079	1,645,745	1,753,424
Other crops	36,320	48,520	82,700	87,973	90,290	84,997	101,252	99,851	110,082
Grass and green fodder	740,620	734,760	731,740	721,821	715,298	673,598	606,373	549,875	470,382
Fallow	51,820	36,700	18,760	12,903	6,445	5,283	3,986	2,574	2,181
Permanent grassland and grazings	527,788	547,240	512,680	475,256	407,920	376,971	340,761	315,932	294,960
Total agricultural area	3,212,648	3,252,820	3,213,680	3,154,561	3,121,118	3,108,070	3,085,634	2,985,277	2,927,021

Source: Danmarks Statistik, *Statistiske undersøgelser nr. 22*, Danmarks Statistik, *Statistisk tiårsoversigt 1975*.

Within this picture, significant changes also happened in the relative importance of different grains and root crops. Barley, which had always been significant and was primarily used for animal feed, became the dominant cereal. At the end of the period, it occupied as much land as all the other cereals put together. The expansion of barley was due to new variants that gave higher yields and were more climate tolerant. On the other hand, less land was used for oats and wheat. The first change was due to a decline in working horses after the war, while the second is related to the fact that, despite the introduction of new varieties, Danish wheat made poor flour for baking, making it difficult to produce for this market.[28] With regards to yields, these increased by almost 65 per cent for grains as a whole between the early 1930s and the early 1970s.[29] All in all, the increase in production led to first to a decline in imports and even cereal exports, thereby changing a part of the classical production structure.[30] The picture is more complex for the root crops. The main changes were that first mangolds and later kohlrabi declined in importance, while beets used for cattle feed and beets for sugar production increased in importance. The increase in the yields of roots was smaller than for cereals, but the average yields per hectare increased by 39 per cent for root crops as a whole between the 1930s and the 1970s, while the figure for beets used for animal feed was 35 per cent.[31] These figures, however, only reflect the yields of the roots.

Ensilage of the green leaf top of roots became widespread after the Second World War, and so the total yield of root crops increased by more than is indicated by the numbers for the roots alone. With this, proteins in the silage also became available, and it was estimated that the ensilage taking place at over 90,000 farms in the early 1950s saved 100,000–135,000 tons of oil cakes annually.[32] The increase in yields was not only the result of new varieties being introduced but also of a growth in fertiliser usage.[33] Table 8.2 shows that this was the case for both manure and artificial fertilisers, but the growth of the latter was much steeper than the former.

28 Bettina Buhl, 'Planteproduktionen', in *Dansk Landbrug, 1945–2020,* Gudrun Gormsen (ed.) (Copenhagen: Gads Forlag, 2022), 159–60.

29 The figures for barley, oats and mixed grains were some 40 per cent, wheat 62 per cent and rye 98 per cent.

30 Pedersen, *Det danske landbrugs historie,* IV, 227–9.

31 Author's calculation based on data in Danmarks Statistik, *Statistiske undersøgelser nr. 22*; Danmarks Statistik, *Statistisk tiårsoversigt 1975* (Copenhagen: Danmarks Statistik, 1975).

32 Døssing, 'Strukturproblemer i dansk landbrug', 292.

33 Commercial fertilisers first appeared in the 1820s in the form of bone meal and night-soil, while guano and its derivatives arrived in the 1840s. Bjørn, '1810–1860', 86. Use of commercial fertilisers increased significantly after 1900, and manure handling improved in the late nineteenth and early twentieth century. Rasmussen *et al.*, '1860–1914', 288–91.

TABLE 8.2. Consumption of fertilisers (kg of pure nutrients/ha) (1929/30–33/4 to 1969/70–73/4).

	Nitrogenous fertilisers			Phosphorus fertilisers			Potassium fertilisers		
	Commercial	Manure	Total	Commercial	Manure	Total	Commercial	Manure	Total
1929/30–33/34	9	38	47	8	13	21	6	52	58
1934/35–38/39	11	38	49	9	12	21	9	51	60
1939/40–43/44	12	32	44	3	11	13	14	48	62
1944/45–48/49	12	35	47	6	11	18	13	50	63
1949/50–53/54	23	39	62	12	13	25	33	53	85
1954/55–58/59	30	41	71	14	14	29	41	53	93
1959/60–63/64	44	44	88	17	15	32	47	53	100
1964/65–68/69	70	50	120	18	17	35	50	56	106
1969/70–73/74	106	47	154	20	17	37	55	49	104

Source. Danmarks Statistik, *Statistiske undersøgelser nr. 22*, Danmarks Statistik, *Landbrugsstatistik (1974)*.

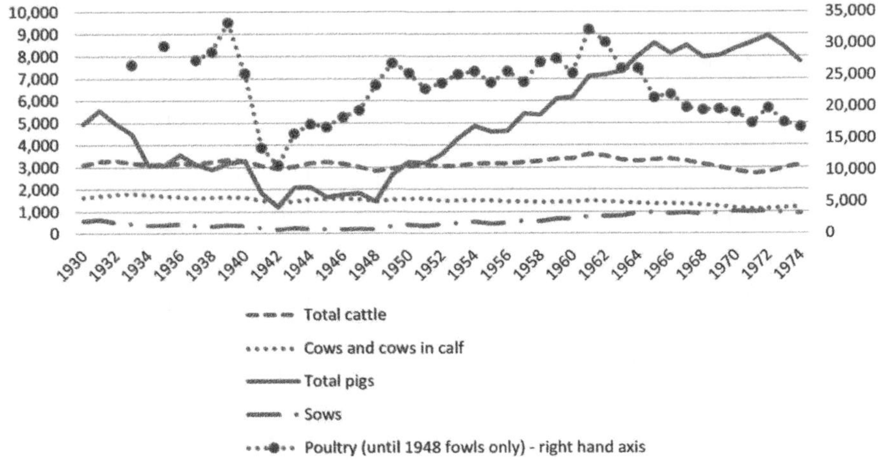

FIGURE 8.2. Numbers of main farm animals, 1930–74.

Hence, at the end of the period more than 50 per cent of the fertiliser applied to the land came from commercial fertilisers. Pesticides were also introduced in the 1950s but no data on usage exists before 1970.[34]

Although the increase in arable production was important, the main economic driver of the sector was animal products.[35] Figure 8.2 shows developments in the number of production animals, which was not uniform across species. First, the number of pigs was negatively influenced by the economic crises and political upheavals of the 1930s and 1940s, but the post-war recovery was fast.[36] On the other hand, the number of cattle was much less affected by the crises of the 1930s and the German occupation. In fact, it remained stable until a decline set in at the end of the period. Third, poultry was kept mainly to produce eggs for the export trade to the United Kingdom. Much less important than milk and butter, it was nevertheless a constant until the 1960s.

34 Peter Bavnshøj, 'Redskaber, maskiner og følgeindustrier', in *Dansk Landbrug 1945–2020*, Gormsen (ed.), 110.

35 Until 1965 income from animal products equalled close to 80 per cent of the sector's gross income. Pedersen, 'Det danske landbrugs historie', 28–30.

36 Christiansen, 'From Food Surplus to Even More Food Surplus', 126–32.

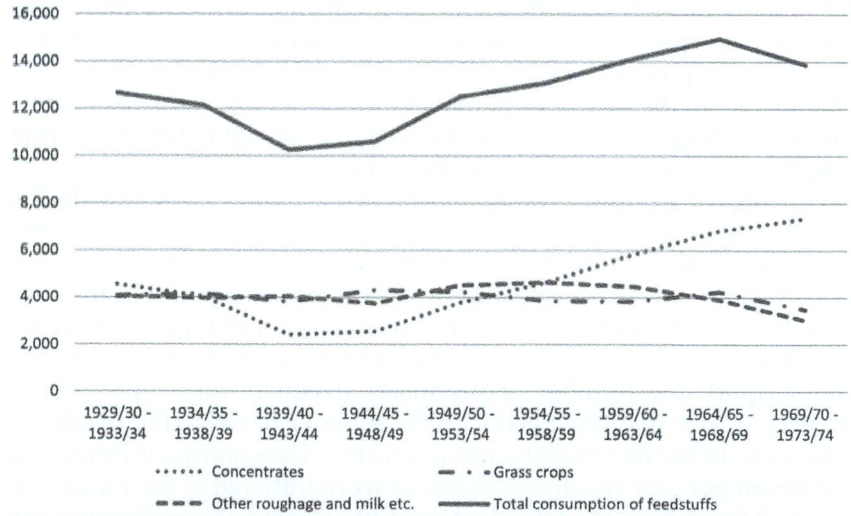

FIGURE 8.3. Composition of feedstuff usage by main categories, 1929–30 to 1973–4 (averages over five-year periods). Source: *Danmarks Statistik, Statistiske undersøgelser nr. 25*, Danmarks Statistik, *Landbrugsstatistik (1973, 1975)*.

The different trajectories in the number of pigs and cattle during the 1930s and 1940s reflects different production logics. For pigs, piglets were the product, while for cattle it was milk rather than calves. Moreover, reproduction speed is much faster for pigs than cows, making it easier and cheaper to replenish the stock of pigs than cattle.

Concerning feed consumption, Figure 8.3 demonstrates that concentrates, grass crops and other roughage, as well as milk and so on, each accounted for approximately one-third of total feed usage at the beginning of the period. During the Second World War relatively less concentrate was used due to the stop on the imports of oil seeds used for vegetable oil production, the by-products of which were made into oil cake for cattle, and this negatively impacted milk production. The composition of the feeding stuffs utilised changed again in the post-war years, and concentrates became relatively more important than the two other categories. Yet over these years there was no clear trend in feed consumption per livestock unit.[37] The amount peaked in the 1950s but by the early 1970s it was only 5 per cent higher than in the early 1930s.[38] This might indicate

37 One 'livestock unit' is the number of animals of a given species that consumes an equal amount of feed to one milking cow, for example, one horse, two sows, twenty-five piglets and fifty chickens. Danmarks Statistik, *Statistiske undersøgelser nr. 25*, 10.

38 Ibid.; *Danmarks Statistik: Landbrugsstatistik (1967, 1971, 1972).*

that initially farmers increased animal production by using more feed. Nonetheless, optimising feedingstuff consumption was an important part of the empirical research carried out by the Agricultural Research Laboratory.[39] In the case of pigs, more efficient feeding plans reduced the required feedingstuffs to increase the weight of an animal by 1 kilo from 5.4 feed units in the 1920s to 4.4 in the 1950s.[40]

With regard to milk production, Figure 8.4 shows a slight decline from the 1930s to the 1970s.[41] This long-term trend was the result of a fall in the number of production animals and an increase in the yield per cow. Each cow produced almost 30 per cent more milk in the early 1970s than forty years earlier. The increase in yield per cow in the 1960s and 1970s happened in a difficult market situation, and despite state support, the number of producers declined. Since this process happened faster than the decline in the number of cows, the result was an increase in the number of cows per farm.[42] The continued increase in production per cow was the outcome of work initiated in the nineteenth century.[43] Until the 1960s the dominant breed for milk production was the Red Danish Dairy breed – *Rød Dansk Malkerace* – which was defined in 1878. Pedigree control started in 1881, breeder competitions in 1884, and the first control association emerged in 1895. Breeding activities increased milk production per cow and the favoured characteristics, such as ease of milking, a calm temper and the ability to eat and convert coarse fodder.[44]

39 Lampe and Sharp, *Land of Milk and Butter*, 202. Holger Ærsøe, *Husdyrbrugsforsøgsvirksomheden i Danmark. En redegørelse for Landøkonomisk Forsøgslaboratoriums Oprettelse, Udvikling og Virksomhed i tiden 1882–1942* (Copenhagen: Statens Husdyrbrugsudvalg, 1943), 166–205.

40 Danmarks Statistik, *Landbrugsregnskaber i 100 år*, 19.

41 The wartime production decline was mainly the result of a smaller production per animal due to a lack of protein feed. Pedersen, 'Det danske landbrugs historie', 139 and 175.

42 Jacob A. Buksti, 'Dansk mejeribrug 1955–1982', in *Dansk mejeribrug, 1882–2000*, Bjørn (ed.), 339.

43 The Agricultural University – *Landbohøjskolen* – was established in 1858, and the possibility of conducting research into rational feed consumption for cattle was subsequently discussed several times. The Agricultural Research Laboratory – *Landøkonomisk Forsøgslaboratorium* – was established in 1883 building on previous practical research work by N. J. Fjord from The Agricultural University. Ærsøe, *Husdyrbrugsforsøgsvirksomheden i Danmark*. The guiding principle of the Agricultural Research Laboratory was 'mobile laboratories' – a cooperation with selected farms and creameries – establishing a direct link between research, farmers and creameries. Research results were published in periodical reports.

44 Arne Nielsen and Bernt Bech Andersen, 'RDM i 125 år', in *Rød Dansk Malkerace: Avlsmæssigt og kulturhistorisk belyst*, Lars Gjøl Christensen *et al.* (eds) (Holstebro: Rounborgs grafiske hus, 2003), 15–28.

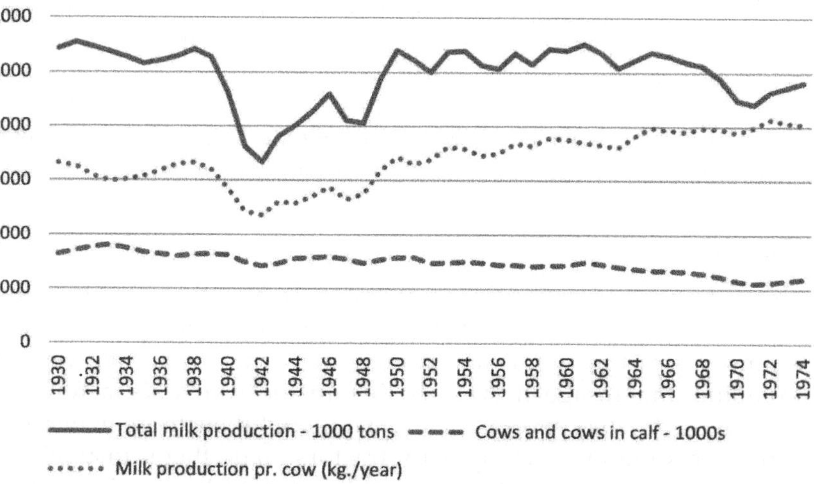

FIGURE 8.4. Number of cows and cows in calf, total milk production and average milk production per cow, 1930–74 (annual data). Source: *Danmarks Statistik, Statistiske undersøgelser nr. 25*, Danmarks Statistik, *Landbrugsstatistik (1967, 1971, 1972, 1974).*

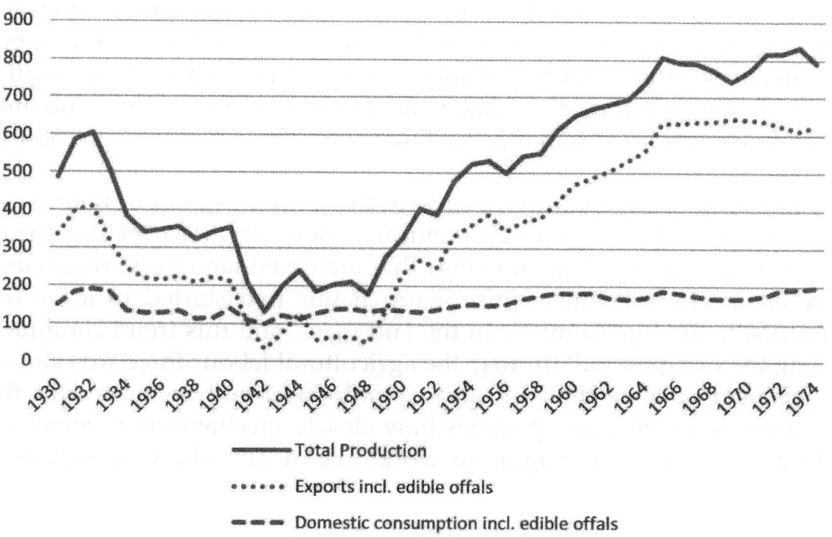

FIGURE 8.5. Production, export and domestic consumption of pig meat, 1930–74 (1,000 tons) (annual data). Source: *Danmarks Statistik, Statistiske undersøgelser nr. 25, Danmarks Statistik, Landbrugsstatistik* (1967, 1969, 1972, 1974).

In the case of the pigs, Figure 8.5 demonstrates a larger variation in production.[45] This was the case during the war, where there was a drop in pig meat production. Yet production recovered quickly in the following years and soon surpassed pre-war levels by a wide margin. Figure 8.5 also underlines that it was the export market that drove production, while the domestic market only shows a slight increase over time.

8.3 Mechanisation

An important part of the Green Revolution was the introduction of powered machines and tools. This also happened in the post-war years in Denmark, starting with the introduction of tractors, followed later by combine and forage harvesters. Before the war, only a few large farms had tractors, as several factors hampered their more general use. The iron tyres found on many early tractors made them unsuitable for use on roads, meaning that farmers still required horses. Moreover, a hefty price tag made them an unattractive investment at a time when farm incomes were depressed, access to export markets was restricted, and many farmers struggled with debt.[46] Yet, Figure 8.6 shows a fast post-war growth, going from fewer than 5,000 tractors around 1945 to approximately 100,000 in 1960. The number continued to increase for another decade until it stabilised at a number above the total number of farms, indicating that the tractorisation was then complete.[47] Figure 8.6 also shows a close inverse relation between tractorisation and a 90 per cent decrease in the number of horses in less than twenty years. Finally, Figure 8.6 shows that after electricity arrived in the 1930s, it became possible to introduce milking machines, and these became common in the late 1940s.

There were three main reasons why the mechanisation of field work and transportation became economically more attractive in the 1940s. The first was the shortage of labour that increased labourers' wages and gave an incentive to mechanise. Farm hands had started to leave the countryside in large numbers in the late 1930s, and this trend continued during the occupation.[48] By 1947 the agricultural labour force was almost 30 per cent smaller than in 1933–4, and this trend continued in the following years. Figure 8.7 shows how closely mechanisation coincided with a reduction in the agrarian workforce. It also shows a reduction

45 Figure 8.5 does not allow for negligible yearly stock changes.

46 Døssing, 'Strukturproblemer i dansk landbrug', 289; Jens Skriver, 'Traktordriftens gennembrud i Danmark 1945–65', *Bol og By* 2 (1986), 133.

47 It has been estimated that around 1960 the economic limit for buying a tractor was a farm with 10 hectares. Smaller farms, though, could hire tractors from machine stations. Ibid., 138–9.

48 Døssing, 'Strukturproblemer i dansk landbrug', 293.

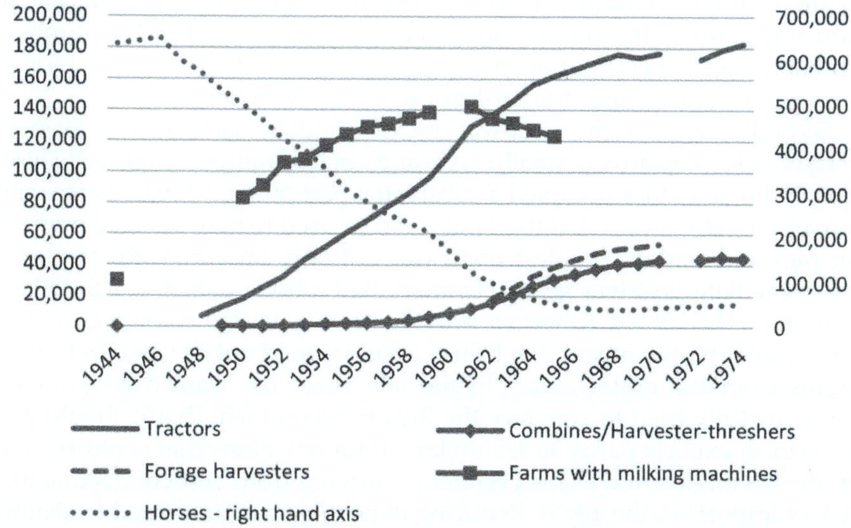

FIGURE 8.6. Farm machinery and horses, 1944–74 (annual data). Source: Danmarks Statistik, *Statistisk årbog* (various years).

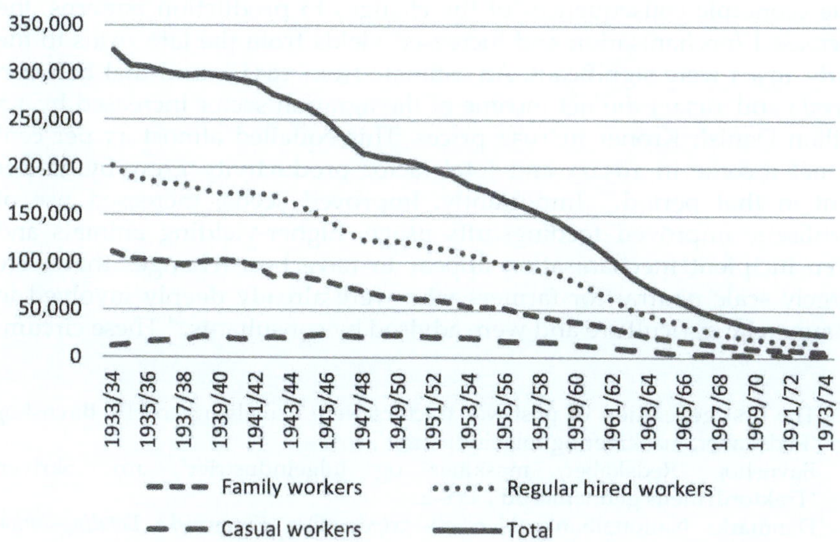

FIGURE 8.7. Agricultural labour 1933–4 to 1973–4 (man years) (annual data). Source: Danmarks Statistik, *Landbrugsstatistik* (1969, 1973, 1975).

in the number of family workers. This indicates the consolidation of farms, which will be analysed in the next section. Moreover, the numbers probably also reflect that farmer's wives and children gradually moved their primary occupation to off-farm work and education.

Second, many of the post-war tractor models, such as the Massey-Ferguson, were relatively small, cheap and apt for family-size farms.[49] Third, oats for horse fodder occupied a substantial part of the cultivated area, and buying a tractor meant that this land could be used to produce feedingstuffs for pigs and cattle.[50] This last point was not only important for farms. In the immediate post-war years, Denmark had a trade deficit in US dollars. Exports to the United Kingdom provided much needed foreign currency, but inconvertibility meant that British pounds could not be used for buying inputs from the dollar area.[51] In the late 1940s the Danish government unsuccessfully tried to convince the British government that it should pay for Danish exports partly in US dollars. With few items that could be sold on the US market, the Danish economy suffered from bottlenecks due to a lack of imports in the 1950s. Reducing dependency on imported feedstuffs by reducing oat production for horses was an important motive for the state to import tractors as part of the Marshall Plan.[52]

8.4 Consolidation

The economic consequences of the changes to production patterns, the increased mechanisation and increased yields from the late 1930s to the early 1950s were significant. An estimate from 1953 found that between 1935/9 and 1952/3 the net income of the agrarian sector increased by 1.3 billion Danish Kroner in 1952 prices. This equalled almost 45 per cent of net income in 1952/3 and total factor productivity grew by 32 per cent in that period.[53] Importantly, improved seeds, increased use of fertilisers, improved feedingstuffs usage, higher-yielding animals and even incipient mechanisation appear to have been changes that were largely scale neutral for farmers who were already deeply involved in commercial agriculture and were advised by consultants.[54] These circum-

49 The first generation of post-war tractors were usually 14-20 HP. Bavnshøj, 'Redskaber, maskiner og følgeindustrier', 101.

50 Bavnshøj, 'Redskaber, maskiner og følgeindustrier', 101; Skriver, 'Traktordriftens gennembrud', 151–2.

51 Danmarks Nationalbank, *Marshall-hjælpen. Den Europæiske Betalingsunion* (Copenhagen: Danmarks Nationalbank, 1999), 29.

52 Vibeke Sørensen, *Denmark's Social Democratic Government and the Marshall Plan* (Copenhagen: Museum Tusculanum Press, 2001), 184–90.

53 Døssing, 'Strukturproblemer i dansk landbrug', 294.

54 It has been stated that 'The interwar period and the first post-war years were probably the period in our entire agrarian history, when economy of scale was the smallest, maybe even non-existent'. Niels Kærgård and

stances allowed many farmers to stay in business well into the post-war years. The number of farms in 1960 was almost 95 per cent of the pre-war level. The raw statistics, though, are probably a bit misleading.[55] Even so, the economic situation became more complicated by the late 1950s. As a professor of Agrarian Economics, Kristen Skovgaard, said in 1957, the issue was that Danish agriculture was very modern but also highly specialised. This had been an advantage, but things were now becoming more difficult. Protectionist policies restricted access to new markets, and it was difficult to diversify production.

In Skovgaard's view, there were only two options. The first was to increase domestic sales, but this was limited by population size. The second and better alternative, according to Skovgaard, was to increase the productivity of labour by further mechanisation and increasing farm size while reducing the overall number of farms. However, the legislation that restricted farm consolidation prevented the immediate implementation of this option.[56] In the long run though, as foreseen by Skovgaard, the solution was to reduce the number of farms, and inevitably it was first and foremost the smaller farms that disappeared. This became possible when farmers took advantage of new technical opportunities based on economies of scale, following a gradual liberalisation of the legislation on farm consolidation.[57]

This is reflected in Figure 8.8, which shows a marked decline in the total number of farms after 1960. More than a third of the farms registered in 1960 were gone by 1975. Consolidation may even have been delayed by farmers expecting that Danish membership of the EEC would increase land prices.[58] But it did take place despite continuous and growing state support in the 1960s. Prices on the home market were allowed to follow the rise in farm costs, while cash payments compensated for the lack of export markets.[59]

Tommy Dalgaard, 'Dansk Landbrugs strukturudvikling siden 2. verdenskrig', *Landbohistorisk Tidsskrift* 11 (2014), 11.

55 The first census distinguishing between full-time and part-time farms – from 1964 – showed that 40,000 farms (25 per cent of total) were part time. Jørgen Skovbæk, 'Dansk landbrug siden Den 2. Verdenskrig', *Landbohistorisk Tidsskrift* 3 (2006), 17. This phenomenon had already existed for some time. Det Økonomiske Råd, Formandsskabet, *Strukturproblemer*, 14.

56 K. Skovgaard, 'Landbrugets tilpasning til skiftende økonomiske vilkår', *Nationaløkonomisk Tidsskrift* 95 (1957), 55–6. The Economic Council reached similar conclusions in 1964. Det Økonomiske Råd, Formandsskabet, *Strukturproblemer*, 19.

57 Danmarks Statistik, *Landbrugsregnskaber i 100 år*, 20.

58 Erik Mortensen, 'Landbrugets strukturproblemer', *Nationaløkonomisk Tidsskrift* 102 (1964), 287.

59 Buksti, 'Dansk mejeribrug, 1955–1982', 382; Christiansen, 'From Food Surplus to Even More Food Surplus', 136–7; Skovbæk, 'Dansk landbrug siden Den 2.

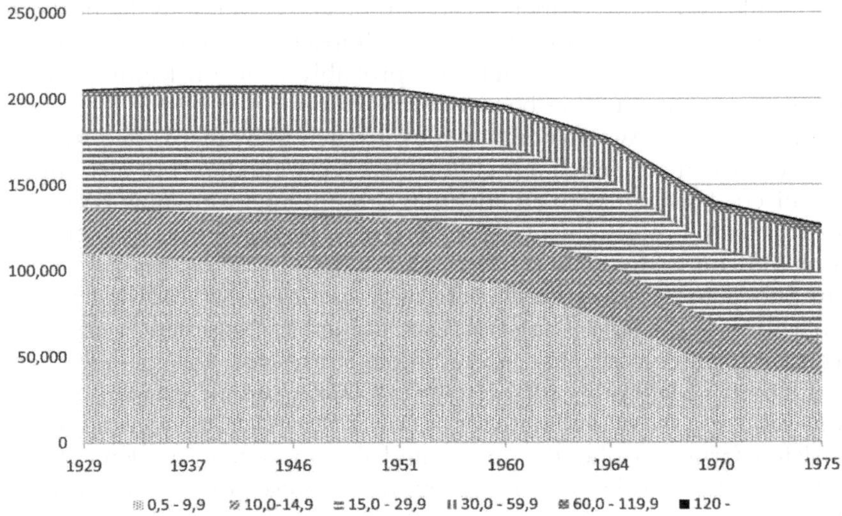

FIGURE 8.8. Number of farms according to size, 1929–75 (select years as shown). Source: Danmarks Statistik, *Statistiske undersøgelser nr. 22*, Danmarks Statistik, *Statistisk tiårsoversigt 1975*.

The process of farm consolidation brought about a decline in the number of farms that was faster than the decline in the total cultivated area. Many farms smaller than 30 hectares disappeared, while farms of more than 30 hectares increased first in relative numbers and from 1970 also in absolute numbers.[60] Still, this was only the beginning. In the early 2020s only about 8,000 full-time farms remained, which is a reduction of 95 per cent compared to 1945. Consolidation also happened among the creameries and slaughterhouses. By the mid-1950s the structure of creameries established around 1900 was largely intact.[61] Then, a rapid process of transformation took place with 1,480 creameries in 1955 reduced to 348 in 1972.[62] In parallel with the reduction in the number of creameries, the 1960s also witnessed the first mergers, where several cooperatives

Verdenskrig', 30; Det Økonomiske Råd, Formandsskabet, *Strukturproblemer*, 11–12.

60 Until 1964 there were between 23,000 and 26,000 farms larger than 30 hectares. This increased to 29,000 in 1975, equalling 23 per cent of total farms. Only 12 per cent of the farms were that large in 1929.

61 The number of creameries peaked at 1,711 in 1935.

62 As a result, the average amount of milk received in the creameries exploded. Cooperatives went from 3.4 million kilos in 1955 to 16.5 million kilos in 1973, while private creameries went from 2.0 million kilos in 1955 to 7.5 million kilos in 1973. Hansen, *Andelsbevægelsens evne til forandring*, 29–30.

merged into one commercial unit with several sites.[63] By the early 1960s it was recognised that local mergers were insufficient, and the idea of 'Creamery Denmark' was born. *Mejeriselskabet Danmark* – later *Arla* – was created in 1970 with forty creameries, and the consolidation was completed in 1999, when *Mejeriselskabet Danmark* absorbed its last large competitor, *Kløvermælk*.[64] A similar process of consolidation and fusions also took place among the slaughterhouses. By the end of 1972, there were thirty cooperatives and only four private slaughterhouses left, down from sixty-two cooperatives and fifteen private ones in 1951.[65]

8.5 Specialisation: Incipient revolution

The last part of the 'Green Evolution' was that of increasing farm specialisation that proceeded in parallel with farm consolidation. As mentioned initially, the traditional production units were small to medium integrated farms, and this was still the case by the late 1960s. In 1968 94 per cent of cattle and 84 per cent of pigs were found at farms that had both types of animals.[66] Yet, at the end of the period, it is possible to see a growing specialisation in cattle, pigs or arable products.[67] Figure 8.9, which extends until 1990, shows that this specialisation process continued. Hence, the process from the 1960s onwards presaged the next 'revolution', which happened in the following decades. In 2020, only 2 per cent of farms had both cattle and pigs, while 62 per cent had neither.

The change to specialised farms was a consequence of ever-increasing capital requirements for ever-growing production facilities but was also facilitated by new crops and more efficient cultivation methods.[68] Moreover, heavier tractors and increased use of artificial fertilisers, irrigation and pesticides reduced the risk of failed harvests, while the use of milk proteins to produce cheese and powdered milk reduced the incentive to combine cattle and pigs on farms.[69] Finally, the price policy of the EEC probably also increased specialisation as there was less need to spread risk over various product lines.[70]

63 Buksti, 'Dansk mejeribrug, 1955–1982', 387–92.

64 Ibid., 394, 400–2.

65 Pedersen, 'Det danske landbrugs historie', 236.

66 The first statistics on animal distribution on farms is from 1968, but the situation appears to have changed little between 1950 and 1968. Skovbæk, 'Dansk landbrug siden Den 2. Verdenskrig', 24.

67 The specialisation also included a geographical specialisation, where the farms on Zealand tended to specialise in non-animal production, while milk and butter was predominantly produced in Jutland. Buksti, 'Dansk mejeribrug, 1955–1982', 339.

68 Det Økonomiske Råd, Formandsskabet, *Strukturproblemer*, 17

69 Skovbæk, 'Dansk landbrug siden Den 2. Verdenskrig', 15.

70 Danmarks Statistik, *Landbrugsregnskaber i 100 år*, 17.

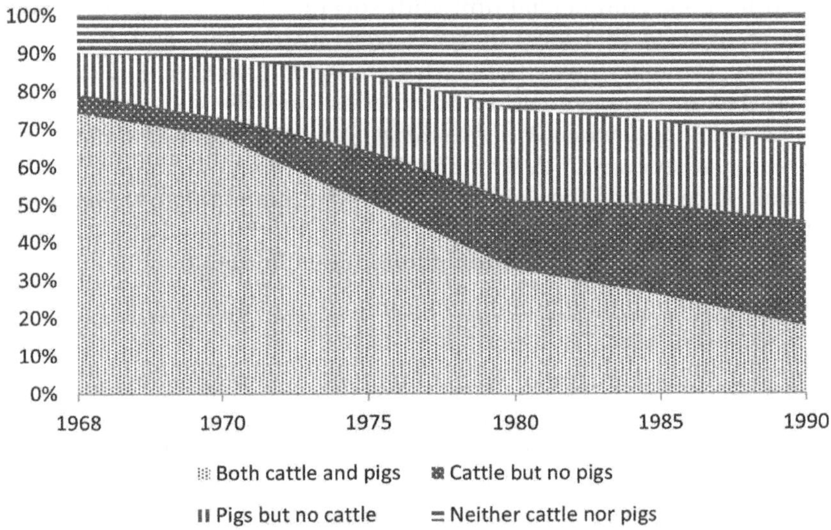

FIGURE 8.9. Process of farm production specialisation, 1968–90 (select years as shown). Source: Danmarks Statistik, *Landbrugsstatistik (1968, 1970, 1975, 1980, 1985, 1990).*

8.6 Conclusions

All in all, we have demonstrated that Danish farmers continuously adapted their arable and animal production to changing conditions. Post-war developments in production were to a large degree a continuation of pre-war trends. Farmers switched crops due to relative costs of input. Until the 1960s they continuously increased output through changes to the crop mix, intensification of land use, new varieties of well-known crops and an increase in the use of manure, artificial fertilisers and pesticides. When production levelled out, it was due to a decline in the total cultivated area and further changes in the crop mix.

In the case of animal production, the continued improvement in the productivity of the *Rød Dansk Malkerace* obtained through a sustained breeding scheme and better understanding of optimal feed composition increased milk production per animal. In the case of pigs, the improvements were twofold: a decline in the amount of feedingstuffs required to increase living weight and an increase in the number of piglets per sow-year.

The improvements appear to have been largely scale neutral well into the 1960s, allowing farmers to adapt to the combination of new possibilities and changes in market conditions. Hence, most of the basic production structure was stable, but not static, between 1930 and the late 1960s or early 1970s, meaning that the sector did not experience a Green Revolution but rather a 'Green Evolution'. This happened even though the sector implemented many of the Green Revolution's technological principles.

This adaptability seems to be related to the fact that the Danish agrarian sector had already experienced a 'first Green Revolution' in the late nineteenth century. This had led to a strong commercial focus and experience with a largely farm-managed continuous improvement of the production system, both on and off the farm. Hence, the underlying Green Revolution logic of increasing farmers' integration into the market was a well-established fact by the 1930s. The 'traditional' small- and medium-size integrated farms were already a modern capitalistic enterprise firmly established in an export-orientated market system.

A supplementary explanation for the adaptability of Danish farmers might be related to a comment made by Cabral *et al.*, 'The "regime of truth" associated with the Green Revolution epic privileges science over experiential knowledge, technological over social innovations, and national goals over local needs'.[71] The developments described here point to the peculiarity that in the Danish case the 'regime of truth' combined science *and* experiential knowledge, technological *and* social innovation, and national *and* local needs, thereby differing from the Green Revolution.

There are many differences between 'traditional' twentieth-century Danish agriculture and 'traditional' Global South agriculture in the twenty-first century. Nevertheless, this might be an area where the Danish experience has relevance across borders and centuries. Even so, the Danish farmers could not in the long run resist the implications of their modernisation, and this led to a second profound revolution. The first signs of this appeared in the 1960s, but the main part took place several decades later, where a few large, specialised farms replaced the traditional small- and medium-size integrated farms. An entire social group and a culture that had defined an important part of Danish history in the nineteenth and twentieth century has now disappeared.

71 Cabral, Pandey and Xu, 'Epic narratives', 252.

9

The 'Green Revolution' in the Red Zone: the case of socialist Hungarian agriculture

Zsuzsanna Varga

In Hungary the narrative of agricultural modernisation cannot be said to have started with the Green Revolution. It was preceded by the transfer of the socialist model of large-scale industrialised agriculture on the country. This was part of a wider process by which the Soviet Union, in the second half of the 1940s, imposed its political and economic system onto the East Central European countries, of which Hungary was one. The aim of the Sovietisation of agriculture was to create large-scale production entities (state farms, collective farms) in the place of family-owned peasant farms, which – according to communist ideology – were considered underdeveloped. Following from this logic, motorisation and chemicalisation were promoted only on these large-scale farms; that is, the main players of socialist agricultural modernisation. However, those processes could not lead to increased production for a long time because of the negative consequences of the dramatic structural intervention made into traditional peasant farming. The Green Revolution only came with the second trans-systemic transfer from the late 1960s when the capitalist model of industrialised agriculture was transplanted into socialist large-scale agriculture. As a result, the decade of the 1970s brought a quick boom in Hungarian agriculture. In per capita value of agricultural production, Hungary rated sixth in the world by the early 1980s.[1]

After a brief introduction to the capitalist period of Hungarian agriculture, the first part of this chapter discusses the coerced transition from small-scale agriculture to large-scale socialist agriculture between 1949 and 1961 under the specific conditions of the Cold War and the

1 Központi Statisztikai Hivatal, *A magyar mezőgazdaság nemzetközi összehasonlításban* ['Hungarian agriculture in international comparison]' (Budapest: KSH, 1987).

planned economy. The second part analyses the paradigmatic shift within socialist agriculture that led to the Western technology and know-how transfer known as the Green Revolution being adopted. Studying both transfers, special attention is paid to the political and agro-industrial imperatives, the actors of the diffusion and the impacts (both results and limits). Besides archival and statistical data sources, the chapter also draws on oral history and the contemporary press.

In undertaking the analysis of the Hungarian experience, a concept elaborated by Auderset and Moser has proved to be fruitful. They speak of an 'agrarian-industrial knowledge society' from the last third of the nineteenth century to the mid-twentieth century, when the use of biotic and the consumption of fossil resources were dominant in the agriculture.[2] The post-war transition from an 'agrarian-industrial knowledge society' to an 'industrial-agrarian knowledge society' was characterised by the processes of motorisation and chemicalisation.[3] Discussing the two above-mentioned trans-systemic transfers in Hungary might contribute to our understanding of the similarities and differences of state-enforced 'high modernism'[4] on both sides of the Iron Curtain.

9.1 Historical introduction

Hungary inherited from the nineteenth century a dual agricultural structure characterised by large estates (latifundia-system) on the one hand, and a vast number of small peasant holdings on the other. The land reform of 1920 barely changed the bimodal distribution of land.[5] Nearly half of the country's total land was owned by a few dozen aristocratic families, yet the proportion of non-aristocratic large estates was high. As a contrast, only about 20 per cent of the total land belonged to small peasant farms of less than 5.7 ha (10 kh),[6] which made up some four-

2 Juri Auderset and Peter Moser, *Die Agrarfrage in der Industriegesellschaft: Wissenskulturen, Machtverhältnisse und natürliche Ressourcen in der agrarisch-industriellen Wissensgesellschaft (1850–1950)* (Wien: Böhlau Verlag, 2018).

3 See also the contribution by Auderset and Moser in this volume.

4 A phrase used by James C. Scott, *Seeing Like a State: How Certain Schemes to Improve the Human Condition Have Failed* (New Haven, CT: Yale University Press, 1998).

5 Paul Brassley, 'Land Reform and Reallocation in Interwar Europe', in *Contexts of Property in Europe: The Social Embeddedness of Property Rights in Land in Historical Perspective,* Rosa Congost and Rui Santos (eds) (Turnhout: Brepols, 2010), 151.

6 In Hungary before 1972 the official unit of land measurement was the *kataszt-rális hold.* One katasztrális hold (kh) = 0.57 hectare (ha). In this chapter I calculate land measurement in hectares to facilitate comparison with other countries.

fifths of all agricultural holdings.[7] The dual structure of a few latifundia and a mass of tiny peasant holdings was unique in inter-war Europe.

This highly disproportionate distribution of landed property explains why only about 30 per cent of the agrarian population was able to maintain a family from the product of their own land. In the mid-1930s about 70 per cent of agrarian society consisted of people with very little or no landed property who, consequently, were compelled to seek waged labour.[8] The situation of the peasants was made more difficult as a result of the inheritance system by which land was divided among descendants. Each generation farmed on smaller plots of land than their ancestors. The dwindling estates did not provide a sufficient livelihood, so their owners also entered the labour market. In the first half of the twentieth century, opportunities for mass migration to the USA emigration narrowed, and industry could not absorb the surplus agricultural labour force. Due to the cheap and abundant supply of labour, mechanisation made little progress. Non-mechanised capstan threshers were replaced gradually by steam and oil- or petrol-driven threshers. Between 1925 and 1929 the number of tractors increased from 1,189 to 6,800, but in the first half of the 1930s barely more than 100 vehicles were added to the tractor fleet. The spread of harvesting machines was also hindered by the availability of a very cheap labour force.[9]

The dual farm structure mentioned above was formed in the last third of the nineteenth century as a result of the emancipation of serfs. Ideas for the modernisation of both large estates and small family farms were already in circulation. Due to the dissolution of the Austro-Hungarian Monarchy after the First World War, new macro-level strategies of adaptation became necessary. Agricultural science provided the necessary base for this. In this field, there was a strong continuity going back to the high-quality scholarship developed during the dualistic period of the Monarchy.[10]

In the 1920s there were proposals for how to foster a more diversified agricultural production in order to create a greater scope for growth and flexible adjustments after the loss of the protected markets that had existed under the Monarchy. However, state economic policy prioritised

7 Péter Gunst, 'Hungarian Agrarian Society during the Inter-War Period (1919–1945)', in *Hungarian Agrarian Society from the Emancipation of Serfs (1848) to the Re-Privatisation of Land*, Péter Gunst (ed.) (New York: Columbia University Press, 1998), 199–231.

8 Ibid.

9 Miklós Szuhay, 'Evolution of Hungarian Agriculture during the Inter-War Years (1918–1945)', in *Hungarian Agrarian Society*, Gunst (ed.), 179–80.

10 István Orosz, 'A modernizációs kísérletek főbb szakaszai a magyar mezőgazdaságban a XIX–XX. században' ['The main stages of modernisation experiments in Hungarian agriculture were in the nineteenth and twentieth centuries'], *Múltunk* 28 (2003), 250–2.

missing or underdeveloped industries by a mainly tariff-based import-substitution-policy, which favoured the industrial at the expense of the agricultural sector.[11]

In the inter-war period in Hungary, amid the general lack of capital, we can find only a few examples of agricultural modernisation. Some large-scale, wage-labour based estates started modernisation efforts, as was indicated by their specialisation and the appearance of processing industries connected to agriculture (alcohol distilleries, sugar factories, mills, lumberyards). However, in the majority of large estates the farming methods changed very little. There were also regions where peasant farms with good market opportunities started to intensify and specialise their farming practice, especially around the capital and other major cities. For the most part, we do not witness the Western European-style transformation that prioritised fodder production over grain cultivation in favour of animal husbandry. In Hungary, the proportion of cereals by acreage remained around 54 per cent. The most successful state initiative was linked to this sector. Relying on the results of Hungarian wheat breeding, in 1931 the Ministry of Agriculture decided to improve the quality of wheat production nationwide. Responding to the regional features of wheat production, seven districts were created. Those producers who wanted to participate in the campaign were given free high-quality wheat seeds.[12]

It can be concluded that in the inter-war period Hungary remained an agrarian-industrial country. The share of agrarian population did decline somewhat to 50 per cent in 1940 while the share of those engaged in industry rose from 32 per cent in 1930 to 35 per cent in 1940. The proportion of agriculture's contribution to the national income was 32 per cent in 1930. By 1940 it had fallen marginally to 30 per cent. Exports continued to be dominated by agricultural commodities, which formed 67 per cent of the total in 1935–8.[13]

9.2 Copying the Soviet model of large-scale socialist agriculture

Unlike other European countries, where large estates were generally liquidated by reforms after the First World War, the system of latifundia

11 Michael Kopsidis, 'Agricultural Development and Impeded Growth: The Case of Hungary, 1870–1973', in *Agriculture and Economic Development in Europe Since 1870*, Pedro Lains and Vicente Pinilla (eds) (London and New York: Routledge, 2009), 286–94.

12 Szuhay, 'Evolution of Hungarian Agriculture', 184–5.

13 In most cases the statistical data employed in this chapter is taken from Hungarian Central Statistical Office, *Hungarian Agriculture 1851–2000* (CD-ROM, Budapest: Hungarian Central Statistical Office: 2000).

was abolished in Hungary only in 1945.[14] As a result of the radical land reform in 1945, the proportion of the population employed in agriculture even increased, reaching 54 per cent in 1949. Consequently, the proportion of landless groups within the peasantry fell from the pre-war level of 46 per cent down to 17 per cent, while those in the category of smallholders rose from 47 per cent to 80 per cent, but the new landowners received on average five kh a piece – less than 3 ha. Most of the small farms were self-sufficient. They were based on human and draft animal power, as before 1945. Motorisation – as in the majority of European countries – was mostly employed in threshing.[15]

That at the end of the Second World War, Hungary, as part of the losing side, fell into the zone of influence of the Soviet Union, had a far-reaching impact on political, economic and social life.[16] The process of Sovietisation accelerated from 1947–8 with the increase of Cold War tensions. There were differences in the timing and the methods applied by the different East Central European countries, but the main elements of this model were the same everywhere: introduction of the one-party system, nationalisation leading to the dominance of state ownership and introduction of the planned economy in place of the market economy.[17]

As part of the communist takeover, other political parties, including the agrarian parties, were weakened and their leaders were imprisoned or forced into exile.[18] The communist parties' promised that, by adopting the Soviet model, the underdeveloped agrarian and agro-industrial countries of East Central Europe would quickly become industrial ones.[19] In reality, the Soviet Union aimed to create a well controllable and autarchic bloc, which on the one hand would become independent of the

14 Kopsidis, 'Agricultural development', 286–310.

15 Sándor Szakács, 'From Land Reform to Collectivization (1945–1956)', in *Hungarian Agrarian Society*, Gunst (ed.), 260–4.

16 László Borhi, *Dealing with Dictators: The United States, Hungary, and East Central Europe, 1942–1989* (Bloomington, IN: Indiana University Press, 2016), 82–136.

17 Iván T. Berend, *Central and Eastern Europe, 1944–1993: Detour from the Periphery to the Periphery* (Cambridge: Cambridge University Press, 1996), 3–39.

18 Nigel Swain, 'The Fate of Peasant Parties during Socialist Transformation', in *Bauerngesellschaften auf dem Weg in die Moderne: Agrarismus in Ostmitteleuropa 1880 bis 1960*, Helga Schultz and Angela Harre (eds) (Wiesbaden: Harrasowitz, 2010), 163–76. See also the contribution by Miguel Cabo in this volume.

19 On the issue of the existence of the Soviet model, I agree with Nigel Swain's interpretation: until Stalin's death the Soviet model was a Stalinist model. However, after 1953 this model changed, it became a 'moving target', a changing set of features, due to the Khrushchev's reforms. Nigel Swain, 'Eastern European Collectivization Campaigns Compared, 1945–1962', in *The Collectivization of Agriculture in Communist Eastern Europe: Comparison and Entanglement*, Constantin Iordachi and Arnd Bauerkämper (eds) (Budapest-New York: CEU Press, 2014), 506–13.

capitalist West, and on the other hand develop a significant base of heavy and military industries. Preparations for the anticipated next world war played a significant role in both endeavours.[20]

The political context is vital to understanding the Sovietisation of agriculture; that is, the copying of the Stalinist system of agriculture. The major feature of the Stalinist model was the subordination of agriculture to industry.[21] Stalin treated agriculture as an 'inner colony', from which both material and human resources were extracted.[22] In the Soviet Union through the forced collectivisation of the 1930s, peasant farms were liquidated, and new large-scale production entities were created. They ensured the concentrated accumulation of income, as well as the control and subjugation of agricultural producers.

Copying the Stalinist model, two types became typical in large-scale farming: state farms (*sovkhozi*); and collective farms (commonly known as *kolkhoz*).[23] At the top of the hierarchy of Stalinist agriculture were the sovkhoz. According to communist ideology, these were the embodiment of the highest form of property: state property. They received the majority of agricultural investments for motorisation, so the use of fossil fuels progressed fastest on the state farms. They were seen as symbols of modern socialist agriculture.

Collective farms were deemed to be of a lower order because they remained the property of the peasants. It is important to emphasise that during the collectivisations, peasants' land remained privately owned within most of East Central Europe. However, this was merely a formality, as once the peasants joined the collective farm, their land could not be freely sold or rented.[24]

Unlike state farms, collective farms could not own agricultural machinery. Instead, their machine supply was provided by the network

20 János Kornai, *The Socialist System: The Political Economy of Communism* (Oxford: Clarendon Press, 1992), 62–90.

21 The subordination of agriculture to industry is not only characteristic of the socialist model. As Moser and Varley have pointed out, integrating agriculture into the realm of an industrial society required its subordination to the hegemonic conceptions of industrial progress. Peter Moser and Tony Varley 'The State and Agricultural Modernisation in the Nineteenth and Twentieth Centuries in Europe', in *Integration through Subordination: The Politics of Agricultural Modernisation in Industrial Europe,* Peter Moser and Tony Varley (eds) (Turnhout: Brepols, 2013), 13–39.

22 Stephan Merl, 'The Role of Agriculture in Soviet Industrialization', in *Communist Agriculture: Farming in the Soviet Union and Eastern Europe,* Karl-Eugen Wädekin (ed.) (London-New York: Routledge, 1990).

23 Lynne Viola, 'Collectivization in the Soviet Union: Specificities and Modalities', in *Collectivization of Agriculture in Communist Eastern Europe,* Iordachi and Bauerkämper (ed.), 52–61.

24 Swain, 'Eastern European Collectivization Campaigns', 506–7.

of Machine and Tractor Stations (MTS). Collective farms thus became highly dependent on MTS. The control of collective farms by the state was secured by their management by reliable party members – usually with an industrial workers' background – sent from towns to the villages or poor local peasants elevated to leading positions.[25] All this was a clear sign that political trust and ideological commitment were more important than professional competence. It is also important to add that, while the Communist Party[26] did not recognise the value of the knowledge accumulated in the sector before 1945, there was a shortage of specialists familiar with Soviet agriculture.

Hungarian communist leaders faithfully copied Stalinist economic policy, which based forced industrial growth on internal accumulation. In addition to restricting consumption by the population, it was hoped that the necessary means for growth could be created by draining income from agriculture. The system of compulsory deliveries and the distorted pricing system together played a significant role in securing peasants' income for the state but it should not be forgotten that classical income-extraction was also in operation in the form of discriminative taxation.[27] Following the Stalinist model, agriculture in Hungary became an 'inner colony'. This is implied by the fact that the need for agricultural inputs were ignored by both investment policy and machine industry. While tractors became the iconic symbol of modern socialist agriculture, in Hungary, of the 22,000 planned new tractors, only around half had been delivered by the end of the first five-year plan (1950–4). Quality problems and lack of spare parts were everyday phenomena in these years. An important characteristic of this period was that the available scarce resources – motorised technology, artificial fertilisers, pesticides and so on – were distributed unequally, with priority being given to state farms. Peasant farms labelled as 'backward' were excluded from the process of tractorisation.[28]

On 3 March 1949, the Political Committee (PC) of the Hungarian Workers' Party passed a resolution declaring that the transition from small peasant farming to large-scale collectivised farming was to be

25 R. W. Davies, *The Soviet Collective Farm, 1929–1930* (London: Palgrave Macmillan, 1980), 75–97.

26 The name of the Communist Party in Hungary between 1945–8 was the Hungarian Communist Party (HCP), between 1948–56 the Hungarian Workers' Party (HWP) and between 1956–89 the Hungarian Socialist Workers' Party (HSWP).

27 Zsuzsanna Varga, 'Wartime Agricultural Policy in Peacetime: A Case Study of Hungary, 1940–1956', in *War, Agriculture, and Food: Rural Europe from the 1930s to the 1950s*, Paul Brassley, Yves Segers and Leen Van Molle (eds) (New York: Routledge, 2012), 102–6.

28 Szakács, 'From Land Reform to Collectivization', 287–91.

accomplished in the course of the first five-year plan.[29] The Hungarian party leadership, following Stalin's instructions, wanted to implement this profound structural change in a very short time. Most countries of the Soviet bloc began their full-scale collectivisation campaigns in 1948 or 1949.[30] In Hungary, as in other socialist countries, a huge conflict had emerged between the communists and peasant society. Only a small group of landless peasants and part-time farmers were attracted to collective farming in the early 1950s. The vast majority of the landed peasantry had no intention whatsoever of giving up their land. What they had seen as POWs in the Soviet Union or heard about the functioning of the *kolkhoz* was completely alien to them. Signing the declaration of entry meant the loss of economic independence, since those who joined the *kolkhoz* were obliged to surrender both their tools and livestock to the collective and to carry out all work tasks (apart from work on household plots) as members of brigades and work teams.[31] The model charters of collective farms strictly defined their operational mechanisms, just as they did the rights and duties of membership.[32]

Despite the fact that propaganda emphasised the expected benefits, and some progress had been made in the area of motorisation and the introduction of new high-yielding varieties and specialised breeds of livestock, the resistance of the peasantry was so strong that over time collectivisation involved more and more state violence.[33] Nevertheless, the first two collectivisation campaigns failed. The first one was stopped in 1953, after Stalin's death. By this time, the catastrophic consequences of collectivisation (dramatic decline in production, increase of uncultivated land, outflow of peasants from agriculture) could not be concealed. Hungary's natural features – climate, soil and water supply – afford

29 Magyar Nemzeti Levéltár Országos Levéltár [National Archives of Hungary, hereafter cited as MNL OL], M-KS 276. f. 53. cs. 22. ő. e. Jegyzőkönyv a Politikai Bizottság (PB) 1949. március 3-i üléséről. [Minutes of the PC of HWP] 3 Mar. 1949. Agenda 2. Javaslat a mezőgazdaság ötéves tervére. ['Proposition on the agricultural part of the first five-year plan'].

30 Swain, 'Eastern European Collectivization Campaigns', 499–508.

31 In Hungary the full name of the kolkhoz-type collective farm was '*mezőgazdasági termelőszövetkezet*' ('agricultural producers cooperative'). In Western academic literature there is another widely used term: 'collective farm'. In my chapter the term collective farm will be used, while drawing attention to the difference between a socialist cooperative and a Western-type cooperative.

32 Karl-Eugen Wädekin, 'The Soviet Kolkhoz: Vehicle of Co-operative Farming or of Control and Transfer of Resources', in *Co-operative and Commune,* Peter Dorner (ed.) (Madison, WI: University of Wisconsin Press, 1977).

33 József Ö. Kovács, 'The Forced Collectivization of Agriculture in Hungary, 1948–1961', in *Collectivization of Agriculture in Communist Eastern Europe,* Iordachi and Bauerkämper (eds).

excellent potential for agricultural cultivation, yet in 1952, for the first time, it became a net grain importer.[34]

As a consequence of de-Stalinisation, in 1953–4 a more peasant-friendly policy was adopted to revitalise agricultural production. However, this period of relief did not last long, and the second collectivisation campaign was launched by the Hungarian Workers Party (HWP) in the fall of 1955. It met such resistance that within half a year agricultural crisis recurred nationwide. Accumulated food supply problems contributed in large measure to the outbreak of the 1956 Hungarian Revolution.

This was the situation that confronted the Kádár government once it came to power, with Soviet assistance, following the bloody defeat of the Revolution of 1956. Food supply became a strategic issue for the new regime, which attempted to compensate for its lack of political legitimacy through promises to increase living standards. As János Kádár, the chief secretary of the HSWP, pointed out at the meeting of the Party's Provisional Central Committee of 2 December 1956: 'Our policy in economic questions, and especially in questions of redistribution, is that the priority should be a gradual rise in living standards.'[35]

Fulfilling the aims of the living standards policy at that time depended mainly on food supplies. To increase agricultural production and provide incentives for producers, the Kádár government decided on an alteration in agrarian policy. Among its first steps, the government halted the second collectivisation campaign and abolished the compulsory delivery system that had been one of the fundamental elements of the Stalinist agricultural system. Hungary was the first socialist country to take this step, the most enduring impact of which was the revival, albeit to a limited degree, of market mechanisms in agriculture.[36]

In late 1958, the leadership of the HSWP took the decision to resume collectivisation as a way of demonstrating its allegiance to Moscow and its conformity with the other countries of the bloc. Bulgaria completed the process of collectivisation in 1958, Czechoslovakia in 1959, East Germany in 1960 and Romania in 1962. The latest research has emphasised that Khrushchev did not insist on the Stalinist model being implemented in its fullest form during the completion of collectivisation in East Central Europe.[37] Thus, it is understandable why Yugoslavia and Poland could

34 Szakács, 'Evolution of Hungarian Agriculture', 287–91.

35 MNL OL, M-KS 288. f. 4. cs. 6. ő. e. Jegyzőkönyv a Magyar Szocialista Munkáspárt Ideiglenes Központi Bizottságának üléséről '[Minutes of the Provisional CC of HSWP'], 2 Dec. 1956.

36 Zsuzsanna Varga, 'The Impact of 1956 on the Relationship Between the Kádár Regime and the Peasantry, 1956–66', *Hungarian Studies Review* 34 (2007), 155–76.

37 Swain 'Eastern European Collectivization campaigns', 503–13.

be omitted under Khrushchev. Such a 'separate path' under Stalinism was unimaginable.

Hungary completed collectivisation in 1961. There were 271 state farms, approximately 4,200 collective farms and almost 165,000 individual farmers registered.[38] The collective farms used almost 70 per cent of the country's arable land and employed three-quarters of the total number of agricultural labourers. The success of the collectivisation in statistical terms was not automatically accompanied by the rapid consolidation of collective farming. Between 1959 and 1961 the number of active agricultural labourers fell by 350,000 and the composition of collective farm membership in terms of age and gender became increasingly disadvantageous. At the end of 1961, three-quarters of the members were over forty years old, and almost 40 per cent were women. During the 1950s, as a consequence of the collectivisation campaigns, huge numbers of peasants (mostly men) abandoned agriculture. The rate of this outflow of labour exceeded the rate of mechanisation. In this context the remaining (largely) female workforce turned out insufficient. Moreover, in the first half of the 1960s most agricultural investment had to be spent on the construction of new large-scale buildings (stables, storage houses, offices). For this reason, there was not enough resource to buy new machinery to counterbalance the decreasing manpower. The newly collectivised agriculture, which according to ideological assumptions was a fundamental step towards an industrial-like and 'productivist' agriculture, for years failed to produce the expected impressive increase in production.[39] The food base of the standard-of-living policy was therefore in danger.

The changing international environment under Khrushchev created the opportunity for the Hungarian party leadership to develop a new strategy to handle these problems. A special intermediary group, the agrarian lobby, became the key player in this. Its members entered the political leadership after the 1956 Revolution. Thanks to their rural origin and their experience of the party-state apparatus during the 1950s, they were able to become mediators between the party leadership and the collective farm membership.[40] Among the members of the agrarian lobby, Lajos Fehér stands out. He had the trust of János Kádár due to their activities in the communist underground movement before 1945.

38 Data taken from Hungarian Central Statistical Office, *Hungarian Agriculture 1851–2000*.

39 MNL OL, M-KS 288. f., 28. cs., (1962) 3. ő. e. A KB Mezőgazdasági Osztály tájékoztató jelentése a PB számára a termelőszövetkezetek 1961. évi zárszámadásáról. ['Report of the HSWP Agricultural Department to the Political Committee on the end-of-year accounts of the agricultural producer cooperatives in 1961'].

40 Zsuzsanna Varga, *The Hungarian Agricultural Miracle? Sovietization and Americanization in a Communist Country* (New York: Rowman and Littlefield, 2021), 107–14.

In the first half of the 1960s, as a result of the agrarian lobby's negotiations, an increasing number of local initiatives were transferred from the category of 'banned' or 'tolerated' into the category of 'favoured'. This measure significantly widened the scope of collective farms. The collective farm membership, for example, won the right to keep more animals on their household plots, to undertake share-cropping, to receive premiums in kind, and so forth, The 'good practices' of work organisation and remuneration differed from the Soviet *kolkhoz* model but served to stimulate the self-interest of the collective farm members. The creative adaptation of state-imposed collectivisation by local actors highlights the potential of bottom-up initiatives from the rural society. As a result of the interactions between the HWSP leadership and collective farms mediated by the agrarian lobby, a gradual deviation from the Stalinist model started from the early 1960s in Hungarian agriculture.[41]

9.3 Technology and know-how transfer from the West: the hidden Green Revolution

Learning from capitalist countries represented the other means of addressing post-collectivisation problems in socialist Hungary. The agrarian lobby played an initiating role in this process as well. It is worth mentioning that among the members of the agrarian lobby, there were quite a few who had visited Western Europe in the inter-war period, mostly during their studies. Such a figure was Ferenc Erdei who was counted among the most influential members of the lobby. During his study trips to Western Europe in the 1930s, he visited countries (the Netherlands, Switzerland) that could serve as examples due to their advanced agriculture and cooperative movements.[42]

After 1956, maintaining contacts with the Western world became difficult again because of Hungary's partial international isolation. The leaders of the agrarian lobby, Lajos Fehér and Ferenc Erdei were in agreement that the only way out of this situation was to promote the exchange of scientific experience and know-how. The Institute of Agricultural Economics, led by Erdei, played a prominent role from its establishment in 1957 in the dissemination of the results of Western agricultural science. On the one hand, Institute staff closely followed up-to-date research literature, and, when possible, took part in the activities of international organisations; on the other, Erdei, as general secretary of the Hungarian Academy of Sciences, collected and forwarded

41 Zsuzsanna Varga, 'Conflicts and Compromises Between the Hungarian Socialist State and the Peasantry: Contextualising the "Hungarian Agricultural Miracle"', in *Integration through Subordination*, Moser and Varley (eds).

42 Tibor Huszár, *Erdei Ferenc 1910–1970: Politikai életrajz* ['Ferenc Erdei 1910–1970: Political biography'] (Budapest: Corvina, 2012), 386–96.

information from other research institutes to the Party centre, primarily to Fehér, who supervised agriculture in various positions during the 1960s.[43] By this process, a channel was formed through which the results of scientific research reached the level of decision-makers.

The top-priority information was any that would allow the Party leadership to obtain a quick increase in production, especially meat production, which is why most expert delegations were sent to those West European countries that were leaders in this field. Western poultry and egg production had developed at an exceptionally quickly since the Second World War. This sector was the first to employ 'industrial' solutions by combining the results of biological and technical sciences. As the term indicates, a closed system was created in which all the factors influencing production – light, air, water supply, hygienic conditions, compound feed and so on – were regulated automatically. By regulating light and temperature, the animals' biological rhythms could be separated from the change of seasons. As a result, the new technology was capable of producing massive quantities of meat year on year.

This was exactly what was needed by a Hungarian leadership that had adopted the standard-of-living policy, but at the same time was faced by the weak performance of collectivised agriculture. The political decision to initiate the poultry programme, that is to adopt the Western model of poultry and egg production, was therefore made at the highest level of the HSWP.[44]

It is important to highlight that this early adoption of western technology could not have taken place without the approval of the Soviet leadership. Following the defeat of the 1956 Revolution, Moscow accorded the Hungarian leadership greater room for manoeuvre in some areas to prove the superiority and viability of the socialist system. The impact of this kind of 'exceptionalism' made itself felt particularly strongly in agrarian policy, to which Khrushchev's own interest in agriculture also contributed.[45]

The first success dates back to 1960, when a Hungarian delegation purchased what was then one of the most modern poultry and egg production systems from West Germany.[46] The Lohmann company not only supplied breeding animals and complete poultry sheds, but also, in

43 Varga, *Hungarian Agricultural Miracle?*, 153–62.

44 MNL OL M-KS 288. f. 5. cs. 200. ő. e. Jegyzőkönyv az HSWP Politikai Bizottság 1960. szeptember 13-i üléséről. ['Minutes of the PC of HSWP'] 13 September 1960.

45 János M. Rainer, 'The Sixties in Hungary: Some Historical and Political Approaches', in *Muddling Through in the Long 1960s: Ideas and Everyday Life in High Politics and Lower Classes of Communist Hungary*, György Péteri (ed.) (Trondheim: Norwegian University of Science and Technology, 2005).

46 MNL OL M-KS 288. f. 17. cs. 5. ő. e. Keserű János feljegyzés Fehér Lajos részére a nyugat-németországi tanulmányútról. 1960. május 17. ['Memo from János Keserű to Lajos Fehér on his study trip in West Germany', 17 May 1960].

addition, the training in West Germany of Hungarian experts (architects, mechanical engineers, veterinary surgeons, chemists, animal breeders, feed providers). The three-year pilot poultry programme, led by the Bábolna State Farm, was a great success. Bábolna was the first farm – not only in Hungary but also in the Soviet bloc – to adopt the methods of industrialised poultry meat and egg production. When Khrushchev paid a visit to Hungary in spring 1964, the first place he wanted to visit was Bábolna and he expressed his interest in transferring its innovative technology into Soviet agriculture. Bábolna made several attempts to establish chicken factories there, but for several reasons (a different work ethic, the acute problems of a shortage economy, among others) they could not produce the expected results.[47]

The next step in Hungary was for Bábolna, as a system centre, to start to disseminate this technology for modern poultry production to the less capital-rich state farms and collective farms. In 1964, there were sixty-three partner farms, but in 1966 the number was 158, and in 1967 as many as 217.[48] This was of exceptional importance to the agrarian lobby because it proved that Western technology could be successfully adopted in a socialist economic environment. It provided an excellent basis for further lobbying for the expansion of capitalist relations.

Later, the intensification of the Western technology and knowledge transfer was connected to a radical economic reform: the New Economic Mechanism (NEM). The goal of the reform introduced on 1 January 1968 was to alleviate the problems of the planned economy, implementing certain supply-demand mechanisms. It was intended that this would be achieved partly by reducing the role of central planning, and partly by increasing companies' independence. These were the main features that distinguished the Hungarian economic reform from those of other socialist countries in the 1960s.[49]

Opening up to the West became the HSWP's priority during the preparations for the economic reform. It proved to be crucial for the agrarian sector that Hungary managed to join the UN Food and Agriculture Organization (FAO) a year before the introduction of the New Economic Mechanism, in 1967.[50] At that time, Poland, Yugoslavia and Romania were the only socialist countries to be members. The Soviet Union distanced itself from this 'dangerous imperialist' organisation.

47 Zsuzsanna Varga, 'Between East and West: A Cultic Place of the Hungarian Agriculture – Bábolna Farm', in *Cultic Revelations: Cult Personalities and Phenomena*, Anssi Halmesvirta (ed.) (Jyväskylä: Historietti Oy, 2011).

48 Ibid.

49 Kornai, *Socialist System*, 474–510.

50 Hungary had been a member of the organisation between 1946 and 1951, but under Soviet pressure decided to quit, as did Poland and Czechoslovakia. Varga, *Hungarian Agricultural Miracle?*, 199–201. See also the contribution by Jonathan Harwood in this volume.

Meanwhile, the agrarian lobby, as part of the preparations for the NEM, eliminated the remaining elements of the Stalinist agricultural system and at the same time lifted the sector, economically and socially, out of its role as an 'inner colony'.[51] Comparison of Hungary's 1967 Cooperative Law with the revised rules of operation for Soviet *kolkhozi* in 1969 clearly demonstrates the differences that had emerged by this time. The Cooperative Law (Law IV of 1967) gave legal status to the 'good practices' mentioned at the end of the previous section. The collective farms gained increased autonomy. In addition to having more control over their input plans, they also gained the right to make contracts independently with other collective farms and with state farms, including contracts for marketing their output. Moreover, the agrarian lobby claimed that the proportion of agricultural investments – for the first time in socialist Hungary – rose above 20 per cent. A turnaround could be detected in investment structure as well: the balance shifted from construction to motorised technology. Taking advantage of imported socialist-origin machinery, the motorisation of grain harvesting and threshing reached 100 per cent by the late 1960s. In the case of other crops, this level was reached quite a few years later, already within the context of the Western technology transfer.

Membership of the FAO opened many opportunities.[52] For the Hungarian delegations, participation during FAO conferences made it easier to establish relationships with politicians and agricultural experts from capitalist countries, including the United States. It is also important to add that from the mid-1960s important changes took place in international relations, thanks to the fact that in 1964 President Johnson announced his policy of 'bridge-building' towards East European states.[53] This made it possible for Hungarian agriculture, which was struggling to assure a well-balanced and cost-effective supply of fodder for its livestock sector, to buy world-class technology from the United States. This was the so-called 'technically operated production system', whose goal was to optimise yield, minimise costs and maximise performance in specialised areas of production, such as corn (maize), wheat or livestock operations.[54]

51 Author's interview with István Szabó, 12 November 2011. For many decades he was the president of one of the biggest collective farms, the Red Star Collective Farm, Nádudvar, and from 1967 he was also the president of the National Council of Collective Farms.

52 Juan Pan-Montojo, 'International Institutions and Agriculture: From the IIA to the FAO', in *Agriculture in Capitalist Europe: From Food Shortages to Food Surpluses*, Carin Martiin, Juan Pan-Montojo and Paul Brassley (eds) (London: Routledge, 2016). See also the contribution by D'Onofrio in this volume.

53 Borhi, *Dealing with Dictators*, 138–83.

54 Paul Marer, *East-West Technology Transfer: Study on Hungary 1968–1984* (Paris: Organisation for Economic Cooperation and Development, 1986), 159–60.

The first high-ranking delegation travelled from Hungary to the United States in 1969. It visited the following companies: FMC, Northrup King, Ralston Purina, De Kalb, and John Deere. At the end of the study visit, the Bábolna State Farm was able to purchase John Deere machinery complexes capable of cultivating 6,000 hectares of corn (maize). Via the 1969 cooperation agreement, Bábolna entered into partnership with Corn Production Systems of Chicago, on the basis of which American technology and know-how and local management and inputs were synthesised into a large-scale crop management model.[55]

Here, and unlike the transfer of Stalinist agricultural methods, non-party or state institutions became the mediators of transfer. It was the large-scale farms or their associations that established business contacts with Western companies, and later they acted as system centres and transmitted the developed Western technology to less capital-rich state farms and collective farms. In the case of maize, for example, the system centre coordinated all areas of technology and know-how: genetics, plant protection, soil management (fertiliser, irrigation, drainage); specification of machinery and efficient handling of its maintenance and services; grain handling and storage; selection and training of all personnel; and financing and financial management.

Another disparity between the two model transfers was that when farms adopted Western production systems, they had the possibility of choosing between several possible models, economic performance and efficiency being the decisive issues. It is important to emphasise that state farms and collective farms were not under pressure to join. They could be members of many types of production system at the same time. By the end of the 1970s, a total of seventy-two production systems were functioning in Hungary: including twenty-one with crop production, thirty-one with horticulture, seventeen with livestock and three with a mixed profile. By 1981, 96 per cent of all state and collective farms were participating in some form of agricultural production system and 90 per cent of the country's corn (maize) and 88 per cent of its wheat crop were produced by such integrations.[56] The emergence of a both Sovietised and Americanised mode of farming in Hungary by the 1970s resulted a specific hybrid agriculture. Beside the tractors, combines and so forth of socialist origin, the latest Western machinery cultivated the land under socialist agriculture. Importing this machinery was closely linked to know-how transfers, and the necessary conditions for this had been provided by the modernisation of agrarian education.

55 MNL OL, XIX-K-9-ab 34. d. Tájékoztató jelentés a Magyar Forradalmi Munkás-Paraszt Kormány részére a mezőgazdasági szakdelegáció tanulmányútjáról ['Guiding report on the study trip made by the agricultural delegation to the Hungarian Workers' and Peasants' Government'] 1969.

56 András Schlett, 'Success and failure of the Hungarian Agrarian Model 1960–1990', *Arhivele Totalitarismului* 74–5 (2012), 97–101.

Imre Dimény, as an influential member of the agrarian lobby and minister of Agriculture and Food between 1967 and 1975, played an important role in the production and circulation of knowledge during the application of the Green Revolution in Hungary. He told me in an interview given in 2012 that he and his colleagues never officially used the term 'Green Revolution' in the Hungarian context because initially the United States had been its active protagonist. He recalled that in the opinion of the Soviets, the goal of the Green Revolution was not only to put an end to world hunger, but also to neutralise the revolutionary activities of the poor in the Third World.[57]

The agrarian lobby considered it a priority that the Ministry of Agriculture and Food (MAS) (and not the Ministry of Education) supervised secondary and higher agricultural education. The importance of this can be understood when we recall that under Stalinism, pre-war expertise was not only devalued, but its representatives – agricultural professionals, members of the state administration or even scientists – were treated as enemies and expelled from their positions. Agrarian relations with the West were broken in the atmosphere of the Cold War. In the new or reorganised institutions of agricultural education, classes were based on textbooks translated from Russian. At the same time, many young Hungarians were sent to study at the agricultural universities of the Soviet Union. After 1956 the agrarian lobby paid a lot of attention to informing the wider professional audience about the achievements of Western agricultural development. Their channels were the agricultural press, book publishing and radio programmes.[58] The journal *Gazdálkodás* [Farming], established by Ferenc Erdei, had three regular columns that effectively promoted the diffusion of up-to-date Western professional results and reported scientific debates.

After 1967 the agrarian lobby via the MAS was able to speed up the integration of Western know-how into the curricula of agricultural education. Multifaceted forms of cooperation were developed between universities and leading farms of the production systems in the field of professional secondments, research projects and further training.[59] The technical and technological renewal of agricultural production proceeded so quickly that it was only through these intensive cooperations that it was possible to ensure that specialists would be well trained.

***

The following series of data clearly outlines the achievement of the Green Revolution in Hungary. Fertiliser usage rose from 118 kg per ha on collective farms in 1968 to 322 kg per ha in 1982, and standardised tractor capacity rose from 349 units per 1,000 ha in 1968 to 552 in 1982.

57 Author's interview with Imre Dimény, 31 January 2012.

58 Varga, *Hungarian Agricultural Miracle?*, 169–73.

59 Ibid., 187–90.

The broad dissemination of multifunctional, oil-fuelled tractors and other motorised technologies, together with the growing use of chemical implements such as artificial fertilisers, pesticides and herbicides, increased the agrarian sector's dependence on mineral and fossil resources. The other consequence was a rapid increase in agricultural productivity, especially in wheat and corn production. Over the course of the 1970s, a complete replacement of wheat varieties took place, while the preferred maize hybrids changed twice. As a result of all these factors, average wheat yields rose from 2,100 kg per ha in the early 1970s to 4,000 kg per ha by the end of the decade, while corn yields rose from 3,380 to 5,300 kg.

TABLE 9.1. The average yield of key crops in Hungary, select years 1935–89 (kg/ha).

Year	Wheat	Corn	Barley	Sunflower	Sugar beet
1935	1,340	1,200	1,270	810	16,100
1945	870	1,440	810	720	8,930
1950	1,520	1,570	1,260	850	14,600
1953	1,650	2,240	1,860	1,180	20,220
1960	1,910	2,030	1,890	820	18,120
1970	2,130	3,380	1,950	1,010	28,730
1980	4,760	5,320	3,770	1,660	37,640
1989	5,240	6,440	4,690	1,950	43,980

Source: *Magyar mezőgazdaság 1851–2000*, CD-ROM.

The dynamic increase in average yields of wheat and corn created the foundations for the rapid development of livestock yields. Between 1970 and 1985, total meat production rose by 37 per cent, from 957,000 tons to 1,300,000 tons. Measured in terms of per capita grain production, Hungary ranked fifth in the world in 1980. In the same year, in terms of meat production, Hungary took third place after Denmark and Australia. The results achieved in grain and meat production made it possible for Hungarian agrarian exports to triple between 1965 and 1975.[60] It was a unique achievement within COMECON.[61] Compared to the hymns

60 The traditional export orientation of Hungarian agriculture was revived. In the 1980s, export orientation turned into export compulsion because a growing amount of 'hard currency' (for example, US dollars) was needed to repay the national debt. Agricultural exports to the West could not be replaced by other products or branches. As a result, the quantitative development of production always took precedence over the management of environmental problems.

61 Gregor Lazarcik, 'Comparative Performance of Agricultural Output, Inputs and productivity in Eastern Europe, 1965–83', in *Socialist Agriculture in*

of praise sung at the time, today's assessment is more critical due to the negative environmental consequences (for example, the nitrification of groundwater, soil erosion, soil compression, among others) At that time, food-supply issues and export earnings took precedence over any environmental problems. These could be discussed only in reports 'for internal use'.[62]

These results may suggest that the Green Revolution culminated in a fully industrialised and homogenised agriculture in Hungary. However, looking under the surface, an interesting duality can be discovered that resembled the pre-war dual structure of latifundia and small part-time farms.[63] In socialist agriculture the duality appeared through the division of labour. Production of grain crops came almost completely under the control of the industrialised collective farm, while more labour-intensive vegetable and certain livestock tasks were increasingly transferred to the household farming sector.[64]

Collective farm members, after performing a certain amount of work per year on the collective farm, were entitled to a household plot of up to 0.57 hectares (1 kh). For a long time there was a sharp distinction between the collective farm and the household plot, as the latter was regarded by the communist ideology as a concession to the individualism of the peasants. It was expected to be a temporary arrangement that would disappear over time. Instead of disappearing, household production was expanded. It became an integral and very important part of Hungarian agriculture. In the 1970s approximately 40 per cent of net agricultural production was derived from household-plot farming. The collective farms were encouraged to subcontract the raising of young livestock to households, to provide households with increased feed conversion and technical assistance, and to purchase and market their production. Although there were mechanisms by which elements of industrial agriculture reached household farms, in most of them production remained at pre-industrial levels.[65]

Households' potential for expansion was limited by difficulty of acquiring agricultural land and access to capital. The more prosperous, commercially orientated households could not expand production, and their income was not invested for further productive use but was

Transition: Organizational Response to Failing Performance, Karl-Eugen Wädekin and Josef C. Brada (eds) (Boulder, CO, and London: Westview Press, 1988), 313–32.

62 Jonathan Harwood, 'Was the Green Revolution Intended to Maximise Food Production?' *International J. Agricultural Sustainability* 17 (2019), 312–25.

63 Kopsidis, 'Agricultural development', 286–310.

64 Imre Kovách, 'Hungary: Co-operative farms and Household Plots', in *Many Shades of Red: State Policy and Collective Agriculture,* Mike Meurs (ed.) (New York-Oxford: Rowman and Littlefield Publ., 1999), 125–50.

65 Nigel Swain, *Collective Farms Which Work?* (Cambridge: Cambridge University Press, 1985), 25–150.

channelled into ever higher levels of consumption. On the other hand, the state did not allow the poorly performing collective farms or state farms to go bankrupt, nor to sell part of their land to individual farmers, because this would have meant a step back from the superiority of state property over private property. This was the reason why the agrarian lobby in the mid-1980s could not obtain political support for introducing new, flexible organisational forms into hybrid agriculture.[66]

9.4 Concluding remarks

The 1950s in Hungary were the decade of a forced agricultural modernisation within the socialist planned economy in the Cold War era. Motorisation and chemicalisation were key elements of socialist large-scale agriculture. As the decade-long forceful collectivisation overturned property and production relations, devalued and even destroyed pre-1945 knowledge, socialist agriculture in Hungary failed to meet growth expectations for many years.

Within the transition from an 'agrarian-industrial knowledge society' to an 'industrial-agrarian knowledge society', a new period can be said to have begun when the transfer of Western technology and know-how started. Analysing the Hungarian case, all the main elements of the modernisation programme known as the Green Revolution could be identified. So, for example, high-yielding varieties, specialised breeds of livestock, industrial fertilisers and pesticides, and the motorisation of most parts of the productive cycle can all be observed. At the same time, the Green Revolution did not come to Hungary as an American aid programme, but as a result of individual business agreements. The actors of socialist Hungarian agriculture entered into direct contact with American companies.

An additional distinguishing feature of the Hungarian case is that, while in the countries affected by the Green Revolution, the recipients were peasant farms, in Hungary they were state farms and collective farms. In this context, it is important to point out that while the transfer of knowledge related to new production technology was a constant problem on peasant farms, the dissemination of knowledge in Hungarian large-scale agriculture was soon institutionalised. The training of agricultural engineers increased both quantitatively and qualitatively. This was one of the key factors behind the rapid and durable production increase.

66 Iván Harcsa, Imre Kovách and Iván Szelényi, 'The Hungarian Agricultural Miracle and the Limits of Socialist Reforms', in *Privatizing the Land: Rural Political Economy in Post-Communist Societies*, Iván Szelényi (ed.) (London and New York: Routledge, 1998), 21–42. Varga, *Hungarian Agricultural Miracle?*, 254–64.

The importance of expertise is also key because the soil and climatic conditions for crop cultivation differ locally, so the adaptation of imported technology was not just mechanical copying but had to be tailored to each specific farm. To improve local adaptation, system centres in Hungary also organised continuous data collection. This also attracted the interest of American companies, because at that time they had not been able to collect data on a similarly large area from American farmers. This proves that the circulation of knowledge across the Iron Curtain operated not only in the West–East direction, but also from the East to the West.

All this leads from the economic effects to the social ones. Contact with Western European and American companies operating in the market economy (study trips, professional meetings) initiated changes in the work culture and value system of the participating Hungarian professionals engaged the agriculture. After a while, these divergencies provoked the criticism and frustration of the sectors that continued to operate exclusively in the context of the Hungarian planned economy and COMECON.[67]

The Hungarian planned economy was modified in 1968, but the one-party system itself was not, and neither were the basic tenets of communist ideology. Thus, referring to the interests of state-owned industrial companies, the importance of industrial workers, or even to the superiority of state property legitimated occasional arguments that agriculture was receiving too much investment, and intensive relations with the West would lead to dangerous consequences. In Moscow, during Brezhnev's time, the performance of Hungarian agriculture was evaluated particularly critically. By the 1980s, parallel to the deepening crisis of the Soviet Union and the bloc countries, the Soviet perception of Hungarian agriculture had changed a lot, and it was cited as an example to be followed.[68] At the same time, as has been discussed, the rigid axioms of ideology raised obstacles to the renewal of hybrid agriculture that would not be removed until the fall of the socialist system.

67 Ibid., 221–40.
68 Ibid., 248–9.

10

Reordering rural Congo: Agricultural development and the *paysannats indigènes* in the Belgian Congo, 1930s–1950s

Yves Segers

'En effet, on est arrivé à la limite de ce qui peut être demandé aussi bien du personnel de propaganda qu'aux paysans …'[1]

The quotation with which we begin comes from a confidential inspection report, written in 1954, in which an employee of the *Service agricole de la Colonie* refers to the limits and difficulties encountered in the management and functioning of the *paysannats indigènes*, both for the staff of the Service and for the Congolese farmers who endured the imposition of coerced hard labour. With this large-scale settlement scheme, the colonial authorities, supported in this by the INEAC (*Institut National pour l'Étude Agronomique du Congo Belge*; the National Institute for Agronomic Research of the Belgian Congo), wanted to improve and 'westernise' the agricultural practices of the indigenous population to increase productivity and improve living standards. At least, that was the official discourse, because in practice there was a huge gap between theory and reality, between plans and their realisation.

The paysannats indigènes were founded at the end of the 1930s. They were initially very small-scale. Drachoussoff, writing in 1956, reported that:

> In 1937 there were barely six families involved in the settlement schemes. By 1946 this had increased to 50,000 and in 1958 to no less than

1 AA (Archives Africaines), AGRI-AIMO, GG7758, 'Confidentiel: rapport d'inspection de monsieur le conseiller technique agricole Nelis – territoire de Budjala: paysannat indigène Banza de la Lua, April 1954', 3. All other quotes in this chapter are translated from French.

> 200,000 families. In the latter year the paysannats comprised approximately 86,000 hectares, the largest part of which was taken up by the production of oil palm (57,000 hectare), [but] Robusta coffee (16,000 hectares) and rubber (10,000 hectares) were also grown. The plan was to take an additional 66,000 hectares into production in the short term.[2]

For the crops grown see Table 10.1.

TABLE 10.1. Area of crops grown under the *paysannats* system in 1958, hectare per province.

	Leopoldville	Equateur	Oriental	Kivu	Katanga	Kasai	Total
Palm Oil	12,020	15,581	10,217	4,214	895	13,807	56,734
Robusta coffee	607	1557	1489	588	0	11,631	15,872
Arabica coffee	0	0	212	2772	154	0	3,138
Rubber	328	3961	1932	0	0	3765	9986
Tea	0	0	0	335	0	0	335
Total	12,995	21,099	13,850	7,909	1,049	29,203	86,105

Source: V. Drachoussoff, 'Agricultural change in the Belgian Congo, 1945–1960', *Food Research Institute Studies* 5 (1965), 154.

The *paysannats* were intended to be an answer to the structural problems of Congolese agriculture and the socio-economic challenges of the Great Depression. On the eve of independence in 1960, about 10 per cent of the total rural population in the Belgian Congo lived and worked within the contours of this system. It gave Congolese farmers individual titles to collectivised land holdings. According to Piet Clement, this initiative heralded a third phase of colonial agricultural policy, following an initial period of *Raubwirtschaft* (characterised by unbridled plundering of Congolese natural resources such as ivory and rubber), which was followed by the introduction of compulsory cultivation in 1917 to significantly increase cash crop production.[3] The central idea of the paysannats was to replace the traditional Congolese villages scattered across the vast countryside with organised allocations of agricultural land. The local population was encouraged to move to these paysannats. Each household was allocated a piece of land where crops for export such as cotton, groundnuts or palm

2 Vladimir Drachoussoff, 'Agricultural Change in the Belgian Congo, 1945–1960', *Food Research Institute Studies* 5 (1965), 152–5.

3 Piet Clement, 'Agricultural Policies and Practices in the Belgian Congo. The Origins and Implementation of the "Indigenous Peasantry" Scheme (1917–1959)', in *The Belgian Congo Between the Two World Wars*, Jacques Vanderlinden (ed.) (Brussels: Royal Academy for Overseas Sciences, 2019), 83–128.

oil had to be cultivated, as well as food for their own use. In this way, the *Service Agricole* and INEAC wanted to replace traditional agricultural methods with Western, scientifically based cultivation practices.

Congolese agriculture was traditionally organised on collective principles. The land belonged to the village community and families were allowed to cultivate the plots allocated them as they saw fit. They owned the usufruct but had no individual property rights. More than seventy crops were grown in the Congo Basin around 1900, including rice, cassava, plantain, groundnuts and soy. Both agricultural practices and eating habits were adapted to the tropical environment. The women were responsible for all the work on the land; the men focused on hunting, fishing and gathering foodstuffs. When the soil became less fertile, which could happen within a few years due to a lack of manure, new plots were brought into use (slash and burn). Over time, these new lands became situated so far from the village that it was moved. The colonial government discouraged this form of semi-nomadic agriculture, in part because it produced lower yields, but primarily because it wanted to strengthen its grip on the population and manage most of the land itself. The paysannats fulfilled this aim. At the same time, they aspired to improve sanitary and housing conditions, and to set up a large-scale form of social engineering.[4]

The *paysannats* project in the Belgian Congo was certainly not unique on the African continent. Other European countries too started and developed large-scale settlement schemes from the inter-war period onwards – among others in Angola, Togo, Kenya, French Sudan (Niger), Mozambique, British Tanganyika – and in many cases they continued this policy until independence.[5] However, without a doubt the indigenous peasantry scheme implemented in the Belgian Congo was the most comprehensive and ambitious of such programmes. Viewed more broadly, these initiatives fit into a global project of colonial reform and internal or 'native colonisation' (*colonization indigène*), a concept that implied the resettlement and sedentarisation of local peasants in fertile regions, which mirrored practices of white European settlement in the colonies and, to a certain extent, even of internal colonisation in Europe.[6]

4 Yves Segers and Leen Van Molle, 'L'agriculture dans le Congo colonial. Un succès aux dépens de la population rurale?', in *Le Congo colonial. Une histoire en questions,* Idesbald Goddeeris, Amandine Lauro and Guy Vantemsche (eds) (Waterloo: Renaissance du Livre, 2020), 167–81.

5 Frederik Cooper and Randall Packard, *International Development and the Social Sciences: Essays on the History and Politics of Knowledge* (Berkeley, CA: University of California Press, 1997), 7; and *Developing Africa: Concepts and Practices in Twentieth-Century Colonialism,* Joseph Morgan Hodge, G. Hold and M. Kopf (eds) (Manchester: Manchester University Press, 2014).

6 Liesbeth Van de Grift, 'On New Land a New Society: Internal Colonisation in the Netherlands, 1918–1940', *Contemporary European History* 22 (2013),

Various objectives and practices associated with the paysannats system and other large-scale colonial development programmes can be found in the Green Revolution. This global aid programme for what was then called the 'Third World', set up in the 1950s–1970s by private companies and governments in Latin America and South Asia, also wished to modernise indigenous, local agriculture through the introduction of Western practices and inputs, with the aim of avoiding hunger and food shortages and improving the precarious living conditions of the rural population while producing tradable crops for export.[7]

Over the past two decades, historians, anthropologists and other academics have investigated several of these development initiatives on the African continent. Christophe Bonneuil analysed the role of science in the emergence of a post-war development regime in Sub-Saharan Africa, which he identified as the start of a *developmentalist state*, in which improving the living standards of the African population was central to the discourse. From the 1930s, colonial governments developed a strong interventionist policy, including setting up small and large colonisation projects and settlement schemes.[8] Bonneuil considered the paysannats as the ultimate example of social engineering. According to him, the paysannats' main purpose was taming agrarian societies and turning them into objects of development. As Helen Tilley would later argue in her study of the African Research Survey (1929–1938), Bonneuil described the newly created villages as 'social laboratories' in which Western scientists could test and impose their knowledge from above.[9] Monica Van Beusekom in turn examined the development policy of the *Office du Niger* in the French Sudan (Mali), an institution that specialised in rural water management.[10] Despite the application of Western knowledge, the irrigation scheme was inefficient and unsuccessful.

609–26; Charlotte Vekemans and Yves Segers, 'Settler Farming, Agricultural Colonisation and Development in Katanga (Belgian Congo)', *Historia Agraria* 81 (2020), 195–226.

7 Jonathan Harwood, *Europe's Green Revolution and Others Since: The Rise and Fall of Peasant-Friendly Plant Breeding* (Abingdon and New York: Routledge, 2016), 115–18.

8 Christophe Bonneuil, 'Development as Experiment: Science and State Building in Late Colonial and Postcolonial Africa, 1930–1970', *Osiris* 15 (2000), 259; Christophe Bonneuil, 'Penetrating the Natives: Peanut Breeding, Peasants and the Colonial State in Senegal (1900–1950)', *Science, Technology & Society* 4 (1999), 273–302.

9 Hellen Tilley, *Africa as a Living Laboratory: Empire, Development and the Problem of Scientific Knowledge, 1870–1950* (Chicago, IL: University of Chicago Press, 2011).

10 See the works of Monica Van Beusekom, 'Disjunctures in Theory and Practice: Making Sense of Change in Agricultural Development at the Office du Niger, 1920–1960', *J. African History* 41 (2000), 79–99; *Negotiating Development: African Farmers and Colonial Experts at the Office du Niger* (Oxford:

Recognising that their plans had to a degree failed, from the late 1940s onward, the agronomists involved took more account of the tacit knowledge of local farmers. Samuel Coghe studied the plans for model villages in Portuguese Angola during the inter-war period, which according to colonial administrators, embodied the solution for sanitary, demographic and agricultural problems. Furthermore, Coghe underlined that these were part of larger and transnational debates about rural development in colonial Africa and Asia. It is interesting that he found that the Portuguese colonial administration drew inspiration from the agricultural projects in the Belgian Congo.[11] The impact of British development theories and policies on agricultural colonisation in British colonies from the late 1890s to its (seeming) demise in the 1960s is studied by Joseph Morgan Hodge. He analysed the growing prominence of scientific knowledge and technical experts in shaping colonial development policy, the resulting tensions between these technocrats and political officers, and the experience and reactions of the indigenous population. Hodge concluded that scientific experts and technical officers became the principal conduit for new ideas and influence. Furthermore, he emphasised that local farmers resisted the colonial administration's directives in several ways.[12]

Agricultural policy in the Belgian Congo and the interaction between traditional and Western agricultural knowledge has recently been studied by Yves Segers, Leen Van Molle and Wemo Menge, among others.[13] They underlined how much industrial interests prevailed in the colony and the ways in which the traditional practices and techniques of the Congolese farmers were scorned and suppressed by state-employed agronomists.[14] Mobili Danga Kassa went even further, by linking contemporary poverty in the Congolese countryside to Belgian agricultural colonisation.[15] In

James Currey, 2002); 'Individualism, Community, and Cooperatives in the Development Thinking of the Union Soudanaise – RDA, 1946–1960', *African Studies Review* 51 (2008) 1–25.

11 Samuël Coghe, 'Reordering Colonial Society: Model Villages and Social Planning in Rural Angola, 1920–1945', *J. Contemporary History* 52 (2017), 16-44.

12 Joseph Morgan Hodge, *Triumph of the expert: Agrarian doctrines of development and the legacies of British colonialism* (Athens, OH: University of Ohio Press, 2007).

13 Yves Segers and Stephanie Kerckhofs, 'Crisis in de tropen. Landbouwpolitiek en agrarische wetenschap in Belgisch Congo (1900–1940)', in *Overheid & economie: Geschiedenissen van een spanningsveld,* Bruno Blondé *et al.* (eds) (Antwerp: Antwerp University Press, 2014), 145.

14 Leen Van Molle, Yves Segers and Stephanie Kerckhofs, '"C'est par la science qu'on colonise". Over de relatie tussen de Grote Depressie en de landbouwpolitiek in Belgisch-Congo', in *The Belgian Congo Between the Two World Wars,* Vanderlinden (ed.), 159–89; Wemo Menge, *Transfert du savoir agricole au Congo-Zaïre. Héritage colonial et recherche agronomique* (Paris: L'Harmattan, 2001).

15 Jeannôt Mobili Danga Kassa, *Politiques agricoles et promotion rurale au Congo-Zaïre (1885–1997)* (Paris: L'Harmattan, 1998).

addition, the publications of Osumaka Likaka and more recently Reuben Loffmann opened up new research perspectives and insights: in an exercise of oral history, they collected stories and testimonials from Congolese farmers and rural dwellers.[16] The result is a combination of striking testimonies about violence and resistance, which provide evidence that Congolese *agency* played a central role in the history of the Belgian Congo. The agrarian policy and the colonisation projects in particular were simply not welcomed by the local population.[17] Finally, reference should be made to the publications of historian Piet Clement: he analysed in great detail the general history of the paysannats in the Belgian Congo and concluded that the system did not achieve the expected results and significantly perturbed and even destroyed local agricultural knowledge and traditions.[18]

In other words, the historiography is predominantly negative about the achievements of colonial agricultural initiatives and the paysannats system in particular. The question then arises as to how this system was explained and propagated by the colonial government and its agronomists and experts. What objectives did they put forward? With what arguments did they justify their policies and practices? To answer these questions, I analyse the discourse and opinion of Belgian colonial experts, through a close reading of the *Bulletin agricole du Congo belge*. This scientific journal appeared between 1910 and 1961 and was published by the *Service agricole de la Colonie* (Ministry of Colonies). The readership consisted of colonial officials and settler farmers (the so-called *colons*), agronomists and other experts active in the Belgian Congo and other colonies worldwide. I mainly analysed the articles that discuss socio-economic aspects of the paysannats and paid less attention to agronomic and technically orientated contributions. A total of thirty-one articles were published between 1938 and 1960. The lion's share was published in the 1950s, which should come as no surprise, as this decade marked the apogee of the paysannats system. As elsewhere in the colonial world, several development plans saw the light from the late 1940s onward, when colonial administrations succeeded in penetrating society more deeply than ever before. Low and

16 Osumaka Likaka, 'Rural Protest: The Mbole Against Belgian Rule, 1897–1959', *International J. African Historical Studies* 27 (1994), 589–617; Osumaka Likaka, *Naming Colonialism: History and Collective Memory in the Congo, 1870–1960* (Madison, WI: University of Wisconsin Press, 2009).

17 Rueben Lofmann, 'Belgian Rule and its Afterlives: Colonialism, Developmentalism, and Mobutism in the Tanganyika District, Southeastern DR-Congo, 1885–1985', *International Labor and Working-Class History* 92 (2017), 56–9.

18 Piet Clement, 'The Land Tenure System in the Congo, 1885–1960: Actors, Motivations and Consequences', in *Colonial Exploitation and Economic Development: The Belgian Congo and the Netherlands Indies Compared,* Frans Buelens and Ewout Frankema (eds) (London: Routledge, 2013), 88–108.

Lonsdale termed this period rightly as 'the second colonial occupation'.[19] The majority of the articles in the *Bulletin agricole* were written by agronomists employed by the colonial administration and the INEAC. I compare their opinions in the *Bulletin* with unpublished sources and reports from the Africa archive (kept at the Ministry of Foreign Affairs, Brussels), and with the available secondary literature.

This contribution consists of five sections. In the first I explain how the paysannats system came about, and what the official motives and objectives for it were. In the following sections I discuss in more detail a specific objective or problem/challenge that confronted the colonial agricultural administration and that was discussed in the *Bulletin*: modernising and improving agricultural production and productivity; combating rural exodus; respecting local traditions; and finally, I reflect on the resistance against the paysannats system by Congolese farmers. In the conclusion, the similarities and differences between the paysannats and the Green Revolution are unravelled.

10.1 From *Raubwirtschaft* to paysannats indigènes

As already mentioned above, the start of the paysannats indigènes in 1937 marked a striking break with the agricultural policy of the previous decades, characterised by *Raubwirtschaft* and the system of compulsory cultivation. From the early 1930s, the destructive consequences of years of economic and agricultural exploitation became increasingly apparent. The revolution of the Pende, a tribe in the Kwilu province, in 1931 brought the miserable living and working conditions of the indigenous population onto the political agenda. The Pende revolt was one of the largest uprisings during the inter-war period and was inspired by the violent recruitment of labour by Western companies, such as the Huileries du Congo Belge (HCB), a subsidiary of Lever Brothers. The situation was further worsened by the sharply falling prices of, for example, palm nuts, which meant that the population had to work much longer to pay their taxes.[20] A small group of intellectuals and elitist-reformers, including Crown Prince Leopold (the later King Leopold III), denounced the abuses in the colony and advocated a new agricultural policy centred on the emancipation of Congolese farmers. A whole range of proposals were considered: easier access to farmland, the provision of modern tools and credit, investments in the education of the rural population and the abolition of compulsory cultivation. These ideas were largely legitimised by the speech given by the Crown Prince in the Senate in July 1933 following his long journey through the Congo. Leopold broke a lance

19 Hodge, *Triumph of the expert*, 209.

20 Louis-François Vanderstraeten, *La répression de la révolte des Pende du Kwango en 1931* (Brussels: Académie royale des sciences d'outre-mer, 2001).

for the establishment of an independent Congolese farming class and a reorganisation of the scientific research into tropical farming. Leopold's trip to the Dutch and British colonies in south-east Asia a year earlier had convinced him that indigenous agriculture was crucial to the economic recovery of the colony.[21]

However, his speech did not immediately lead to concrete initiatives, while in the meantime the economic situation worsened. The oversupply of colonial products on the global market, caused by a shrinking demand, led to sharp price drops, falling wages and rising unemployment in the Congolese industries and on its plantations. In rural regions, the situation became even more difficult because many workers returned from the cities to their native villages. Added to this, the global crisis in the Belgian Congo was reinforced by internal, structural issues, such as soil erosion and deforestation, low productivity, a lack of technical assistance and labour shortages. The colonial authorities initially responded with short-term measures. Thus, transport costs for agricultural products were reduced significantly and a temporary fund for agricultural credit was set up as a mechanism to help farmers get through the difficult period. However, according to historian Bogumil Jewsiewicki, these initiatives primarily benefitted export-orientated plantations and the colons. The colonial authorities shifted the effects of the crisis onto rural society. What is more, the Congolese farmers suffered a great deal more under the economic recession than did other colonies on the African continent such as the Gold Coast and Uganda, where agrarian production was much more in the hands of indigenous producers.[22]

The establishment of the INEAC by the colonial authorities on 22 December 1933 aimed to tackle the structural problems in the agricultural sector. As a scientific mission, the new institution's task was to support not only European commercial agriculture (concession companies and settlers), but also Congolese farmers. Shortly before the Second World War, INEAC managed about fifteen research stations and plantations, each of which specialised in a specific theme or crop, spread over the vast Congolese territory. It deployed some eighty European experts, the majority with a university degree. INEAC organised training courses for the agronomists and technical personnel of the Service agricole and

21 Piet Clement, 'Agricultural Policies and Practices in the Belgian Congo: The Origins and Implementation of the "Indigenous Peasantry" Scheme (1917–1959)', in *The Belgian Congo Between the Two World Wars*, Jacques Vanderlinden (ed.), 83–128; Van Molle, Segers and Kerckhofs, 'C'est par la science qu'on colonise', 159–89.

22 Clement, 'Agricultural Policies and Practices in the Belgian Congo', 83–128; Menge, *Transfert du savoir agricole au Congo-Zaïre*; Bogumil Jewsiewicki, 'The Great Depression and the Making of the Colonial Economic System in the Belgian Congo', *African Economic History* 4 (1977), 153–76.

aimed for a more rational implementation of compulsory cultivation. At the same time, INEAC reinforced cooperation with private companies. Furthermore, an important new responsibility was the reorganisation on a scientific basis of indigenous farming. The aim was to encourage the Congolese farmers to adopt modern Western methods without breaking entirely with valuable time-honoured practices, and to farm on individual plots (and thus no longer on a collective basis).[23]

INEAC started to experiment with paysannats indigènes in 1937; no more than six families took part in the trial project. Although the impact was minimal at first, this initiative inaugurated an important new phase in the Congo's colonial agricultural policy. During the Second World War, additional paysannats were established, involving dozens of families; but after the war, the paysannats system went up a gear.[24] Fundamental to this was a successful cooperation between INEAC and cotton giants Cotonco and Colocoton, who were increasingly concerned about soil exhaustion and erosion. In his study *Afrique, terre qui meurt*, the colonial scientist Jean-Paul Harroy had raised the alarm because of European farming methods' shortcomings and negative effects on African land and soil. It was not the traditional practices, as many Western agronomists claimed, but colonial imperialism and monocultures that had disturbed the equilibrium between soil, fauna, flora and human activities.[25] In 1946, Cotonco made a proposal to the INEAC to extend the *paysannats* system near the station of Bambesa to 7,000 km^2 and thus include almost 50,000 Congolese people in agricultural colonies. At the end of 1948, more than 5,000 plots had been divided among the selected families. Through the experiments of the previous years, INEAC personnel believed themselves to have acquired the necessary expertise to further develop organised agricultural colonisation, both in a theoretical and practical sense.

From the late 1940s onwards, the colonial authorities made the paysannats indigènes a key element in their agricultural policy. The ambition was to integrate into the *paysannats* system no fewer than 500,000 Congolese farmers and their families (altogether around 2.5 million or a quarter of the entire population) by 1959. In the Ten-Year Plan (1949–1959), 25 billion francs had been reserved for the development of the colony. However, more than half of this budget went into the expansion of transport infrastructure, and the actual agricultural programme was only allocated 1.4 billion francs, barely half of which was earmarked for stimulating Congolese farming itself. Consequently, the ambitions turned out to be unattainable. In 1959, only around 210,000

23 Clement, 'Agricultural Policies and Practices in the Belgian Congo', 83–128.

24 *Le développement rurale en Afrique centrale. Synthèse et réflexions*, Vladimir Drachoussoff, Alexandre Focan and Jacques Hecq (eds) (Brussels: Foundation Roi Baudouin, 1991).

25 Jean-Paul Harroy, *Afrique, terre qui meurt. La dégradation des sols africains sous l'influence de la colonisation* (Brussels: Marcel Hayez, 1949).

farmers and their families were participating, and meanwhile the system of compulsory cultivation continued to exist. Independence in 1960 and the turbulent years that followed put an end to the system of *paysannats* as developed by the colonial government and INEAC.[26]

10.2 Higher agricultural production and modernisation through Western knowledge

The *paysannats* were initially an economic and agricultural project with the aim of modernising or rationalising Congolese farming methods to increase production and productivity, mainly of cash crops such as cotton, coffee and palm oil. After all, in the opinion of INEAC agronomists, the Congolese way of farming was 'primitive'.[27] In their publications the state agronomists frequently emphasised the distinction between the 'inefficient' indigenous agriculture practised before colonisation and the rational agriculture on the *paysannats*.[28] In reality, however, agriculture on the *paysannats* was based on precolonial techniques such as crop rotation, more than had been the case in previous decades, which resulted in a mixed system and hybrid knowledge.[29] Nevertheless, that insight prevailed no earlier than the late 1950s, when it became accepted that Western techniques had contributed to soil degradation and even food shortages.[30] It is also striking how Eurocentric their vision of Congolese agriculture was. According to the INEAC experts, it was inefficient because local farmers focused heavily on the production of food for their own consumption (such as cassava, maize, groundnuts and vegetables) and hardly produced any cash crops of their own accord. Clearly, the agronomists evaluated agriculture on the basis of European or Western criteria such as market orientation, the production of export crops and the pursuit of financial profit, while ignoring the fact that securing an adequate food supply was one of the main goals of the local population.[31]

According to the agronomist J. Henry writing in 1952, the basic problem was that the Congolese looked down on farming. The evidence for this lay in the fact that it was mainly women who worked the land. Henry argued

26 Guy Vantemsche, *Genèse et portée du 'Plan décennal' du Congo belge (1949–1959)* (Brussels: Mémoire Académie Royale des Sciences d'Outre-Mer, 1994).

27 G. Dubois, 'Politiques agricoles en milieux ruraux', *Bulletin Agricole du Congo Belge* 42 (1952), 267.

28 A. Loeckx, 'Plan de cultures de la famille Jupaliri', *Bulletin Agricole du Congo Belge* 40 (1949), 298.

29 J. Clement, 'Etude relative au paysannat indigène', *Bulletin Agricole du Congo Belge* 42 (1952), 258; Hellen Tilley, *Africa as a Living Laboratory: Empire, Development and the Problem of Scientific Knowledge, 1870–1950* (Chicago, IL: University of Chicago Press, 2011).

30 Likaka, *Rural Society and Cotton in Colonial Zaïre*, 3.

31 Clement, 'Agricultural Policies and Practices in the Belgian Congo', 106–7.

that Congolese men could only be motivated to engage in agriculture through the introduction of the *paysannats* system; a comment that can be seen as a justification for the further colonisation of the countryside.[32] According to Staner, the Congolese refusal to adapt to European customs and adopt Western farming techniques was obvious evidence of their 'primitiveness'. He therefore suggested a drastic solution: 'It is essential that old structures be replaced'.[33]

A strategy for bringing about change involved organising agricultural education and starting propaganda initiatives with the aim of 'educat[ing] the peasants and turn them into men in every sense of the word'.[34] Thanks to the agricultural schools on the paysannats, the Congolese would, according to agronomist Henry, be taught a 'true peasant character'.[35] Oswald Liesenborghs, education inspector at the Ministry of Colonies, wrote in 1941 that Congolese men considered it a humiliation to engage in agriculture because this was traditionally the job of women.[36] Educational initiatives were therefore needed to make the Congolese realise that agriculture was also a man's business and that this could help in the 'improvement of their species'.[37] In addition, greater male participation would release Congolese women from heavy physical work and thus allow them to spend more time on family and household tasks.[38] It also shows how deeply the *paysannats* permeated the farmers' daily lives, which, incidentally, also happened in other colonies. Bonneuil described such policies as a 'Trojan horse', which through cognitive penetration made farmers more receptive to state intervention in agriculture.[39]

In addition to education, the added value of propaganda was also regularly discussed in the *Bulletin*, often looking at foreign examples. Colin Maher, a British agricultural researcher, wrote in 1949 that Kenyan farmers had no sense of initiative because they attributed crop failures to the wrath of malevolent gods and consequently refused to adopt new

32 J. Henry, 'Les bases théoriques des essais de paysannat indigène, entrepris par l'INEAC au Congo Belge', *Bulletin Agricole du Congo Belge* 42 (1952), 181; Likaka, *Rural Society and Cotton in Colonial Zaïre*.

33 Pierre Staner, 'Les Paysannats Indigènes du Congo Belge et du Ruanda-Urundi', *Bulletin Agricole du Congo Belge* 46 (1955), 474.

34 George Sladden, 'Evolution possible du paysannat indigène au Congo belge', *Bulletin Agricole du Congo Belge* 43 (1952), 12.

35 Henry, 'Les bases théoriques des essais de paysannat indigène', 162.

36 Oswald Liesenborghs, 'Side Drawings on Agricultural Education in the Congolese Folk School', *Bulletin Agricole du Congo Belge* 32 (1941), 316.

37 J. Deheyn, 'L'action scolaire en milieu rural', *Bulletin Agricole du Congo Belge* 43 (1952), 50.

38 N. Thiry, 'Note sur la conduite d'un paysannat', *Bulletin Agricole du Congo Belge* 42 (1952), 246.

39 Bonneuil, 'Development as Experiment', 271.

farming techniques. Propaganda and education were therefore essential, according to him, for penetrating the minds of Africans.[40]

10.3 Fighting the rural exodus

Another important objective of the paysannats was to limit the mobility of the rural population by making them more familiar with the principles of individual property. In this way, the agronomists hoped to provide an answer to the mass rural exodus. More generally, according to the agronomist J. Muller in 1953, this policy would lead to social improvement for the Congolese in a 'sound economic framework'.[41] Policymakers described curbing the rural exodus as a top priority because the resulting labour shortages prevented cash-crop production from increasing in a sufficient manner.[42] According to the INEAC, the Congolese would not so easily abandon the paysannats when they could work their own plot of land or even could become owners. The traditional collective farming system therefore had to be replaced, although according to Staner this would not be an easy task: 'To reform the property system, we must destroy one of the fundamental concepts of the psychology of the native'.[43] It would also broaden their sense of responsibility, because, according to many agronomists, this was just what was missing in the personality of Congolese rural dwellers.[44] On the other hand, some agronomists pointed to an anticipated negative impact of this new land policy: 'Objective and valuable studies have shown that, on the contrary, the immediate introduction of private property in the native environment would rather be a brake and an obstacle.'[45]

In practice, this policy of sedentarisation generated unintended side effects. For example, the male population could devote less time to hunting, which had a negative impact on the size and diversity of rural households' daily diet.[46] Moreover, young men in particular continued to seek refuge in the city or in industrial regions, where wages were higher and life more modern. It is no coincidence that the colonial authorities tightened their migration policy after the Second World War and special courts were established to bring refugee farmers back to the paysannats.[47] The *Bulletin* hardly refers to this, but this strict policy is reflected

40 Colin Maher, 'Study of the Methods of Propaganda and Education', *Bulletin Agricole du Congo Belge* 40 (1949), 246–7.

41 J. Muller, 'Paysannat et Coopérative Turumbu', *Bulletin Agricole du Congo Belgium* 44 (1953), 114.

42 Clement, 'Land Tenure system in the Congo', 102.

43 Staner, 'Les Paysannats Indigènes du Congo Belge et du Ruanda-Urundi', 473.

44 Sladden, 'Evolution possible du paysannat indigène au Congo belge', 9.

45 Henry, 'Les bases théoriques des essais de paysannat indigène', 175.

46 Clement, 'Rural Development in the Belgian Congo', 264–5.

47 Likaka, *Rural Society and Cotton in Colonial Zaïre*, 115.

in unpublished source material. For example, S. Opsomer, territorial administrator in the Equator Province, wrote a letter in 1948 asking for the names of the 'deserters' who had fled his *paysannat*.[48]

It is clear that the *paysannats* system also aimed, as in other African colonies, to better control and discipline the population and to detect and suppress any anti-colonial resistance more quickly.

Given the need for cheap Congolese labour, one of the main goals of the *paysannats* was to control farmers' daily lives as much as possible, to minimise dissent and maximise output.[49] The Belgian agronomists posited several times the conviction that this was necessary to 'civilise' the local population: 'These primitive peasants must therefore be followed very closely', wrote vice-governor-general Hendrik Cornelis in a letter in 1954.[50] The control of daily life was also reflected in the ban on performing religious rituals. The INEAC legitimised this policy by emphasising that leisure and entertainment were obstacles to productivity; which again proves that economic motives took precedence over social and humanitarian objectives.[51]

All this was done voluntarily and without the use of force, emphasised the INEAC agronomists in their publications: 'Emphasis is placed on the fact that the natives are in no way forced to be included in the native farms', Staner wrote in 1955.[52] According to agricultural engineer G. Tondeur, 'voluntarism' was the basic principle of the *paysannats*, and he continued: 'This system of freedom offers the great advantage of placing the responsibilities on the side of the farmers.'[53] This discourse went hand-in-hand with emphasising the break with the widespread system of compulsory cultivation of the past. For example, Albert Gille stated that the INEAC had 'cast off' previously existing colonialism.[54] J. Collier even observed that, given the low workload, the Congolese were 'far from hard-working men'.[55] However, two remarks are appropriate here. First, as mentioned before, the compulsory cultivation system lasted until independence in 1960 (with thirty compulsory days of free work still being required). Secondly, practice clearly contradicts these

48 AA, AGRI-AIMO, GG7758, Letter from Budjala Territorial Administrator S. Opsomer to District Commissioner, 1948.

49 Likaka, *Rural Society and Cotton in Colonial Zaïre*, 45.

50 AA, AGRI-AIMO, GG7758, Letter entitled 'paysannats indigènes' by H. Cornelis, Vice Governor-General, 27 April 1954, 2.

51 Likaka, *Rural Society and Cotton in Colonial Zaïre*, 47.

52 Staner, 'Les Paysannats Indigènes du Congo Belge et du Ruanda-Urundi', 554.

53 G. Tondeur, 'Surpopulation et displacement des populations', *Bulletin Agricole du Congo Belge* 40 (1949), 2341.

54 Albert Gille, 'De Technique à l'Humain', *Bulletin Agricole du Congo Belge* 42 (1952), 264.

55 J. Collier, 'Les Paysannats de Nord-Sankuru', *Bulletin Agricole du Congo Belge* 50 (1959), 621.

claims. A confidential report from 1952, for example, concluded that the heavy workload on many *paysannats* had led to malnutrition among the Congolese rural population.[56] Furthermore, the author of an inspection report two years later stated: 'Indeed, we have reached the limit of what can be asked of both propaganda personnel and peasants.'[57] Other agronomists took a less pessimistic view: in 1952 J. Clement described the *paysannats* as '*villages heureux*'.[58] A few years later Staner wrote: 'Finally, the indigenous agricultural business is not an end in itself: it is a starting point for a thorough improvement of the state of Congolese farmers and should lead to their economic freedom.'[59] More in-depth and comparative research in the future on the operation and impact of the *paysannats* could shed more light on this.

10.4 Respect for traditions?

Several agronomists, among which Staner was one of the most active, emphasised in their publications that understanding and respect for the mentality of the Congolese population was crucial for the success of the *paysannats*.[60] Local traditions therefore had to be respected as much as possible. The agronomist George Dubois endorsed this premise as follows: 'The native must be able to feel at home.'[61] This was a somewhat contradictory statement, since the Congolese farmers had worked the land for centuries and the *paysannats* system had been introduced no more than two decades earlier. In practice, agricultural colonisation disturbed and even destroyed local values, traditions and customs. The historian and anthropologist Jan Vansina investigated the impact of the *paysannats* on the Kuba Kingdom in eastern Congo, where colonial administrators arrived unannounced to fence and divide land for forced labour. Their behaviour was even expressed in the language of the Kuba, which called the *paysannats* 'mpiki', referring to the French word *piquet* ('picket' in English), the fences with which the INEAC staff fenced the agricultural plots. Although land ownership in Kuba culture actually

56 AA, AGRI-AIMO, GG7758, Letter entitled 'Commentaires du Conseillers des Paysannats et Coopératives du District', Brichard to Thielens, 17 February 1953, 2.

57 AA, AGRI-AIMO, GG7758, 'Confidentiel: rapport d'inspection de monsieur le conseiller technique agricole Nelis – territoire de Budjala: paysannat indigène Banza de la Lua', April 1954, 3. For the text in French, see the opening quotation.

58 Clement, 'Etude relative au paysannat indigène', 137.

59 Staner, 'Les Paysannats Indigènes du Congo Belge et du Ruanda-Urundi', 553.

60 Ibid., 476.

61 G. Dubois, 'Politiques agricoles en milieux ruraux,' *Bulletin Agricole du Congo Belge* 42 (1952), 37.

belonged to the village community, this redistribution was effected alongside the implementation of individualism and private property. In other words, the INEAC experts adapted the traditional property rights system to the Western model of private property.[62]

If one wanted to show respect for Congolese traditions, one had to know them sufficiently and (want to) understand them. It is noticeable that after the Second World War, more and more voices argued within the INEAC for scientific research into Congolese society and culture. For example, in 1949 Tondeur emphasised the importance of research into the social structure of Congolese clans. This was important to prevent families from taking all their relatives with them when they had to move to the *paysannats*, which would lead to uncontrolled overcrowding.[63] Also according to Staner, a better knowledge of the local population and culture was crucial for organising life in the model villages. The staff had to 'really understand' the farmers to gain their trust.[64] The agricultural engineer Albert Gille even described the available social studies on the agricultural allotments as an example of 'excellent empiricism', and the insights had been immediately and warmly welcomed by local chiefs.[65]

However, ultimately, the reality in the Congolese countryside and *paysannats* looked very different. Social research was hard because experts and state consultants had to study large areas; communication and transport was slow and often problematic. Moreover, obtaining the cooperation of the rural population was difficult in many cases.[66] Although in the 1950s about 10 per cent of the rural population lived and worked in the *paysannats*, the growth of agricultural production remained limited and, out of necessity, more and more food had to be imported. According to state agronomists this was due to the 'laziness' of the Congolese, but in practice there was simply too little agricultural expertise available among the agronomists of the INEAC and in the colonial administration.[67] In the internal documents of the Ministry of Colonies, the lack of social and cultural knowledge is increasingly addressed. For example, in a letter of 1957, the agronomist A. Delire expressed his concern about this and suggested that the agronomists should learn the local languages, and their proficiency should be proven by examination.[68]

62 Jan Vansina, *Being Colonized: The Kuba Experience in Rural Congo, 1880–1960* (Madison, WI: University of Wisconsin Press, 2010), 173 and 219.

63 G. Tondeur, 'Surpopulation et displacement des populations', *Bulletin Agricole du Congo Belge* 40 (1949), 23–46.

64 Staner, 'Les Paysannats Indigènes du Congo Belge et du Ruanda-Urundi', 477.

65 Gille, 'De Technique à l'Humain', 263.

66 Clement, 'Rural Development in the Belgian Congo', 266.

67 Likaka, *Rural Society and Cotton in Colonial Zaïre*, 103.

68 AA, AGRI-AIMO, GG7758, Report by A. Delire entitled 'Intensification de l'Agriculture – Affectation du personnel agricole', 1957, 5. In reality, there was not one Congolese language, but several.

10.5 Resistance

The use of coercion, the lack of agronomic and social knowledge and the disappointments that followed, caused a lot of frustration and anger among the Congolese population. How did they react against this situation and the *paysannats* system? There is little to be found about this in the *Bulletin*. The agronomists associated with the INEAC and the colonial administration did not openly write about protests or resistance by Congolese farmers. Criticism of the functioning of the *paysannats* was also scarce. Perhaps they honestly believed that the *paysannats* only offered benefits. Or maybe they had not noticed silent forms of protest? However, there was severe resistance to the *paysannats*, both individually and collectively, and this manifested itself in both passive and active ways.

Likaka examined the resistance of the Mbole community in eastern Congo in the 1950s and concluded that their folk culture had numerous puns and metaphors reflecting their hostility to agricultural colonisation. The word for 'weight loss', for example, was the same as the one they used for forced labour at the *paysannats*.[69] Also, in the Chokwe community in Katanga province, the word '*paysannat*' simply meant 'compulsion'.[70] Both examples illustrate how much reality differed from the development rhetoric of the colonial authorities and the experts of the INEAC. The soft resistance through language and naming was not a specific Congolese phenomenon. In French Sudan, for example, the inhabitants of the model villages described themselves as 'tubabu jonw', meaning 'slaves of the white man'.[71]

The main form of active resistance was flight. The resident population always had to ask permission to leave the *paysannats*, whether to visit family or the nearest city. Since the Congolese were not given formal opportunities to express their displeasure and frustrations (although in some *paysannats Conseils des Paysannats* were organised between Congolese farmers and state agronomists during the 1950s), they tried to make their voices heard indirectly. In 1950, 20 per cent of the Mbole population fled or 'voted with their feet', as Likaka formulated it.[72] Despite these figures, many Congolese failed to flee, as the counter-measures were highly repressive and the colonial government even engaged spies to detect any signs of resistance.[73] Through interviews,

69 Likaka, 'Rural Protest: The Mbole Against Belgian Rule, 1897–1959', 606. See also Likaka's study *Naming Colonialism*, in which he elaborates on the linguistic aspect of resistance strategies.

70 Clement, 'Land Tenure system in the Congo', 103.

71 Monica Van Beusekom, 'Disjunctures in Theory and Practice', 84.

72 Likaka, 'Rural Protest: the Mbole against Belgian Rule', 614.

73 Jewsiewicki, 'The Great Depression and the Making of the Colonial Economic System', 169.

Likaka was able to collect many testimonies that reveal other forms of agency in addition to flight. For example, the food shortage caused by the policymakers' obsession with investing mainly in cash crops provoked subtle forms of resistance such as cutting the plants' roots so they died.[74] The farmers also secretly sang derogatory songs about the Belgians and falsified the weight of, for example, cotton, by adding stones. Local medicine men were asked for drugs to lose body weight so that whoever took them would not be chosen for the hardest work.

Silence was also an important form of agency. For peasants, being silent did not mean the absence of thoughts and defiance. In fact, peasants were engaged in many forms of struggle that were often perceived by colonial administrators as expressions of 'African laziness'.[75] Silence was a deliberate strategy to hide hostility and to prevent the colonists from penetrating any deeper into the Congolese's daily lives. Likaka therefore described it as 'veiled refusal'. So, it is clear that the rhetoric in the *Bulletin agricole* about the laziness and passivity of the Congolese was mistaken and that the agronomists did not realise that in many cases this trait was itself a form of resistance. This hidden protest is closely related to the desire for cultural autonomy among the local population, who tried to preserve their traditions as much as possible through subtle disobedience. Although this was strictly forbidden, they sometimes still organised night-time religious gatherings. Another interesting illustration of their resistance is the founding of *Atongu*: these were village communities that the 'deserters' set up deep in the forest to plan attacks. The *Atongu* were a catalyst for the emergence of a wider resistance movement that even attacked *paysannat* supervisors. This tactic was effective because it undermined the prestige of policymakers and made farmers realise that the colonial government was not invincible.[76]

Finally, what about the presence of critical voices in the *Bulletin*? They were not completely absent, but scarce and rather subtly worded. For example, in 1952, Thiry expressed his concerns about an active form of resistance; namely, arson. Although the farmers knew that this was strictly forbidden and, if caught, there were very severe penalties, the Congolese continued doing it to Thiry's great surprise: 'I believe that the native is not afraid of sanctions; he does not fear the payment of a transactional fine, nor a stay in prison following a guilty verdict. In other words, the current legal provisions do not seem to be sufficiently effective.'[77] He suggested the use of even more severe punitive measures, which clearly shows that resistance was a real feature of life on the *paysannats*.

74 Vansina, *Being Colonized*, 219.

75 Likaka, *Rural Society and Cotton in Colonial Zaïre*, 108.

76 Likaka, 'Rural Protest: The Mbole Against Belgian Rule', 616.

77 N. Thiry, 'Note sur la conduite d'un paysannat', *Bulletin Agricole du Congo Belge* 42 (1952), 260.

10.6 Conclusion

In numerous African colonies, a developmentalist state was imposed from the 1930s onward in response to structural problems such as labour shortages and soil erosion and the impact of the Great Depression on trade. The *paysannats indigènes* system in the Belgian Congo, which only really took off over the course of the 1940s, fits into this international movement, which clearly anticipated what would later be referred to as the Green Revolution.[78] When we compare the two, a number of similarities and differences stand out.

Both aimed to modernise and improve agriculture and rural living standards via the transformation of traditional practices, employing scientific insights and new technology provided by Western experts and institutions. The Western research model, which is based on the development of agricultural universities and extension initiatives, provided guidance. Both the *paysannats* and the Green Revolution had the ambition to solve regional and (inter)national food shortages and famines. Especially during the first phase, the public and private initiators gave priority to improving production. Much less attention was paid to the social and cultural consequences of this policy. Another common (but less officially pronounced) objective was to prevent political and social unrest. The colonial authorities in the Belgian Congo in particular wished to discipline and control the local population. Western countries and private donors, especially from the United States, used the Green Revolution during the Cold War to curb the popularity of communism and the demand for land reforms. In addition, it was also a useful way to provide the Western companies who were active in the agro-industry with larger markets for their products (such as improved seeds, plants and fertilisers). In this way, investments in aid programmes could be earned back. Belgian and European companies benefited from the *paysannats* thanks to the availability of cheap labour, raw materials and agricultural products. Furthermore, it is clear that both the *paysannats* system and the Green Revolution were characterised by a considerable distance between theory and practice. In reality, both were less successful than the official discourse suggested. Over time, they were also criticised for their negative impact on the environment: erosion, the large-scale use of water, the contamination of soil, ground and surface water due to an excessive use of fertilisers and crop-protection products (although this was less the case in the *paysannats* due to high transport costs). Their positive influence on the social situation and the fight against hunger and poverty would also increasingly come into question.

78 Harwood, *Europe's Green Revolution and Others Since* and his chapter in this volume.

Despite the numerous similarities, some differences are also noticeable. In many cases, the Congolese rural population was forced to join the *paysannats* system. This top-down enforcement was generally absent in the Green Revolution. The *paysannats* were part of a colonial agricultural and economic policy that focused primarily on the production of cash crops and much less on the cultivation of staple foods that were important for the food supply of the rural and urban population. It is one of the reasons why historians regard the *paysannats* system as a missed opportunity, especially from a social perspective. The share of export crops in total agricultural production continued to increase during the 1950s, as did their yields. The production of food for the local Congolese population came under increasing pressure. It is therefore not surprising that more and more food had to be imported into the colony before independence in 1960.

For the colonial authorities and Western agronomists and experts, the *paysannats* system was an ideal framework in which to experiment, to see how and with what success local farmers could be transformed into modern, productive farmers. The *paysannats* were an ideal lab for technical and social engineering: to test the efficiency of state intervention, to check to what extent Congolese rural society was malleable. Similar plans and initiatives in other African and Asian colonies served as inspiration, while at the same time the achievements in the Belgian Congo functioned as an example elsewhere. Further research into this knowledge exchange and the impact on the architects of the Green Revolution is desirable. How can we explain that so little was learned from colonial failures and the same mistaken assumptions and strategies were embraced by the next generation?

The evolution of the Belgian Congo's agricultural policy and the introduction of the *paysannats* system illustrates the colonial authorities' quest to mould the colony's primary sector and rural society on a Western model. Many obstacles had to be negotiated, and this happened with varying success. Colonial agricultural politics got no further than a sub-optimal compromise. In many cases, this was the result of a difficult balancing act between diverse and evolving objectives, views and interests. Even within the colonial administration and among the agronomists associated with the INEAC, different opinions existed, for example about how the knowledge of local farmers should be treated and valued. On the whole, the government's initiatives and measures only partially achieved the ambitions set and generated countless undesirable side effects that the authorities were not always able to control or even monitor. The Congolese territory was huge (approximately seventy times the size of Belgium), staff and field expertise remained limited, and financial resources were always insufficient or were used inefficiently. The *paysannats* system was therefore confronted with several problems and challenges, among them limited increases in production, resistance (whether tacit or not) to the imposition of Western agronomic practices and societal norms, flight to the city and industrial regions. This resistance resulted, among other things, in a negative image of the Congolese farmer in the eyes of the agronomists: he was lazy, stupid and unable to farm efficiently without the assistance of Western agronomists.

However, as the 1950s progressed, understanding of indigenous culture and agricultural practices increased. Some agronomists advocated far more research into the social and cultural customs of the local population. The operation of the *paysannats* was adapted in some regions in response to resistance and protest. This resulted in modest efforts to strengthen the connection and cooperation between Western agronomists and civil servants on the one hand, and local farmers on the other, or at least to integrate indigenous knowledge into Western-orientated agricultural practices, as a result of which new, hybrid agricultural knowledge emerged. However, these new insights only very gradually gained a foothold in the scientific world. This occurred not only in the Congo, even after independence, but also elsewhere in the world and in the context of the Green Revolution. How this is to be explained and understood can only be uncovered through further research that will bring together the histories of colonial, agricultural and development sciences.

11

Back to the future: international agrarian development in Ethiopia and the legacy of Italian colonialism

Michele Sollai

From the point of view of agricultural growth, contemporary Ethiopia appears to be a country on the rise, developing towards an ever-brighter future. Despite recurrent political instability, ethnic tensions and armed conflicts, since the mid-1990s Ethiopia's agricultural sector has figured among sub-Saharan Africa's largest and fastest-growing, in terms of both food (especially grains) and cash crop production (especially coffee), for export as well as internal consumption, on large-scale mechanised plantations as well as in small-scale subsistence farming.[1] Albeit assisted by the increasing role of private agribusiness, the state remains the pivotal actor in Ethiopia's agricultural growth and modernisation. From the start of the Ethiopian Peoples' Revolutionary Democratic Front (EPRDF) regime under Meles Zenawi in the early 1990s until Abiy Ahmed's current government, development has become a state ideology in Ethiopia.[2] Still, the Ethiopian developmental state did not – and does not – act in isolation from international actors. International organisations – such as the Food and Agriculture Organization (FAO), the World Bank and the International Fund for Agricultural Development (IFAD) – as well as NGOs (for example, the Alliance for a Green Revolution in Africa, AGRA) and bilateral programmes (for example, the United States Agency for International Development [USAID]) continue to provide an essential contribution to the planning, financing, implementation and monitoring of agricultural and rural development in Ethiopia.

1 Emelie Rohne Till, *Agriculture for Economic Development in Africa: Evidence from Ethiopia* (Cham: Palgrave Macmillan, 2022).

2 Christopher Clapham, 'The Ethiopian Developmental State', *Third World Quarterly* 39 (2018), 1151–65.

The global significance of agricultural growth in Ethiopia and the contribution of international assistance are well reflected in academic scholarship. Agricultural economics, development studies, political science and ethnographic research have all devoted research time to the description of the dynamics, impact and pitfalls of recent and current agrarian development policy in Ethiopia.[3] While some of these studies seek to provide a historical perspective on the evolution of state and international agrarian development efforts, the contribution of historians has – so far – been slight. A few remarkable works not directly focused on development offer a long-term perspective on the whole or sections of Ethiopia's agriculture in the twentieth century.[4] With respect to agrarian development specifically, a bird's-eye view of the relevant literature tends to indicate the late 1950s – and the launching of Ethiopia's Five-Year Development Plans – as the moment at which the modern agrarian development in Ethiopia began.[5] Among the studies focusing on the 'initial' phase of Ethiopia's development planning from that date until the downfall of Haile Selassie's Imperial government in 1974, a few concentrate on the concurrent rise of international technical assistance programmes and large-scale private commercial agriculture.[6] Beyond the dramatic disruption of Ethiopia's farming and land tenure brought about by the DERG military junta and the parallel intensification of international humanitarian aid between 1974 and 1991, some attention is given to the transformation of previous agricultural development schemes during this regime.[7] As for the following years until the present day, most of the available literature consists of contemporary accounts

3 See, for example, Tom Lavers, '"Land grab" as Development Strategy? The Political Economy of Agricultural Investment in Ethiopia', *J. Peasant Studies* 39 (2012), 105–32; Davide Chinigò, 'Decentralization and Agrarian Transformation in Ethiopia: Extending the Power of the Federal State', *Critical African Studies* 6 (2014), 40–56.

4 See, for example, James C. McCann, *People of the Plow: An Agricultural History of Ethiopia, 1800–1990* (Madison, WI: University of Wisconsin Press, 1995); Getnet Bekele, *Ploughing New Ground: Food, Farming, and Environmental Change in Ethiopia* (Woodbridge: James Currey, 2017); Luca Puddu, 'A pragmatic High Modernism? Rural Development and State Building in the Ethiopian Lowlands, c. 1960–2019', *Critical African Studies* 14 (2022), 311–29.

5 Warren Robinson and Fumiko Yamazaki, 'Agriculture, Population, and Economic Planning in Ethiopia, 1953–1980', *J. Developing Areas* 20 (1986), 327–38.

6 Karl Bruno, 'An Experiment in Ethiopia: The Chilalo Agricultural Development Unit and Swedish Development Aid to Haile Selassie's Ethiopia, 1964–1974', *Comparativ* 27 (2017), 54–74.

7 Paul H. Brietzke, *Law, Development, and the Ethiopian Revolution* (Lewisburg, PA: Bucknell University Press, 1982); Alemneh Dejene, *Peasants, Agrarian Socialism, and Rural Development in Ethiopia* (Boulder, CO, and London: Westview Press, 1987).

revolving around the Agricultural Development Led Industrialization (ADLI) strategy and the EPRDF's developmental state.[8]

This peculiar periodisation – starting off no sooner than in the late 1950s, interspersed by multiple regime changes – quite markedly sets Ethiopia's path to agrarian development apart from the rest of sub-Saharan Africa. In recent decades, a growing number of historians have highlighted the connections between colonial development and state-led and international development in Africa during and after the Cold War.[9] Ethiopia has been remarkably absent from this historiographical wave. Due to the still prevalent representation of Ethiopia as a 'never colonised' country and to its long independent status under Haile Selassie's Imperial government between 1930 and 1974[10], few – if any – attempts have been made to place the Ethiopian case in dialogue with the colonial/post-colonial framework now established by the historiography of development.

In view of a more comprehensive and rigorous historicisation of Ethiopia's path to agrarian development and rural modernisation, this chapter problematises and challenges this periodisation. First, it shows that the origins of international agrarian development in Ethiopia can be traced to before the onset of official state planning in the late 1950s. Starting in the transition from the British Military Administration (1941–4) to the full reinstatement of the Imperial Ethiopian Government in the mid-1940s, Ethiopia's agriculture became the subject of international technical assistance missions of the US Foreign Economic Administration (FEA), the United Nations Relief and Rehabilitation Administration (UNRRA), the FAO and the US Point Four Program. Most importantly, the chapter argues that colonial development and rural modernisation during the Italian fascist occupation (1936–41), albeit short-lived, left a substantial legacy and had a wide-ranging impact on and beyond this early phase of international agrarian development in Ethiopia.

By tracing these deeper roots while not contesting the peculiarity of Ethiopia's historical trajectory in the twentieth century, the chapter moves beyond Ethiopia's 'exceptionalism' to show the possibilities of establishing parallels and connections between it and other colonial/post-colonial contexts commonly treated in the historiography of development.

8 The basic premise of ADLI was that agricultural growth – including that of small-scale farming – should constitute the driver of economic progress and industrialisation in Ethiopia. See Tilahun Sisay, 'Review: Agriculture-industry Linkage and Technology Adoption in Ethiopia: Challenges and Opportunities', *Tropical Drylands* 2 (2018), 18–27.

9 Joseph Morgan Hodge, *Triumph of the Expert: Agrarian Doctrines of Development and the Legacies of British Colonialism* (Athens, OH: Ohio University Press, 2007); Frederick Cooper, 'Writing the History of Development', *J. Modern European History* 8 (2010), 5–23.

10 Aaron Tesfaye, *State and Economic Development in Africa: The Case of Ethiopia* (Cham: Palgrave MacMillan, 2017).

The chapter views in a larger perspective the ideological and operational novelty of post-Second World War international development. In parallel with the Ethiopian Imperial State, the FEA, UNNRA, the FAO and Point Four agents all presented and sought to implement complex, sometimes diverging visions of Ethiopia's agrarian future. Planning the future, however, does not always amount to the obliteration of past experiences. As this chapter shows, early post-war foreign experts often reverted to imaginaries, plans and material leftovers of Italian colonial agrarian development to frame proposals for Ethiopia's path towards rural modernity.

11.1 Material legacies: Italian assets and Ethiopia's agrarian futures

After the end of the Italian occupation, Ethiopia was left with an uncertain future. Aided by the uprising of Ethiopian resistance fighters, British forces invaded the country and overthrew the Italian colonial government in late 1941. Haile Selassie returned from exile and was reinstated as Emperor soon after, but it was only in 1944 that the British started withdrawing from their supervision over important sectors of the national economy.[11] The relationship between the Ethiopian authorities and their British counterparts grew progressively tenser during this critical conjuncture, due to the latter's constant meddling in the former's internal affairs.[12] To secure its independence in the face of such interferences, the Ethiopian government opted for strengthening its alliance with the United States and the emerging United Nations.[13] This strategy had economic and developmental reasons apart from political and diplomatic ones. Roosevelt's government had extended lend-lease aid to Ethiopia in 1942–3, and, under the aegis of the FEA, an American Technical Mission headed by US engineer Perry Fellows was invited to reside in Ethiopia in 1944–5 with the aim of preparing a ten-year development plan.[14] In parallel to direct US involvement, Ethiopia was included in the programme of operations of UNRRA. In 1944, UNRRA sent a preliminary mission to determine the aid and technical assistance needs

11 Harold G. Marcus, *The Politics of Empire: Ethiopia, Great Britain and the United States, 1941–1974* (Lawrenceville, NJ: The Red Sea Press, 1983), 8–78.

12 Saul Kelly, 'Desert Conquests: Early British Planning on the Future of the Italian Colonies, June 1940–September 1943', *Middle Eastern Studies* 50 (2014), 1006–26.

13 Getnet Bekele, 'Food Matters. The Place of Development in Building the Postwar Ethiopian State, 1941–1974', in *International J. African Historical Studies* 42 (2009), 29–54.

14 Jacqueline Swansinger, 'A Three-Legged Race: Ethiopian Reconstruction, 1940–1944', *J. World History* 2 (1991), 175–200.

of the country, which was followed by a second fully fledged mission of nineteen technical experts in 1946.

One of the key components of the mandate of these international technical assistance missions was to devise a path for the agrarian development of Ethiopia. To this end, Fellows' mission included two agricultural experts, Wayne W. Adams and A. T. Semple. The UNRRA missions featured a Welfare Division – largely dedicated to rural welfare – and an Agricultural Rehabilitation Division, initially led by Wynant D. Hubbard and then managed by Angel G. Sandoval and Jack Torosky. The two missions started by ascertaining the conditions of Ethiopia's agriculture and identifying the key resources on which to base the country's agrarian future. As this task naturally implied an assessment of the impact of the Italian occupation, the FEA and UNRRA representatives did not hesitate to affirm that the Italian presence had not caused any fundamental disruption to Ethiopian agriculture. Reportedly, large territories had not been affected at all by the occupation. Rural displacement was limited, and the production of food and cash crops in some cases had increased and even thrived since the start of the war.[15] The material advancements made by the Italians were often presented as a clear testimony to how Ethiopian rural areas had progressed in the recent past in terms of trade capacity and overall agricultural production. Echoing British views on the matter, FEA local representative Hickman Price Jr affirmed that 'in no other similar period of time has a backward nation ever received the material legacy that the Ethiopians obtained from the Italians'.[16] Besides the countrywide development of a road network and of modern cities, the Italian colonial regime invested heavily in rural infrastructure and the importation of new agricultural materials.[17] Research farms, dams, bridges, as well as all the agricultural machinery brought to the country during the occupation appeared to the foreign eye as a demonstration of the progress the Italians had made in the rural modernisation of Ethiopia.

These observations posed a paradox for the UNRRA mission. Ethiopia's appeal to UNRRA was based on an interpretation of Italy's invasion and occupation as a continuous state of warfare that had debilitated the country's prevalently agricultural economy. Hence, debilitation

15 United Nations Archives (henceforth UNA), New York. S-1245-0000-0140, George Xanthaky to Michail Menshikov, 'Preliminary Memorandum on Ethiopia', 14 August 1944.

16 The National Archives (henceforth TNA), Kew, FO 922/312, Hickman Price Jr. to MESC Addis Ababa, 'The Fundamental Welfare of Ethiopia: How Can It Be Achieved?, pt 1', 18 November 1944.

17 On road construction during the Italian occupation, see Caitlin Alexandra Collins, 'Paving the Way to Empire: Roads in Ethiopia from Menelik II to Mussolini' (PhD dissertation, University of Pennsylvania, 2022).

required 'rehabilitation'; namely, the restoration of the conditions characterising Ethiopia's agriculture prior to the war with Italy. UNRRA agents' conviction that Ethiopia's agriculture had experienced growth rather than decline in the previous years were clearly at odds with such a strict interpretation of their 'rehabilitation' mandate: it would be not only unfeasible, but especially counterproductive to reverse the substantial legacy left by the occupation in the field of agriculture.[18] What may have turned into an impasse over principles was averted by the sense of pragmatism and opportunity of both the UNRRA mission and the Ethiopian government. 'Rehabilitation' quickly shifted from its backward-looking original meaning to a forward-looking one as 'development'. UNRRA officers clearly operated within a framework orientated towards laying the foundations of Ethiopia's agrarian future. Still, planning the future did not necessarily equal undoing the past. After all, the foundations of Ethiopia's development were already there; they just had to be restored. UNRRA agrarian experts agreed that the material legacy of the occupation represented an ideal starting point to build the development of post-war Ethiopian agriculture. Far from being just relics of past oppression, the leftovers of colonial agriculture in fact embodied a road to the future that could be re-orientated towards the welfare and productivity of Ethiopia's agricultural sector.[19]

Experiment stations, farmhouses, food and cash crop processing plants, warehouses and grain storage facilities, as well as lorries, tractors, ploughs, seeds and all other sorts of agricultural tools and implements – the Italians had developed a vast rural infrastructure and imported numerous technological inputs to support the expansion of agrarian colonisation and of commercial agriculture in the previous years.[20] It is no surprise that all these materials continued to be considered as valuable assets. The ownership and utilisation of the Italian material legacy had been one of the main sources of tension between Haile Selassie's government and British authorities in the aftermath of the occupation. British occupying forces undertook detailed reconnaissance tours to assess what the Italians had left behind and its serviceability. Considering these materials as enemy property,

18 UNA, S-1245-0000-0143, Gerard F. Price to Conrad Van Hyning, 'Supplementary Report', 24 April 1945.

19 UNA, S-1210-0000-0046, US Technical Project in Ethiopia, 'Interim Draft. Summary of Recommendation', 22 December 1944.

20 Comprehensive data on Italian imports of agricultural machinery is lacking but both Italian and British sources attest that the number of tractors introduced to Italian East Africa was around 700, of which around 350 were in Ethiopia. See Centro di Documentazione Inedita dell'Istituto Agronomico per l'Oltremare (henceforth, IAO), File No. 1800 'Promemoria per il Prof. Maugini', 1940 and Oxford, Bodleian Library, 'Papers of F. de V. Joyce', MSS. Afr. s. 2157, b. 12, F. de V. Joyce, 'Report', n.d.

they claimed, dismantled and relocated several of these assets – from tractors to entire plants – from Ethiopia to British colonies to aid the war production effort.[21] Haile Selassie viewed this behaviour as a clear violation of sovereignty and as an illicit appropriation of Ethiopian economic resources. British policy towards former Italian agricultural assets gradually changed in the course of 1942, when Ethiopia itself was included in the Middle East Supply Centre, an Allied organisation meant to coordinate the production and distribution of supplies to areas of the Middle East and the Gulf afflicted by wartime famine. In this context, Italian assets were mobilised to support Ethiopia's own food production and processing. For example, the Italian flour mill and pasta factory 'Colonalpi' in Addis Ababa was put back into use. Italian lorries proved essential for transporting cereals from fields to sorting facilities.[22]

Despite this mobilisation of Italian agricultural assets, UNRRA surveys revealed how only a fraction of Italian tractors, threshers, ploughs and other farm tools had actually been collected and re-distributed. In dire need of modern technological inputs and aware of the high costs of importing them, the Ethiopian government set the repurposing of Italian machinery as a key economic priority, not least due to the importance that it attributed to agricultural mechanisation for the modernisation of Ethiopian farming. The UNRRA Agricultural Rehabilitation Division was entrusted with carrying out this task and hired two other farm machinery experts from the UNRRA Field Services Branch specifically for this purpose.

According to the 1947 final report of UNRRA's main farm machinery expert Lada-Lobarzewski, the diffusion of mechanisation in Ethiopian agriculture presented undeniable advantages. The large number of Italian-made and US-made tractors would make it possible to quickly start a mechanisation programme. Moreover, mechanisation would in time enhance productivity levels and promote the development of export-orientated commercial agriculture. Still, while Lada-Lobarzewski did not doubt that Ethiopia's agrarian future would sooner or later welcome mechanisation on a large scale, he warned against having blind faith in its indiscriminate adoption. The abundance of animal draft power and manual labour in Ethiopia posed few economic incentives for switching *en masse* to mechanised farming. As previously noted by FEA experts, rushing to discard Ethiopian farmers' common tools and farming techniques in favour of modern machinery could be

21 Richard Pankhurst, 'Post-World War II Ethiopia: British Military Policy and Action for the Dismantling and Acquisition of Italian Factories and Other Assets, 1941 2', *J. Ethiopian Studies* 29 (1996), 35–77.

22 TNA, WO 230/57, D.C.P.O. Office (Addis Ababa) to Major Trade Officer, 8 December 1941.

economically disruptive in the short run.[23] Lada-Lobarzewski, in line with other agrarian experts of the UNRRA mission, did not conceive his role as a development agent simply as that of championing modernisation, but urged gradualism, caution and attention to local conditions.[24]

Moreover, UNRRA agents quickly realised how most of the abandoned Italian tractors and machinery needed repair to become usable again, yet very few repair facilities with trained personnel and supplies of spare parts existed at that time in Ethiopia.[25] To this end, UNRRA concentrated on the establishment of repair centres, machinery pools and above all three training programmes for Ethiopian mechanics and tractor drivers. Soon enough, it became clear how even these initial projects were too big to handle for the small staff of the UNRRA mission. The Brethren Service Committee – the operational wing of the US-based Church of the Brethren dedicated to humanitarian aid during the Second World War – sent six mechanics to assist in the establishment and running of the training programmes.[26] With insufficient funding and time at its disposal, however, the UNRRA Farm Machinery Program did not manage to become the fountainhead of agrarian mechanisation as hoped by the Ethiopian government. When the UNRRA mission closed operations in 1947, a large proportion of the Italian agricultural machinery was still in warehouses, and pools of Italian tractors had received few if any requests for their use from Ethiopian farmers.[27]

11.2 Planning legacies: lives and afterlives of Italian colonial development

Beyond the emphasis of the UNRRA mission and Haile Selassie's government on Italian agricultural machinery, other aspects of the Italian material legacy continued to play an important role in the evolution of international technical assistance in Ethiopia in the early post-war years. During the occupation, one of the fascist colonial regime's key strategies of agrarian development was the establishment of 'colonisation centres'; that is, state-led settlements of Italian farmers equipped with modern

23 The National Archives at College Park, Maryland, United States (henceforth NARA II), RG 469, Ethiopia Desk Subject Files, 1951–1961 (UD 394), b. 1, f. 7, Arthur T. Semple, 'Report on the agriculture of Ethiopia', 1944.

24 UNA, S-1347-0000-0018, Lada-Lobarzewski, 'The Use of Farm Machinery in Ethiopian Agriculture', April 1947.

25 UNA, S-1209-0000-0211, J. Torosky to M. C. Wilson Lucom, 'Report of Agricultural Rehabilitation Division, month of September', 30 September 1946. UNA. See also S-1210-0000-0045, Lada-Lobarzewski, 'Closing Report on Farm Machinery Program for Ethiopia', n.d.

26 UNA, S-1303-0000-3156, A. G. Sandoval, 'Report of Agricultural Rehabilitation Division for 11/1946', 5 December 1946.

27 UNA, S-1350-0000-0016, Anne Laughlin to Makonnen Habte Wold, 2 June 1947.

infrastructure and guided by Italian expertise. The Italian parastatal agency *Opera Nazionale Combattenti* (ONC) coordinated the development of two extensive colonisation centres in Holeta and Bishoftu, respectively north-west and south-east of Addis Ababa. Following the British takeover in late 1941, the vast majority of the centres' managers, technicians and settler farmers were evacuated. Still, despite the loss of their original colonisation purpose, the Holeta and Bishoftu farm complexes continued to have strategic importance in Ethiopia's agrarian development. The Ethiopian government authorised some Italian experts and farmers to stay and keep running local farming activities, working in particular on wheat experimentation and agricultural education for Ethiopian pupils.[28] In 1945 two UNRRA Welfare officers even proposed to convert the Bishoftu and Holeta centres into fully fledged agricultural schools.[29] According to this plan, UNRRA would kickstart the management and then hand them over to the Near East Foundation, an important US-based non-governmental development organisation that was already involved in south-eastern Europe, the Levant and the Middle East, and looked to extend its operations to Ethiopia.[30]

This project was not implemented, but the two former colonisation centres remained central to international development planning. In 1947, the FAO started its operations in Ethiopia by taking over most of UNRRA's agricultural and rural welfare projects and launching a series of new initiatives. One of these consisted of a seed experimentation programme based at the former colonisation centre at Holeta – by then turned into government farm. Soon after the establishment of the US Point Four Mission to Ethiopia in 1952, US agronomists too participated in the trial of new varieties of cereal crops at Holeta.[31]

US Point Four agents had more ambitious plans in mind for the former Bishoftu colonisation centre. One of the main components of the US development mandate in Ethiopia was a 'Cooperative Agricultural Education Program' centred on the establishment of an agricultural institution of higher education. The representatives of the Oklahoma A&M College – entrusted by the US Technical Cooperation Administration (TCA) with carrying out most of the Point Four agricultural projects in Ethiopia – soon identified the territory of the former colonisation centre in Bishoftu as their preferred site for the constitution of the 'Imperial College of Agricultural

28 NARA II, RG 469, Ethiopia Desk Subject Files, 1951–61 (UD 394), b. 1, f. 7, Arthur T. Semple, 'Physical facilities of the Ministry of Agriculture', 9 May 1945.

29 TNA, FO 922/312, Hubbard to Ethiopian Minister of Foreign Affairs, 14 January 1945.

30 UNA, S-1245-0000-0140, Leasure to Gerard F. Price, 9 March 1945.

31 Alexander Elliott, 'Role of Agricultural Education in the Development of Agriculture in Ethiopia' (PhD dissertation, Iowa State College, 1957), 232.

and Mechanical Arts'.[32] While it was eventually decided that the College would be built in Haramaya in the eastern region of Harar, Bishoftu was turned into the main centre of Point Four agricultural research in the central Ethiopian highlands. Headquartered in Bishoftu, the 'Central Experiment Station' from the mid-1950s concentrated on cereal crops and wheat in particular, which since the Italian occupation, had become one of the main crops cultivated in the region. Moreover, Italian agricultural research remained an important source of inspiration for the Bishoftu Central Experiment Station. Local Point Four agronomists orientated their wheat experimentation programme along very similar lines to that undertaken by Italian colonial scientists during the occupation.[33]

Besides grain farming, early post-war international development programmes in Ethiopia paid particular attention to cash crops. Due to Ethiopia's heavy dependence on cotton imports, Haile Selassie's Imperial government was particularly keen on receiving technical assistance on the development of this commodity. Ethiopia's cotton production took off in the 1960s following the FAO and World Bank-backed expansion of commercial cotton plantations in the lower valley of the Awash River in north-eastern Ethiopia.[34] However, the close links between state and international development policy in the expansion of cotton production in Ethiopia had started much earlier. Since the aftermath of the occupation, British businessmen, UNRRA, the FEA, the FAO and US Point Four agents had all canvassed plans to turn Ethiopia into a modern cotton-producing country. Compared to the evolution of Ethiopia's cotton sector from the 1960s until the present day; however, all these early post-war cotton projects sought to advance a peculiar development model, one based on the co-ordination and improvement of small-scale rainfed cotton farming rather than on the promotion of plantation-style irrigated agriculture. Albeit with different modalities and rationales, this model took clear, direct inspiration from colonial cotton development during the Italian occupation.

Based on the example of state-disciplined cotton schemes in British Uganda, Portuguese Mozambique and the Belgian Congo,[35] the Italian

32 Amanda Kay McVety, *Enlightened Aid. U.S. Development as Foreign Policy in Ethiopia* (Oxford and New York: Oxford University Press, 2012), 123–60; Oklahoma State University in Ethiopia, *Terminal Report, 1952–1968* (Oklahoma State University, [Addis Ababa], 1969), 20.

33 Michele Sollai, 'How to Feed an Empire? Agrarian Science, Indigenous Farming, and Wheat Autarky in Italian-Occupied Ethiopia, 1937–1941', *Agricultural History* 96 (2022), 379–416.

34 Luca Puddu, 'State Building, Rural Development, and the Making of a Frontier Regime in Northeastern Ethiopia, c. 1944–75', *J. African History* 57 (2016), 93–113.

35 Cyril Ehrlich, 'Some Social and Economic Implications of Paternalism in Uganda', *J. African History* 4 (1963); Allen Isaacman, 'Coercion, Paternalism

colonial regime had launched an ambitious scheme of cotton development revolving around the establishment of 'Cotton Districts' in specific areas of Ethiopia (as well as Eritrea and Somalia) that were deemed economically and ecologically suitable for cotton farming. The Cotton Districts were divided up between two *ad hoc* parastatal companies, which were not meant to take direct control of the land but rather acted as coordinators and promoters of small-scale local cotton farming in their respective area. With the scientific assistance of the Italian colonial agrarian services, local agents of the two companies were to incentivise the diffusion of modern technological inputs throughout the area of each Cotton District and progressively affirm the cultivation of cotton as a stable component of local indigenous farming.[36] Overall, the implementation of this model was probably one of the major economic fiascos of the Italian colonial regime in Ethiopia.[37] As various episodes in the history of development show, however, failed projects could leave a greater and longer legacy than the ones branded as successes.

British business representatives had taken advantage of the British military occupation to investigate potential economic opportunities in Ethiopia during the war. In 1943, Patrick Keown-Boyd – a British cotton expert from Anglo-Egyptian Sudan – came to Ethiopia to evaluate the possibility of reviving large-scale cotton production in the country.[38] Keown-Boyd's plan was largely based on the resumption of the old Cotton Districts model under the management of a new, *ad hoc* Ethiopian national corporation. According to this plan, moreover, the processing of cotton would be undertaken in the Italian-built cotton factory in Dire Dawa, which in the meantime had been taken over by the Anglo-Egyptian Sabean Utility Corporation.

Following this, it was the FAO – and in particular its main cotton expert G. Edward Nicholson – which placed the most emphasis on the Cotton Districts development model as the soundest strategy for laying the foundations for modern cotton farming in Ethiopia. In conjunction with the arrival of two FAO experts in Ethiopia in 1948, the FAO requested and obtained a report provided for the occasion by the Agronomic Institute for Italian Africa – Italy's main centre of colonial agricultural research during the occupation – outlining the programme of the Cotton Districts with

and the Labour Process: The Mozambican Cotton Regime 1938–1961', *J. Southern African Studies* 18 (1992), 487–526; Osumaka Likaka, *Rural Society and Cotton in Colonial Zaire* (Madison, WI: University of Wisconsin Press, 1997).

36 IAO, File No. 1761, Farsetti, 'Relazione finale campagna cotoniera anno 1939–1940', April 1940.

37 Haile Larebo, *The Building of an Empire: Italian Land Policy and Practice in Ethiopia, 1935–1941* (Oxford-New York: Clarendon Press, 1994), 259–83.

38 NARA II, RG 469, Unclassified Central Files, 1953–1961 (P 248), b. 1, f. 16, Patrick V. Keown-Boyd, 'Report on the Cultivation of Cotton in Ethiopia', 1943.

data unobtainable elsewhere.[39] This information played an important role in the cotton development recommendations that Nicholson made to the Ethiopian government in the early 1950s.

The co-ordination and management of small-scale cotton farmers was once again presented as the most reliable way forward.[40] Although Nicholson identified various areas of Ethiopia as agro-climatically suitable for cotton production, he recommended concentrating initially on three regions that had formerly comprised the Italian Cotton Districts, Awash, Soddu and Alomata, respectively in central, south-western and central-northern Ethiopia. A degree of pragmatism was likely to have informed his suggestion. To rapidly increase production, it made sense to Nicholson to build on pre-existing infrastructure and rely on consolidated practices, before expanding into territories untouched by modern agricultural practices. Overall, Nicholson showed a certain intellectual proximity to the developmental logic of the Cotton Districts. The Italian experience, often mentioned in Nicholson's reports, were clearly put in direct connection with future plans of cotton development in Ethiopia. The Italian cotton scheme was depicted as if it had had few fundamental problems: it had failed because of the way it had been implemented, not because of any inherent flaws in its conception.[41]

Although this plan remained on paper for the most part, Nicholson provided key assistance and collaborated closely with Point Four experts and the Ethiopian government in the planning of the 'Agricultural Improvement Centres', the main international project of cotton development in mid-1950s Ethiopia.[42] This scheme was meant to take place in particularly promising agricultural regions of the country, where US and Ethiopian extension agents would promote the diffusion of 'improved' practices among local farming communities. In 1953, Point Four personnel constituted the first pilot Agricultural Improvement Centre on the Kobo-Alomata plain, as mentioned before, the same area of one of the main Italian Cotton Districts. This choice was based on practical considerations. Point Four agents' preliminary survey trips to Alomata in 1953–4 largely concentrated on the reconnaissance of the leftovers of the Italian scheme: buildings and infrastructure that could be re-used, cotton

39 IAO, File No. 1106, Istituto Agronomico per l'Africa Italiana to FAO, 'Rapporto schematico sulle attività cotonicole svolte dall'Italia in Etiopia', 11 July 1949.

40 G. Edward Nicholson, *Cotton in Ethiopia* (Addis Ababa: Imperial Ethiopian Government, Ministry of Agriculture, 1956).

41 Archives of the Food and Agricultural Organization (henceforth FAOA), Rome, RG 71.20, Series G3, 'Missions to Ethiopia. Reports by Experts, 1948–1956', G. Edward Nicholson 'Interim Report to the Government of Ethiopia on Cotton Production', December 1953.

42 FAOA, 10AGP151 Plant Division – Mr Whyte's files - Cotton – Ethiopia, Mulatue Debebe to G. E. Nicholson, 1953; 'Minutes of meeting of FAO-Point 4 Cotton Sub-Committee', 8 April 1953.

machinery laying idle but only partially worn out by time. Moreover, farmers in the surroundings reportedly still cultivated cotton varieties originally introduced by the Italians.[43] The material legacy and practical imprint of the Cotton District clearly made Alomata a privileged location in view of the constitution of the Agricultural Improvement Centre.

The Kobo-Alomata Centre was officially launched in 1954. Headquartered in the old premises of the Italian Cotton District, it organised field demonstrations of modern cotton growing techniques and the distribution of modern implements and high-yielding seeds, but also included educational and extension activities not directly related to cotton. Not too dissimilar from the earlier Italian scheme or the later FAO plans, the experience of the Point Four cotton project was very soon fraught with difficulties that made it fail in its promise to increase the quality and productivity of small-scale cotton farming.[44] Insufficient funding and staff on the ground represented a major limiting factor. Moreover, the almost immediate malfunction of this development model was due to foreign experts' misunderstanding of the social, political and economic dynamics of Ethiopian small farming and of the local environment. The poor results of this pilot scheme eventually led to the abandonment of the plan for a second Agricultural Improvement Centre in Soddu, another area previously under an Italian Cotton District. US technical assistance gradually withdrew from the whole project in the late 1950s.[45]

11.3 Conclusion

As Hodge pointed out, historians of development should be careful not to overemphasise the colonial origins of post-Second World War plans and practices of development.[46] This is far from being the case with respect to Ethiopia. The short duration and peculiar dynamics of the Italian occupation – for which it is indeed commonly referred to as *occupation* rather than colonial rule – certainly place it on a different scale *vis-à-vis* long-term Italian colonial rule in Libya, Eritrea and Somalia, as well as British, French, Belgian or Portuguese colonialism in Africa as a whole. Moreover, the very incomplete – to say the least – state of archival holdings on the Italian occupation in both Italian and Ethiopian archives

43 NARA II, RG 469, Unclassified Central Files, 1953–1961 (P 248), b. 6, f. 8, D. B. Jeffrey to Gordon, 4 June 1954.

44 NARA II, RG 469, Unclassified Central Files, 1953–1961 (P 248), b. 27, f. 22, J. L. Bridges, 'Report of Findings at the Agricultural Improvement Center, Alomata', 9 October 1957.

45 NARA II, RG 469, Unclassified Central Files, 1953–1961 (P 248), b. 18, f. 4, B. E. Wilson to L. H. Brannon, 'Inspection trip to Soddu', 3 January 1956.

46 Joseph M. Hodge, 'Writing the History of Development (Part 2: Longer, Deeper, Wider)', in *Humanity: An International Journal of Human Rights, Humanitarianism, and Development* 7 (2016), 125–74.

has hindered the full reconstruction of the social, economic and environmental legacy of Italian colonial rule.

As briefly shown in this chapter, however, we can still find the means to do more in this regard, not least in order to challenge and problematise what may be called the 'exceptionalisms' that have, until not so long ago, characterised Italian and Ethiopian historiography. In Italy, historical investigation into Italian colonialism has amounted to colonial apologism.[47] The impact of the Italian colonial rule was consistently sanitised to obscure its widespread violence and racism. Italian colonial apologists appropriated the originally derogatory representation of Italian colonialism as 'ragamuffin imperialism' and turned it into one largely innocuous imperialism having little similarity with the wrongdoings of other colonial Empires.

Since the pioneering work of Angelo Del Boca, Italian historiography has made giant strides towards dismantling this representation. Italian colonial rule – especially but not only in occupied Ethiopia – was in fact as, if not more, inhumane and destructive as that of other European empires. The peculiar positioning required by urgency of such historiographical – and political – reckoning has in some cases led historians to slide into a sort of Italian colonial exceptionalism in reverse. Especially in the case of the occupation of Ethiopia, the historiographical focus has been mostly on the peculiarly *fascist* dimension of the undertaking rather than on its broadly *colonial* character. The inadvertent consequence of this approach is that we still tend to emphasise what makes the Italian occupation of Ethiopia *distinct* from rather than *comparable* or *connected* to the history of other colonial case studies.

Ethiopian historiography has largely downplayed the Italian occupation as a transient moment in the country's historical trajectory. In his much-cited *History of Modern Ethiopia*, Bahru Zewde dedicates to the occupation five pages out of more than 200. For Bahru, in fact, the occupation had an 'episodic character', it was essentially 'an interlude in the course of modern Ethiopian history'.[48] From the viewpoint of agrarian development, there seems to be an implicit understanding that since all Italian projects failed, they were largely inconsequential in the short as well as in the long run. This interpretation plays well into Ethiopian exceptionalism, as it allows to maintain the notion of a practically seamless history of independence and of a unique path to modernisation.[49]

47 Antonio M. Morone, 'I custodi della memoria. Il Comitato per la documentazione dell'opera dell'Italia in Africa', *Zapruder* 23 (2010), 24–38.

48 Bahru Zewde, *A History of Modern Ethiopia, 1855–1974* (London, Athens, OH, and Addis Ababa: James Currey, Ohio University Press, Addis Ababa University Press, 1991), 160–5.

49 Sara Marzagora, 'Nationalism: The Italian Occupation in Amharic Literature and Political Thought', in *The Horn of Africa and Italy: Colonial, Postcolonial and*

By highlighting (parts of) the Italian colonial legacy on early post-war international agrarian development in Ethiopia, this chapter has shown how the Italian occupation can indeed be analysed together with other case studies within the historiography of development. As highlighted in the chapter, the same can be said of Ethiopia's development path. Without disregarding the important elements that distinguish the political, social and economic trajectory of Ethiopia over the twentieth century, the legacy of Italian colonial artefacts and plans of rural modernity in Cold-war era international agrarian development is but one important example of connections that can be made between this and other more widely explored case studies in British and French (post-)colonial Africa.[50]

Transnational Cultural Encounters, Simone Brioni and Shimelis Bonsa Gulema (eds) (Oxford: Peter Lang, 2018), 141–66.

50 Joseph M. Hodge, 'British Colonial Expertise, Post-Colonial Careering and the Early History of International Development', *J. Modern European History* 8 (2010), 24–46; Damiano Matasci, *Internationaliser l'éducation: La France, l'UNESCO et la fin des empires coloniaux en Afrique (1945–1961)* (Villeneuve d'Ascq: Presses universitaires du Septentrion, 2023).

12

New models for agriculture in the post-war American Southern Cone

Luis Ernesto Blacha

The discourses on agricultural modernity that circulated in the countries of the American Southern Cone at the beginning of the twentieth century differed from country to country in their contents and the actors they addressed.[1] Both experimental practices in the 1920s and public policies in the 1930s offered a variety of ways in which the agricultural sector in each country could advance. After the Second World War, a single common discourse – which in the 1960s came to be called the Green Revolution – emerged as the sole route to modernisation. Agriculture, however, had to compete with industry to attract foreign currency, since Import Substitution Industrialisation (ISI) policies required imports of foreign machinery and technology. This competition for resources enhanced the importance of international organisations like the Economic Commission for Latin America and the Caribbean (ECLAC) and the Food and Agriculture Organization of the United Nations (FAO) since they could offer regional solutions. All the countries in the region were torn by these contradictory necessities and resorted to similar formulae in their agricultural policies, as the Brazilian, Argentinian and – to a lesser degree – Uruguayan cases we shall discuss in this chapter will show. The enforcement of common practices and discourses on local

1 Argentina, Brazil and Uruguay were selected as representative case studies of agricultural modernisation in the Southern Cone due to their role as major producers of primary goods for the global market since the late nineteenth century. Chile is excluded due to the dominance of its mining production, and Peru focuses its agriculture mainly on the domestic market, primarily to improve the internal food supply, but not for export. In Ecuador, Chile and Colombia, the Rockefeller Foundation worked to modernise agriculture but primarily to improve the internal food supply.

producers during the post-war period reflected international demands and concealed the diversity of pre-existing projects for modernising agriculture. Was it possible for agriculture alone to trigger modernisation? How could industrialisation co-exist with a modernised rural world? Southern Cone governments were confronted by these questions and gave relatively similar answers through their public policies and the discourses that justified them. Disentangling policies and discourses developed under the influence of international organisations and the pressures imposed by ISI policies will be the object of this chapter.

12.1. Argentina: a modernisation orientated towards the world

Argentina's integration into the global market stands out as one of the most successful stories of the first wave of globalisation (1870–1930). It was a process of productive integration that accounted for an annual growth rate of 3.5 per cent in Latin America between 1850 and 1914.[2] Due to the volume and diversity of its agricultural exports, the Argentinian case becomes crucial in explaining the impact of the first wave of globalisation in the Southern Cone of the Americas. Together with Uruguay, it led the export-driven growth, while Brazil struggled to regain the significant role it had held earlier.

In Argentina, a combination of factors contributed to its success between about 1880 and the onset of the Depression in 1929–30: the natural fertility of the soils in the Pampas region, infrastructure (the railway network), improvements in pastures, and animal genetics, European immigration and the ability to alternate between arable and pastoral regimes to meet the demands of the major European metropolises.[3] Despite being the southernmost country in the American Southern Cone, the reduction in maritime freight costs and the presence of rural tenants ('chacareros') who embodied the 'revolution in the Pampas' help explain why Argentine exports represented 4 per cent of world trade in 1920.[4]

Natural conditions played a significant role in the first three decades of the twentieth century in both Argentina and Uruguay. For Uruguay, its livestock production was also based on natural pastures that required only minor improvements to provide suitable forage for the cattle processed by its meatpacking industry. In the same way as Argentina, genetic enhancements were introduced into the cattle herds. However,

2 Luis Bértola and Jeffrey Williamson, 'Globalization in Latin America before 1940', in *Cambridge Economic History of Latin America, II: The Long Twentieth Century* (Cambridge: Cambridge University Press, 2006), 28.

3 Osvaldo Barsky and Jorge Gelman, *Historia del agro argentino. Desde la conquista hasta comienzos del siglo XXI* (Buenos Aires: Sudamericana, 2012).

4 Vicente Pinilla and Agustina Rayes, 'How Argentina Became a Super-Exporter of Agricultural and Food Products During the First Globalisation (1880–1929)', *Cliometrica* 13 (2019), 443–69.

Uruguayan livestock production stagnated from the 1929 crisis until the 1990s and revived only after new grass varieties were introduced from New Zealand. Both Uruguay and New Zealand shared ecological conditions and a specialism in cattle production, but while New Zealand embraced new technologies such as the pasture improvements and subsidies for the use of fertilisers throughout the twentieth century, their adoption was delayed in Uruguay and taken up only sporadically.[5]

The natural advantages stemming from the ecological characteristics of the countries of the American Southern Cone were not always accompanied by the adoption of technologies aimed at maximising their exploitation. The extensive characteristics of Argentine production predominated, as well as an alignment with the demands of the major European markets. The inability to expand into new territories with the same levels of soil fertility placed a limit on the growth of the Argentinian economy. By 1912, this extensive territorial model began to show signs of stagnation, but the turning point would only come with the global crisis of 1929, which marked the 'end of outward growth'. As in other Latin American countries, it was during this period that natural conditions had to be complemented with the adoption of more productive technologies in rural areas, allowing for increased yields and alignment with the specific demands of core countries prioritising their industrial growth.

The crisis of 1930 had a dual impact on the American Southern Cone. The economic situation in Europe and the United States reduced their demand for both foodstuffs and raw materials for industry, significantly affecting global trade. Consequently, all countries in the region reduced their exports, which in turn reduced their capacity to import. The decreased supply of imported industrial goods was gradually replaced by local products, which were often more expensive and of lower quality. The lack of foreign earnings made it harder to secure new foreign technologies such as hybrid seeds and machinery to modernise agricultural production. The reduced demand from traditional markets for exports from the American Southern Cone discouraged investment in primary production. While in the medium term, state policies prioritised ISI, the primary source of foreign exchange continued to be exports of agricultural and livestock products. Finding new markets for these traditional products did not seem to be a priority for the various stakeholders – entrepreneurs, government officials and associations – in this sector throughout the American Southern Cone.

The modernisation of agriculture in Argentina resulted in a deepening of regional inequalities that had begun during the first wave of

5 Jorge Álvarez Scanniello, 'Technological Change and Productivity Growth in the Agrarian Systems of New Zealand and Uruguay (1870–2010)', in *Agricultural Development in the World Periphery*, V. Pinilla and H. Willebald (eds) (Cham: Palgrave, 2018), 479–81.

globalisation, even when technologies related to exports could be incorporated into products for the domestic market. The case of the railway system is an important indicator because it led to an energy transition without an Industrial Revolution.[6] The interventionist policies of the 1930s lacked the necessary political support and social and productive impact for the implementation of systems of intensive agriculture. However, it is possible to identify a turning point in Argentina's agro-export growth that demanded the adoption of new technologies, including organisational ones.

The National Board to Combat Unemployment (Junta Nacional para Combatir la Desocupación; JUNALD), established in 1934, is one of the public institutions that from the mid-1930s aimed at improving production by promoting regional economies while also encouraging social control. The Board encouraged the seasonal migration of labour to assist with the harvest. This had two objectives. It served as a way to address the problem of limited mechanisation in crops destined for the domestic market such as cotton and sugar cane. But it also aimed to reduce the impact of the unemployment that emerged after 1931 as a result of the 1929 Wall Street financial crash.

Regional differences became more pronounced during the period of crisis because the production regimes in different territories reacted in different ways to the challenge of depression. These had an impact on the population. Between 1920 and 1940, the percentage of individuals called for mandatory military service and rejected due to physical incapacity increased from 30 per cent to 42.2 per cent.[7] The increase in the number of 'unfit' individuals reflects the inability of some citizens to access to adequate nutrition. It also suggests that agriculture, even in the main productive regions, required modernising to increase yields to serve the domestic population.

The implementation of systems of intensive agriculture in Argentina was interrupted several times during the twentieth century. These interruptions can be attributed to both local political factors and variations in the global demand for raw materials. It took forty years for the modernisation of agriculture to become a systematic public policy. This only occurred with the emergence of the policy of 'Return to the Countryside' (*la vuelta al campo*) initiated by Peronism in 1950 as a way to manage large agricultural producers. Until then, industry, as in the 1930s, was a minor player dependent on the surpluses generated by the agro-export

6 Sandra Kuntz-Ficker, 'Latin America's First Export Era: Reassessing its Economic Contribution', in *The First Export Era Revisited: Reassessing its Contribution to Latin American Economies*, Sandra Kuntz-Ficker (ed.) (Cham: Palgrave, 2017), 26.

7 Josué de Castro, *Geopolítica del hambre. Ensayo sobre los problemas de la alimentación y la población del mundo* (Remedios de Escalada: De la UNLA, 2019), 17.

model, a situation institutionalised by the Economic Plan presented in 1940 by the Minister of Finance, Federico Pinedo. Industry was protected and relied on the earnings of foreign exchange in primary agricultural and livestock sectors. It did not prioritise the supply of agricultural machinery to enhance the mechanisation of the Argentine rural sector, which would have allowed for increased productivity.

Due to its technological backwardness and a land tenure system primarily based on leasehold, agriculture could only re-achieve the production levels of the first decade of the century under exceptional conditions. This technological lag reduced the diversity of production, which had been an advantage in the first wave of globalisation compared to other actors in the Southern Cone of the Americas.

So, unlike Brazil, there was a failure in Argentina to integrate agricultural needs with industrial development. Rural technological backwardness was only addressed when there was a shortage of foreign exchange to keep light industry functioning. The tension between promoting industry and promoting agriculture translated into two distinct national projects based on opposed political identities. Industrialisation was seen as a way to favour the urban working class, while large-scale intensive agriculture was associated with support for the traditional Argentine elites. However, industries initially established in Argentina were directly related to the rural sector: salting plants, meat packing plants, flour mills. The industrial growth that began in the 1930s did not start from these existing capacities but rather relied on a transfer of foreign exchange from agriculture to new emerging industries such as food processing, textile and the metallurgic industries. This was one of the main reasons for technological backwardness in the rural sector. The vastness of the country did not facilitate the coordination of federal policies that promoted integrated intensive productions. The growth of light industry, which proceeded quickly in the mid-1940s, stimulated internal migration from rural areas to cities, a trend that had been developing since the 1930s.[8] The expansion of agricultural production for the domestic market in a vast country with a small population was not a nationwide project as in the Brazilian case. Instead, it arose out of the need to feed the industrial workforce, which increased in numbers during the Peronist era (1945–55).

The modernisation of the rural world came to be seen as a political objective shared by both Peronists and 'anti-Peronists' in the late 1940s. Agricultural mechanisation was seen as an extension of the industrial practices of the major port cities into the countryside. However, coordination between the urban and rural worlds was not always a part of Peronist public policies. While the *descamisados* ('shirtless', the name

8 Jorge Schvarzer, *La industria que supimos conseguir. Una historia político-social de la industria argentina* (Buenos Aires: Grupo Editorial Planeta, 1996).

applied in Peronist jargon to its popular base) gained social citizenship benefits from the Secretariat of Labour and Social Welfare (Secretaría de Trabajo y Previsión) in 1943, these rights were extended to agriculture with the Rural Worker Statute for permanent workers in 1944, and for seasonal workers in 1947 with the reorganisation of the Centre for Various Trades (Centro de Oficios Varios).

12.2 Uruguay: dynamic stagnation

The modernisation of Uruguayan agriculture presents significant differences when compared to Brazil and Argentina, not only because of its smaller scale of production but also due to its prioritisation of livestock production. In the first globalisation, it made intensive use of the natural conditions of its soils to feed cattle and sheep, the products of which formed 80 per cent of the country's exports.[9] Uruguayan livestock production grew at an annual rate of 3 per cent between 1870 and 1913, without being able to incorporate new land (as occurred in Argentina). The railway and the enclosure of production units during this period were important factors in achieving this rate of growth. Genetic improvements in sheep began to be made in 1860 and in cattle in 1880, driven by learning-by-doing. However, pasture was not improved despite the fact that 90 per cent of Uruguay's productive land was dedicated to livestock farming. In this period, large landowners and small producers co-existed. During the presidency of José Batlle y Ordoñez (1904–16), the state, which had supported the expansion of livestock farming, distanced itself from ranchers. His anti-latifundia reforms were seen as favouring the modernisation of agriculture but lacked the support of the main livestock producers. Demands for access to land are one of the factors that explains the delay in improving pastures.

These social tensions, as well as the depletion of natural resources that had established Uruguay as a global meat producer, led to a dynamic stagnation of livestock production between 1930 and 1980. To modernise its livestock farming, after 1980 Uruguay adopted varieties of grass developed in New Zealand in the 1950s. This differs from the North American technologies adopted in Argentina and Brazil, but also from the French organisation used by some medium-sized Argentine producers in the 1960s.[10] The stagnation of Uruguayan livestock farming was linked to the failure to improve its pastures, not to a lack of mechanisation. However,

9 M. I. Moraes, 'El capitalismo pastor. Dinámica tecnológica e institucional de la ganadería uruguaya entre 1870–1930', *Historia Agraria* 29 (2003), 13.

10 The Consorcios regionales de experimentación agrícola [Regional Agricultural Experimentation Consortia] are the Argentinian version of the French Groupes de Développement Agricole (GDA).

Uruguay reduced its arable land by 0.5 per cent between 1950 and 1973. During the same period, both Brazil (with 3.6 per cent) and Argentina (2 per cent) expanded the land area dedicated to agriculture. The Green Revolution also impacted the percentage of the active population in agriculture. While Argentina's active agricultural population decreased from 1.623 million in 1950 to 1.448 million in 1973 (a reduction of 0.5 per cent per annum), Uruguay's reduction was 0.8 per cent per annum over the same period (from 216,000 to 178,000 active agricultural workers). In contrast, Brazil's active agricultural workforce increased from 9.887 million in 1950 to 14.497 million in 1973 (an increase of 1.7 per cent per annum).

12.3 Brazil: a modernisation with internal development

In Brazil, despite its vast territorial expanse and large population, rural production was heavily concentrated in a few regions in the early twentieth century. Coffee was then the country's leading export, as it had happened since independence. For this reason, the coffee elite in São Paulo had played a prominent role within the Brazilian state from its inception. Until 1930, coffee was the primary focus of agricultural policies. The second most important crop, cotton, was seen as the 'crop of the poor man' in the early twentieth century and continued to lag behind coffee, even as the Brazilian textile industry developed into a major domestic player. Coffee plantations were able to serve American markets without competing with agricultural production in the United States. In contrast to Argentina's policy of neutrality, Brazil actively supported the Allies during both world wars and this granted it access to more favourable international agreements. It was also translated into American aid after the Second World War for the implementation of the Green Revolution, integrating its industrial capacity.

The modernisation of rural Brazil demanded a re-assessment of the central role of the coffee elite in São Paulo. The regions dedicated to coffee cultivation were concentrated along the railway lines, a much smaller network than Argentina's, even though Brazil has a significantly greater land area. In the 1930s, a series of steps were taken to prioritise agricultural diversity. The establishment of the National Agriculture Society (Sociedade Nacional de Agricultura; SNA) played a pivotal role here and in subsequent developments related to the adoption of Green Revolution technologies.[11] The objectives of the SNA encompassed both production

11 Sonia Regina de Mendonça, 'Conflictos intraclase dominante agraria y políticas agrícolas bajo el varguismo (1930–1954)', in *Agro y política a uno y otro lado del Atlántico. Franquismo, salazarismo, varguismo y peronismo*, Noemi Girbal-Blacha, María López Ortiz and Sonia Regina de Mendonça (eds) (Buenos Aires: Imago Mundi, 2016), 80.

and politics because they aimed to reduce Brazil's dependence on imports of wheat and Argentine beef.

Unlike the other cases within the American Southern Cone discussed in this chapter, Brazilian industrialisation emerges as a pivotal force in the modernisation of its rural sector. The difference lies in Brazil's access to American technical cooperation and in the existence of a more diversified bourgeoisie. Its primary objective was not only to sustain the urban industrial workforce within the nation but also to evolve into a vital supplier of raw materials for industries. The significance of its domestic market represented a distinctive aspect of the Brazilian experience. The conflict between ISI and rural modernisation appears to have had a less pronounced impact here than in Argentina, where industry's reliance on foreign exchange competed with the rural sector's imperatives for modernisation. In Brazil, there wasn't a time when the 'backwardness' of rural production limited the provision of foreign exchange at the pace and intensity required for its light industrial growth. For a short period in the 1950s a high growth rate was achieved.

The state interventionism of the 1930s encouraged a domestic market for agricultural products, and with this goal in mind, it had to challenge the hegemony of the São Paulo coffee elite. The public corporations established at this time planned a production strategy guided by public policies rather than private interests. They reinforced the importance of the newly created associations of large 'non-coffee' agricultural producers. During the first government of Getúlio Vargas (1930–4), agriculture was diversified for nationalist purposes and to improve the food supply of the urban-industrial masses. This change occurred within the global order, both internally and externally, as the country aligned itself with American policies for the region. The limited agricultural capacity in place amplified the impact of the public organisations as a means of modernising agriculture through diversification.[12]

In contrast to the Argentine case, this was a productive change initiated by the state and was not simply a strategy to defend prevailing economic interests. It led to the emergence of new productive actors that would have a significant impact in the following decades of the twentieth century.

12.4 Was every past time better?

Beyond the various levels of integration into the global market that had already taken place in Argentina, Uruguay and Brazil, the New York stock market crash of 1929 revealed the constraints on the growth of the productive model of the first wave of globalisation. Its consequences were

12 Fiona Gordon-Ashworth, 'Agricultural Commodity Control under Vargas in Brazil, 1930–1945', *J. Latin American Studies* 12 (1980), 88.

not only economic but also social and political. If integration into the global market underpinned the leadership of the ruling classes, changes in the international context had a significant impact on the different national economies.

The crisis questioned the efficiency of relative advantages based on 'natural' factors. Productive diversity and state intervention were part of the strategies implemented to adapt to a period of rapid transformation. The contraction of global trade not only reduced potential consumer markets but also decreased imports of industrial goods into the American Southern Cone. Liberalism as a political practice with economic consequences was called into question. A growing tendency towards authoritarianism threatened democracy.

As late as 1937, 48.7 per cent of agricultural land in Argentina was held by small farmers. But large landowners had more land and a stronger political influence. The way in which access to land remained uneven can be demonstrated in two distinct periods. Mortgage credit in the 1920s favoured tenants, but after 1930, when many small farmers could no longer afford to pay their mortgages, public policies ensured that the land returned to the hands of large landowners.

This situation did not provide incentives to incorporate new technologies into production. However, in 1935, Argentina began assembling tractors, threshers and mowers. In 1941 though, non-mechanised ploughs called *arados de mancera* still remained the usual agricultural implement employed in Argentina. State support focused on modernising port infrastructure, and, in 1932, Argentina began shipping its production using grain elevators in the ports of Buenos Aires and Rosario. By this time, the country had lost much of its 'comparative advantage', and the introduction of the Grain Elevator Network came late when compared to developments in the United States and Canada.

In the Brazilian case, the limited diversification of production exacerbated the depression caused by the crisis. The dangers posed by over-reliance on coffee had already been anticipated during the First World War. At that time, state aid implemented a coffee support programme that continued throughout the 1920s as the National Coffee Council (Conselho Nacional do Café).[13] These public policies served the interests of the São Paulo coffee elite but offered nothing for the development of agricultural production in the remainder of the country. However, the Brazilian government tackled the 1930 crisis in a very different way to Argentina, as its ties with the United States and its participation in the First World War gave it a degree of political credit with the United States that the Argentina lacked.

13 Christopher Absell and Antonio Tena-Junguito, 'The Brazilian Export Economy, 1822–1913', in *First Export Era Revisited*, Kuntz-Ficker (ed.), 141.

Whereas in Argentina the Regulatory Boards of Production (Juntas Reguladoras de la Producción), established from 1932 onwards, had a defensive character and were orientated towards subsidising agriculture, the Brazilian public authorities after 1930 diversified production and promoted domestic consumption, facilitating their integration with ISI.[14] Consequently, there was a shift that broadened the composition of the ruling classes, even though the government was essentially authoritarian.

In contrast, the 1930s in Argentina were marked by a return of the traditional political class linked to the agro-export model after a period in which middle classes had been involved in national government. Leaders such as Agustin P. Justo in Argentina and Getúlio Vargas in Brazil were economically liberal but politically conservative, and saw state interventionism as a defensive strategy to protect their economic interests. As we saw, despite the establishment of Regulatory Boards of Production to ensure minimum price support for exports and JUNALD, which financed the relocation of labour to specific areas of production, the Argentinian government did not approach the crisis as an opportunity for change in Argentina. Palliative measures were introduced for agriculture, given the contraction of exports, and for the industry to sustain the demand for industrial products that could not be met through imports. In this defensive stance, there was no opportunity to incorporate new technologies or promote new linkages between productive sectors.

Following the conclusion of the Second World War, more process technologies were integrated as part of state interventionism in Argentina. ISI focused on light metallurgical industry production, directed towards urban applications. Agricultural machinery production was not among its priorities. 'Rural enabling loans' were a component of public policies for the rural sector and can be viewed as process technologies. However, starting from 1946, fixed investments in infrastructure were reduced. These loans, characterised by extended repayment periods and low interest rates, had been aimed at small and medium agricultural producers since 1945. With the return of workers to rural areas in 1950, these loans were extended to all rural sectors (large and small landowners, tenants, livestock and dairy sectors) with the aim of promoting the capitalisation of the agricultural sector as a whole.

14 Vanderlei Vazelesk Ribeiro, 'Brasileños de cuerpo y alma y argentinos fervientes: trabajadores rurales ante el varguismo y el peronismo', in *Agro y política a uno y otro lado del Atlántico*, Girbal-Blacha, Ortiz and de Mendonça (eds), 102.

12.5 Technologies: artefacts, industrialisation and organisation

The pessimism that marked the early 1930s had largely passed by the middle of the decade when signs of recovery and an increase in international agricultural prices could be observed. However, the situation became complicated once again with the onset of the Second World War in 1939. Argentina and Uruguay's established capacity in the production of *tasajo* (salted meat) aligned well with the provision of rations for the troops fighting in Europe. And Brazil became a strategic ally of the USA, which facilitated its industrial growth.

For Latin American Structuralism in the 1940s and 1950s, industrialisation was seen as something that had to be pursued even at the expense of agriculture. State intervention implemented a transfer of resources from agriculture to manufacturing, which not only led to significant social changes but also diminished the competitive edge of primary goods exports, a trend that had been apparent since the late 1920s.[15] The capital and resources needed for modernising agriculture (such as machinery and fertilisers) were instead directed towards ISI, resulting in a disjointed process compared to the coordinated approach seen in core countries.

By the end of the Second World War in 1945, the policy of ISI in Argentina had started to show its limitations, especially when agricultural products were excluded from the General Agreement on Tariffs and Trade (GATT) in 1947. The national and popular government led by Juan Perón opted for a closed economy and income redistribution. This further complicated access to the international markets that had long been crucial for the region's exports. The implementation of ISI policies reduced the importance of agricultural exports within the national economy. This was because foreign exchange was primarily allocated to the nascent industrial sector, at least until 1949, while the modernisation of rural industries was given a lower priority. However, exceptions existed, and official credit continued to benefit the agricultural sectors.[16]

This sense of neglect of the rural world was also present in Brazil, despite its greater alignment with ISI. The National Agriculture Society (SNA) in Brazil highlighted this issue, despite its support for state intervention in the economy. American support for the modernisation of Brazilian agriculture played a crucial role in this process.

Machinery, chemical products and scientific knowledge are all elements in modern production in both rural and urban industries. However,

15 Arturo O'Connell, 'La Argentina en la depresión: Los problemas de una economía abierta', *Desarrollo Económico* 23 (1984), 479–514.

16 M. Martín-Retortillo *et al.*, 'The Goose That Laid the Golden Eggs? Agricultural Development in Latin America in the 20th Century', in *Agricultural Development in the World Periphery*, Pinilla and Willebald (eds), 348.

in the modern projects of Latin America in the first half of the twentieth century, it seemed that only urban businesses had the potential for transformation. Argentina illustrates this tendency, not only due to its significant regional differences but also because of the cosmopolitan nature of its cities. Universal free public education, thanks to which the population enjoyed a high rate of literacy, set Argentina apart from other countries in the region. So too did the opportunities for political participation. The abundant and cheap labour force in Argentina and Uruguay was buoyed by immigration from Europe until 1914. In the case of Argentina, domestic mobility tended to replace immigration after 1945. Immigration though has had a much smaller impact on the Brazilian workforce. Tractorisation occurred in both countries after the Second World War. In Brazil, it was promoted with American support and integrated into the ISI project. In Argentina and Uruguay, tractorisation was slower because it took place in the context of infrastructures inherited from the first era of globalisation.

The establishment of the National Agricultural Council (Consejo Agrario Nacional, CAN) in Argentina in 1940 promised a future land redistribution. In 1946, the Peronist government turned this land reform into a modest programme of mortgage loans facilitated through the nationalised banks. In Brazil, both the Land Statute of 1964 and the National Agrarian Reform Plan (Plano Nacional de Reforma Agrária) of 1986 were never implemented. Uruguay, on the other hand, passed Law No. 7377 in 1921, authorising the Mortgage Bank of Uruguay (Banco Hipotecario del Uruguay) to carry out a colonisation plan that offered applicants productive units of up to 73 hectares. In fact, neither Argentina nor Uruguay implemented land reforms, nor did agrarian movements actively agitate for land access until the 1960s.

In contrast to Brazil's alignment with the United States in its agricultural policy and industrial production, Argentina experienced a period of relative international isolation from 1939 to 1955 during which it encountered difficulties in securing some types of industrial equipment and military supplies. However, the challenge that this posed did not have the same effect on agricultural machinery and agrochemicals because subsidiaries of transnational companies producing these goods were established in the country in the 1950s. Argentina's openness to American capital was a means to remediate the technological lag experienced in the rural world.

In addition to transnational corporations establishing themselves in Argentina, the state also played a prominent role as a disseminator of new technologies. In 1957, the National Institute of Farming Technology (Instituto Nacional de Tecnología Agropecuaria; INTA) began its operations, adapting imported machinery to local conditions.[17] The growth of

17 M. Martín-Retortillo *et al.*, 'The Dynamics of Latin American Agricultural Production Growth, 1950–2008', *J. Latin American Studies* 51 (2019), 593.

the domestic market, which stimulated consumption and reduced the exportable surpluses, along with the reduced demand for Argentinian products in post-war European markets, are all factors explaining why the adoption of new technologies did not translate into a significant increase in exports. The foreign policy of the United States reinforced its control of the region by transferring technologies adapted to American conditions. Argentina incorporated these technologies into its local production, but the country's political position acted to limit its exports of both beef and corn to US markets.

The American Southern Cone as a whole would continue to play a significant role in the Great Acceleration,[18] a novel form of global integration where the region contributed a substantial quantity of raw materials – not limited to agricultural ones – which were processed into industrial products in other parts of the world. The Green Revolution not only carried political implications but was also founded on resecuring a share of the global market that had been lost in the depression of the early 1930s. American support served as a stabilising force in geopolitical relations by enabling access to specific technologies. However, the differing financial capacities of the region's productive actors hindered the full adoption of the technological package.

The adoption of hybrid seeds, particularly for wheat, resulted in a standardisation of production. Although these seeds were available to farmers, the intensive irrigation and machinery that were also part of the Green Revolution could not always be adopted. The failure to implement the complete technological package hindered the increase in productivity in the region. The discourse surrounding the actors driving the change is emblematic of the diversity characterising the modernisation process in the American Southern Cone. In the case of Argentina, it was not the small-scale producers but rather the medium and large-scale ones with the required capital who drove modernisation.

12.6 Change of actors

The process of rural modernisation in the beginning of the second postwar period in Latin America encompassed a diverse array of actors, including peasants, small-scale producers, the global market, credit organisations (both national, regional and international) and private corporations such as the Rockefeller Foundation. The initiatives of the latter institutions introduced top-down technologies, and excluded any involvement of the

18 The Great Acceleration refers to the exponential increase in industrial production that occurred after the Second World War, leading to a significant expansion of international trade to meet urban consumption demands. Its scale was so extensive that it fundamentally transformed the impact of human activity on global ecosystems.

stakeholders, often referred to as 'peasants'. They generally did not incorporate national institutional actors like INTA in Argentina or CNEPA (Centro Nacional de Pesquiza Agrícola) in Brazil, which promoted self-directed processes that aimed at facilitating the engagement of these stakeholders in the programme's formulation stages. These institutions functioned as key intermediaries in adapting American technologies for implementation in the Southern Cone.

In the Argentine case, the Regional Experimentation Consortia (Consorcios Regionales de Experimentación; CREA), formed by middle-class elements of the Pampas rural world, were the actors most actively involved in this modern agriculture, influenced to some extent by the French experience. In the government sector, the American model, particularly the Maize and Wheat Improvement Centre (CIMMYT), which internationalised itself starting in 1963, gained greater prominence.

The dissemination of knowledge and professional training was another ambition of the CREA, but its impact and resources were relatively small when compared to the Rockefeller Foundation's activities on a Latin American scale. In both cases, training was focused on agriculture and soil management to increase productivity in the Great Acceleration. In the case of Argentina, only four scholarships were awarded out of a total of 297 granted by the Foundation in its regional programme, whereas Colombia received fifty-two and Brazil forty.[19]

These training programmes failed to consider regional nuances or the differing economic capabilities of the target producers. They did not differentiate between small-scale rural producers ('chacareros') in Argentina, who operated as tenants, and impoverished peasants in Brazil. Modernisation efforts aimed to enhance productivity often resulted in costs that the actors could not afford. While state aid or assistance from international organisations might offer temporary relief initially, once it was withdrawn, sustaining programmes for hybrid seeds and access to mechanisation might become impossible. Moreover, geopolitics also played a role in how these technologies were implemented. In the Brazilian context, there was apparently no direct competition with American producers, whereas Uruguay, and Argentina in particular, were seen as direct competitors. In Brazil, the contribution of American technicians was deemed crucial, whereas in other countries in the American Southern Cone, the modernisation process had a more pronounced local component in the way it incorporated new techniques and devices.

19 M. Heinz, F. A. P. Korndörfer and C. E. de Brum, 'The Rockefeller Foundation and the Training of Agricultural Specialists for Latin America: A Profile of Scholars from Latin American Scholarship Program in Agriculture (1951–1962)', *Historia Ambiental Latinoamericana Y Caribeña (HALAC) Revista De La Solcha* 12 (2022), 315.

Technologies designed for other contexts and actors often required a series of adaptations to function effectively. The implementation of the state tractor pool initiative in Brazil during the 1950s is a significant case. Between 1950 and 1973, Brazil had two tractors per 1,000 agricultural workers, while Argentina had fifteen, and Uruguay had forty-eight tractors for the same number of workers. In 1953 the Ford Company opened a factory making rural machinery (Fordson) in Brazil, from where they were also exported to Argentina. The tractor pool initiative not only represented a way for capital-deprived producers to utilise expensive technologies but also served as a solution for the state when it subsidised not the purchase of equipment but its usage. A similar approach to these problems can be seen in Argentina where JUNALD, funded the transportation of labour to harvests in marginal regions.

12.7 Epilogue

The modernisation of agriculture in the American Southern Cone involved different starting points. For this reason different implementation strategies had to be devised. In all cases, US influence and the role of the state were central to determining how actors – large, small and medium-sized – accessed technology. A significant role in the global economy before the 1930s crisis did not guarantee successful integration into the Great Acceleration. The Green Revolution was not just a technological package but also a geopolitical project. The standardisation of crops and production processes did not equalise the actors but rather made their differences more noticeable.

The tension between serving the domestic market and foreign exports took on a new importance in the American Southern Cone after the Second World War. Agriculture not only had to feed the urban population but also needed to generate foreign currency to support policies of ISI. Hybrid seeds, which were more productive and resilient, were the first component of a technological package that it was not always possible to adopt in its entirety. Even countries with extensive mechanisation underpinning their agriculture did not achieve integration with their industrial sectors, nor did they develop forms of organisation that connected with global financial capital. In Brazil, which did not compete with American production, its agriculture was modernised in ways that provided a way to meet domestic demand for both food and raw materials for industry. The state played a key role in Brazil, the integration of industry and agriculture here was not part of a tension-filled process as it was in Argentina. In Argentina, a large proportion of the tractor supply was directly imported from the United States. Even those manufactured domestically contained a large proportion of imported components. The state played an important role by transferring foreign currency from agriculture to industry, but also through protectionist policies that made rural machinery imports difficult. In the case of Uruguay, the solution to these issues included the adoption of practices developed in other countries that were designed for a very different scale. The creation of its Agricultural Technology Institute in 1989 also helped bring about Uruguay's late modernisation.

Despite the local experiences and different strategies involved, the paths leading to agricultural modernisation would eventually converge until, by the end of the twentieth century, corporate agribusiness had become the dominant production model. Hybrid seeds were eventually replaced by genetically modified organisms (GMOs). More technologically advanced rural machinery allowed for precision agriculture with geo-referencing and more efficient soil management practices, such as no-till farming. With the general adoption of this (American) technology, the different routes taken by the countries of the American cone to modernisation were effaced and became one.

13

'Taking risks to create value': agricultural modernisation and the making of 'Progressive' Indian farmers, 1947–1967

Madhumita Saha

In the summer of 1966, very few believed a technological revolution could happen in Indian agriculture. This was the moment when devastating drought in the states of Bihar and eastern Uttar Pradesh led to the worst crop failure in the history of those places. Droughts imperilled the Indian state, leading to a situation that anthropologist Akhil Gupta described as a 'crisis of sovereignty'.[1] While the international agencies struggled to send aid to tide over the crisis, Dr Prem Lai Gautam, who was then heading the Department of Agronomy at the Indian Agricultural Research Institute (IARI), announced a 'new development' in Indian agriculture at the annual meeting of the Indian Agronomy Society in Udaipur. Roughly 650 km away from Udaipur, on the experimental fields of IARI at New Delhi, scientists were testing the first batches of high-yielding variety (HYV) seeds like Sonora 63, Sonora 64 and Lerma Rojo 64A. As an agronomist, it was clear to Dr Gautam that 'we now had a wheat which, in the hands of a farmer following good husbandry, could give double the yield and four times the profit'. With a '200 per cent to 400 per cent increase in crop intensity' appearing to be a real possibility, Dr Gautam was confident that 'a major breakthrough' has been achieved in agricultural sciences. It would be a further year before the USAID official William Gaud would christen the 'major breakthrough' in cereal yields as the Green Revolution.[2]

1 Akhil Gupta, *Postcolonial Developments: Agriculture in the Making of Modern India* (Durham, NC: Duke University Press, 1998).

2 M. S. Swaminathan (ed.), *Wheat Revolution: A Dialogue* (New Delhi: Macmillan, 1993), 5. For Gaud's coinage, William S. Gaud, 'The Green Revolution:

However, Dr Gautam's promise of 'Double yield; fourfold profit' would not be easily realisable for many farmers. Even when the yield rose, the very high cost of buying the biochemical and mechanical components of the technological package meant that the prospect of profit out of the reach of many farmers. The celebrations over achieving food self-sufficiency could not obscure the new challenges that the Green Revolution brought to Indian agriculture. By the 1980s, the high cost of production, falling crop prices and increasing indebtedness ignited large-scale peasant movements in India.[3] After introducing the new seeds, it did not take technocrats long to realise that the 'risks and uncertainty' involved in HYV cultivation were a disincentive to peasants, particularly, small farmers with limited means.[4] Environmental uncertainties and market risks bedraggled any neat planning of agricultural development: rainfall failure shrivelled crops, pest attacks impaired productivity, disease destroyed plants over vast swaths of land, and the high expenses incurred in buying the inputs often didn't give a remunerative return because of the low price at which the grain was sold.[5] These factors made the peasants doubt whether they would recover their investment in buying new farming technologies: the potential risk factors involving the market and the environment deterred expensive technological adoption.

Alongside works that studied the factors guiding users' responses to technological innovations, substantial research exists on the government initiatives for promoting the adoption of new technologies.[6] In the case

Accomplishments and Apprehensions', paper to the Society for International Development, Washington, DC, 8 March 1968, www.agbioworld.org/biotech-info/topics/borlaug/borlaug-green.html (accessed 30 March 2025).

3 Social scientists have studied the history and politics of the peasant movements that broke out in states such as Uttar Pradesh, Karnataka and Maharashtra. See Tom Brass (ed.), *New Farmers' Movements in India* (New Delhi: Routledge, 1995); and Ashutosh Varshney, *Democracy, Development, and the Countryside: Urban-Rural Struggles in India* (Cambridge: Cambridge University Press, 1998).

4 Sumit Roy, *Agriculture and Technology in Developing Countries* (New Delhi: Sage Publications, 1990), 143; Francine Frankel, *India's Green Revolution: Economic Gains and Political Costs* (Princeton, NJ: Princeton University Press, 1971); Andrew Pearse, *Seeds of Plenty, Seeds of Want: Social and Economic Implications of the Green Revolution* (New York: Oxford University Press, 1980).

5 Paucity of rain especially impacted small and marginal farmers who lacked resources for countering inadequate levels of rainfall through artificial irrigation. Similarly, the option of fighting pests and diseases through use of pesticides was financially straining for them. Moreover, farmers had to have access to reliable information for the proper doses of pesticides. In absence of rigorous extension services, farmers could not easily access this information.

6 R. S. Cowan, 'The Consumption Junction: A Proposal for Research Strategies in the Sociology of Technology', in *The Social Construction of Technological Systems*, W. E. Bijker, T. P. Hughes and T. J. Pinch (eds) (Cambridge, MA: MIT Press, 1987), 261–80; Josh Lauer, 'Visualizing Black Telephone Users:

of the Green Revolution technological package, for instance, scholars have looked into how the Indian government focused on motivating farmers to choose dwarf/semi-dwarf seed varieties for cultivation.[7] Such studies look into economic measures, such as price support, high procurement prices and the state subsidies given to farmers over the years. These analyses are crucial for comprehending the developmental history of the country and the political and social impacts that they left on villages.

Technocrats endorsed these economic strategies, arguing that the technological revolution would not materialise without conducive infrastructure or fiscal policy measures. This is not to claim that the policymakers were unequivocal in supporting these measures. Francine Frankel and Ashutosh Varshney recorded sharp differences of opinion between the planners and members of the agriculture ministry on various aspects of India's agricultural policy. However, despite, the grave allegations of 'inequality' labelled at these measures, these helped maintain the tempo of agricultural reforms until the mid-1970s.[8]

Along with planned economic measures to incentivise farmers and inspire them to use new technologies, the state focused on augmenting crop production by making food producers receptive to the latest technologies – an openness to change that the developmental state saw as a mark of the 'modern' farmer. After independence, the development regime insisted that without modernising the farmers' way of thinking, it would not be possible to modernise the agricultural sector because, arguably, one of the principal causes of India's underdevelopment was the latter's backward mentality.[9] In both cases of the land and the tillers, techno-

Technological Whiteness and Racial Exclusion in Bell System Advertising', *Technology and Culture* 65 (2024), 899–931; Ronald Kline and Trevor Pinch, 'Users as Agents of Technological Change: The Social Construction of the Automobile in the Rural United States', *Technology and Culture* 37 (1996), 763–95; Christane Berth, 'Interrupted Conversations: Gender and Telephone Use in Mexico, 1930s–70s', *Technology and Culture* 64 (2023), 124–48.

7 Varshney, *Democracy, Development, and the Countryside; Frankel, India's Green Revolution*; Pearse, *Seeds of Plenty; Science, Politics, and the Agricultural Revolution in Asia*, Robert S. Anderson, Paul R. Brass, Edwin Levy and Barrie M. Morrison (eds), AAAS Selected Symposium 70 (Boulder, CO: Westview Press, 1982); Tim P. Bayliss-Smith and Sudhir Wanmali, *Understanding Green Revolutions: Agrarian Change and Development Planning in South Asia* (Cambridge: Cambridge University Press, 1984); *The Green Revolution Revisited*, Bernhard Glaeser (ed.) (London: Allen & Unwin, 1987); Surinder S. Jodhka, *The Indian Village: Rural Lives in the 21st Century* (New Delhi: Aleph Book Company, 2023).

8 Varshney, *Democracy, Development, and the Countryside*; Francine Frankel, *India's Political Economy, 1947–2004: The Gradual Revolution* (India: Oxford University Press, 2005).

9 Accusing Indian farmers of laziness and a reluctance to innovate dates back to colonial times. There was a strong entrenched belief in all supporters of

scientific knowledge became a tool in the hands of the regime to increase the productivity of the soil and modernising people cultivating it.

It is not uncommon to find instances in Indian history where the colonial state, missionaries and even individuals, set out to reform the mentality of cultivators to advance their moral and economic agenda. At different historical junctures, farming practices were associated with either personal virtues like 'toil', 'sacrifice' and 'risk-taking', or linked to goals of national development and ideas of progress.[10] The emphasis on 'revolutionising' the mentality of farmers was never more important than during the Green Revolution. When Norman Borlaug, the 'Father of the Green Revolution', wrote to J. A. Pelissier, the Head of the Product Research Division of the ESSO Research and Engineering Company, that he and his researchers were on the verge of 'trigger[ing]' a 'real revolution' in wheat production, he meant accomplishing more than raising the crop yield; he believed that the Mexican seeds would introduce 'dynamic new methods in one stroke … [and] kill old ideas and methods', transforming farmers into productive modern citizens of a developed nation.[11]

Within the political context of the Cold War in Asia, the US considered it politically prudent to stand by the peasants of the recently decolonised countries lest they fell for the lure of communism. The capitalist bloc in general feared that communist propaganda would prey on the economically vulnerable peasants of the East and, thus, one of the key objectives of the American rural development programme in India included transforming farmers into an asset for the capitalist world. Becoming an asset implied that Indian tillers would cultivate 'efficiently and abundantly' like American farmers by adopting into use the latest technological innovations that the First World nations like the US transferred to India for widescale dissemination.[12]

---

agrarian improvement that Indian villages and villagers were unchanging and unwelcoming of change. For a discussion of the allegedly unchanging nature of Indian villages see Ronald Inden, 'Orientalist Constructions of India', *Modern Asian Studies* 20 (1986), 401–46; Ronald Inden, *Imagining India* (Oxford: Basil Blackwell, 1990), particularly chs 3 and 4; Jodhka, *Indian Village*. On the alleged physical laziness of Indian labourers see Jayeeta Sharma, '"Lazy" Natives, Coolie Labour, and the Assam Tea Industry', *Modern Asian Studies* 43 (2009), 1287–324.

10 For a classic account, see Anand Pandian, *Crooked Stalks: Cultivating Virtue in South India* (Durham, NC: Duke University Press, 2009); also Neeladri Bhattacharya, *The Great Agrarian Conquest: The Colonial Reshaping of a Rural World* (New Delhi: Permanent Black, 2018).

11 Iowa State University (hereafter ISU), Special Collections, Norman Borlaug Papers, box 5, folder 20, Borlaug to J. A. Pelissier, 26 July 1965.

12 Nick Cullather, *The Hungry World: America's Cold War Battle against Poverty in Asia* (Cambridge, MA: Harvard University Press, 2013); David C. Engerman, *The Price of Aid: The Economic Cold War in India* (Cambridge, MA: Harvard University Press, 2018), 22–37.

This chapter will unpack the developmental narrative of the Green Revolution period, when technocrats scripted ways of improving cultivators' conditions by attempting to change their mentality and giving new directions to their farming practices. The state considered the making of 'progressive farmers' – requiring cultivators to embrace a new set of values – as indispensable for the wide dissemination of the new technology. The most coveted value required of a farmer was his openness to the latest developments in agricultural technologies. Development experts advocated receptivity to technological modernisation to the extent of urging farmers to take 'risks'. A risk-taking farmer was the ideal, and even a risk-neutral farmer, who was not entirely averse to taking risks, fitted the requirements of a development-orientated regime. This chapter analyses the concept of a progressive farmer that evolved in conjunction with efforts to turn Indian farming into a capital-intensive activity and that shared close ties with the developmental goals of the Indian state.

Mainstream developmental narratives noted no contradictions between the cultivators' psychological and material growth on the one hand, and the economic aspirations of the state on the other. The state's developmental path included the following milestones: modernisation of the countryside, growing the required amount of food for national self-sufficiency, and producing cheap food for the country's growing industrial labour force. By keeping the food prices low, the government wanted to ensure that workers, who were moderately paid, could afford their daily meals.[13] Farmers, as the citizen-cultivators, were expected to embrace and contribute to the state's planned objectives. A farmer must not aim to produce for mere subsistence; the goal was to grow more and, thereby, contribute to India's war against hunger and underdevelopment. The agendas could only be realised when farmers adopted productive technologies and moved beyond their subsistence-driven existence. By doing so, it was claimed that the farmer would also attain prosperity for himself.

The first half of the chapter discusses the aspersions of backwardness that the colonial state and the middle-class nationalists cast on the peasants. In their dealing with the rural population, educated Indians and the colonial machinery exhibited a curious combination of racism and paternalistic imperialism. The chapter brings out the fragmented nature of Indian nationalism itself, exposing the middle-class mentality of seeing itself as the enlightened custodian of its less privileged countrymen.[14] The Indian modernisers perceived farmers as 'lazy' and 'backward', ignoring the challenges colonialism posed to Indian agriculturalists.

13 Sukhamoy Chakravarty, *Development Planning: The Indian Experience* (Oxford: Clarendon Press, 1987), 21–2.

14 This was very similar to how the 'white' men saw themselves as harbingers of improvement.

Heavy taxation, lack of infrastructure and inadequate credit facilities held back the peasants while the lack of extension services led to a failure to disseminate techno-scientific knowledge from the laboratories to the fields.

The second part of the chapter explores the development discourse of the Green Revolution that charged farmers with the responsibility for increased production, making the achievement of state's developmental goal their personal ambition. Whether the state's developmental goals and expectations of the farmers matched the social context of farming is the question that drives the third and remaining part of the chapter. The historical explorations undertaken by the paper across the Green-Revolution divide show how a farmer's choice of technology was deeply influenced by the social context of farming that included material concerns but was not solely driven by the quest for commercial profit. This did not imply that farmers, who did not readily adopt the new technology, were against farming for the markets, as had been so often assumed by proponents of improvement/development. Even farmers who produced global market crops, the anthropologist Tania Murray Li has argued, only did so when conditions were amenable and provided farmers with opportunity and security.[15]

In exploring the social context(s) of farming, this chapter investigates what it meant for the tillers to have 'opportunity' and 'security' regarding economic and environmental factors. Generally, farmers were discerning about environmental risks before opting for something new because rain and pests, diseases and soil health impacted on their income and therefore prosperity, often irreversibly. Here we argue that modernisers largely missed these agroecological variations; the key principle of the technological efforts of the Green Revolution was attaining a 'wide adaptability' that discounted agroecological variabilities.[16] Technocrats repeatedly underlined the material benefits of growing the new seeds with heavy applications of fertilisers and pesticides, while playing down the potential environmental risks that the farmers faced. The farmers' cautious response towards HYV seeds did not stem from their awareness of the environmental harms posed by energy-intensive farming, as little was done at the official level to inform them about the damage intensive farming might cause the environment. Rather farmers were concerned about the environmental consequences if they shifted from traditional,

15 Tania Murray Li argued that whether farmers would 'enthusiastically' participate in the production of global market crops – a sure sign of capitalist farming – depended on several 'conditions', which she identifies as desire, opportunity and security. 'Dynamic Farmers, Dead Plantations, and the Myth of the Lazy Native', *J. Peasant Studies* 50 (2023), 519–38.

16 Marci R. Baranski, *The Globalization of Wheat: A Critical History of the Green Revolution* (Pittsburgh, PA: University of Pittsburgh Press, 2022).

well-known and long-tested ways of crop cultivation. The development experts argued that farmers suffered from anxiety of incurring losses, and it was that fear that kept them from embracing the Green Revolution technological package. Despite their optimistic stance, experts knew that threats from pests, diseases and drought were real, but as they did not have the necessary remedies at their disposal, the only way left for the experts was to urge the farmers to accept an element of risk.

13.1 The 'mentality' of peasants and the realities of farming

The belief that the 'mentality' of Indian farmers was not conducive to the productivity-orientated practices of modern agriculture was as old as colonialism itself. The colonial rulers created in Bengal a class of 'zamindars' (landlords) and introduced a 'Rule of Property' through the Permanent Settlement Act of 1793 so that these landowners, created in the image of their British counterparts, would assist the colonial rulers in the expansion of Indian agriculture.[17] However, as agricultural prosperity remained elusive, the British Raj shifted the blame onto the Indian peasants, accusing them of being the embodiment of the Oriental attributes of 'laziness' and 'otherworldliness', which made them ill-equipped for agricultural entrepreneurship.[18] There were a few exceptional British experts, such as the scientists Augustus Voelcker (1854–1937) and Albert Howard (1873–1947), who tried to understand the challenges of farming in India and who valued collective farming knowledge, but largely the colonial interpretation of the Indian rural life smacked of racism.[19]

Indian nationalists, who vehemently criticised the British Raj for its lack of agricultural improvements, also showed little faith in the ability or willingness of their countrymen when it came to the cause of agricultural growth. Along with their criticism of the colonial rent policy, which they argued had stifled all entrepreneurship among peasant cultivators, the Indian middle-class liberal intelligentsia considered it largely their duty to take the lead in rural development matters. A classic example in this matter was Rabindranath Tagore (1861–1941), a world-renowned

17 Ranajit Guha, *A Rule of Property for Bengal: An Essay on the Idea of Permanent Settlement*, 2nd edn (New Delhi: Orient Longman, 1982).

18 In the colonial period the notion of farmer incapacity was entrenched in the 'myth of the lazy native'. Syed Hussein Alatas analysed it as a profoundly racialised ideological formation: *The Myth of the Lazy Native: A Study of the Image of the Maylays, Filipinos and Javanese from the 16th to the 20th century and its Function in the Ideology of Colonial Capitalism* (London: F. Cass, 1977).

19 Augustus Voelcker, *Report on the Improvement of Indian Agriculture* (India: Office of the Superintendent of Government Printing, 1897); Sir Albert Howard, *The Soil and Health: A Study of Organic Agriculture* (Indore: Banyan Tree, 2013 [1947]).

poet-novelist-songwriter, who was also an entrepreneur and owned considerable land. This gave him a unique connection with rural Bengal, whose beauty he adored and constantly wrote about, but he found the poverty and backwardness of rural India demeaning and dehumanising. He wrote relentlessly about the sad condition of Indian villages and ways to improve them.[20] First in Patisar in eastern Bengal and then in Sriniketan in western Bengal, Tagore's rural cooperative programmes were an example of 'eminent public intellectuals engaged in the culture of supporting experimental farms to advance the knowledge of modern science and technology to the cultivating classes of Bengal'.[21] As more and more Bengali youth returned from abroad, trained in agricultural science, intellectuals like Tagore, who took an interest in improving the standard of rural life became increasingly common. Members of the liberal intelligentsia came to see it as the role of the educated and wealthy to participate in agricultural improvement.[22] However, as far as the possibility of modernising agriculture with the help of the peasantry was concerned, contemporary Bengalee periodicals dismissed the 'traditional chasha' as 'foolish, illiterate, unable to count, and dependent on others in every way'.[23] This dismissive approach towards peasants was not unique to colonial India but was also applied to cultivators in other Asian countries during the 1950s. After the British, it was the Americans who furnished stereotypical portrayals of peasants from the global south as mired in poverty and debilitated by apathy and inefficiency.[24]

In the mid-twentieth century, many of the national and transnational development initiatives embraced these stereotypical portrayals of the peasants. The development experts came to believe in the transforming power of science and technology, allowing the peasants to have a more economically rewarding life. The accusations of physical laziness became accusations of peasants being mentally lazy – a trait that needed curing if a newly independent country wanted to launch into an age of economic prosperity.[25] Scholars have noted a serious disjuncture

20 Rabindranath Tagore, 'Swadeshi Samaj', in *Rabindra Rachanabali Centenary*, XII (Kolkata: Government of West Bengal, 1989), 683–702.

21 Arnab Roy, *Contextualising Modern Science*, 50.

22 Arnab Roy, 'Agriculture and the "Literati" in Colonial Bengal, 1870 to 1940', *Review of Agrarian Studies* 6 (2016), 80–97.

23 'Development of Indian Agriculture', *Krishitatva* 6/11 (1884), 206.

24 Examples of such portrayals of Asian peasants can be found in USDA, Office of Foreign Agricultural Relations, Washington DC, Stanley Andrews Papers, 6. Box 3, International Round-up: Summary of Remarks by Stanley Andrews, 22 August 1950; Government Service File 1950, Speech File. Production Credit Associations, St Louis, Missouri.

25 For a detailed discussion of the 'myth' of physical laziness as propounded by the colonial plantation economy to subject tea garden workers, see, Sharma, '"Lazy" Natives, Coolie Labour, and the Assam Tea Industry', 1291–4.

between the modernising intent of the state and the peasants' preferred ways of farming. James Scott explained cultivators' behaviour in the nineteenth century in south-east Asia in terms of 'subsistence ethics'. He showed how the cultivators there, living – as their counterparts did elsewhere – close to the subsistence margin and subject to the vagaries of weather and the claims of outsiders, were left with 'little scope for the profit maximisation calculus of traditional neoclassical economics'.[26] In the so-called first-world states, similar contradictions between farmers and technocratic regimes are known to have occurred. In the early twentieth-century United States, farmers resisted standardised farming practices, an essential feature of the modernisation process, as it was done with little consideration of the social, economic as well as agroecological context of farming.[27] However, farmers' response to a newly introduced technology cannot simply be framed in binaries of acceptance and refusal. Rather, the objective should be to find out the material factors that shaped the responses of a peasant cultivator towards an innovative farming technology.[28] For instance, the anthropologist Akhil Gupta discussed how farmers of a village in north-west India ('Alipur') started using chemical fertilisers in high doses while cultivating HYV seeds despite their reservations about the chemicals. That artificial fertiliser made the soil 'weak and deficient' and 'diminished' the taste of crops were common complaints from farmers in the area. Yet they took to the new seeds and the associated technological inputs because 'the output is better and the prices are good'.[29]

Obtaining 'good prices' for 'higher outputs' was a crucial consideration that inspired a cultivator to produce beyond his subsistence needs. But neither higher outputs nor good prices came at the cost of consistency. If the 'risk' element had a higher cost than the pecuniary potential of a technology, the likelihood was that farmers would be reluctant to adopt it. The greatest challenge to the technocrats involved

26 James Scott, *The Moral Economy of the Peasant: Rebellion and Subsistence in Southeast Asia* (Hartford, CT: Yale University Press, 1976), 3.

27 Deborah Fitzgerald, 'Accounting for Change: Farmers and the Modernizing State', in *The Countryside in the Age of the Modern State*, Catherine McNicol Stock and Robert D. Johnston (eds) (Ithaca, NY: Cornell University Press, 2001), 192.

28 Tania M. Li has argued that with the growth of peasant studies as a field of research, Scott's concept of a 'static peasantry' governed by a distinct 'moral economy' orientated towards subsistence has been subjected to significant critiques. She argued that instead of imagining peasants as a 'static' entity who preferred 'natural economy' over 'market economy', the goal should be to understand how cultivators responded to new circumstances in 'dynamic' ways. Li, 'Dynamic Farmers, Dead Plantations, and the Myth of the Lazy Native', 1–3.

29 Gupta, *Postcolonial Developments*, 2 3.

with the Green Revolution project was popularising the seeds among the farmers as the HYV seeds came with several risk scenarios. These were not figments of the imagination of a subsistence-driven peasantry for they were substantiated by the observations of scientists closely involved with the technological project.

Closely braided with HYV's promises of high yields was the threat of losses from disease and pest attacks. It became a matter of great concern when cultivators discovered to their dismay that a large number of dwarf wheat varieties, such as Kalyansona, PV 18 and Sonalika, though highly resistant to rusts under field conditions at the time of their release, proved to be susceptible to a new strain of the rust pathogen. With little or no infrastructure to fight widespread pest or disease incidence, many were alarmed that such attacks carried the risk of spiralling out of control and causing widespread crop loss. In 1966 a deeply anguished A. H. Moseman, the Assistant Administrator for Technical Cooperation and Research, observed that although important people in the Indian administration, such as the Agricultural Secretary B. Sivaraman, might think that availability of the Taiwan rice and Mexican wheat varieties had largely resolved India's food problems, the country was facing a potentially 'unhealthy situation' caused by practising large-scale 'one variety' agriculture.[30]

Threats from pests and rust constituted significant risks for farmers. Agricultural scientists learnt over the years that farmers would reject even a potentially HYV if susceptible to such attacks. The scientist S. Gandhi became aware of the Mexican wheat in the crop season of 1963–4.[31] He found the plants' stature impressive, with EA-222-1 being 'exceptional' with its tillering and 'good heads'. As a 'triple dwarf', EA-222-1 was the ideal wheat for the Green Revolution scientists who saw it as a 'progression' from the two-gene type. Being 'shorter and stiffer', it had greater immunity to lodging and could take in more fertilisers than the two-gene type.[32] The belief among scientists that they could overcome the 'yield plateau' of previous varieties with EA-222-1, however, could not be realised. When the new variety was distributed among farmers in the winter of 1968–9, there was unexpected heavy rain in February, leaving the entire crop of that season badly affected by rust. As a sombre

30 ISU, Special Collections, Norman Borlaug Papers, Box 5/34, A. H. Moseman to Borlaug, 29 September 1966.

31 The scientist S. Gandhi had been associated with wheat research for three decades, working in all the pioneering wheat-growing states and with some 'very eminent leaders in the field of wheat research' including Chaudhuri Ramdhan Singh in Punjab, Mr Bhatnagar in Rajasthan, Dr Ekbote in Madhya Pradesh and Dr T. R. Mehta in UP. These scientists produced excellent wheat varieties, such as Jaipur local and C.591. These varieties combined quality, yield, early maturity and wide adaptability.

32 Scientific Report of IARI, Division of Genetics (New Delhi: IARI, 1968), 58.

Dr Gandhi reflected, the 'rust disaster' of 1968–9 pushed the triple dwarfs into the background.[33]

Water was a prime requirement for the successful cultivation of HYV seeds. High fertiliser application tripled the water requirements of the new seeds, without which the plants withered. More importantly, the new technological regime required water to be distributed on a mammoth scale and at the right moments. In 1965–6, only 20.9 per cent of the cultivated area of India was irrigated, and thus the introduction of the new technology was limited to those areas with adequate surface irrigation.[34] C. Subramaniam, who oversaw the introduction of Green Revolution technology as the Union Food and Agricultural Minister, admitted: 'we selected the irrigated areas and particularly Punjab [of which Haryana was then a part] and western Utter Pradesh'.[35] The scientist J. P. Tandon, who played a pioneering role in the introduction of the new seeds, observed years later that the availability of water had become one of the 'biggest constraints' because 60–70 per cent of the new varieties of wheat were sown in December at a time of very little precipitation. Tandon pointed out in no uncertain terms that even lands classified as 'irrigated' were 'getting less than 50 per cent of the required amount of irrigation'.[36]

Scheduling of water was critical for HYV crops – a condition that the farmers found hard to meet. Even for Uttar Pradesh – located at the heart of Gangetic doab – where the Green Revolution technological package was introduced in its first phase, scientists observed that 'synchronising the release of water for irrigation has been practically impossible'. Agricultural scientists complained of the great difficulty in bringing about any systemic changes in water management.[37] Scientists' reflections and observations make it clear that the Green Revolution seeds came with several challenges that could not be instantaneously resolved. For farmers with limited means or cultivators of semi-arid and arid regions, these challenges further threatened their subsistence base, making the new technology too risky to adopt.

The Green Revolution technology required farmers to invest more. Farmers without the means to buy fertilisers and pesticides and with limited access to irrigation had little chance of succeeding with the new seeds. Even with all these inputs in place, there was always the

33 *Wheat Revolution*, Swaminathan (ed.), 15–17.

34 Government of India, Ministry of Agriculture and Farmers Welfare, Department of Agriculture, Cooperation and Farmers Welfare, Directorate of Economics and Statistics, *Agricultural Statistics at a Glance 2016* (Government of India, Controller of Publication, 2017), 83.

35 *Wheat Revolution*, Swaminathan (ed.), 84.

36 Ibid., 85.

37 Ibid., 51–2.

danger of crop losses from diseases and pest attacks. However, with the new technological turn in Indian agriculture and the capitalist ethics slowly sinking its roots in the foodcrop sector, a risk-taking attitude was encouraged among farmers. The advocates of the Green Revolution believed that innovations would be widely disseminated if only farmers were willing to take risks with the new technology. Just as the moral precepts of toil became crucial for the British colonial regime to motivate the Kallar farming community in south India to accept agricultural reforms, similarly, the principle of risk-taking was evoked to persuade farmers into sowing the new seeds even when technocrats knew their use came with unresolved challenges.[38]

13.2 Risks, profits and service to the nation

With the introduction of the Green Revolution technological package in the second half of the 1960s, various agricultural economists collaborated with practitioners of other branches of agricultural science to develop a new framework of persuasion based on economic profitability. Agricultural economists in India were part of a transnational 'rationalising elite' who worked to convince cultivators of the economic benefits of the new technology. The economists undertook a series of studies examining heavy applications of fertiliser. The goal of these studies, Deborah Fitzgerald observed, was to marshal evidence that would persuade ordinary farmers 'to change the way they did things'.[39] P. N. Saxena, an agricultural economist working with IARI, made a comparison between the traditional and the Mexican varieties and concluded that Indian farmers would achieve the highest return by cultivating the Mexican variety, S-227, which would return Rs 6 for every rupee invested.[40] Experiments revealed that farmers cultivating traditional varieties would be making on average Rs 600–700 less per hectare. The nature of the experiments indicates that the agricultural economists were primarily motivated by the idea of bringing quantitative insights to bear on agricultural questions to overcome the 'romantic and impractical ideas' of existing farm practices.[41] The experts argued that the deliverance of the country and its people from hunger and poverty lay in discarding the ways of subsistence agriculture and in working for high yields and high economic returns.

38 Anand Pandian, *Crooked Stalks: Cultivating Virtue in South India* (Durham, NC: Duke University Press, 2009), 141–71.

39 Fitzgerald, 'Accounting for Change', 192.

40 P. N. Saxena, 'Fertilizer Needs of Mexican Wheats', *Indian Farming*, August 1967, 40–2.

41 Fitzgerald, 'Accounting for Change', 194.

Throughout this period, the print media widely reported instances of farmers securing unprecedented yields of crops. Scientists, such as Dr M. S. Swaminathan, repeatedly referred to these achievements to demonstrate what the new technology could do to transform the productivity of Indian farms. To win the war against hunger, experts urged, farmers needed to become heroes by adopting the improved varieties and by producing more in their fields. Such a farming hero was Kanwar Mohinderpal Singh. A farmer from the Delhi region, Singh became a familiar name to many. His claim to fame rested in the fact that he harvested nearly 8.4 tons of crops per hectare – the highest yield ever recorded anywhere in the world in 1967 for a crop of 150 days' duration. Eager to project Singh's achievement as an instance worthy of emulation by other farmers, Swaminathan, then Director of IARI and Dr S. P. Kohli, the Coordinator of the All India Coordinated Trial, often referred to him in their writings. Mohinderpal Singh came to represent all those 'progressive' farmers who adopted the high-yielding varieties to improve their financial position.[42] The vision of a hunger-free India came to revolve around these progressive farmers who, development experts believed, by discarding traditional ways of farming, showed the way to overcome backwardness. Equating progressivism with the adoption of new technology, however, amounted to reducing the whole reality of a person's life to a single feature or trait.[43]

The prevalent discourses on hunger did not analyse local situations to understand what kept some farmers from adopting dwarf seeds. Escobar observed in his critique of development that these accounts concentrated on providing an expert's view of the subject rather than dwelling on the peasants' perspective. 'One never finds … consideration given to peasants' struggle and oppression, nor accounts of how the peasants' world may contain a different way of seeing problems and life.'[44] Risk-averse farmers were as much a problem as malnourished ones were, and often the two categories coincided. The only solution was to fix them through effective development.

The agenda of effective development involved characterising farmers as either risk taking or risk averse. It involved fragmenting their

42 The commendation given to exemplary farmers continued until recent times as may be seen in the compilation published by National Institute of Agricultural Extension Management of farmers who stood out from the general milieu in terms of education, commitment to the war against hunger, in openness to receive technical guidance, in the rapport they enjoyed with members of the scientific establishment. *Inspiring Stories from Innovative Farmers*, B. K. Muttanna, Lakshmi Murthy and Saravanan Raj (eds) (Hyderabad: MANAGE, 2018).

43 Arturo Escobar, *Encountering Development: The Making and Unmaking of the Third World* (Princeton, NJ: Princeton University Press, 1995), 110.

44 Ibid., 111.

experiences and labelling farmers on a single criterion. Whether farmers were willing to take 'risks' or at least approach the question of investing in new technology with a measure of neutrality (not outright rejection) became an important topic of discussion during the Green Revolution. A 'risk-neutral' farmer might be won over for capitalist development in agriculture in the future. Even if such a farmer would not be an early adopter of the new technology, once convinced through demonstrations and reports of the experience of others of the profitability of new ways of farming, he might be sufficiently persuaded to agree to try it. In contrast, a 'risk averse' farmer would be unwilling to invest if there was any danger of making a loss; his preference was to forego higher returns if it meant increasing the risk to his income. As instilling higher production through investment in new technologies was slowly gaining ground among agricultural scientists and economists, the 'risk-neutral' farmer became increasingly important in the thinking of the advocates of technological progress.

This essentialising of the farmers' approach to the new technologies and definition of their identity according to their attitude helps explain the importance that scientists accorded to farmers like Kunwar Mahinderpal. He, and others like him, who successfully invested in dwarf seeds and chemical fertilisers, became a representative example of a 'risk-taking' farmer.[45] More than anything else, the labelling depended on a farmer's response to new technology; his identity was determined by his role as a user of the latest technology. The agricultural growth strategies did not consider the interests, needs and concerns of the farmers who chose not to (or were unable) to adopt the new technological package.

Economists such as Sudhir Sen, who saw the promises of a 'richer' harvest as opening up new horizons for developing countries, urged farmers as well as the government to take risks and dispense with the much longer process of trials and experiments conducted under local conditions to discover which diseases the new varieties might be susceptible. He considered it 'perfectly sensible' to 'trade-off-traditional safety' for India and, especially, urged its farmers to do everything to win the 'fateful race between population growth and economic development'.[46] Sudhir Sen's point of view is a typical example of how

45 In a study conducted towards the later years of the 1970s, agricultural economists strongly argued that to encourage greater investment in agriculture, there should be an effective crop insurance system, which would enable farmers to shift the risks to the insurance system as a whole rather than bearing the brunt of them on their own shoulders. Hans. P. Binswanger, 'Risk Attitudes of Rural Households in Semi-Arid Tropical India', *Economic and Political Weekly* 13/25 (24 June 1978), A49–A62.

46 Sudhir Sen, *A Richer Harvest: New Horizons for Developing Countries* (India: Tata McGraw-Hill, 1974), 72.

experts' strategies to secure high yields were remote from the realities of farmers' lives in India.

In the case of cultivating dwarf varieties, a farmer's susceptibility to losing crops to pest attacks was an undeniable reality, especially if he lacked the means to purchase those chemical pesticides on which the crop protection measures of the new seeds were primarily dependent. Considering the difficulties of breeding pest-resistant varieties, the Ford Foundation-sponsored review team of 1971 endorsed the extensive use of pesticides. In practice, however, farmers' use of pesticides remained far from adequate. By March 1974, the annual consumption was only 45,000 tonnes.[47] Moreover, the non-availability of dusting and spraying equipment also discouraged the use of pesticides. Although local administrative officials frequently made arrangements to keep some equipment in their offices for loan to farmers, there were complaints that there was too little of it, that its breakdown rate was high, and that users did not return it on time.[48] In distinguishing the entrepreneurs from others who allegedly displayed a lack of confidence in the 'seeds of plenty', experts discounted the material factors, including infrastructure shortcomings, that guided a farmer's decision.

13.3 Conclusion

It was not farmers who called for the Green Revolution technological package to be introduced in India, it was the Agriculture and Food Ministry and influential members of the Indian Council of Agricultural Research who took the initiative to introduce the Mexican HYV seeds. The Indian state promoted the introduction of the technological package as a response to the challenges it faced of recurrent famines and episodes of food scarcity. For the technological package to succeed in India, it was necessary for farmers to become willing users of the technology. For resourceful farmers, who possessed fertile land and operated in regions with good infrastructure, the new seeds brought to them the 'promise of plenty'. The technocratic regime ignored the contexts required for the new varieties to achieve their full potential. Rather they normalised successful farming experiences to push others towards them. The state introduced economic measures and built infrastructure to encourage the adoption of the technology and, along with these measures, urged

47 In a sample taken from West Godavari, Andhra Pradesh, only 30 per cent of the total stock of fungicides and insecticides had been sold, and in another sample from Tikamgarh, Madhya Pradesh, only 20 per cent. Biplab Dasgupta, *Agrarian Change and the New Technology in India* (Switzerland: United Nations Research Institute for Social Development, 1977), 67.

48 AERC, *A Study of the High-Yielding Varieties Programme, Rabi 1968–69* (Waltair, December 1969).

farmers to take risks in the name of national growth. Any sign of unwillingness or scepticism towards the new technologies was branded as a sign of backwardness. Though the supporters of the Green Revolution found it persuasive to see farmers' responses in terms of binaries, historical analysis sheds light on the complex web that constituted a farmer's world; a tiller's relationship with technology was embedded within this network and could not possibly exist outside it.

In exploring the relationship between the technocrats and the tillers, this chapter has shed light on the gap between expert strategies and the intricate fabric of farmers' lives. The challenges farmers faced in adopting the new technologies were often overlooked in the mainstream discourse on development. A farmer's decision to grow (or not) a particular variety was contingent on factors such as disease susceptibility and water requirements of the HYV seeds, their susceptibility to pest attacks and the high cost of farming. Economic and ecological variabilities were ignored, with peasants being encouraged to grow the crops irrespective of challenges. Just as the colonial government used the 'myth of lazy peasants' to serve their economic goals, the national government utilised the myth of progressive and risk-taking farmers to implement its development projects. Agricultural economists played a prominent role in persuading farmers with their argument on economic profitability; tillers not acting in line with the expectations of the development regime were deemed to be 'risk averse', a derogatory term in the decades of the Green Revolution. The media, by retailing the success stories of risk-taking farmers, played a pivotal role in feeding the development narrative, and facilitated public celebration of 'heroes'. The state's chosen path of agricultural modernisation was neither smooth nor universally approved. All the same, it successfully created a support base for the Green Revolution by laying down what constituted acceptable economic behaviour for farmers. In growing the HYV crops, farmers would keep the development vision alive until the cost exceeded the return. It was the allies of modernisation who would ultimately turn out to be the development regime's biggest critics as we see in the numerous farmers' movements that are currently active in India.

PART III

THE TRIUMPH OF THE MODERNISING LOGIC AFTER 1945

14

Agricultural modernisation from a biophysical point of view: Spain, *c.* 1900–2008

Manuel González de Molina

The prevailing narrative of agricultural modernisation continues to provide a positive view of the economic growth experienced by the agricultural sector, especially since the 1960s, when the technologies of the so-called Green Revolution began to be adopted. The case of Spain is paradigmatic. According to the conventional economic approach, based solely on monetary values, the industrialisation of Spanish agriculture multiplied the availability of food for human consumption, increased the number of citizens who could be fed and the caloric content of their diet. It is even claimed that the sector contributed to the country's economic growth, refuting the traditional idea that it had been a hindrance to its development. However, if agrarian modernisation is analysed using not only a monetary approach but a biophysical one as well, our assessment changes. The socio-metabolic approach provides compelling evidence showing that the growth of agricultural production in Spain had significant economic, social, environmental and even public health consequences. This modifies the traditional narrative in a more pessimistic and critical sense, and helps explain the eco-social crisis we are going through.[1]

1 The main data and conclusions of this chapter are taken from the more comprehensive study by Manuel González de Molina, David Soto Fernández, Gloria Guzmán Casado, Juan Infante-Amate, Eduardo Aguilera Fernández, Jaime Vila Traver and Roberto García-Ruiz, *The Social Metabolism of Spanish Agriculture, 1900–2008: The Mediterranean Way Towards Industrialization* (Cham: Springer, 2020).

14.1 Evolution of land use

Spanish agriculture multiplied its production by 3.3 times between 1900 and 2008, reaching a peak at the start of this century, when its annual output was over 104.2 million tonnes of plant agricultural products measured as fresh matter. These figures emerge from an analysis of agricultural production without allowing for the water content of agricultural products. All crops increased their yields whilst their cultivated areas decreased in size. The production of cereals, fruits and vegetables, forage plants and olive groves grew particularly sharply, reflecting Spain's progressive specialisation. Livestock production grew even further, multiplying by a factor of 8.2 over the same period. It also generated a larger share of total agricultural output, increasing from 7 per cent to almost 17 per cent. Growth in agricultural production seems even more remarkable when measured in monetary terms: the value of Final Agricultural Production multiplied by 5.1 times at constant prices between 1953 and 2003, while its share of total employment and Spanish GDP declined.

These outcomes are generally viewed as a positive achievement. They are characteristic of modern agricultural growth and industrialisation, and common to most economically advanced countries. Major productivity improvements facilitated the transfer of labour from rural areas to urban-industrial activities. Between 1960 and 2008, the active agricultural population fell from almost 5 million to just over 1 million individuals. This population transfer from the countryside to cities has also been judged as a highly positive contribution of the agricultural sector to Spain's economic growth. Overall, the role of agriculture was redefined during its industrialisation process. Agriculture shifted from providing food and labour to becoming mainly a supplier of raw materials to an agri-food complex, a business made up of the agro-industry, food distribution and agrarian input manufacturers. This shift is considered to be another notable contribution to Spain's economic growth. In fact, the agri-food trade has been generating a surplus in monetary terms since the beginning of the 1980s, based on quality differentiation and greater external competitiveness. A biophysical approach, however, reveals a less comfortable picture.

In Figure 14.1, changes in land uses are summarised based in six categories. The most obvious change emerged from the changing balance between cultivated areas and forest. Cultivated areas grew continuously from 1900 to the 1970s, reaching almost 21 million hectares. They have steadily declined ever since, covering a little more than 16 million hectares today. The fall in cultivated areas is attributable to the drop in the surface area devoted to cereals: at the same time there has been an increase in the area given over to uses such as olive growing or industrial crops. This does not imply a fall in cereal production. Rather, unirrigated lands in the interior of the country, with low yields, have largely abandoned cereal growing. Forest, however, has followed the opposite

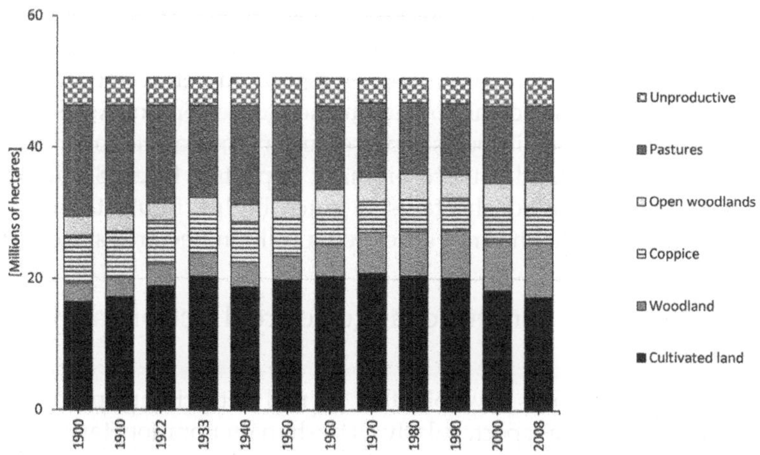

FIGURE 14.1. Evolution of types of land uses, in thousands of hectares, 1900–2008 (select years). *Source*: González de Molina *et al.*, 2020.

trend. Now here it needs to be explained that by forest we mean the sum of wooded areas, bush as well as timber woodlands and coppice, but forest also includes other categories of land that are not cultivated under arable regimes, such as natural meadows, pastures, wasteland pastures, esparto fields and areas with a variety of shrubs. By 1900, Spain's total forested area was 29.85 million hectares. In 1960, the figure was 25.92 million hectares and 28.05 in 2000. The total forest area fell during the first half of the twentieth century by 3.38 million hectares, of which only 0.86 were forested. Deforestation during these years did not imply, therefore, a big loss of trees. Spanish woodlands began to specialise in timber, a trend that greatly intensified in the second half of the twentieth century. The surface area of timber woodlands increased from 2.84 million to 3.70 million hectares between 1900 and 1950. Forest policies increasingly focused on the planting of conifers and fast-growing timber species to serve the demand of the Spanish economy for increasing amounts of timber while firewood scrubland lost its value.

This growth of woodlands is a paradigmatic case of the forest transition,[2] that is, a shift from a *declining* area of forest to an *increasing* one. The process can often be explained by the fact that the cultivated areas on which the domestic economy relied have been shifted to other countries. For example,

2 Eric F. Lambin and Patrick Meyfroidt, 'Global Land Use Change, Economic Globalization, and the Looming Land Scarcity', *Proceedings of the National Academy of Sciences* 108 (2011), 3465–72.

soya beans, an important source of protein for livestock, are now grown on forest land in Argentina and Brazil, which has allowed some low productivity arable land in Spain to be converted into timber forest. Countries that have increased their forest areas have often displaced deforestation to other parts of the world.[3] This seems to true in the case of Spain. As estimated in another study, Spanish imports represented in 1900 a little over 700,000 hectares of embodied land (due to biomass imports).[4] In 2008, the figure had reached over 11 million hectares, a much higher figure than that of woodland growth, which has not exceeded 3 million hectares since 1900.

14.2 Evolution and content changes of real net primary productivity

Agricultural production as a whole, that is, real net primary productivity (NPP_{real}), did not grow as spectacularly as fresh matter or monetary statistics seem to imply. NPP_{real} grew by only 28.5 per cent between 1900 and 2008, though not in a uniform way over the period. Therefore, agricultural industrialisation did not lead to greater yields per unit area if we consider the agroecosystems' overall capacity to produce biomass. This observation should challenge the view that industrialisation is associated with massive yield increases achieved with the lavish use of external inputs.

Table 14.1. Net primary productivity according to land use types, in millions of tonnes of dry matter.

	1900	1933	1950	1970	1990	2008
Farmland	66	91	73	84	99	104
Pasture	122	111	131	127	117	130
Woodland	57	54	54	73	76	81
Total	245	256	258	283	293	314
NPP_{real} /ha (tonnes of plant biomass produced per ha.)						
Farmland	4.0	4.5	3.7	4.0	4.9	6.0
Pasture	4.5	5.0	5.7	6.4	6.1	6.3
Woodland	1.9	2.1	2.0	2.8	2.9	2.8
Total	4.8	5.1	5.1	5.6	5.8	6.2

Source: Spanish Agrarian Statistics.

3 Patrick Meyfroidt, Thomas K. Rudel and Eric F. Lambin, 'Forest Transitions, Trade, and the Global Displacement of Land Use', *Proceedings of the National Academy of Sciences* 107 (2010), 20917–22.

4 Juan Infante-Amate, Eduardo Aguilera, Francesco Palmeri, Gloria Guzmán, David Soto, Roberto García-Ruiz and Manuel González de Molina, 'Land Embodied in Spain's Biomass Trade and Consumption (1900–2008): Historical Changes, Drivers and Impacts', *Land Use Policy* 78 (2018), 493–502.

The NPP_{real} increased more in cultivated areas (57 per cent) and in woodlands (42 per cent) than in the pastures, which grew by only 6 per cent. (Table 14.1) This means that human pressure to increase production was concentrated mainly in cultivated areas, where biomass utility is greater. This land use accounted for essentially the same surface area in 2008 as in 1900. In fact, by 2008 productivity per hectare over land in general had grown by 50 per cent compared to 1900. The increase in woodland biomass, however, was due to the increase in the surface area of woodland, improved management and, paradoxically, the cessation of many traditional types of use, especially firewood collection. The small increase in pasture NPP_{real} can be explained both by the decrease in surface area and, again paradoxically, by Spain's abandonment and underusage of lands dedicated to this use. This becomes more evident when looking at productivity per hectare of pasture, which increased by almost 40 per cent from 1900.

TABLE 14.2. Net primary productivity according to origin, in millions of tonnes of dry matter.

	1900	1933	1950	1970	1990	2008
Total accumulated biomass	11.7	10.8	12.0	21.7	23.4	23.7
% of NPP_{real}	4.8	4.2	4.6	7.7	8.0	7.5
Total non-harvested biomass	183.4	184.3	184.2	203.5	202.9	222.1
% of NPP_{real}	75.0	72.0	71.4	71.8	69.3	70.7
Domestic extraction	50	61	62	58	66	68
% of NPP_{real}	20.2	23.7	23.9	20.5	22.6	21.8
Total NPP_{real}	245	256	258	283	293	314

Source: Spanish Agrarian Statistics and author's own calculations.

Interesting aspects of the evolution of NPP_{real} come to light when it is broken down into different categories (Table 14.2). As we have already observed, the net primary productivity of woodlands grew the most after farmlands. This was largely due to a notable growth of forested areas and accumulated biomass, which doubled over the period, revealing a growing percentage of total net primary productivity, from 4.8 per cent to 7.5 per cent. Accumulation of biomass in the aerial parts of woodlands (the trunks and branches of trees), which multiplied almost twenty-fold, was the main factor. Biomass accumulated in trees and in forests in general because it was no longer gathered for firewood. This

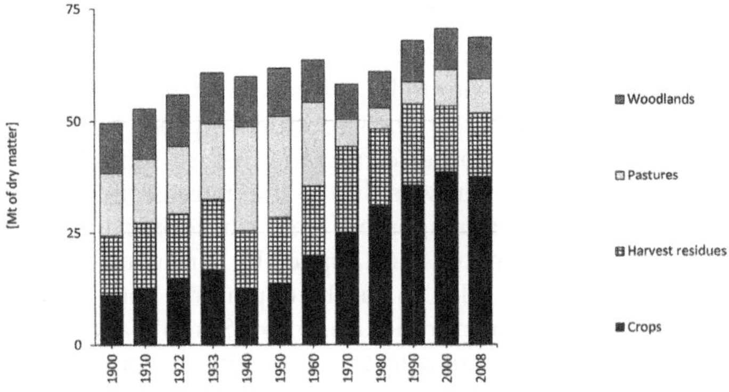

FIGURE 14.2. Domestic biomass extraction by origin, in millions of tonnes of dry matter, 1900–2008 (select years). *Source*: González de Molina *et al.*, 2020.

accumulation greatly intensified from the 1960s onwards and explains the proliferation of forest fires in public woodlands ever since.[5] Unharvested biomass (that is, biomass that is not removed for human use) supports trophic food chains. It provides food for the herbivorous species inhabiting the agroecosystems and therefore it also helps to sustain their diversity. Its evolution throughout the period reflects the deterioration of the soil biological life. Overall, this biomass type grew by 21 per cent in absolute terms, but in relative terms it contributed the least to the growth of total NPP_{real}, being clearly below the average. This means that its importance dropped in relative terms from 75 per cent to 70.7 per cent. This drop was worse in pastures and farmlands.

Only approximately one fifth of total NPP_{real} was appropriated throughout the period by humans; that is to say, it was extracted from agroecosystems. The quantity of this biomass is called Domestic Extraction (DE). Figure 14.2 shows the evolution of vegetal biomass extracted from Spanish agroecosystems between 1900 and 2008, measured in megatonnes of dry matter. As pointed out earlier, dry matter is the most suitable way of measuring the real magnitude of the changes. This is because current varieties have a higher water content than those grown previously and there has been a shift towards crops that require more water for growth,

5 Francisco Casero Rodríguez and Manuel González de Molina, 'Mito y realidades de los incendios forestales en Andalucía', in *El fuego. Mitos, ritos y realidades*, José Antonio González Alcantud and Manuel González de Molina (eds) (Barcelona: Anthropos, 1977), 377–410.

which this affects total production weight. In addition, irrigation allowed for the multiplying of yields per unit area. The DE of biomass (that is, biomass appropriated directly or indirectly by Spanish society) grew by 38 per cent throughout the period (that is, more than NPP_{real} (28 per cent)).

The increase in agricultural production based on our measurements differs from the increase obtained using conventional calculations: while in monetary terms 'agricultural production' grew almost six-fold, it grew only by 38 per cent in physical terms. Agriculture's great leap forward following its industrialisation can be put into perspective if we consider not only commercial biomass, but all the biomass appropriated by Spanish society: both that with end uses in society and biomass reused in agroecosystems to feed livestock, used as seeds, etc. The difference is even more notable when considering the total biomass necessary to reproduce the fund elements that maintain agroecosystems' production capacity; that is, the NPP_{real}. These 'costs' are usually not included in national accounts nor, therefore, in agricultural sector accounts.

A disaggregated analysis shows that DE growth was concentrated in the cultivated plants trade, increasing by 236 per cent when 2008 is compared to 1900, due to a small (8 per cent) growth in residues (the parts of the crop for which there is no market outlet). In contrast, biomass appropriated by pastures and forests decreased respectively by 46 per cent and 17 per cent. Main crop productivity increased threefold, while residue productivity only increased by 40 per cent. Pasture abandonment and underuse explain an extraction drop of up to 81 per cent for these lands, below 1 tonne per hectare, despite having reached more than six tonnes in the 1940s and 1950s. Forest conservation policies and household energy transition, as mentioned above, explain the decrease in woodland extraction per hectare (17 per cent).

The industrialisation of agriculture led to a significant increase in produced biomass, but this increase was concentrated in cultivated lands and more specifically in the most commercially orientated crops. In fact, extraction from these lands went from 22.5 per cent of total DE in 1900 to 54.8 per cent in 2008, reflecting Spanish agriculture's production specialisation.

Important changes also took place in DE types of end uses (Figure 14.3). Biomass aimed at human food accounted for 9 per cent in 1900, rising to 14 per cent in 2008. Similarly, use of biomass as a raw material went from 1 per cent in 1900 to 4 per cent today. The major change, however, concerned biomass intended for stockfeed for animals. As early as 1900, it represented 56 per cent of extracted biomass, which is logical because the main agricultural tasks were carried out using farm animals. In 2008, that percentage was at 57.5 per cent, having risen to its highest percentage in 1960 with a share of almost two-thirds. Since that decade, around 40 million tons of dry matter have been used annually to feed

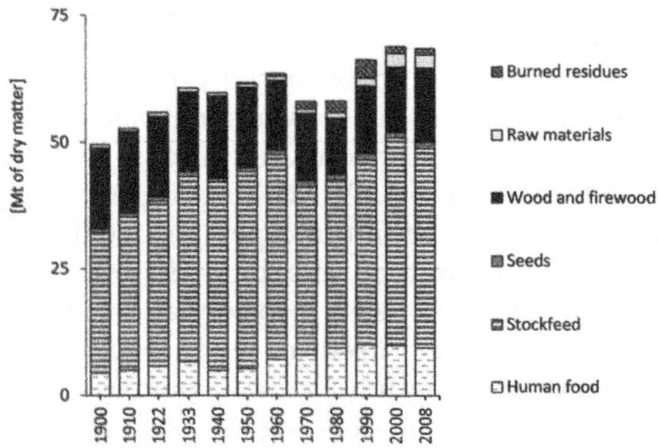

FIGURE 14.3. Destination of biomass domestic extraction, in millions of tonnes of dry matter, 1900–2008 (select years). *Source*: González de Molina *et al.*, 2020.

livestock, despite animal traction no longer being used. As we will see below, growth of livestock numbers has reached unprecedented levels in recent decades, linked to notable diet changes, specialising in meat and dairy products.[6]

On the other hand, the proportion of DE drawn from timber and firewood decreased considerably, from 32 per cent in 1900 to 21 per cent in 2008, mainly due to the lower weight of biomass energy use thanks to the supply of gas to Spanish households. However, the drop in firewood use, especially from woodlands, was partially offset by the use of wood as a raw material. This fact is consistent with the growth of forested woodlands mentioned previously. Spanish forest DE thus dropped by only 17 per cent, less than firewood consumption based on this source. Strikingly, starting from the 1950s, burnt harvest residues eventually reached 3.6 megatonnes in the 1990s – that is, 5.5 per cent of total DE – a real wastage.

6 Manuel González De Molina, David Soto, Juan Infante-Amate, Eduardo Aguilera, Jaime Vila Traver and Gloria Inmaculada Guzmán, 'Decoupling Food from Land: The Evolution of Spanish Agriculture From 1960 to 2010', *Sustainability* 9 (2017), 2348.

Table 14.3. Crop domestic extraction (without residues) in Spain, in millions of tonnes of dry matter.

	1900	1910	1922	1933	1940	1950	1960	1970	1980	1990	2000	2008
Cereals	5.5	6.3	6.8	7.9	5.0	5.9	7.6	10.7	13.1	16.5	18.6	20.2
Legumes	0.5	0.6	0.7	0.7	0.5	0.5	0.7	0.6	0.3	0.2	0.3	0.2
Grapes	1.1	0.8	1.1	1.0	0.9	0.7	0.8	1.2	1.8	1.6	1.8	1.6
Olives	0.6	0.6	0.9	1.0	0.8	0.9	1.1	1.1	1.4	1.6	2.8	3.4
Potatoes	0.5	0.7	0.7	1.1	0.8	0.8	1.0	1.1	1.3	1.2	0.7	0.5
Fruit and vegetables	0.7	0.9	1.1	1.5	1.5	1.2	1.5	1.7	2.0	2.5	2.6	2.7
Industrial and other	0.5	0.5	0.6	0.7	0.5	0.7	1.3	1.9	2.4	3.5	3.2	2.4
Artificial meadows and fodder	1.8	2.3	3.0	2.9	2.7	3.1	6.1	6.5	8.5	8.5	8.5	6.7
Total	11.2	12.6	14.9	16.7	12.7	13.8	19.9	24.8	30.8	35.6	38.7	37.5

Source: Spanish Agrarian Statistics and author's own calculations.

As Table 14.3 shows, virtually all crops increased their production throughout the twentieth century. The crop that grew the most was olives.[7] On the opposite side were legumes, which went from 4 per cent of total production at the beginning of the century to becoming marginal. Dry matter figures draw a quite different picture of specialisation compared to that of fresh matter. The most commercial and export-orientated crops (horticultural crops above all) incorporate water, and are demanding of water when growing to a much greater degree than crops such as cereals, which also have a much higher content of dry matter. In 2008, cereals accounted for 53.8 per cent of dry matter, compared to 21.9 per cent of fresh matter. This different way of presenting the data shows that Spanish agricultural specialisation has been based on water export and the increasing use of water resources in an eminently semi-arid country.[8]

14.3 Spanish livestock in the twentieth century

Spain's livestock changed fundamentally over the twentieth century, shifting from organic-based livestock, closely linked to the territory in which the animals were being raised, to livestock farming of an industrial nature, mostly housed indoors, landless and thus much more dependent on stockfeed, industrial inputs and imported feeding stuffs. These changes brought about a notable growth of total herds, from 54 million heads in 1900 to 838 million heads in 2008, with significant transformations in their composition, destination of products and services, management and feeding (see Figure 14.4). In terms of live weight, livestock multiplied 2.4 times, from 2.8 million tonnes at the beginning of the twentieth century (with peaks of around 3.4 million in the 1930s), to almost 7 million in 2010. This huge increase would also have considerable environmental impacts, especially those generated by intensive livestock farming and the increase of greenhouse gas emissions.[9]

7 Juan Infante-Amate, *¿Quién levantó los olivos? Historia de la especialización olivarera en el sur de España (s. XVIII–XX)* (Madrid: Ministerio de Agricultura, Alimentación y Medio Ambiente, 2014).

8 Ignacio Cazcarro, Rosa Duarte, Miguel Martín-Retortillo, Vicente Pinilla and Ana Serrano, 'How Sustainable is the Increase in the Water Footprint of the Spanish Agricultural Sector? A Provincial Analysis between 1955 and 2005–2010', *Sustainability* 7 (2015), 5094–119; Rosa Duarte, Vicente Pinilla and Ana Serrano, 'The Water Footprint of the Spanish Agricultural Sector: 1860–2010', *Ecological Economics* 108 (2014), 200–7.

9 Luis Lassaletta, Gilles Billen, Estela Romero, Josette Garnier and Eduardo Aguilera, 'How Changes in Diet and Trade Patterns have Shaped the N cycle at the National Scale: Spain (1961–2009)', *Regional Environmental Change* 14 (2014), 785–97.

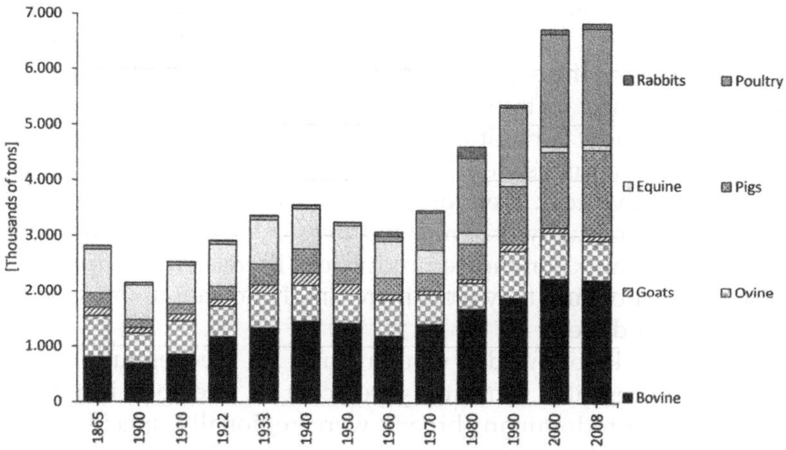

FIGURE 14.4. Evolution of live livestock weight in thousands of tonnes, 1865–2008 (select years). *Source*: González de Molina *et al.*, 2020.

The pace of change during the twentieth century, however, was irregular. Livestock numbers increased by 55.6 per cent between 1900 and 1940, stalled between 1950 and 1960 and rose by 97 per cent between 1970 and 2008. Livestock's internal composition and its end uses underwent considerable transformations. The first of these is related to labour and traction livestock, on which agriculture was heavily reliant prior to mechanisation. Livestock used for these ends lost ground to other livestock species and, within this category, to livestock aimed at human food. The reason is that livestock was replaced by internal combustion engines, both for mechanisation and transport. In fact, equine livestock became almost marginal over time. The second major transformation was the loss of traditional livestock species. Sheep and goats, once tied to pasture and forest lands according to their feeding needs and breed and thus better adapted to land and climate conditions, shrank in numbers and importance throughout the century. At the beginning of the twentieth century, both types of herd together represented 29.1 per cent of live weight. In 2008, sheep accounted for little more than 10 per cent by live weight, specialised in the production of lambs and, to a lesser extent, of milk for cheese. Goats formed only 1.3 per cent and also produced meat and cheese.

The third transformation was that experienced by cattle. In 1900 beef cattle represented 31.9 per cent of live weight and represented the main species. Today, cattle's relative weight has increased slightly, reaching almost one-third of the total. However, big changes have taken place within this category, related to breeds, specialisation and feeding. A large share of cattle used to be employed in field work and to a lesser extent transportation. The use of teams of oxen was very common for tillage or threshing at the beginning of the last century. Oxen-pulled carts were commonly used to transport goods. Cows were chiefly used for breeding and sporadic agricultural tasks. Most of their milk was used to feed calves. Young animals were rarely slaughtered for meat production. The life cycle of livestock therefore exceeded ten or twelve years. This diversity of uses gradually declined and livestock came to be optimised for either meat or milk for cheese production. Breeds were improved to maximise production and they were increasingly housed undercover and fed with compound feed.

Porcine livestock followed a similar path. At the beginning of the century pigs represented almost 6.5 per cent of livestock in terms of live weight. The predominant breeds were regionally specific. Today porcine herds represent 22.7 per cent of livestock, coming after cattle and poultry in total livestock weight. Pig breeding has now become a highly industrialised activity that provides meat at affordable prices. Pig meat is now one of the pillars of the Spanish diet. The pigs are bred in large intensive farms, are housed in temperature-controlled structures on a permanent basis, fed on compound feed and undergo frequent veterinary treatments.

The fourth and final series of transformations concerned poultry. At the beginning of the twentieth century, chickens were raised to produce eggs and, when their production declined, they were slaughtered for meat. The chickens' diet competed with human food, as in the case of pigs, hence their limited numbers. They were fed organic household waste or grain. Today, breeding, especially that of poultry, is a major livestock activity that also involves intensive production and permanent housing. In 2008, poultry represented 30.4 per cent of total livestock live weight, with almost 737 million birds dedicated to the production of meat and eggs, with increasingly shorter breeding cycles and fed with grains and concentrates. In this way, poultry breeding, feeding and use have radically changed. Rabbits followed a similar trend, but to a lesser extent. Once the product of hunting, they too became farmed animals.

Livestock feeding thus depended mainly on pastures and harvest residues (45 per cent and 25 per cent respectively) until the 1960s. From then on, it began to depend on quality feed from crops and the industrial manufacture of concentrates. Since the 1980s, an increasing share of this feed has come from imports. In 2008, 48 per cent of stockfeed came from primary crops and 15 per cent from net imports. Meanwhile, a large part of the agricultural area was abandoned or, in the case of pastures, were underutilised, as shown by the drastic reduction in grazed

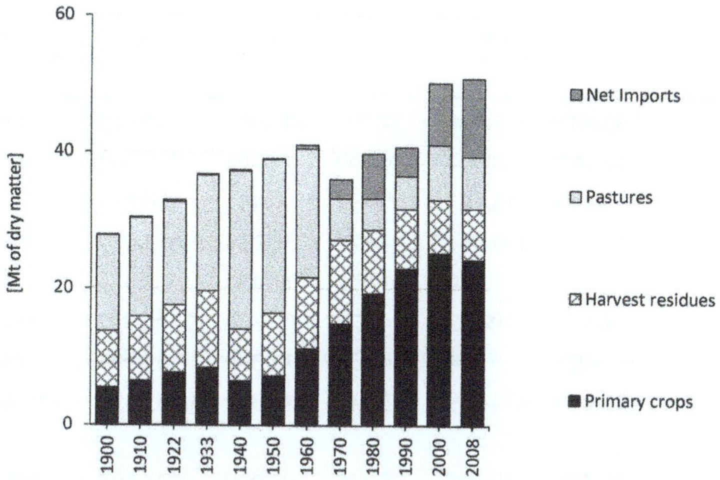

FIGURE 14.5. Origin of animal feed, in millions of tonnes of dry matter, 1900–2008 (select years). *Source*: González de Molina *et al.*, 2020.

biomass. DE for stockfeed went from 27.8 megatonnes of dry matter in 1900 to 39.4 megatonnes in 2008, from 56 per cent to 57.5 per cent of total extraction. Furthermore, livestock has grown at a much higher rate than the domestic supply of stockfeed (a 215 per cent increase in live weight between 1900 and 2008 compared to an 82 per cent increase of stockfeed). As a result, levels of DE have shown to be insufficient to maintain the livestock growth rate and its food requirements, explaining the reliance on imported feedstuffs.

The evolution of livestock production logically reflected the transformations reviewed above. We can decompose its analysis into three major periods: the first, a period of continuous production growth until the mid-1930s, marking the end of the agrarian crisis at the end of the nineteenth century; second, the period of crisis including the Civil War and dictatorship that lasted until the mid-1960s; and a third and final period of accelerated production growth, especially of meat and milk, from the 1960s until today.

Table 14.4. Livestock production in tonnes of dry matter, 1900–2008.

	1900	1933	1950	1970	1990	2008
Meat:						
Beef	53,838	105,626	52,763	148,877	256,673	330,754
Lamb	44,487	52,892	39,289	74,284	128,693	97,780
Goat	9,468	14,121	6,857	6,401	8,819	5,203
Pig	40,641	104,444	82,522	256,874	1,013,979	1,888,429
Horse	0	0	1,682	5,458	2,325	2,216
Poultry	4,115	6,403	4,673	207,108	388,947	604,380
Rabbit	491	764	4,453	11,306	35,895	30,600
Total	153,040	284,249	313,347	710,308	1,835,332	2,959,362
Eggs	12,728	19,805	31,435	97,860	131,665	154,882
Wool	21,933	25,442	24,762	21,660	23,981	23,191
Milk:						
Cow	104,417	177,739	259,956	523,777	718,461	751,934
Sheep	17,147	8,672	13,610	30,326	35,685	56,314
Goat	36,577	38,223	33,155	28,458	46,694	56,372
Honey	3,897	4,908	5,391	6,816	18,255	25,081

Source: Spanish Agrarian Statistics and author's calculations. The meat is expressed in live weight.

Livestock production growth is clearly correlated with the evolution of livestock herds (Table 14.4 and Figure 14.5). As we saw, sheep and goats lost relative weight in overall livestock. Although livestock grew by 75 per cent between 1965 and 2008, poultry (354 per cent) and pigs (452 per cent) grew the most because of rising domestic demand for low-priced meat and export opportunities.[10] The industrial model undeniably permitted market-orientated livestock production to grow to an extent that would have been unthinkable in traditional organic agriculture. However, this growth came at the expense of a more or less complete rupture of the ties between livestock and the land, as well as the almost entire loss of traditional animal multifunctionality.

10 González De Molina, Soto, Infante-Amate, Aguilera, Vila Traver and Guzmán, 'Decoupling Food from Land'.

14.4 Spanish agricultural modernisation from a biophysical point of view

In summary, Spanish agriculture over the past century has evolved towards increasing production commodification and significant changes in the patterns of biomass use. Both production and technological efforts have been directed towards maximising the share of biomass of highest commercial value, entailing, as we will see, the reduction of crop multifunctionality. In other words, agricultural production growth has been much greater than the growth of agroecosystems' NPP_{real}. Considering the dimensions of the natural environment or agroecosystem, Spanish agriculture's industrialisation led to increasingly segregated land uses, production loss and the loss of functional synergies based on the integration of agriculture, livestock and forestry. This resulted from certain land use types taking over others and the rupture of the previous ecosystemic equilibrium, in turn reflecting growing specialisation. Livestock growth mainly relied on intensive landless farms, which lacked any connection to the land. In this way, close ties within agroecosystems between agricultural and livestock activities, not only in terms of food but also in terms of maintaining soil fertility and the supply of traction, were broken. The introduction of synthetic chemical fertilisers and mechanisation made use segregation viable. The same phenomenon affected forest lands, dedicated to forestry or conservation policies that often excluded or restricted other possible uses. In short, the trend towards production specialisation and intensification has been a growing requirement of Spanish agriculture's growth model. This has tended to impose specialised land uses on the territory based on market demands rather than land capacity or the endowment of natural resources. The result is a loss of geodiversity and spatial heterogeneity. Flows of energy and materials, once more local and contained, have ended up being globalised and of fossil origin.

At a farm scale, production specialisation led to the following consequences: a strong tendency to suppress crop and polyculture associations; the simplification of rotations and their later suppression; the elimination of fallows or their substantial reduction; and the fostering of crop alternations governed by market demands. Agriculture shifted from crop and plant heterogeneity and their layout adjustments to monocultures, entailing significant reductions of genetic, structural and functional diversity.[11] At the agroecosystem scale, this phenomenon progressively reduced the capacity of agroecosystems for autonomous replacement fertility. At the farm level, the relative demand for fertilisers significantly

11 Infante-Amate, *¿Quién levantó los olivos?*; Stephen R. Gliessman, *Agroecology: The Ecology of Sustainable Food Systems* (New York, USA: CRC Press, Taylor & Francis, 2007).

increased: the spread of chemical fertilisers made this fundamental change possible. It sparked, in turn, the desire to suppress fallow and legume sowing. Cultivation was reduced to less than half of its original level between 1900 and 2008. This led to a reduction in the flow of nitrogen from symbiotic fixation and the loss of the ability of agroecosystems to replenish soil fertility by themselves.

At the crop level, very important transformations affected both plants' morphologies and their uses. This evolution also applies to different livestock species. At the beginning of the twentieth century, when agriculture and livestock were still organic, cultivated plants and livestock species each served different purposes. Livestock provided meat and milk, but also carried out agricultural tasks or transported goods. High cereal stalks were aimed at producing large quantities of straw, the basis of horse provender (and that was returned to the soil as manure). Progress in crops allowed the development of livestock that could feed on farmlands without competing with human food.

The aim of farmers was to maximise the harvestable parts of plants, especially those with the highest commercial value; in turn, the aim of cattle farmers was to select the species and breeds generating the largest quantity of meat and milk. Thus, in the case of phytomass, seeds were selected and improved to concentrate photosynthetic capacity in the marketable part of cultivated plants, for example, by modifying cereals' morphology to concentrate more biomass in grains and less in straw. The process was applied to most arable crops and led to the considerable growth in grain yields per hectare. The Green Revolution was largely based on the genetic change that produced crop types with a lower 'waste' weight. This phenomenon is visible in the changing relationships between grain and straw in cereals and legumes. Traditional cereal and legume varieties had high straw stems, therefore less grain, and, as we mentioned, were an essential part of animal feed. With the industrialisation of agriculture, these were replaced with varieties that produced more grain and less straw. In the case of woody plants, improvements and changes to management practices consisted of translocating stem and leaf biomass to the harvestable fruit. Multifunctional usage has been superseded by a preference for the commercial use of fruits. The case of olive-growing is paradigmatic: from producing firewood, foliage and olive kernel oil for livestock, table olives, domestic lighting and edible oil, olive groves now almost exclusively produce oil, leading to changes in grove management and tree morphology.[12]

12 Infante-Amate, *¿Quién levantó los olivos?*; Juan Infante-Amate, Manuel González de Molina, Tom Vanwalleghem, David Soto, José Alfonso Gómez, 'Erosion in the Mediterranean, from a Historical Perspective: The Case of Olive Groves in the South of Spain (1752–2000)', *Environmental History* 18 (2013), 1–23.

All these changes explain the remarkable increase of some crop yields (620 per cent in the case of corn – maize – between 1900 and 2008 or 332 per cent in the case of wheat), a much higher growth than that of NPP_{real} per hectare in cultivated areas (50 per cent) or DE per cultivated hectare (102 per cent). In other words, the land's biophysical productivity has grown at a much lower rate than grain or fruit yields per hectare. The reason is the concentration of biomass in grain or harvestable fruit and, therefore, the reduction of harvest residues. Another factor is the removal of weeds by mechanical means or herbicides. Moreover, the introduction of improved and hybrid seeds, in the quest for maximum grain yields or the selection of woody plants varieties with high yields, has led to a substantial loss of genetic diversity. This process has favoured the intensive use of fertilisers. The result has been the abandonment of seed varieties that were better adapted to soil and climate conditions and that, as far as we know, demanded less nutrients.[13]

In the case of livestock, a radical transformation has taken place. As livestock production grew, extensive stock-farming became less important and there has been a resort to feedstuffs produced off-farm. The bulk of livestock has lost its land ties and is housed in intensive farms. Feed from abroad is often used, and breeds suited to the production of meat or milk have been introduced from other countries. Traction livestock has almost completely disappeared and thanks to cheaper feed, monogastric livestock (poultry and pigs) now have an unprecedented prominence in agriculture. Ever bigger quantities of straw have been either burned or left on the farm. Extensive livestock farming, where it is still practised, is often the last refuge of traditional livestock breeds.

14.5. Some impacts of Spanish agricultural modernisation

As we have seen, Spanish agroecosystems experienced significant intensification and productive specialisation. Given that land uses were segregated, the many connections between them broke down, and agroecosystems increasingly needed inputs from outside the agricultural sector. Organic inputs produced on the farms themselves and in the local environment, such as manure and animal traction, were replaced by large quantities of inorganic inputs manufactured with fossil fuels, among them synthetic fertilisers and pesticides, machinery, fuel and electricity (Figure 14.6). Industrial inputs and their energy costs began to grow strongly in the 1960s, first with the use of chemical fertilisers and irrigation, then by

13 Guiomar Carranza-Gallego, Gloria Inmaculada Guzmán, David Soto, Eduardo Aguilera, Inmaculada Villa, Juan Infante-Amate, Antonio Herrera and Manuel González de Molina, 'Modern Wheat Varieties as a Driver of the Degradation of Spanish Rainfed Mediterranean Agroecosystems throughout the 20th Century', *Sustainability* 10 (2018), 3724.

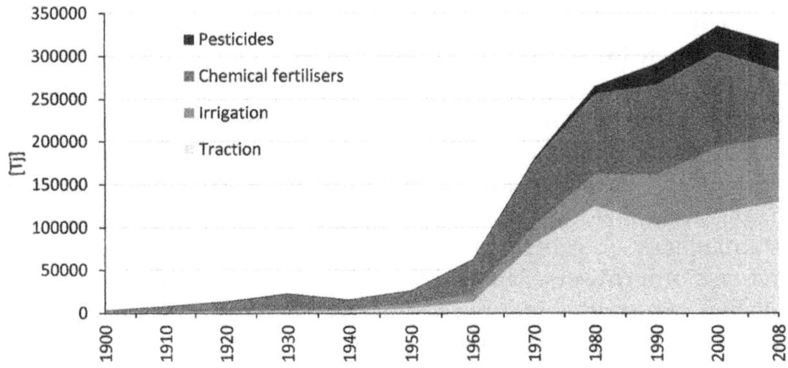

FIGURE 14.6. Energy value of inputs used in Spanish agriculture, in terajoules (Tj), 1900–2008. *Source*: González de Molina *et al.*, 2020.

mechanisation followed by crop protection. Overall efficiency declined significantly. Specifically, efficiency in relation to external inputs went from providing 17 joules for each invested joule in 1900, to 1.2 in 2008.[14] The graph clearly shows the enormous amount of energy originating from outside the agricultural sector that it was necessary to inject into agroecosystems to maintain the continuous growth of agricultural production. While biomass DE grew by 38 per cent, the use of external energy multiplied by 100. In 1900, industrial inputs from outside the agroecosystem and used for production represented only 14.5 per cent of total invested energy; in 2008, that percentage had risen to 62 per cent,

14 Gloria Guzmán, Manuel González de Molina, David Soto, Juan Infante-Amate and Eduardo Aguilera, 'Spanish Agriculture from 1900 to 2008: A Long-Term Perspective on Agroecosystem Energy from an Agroecological Approach', *Regional Environmental Change* 18 (2018), 995–1008; Gloria Guzmán and Manuel González De Molina, 'Energy Efficiency in Agrarian Systems from an Agro-Ecological Perspective', *Agroecology and Sustainable Food Systems* 39 (2015), 924–52; Enric Tello, Elena Galán, Vera Sacristán *et al.*, 'Opening the Black Box of Energy Throughputs in Farm Systems: A Decomposition Analysis Between the Energy Returns to External Inputs, Internal Biomass Reuses and Total Inputs Consumed (the Vallès County, Catalonia, c.1860 and 1999)', *Ecological Economics* 121 (2016), 160–74; Gloria Inmaculada Guzmán and Manuel González De Molina, *Energy in Agroecosystems: A Tool for Assessing Sustainability* (Boca Raton, FL: CRC Press, 2017).

and if we add the feed from Latin America, it reached 99.4 per cent of total energy invested in agricultural production; that is, practically all the energy invested came from outside the agricultural sector.

All these transformations have led to a serious deterioration of the basic fund elements not only of Spanish agroecosystems but also of those of third countries.[15] The fund elements that maintain ecosystem services, such as soil fertility, biodiversity, carbon sequestration, water quality, and so on, have all been degraded. In addition, agricultural and livestock activities have become an active source of pollution and cause the depletion of scarce resources such as fossil fuels and mineral nutrients. The dissipative profile of livestock has risen disproportionately, consuming almost 60 per cent of biomass from both DE and foreign trade and requiring a similar amount of inputs. Or, to put this another way, livestock production is an inefficient way of converting plant biomass into meat or other animal producers. *Intensive* livestock has increased this inefficiency. Moreover, livestock farming is in every practical way disconnected from its surroundings. It is the sector's major source of emissions and pollution from slurry.

But perhaps the most significant deterioration is that suffered by the agricultural population. The number of farmers is constantly decreasing and those who survive are aging and threatened by the lack of individuals to succeed them. Agricultural income declined by 17.2 per cent between 1960 and 2017 (measured in constant euros) and the number of people employed in the sector decreased from 5.1 million in 1950 to just over 774,500 in 2016. The other side effect has been the increase in the size of the technical means of production, which have acquired an excessive weight, requiring a growing supply of energy, mostly from fossil sources. The industrialisation of agriculture has therefore been based on an operating model that jeopardises not only the environmental health of agroecosystems but also the very viability of the agricultural activity that has emerged over the past half century.

15 Basic fund elements are the biophysical assets with which an agroecosystem is endowed.

15

The 'modernisation' of agriculture in the Global South after 1945: Green Revolution as 'American revolution'[1]

Jonathan Harwood

During the twentieth century 'agricultural modernisation' has had a variety of meanings. The central thesis of this volume, nevertheless, is that over the course of that century the range of strategies adopted for alleviating rural poverty narrowed drastically. After the Second World War social, economic and political measures were largely displaced by a productionist model in which new technology was expected to play the key role. Such 'high-input agriculture' relied on the use of improved seed, synthetic fertiliser, pesticide (and often mechanisation), all of which were usually supplied by the private sector. The aim, accordingly, was to transform the 'peasant' into an entrepreneurially minded 'farmer'. Because this shift to the new technology was relatively abrupt, and its impact on production was substantial, economic historians often refer to this transition as the 'agricultural revolution' of the 1950s.[2]

How is this shift to be explained? Significantly, it cannot be attributed to the *invention* of new agricultural technologies during the Second World

1 I was able to draw on the resources of the University of Sussex's main library, thanks to the support of Jeremy Kent Hall (Director, Science Policy Research Unit, University of Sussex). An earlier version of this chapter was given to a seminar at Shiv Nadar University (Uttar Pradesh, India) whose participants I thank for their comments. I am also indebted to Juan Pan-Montojo and Inderjeet Parmar for helpful advice.

2 David B. Grigg, 'The Agricultural Revolution in Western Europe', in *Understanding Green Revolutions: Agrarian Change and Development Planning in South Asia*, Tim P. Bayliss-Smith and Sudhir Wanmali (eds) (Cambridge: Cambridge University Press, 1984), 1–17; Paul Bairoch, 'Les trois revolutions agricoles du monde developpé: rendements et productivité de 1800 a 1985', *Annales: Histoires, Sciences Sociales* 44, (1989), 317–53.

War or in the immediate post-war years. As is well-established, the technologies involved were all available and in use well before the war.[3] It appears, therefore, that pre-existing technological potential was *unleashed* after 1945, making a greater impact than it had before the war. Moreover, this process of 'unleashing' cannot be understood by focusing solely upon high-input approaches since prior to the war there were other competing technologies in use. As Auderset and Moser's analysis of modernisation in Europe has shown, most of the alternatives to industrial agriculture on the modernisation agenda up to the 1940s were progressively marginalised after the war.[4] Unleashing, therefore, involved a shift in the balance of power among different technical approaches to boosting productivity.

Histories of agricultural modernisation have so far been based largely on the transformation in Europe and North America, but it is important to recognise that much the same process also took place in the Global *South* after 1945. Those development programmes, commonly referred to as the 'Green Revolution', are generally said to have begun in Mexico in the 1940s, spreading elsewhere in Latin America during the 1950s, and to South Asia during the 1960s.[5] And just as in the North, it is not that the technologies of industrial agriculture were unknown in the South before 1945; in some places they were introduced already during the inter-war period. It is rather that at various points following the Second World War Green Revolution technology gradually displaced alternative approaches to modernisation.[6]

3 Arnaud Page, '"The greatest victory which the chemist has won in the fight (…) against Nature": Nitrogenous Fertilizers in Great Britain and the British Empire, 1910s–1950s', *History of Science* 54 (2016), 383–98. While true in a strict sense, this claim requires qualification. As Juan Pan-Montojo has reminded me, although several of the technologies in question were *invented* well before the Second World War (for example, tractors, synthetic fertilisers, advanced plant-breeding methods), some of them underwent substantial *improvement* during the 1930s and the war. That means that technological *innovation* may have been one of the factors that contributed to the upsurge of high-input agriculture after 1945.

4 Juri Auderset and Peter Moser, *Die Agrarfrage in der Industriegesellschaft: Wissenskulturen, Machtverhältnisse und natürliche Ressourcen in der agrarisch-industriellen Wissensgesellschaft (1850–1950)* (Vienna: Boehlau Verlag, 2018).

5 Robert S. Anderson, Edwin Levy and Barrie M. Morrison, *Rice Science and Development Politics: Research Strategies and IRRI's Technologies Confront Asian Diversity (1950–1980)* (Oxford: Clarendon Press, 1991); John Perkins, *Geopolitics and the Green Revolution: Wheat, Genes and the Cold War* (New York: Oxford University Press, 1997); Nick Cullather, *The Hungry World: America's Cold War Battle against Poverty in Asia* (Cambridge, MA: Harvard University Press, 2010).

6 Lane E. Holdcroft, 'The Rise and Fall of Community Development, 1950–1965: A Critical Assessment', in *Agricultural Development in the Third World,* Carl Eicher and John M. Staatz (eds) (Baltimore, MD: Johns Hopkins University Press 1984), 46–58. As one development expert observed, 'Agricultural

In this chapter I ask why the use of high-input agricultural technologies in the South accelerated rapidly after 1945. As we shall see, the explanations that historians have usually given for this are deficient for several reasons. I will argue that an adequate account requires us to consider the influence of American 'soft power'.

15.1 Accounting for the emergence of the Green Revolution

The usual explanations that historians have given for the rise of the Green Revolution are either economic or geopolitical in nature. In the case of the former, a few authors argued many years ago that the Green Revolution found support from western agribusiness corporations who saw it as a way to expand the global market for inputs.[7] Recently this thesis has begun to attract renewed historical attention.[8] But most historians of the Green Revolution have instead emphasised the importance of geopolitical context; namely, the emergence from the late 1940s of the Cold War.[9] Confronted with the growing power of the Soviet Union, a successful peasant revolution in China, and growing support for communism among impoverished rural populations elsewhere in Asia, western politicians sought ways to counter the attractions of communism. Many were thus inclined to lend their support to Green Revolution programmes, it is argued, in the belief that a powerful new agricultural

development, envisaged only fifteen years ago as a process of socio-economic advance, has been narrowed to the scope of increased agricultural output'. Erich H. Jacoby, *Man and Land: The Fundamental Issue in Development* (London: Andre Deutsch, 1971), 13.

7 Harry M. Cleaver, 'The Origins of the Green Revolution' (PhD diss., Stanford University, 1974). Susan George, *How the Other Half Dies: The Real Reasons for World Hunger* (Harmondsworth: Penguin, 1977).

8 Corinna Unger, *Entwicklungspfade in Indien: eine internationale Geschichte, 1947–1980* (Goettingen: Wallstein, 2015); Jonathan Harwood, 'Was the Green Revolution Intended to Maximise Food Production?', *International J. Agricultural Sustainability* 17 (2019), 312–25; Karin Bugow, 'The Role of Multinational Corporations in the Green Revolution, 1960s and 1970s', (PhD diss., Jacobs University, Bremen, 2020).

9 Perkins, *Geopolitics and the Green Revolution*; Cullather, *Hungry World*; Nick Cullather, 'The War on the Peasant: The United States and the Third World', in *The Cold War in the Third World*, Robert J. McMahon (ed.) (New York: Oxford University Press, 2013), 192–207. To be sure, the Cold War was not the only political factor prompting Green Revolutions after 1945. In several Latin American countries internal political dynamics also affected the timing of the new technology's introduction. Cynthia Hewitt d'Alcantara, *Modernizing Mexican Agriculture: Socioeconomic Implications of Technological Change, 1940–1970* (Geneva: UN Research Institute for Social Development, 1976); Antonio Chamorro, 'Expanding the Green Revolution to Small Farmers in Ecuador (1970 to 1990s)', *Etudes rurales* 205 (2020), 162–81.

technology promised to alleviate rural poverty without the need for social revolution.[10] As one US civil servant put it, the West's offer of a 'green revolution' would make 'red revolutions' unnecessary.[11]

Although both economic and geopolitical explanations are probably part of the story of the Green Revolution's emergence, it is important to recognise their limitations. The problem with the former, for example, is that while corporate interests almost certainly provided substantial support for Green Revolution programmes, it is not clear how such interests could account for the rise of the Green Revolution in a *specific* period. Assuming that inputs industries were searching for expanded markets throughout the twentieth century, for example, why should the Green Revolution have emerged at the particular time it did rather than earlier or later? Corporate interests, therefore, should better be treated as an accessory cause, strengthening support for a movement whose emergence was triggered by historically specific causes.

Relying upon the Cold War – as a historically specific explanation – also runs into difficulties, one of which concerns timing; namely, the fact that various programmes of US technical assistance for agriculture in the South – largely indistinguishable from the better-known Green Revolution programmes – date from *before* the Cold War. More fundamentally, what the Cold War thesis overlooks is that Green Revolutions were not simply imposed on the Global South. They were introduced with the host countries' *consent*. This means that although the Cold War is useful for understanding why the Green Revolution attracted support from politicians and voters in the *North* (who were preoccupied with the spread of communism), it fails to explain why the Green Revolution's technologies were viewed favourably by many governments in the South.

Consider these difficulties in more detail. The first problem with the Cold War thesis is that programmes of technical assistance very like the Green Revolution[12] were already underway well before 1947 when the

10 As Westad's analysis makes clear, however, the Green Revolution was merely part of a wider US strategy. Committed to extend US values and prosperity abroad, both academic advisors and politicians in the US believed that 'developing' poor countries would require not just social and political reform, but practical assistance in areas such as health and education. And the key to this was US knowledge and technology. Odd Arne Westad, *The Global Cold War: Third World Interventions and the Making of Our Times* (Cambridge: Cambridge University Press, 2007), 32–8.

11 William S. Gaud, 'The Green Revolution: Accomplishments and Apprehensions', paper to the Society for International Development, Washington, DC, 8 March 1968, http://www.agbioworld.org/biotech-info/topics/borlaug/borlaug-green.html (accessed 30 March 2025).

12 Admittedly, it is difficult to know just how closely inter-war US technical assistance for agriculture resembled the Green Revolution's 'technological package' since the programmes after 1945 are far better documented than

Cold War is usually said to have begun. US technical assistance to various countries in the South dates from the nineteenth century.[13] After acquiring colonies in the Philippines and the Caribbean in 1898, for example, the US introduced agricultural machinery, fertiliser and experiment stations as part of its 'civilising mission'.[14]

As Picado and Fernández have pointed out, however, perhaps the most important institutional antecedent of the Green Revolution was the Institute for Inter-American Affairs through which the US provided technical assistance for Latin American agriculture.[15] To be sure, the origins of the IIAA were also geopolitical. But the source of US concern in

---

their pre-war counterparts. Nevertheless, existing sources indicate that during the inter-war period the US provided high-yielding varieties to Mexico (Joseph Cotter, 'The Origins of the Green Revolution in Mexico: Continuity or Change?', in *Latin America in the 1940s: War and Postwar Transitions,* David Rock (ed.) (Berkeley, CA: California University Press, 1994), 224–41, at 229 and 236); improved plant varieties and knowledge about irrigation technology to Colombia (Timothy W. Lorek, 'Developing Paradise: Agricultural Science in the Conflicted Landscapes of Colombia's Cauca Valley, 1927–1967' (PhD diss., Yale University, 2019, ch. 2); and tractors plus advice on 'scientific agriculture' to Turkey (Heinrich Hartmann, *Eigensinnige Musterschueler: laendliche Entwicklung u. internationales Expertenwissen in der Tuerkei (1947–1980)* (Frankfurt: Campus, 2020), 48 and 84, 78 and 93). During the 1920s, similarly, the International Education Board funded plant breeders from Cornell University to work at China's University of Nanking: see Harry Houser Love and John Henry Reisner, *The Cornell-Nanking Story* (Cornell International Agricultural Development Bulletin no. 4, Ithaca, NY: New York State College of Agriculture, 1964); Randall E. Stross, *The Stubborn Earth: American Agriculturalists on Chinese Soil, 1898–1937* (Berkeley, CA: University of California Press, 1986); and Seung-Joon Lee, 'Rice and Maritime Modernity: The Modern Chinese State and the South China Sea Rice Trade', in *Rice: Global Networks & New Histories,* Francesca Bray, Peter A. Coclanis, Edda L. Fields-Black and Dagmar Schäfer (eds) (Cambridge: Cambridge University Press, 2015), 99–107, at 106–7.

13 Merle Curti and Kendall Birr, *Prelude to Point Four: American Technical Missions overseas, 1838–1938* (Madison, WI: University of Wisconsin Press, 1954).

14 Michael Adas, *Dominance by Design: Technological Imperatives and America's Civilizing Mission* (Cambridge, CA: Harvard University Press, 2009), 30–2; Michael E. Latham, *Modernization as Ideology: American Social Science and 'Nation Building' in the Kennedy Era* (Chapel Hill, NC: University of North Carolina Press, 2000), 13–17. On early twentieth-century US technical assistance for agriculture in other developing countries see Gary R. Hess, 'American Agricultural Missionaries and Efforts at Economic Improvement in India', *Agricultural History* 42 (1968), 23–34; and David Ekbladh, *The Great American Mission: Modernization and the Construction of an American World Order* (Princeton, NJ: Princeton University Press, 2010), ch. 1.

15 Wilson Picado and José A. Fernández Molina, 'On the Institutional Cloning Hypothesis: US Agricultural Cooperation Programs in Latin America since WWII', *TransRuralHistory* (2nd international meeting of the Spanish and

this case was not communism but fascism. During the 1930s Washington began to worry about the expansion of Latin America's trade with Nazi Germany, Italy and Japan and subsequently took measures to secure its supplies of food and raw materials from the region.[16] In 1939 an Office of Inter-American Affairs was created within the State Department with Nelson Rockefeller as director.[17] Although focusing initially on countering Nazi ideology, the Office also provided technical assistance.[18] Then in 1942 a distinct institution was created to manage and coordinate the Office's technical assistance programmes: the Institute for Inter-American Affairs.[19] The IIAA worked with Latin American governments to enhance public health facilities and improve infrastructure but also to boost agricultural production.[20] Working collaboratively with host country experts as well as the private sector, IIAA institutes taught local farmers and experts how to use improved seed and new cultivation techniques but also offered scholarships that allowed promising locals to attend US universities. Although jointly funded and formally accountable to the host country's Ministry of Agriculture, it is worth noting that these institutes were usually directed by a US citizen, and their research and extension work was controlled by US personnel.[21] Many of the institutes ran subsidiary projects that imported and sold seeds, fertiliser and insecticides to farmers.[22]

Portuguese Rural History Societies), Santiago de Compostela, 2018. Cf also the chapter by both authors in this volume.

16 Javier Gonzalo Alcalde, *The Idea of Third World Development: Emerging Perspectives in the US and Britain, 1900–1950* (Lanham, MD: University Press of America, 1987); Eric Helleiner, *Forgotten Foundations of Bretton Woods: International Development and the Making of the Postwar Order* (Ithaca, NY: Cornell University Press, 2014), 31–2.

17 Alcalde, *Idea of Third World Development*, 122–4; Stephen J. Macekura, 'The Point Four Program and US International Development Policy', *Political Science Quarterly* 128 (2013), 127–60, at 134.

18 Craig Murphy, *The UN Development Programme: A Better Way?* (Cambridge: Cambridge University Press, 2006), 37.

19 Kenneth R. Iverson, 'The "Servicio" in Theory and Practice', *Public Administration Review* 11 (1951), 223–8.

20 Claude C. Erb, 'Prelude to Point Four: the IIAA', *Diplomatic History* 9 (1985), 249–69; Macekura, 'Point Four Program'.

21 Darlene Rivas, *Missionary Capitalist: Nelson Rockefeller in Venezuela* (Chapel Hill, NC: University of North Carolina Press, 2002), 53; Picado and Fernández, 'On the Institutional Cloning Hypothesis'; Arthur T. Mosher, *Technical Co-operation in Latin-American Agriculture* (Chicago, IL: Chicago University Press, 1957).

22 Mosher, *Technical Co-operation*, 17. Wartime programmes such as the IIAA are important, but one wonders to what extent the war itself may have shifted public perceptions of 'scientific agriculture'. By putting pressure on farmers to maximise output, for example, the war fostered the extensive use of synthetic fertilisers and mechanisation, and the resulting jump in productivity was in

Nor were government bodies and the Rockefeller Foundation the only US sponsors of early technical assistance. Soon after the war various private organisations also established programmes for agriculture in Latin America. Brazil, for example, was the site of several private organisations established by Nelson Rockefeller with the aim of promoting modernisation via 'scientific agriculture' (including improved seed).[23] In addition to the American International Association (AIA, established 1946), Rockefeller also established a profit-making organisation, the International Basic Economy Corporation (IBEC), which focused on increasing productivity using high-tech methods such as synthetic fertilisers and tractors.[24] The impact of these organisations was considerable. Between 1949 and 1964 AIA funded the training of 200 Brazilian extension workers in the US, while the US government funded more than thirty US agronomists to go to Brazil to train extension agents and set up extension services.[25]

Rockefeller's organisations are important partly because they demonstrate that post-war technical assistance was not provided just by programmes that are conventionally regarded as part of the Green Revolution. But they are also significant for another reason: their existence further weakens the Cold War thesis. For historians of US-Latin American relations are agreed that, in the eyes of US politicians and officials, communism did *not* pose a serious threat in Latin America during the 1950s.[26] The US's Cold War concerns were focused instead on western Europe (giving rise to the Marshall Plan) as well as on Asia. As a result, although various Latin American governments appealed to the US for development aid after 1945, they got little response.[27] This suggests that US programmes of technical assistance for Latin America after 1939 and throughout the 1950s are unlikely to have been driven by Cold War concerns.[28]

---

effect a gift to the inputs industry, demonstrating the power of its approach to agriculture (Philip Conford. 'Science, Organic Husbandry and the Work of Dr. David Hodges', *Agricultural History Review* 59 (2012), 217–36, at 218). Moreover, the wartime invention and introduction of other technologies perceived as deriving from 'science' – for example, DDT, penicillin, the atomic bomb – is apt to have encouraged the belief that cultivation practices allegedly based on agricultural science (for example, synthetic fertiliser, high-yielding varieties) might similarly be the most effective way to modernise.

23 Elizabeth Anne Cobbs, *The Rich Neighbor Policy: Rockefeller and Kaiser in Brazil* (New Haven, CT: Yale University Press, 1992).

24 Ibid., 146–8.

25 Brazil was not the only Latin American country where Rockefeller's organisations championed 'scientific agriculture'. On similar organisations in Venezuela, see Rivas, *Missionary Capitalist*.

26 Ibid., 215; Helleiner, *Forgotten Foundations of Bretton Woods*, 262.

27 Until 1959 when the Cuban revolution focused US minds. Alcalde, *Idea of Third World Development*, 178–81; Cobbs, *Rich Neighbor Policy*, 3, 12–13; Rivas, *Missionary Capitalist*, 174–5.

28 Cobbs, *Rich Neighbor Policy*, 136.

Thus, although historians commonly regard the Green Revolution as having been driven by the Cold War, this linkage is much weaker than is often claimed. For not only were Cold War concerns insignificant in Latin America during the 1950s, but various US-funded programmes of technical assistance for agriculture were set up well before the onset of the Cold War.

15.2 The importance of soft power

There is a more fundamental reason, however, why the explanatory power of the Cold War has been overemphasised. To be sure, against the backdrop of the Cold War it is easier to understand why US politicians, foundation trustees and other donors were willing to support Green Revolution programmes. But donor support of itself is insufficient to explain why such programmes actually went ahead because the decision to proceed did not depend on donors alone. For a key feature of technical assistance programmes including the Green Revolution is that they were *cooperative* in character.[29]

Whether funded by the Rockefeller Foundation or other donors, these programmes were based on a contract between donor organisation and recipient that specified what work was to be carried out, over what period, and who would fund it.[30] As a result, such programmes could not proceed without the host government's agreement, and a striking feature of technical assistance programmes in the 1940s and 1950s was their popularity.[31] Why, then, were host countries so keen on foreign technical assistance? The answer, as we shall see, had little to do with the Cold War.

29 During the 1950s technical assistance by both the US and the United Nations was provided via what were called 'technical cooperation' programmes.

30 Murphy, *UN Development Programme*, 97, 102; Perkins, *Geopolitics and the Green Revolution*, 106–8; Macekura, 'Point Four Program', 135–6; Amanda Kay McVety, *Enlightened Aid: US Development as Foreign Policy in Ethiopia* (Oxford: Oxford University Press, 2012), 109–11.

31 Lester Brown, *Seeds of Change: The Green Revolution and Development in the 1970s* (New York: Praeger, 1970), 8–9. On inter-war China's interest in drawing upon the advice of Western economists, see Margherita Zanasi, 'Exporting Development: The League of Nations and Republican China', *Comparative Studies in Society and History* 49 (2007), 143–69. On the enthusiasm for technical assistance from the UN, see David Webster, 'Development Advisors in a Time of Cold War and Decolonization: The UN Technical Assistance Administration, 1950–1959', *J. Global History* 6 (2011), 249–72, at 252; Ruth Jachertz, '"To keep food out of politics": The UN Food and Agriculture Organisation, 1945–1965', *International Organisations and Development, 1945–1990*, Marc Frey, Sönke Kunkel and Corinna Unger (eds) (Basingstoke: Palgrave-Macmillan, 2014), 75–100, at 84–5; Murphy, *UN Development Programme*, 51–3. On Colombia's request to the Rockefeller Foundation in 1948, see Lorek, 'Developing Paradise', 248.

In attempting to account for this shift it will be useful to distinguish three kinds of power that appear to have influenced the outcome. To be sure, forms of geopolitical and economic power played a role in the turn towards high-input agriculture after 1945. But as various authors have argued, conventional forms of power – military force, political pressure, economic pressure – are rarely sufficient to explain major shifts of policy.[32] 'Soft power' – that is, exercising influence or persuasion through non-coercive means to induce others to align their views with yours – is equally important.[33]

According to Nye, soft power can be exercised in several ways. One vehicle thought to be effective in promoting an attractive image of the power-seeking group is popular culture (for example, film, television, commercial products). But another medium for the exercise of soft power (which Nye mentions but does not pursue in detail) is what is sometimes called 'high culture'. This category includes the perceived quality of a nation's scholarship, the innovativeness of its science and technology,[34] and the attractiveness and accessibility of its higher education system to students and staff from abroad. That most European countries attach importance to this form of soft power is evident from the existence of such organisations as the British Council, the Alliance Française or the Goethe-Institut. It seems plausible, therefore, that aid donors in the North have influenced developing countries through the perceived quality of the donor's technical expertise as well as its accessibility.[35]

Although Elizabeth Cobbs' illuminating study of Nelson Rockefeller's organisations in Brazil does not employ the concept of soft power, it nicely illustrates nonetheless how technical expertise was deployed in an attempt to acquire such power. She argues that these organisations represented a continuation of the 'Good Neighbour Policy' that President

32 John Agnew, *Hegemony: The New Shape of Global Power* (Philadelphia, PA: Temple University Press, 2005).

33 Joseph Nye, *Soft Power: The Means to Success in World Politics* (New York: Public Affairs, 2004).

34 On US attempts to exercise soft power after 1945 by exploiting its dominance in science and technology, see John Krige, 'Technological Leadership and American Soft Power', in *Soft Power and US Foreign Policy*, Inderjeet Parmar and Michael Cox (eds) (London: Routledge, 2010), 121–36. On the foundations' efforts to alleviate anti-US sentiment by attracting foreign scholars to knowledge-networks in the social sciences, see Inderjeet Parmar, *Foundations of the American Century: The Ford, Carnegie and Rockefeller Foundations in the Rise of American Power* (New York: Columbia University Press, 2012).

35 In a similar vein, Geiger has argued that the Marshall Plan's technical assistance programmes contributed to the acceptance by Western European governments of the American vision of a new international economic order after 1945; Till Geiger, '"The Power Game", Soft Power and the International Historian', in *Soft Power and US Foreign Policy*, Parmar and Cox (eds), 83–107, at 87–8.

Roosevelt had introduced in the 1930s.[36] Judging that the customary US reliance on military intervention in Latin America was having diminishing returns, Roosevelt had opted to develop a system of friendly alliances with which to influence policy in the region. Rockefeller shared this view, she argues, hoping that his organisations' technical assistance and other forms of development aid would foster good relations with the host countries and bring about shifts of policy more conducive to US business interests. Cobbs' thesis appears to characterise, not just Nelson Rockefeller's organisations, but the whole range of US-funded technical assistance programmes after 1939.

The argument that follows, therefore, is that US soft power was crucial for the spread of the Green Revolution from *c.* 1940 into the 1960s. The war's outcome, leaving European economies shattered and the US as the strongest country militarily and economically, gave the US the leading role in shaping international politics (in the non-communist world). A new feature of this post-war scene was the formation of 'development policy' through which rich countries in the Global North offered technical assistance to 'underdeveloped' countries in the South. Because of the dominant role of the US in this area, nearly all the early programmes for agricultural 'development' from the 1940s were staffed by American experts (or by host country scientists who had been trained in the US). These experts, naturally enough, brought their own vision of how best to 'modernise' agriculture. Promoted by state agencies in the US since the late nineteenth century, it was an approach that relied heavily on commercial inputs. For this reason, the early Green Revolution can fairly be described as an 'American revolution'.

Central to this argument, therefore, is the *scale* of US technical assistance for agriculture after the war: how widespread were US experts in the Global South? We have already encountered above several US organisations providing technical assistance that are not usually regarded as part of the Green Revolution (IIAA, AIA, IBEC). If we now consider those programmes that are commonly associated with the Green Revolution, we find that every one of them was funded by a US organisation. The Mexican Agricultural Program and others modelled upon it in Colombia, Ecuador and Chile during the 1950s were funded by the Rockefeller Foundation. The Indian Green Revolution from the 1950s was funded by both Ford and Rockefeller Foundations. Green Revolutions elsewhere in South Asia during the 1960s and 1970s were funded by the Ford Foundation. Finally, new studies of the Green Revolution in Brazil from the late 1940s into the 1960s demonstrate its reliance on support from the US government and US private organisations.[37]

36 Cobbs, *Rich Neighbor Policy*, 237–8.

37 Ryan Nehring, 'The Brazilian Green Revolution', *Political Geography* (2022),

But foundation-supported programmes were not the only form that post-war technical assistance took. Although they have attracted much less attention from historians, the so-called 'Point Four' programmes – first proposed in President Truman's 1949 inaugural speech – were more numerous and arguably just as important as foundation programmes.[38] Moreover, Point Four programmes were similar in character to Green Revolution programmes, partly because they provided the technologies of high-input agriculture,[39] but also because the Rockefeller's programme in Mexico was one of the institutional models for Point Four.[40]

As Truman explained, 'we must embark on a bold new program for making the benefits of our scientific advances and industrial progress available for the improvement and growth of underdeveloped areas'.[41] Although the proposal to provide 'technical assistance' to poor countries was a last-minute inclusion in Truman's speech, some historians have subsequently come to regard this provision as marking the beginning of 'the development age'.[42] Like most aid programmes – then as now – however, Point Four programmes were not motivated solely by humanitarian concerns. In part they were designed to further US Cold War aims,[43] but the act establishing the programme envisioned that small-scale government-funded projects would also pave the way for capital investment by firms and other organisations.[44] Politicians had an eye on the prospects for new global markets, so Nelson Rockefeller sought to make Point Four attractive, arguing that 'the security and continued prosperity of the US and other relatively industrialized nations can be maintained only if there is complementary progress in the economically

https://www.sciencedirect.com/science/article/abs/pii/S0962629821002341 (accessed 30 March 2025).

38 David Ekbladh, *The Great American Mission*, 77ff; Macekura, 'Point Four Program'.

39 Jonathan Bingham, *Shirt-sleeve Diplomacy: Point Four in Action* (New York: John Day, 1954).

40 Cotter, 'Origins of the Green Revolution in Mexico', 248; Shane Hamilton, *Supermarket USA: Food and Power in the Cold War Farms Race* (New Haven, CT: Yale University Press, 2018), 49.

41 Quoted in Ekbladh, *Great American Mission*, 77.

42 Gilbert Rist, *The History of Development: From Western Origins to Global Faith*, 3rd edn (London: Zed Books, 2008), 71; Macekura, 'Point Four Program', 130. The claim is somewhat misleading. To be sure, Point Four represented the first explicit policy *in the US* to provide development aid for the global South, and in 1961 the agency initially responsible for Point Four programmes was renamed the US Agency for International Development (USAID). But as several historians have shown, the concept of 'development' and programmes of aid for the South had been a part of British colonial policy from the 1920s.

43 Alcalde, *Idea of Third World Development*, 205–6.

44 Macekura, 'Point Four Program', 140, 143–4.

backward areas'.[45] The low cost of technical assistance (compared to large-scale infrastructure projects) was another selling-point in Congress at a time when 'development aid' had not yet become a standard item of government expenditure. From the US point of view, therefore, Point Four was a bargain: 'How can we help get more buying power in the hands of the other peoples of the world? How can we help them get more dollars without just giving it to them?'[46]

The answer to his question, in the eyes of many in the US, was that knowledge and expertise were key to the strength of the US economy. Potential recipients of Point Four assistance seem to have agreed, for the programme was decidedly popular among poor countries. Within a year of starting, there were projects underway in twenty-two countries,[47] and by 1953 Point Four had placed more than 2,000 technical experts in thirty-five countries.[48]

Of course, technical assistance during the 1940s and 1950s was not provided just by US organisations. How significant, then, were other donors? If we consider Western Europe, for example, assessing the significance of its technical assistance is not straightforward since the literature on that subject is still relatively small. For the moment, however, the scale of such support appears to have been substantially lower than US aid. If this was the case, it would not be surprising. Britain was effectively bankrupt in 1945, and German industry was largely destroyed. As a result, West Germany only began to fund development aid from the late 1950s, and its ministry for development was not established until 1961.[49] During the 1950s and 1960s the resources that some imperial powers could afford to spend on economic aid to former colonies – with an eye to maintaining economic and political influence[50] – were limited because the Europeans were elsewhere having to fund colonial wars in an attempt

45 Nelson Rockefeller, 'Widening Boundaries of National Interest', *Foreign Affairs* 29 (1951), 523 and *passim*.

46 Rockefeller, quoted in Cobbs, *Rich Neighbor Policy*, 59.

47 Anon., 'Agricultural Point Four Reaches 22 Countries', *Foreign Agriculture* (Office of Foreign Agricultural Relations, USDA), 15 (2) (February 1951), 34.

48 Perkins, *Geopolitics and the Green Revolution*, 154.

49 Heide-Irene Schmidt, 'Pushed to the Front: The Foreign Assistance Policy of the Federal Republic of Germany, 1958–1971', *Contemporary European History* 12 (2003), 473–507; Hendrik Grote, 'Von der Entwicklungshilfe zur Entwicklungspolitik: Voraussetzungen, Strukturen u. Mentalitaeten d. bundesdeutschen Entwicklungshilfe, 1949–1961', *Vorgaenge* 166 (2004), 24–35; Karsten Linne, 'Personelle Engpaesse: Tropenlandwirte fuer d. "Entwicklungshilfe"', *Zeitschrift fuer Agrargeschichte u. Agrarsoziologie*. 69 (2021), 83–99.

50 Heide-Irene Schmidt and Helge Pharo, 'Introduction', *Contemporary European History* 12 (2003), 387–94 at 390.

to cling on to empires.[51] As a result, in south-east Asia after 1945, for example, the US was 'the predominant power and principal donor of development assistance in the region'.[52] Similarly, multilateral European aid began with the establishment of the EEC's Development Fund only in 1958, and its initial funding was small.[53]

In Eastern Europe a Commission for Technical Assistance was set up in the late 1950s, but its focus was on manufacturing and industrialisation.[54] From the late 1950s the Soviet Union funded technical assistance to agriculture in Sub-Saharan Africa – emphasising mechanisation – but the projects were discontinued within a few years,[55] and at the time Soviet aid was dwarfed by that from the capitalist countries.[56] On present evidence, therefore, it appears that into the early 1960s US agricultural experts greatly outnumbered their European counterparts in developing countries.

To be sure, Europe was not the only non-US source of technical assistance after the war. The UN's Food and Agricultural Organization (FAO; established 1945) initially had a Rural Welfare Division that promoted broadly based rural development through self-help at village level.[57] In 1950 it also created a programme of technical assistance that financed individual experts, fellowships for foreign study, and training programmes for local technicians in various countries,[58] all of which steadily eclipsed its work on rural welfare. Its technical assistance programme was also in great demand from developing countries and continued to dominate the organisation through the 1960s.[59] Despite sending hundreds of experts to dozens of countries and awarding hundreds of fellowships for training,

51 Marc Frey, 'Control, Legitimacy, and the Securing of Interests: European Development Policy in Southeast Asia from the Late Colonial Period to the Early 1960s', *Contemporary European History* 12 (2003), 395–412.

52 Ibid., 409.

53 Veronique Dimier, *The Invention of a European Development Aid Bureaucracy* (London: Palgrave Macmillan, 2014), 16.

54 Sara Lorenzini, 'COMECON and the South in the Years of Detente: A Study of East-South Economic Relations', *European Review of History* 21 (2014), 183–99.

55 Alessandro Iandolo, 'The Rise and Fall of the "Soviet Model of Development" in West Africa, 1957–1964', *Cold War History* 12 (2012), 683–704.

56 Schmidt, 'Pushed to the Front', 476; Eric Burton, 'Socialisms in Development: Revolution, Divergence & Crisis, 1917–1991', *Journal für Entwicklungspolitik* 33 (2017), 4–20, at 11.

57 Amalia Ribi Forclaz, 'From Reconstruction to Development: The Early Years of the FAO and the Conceptualization of Rural Welfare, 1945–1955', *International History Review* 41 (2019), 351–71.

58 Donna C. Mehos and Suzanne M. Moon, 'The Uses of Portability: Circulating Experts in the Technopolitics of Cold War and Decolonization', in *Entangled Geographies: Empire and Technopolitics in the Global Cold War*, Gabrielle Hecht (ed.) (Cambridge: MIT Press, 2011), 43–74, at 56ff.

59 Jachertz, 'To keep food out of politics', 84–5; Murphy, *UN Development Programme*, 51–3; Ribi Forclaz, 'From Reconstruction to Development', 360ff.

however, the UN's budget for technical assistance in the early 1950s was only a tenth the size of US spending on foreign aid.[60]

As a UN organisation, the FAO claimed that its expert teams would be multinational in character and that no single nationality would be overrepresented.[61] To what extent, then, was its technical assistance distinct from that of the US? In 1952 the largest contingent among its experts – about one-third – were from the US,[62] and between 1948 and 1956 both of its directors-general were Americans. One of them, Norris Dodd, had previously worked for the USDA and regarded the FAO as a kind of international department of agriculture that would oversee a global agricultural revolution comparable to that which the USDA had overseen in the US.[63] As far as the nature of FAO technical assistance is concerned, there are several indications that it promoted the use of commercial inputs, including hybrid maize seed, fertiliser and pesticide.[64] In 1959 the FAO met with representatives of the international fertiliser industry, leading to the establishment of a Fertiliser Industry Advisory Board that provided 'expertise' and free fertiliser to host countries.[65] Despite the FAO's claim to a multinational character, therefore, its vision of technical modernisation appears to have been little different from that championed by the US.

Post-war technical assistance, therefore, was heavily dominated into the 1960s by US experts (or by FAO experts recommending similar technology). To understand the impact of the 'Americanisation' of such expertise, however, we must place it in a political and economic context. The central fact is that the US economy had emerged from the war in very good shape. Its gross national product (GNP) had nearly doubled between 1939 and 1945, and no other country's GNP was even one-third of its size.[66] This made for a huge disparity between the US and western European economies. In consequence, until the mid-1950s, in one historian's

60 Webster, 'Development Advisors in a Time of Cold War and Decolonization', 255; Amy Staples, *The Birth of Development: How the World Bank, Food and Agricultural Organisation, and World Health Organisation Changed the World, 1945–1965* (Kent, OH: Kent State University Press, 2006), 100.

61 Mehos and Moon, 'Uses of portability', 59–60.

62 Ribi Forclaz, 'From Reconstruction to Development', 361–2; Webster, 'Development Advisors in a Time of Cold War and Decolonization', 252–3.

63 Staples, *Birth of Development*, 97.

64 Jachertz, 'To keep food out of politics', 80; Staples, *Birth of Development*, 86, 101; Robert W Jugenheimer, 'Hybrid Maize Emigrates to the Old World', *Foreign Agriculture* 18 (1954), 63–6. Pat R. Mooney, *Seeds of the Earth: A Public or Private Resource?* (Ottawa: Inter-Pares, 1979), 48.

65 Jacoby, *Man and Land*; id., 'Agri-business and the United Nations System', *Development and Change* 9 (1978), 331–40; Staples, *Birth of Development*, 112–13.

66 Geir Lundestad, 'Empire by Invitation? The US and Western Europe, 1945–1952', *J. Peace Research* 23 (1986), 263–77, at 264.

judgement, the only country that could afford to set up a system of foreign economic assistance was the US.[67] When one also takes into account the scale of its military strength, some historians reckon that the US emerged from the Second World War 'by far the strongest power on earth'.[68]

Predictably, such geopolitical dominance invites hubris. As European empires began to crumble from the late 1940s, it seems likely that those Americans charged with designing and implementing technical assistance programmes may have felt little inclined to turn to earlier European experience, confident that US agricultural know-how would be as successful in the global South as US science and technology had been in the war.[69] In his wide-ranging study of the transfer of US technology to other countries, for example, Michael Adas remarks that:

> America's emergence as a global power has been consistently driven by a sense of can-do confidence, a faith in scientific and technological solutions, and a missionary certitude that the US was destined to serve as a model for the rest of humanity.[70]

Although Adas' judgement is a sweeping one, it fits the early years of the Green Revolution quite well. Reporting back to the Rockefeller Foundation from a reconnaissance trip to Colombia in 1948, for example, two agricultural scientists wrote that 'What has been done in the US can also be done in other American countries, but only with help from the US'.[71] A year later, as the Point Four programme was announced, another advisor to the Foundation voiced unease, writing that the US government seemed to be taking up development activity with a:

> maximum sense of our own power, our own interest, our own goodness and our own knowledge [but he warned that the US had] very little knowledge of the parties of the second part. Our conceit and

67 Schmidt, 'Pushed to the front', 475.

68 Lundestad, 'Empire by Invitation?', 264; Westad, *Global Cold War*, 110.

69 This inclination to discount the value of European experience is noticeable in the writings of US experts who were involved in the design of Green Revolution programmes in the 1940s and 1950s: Jonathan Harwood, 'Coming to Terms with Tropical Ecology: Technology Transfer in the Early Green Revolution', *International J. Agricultural Sustainability* 19 (2021), 305–18. The Marshall Plan's agricultural experts were similarly disposed. As Bernardi has observed, the Plan's technical assistance concept was supposed to promote an 'exchange' of knowledge, but this exchange 'was not conceived on an equal basis, but on the idea of the superiority of the American system of production compared to Europe'; Emanuele Bernardi, 'Political Stability, Modernization and Reforms During the First Years of the Cold War', in *Agriculture in Capitalist Europe*, Carin Martiin *et al.* (eds) (London: Routledge, 2016), 57–74, at 47.

70 Adas, *Dominance by Design*, 8.

71 Quoted in Lorek, 'Developing Paradise', 281; cf. 275–7.

> our desire for speed gives us very little readiness to study these matters before acting.[72]

This self-confidence seems to have persisted into the 1960s, judging from the reflections of an American agronomist on his days as a graduate student:

> [It] … was a time of scientific euphoria … As scientists we considered that we were masters of our fate and the fate of humankind. Our technologies and our opinions … dominated the formulation of the development paradigm of the day … There was little or no debate during those years, in the biological sciences at least, on development's direction. The success of current technologies was so overwhelming that it stifled serious debate on alternatives.[73]

With US experts predominating and confident in the power of US technology, therefore, it was almost certainly *their* vision of agricultural modernisation that was promoted; that is, the high-input agriculture that had proved so effective in US agriculture.[74]

***

US experts after the war were clearly keen to spread the word about the merits of 'scientific agriculture', but developing countries were also receptive to this message. For one thing, in the 1940s and 1950s, most countries in the South had relatively small agricultural research systems.[75] This was presumably due in part to the cost being prohibitive

72 Quoted in Ekbladh, *Great American Mission*, 104.

73 Richard R. Harwood, 'A History of Sustainable Agriculture', in *Sustainable Agricultural Systems*, Clive A. Edwards *et al.* (eds) (Ankeny: Soil & Water Conservation Society, 1990), 3–19, at 9–11. In a similar vein, Anderson, Levy and Morrison, *Rice Science and Development Politics*, 56 and 265–6; Cullather, *Hungry World*, 188; Amalia Ribi Forclaz, 'Agriculture, American Expertise, and the Quest for Global Data: Leo Estabrook and the First World Agricultural Census of 1930', *J. Global History* 11 (2016), 44–65 at 60. On the naive enthusiasm with which some US experts in Colombia during the 1940s preached the application of American methods, see Lorek, 'Developing Paradise', 244–5, 250, 256.

74 Willard Cochrane, *The Development of American Agriculture* (Minneapolis, MN: University of Minnesota Press, 1979), 122ff; Deborah Fitzgerald, *Every Farm a Factory: The Industrial Ideal in American Agriculture* (New Haven, CT: Yale University Press, 2003). That is not to say that high-input agriculture was 'peculiarly American'. As is well-established, the technologies constituting this approach were invented in several countries and by 1945 had been introduced in many countries. My argument is merely that US experts pushed an approach to agricultural production that they assumed was superior.

75 With exceptions, already by the inter-war period Japan had a substantial network of experiment stations, though it was not yet an industrialised economy.

for a developing country. In the case of colonies and newly independent countries, it was aggravated by the fact that during the colonial era, research funding had been largely allocated to export crops and had neglected staples. Thus, former colonies wishing to boost food production needed to look abroad for technical assistance, but their options were limited. Newly independent countries avoided where possible turning to former European imperial powers for this purpose, suspecting (rightly) that the latter were bent on maintaining economic and political control. The UN was perceived as more attractive, given its multinational character but, as we have seen, it had a relatively limited budget for technical assistance.[76]

This left the US as the best option. In addition to being able to offer technical assistance on a large scale, the US seems not to have been perceived as suspect (despite having possessed colonies since 1898), perhaps because after 1945 its politicians frequently declared their country's opposition to colonialism.[77] Although on occasion even the US government came under suspicion,[78] US foundations seem to have avoided this taint for the most part. Another attraction of US assistance was probably the productivity of its agriculture, since many newly independent countries wanted rapid growth. Boosting production via Green Revolution programmes offered a way to reduce the cost of food imports so as to subsidise industrialisation. Moreover, although few host country leaders during the 1950s seem to have been concerned to forestall communism, technical assistance nonetheless offered political advantages. Some used it to expand electoral support in rural areas,[79] while others – hoping to avoid political conflict – used it as a 'non-political'

76 Webster, 'Development Advisors in a Time of Cold War and Decolonization', 251–2.

77 Already in the 1920s one US economist returned from visits in the Global South with the impression that many countries were turning increasingly to the US for advice, believing that the US was less likely to exploit them; Curti and Birr, *Prelude to Point Four*, 186. After the First World War the Turkish government was also inclined to trust US experts more than Europeans (Hartmann, *Eigensinnige Musterschueler*, 63), while Syria declared its intention to seek US technical assistance because the US, unlike Britain or France, appeared to have no territorial ambitions in the Middle East: cf. Cyrus Schayegh, 'The Interwar Germination of Development and Modernisation Theory and Practice: Politics, Institution Building, and Knowledge Production Between the Rockefeller Foundation and the American University of Beirut', *Geschichte und Gesellschaft* 41 (2015), 649–84, here 653; Lundestad, 'Empire by invitation?', 268.

78 Mehos and Moon, 'The Uses of Portability', 58–9.

79 Wilson Picado, 'Technology, Geopolitics and Institutions: An Evaluation of the Green Revolution Dominant Narrative in Latin America', in *Handbook of the Historiography of Latin American Studies of the Life Sciences and Medicine*, A. Barahona (ed.) (Cham: Springer, 2022), 15–16.

way to increase production without having to introduce land reform.[80] Finally, US advice was often coupled with the offer to train host country agricultural staff at US universities.

The US 'package', therefore, probably looked like a good deal, though as we shall see, it was also clear to some host country experts that it came at a cost. Consider two examples from south Asia. In their analysis of Green Revolution rice research and development politics during the 1960s and 1970s, Robert Anderson and his colleagues examined why East Pakistan (from 1971, 'Bangladesh') decided to accept US advice that the country should adopt a Green Revolution strategy in rice breeding.[81] The reasons were several. To begin with, the Green Revolution strategy was a low-cost option for the Pakistani government since it was largely financed by USAID, the foundations and the World Bank. In addition, both of Pakistan's five-year-plans during the 1960s were largely based on the advice of US-trained economists (both Pakistani and American) who recommended the Green Revolution's 'technological package' (along with supporting projects such as building fertiliser factories and developing the irrigation network). On the other hand, East Pakistan's own rice-breeders had reservations about the wisdom of this strategy (doubts that later turned out to be well-founded). They acquiesced nonetheless, mainly because funding from the Ford Foundation and other donors offered their only hope of getting a well-equipped institute of rice-breeding research.[82] The overall result, therefore, was that 'The government of Pakistan could not afford *not* to buy the new high-yielding rice seed'.[83] Although the proposed Green Revolution strategy was less than ideal, therefore, the host government decided to go along with it, partly because of the donors' considerable economic resources but also because of the dominance of US expertise within the Pakistani planning process.

India seems to have been a similar case. Several historians have offered explanations for why the country in 1965 abandoned its previous reliance on a broad programme of rural development plus land reform in favour of its 'New Strategy'. Most of these accounts assign the primary causal influence to donors' political and economic power: the US government's use of food aid or the World Bank's mission in 1965 that made future funding conditional on the India's adoption of the New Strategy.[84] Thus 'Longstanding pressures by the major aid-giving powers, applied against

80 George, *How the Other Half Dies*, 69ff; Cotter, *Troubled Harvest*, 323–4.

81 Anderson, Levy and Morrison, *Rice Science and Development Politics*, 251ff.

82 Ibid., 262–3.

83 Ibid., 254.

84 Kristin L. Ahlberg, *Transplanting the Great Society: Lyndon Johnson and Food for Peace* (Columbia, MO: University of Missouri Press, 2008), 106ff; Francine Frankel, *India's Political Economy, 1947–1977* (Princeton, NJ: Princeton University Press, 1978), 269–72.

a new and insecure government ... [which was] anxious to deliver on the economic front, were in fact having their effect'.[85]

Various evidence, however, suggests that the significance of donor's hard power has been exaggerated. As Varshney has pointed out, the New Strategy was not in fact new in 1965.[86] Indian agriculture ministers had been calling for such a strategy since 1952, though they had failed to persuade the government at that time.[87] Moreover, the Agriculture Minister appointed in 1964 had already secured cabinet approval of the New Strategy *before* the World Bank mission's report was released and before the US government had begun to exert leverage via food aid.[88] As one Indian official later remarked, foreign experts had been 'pushing at an open door'.[89]

If the New Strategy actually dated from the 1950s, we should ask how it took shape. More particularly, what was the precise role of foreign advice in that process? For such advice was a politically delicate matter in India after 1947. On the one hand, Indian leaders knew that they would need technical assistance to build up the economy, and they actively sought it, especially from the US. On the other, as a newly independent country, they were acutely sensitive about anything that could be seen as foreign interference in Indian decision-making.[90] This meant that foreign advice was accepted when it accorded with what Indian politicians wanted to do anyway and when it came from what appeared to be a politically neutral source.

India actively sought foreign technical assistance as early as 1946.[91] By the late 1960s Point Four had supported 150 projects in India,[92] and

85 Ibid., 273.

86 Ashutosh Varshney, *Democracy, Development, and the Countryside: Urban-Rural Struggles in India* (Cambridge: Cambridge University Press, 1995).

87 George Rosen, *Western Economists and Eastern Societies: Agents of Change in South Asia, 1950–1970* (Baltimore, MD: Johns Hopkins University Press, 1985), 72–3.

88 Varshney, *Democracy, Development, and the Countryside*, 70–2.

89 David C. Engerman, *The Price of Aid: The Economic Cold War in India* (Cambridge, MA: Harvard University Press, 2018), 252–3.

90 Leonard A. Gordon, 'Wealth Equals Wisdom? The Rockefeller and Ford Foundations in India', *Annals of the American Academy of Political and Social Science* 554 (1997), 104–16 at 109.

91 Perkins, *Geopolitics and the Green Revolution*, 146–7; Nicole Sackley, 'Foundation in the Field: The Ford Foundation's New Delhi Office and the Construction of Development Knowledge, 1951–1970', in *American Foundations and the Co-production of World Order in the Twentieth Century*, John Krige and Helke Rausch (eds) (Göttingen: Vandenhoeck u. Ruprecht, 2012), 232–60, at 241; Unger, *Entwicklungspfade in Indien*, 52.

92 Benjamin R. Siegel, *Hungry Nation: Food, Famine and the Making of Modern India* (Cambridge: Cambridge University Press, 2018), 189.

the Rockefeller and Ford Foundations' projects are well-documented.[93] Operating in India was a tricky business, however, in part because Indian scholars did not take kindly to visiting US experts who, despite knowing very little about the Indian context, confidently presented their recommendations.[94] Moreover offering advice was a particularly delicate matter during the 1960s when the New Strategy was highly controversial among Indian politicians and scientists, and US advice was regarded in some circles as suspect.[95] For this reason the Ford Foundation's director made concerted efforts to win the trust of Indian politicians by distancing the Foundation from controversial US government policies and by not funding any projects that might be perceived by Indian politicians as intrusions on Indian sovereignty.[96] As a result, throughout the 1950s and into the early 1960s, the Foundation enjoyed a remarkable degree of trust from Nehru and the Planning Commission.[97]

Once the foundations had their foot in the door, there were numerous channels through which US expertise could have had an impact. The Rockefeller Foundation's funding of short study visits enabled Indian administrators and educators to observe US agricultural education and research while the provision of fellowships allowed promising Indian students of the agricultural sciences to study in the US, and American experts were prominent on the Indian committee that oversaw the founding of new agricultural universities.[98] And although Indian decision-makers did not accept every piece of US advice, in one historian's view, they were nonetheless inclined to see the Rockefeller as 'non-threatening and apolitical' and thus 'tended to accept these experts as a valid source of advice'.[99] Moreover, Ford Foundation officials seem to have used the trust that they, too, enjoyed to exert influence on Indian development policy, persuading Nehru in the late 1950s that India needed to focus more heavily on food production using improved technology. The government's subsequent decision in 1965 to extend this

93 Perkins, *Geopolitics and the Green Revolution*, 152; Goldsmith, 'Rockefeller Foundation's Indian Agricultural Program', 89–92.

94 Rosen, *Western Economists and Eastern Societies*, 35–7 and 53–5.

95 Frankel, *India's Political Economy*, 265–88; Cullather, *Hungry World*, 183–211.

96 Sackley, 'Foundation in the Field', 234–5, 248–9.

97 Perkins, *Geopolitics and the Green Revolution*, 151–2; Rosen, *Western Economists and Eastern Societies*, 10; Gordon, 'Wealth Equals Wisdom?', 115; Sackley, 'Foundation in the Field'.

98 Arthur Goldsmith, 'The Rockefeller Foundation's Indian Agricultural Program: Why it Worked', in *Philanthropy and Cultural Context: Western Philanthropy in South, East, and Southeast Asia in the 20th Century*, Soma Hewa and Philo Hove (eds) (Lanham, MD: University Press of America, 1997), 85–114, at 93–5 and 98–9.

99 Ibid., 106.

approach to the entire country represented the start of what soon became known as the Indian Green Revolution.[100]

Thus, India's desire for foreign technical assistance, combined with the trust that it placed in US experts, created a situation in which experts had many opportunities during the 1950s to influence India's agricultural education, research and development policy. To speak of 'influence', however, is slightly misleading insofar as it suggests that US experts managed to *overcome* Indian reservations. That does not seem to be how soft power is exercised.[101] In his illuminating study of the Turkish government's attempts to modernise its agriculture after 1918, Heinrich Hartmann argues that the influence of US and German agricultural experts on Turkish policy was heavily constrained by the state of Turkish political debate at the time.[102] Only advice that accorded with the government's priorities was taken on board. As a result, Hartmann argues, foreign expertise acted as a 'catalyst' of policy-change rather than as a 'motor'.[103] This may be a useful way to understand the role of US expertise in the Indian case.[104] For the New Strategy had indigenous roots, having been advocated by Indian ministers already in the early 1950s. And when faced in 1965 with considerable political resistance to the New Strategy, the Agriculture Minister and his allies in the Indian government were able to secure cabinet agreement to the policy by arguing that it was advisable, not just because of the US threat to withdraw food aid, but because it was also endorsed by experts: from the World Bank, both foundations, and a younger generation of US-trained Indian agricultural scientists.[105] Thus, although US expertise alone may not have been sufficient to prompt the decision, it provided the Indian Agriculture Minister with useful legitimation for his preferred course of action.[106]

Twenty years later critics of the Indian Green Revolution singled out this reliance on US advice as a serious defect. Both Dinesh Abrol and Ashok Rudra were critical of Indian politicians and the agricultural science elite for placing excessive trust in American advice on the grounds that US recommendations were inappropriate for Indian

100 Sackley, 'Foundation in the Field', 252–3.

101 Geiger, 'Power Game', 95.

102 Hartmann, *Eigensinnige Musterschueler*.

103 Ibid., 93–4, 126, 158.

104 Cf. Rosen, *Western Economists and Eastern Societies*, 99.

105 Varshney, *Democracy, Development, and the Countryside*, 76–7.

106 Although the evidence cited supports this claim, at the moment it should be regarded as a tentative hypothesis since the secondary sources I have used are quite one-sided. As Varshney has pointed out, by relying primarily on published sources, analyses of Indian economic policy have missed the 'forces, considerations, and interests' that actually shape policy decisions; ibid. xi.

conditions.[107] While their critique of US technical advice was well-taken, however, the lesson that Abrol drew from this episode failed to take into account the Indian context at the time. If host countries are to avoid becoming overly dependent on a single donor, he argued, they must seek *diverse* sources of expertise.[108] Though obviously true, this overlooks the fact that US technical advice after 1945 was relatively easy to obtain as well as attractive. Moreover, as in East Pakistan, it is not clear that India had much alternative. And that opened the door to US soft power.

15.3 Conclusion

The question I posed at the outset was why the Green Revolution emerged after the Second World War in the Global South. The answer that I have offered is that this shift was brought about through a combination of hard and soft power. As for the former, the US certainly possessed abundant political power (ultimately exerted via military means) after 1945. In Japan, South Korea and Taiwan, for example, it was able to push through agricultural modernisation via land reform after the war, but in general US governments seem to have avoided relying on coercion to bring about policy change. Similarly, US institutions – governments, foundations and corporations – possessed unparalleled economic resources after 1945, which, as we have seen, funded a plethora of programmes of technical assistance after the war. But neither form of hard power entirely accounts for host countries remarkable willingness to *accept* US offers of technical assistance. The explanation for this, I have argued, lay in the US's possession of soft power. Although experts in some host countries had reservations about the US vision of 'modernisation', the apparent neutrality, efficacy and accessibility of US expertise proved hard to resist. For that reason, it makes sense to think of the early years of the Green Revolution as effectively an 'American Revolution'.

107 Dinesh Abrol, 'American Involvement in Indian Agricultural Research', *Social Scientist* 11/10 (1983), 8–26. A. Rudra, 'Organisation of Agriculture for Rural Development: The Indian Case', in *Agrarian Systems and Rural Development*, Dharam Ghai *et al.* (eds) (London: Macmillan, 1979), 72–112. A. Rudra, 'Technological Choice in Agriculture in India Over the Past Three Decades', in *Macropolicies for Appropriate Technology in Developing Countries*, Frances Stewart (ed.) (Boulder, CO: Westview, 1987), 22–73.

108 Abrol, 'American Involvement in Indian Agricultural Research', 25.

16

US agricultural cooperation programmes in Latin America since the Second World War[1]

Wilson Picado-Umaña and José A. Fernández Molina

In this chapter we analyse the establishment and subsequent evolution of agricultural technical cooperation programmes in Latin America from the Second World War to 1955, emphasising their institutional dynamics. Our hypothesis is that these programmes' efficiency in more than ten countries with diverse ecological, social and political contexts was due to the strategy of institutional cloning. The Institute of Inter-American Affairs controlled this strategy through the creation of *servicios* for technical cooperation, which were formally ascribed to each national government but in practice remained autonomous to execute agricultural research and extension projects under the control of American personnel. These *servicios* shared a common institutional structure, frequently had the same appellative, executed the same projects and had the same goal: the diffusion of the principles, techniques and inputs of American agronomical culture. The *servicios* incentivised a 'supply-induced demand' for agricultural technology in Latin America, including new varieties, chemical fertilisers and pest-control techniques.

This chapter adds new perspectives to the study of the Green Revolution. First, our contention is that American agricultural cooperation programmes constituted a key episode in the 'prehistory' of the Green Revolution in Latin America, linking the latter to the Second World War. Although most literature on the Green Revolution deals with processes of agrarian change in south-east Asia during the 1960s and 1970s,[2] several recent studies have aimed to place the Green Revolution in the

1 The authors wish to express their gratitude to Allan J. Víquez Mora for his contribution to the research and drafting of this chapter.

2 Karim M. Bazlul, *The Green Revolution: An International Bibliography* (New York and London: Greenwood Press, 1986).

long durée.[3] Following Fitzgerald, this chapter aspires to comprehend the Green Revolution as a historical process.[4]

Second, this study of institutional dynamics confronts Ruttan and Hayami's theory on induced institutional change, which is part of their well-known theory of induced technical change.[5] According to these authors, changes in the relative prices of factors of production could have an impact on the role of institutions for agricultural development.[6] Our hypothesis of 'institutional cloning' acknowledges the role of institutions in agrarian change even if the latter's origin was part of a geopolitical dynamic. Thus, in this hypothesis the institutional change under study was a process generated by the 'supply', instead of the 'demand'; it was not the result of a change in the relative price of factors of production.

The argument is divided into three sections. The first section analyses the agricultural programmes set up by the Rockefeller Foundation in Mexico and South America during the 1940s, when this private institution represented the interests of an American government at war. The following section deals with the Office of the Coordinator of Inter-American Affairs, the government's agency in charge of securing Latin American support for the war effort, particularly the organisation of food supply programmes in several countries. Finally, the last leg focuses on the evolution of post-war agricultural cooperation programmes, emphasising their main goals and their shared institutional dynamic.

16.1 The Office of Special Studies and the Rockefeller Foundation in Mexico

The early stages of the Second World War, then mainly a European conflict, led to an American concern to improve diplomatic relations with Mexico, which had been strained by the nationalisation of oil fields in 1938 and the agrarian reform under President Lázaro Cárdenas.[7]

3 Raj Patel, 'The Long Green Revolution', *J. Peasant Studies* 40 (2013), 1–63; Wilson Picado, 'Evaluating the Green Revolution Dominant Narrative for Latin America: Technology, Geopolitics, and Institutions', in *Handbook of the Historiography of Latin American Studies on the Life Sciences and Medicine: Historiographies of Science*, Ana Barahona (ed.) (Cham: Springer, 2022).

4 Deborah Fitzgerald, 'Exporting American Agriculture: The Rockefeller Foundation in Mexico, 1943–1953', in *Missionaries of Science: The Rockefeller Foundation and Latin America*, Marcos Cueto (ed.) (Bloomington, IN: Indiana University Press, 1994), 73–4.

5 Yujiro Hayami and Vernon Ruttan, *Agricultural Development: An International Perspective* (Baltimore, MD: John Hopkins Press, 1971).

6 Hans. P. Binswanger and Vernon Ruttan, *Induced Innovation: Technology, Institutions and Development* (Baltimore, MD: John Hopkins University Press, 1978).

7 Friedrich Schuler, 'Alemania, México y los Estados Unidos durante la Segunda Guerra Mundial', *Secuencia* 7 (1987), 173–86.

Mexican territory was strategic in the defence against any Japanese attack on the Pacific coast and as a refuelling point in the air defence of the Panama Canal.[8] Furthermore, Mexico produced key mineral and agricultural products for the war effort, such as oil, rubber and natural fibres. Miguel Ávila Camacho, elected as president in 1940, favoured a rapprochement with the United States: his government maintained a 'political equilibrium' between the leftist followers of Cárdenas and the pressure from conservative groups. This government reached a consensus in the Mexican political scene through an explicit anti-fascist position, an asset for American diplomacy at the continental level as a counterweight to the ambiguous Argentine position towards Germany.[9]

The war facilitated a solution to the conflicts arising out of the nationalisation of oil fields. Cárdenas expropriated the oil companies' properties in 1938, mainly investments of Standard Oil Co. and Dutch Shell, which began an aggressive strategy of applying economic and political pressures. Despite these corporations' lobbying power, sales of Mexican oil to the Axis Powers and American participation in the war modified the circumstances for an agreement. The oil companies demanded the return of their properties and later exorbitant compensation too, but the war diminished their leverage over American government: national defence and economic security concerns were prioritised above private interests. A joint commission carried on negotiations and finally set the indemnities at $24 million and 5 per cent interest, well below the oil companies' demands.[10] Eventually Mexico paid almost $30 million to settle the oil fields expropriation.

The new climate in diplomatic relations led to the establishment of the Joint Mexican-United States Defence Commission in 1942.[11] The main American concern was a Japanese attack on the Pacific coast; the American Armed Forces wanted a series of radar stations and airports in Baja California, as well as a joint Mexican-American defence plan. Although the danger of a Japanese attack disappeared, this rapprochement was extended to trade relations through a commercial treaty in December 1942. This agreement increased Mexican exports of oil, copper, lead, zinc and other metals, while it regularised migrant labour and increased American loans to stabilise the Mexican economy.[12] In hindsight the improved Mexican-American diplomatic relations during the war legitimised Ávila Camacho's government – as well as the Partido Revolucionario

8 Josefina Vázquez and Lorenzo Meyer, *México frente a Estados Unidos. Un ensayo histórico, 1776–2000* (México: Fondo de Cultura Económica, 2006).

9 Ibid., 181–2.

10 Ibid., 183.

11 Ibid., 185.

12 Ibid., 186–7.

Institucional's hegemony for several decades – while consolidating the industrialisation policy adopted by the Mexican political elite.[13]

The Rockefeller Foundation (hereafter, the Foundation) was a private philanthropic organisation established in 1913 that would prove instrumental in the formulation of American policies towards Latin America. During the early twentieth century, its main contributions were in the areas of health and education, and its involvement in agricultural programmes was limited. Domestically, the Foundation worked with the Department of Agriculture in an educational programme to eradicate hookworm in the South of the United States between 1906 and 1919. Although its role was strictly to provide the funds, this was an early linkage with the American institutional framework of grant-land colleges, the Department of Agriculture and, from 1914, the Agricultural Extension Service. Abroad the Foundation financed a programme of cereal cultivation at Nanjing University, China, in 1924.[14]

The Foundation's involvement in Mexico began with an evaluation of the country's agriculture. The authors of the report were the phytopathologist Elvin C. Stakman of the University of Minnesota, the agronomist and soil scientist Richard Bradfield from Cornell and the geneticist Paul C. Mangelsdorf of Texas A&M. Stakman already had a reputation from working abroad. He had served as agent of the US Department of Agriculture in Latin America, evaluating the impact of wheat rust, and later was scientific advisor for the rubber plantations owned by Firestone in Liberia. Although he was a prospective chairman for the Mexican Programme, Stakman proposed George Harrar as chairman. Harrar worked at Washington State College, Pullman, had undertaken work in Puerto Rico, and was fluent in Spanish. Harrar and Mangelsdorf, with Stakman's advice, chose the research team. They hired the maize expert from Idaho, Edwin Wellhausen, the phytopathologist Norman E. Borlaug, the soil expert William E. Colwell, the entomologist John J. McKelvey, the maize geneticist Lewis M. Roberts and the botanist Dorothy Parker.[15] The new team members were all born in agricultural zones of the United States, had studied in universities with prestigious agricultural sciences departments, and had experience in experimental stations. Several team members had become acquainted while still in education: Stakman had been professor to Harrar and Borlaug, as Mangelsdorf had been to Roberts and, finally, Harrar had taught McKelvey.[16]

13 Ibid., 189.

14 John H. Perkins, *Geopolitics and the Green Revolution: Wheat, Genes and the Cold War* (New York: Oxford University Press, 1997), 103.

15 Fitzgerald, 'Exporting American Agriculture', 77.

16 Ibid., 78; David Sonnenfeld, 'Mexico's "Green Revolution" 1940–1980: Towards an Environmental History', *Environmental History Review* 16 (1992), 29–52; Joseph Cotter, 'The Rockefeller Foundation's Mexican Agricultural

The recently hired research team became the Office of Special Studies (OSS), organised on the model of American experimental stations. The OSS was a semi-autonomous organisation within the Mexican state (which had its own agrarian research institutions), attached to the Mexican Secretaría de Agricultura, but due to its links with the Rockefeller Foundation it occupied a liminal position. The Foundation paid its personnel's salaries, equipment, funded administrative expenses and contributed part of the Mexican agronomists' salaries. The Mexican government gradually increased its share, paying for local personnel in training, labourers, transportation costs, land and experimental stations.[17]

The Mexican institution competing with the OSS during the war was the Sección de Campos Agrícolas Experimentales, created in the 1930s and attached to the Secretaría de Agricultura. The Sección had a profound leftist leaning, inherited from the Cárdenas government, and sought the betterment of the peasantry. The Sección had several agricultural practical schools to train the leaders of the communities founded by the Agrarian Reform; eventually the Sección became the Instituto de Investigaciones Agrícolas (IIA) in 1947.[18] The Sección had also a research programme where the scientist Edmundo Taboada and his colleagues created several hybrid seeds that then became a model for the American scientists. Taboada studied phytopathology at Cornell University and the University of Minnesota in 1932–3. After his graduation, Herbert Kendall Hayes invited him to study the *chahuixtle*, a wheat disease affecting Minnesotan crops, where he worked with Elvin Stakman.[19] In 1934 Taboada was appointed chairman of the Estación Agrícola Experimental del Yaqui, Sonora.

Even after the foundation of the IIA in 1947, the Mexican government gave stronger financial support to the OSS. Although formally the IIA was the official research programme, the OSS received more official support as well as foreign aid from the Foundation in the period 1943–56, given the investment required in infrastructure and salaries. It was not until 1956 that the size of the IIA budget exceeded foreign funding. By then the

Project. A Cross-Cultural Encounter, 1943–1949', in *Missionaries of Science*, Cueto (ed.), 97–125; Jonathan Harwood, 'Peasant Friendly Plant Breeding and the Early Years of the Green Revolution in Mexico', *Agricultural History* 83 (2009), 384–410; Diana Méndez, 'El Programa Cooperativo Centroamericano para el Mejoramiento del Maíz: Una historia transnacional de la Revolución Verde desde Costa Rica y Guatemala, 1954–1963' (master's thesis, Instituto de Investigaciones Dr José María Luis Mora, México, 2018).

17 Cynthia Hewitt de Alcántara, *La modernización de la agricultura mexicana. 1940–1970* (México: Siglo Veintiuno Editores, 1978), 33–4.

18 Ibid., 31–2.

19 Ana Barahona, Susana Pinar and Francisco Ayala, 'Introduction and Institutionalization of Genetics in Mexico', *J. History of Biology* 38 (2005), 279.

Foundation was withdrawing from Mexico and transferred control over the OSS research programmes, which became the Centro Internacional de Mejoramiento de Maíz y Trigo (CYMMIT).[20]

16.2 The Rockefeller Foundation in Central and South America

The Mexican programme was the Foundation's first agricultural experience in Latin America. Its programme there was the research base for new programmes in Colombia (1950), Chile (1955) and Ecuador (1956). However, the Foundation had given funds for specific activities in these three countries since the 1940s, and the new programmes may be seen as the strengthening of those early contacts. There were also less ambitious programmes in Peru, Brazil, Honduras, Bolivia and Costa Rica, as well as a Central American programme that we discuss below.

The Foundation financed agricultural research in Colombia from the late 1940s.[21] It provided funds to the Universidad Nacional, specifically to the Veterinary College in Bogotá, the Agricultural College in Medellín and the Colegio de Agricultura in Cali – which was later attached to the Universidad Nacional – for buildings, equipment, scholarships to study in the United States or internships in the Mexican programme. After the agreement with the Colombian government in 1949, the Foundation took control over the programme and assigned the research to the scientists Lewis M. Roberts and Joseph A. Rupert both of whom had worked in the Mexican programme, the former in maize and the latter in wheat.[22]

Roberts was a well-known expert on maize even before he worked in the OSS. He was trained with Mangelsdorf and Donald F. Jones, both linked to experimental stations in Texas and recognised as first-class experts on the grain. Roberts went to the Finca Experimental Tulio Espina, Medellín, as programme director, while Rupert set his 'fortress' in Estación Experimental de La Picota, Bogotá, close to wheat's agroecological niche. In Bogotá Rupert experimented with local seeds as well as seeds brought from Mexico.[23] According to Stakman, Rupert experimented with almost 7,000 lines of wheat, most of them with genetic material from the Mexican programme. The *Menkemen* variety, brought from Mexico by Rupert, showed promising yields.[24] Roberts followed the same dynamic in maize research. Through the selection of local and foreign seeds, the Colombian agronomist Eduardo Chavarriaga – a former guest researcher

20 Hewitt de Alcántara, *La modernización de la agricultura mexicana*, 51–5.

21 The Rockefeller Foundation, *Annual Report 1947* (New York, 1947), 166–7; Timothy Lorek, *Making the Green Revolution: Agriculture and Conflict in Colombia* (Chapel Hill, NC: University of North Carolina Press, 2023).

22 Elvin C. Stakman *et al.*, *Campañas contra el hambre* (México: UTEHA, 1969), 226.

23 Ibid., 228.

24 The Rockefeller Foundation, *Annual Report 1954* (New York, 1954), 179.

in the Foundation's Mexican research programme – developed the successful *Eto* variety.[25]

The Colombian programme was the first case of institutional cloning. Its activities followed the path established by the Mexican programme: like in Mexico, the consolidated research programme became the Departamento de Investigación Agrícola, a coordination office like the Mexican OSS under the control of American scientists during its early period. Cloning was also present in shaping experimental stations: the experimental station of La Picota was replaced by the experimental station of Tibaitatá, following the blueprint of the Mexican stations. The Foundation sent Edwin J. Wellhausen, a pioneer in the Mexican programme and its future chairman, as advisor to set up the new institution.[26] Colombia became the Foundation's beachhead in South America.

There was a promotional ladder for these scientists, either moving up through directive positions in the new research programmes, emulating the institutional cloning, or in the Rockefeller Foundation. Scientists from the Colombian programme were sent to Ecuador and Chile to launch research stations after the signing of proper agreements. Rupert was appointed chairman of the local Oficina de Estudios Especiales, attached to the Chilean Ministerio de Agricultura.[27] He supported research on cereals, the creation of experimental stations, and increasing meat production through the improvement of forages. In wheat research Rupert followed the proven methodology of crossing local varieties with lines from Mexico and Colombia: according to Stakman about 18,000 lines. Among the best seeds obtained were the hybrids *Orofén, Rulofén, Orofén 60* and *Chifén*,[28] which had the attributes sought by the American scientists in the Mexican OSS. These spring wheat varieties had short, strong stalks that were responsive to the application of chemical fertilisers. Harrar climbed the Foundation's ladder; he served as its Director of Agriculture in 1955–9, rose to Vice-President in 1959–61 and finished his career as Trustee and President, 1961–72.[29]

25 Stakman *et al.*, *Campañas contra el hambre*, 228.

26 Ibid., 229.

27 Fernando Quesada and Benedetta Calandra, 'Exploring the Liberal Transformation: The Rockefeller Foundation and the Green Revolution in Chile', in *US Public Diplomacy Strategies in Latin America During the Sixties: Time for Persuasion*, Francisco Rodríguez-Jiménez, Lorenzo Delgado Gómez-Escalonilla and Benedetta Calandra (eds) (New York: Routledge, 2024).

28 Stakman *et al.*, *Campañas contra el hambre*, 242.

29 John J. Mackelvey, *J. George Harrar (1906–1982)* (National Academy of Science, Washington DC, 1987, http://www.nasonline.org/publications/biographical-memoirs/memoir-pdfs/harrar-j-g.pdf (accessed 12 March 2024).

16.3 The minor programmes: Ecuador and Central America

There were also programmes in Ecuador and Central America, though modest in their scope when compared with the Colombian programme. The early contacts in Ecuador date from 1956 and their goal was to establish a wheat production programme.[30] Dr John Gliber, an expert on this cereal and member of the Colombian programme, went to Ecuador and helped in establishing demonstration farms in Quito, in the area surrounding the Universidad Nacional. Dr Gliber, Stakman and Roberts returned two years later for a tour in the Ecuadoran countryside, and they prepared a blueprint that would be the precedent for the creation of the Instituto Nacional de Investigación Agropecuaria (INIAP).[31]

The Central American Cooperative Corn Improvement Project, which began in 1954, synthesises the Foundation's *modus operandi* in Latin America.[32] Researchers, their scientific culture, and seeds came from abroad and moved within the isthmus. Sterling Wortman and Donald L. Smith, both scientists from the Mexican programme, served as chairmen, while the Costa Rican agronomist Alfredo Carballo served as the Project's regional coordinator. The scientists continued collecting local seeds to cross with seeds brought from Mexico and Colombia. During the first year they worked with more than 1,000 local lines.[33]

To consolidate the scientific culture recently established by the programme, the Foundation financed the formation of human capital and the organisation of scientific meetings. The Foundation created a scholarship programme to send Central American agronomists and technicians to research internships in Mexico and Colombia. It also organised regional meetings to compare research results. The first and second meetings were held in Costa Rica – 1954 and 1955 – while the third was held in Guatemala in 1956.[34] Thus, despite its relatively peripheral character, even the Central American isthmus shared in the worldwide processes of producing and interchanging agricultural knowledge. The simultaneous exchange of genetic material and knowledge – through the agronomists' control of the new technology – prepared that generation to control the growing institutional framework in agricultural research; these practices were the platform for future programmes in the following decades. Thus, the series of conferences held by the Central American programme during the 1950s was the predecessor of the Programa Interamericano de Mejoramiento de los Cultivos Alimenticios, which

30 Stakman *et al.*, *Campañas contra el hambre*, 236–9.

31 The Rockefeller Foundation, *Annual Report 1957* (New York, 1957), 147–8.

32 The Rockefeller Foundation, *Annual Report 1954* (New York, 1954), 183–4.

33 Stakman *et al.*, *Campañas contra el hambre*, 269.

34 Ibid., 269–70.

integrated research programmes on wheat, potatoes and maize during the following decade.

Finally, aside from the above mentioned programmes, the Foundation financed grants in Brazil, Peru, Honduras (to the Escuela Agrícola Panamericana), Uruguay, Bolivia and Costa Rica (to the Instituto Interamericano de Ciencias Agrícolas). Most of these funds were to buy equipment for universities and experimental stations, scholarships to study in the United States, the organisation of conferences as well as internships in the United States, Mexico or Colombia.

16.4 Nelson Rockefeller and the Office of the Coordinator of Inter-American Affairs

The Office of the Coordinator of Inter-American Affairs was the institution that dealt with the war-related problems of Latin America, while at the same time imposing an anti-Axis policy. Given the German victories in Europe and a possible British defeat, the United States feared the conflict would continue in the Western Hemisphere, particularly in Latin America, where the Japanese, Germans, Italians, Spaniards and local fascists would become a 'Hemispheric Fifth Column' supporting the Axis war effort. Once the United States entered the war in December 1941, it depended on Latin America for wild rubber and for quinine to treat malaria. Following the 'associative state' characteristic of the United States, the President created an institution combining state and private interests to coordinate the war policy in Latin America.[35] The American government appointed Nelson A. Rockefeller, a scion of the family supporting the Foundation, as Coordinator.[36] He had been acquainted with Latin America since the 1920s and in 1937 had proposed to President Roosevelt's aides an Inter-American programme, funded with public and private funds, to solve the region's economic and social problems. These initiatives became policy after Rockefeller's appointment as Coordinator of the Office of Inter-American Affairs (which hereafter we refer to as the Office). The new agency faced the problems of a federal bureaucracy straining under the demands of the war. Rockefeller hired several employees from his family business, transforming the Office of the Coordinator into a sort of family fiefdom.

35 David E. Hamilton, 'Building the Associative State: The Department of Agriculture and American State-Building', *Agriculture History* 64 (1990), 207–18.

36 Darlene Rivas, *Missionary Capitalist: Nelson Rockefeller in Venezuela* (Chapel Hill, NC: University of North Carolina Press, 2002); Claiton M. Da Silva, *De agricultor a farmer. Nelson Rockefeller e a modernização da agricultura no Brasil* (Curitiba, Brasil: Editora Unicentro, 2015).

The Office was responsible for avoiding the collapse of Latin American economies and the subsequent social unrest that might be exploited by the Axis supporters. The United States purchased export products previously sold in Europe and, while it remained a neutral power, bought other goods to deny German access to strategic raw materials. After the United States entered the war, its immediate concern was the hypothetical extension of the conflict into the Western Hemisphere. After the First World War experience – when diseases killed more soldiers than bullets did – an improvement in health conditions in those territories where the American army might confront an invasion became a priority. Beside that, there was an urgent need for food production programmes to supply the Canal Zone, several military bases and any military force that might be deployed in the future, while at the same time improving the diet of the local population. Unlike the First World War, states were using the new science of nutrition to shape their policies: the daily requirements of calories, carbohydrates, proteins and other elements of a healthy diet were now understood. This knowledge guided Japanese and German expansionist policies, the American lend-lease programme to Great Britain and, as shown below, it shaped some agricultural programmes in Latin America.

The Office followed the flexible logic of a private business, creating subsidiary corporations to deal with its variegated interests, which included propaganda, solving transport problems, and even education. Among them, the Institute of Inter-American Affairs (IIAA) was created to deal with health and agricultural cooperation programmes in Latin America. This rationale failed to avoid frequent confrontations with the American federal bureaucracy – the State Department and Secretary of Agriculture – and with the agencies created to support the war effort.[37]

The criteria used to establish food production programmes is unclear. For instance, in 1943 Bolivia – the main producer of strategic metals – imported foodstuffs, but no food production programme was ever established there.[38] As a hypothesis to verify in the archives, the creation of food production programmes depended on three processes. First, the lack of a food production programme in Mexico suggests a division of labour between the Office and the Foundation's activities. Second, the 'national committees' – constituted by American citizens living in each country – might have influenced the type of programmes supported. Finally, a country's proximity to a strategic military base or production activity probably influenced the setting up of food production programmes.

37 CIIAA [Coordinator of Inter-American Affairs], *History of the Office of the Coordinator of Inter-American Affairs. Historical Reports on War Administration* (Washington, DC: Government Printing Office, 1947), 10–24.

38 John D. Black, *World Needs for US Food and Fiber* (Washington, DC: National Planning Association, 1943), 21.

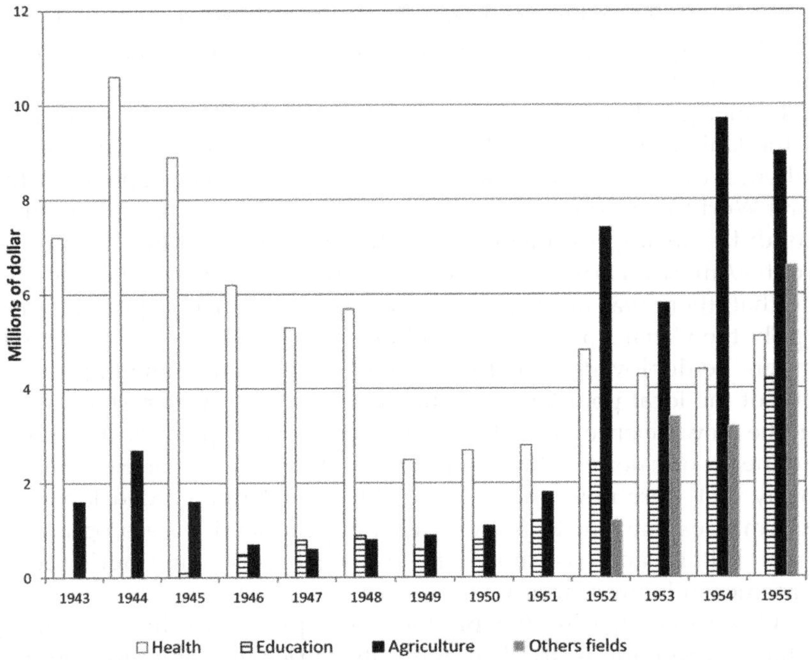

FIGURE 16.1. Distribution of American allocations for technical cooperation programmes in Latin America, 1943–55 (millions of dollars). Source: National Planning Association, 1956, 167.

Thus, the food production programme in Costa Rica supplied food to American troops stationed in the Panama Canal, while its counterpart in Peru provided the American military base at Talara and the personnel of the Rubber Development Commission in the Peruvian Amazon.[39]

The Office of the Coordinator gave priority to the immediate war goals. That was the reason behind an important share of funds going to health programmes during the first years, while funding was later shifted to agricultural programmes, which received most of the funds after 1952 (see Figure 16.1). It is also significant that health and agriculture were the only programmes financed in 1943 and 1944. It was not until 1945 that education became the third item in technical cooperation. Funds for items such as public administration, community development, industry, mines,

39 Arthur T. Mosher, *Technical Co-operation in Latin American Agriculture* (Chicago, IL: University of Chicago Press, 1957); Andrew Nichols, *Development of the Peruvian Extension Service* (Washington, DC: Office of Foreign Agriculture-Institute of Inter-American Affairs, 1952).

transports and others began in 1952 but their share of expenditure was a mere fraction of the above-mentioned main three items.

Food production programmes in Latin American countries began at different times, their duration varied and there were a range of financial agreements (see Table 16.1). The first agreement was signed with Costa Rica on 15 October 1942, while Haiti's was the last, signed on 28 August 1944. There were also substantial differences in the programmes' length: the programme in El Salvador lasted fifteen months, while Costa Rica's was stipulated to last 62.5 months. Finally, as these were commercial agreements between 'allies', the United States and the host governments were supposed to finance them jointly, but there were also substantial differences. The United States financed the 57 per cent of the total costs in Brazil, Haiti, Paraguay, Peru and Venezuela with the respective governments contributing the balance. Although we have no documents explaining the logic behind it, the governments of Costa Rica, El Salvador, Honduras, Nicaragua and Panama were exempted from making any contribution.

TABLE 16.1. Countries with food production programmes, their duration and financial responsibilities, 1942–7 (dollars).

	Duration		Financial responsibilities	
Country	Agreement signature	Closing date	Institute of Inter-American Affairs (dollars)	Host country (dollars)
Brazil	3 Sept. 1943	20 Aug. 1945	2,000,000	1,903,550
Costa Rica	15 Oct. 1942	31 Dec. 1947	151,000	
El Salvador	22 Dec. 1942	1 Apr. 1944	18,798	
Haiti	28 Aug. 1944	31 Dec. 1946	125,000	50,000
Honduras	4 Mar. 1943	30 June 1945	158,250	
Nicaragua	20 May 1943	15 June 1944	31,498	
Panama	20 Nov. 1942	31 Mar. 1946	116,750	
Paraguay	31 Dec. 1942	31 Dec. 1947	250,000	50,000
Peru	19 May 1943	31 Dec. 1946	162,977	162,977
Venezuela	14 May 1943	13 May 1946	500,000	500,000
Total			3,514,273	2,666,527

Source: CIIAA-Coordinator of Inter-American Affairs, 1947, 136.

To prevent the impact on local markets of a growing demand of foodstuffs for American military bases and rubber extraction areas, these programmes had a component promoting new agronomic practices. These included the introduction of agricultural technology, chemical fertilisers and new varieties of foodstuffs to increase output. The programmes in Paraguay and Costa Rica established experimental stations, introduced new varieties of plants and cattle breeds, and created an extension service on the American model.[40] In Haiti the programme faced a large population unable to sustain itself with traditional agricultural practices, a critical situation worsened by the failed programme to produce rubber from *cryptostegia*.[41] The programme implemented projects for irrigation, technical assistance, provisions of seeds and chemical fertilisers.[42] In Venezuela the food production programme worked in the region surrounding Lake Valencia, on lands held by different government agencies.[43] Finally, there were evaluations on the forestry of some countries and a thorough study of nutrition in Paraguay.[44]

16.5 Technical cooperation during the post-war period

Technical cooperation in Latin America went through several transformations once the Second World War was over. The first was a substantial reduction in American funding because the American authorities perceived technical cooperation to be part of the war effort, and so to be brought to an end in peace time. As a result, the budget for the IIAA dropped from $10.6 million in 1945 to $7.4 in 1946 and reached its nadir in 1949 with $4 million. In contrast, the funds from Latin American governments to bilateral programmes rose steadily from almost $5 million in 1945 to $17 million in 1950. Thus, between the last year of the war and the proclamation of Point Four as the core of American foreign policy for developing countries in 1949, the Latin American countries tripled their contributions, while the United States reduced its share by 30 per cent. Aside from these changes in finance, the American state replaced war effort emergency institutions with peacetime policies. The confrontation between the United States and the USSR forced President Truman to announce the so-called Point Four in his inaugural address, offering

40 Rupert H. Porter, *Crop Development in Paraguay* (Washington, DC: Food Supply Division, Institute of Inter-American Affairs, 1947).

41 CIIAA, *History of the Office*, 133–5.

42 SCIAPA (Service Coopératif Inter-Americain de Production Agricole), *Agricultural Progress in Haiti* (Washington, DC: Food Supply Division, Institute of Inter-American Affairs, 1949).

43 IIAA, *The Lake Valencia Region in Venezuela* (Washington, DC: Institute of Inter-American Affairs, Food Supply Division, 1946).

44 IIAA, *The Forest Resources of Paraguay* (Washington, DC: Institute of Inter-American Affairs, Food Supply Division, 1946).

technical assistance to underdeveloped countries, which was approved by Congress as the Act for International Development in 1950. However, a political-bureaucratic confrontation hindered the implementation of the new policy until 1955. Although the technical cooperation programmes in Latin America were not directly threatened by this impasse because the IIAA continued to be the administrating agency, they functioned in an unstable bureaucratic environment.[45]

The technical cooperation programmes in Latin America during the 1950s exhibited new characteristics. Agricultural programmes received a substantial share of the funds, in some countries at least 30 per cent of the available resources, but in other countries double this proportion. Thus, the percentage of funds assigned to agricultural programmes reached 50 per cent in Paraguay and Haiti in 1952, 60 per cent in Peru in 1956, and 75 per cent in Costa Rica in 1952.[46] Furthermore, the agricultural sector was also the main beneficiary of programmes financed by the United Nations and the Organization of American States.[47] The international technical cooperation programmes to Latin America during the 1950s emphasised the agricultural sector. Moreover, there was a significant change in how the programmes used this foreign aid during the 1950s. During the war the largest share of expenses was for equipment and implements, while the remainder paid the salaries of American technicians. Although these items remained important after the war, from 1951 onwards more funds were invested in training local technicians.[48]

A by-product of the technical cooperation programmes was the creation of new markets in the host countries, where American companies found an increasing number of buyers for chemical inputs and agricultural technology. The sudden emergency created by the war had led to the importation of chemical fertilisers and pesticides. At the end of the war the growing increase in the consumption of these products favoured the commercialisation of chemical technology. The authorities of the IIAA considered these new markets a positive consequence of the cooperation programmes.[49]

The propagation of American agronomic culture among local technicians and agronomists led to the formation of new markets. The number of American technicians working in training programmes more than tripled between 1947 and 1954, from 205 to 664. While health programmes had employed most of the staff during the early years, from 1952 onwards

45 National Planning Association (NPA), *Technical Cooperation in Latin America. Recommendations for the Future* (Washington, DC, 1956), 40–2.

46 Ibid., 149–61.

47 Ibid., 183–6.

48 Ibid., 168.

49 Kenneth Iverson, 'The "Servicio" in Theory and Practice', *Public Administration Review* 11 (1951), 223–8.

agricultural programmes were assigned more American technicians than any other field. Between 1952 and 1954 it was almost a third of all technicians. In the same years locally trained technicians formed at least a fifth of the total number of trained technicians in agricultural programmes.[50]

16.6 The Agricultural Cooperation Services

Cooperation programmes in Latin America continued after the war despite declining financial American support, and even grew in size, geographical coverage and fields of action during the early 1950s. By 1955 there were forty-eight technical cooperation programmes in eighteen Latin American countries, of which seventeen were in public health, fifteen in agriculture, with the others in education, industry and other fields. Usually, each country had two or three programmes in different fields, although in exceptional cases such as Peru and Ecuador there were programmes in four or five different fields.

The programmes were a success in many fields and in various countries because the United States utilised a strategy of institutional cloning. This strategy enabled the creation and efficient administration of programmes on education, public health and agriculture in almost all Latin American countries on a common model. In agricultural programmes this was obvious in national programmes that shared a similar administrative structure, name, goals and methodology. The cooperation service – referred to below as *servicio*, the name given it in official reports – was the building block of the institutional cloning strategy. The *servicio* had a core of American technicians and a group of local functionaries, working along the guidelines established in the agreement between the IIAA and the national government. Usually, the IIAA sent a reconnaissance mission to establish the host country's agricultural conditions, and an agreement was signed with the respective government. Both signatories financed salaries, equipment, provisions and installations; the *servicio* administered these resources for projects agreed on with the host country.

The *servicio* had a hybrid administrative character; formally, it was ascribed to the local Ministry of Agriculture – or its equivalent in some countries – but in practice it retained financial and administrative independence, supported by the IIAA. Its director was an American appointed by the IIAA.[51] This ambiguity sometimes brought about conflicts with local institutions, which considered the *servicio*'s status as privileged, autonomous, funded with largesse, under American control, and reluctant to share results or credit. Authorities and functionaries of the IIAA confronted these conflicts by presenting the Institute as apolitical and autonomous, detached from the host country's internal

50 NPA, *Technical Cooperation*, 169.

51 Iverson, 'Servicio', 225–6.

affairs. Declaring the Institute to be apolitical was also an imperative in dealing with complex Latin American power structures, characterised by instability and frequent *coups d'état*.

Given that the same procedure was followed in every country, it is not surprising that they had the same name and acronym, as well as the same antecedents. In three countries – Costa Rica, Honduras and Paraguay – the *servicio* of technical cooperation for agriculture was called STICA; namely, Servicio Técnico Interamericano de Cooperación Agrícola.[52] In two others, Peru and Haiti, it was called SCIPA, in the former the acronym for Servicio Cooperativo Interamericano de Producción de Alimentos, and in the latter the acronym for Service Coopératif Inter-Américain de Production Agricole.[53]

The profile of the American personnel working in the *servicios* was substantially different from the scientists hired by the Foundation during the war. The age of these American technicians ranged between thirty and forty years. Among those with university training most were bachelors, some had masters, and only a few were PhDs. There were also technicians lacking university training, which led to criticism of the Institute's hiring policy. Such a policy was justified by the Institute's interests in hiring technicians with practical knowledge who would be able to face the problems in the host Latin American countries. The technicians hired by the IIAA to work in the *servicios* had a low turnover among programmes and countries, if compared with technicians working for programmes financed by the UN or the OAS. They usually served in two countries for terms of four or five years in each one. The consolidation of the *servicios* depended on the personnel's ability to understand and work in the cultural, political and institutional environment of each country.[54]

The agricultural cooperation services had the same projects in all the countries, despite the differences in social and ecological contexts. The key element in the execution of these projects was a Servicio de Extensión Agrícola according to the American model, opening agencies in the main agricultural areas and training local technicians as extension agents. These agents sold fertilisers and pesticides directly to the farmer. The *servicio* also published technical bulletins, distributed new varieties of plants and introduced demonstration methods at experimental stations and farms to show the new technology to the farmers. A fundamental part of their

52 Anacleto Apodaca, *Enseñando al agricultor. Enseñanza agrícola en un país latinoamericano* (Tegucigalpa, Honduras: Embajada de Estados Unidos, 1954); IIAA-STEA [Institute of Inter-American Affairs y Servicio Técnico de Extensión Agrícola], *A Summary Report. Agricultural Progress in Costa Rica* (Washington, DC: SPI, 1949).

53 IIAA, *Livestock in Peru: Including a Description of SCIPA's Cattle Import Program* (Washington, DC: SPI, 1947); SCIAPA, Agricultural Progress.

54 Mosher, *Technical Co-Operation*, 385–405.

work was soil conservation programmes, which included techniques and tools created by Soil Conservation Science. These programmes were particularly important in slope agriculture or where there was seriously degraded soil.

In many places in Latin America these agents were the first 'experts' that peasants had ever met, and the latter's trust depended on the practical value of the experts' knowledge. The use of pesticides to control ants, locusts and other insects created this peasants' trust. Its effectiveness in the short run demonstrated the practical value of the agent and legitimised the Servicio de Extensión Agrícola in the communities.[55] To broaden the legitimacy of the *servicio*, it created youth clubs, along the lines of the American 4-H Clubs, to include the younger generation in the modernisation of agriculture through lectures on the new technologies and field activities like reforestation. Finally, the *servicio* established home improvement programmes, along the lines of American home economics, with the objective of 'modernising' home management. The underlying assumption was that the family should be an efficient economic unit complementing the farm and housewives ought to be included in the modernising process.[56]

16.7 Conclusion

The analysis of US agricultural programmes during the Second World War focuses mainly on the Mexican experience of the Rockefeller Foundation and the OSS. Most studies have dealt with the improvement of wheat plants by American scientists, which eventually led to the Green Revolution in India two decades later. Conversely, the other American cooperation programmes in Latin America during the 1940s and 1950s have scarcely been mentioned. Although their scientific outcome was less impressive and had less impact in the media, these programmes generated an institutional cloning process as original as plant improvement. The institutional base and adoption of an American agronomic culture led to the modernisation of Latin American agriculture during the 1960s and 1970s. Our contention is that these processes were a 'grey revolution' at the institutional level.

An understanding of the agricultural cooperation programmes in this period – among the first of their type in American history – is an alternative way to understand the history of international cooperation, which would be the cornerstone of American foreign policy after 1960 through

55 Carlos Arroyo, *Origen y desarrollo de la extensión agraria en Costa Rica* (San José, Costa Rica: Tesis de Grado, Universidad de Costa Rica, 1953).

56 Wilson Picado, 'En busca de la genética guerrera. Segunda Guerra Mundial, cooperación agrícola y Revolución Verde en la agricultura de Costa Rica', *Revista de Historia Agraria* 56 (2012), 107–34.

the Agency of International Development (AID). The Latin American experience served as a model for future agricultural programmes established in South-East Asia during the 1960s and 1970s. The comprehension of the logic behind agricultural cooperation programmes sheds light on the dynamic of the Green Revolution's acceptance in the Third World.

Despite the explanatory value of theories of induced institutional change, this study shows that institutional set-up does not depend on changes in the relative prices of factors of production and state intervention. By contrast, the creation of institutions was the product of food demand during war and geopolitical issues, instead of strategic planning. Consequently, these institutions occupied a conflictive environment: they responded both to state and private enterprise interests, while they clashed with homonymous offices in the host state. If during the war there was a boom in plant breeding, during the post-war period there was an intense process of institutional cloning.

The proliferation of US-backed agricultural programmes across Latin America in the Second World War represents one of the first phases in the triumph of the American agronomic model worldwide. However, these programmes were not created in an absolute 'institutional vacuum'. Some Latin American countries already had institutions and programmes for the promotion of modernisation in the agricultural sector. Thus, Argentina had been creating these institutions since the last quarter of the nineteenth century, while Brazil, Colombia and Costa Rica, to cite a few examples, also had their own counterparts.[57] Although there were weak and intermittent connections among these national initiatives, the success in cloning American programmes was possible due to the hegemonic role of the United States after the Second World War, which included geopolitical and market control in the Western Hemisphere.

57 Carolina Da Cunha Rocha, 'Cultivando el Estado, sembrando el progreso: el Ministerio de Agricultura y la formación de la tecnocracia agraria de Brasil (1930–1955)', (PhD diss., El Colegio de México, 2021); Florencia Rodríguez and Federico Martocci, 'Instituciones, agentes y proyectos para el saber agropecuario entre fines del siglo XIX y la revolución verde en Argentina', *Revista Páginas* 15 (37) (2022), https://revistapaginas.unr.edu.ar/index.php/RevPaginas/article/view/731/934 (accessed 3 September 2025); Omar Ruiz-Nieto and Martin Giraldo-Hoyos, 'Semillas sin cosecha: Gestión del conocimiento agropecuario y transformación del paisaje en la Sabana de Bogotá, Colombia (1907–1990)', *Estudios Rurales* 13 (27) (2023) https://estudiosrurales.unq.edu.ar/index.php/ER/article/view/474 (accessed 3 September 2025); Picado, *En busca de la genética guerrera*.

17

Gender and agricultural modernisation: agricultural extension in Spain and France in the 1960s and 1970s[1]

Sylvain Brunier, Ana Cabana Iglesia and Alba Díaz-Geada

In the past two decades, gender has become an increasingly important issue in the analysis of processes of change in the rural world. Studies from women's history, rural sociology and gender anthropology have made evident the importance of including gender as a category of analysis capable of achieving a more holistic approach to the pasts of rural societies.[2] A review of recent literature shows the appearance and consolidation of lines of study that recognise the agency of women and, above all, deny that the generic masculine was an inclusive neuter in historical meta-narratives, and point out the need to make women and other sexual and gender identities visible in historical research.[3]

1 This chapter is supported by AGRIFAMIGEN PID2023-151334NB-I00, funded by Ministry of Science, Innovation and Universities. Also by RYC2021-034738-I financed by the MCIN/AEI/10.13039/501100011033 and by the European Union 'NextGenerationEU/PRTR'; and PID2020-117858RA-100/AEI/10.13039/501100011033.

2 Margreet van der Burg, *'No Second Farmer': Gender, Agricultural Modernisation and Education For Rural Women in the Netherlands* (Hilversum: Verloren, 2002); Berit Brandth, 'Gender Identity in European Family Farming: A Literature Review', *Sociología Ruralis* 42–3 (2002), 181–200; Lise Saugeres, 'The Cultural Representation of the Farming Landscape: Masculinity, Power and Nature', *J. Rural Studies* 18 (2002), 373–84.

3 Ana Cabana Iglesia, 'En femenino plural. La perspectiva de género en la historia rural', in *Del pasado al futuro como problema. La historia agraria contemporánea española en el siglo XXI*, David Soto Fernández and José Miguel Lana Berasain (eds) (Zaragoza: PUZ, 2018), 189–208; Ana Cabana Iglesia *et al.*, 'Gender and Rural History: A Roundtable', *Historia Agraria* 85 (2021) 7–36; Colin R. Johnson, *Just Queer Folks: Gender and Sexuality in Rural America* (Philadelphia, PA: Temple University Press, 2013).

In this chapter we propose to explore the process of agrarian modernisation postulated by public advisory services aimed at farmers ('extensionism') by looking at the gender issue. We will carry out a comparative approach to this topic in the post-Second World War period in two different political contexts: one dictatorial, until the end of the 1970s, in the case of Spain; and parliamentary democracy in the French Republic. We will explore the similarities and differences in imposing the extensionism projects for rural women accomplished by the Domestic Economics Agents of the Agrarian Extension Service (AES), in the Spanish case, and the advisors of the Chambers of Agriculture, in the French case.[4] The aim of this chapter is to establish whether the different political context conditioned the possibilities of negotiated gender roles in this agrarian modernising process. It is necessary to keep in mind that in the following pages we are going to make general considerations, which would undoubtedly require deep explanation if we focused our attention on particulars. Thus, the role of women in rural areas is crossed both by sociocultural differences (class, age, race, and so on) and different agrarian contexts and occupations (day labourers, craftswomen, smallholders, shepherdesses, sharecroppers, among others).

When the extensionist project was adopted as a valid way to achieve the modernisation of rural society and agricultural production, France and Spain were at very different points in their development. In France, the American historian Herrick Chapman proposes the term 'long reconstruction' to describe the unity of the period between the Liberation and the early 1960s.[5] It is well documented that, during the German occupation, the Vichy regime had sought to organise a form of economic upgrading but had failed in its attempt to find an authoritarian corporatist system that would mobilise the already constituted professional groups.[6] At the time of the Liberation, the political and economic elites were preoccupied with a central question: how could modernisation coincide with democratic renewal? In other words, how to bring about an economic revolution without resorting to total state control? The term 'long reconstruction' emphasises the strong political continuities beyond the institutional changes that define the period, from the creation of the Provisional Government at the time of the Liberation in 1944, to the founding of the Fourth Republic in 1946, then to the crisis of 1958, which led to the creation of the Fifth Republic. The creation of the Planning Commission (Commissariat au plan) in the immediate post-war period went hand in hand with the recruitment of social groups who were to

4 Sylvain Brunier, *Le bonheur dans la modernité. Histoire des conseillers agricoles (1945–1985)* (Lyon: Editions de l'ENS, 2018).

5 Herrick Chapman, *La longue reconstruction de la France. À la recherche de la république moderne* (Paris: Presses de Sciences Po, 2021).

6 Pierre Bitoun, 'L'équivoque vichyssoise' [publié en quatre parties], *Bulletin du Mauss* 13 (1985), 11–36; 14 (1985), 127–48; 15 (1985), 101–21; 16 (1985), 151–86.

play a decisive role in the implementation of the modernisation plans drawn up by the State. Beginning in the early 1950s, planners gradually revised their methods of intervention, relying more and more directly on groups such as the employees of large state-owned companies, or the Young Farmers' Union (Centre National des Jeunes Agriculteurs), who embraced the 'battle for productivity' and called for greater regulation by public authorities. The period was thus characterised by strong state intervention in most major sectors, usually supported by professional organisations (unions, associations) that sought to promote technical progress and economic rationalisation throughout society.

For Spain, we need to remember that a dictatorship was imposed in 1939, following the Civil War that resulted from a *coup d'état* led by General Franco against the democratic government of the Spanish Second Republic. During the post-civil war period, economic policy reflected a self-sufficiency ideal and autarkic interventionism, class-based union organisations were prohibited, and a mandatory corporate union structure was created (Union Brotherhood of Farm Workers and Stockbreeders). After the Second World War, in a new international context, the anti-communist nature of the Franco dictatorship meant that it was supported by the new hegemonic power of the United States, regardless of the continuity of the repression or the absence of political freedoms. At the end of the 1950s, the Franco regime re-orientated its economic policy in a liberalising direction (the 1959 Stabilisation Plan). That was an economic requirement of international organisations under the auspices of the United States, as well as an attempt to modernise and reform the mechanisms of dictatorship established to generate internal consensus.[7]

In the case of France, Marshall Plan funds played an important role in financing the first post-war modernisation plans, for example

7 The main discussion of the influence of the North American model on the Agrarian Extension Service in Spain (SEA), can be found in Fernando Sánchez De Puerta Trujillo, *Extensión agraria y desarrollo rural. Sobre la evolución de las teorías y praxis extensionistas* (Madrid: MAPA, 1996). On the influence of the extensionism of the United States in Spain in relation to its influence on the extensionism of countries in south America, Alba Díaz-Geada and Daniel Lanero Táboas, 'Modelos de modernisación para el desarrollismo: el influjo de las propuestas estadounidenses en el Servicio de Extensión Agraria (1955–1975)', *Revista Complutense de Historia de América* 41 (2015), 71–94. In France, the American model exerted an undeniable influence, but it was appropriated differently by different actors: government departments praise the resources allocated to the extension service and its links with agronomic research, while agricultural unionists insist more on the autonomy of each county agent and his proximity to the farmers he advises. Sylvain Brunier, 'A ciascuno la sua America: l'invenzione del conseiller agricole in Francia nel secondo dopoguerra', *Storia e problemi contemporanei* 80 (2019), 116–34.

by promoting the importation of tractors for agriculture. But beyond material goods alone, the spread of the American model also took shape through the organisation of 'productivity missions', made up of senior civil servants, engineers and trade unionists, tasked with observing and importing new methods of work organisation into their countries.[8] The aim of these productivity missions was to install a new state of mind, in which the watchword was the continuous quest for productivity gains. In the agricultural sector, the aim was not only to import new production techniques, but also to consider the means needed to ensure that as many farmers as possible adopted the new methods. The long-standing effort to inform farmers of 'good' practices was now being coupled with an effort to obtain the active support of farmers for modernisation policies. Likewise, popularising technical progress in agriculture was now being rethought in the light of the new benchmark of increased productivity, notably through comparisons between the French and American systems.

Franco's Spain was not included in the Marshall Plan, but in the early 1950s his regime signed a military and economic collaboration agreement with the US (the Madrid Pacts, 1953). This agreement allowed the purchase, through credits from the Eximbank and the Development Loan Fund, of machinery and chemical fertilisers, as well as the importation of agricultural surpluses from the US. After the signing of the pacts, a special US economic mission was established in Spain with the task of supervising its development. In this way, a route to US technical assistance was opened.[9] In the case of the Franco regime, there seems to have been a shift from an initial authoritarian model of modernisation, in which fascist principles had a strong presence, to another with a technocratic profile, more in line with Modernisation Theory.[10] From 1955 to 1971, professionalised extensionism was institutionalised following the US model.[11]

The AES was created in 1955 in Spain. During its early years, based on its founding charter and criteria established in the agreement that was signed with the US government, its agents focused on spreading technical knowledge with the primary objective of increasing agricultural

8 Luc Boltanski, 'America, America ... Le Plan Marshall et l'importation du management', *Actes de la Recherche en Sciences Sociales* 38 (1981), 19–41.

9 Díaz-Geada and Lanero Táboas, 'Modelos de modernización para el desarrollismo', 71–94.

10 Ana Cabana Iglesia and Alba Díaz-Geada, 'Agrarian Fascism in Rural Spain (1936–1951)', in *Agriculture in the Age of Fascism: Authoritarian Technocracy and Rural Modernization, 1922–1945*, Lourenzo Fernández-Prieto, Juan Pan-Montojo and Miguel Cabo Villaverde (eds) (Turnhout: Brepols, 2014), 189–218.

11 Cristóbal Gómez Benito, *Políticos, burócratas y expertos. Un estudio de la política agraria y la sociología rural en España, 1936–1959* (Madrid: Siglo XXI, 1995).

productivity as a means of improving rural standards of living. The 1960s marked the adoption of new theoretical and methodological principles, at a time of expansion for the AES. From a theoretical point of view, it would move from the mere transfer of technology, from top to bottom, to a more social and cultural strategy.[12] In this stage, decentralisation of the AES and autonomy from other institutions concerned with agriculture was promoted, and priority was given to the local level over the regional, working in proximity with farmers, and the training and social – that is to say, not merely technical – profile of the agents.[13]

The American model of agricultural extension, in which most officials worked alongside researchers and agricultural unionists, made a strong impression on French delegations. The dense territorial network, the considerable financial resources deployed, the strong link between research and extension, were all practices that the French officials sent to be trained in America wished to adopt on their return to France. Above all, most of them were impressed by the respect that each County Agent enjoyed with the farmers in his or her area. Although they were civil servants, County Agents boasted considerable freedom of action, and this enabled them to gain the trust of farmers. French Agricultural Service engineers, who had control over the dissemination of technical progress, saw this as an opportunity to assert their need for additional resources and greater autonomy. Conversely, professional leaders emphasised the irreconcilable gap they felt existed between American extension practices and the culture of the French administration, which they considered incapable of adapting to the new situation. The 1950s were thus marked by this competition between government agencies and the main farmers' union for control of extension work. The union won this battle and obtained the allocation of agricultural extension credits to the Chambers of Agriculture, para-public institutions organised at a departmental level, and under its control, to enable the hiring of agricultural advisors. The French model of agricultural development was shaped by this neo-corporatist system. It was based primarily on supporting the most economically dynamic family farms, by encouraging the concentration of land structures and the retirement of older farmers.

12 Cristóbal Gómez Benito and Emilio Luque Pulgar, 'Modernización agraria, modernización administrativa y franquismo. El modelo educativo y administrativo del Servicio de Extensión Agraria (1955–1986)', *Áreas. Revista Internacional de Ciencias Sociales* 26 (2007), 24–5; Sánchez De Puerta, *Extensión agraria y desarrollo rural*, 248–318.

13 Ibid., 412–14.

17.1 When gender matters: agricultural extensionism and women

According to Sánchez de Puerta,[14] the beginnings of extension work with women can be found in the United States in the second decade of the twentieth century. This model was exported to the rest of the world in the 1950s. Thus, Taylorism was introduced into domestic economies to achieve maximum efficiency, including in the rural sphere. In France, the Chambers of Agriculture hired the first women agricultural advisors to support local groups made up exclusively of women in the early 1960s. In Spain, the Home Economics Agents were launched in 1960.[15] But when the first farm advisors were hired, domestic education had already been organised for several decades in both countries. Several institutions provided training for young rural women to prepare them for 'running their own home', by teaching them practical skills (cooking, sewing, small animal husbandry, housekeeping) that defined their role and psychological virtues (temperance, dedication, discretion, meticulousness). In France, since the end of the 1950s, the Agricultural Social Mutuality (Mutualité Sociale Agricole) had been providing a social assistance service that partly covered the tasks of the women's agricultural extension service. It organised small groups of women to act as discussion forums and provide support for the work of the instructors responsible for informing women about the need for hygiene, home improvements, child-rearing and nutrition.

In the case of Spain, the work of the women of the Home Economics Agents overlapped with that carried out by the Rural Instructors of the Feminine Section, the female branch of the Falange (the Fascist Party). Unlike the Rural Instructors, who moved from village to village, the Home Economics Agents worked within the framework of a Local

14 Ibid.; Fernando Sánchez De Puerta Trujillo, 'Estado y agricultura: La extensión agraria', in *Agricultura y sociedad en la España contemporánea*, Cristóbal Gómez de Benito and Juan Jesús González Rodríguez (eds) (Madrid: MAPA, 1997), 913–48.

15 For the training that women received in Franco's Dictatorship to teach rural women, see Sara Ramos Zamora, *Entre lo doméstico y lo público. Capacitación profesional de las mujeres rurales en España (1940–1977)* (Madrid: Biblioteca Nueva, 2016). More specifically, for Rural Instructors, see Ana Cabana Iglesia, Alba Díaz-Geada and Uxía Otero-González, 'Pensar las mujeres rurales. Ser "campesina" para la dictadura franquista', *Studia Histórica, Historia Contemporánea* 40 (2022), 113–34; and for Home Economic Agents in Spain, Silvia Canalejo Alonso, 'Hacerse sitio en el servicio de Extensión Agraria: opositar a agente de economía doméstica (1960–1974)', *International Congress 'Ganarse la vida: Género y Trabajo a través de los siglos'* (Pampaneira, Granada, 2022), and Teresa Ortega López, Ana Cabana Iglesia, Laura Cabezas Vega and Silvia Canalejo Alonso, *Mujeres y agricultura en la política española del siglo XX* (Madrid: Cátedra, 2024).

Agrarian Extension Agency, and, therefore, resided permanently in the area where they worked. Although they were interested in the community as a whole, their interaction was greater with households engaged in productive specialisation processes. The need to propose an integrated improvement strategy between home and farm is an element that was encountered repeatedly by the AES.[16] Home Economic Agents as well as their male counterparts, the Agrarian Extension Agents, addressed both the productive and reproductive spheres during the 1960s, both of which were subjected to new ways of rationalising time and work.

Over the course of the 1960s, ideas stemming from domestic education tended to recede as the training of women advisors improved and their field of intervention became more established. But the model of the good wife and mother continued to be defended at various levels in the name of maintaining a distinctive feminine identity that was endangered by modernity. This socially conservative position was accompanied by a progressive discourse on the liberation of women from the most unacknowledged household tasks thanks solely to the virtues of technical progress. During Franco's dictatorship, the ideal model of the rural woman had gone from the peasant woman as the 'mother' of the social foundations of the new fascist regime in the post-war years to being the guarantor of the reproduction of a harmonious social order of small peasant landowners in the 1950s, to a housewife and companion for the 'agricultural entrepreneur' who must modernise her home from the 1960s onwards.[17]

In France, as proclaimed by the General Assembly of the Fédération Nationale des Groupements familiaux de Vulgarisation Ménagère Agricole in 1967, rural women must be 'liberated' from material and abusive constraints through household information that would enable them to adopt a new lifestyle, and 'integrate rural women into professional and social life' by participating in professional institutions (and thus 'understanding' their husbands better), while 'helping rural women to find their point of equilibrium'; that is, not going too far, not sacrificing social advancement in the name of female emancipation. This approach was close to the ideal of the 'wife working alongside her husband' propagated by the Catholic Female Agricultural Youth (Jeunesses Agricoles Catholiques Féminines) movement. JACF activists gradually moved away

16 'It is often difficult to distinguish where the household economy ends, and the farm economy begins. This is why the Agricultural Extension Service, which is basically intended to improve the living conditions of the rural family, has to be directed towards the rural family, and must therefore address the farmer and his wife in equal measure.' 'La mujer en el campo', *Revista de Extensión Agraria* 1/12 (1962), 1. Also Cabana Iglesia, Díaz-Geada and Otero-González, 'Pensar las mujeres rurales', 120.

17 Cabana Iglesia, Díaz-Geada and Otero-González, 'Pensar las mujeres rurales', 113–34.

from a restrictive view of women's roles that focused solely on the home. Contrary to the opposed stereotypes of the subservient woman on the traditional smallholding and the woman who was completely removed from the functioning of the large farm and had lost all contact with the rural world, the 'wife working alongside her husband' embodied the path of the modernising medium-sized farm, on which the imperative of intensification had to be reconciled with the duty to preserve the cultural heritage of the peasantry. The farm advisors acted as guarantors of this ideal by encouraging the women who best represented it to take on the responsibility for their groups. These advisors were often former members of the JACF. They were sometimes employed in training centres for young people in the countryside. They almost always came from farming families.

The methods used by women extension workers in the 1960s were not radically different from those of their male counterparts in both countries: field experiments, group meetings, testing of materials and so on. But women's groups and extension workers were not involved in farm management issues, which were monopolised by men. Although women have historically played an important role in keeping farm accounts, which often do not separate the domestic and professional spheres, they have been excluded from receiving specialised business advice, which has played an increasingly important role in guiding investment choices and specialising production since the 1960s. From then on, women's agricultural extension groups focused their activities on small and medium-sized farms that were having difficulties, adopting a global approach to problems: the livestock production units for which women farmers were responsible (organisation, working conditions); the consumption problems (purchasing, freezing, self-consumption); and the farm economic environment (opportunities for additional income through crafts).

We can date the beginning of the end for the AES in both France and Spain to the 1970s, mainly because of changes in the economic and social context. In both countries the concentration and specialisation of farms relegated women to menial tasks or to the domestic sphere.[18] In Spain, the agents questioned the extent to which they had contributed to the continuation of small-farm agriculture as opposed to the farm consolidation and enlargement that modernising policies had encouraged.[19] In France, the most senior female advisors continued to work with women's groups, extending their activities to include broader territorial

18 Marie-Catherine Becouarn, *L'évolution des techniques en agriculture et le travail des femmes* (Paris: CNRS/Centre d'Études Sociologiques, 1971), 45. Ana Cabana Iglesia, Elena Freire Paz and Tamara López Fernández, 'From Peasant to Housewife: Feminine Roles and Agricultural Training in Franco's Spain', *History and Anthropology* 34 (2023), 1–22.

19 Sánchez De Puerta, *Extensión agraria y desarrollo rural*, 425–9, 443–4.

management issues. But newly hired female agricultural advisors were assigned to managing male groups. The distinctiveness of women's agricultural extension work gradually disappeared.

Why were chronology and traits in both countries so similar despite the very different political contexts in which extension services were implemented? There are several answers that can be summarised under two main, interlinked heads. First, the hegemonic model proposed by the US was homogeneous and thus the ideal of the rural woman was similar regardless of the initial situations in each country. Moreover, it is not possible to understand the similarity found between two countries with such different political regimes without considering the influence of structural elements that also conferred elements of homogeneity in the economic and gender spheres. Both societies are situated in the orbit of Western capitalism, and this situation came about at a specific moment in the development of the capitalist mode of production. At this specific moment, when the mass consumer society was being built, specific relationships and tensions were established in relation to structural forms of patriarchal domination. For what concerns us here, it is of particular interest to consider the effects of Modernisation Theory, which aims to guide the steps that peasant societies must follow to culminate in the construction of capitalist consumer society.

Modernisation Theory took shape during the 1950s and 1960s, in the geopolitical context of the Cold War. It divided societies into 'traditional' and 'modern'. It attempted to establish parameters to regulate the process by which traditional societies would be transformed into modern ones. This process was understood to be inevitable and extended back to the late nineteenth century. This theory legitimised an active role for states in promoting the process, as well as a leading role for the US as the hegemonic capitalist power in the promotion and implementation of measures that would favour a certain development model, according to capitalist parameters and pursuant to the needs of the political containment of alternative models. Both the Marshall Plan in Europe and the Alliance for Progress in Latin America were initiatives influenced by this conception. At the European level, it was the Organisation for European Economic Creation (OEEC) itself, created with the aim of coordinating the distribution of American aid from the Marshall Plan, which channelled the influence of the North American extension model. In the 1950s, both the Agency for International Development (AID) and the Food and Agriculture Organization (FAO) were already working with extension experts to provide assistance in this area.[20] The influence of the philosophy and practice of extension according to the dominant parameters in the US, both in Europe and in Latin America, was conveyed

20 Ibid., 138.

through two main channels: direct advice from (largely American) experts who travelled to the countries implementing the plan, and the training of personnel from those countries either in the US, or in other places with a developed extension model in tune with the North American one.

In 1962, the journal published by Spain's Agricultural Extension Service reported that the International Agricultural Centre of the Netherlands, in collaboration with the Spanish Ministry of Agriculture and Fisheries had held the tenth international course on 'Programming and methods of agricultural extension and home economics' at Wageningen from 9 July to 5 August. The course was sponsored by the FAO and the OECD, whose delegates were charged with carrying out a comparative analysis of the 'efficiency, influence and cost-effectiveness of each of the extension methods'. The course was attended by representatives from forty countries, including France and Spain, as well as Germany, Belgium, the Netherlands, England, Switzerland, Nigeria, Tunisia and Thailand. The report notes that the programme had been 'intense', that 'interesting topics related to outreach around the world' had been presented and discussed, that working groups had been organised and fieldwork had been carried out in different parts of the Netherlands. The presence of a significantly higher number of women than at previous meetings of this nature was explained as 'a logical consequence of the general trend' to incorporate Home Economics into agricultural extension programmes 'in all those countries where it has hitherto been carried out independently'. In this news report we have the keys to the process of adoption of the US extensionist model in Europe and other parts of the world. Homogeneity was a substantial part of the modernisation model and women did not escape this attempt at standardisation. Women across the board were pushed to aspire to the same ideal of femininity, which included sanctioning inequality between men and women through gendered repertoires of action.[21] Each gender was assigned roles within the agrarian space, in which rural women were entrusted with the task of taking care of the household and given the responsibility of ensuring the smooth running of the family (farm) business as collaborators with their husbands and as guarantors of a 'peasant culture' that should be maintained *unless* it contradicted the modern values of extensionism.

17.2 Home Economic Agents and feminism?

Never truly detached from its household origins, women's agricultural extension work is open to criticism. It can be painted as a vast campaign

21 Sylvain Brunier, 'Les techniques de conseil ont-elles un genre? Le métier de conseillère agricole dans les années 1960', in *Genre et techniques, XIXe–XXIe siècle*, Fabien Knittel and Pascal Raggi (eds) (Rennes: Presses Universitaires de Rennes, 2013), 85–100.

to acculturate rural women to new urban standards of comfort, opening new rural markets for industrialists, the nascent mass retail sector, banks or insurance companies. And certainly, the information delivered at extension meetings resonates with the same forms of persuasion that were addressed to rural women by sales representatives or in press or radio advertisements. They all urged women to adopt a new, modern way of life, which required them to break with their old habits and tastes in terms of food consumption or clothing, household equipment and entertainment. But initiatives as resolutely political as local meetings cannot fail to have effects beyond the mere dissemination of the normative models of urban and industrial society. Admittedly, women's extension meetings did not have the spectacular dimensions of public demonstrations. But they were nonetheless undeniable opportunities for women to assert their presence in semi-public or professional spaces from which they were traditionally excluded, such as squares, cafés and town halls. Each time they took part in a meeting, it was a small victory that required them to organise their work accordingly; that is, to participate in collective action without contravening social and moral norms, to overcome the silent (or noisy) disapproval of their family circle, to make the journey to the meeting place and to find their place within a women's collectivity. For some women, leaving the farm for a day meant leaving their husbands alone to eat at lunchtime. Some women found it hard to envisage doing this and needed a great deal of reassurance from the advisor before they dared. In France, some women, mischievously, asked the advisor to schedule an activity that required them to leave the farm very early in the morning and return late at night, forcing their husbands to do the milking. These manifestations of independence can be described as a form of 'silent feminism', which, without actually overturning the established order, imperceptibly and continuously subverted gender relations within the agricultural world.[22]

Female agricultural extension thus appears two-faced. As American studies on the development of Home Economics have shown, in the first half of the twentieth century, the introduction of 'domestic science' in schools – in this case on farms – was primarily aimed at reinforcing the distribution of roles according to gender, rather than seeking the emancipation of women.[23] But the work carried out by women's extension groups also broke down isolation and encouraged members to engage in collective action, both on the farm and in local communities. The concept of social feminism is used to describe these actions, which, whether or not the actors were conscious of their scope, helped to transform patriarchal

22 Rose-Marie Lagrave, *Celles de la terre. Agricultrice: l'invention politique d'un métier* (Paris: Éditions de l'École des hautes études en sciences sociales, 1987).

23 Robert Stamp, 'Teaching Girls Their "God-Given Place in Life": The Introduction of Home Economics in the Schools', *Atlantis* 2 (1977), 18–34.

structures and the values associated with them.[24] Such work is not overtly anti-establishment, still less revolutionary, but it is undeniably political when it creates spaces in which singular experiences can find expression as part of a minority. And it was crucial in cases such as Spain's, where the dictatorship was still in force, and it is probable that these formative spaces also became spaces for female sociability that could create the conditions to carry out joint initiatives that exceeded the initial objectives of the agents.

17.3 Conclusion

To address the study of the personnel of the AES and, more specifically, the teachers of Home Economics to rural women in France and Spain, it is necessary to consider the evolution of the political and social framework in which it was developed, as well as the specific local universes in which modernisation projects become realities of change (resisted or negotiated). As we try to show in this chapter, it is also important to pay attention to the structures of ideological and international relations in which the organisation of numerous AES expanded worldwide.

What makes the difference when the model of agrarian modernisation and the dissemination mechanisms used to transform the role of rural women are essentially the same, is, in our opinion, the existence or absence of spaces for dissent. The key difference between the French and Spanish imposition of the extensionist model was the existence (or not) of spaces where women could express their disagreement without incurring a penalty for expressing their views. While the French state was more concerned to convince people of the benefits of the extensionist model both in the figure of the male agricultural entrepreneur and in that of the 'modern but not so modern' woman, Spain did not have to convince its citizens, but used all the leverage at its disposal (institutions, local authorities, priests, and so on) to impose the female model it had adopted.

What is the difference between the imposition of gender roles by a democratic state convinced of this archetype and acting alongside agricultural unions versus the imposition of this gender ideal by a dictatorial state? If rural women in France or Spain had been able to 'negotiate' the gender model exported by the US, then it would not be necessary to pose the question. But they had no more room for manoeuvre than rural or urban women in other countries or than their male counterparts. What they had, depending on the existence or lack of democratic guarantees, was a greater or lesser margin to 'appropriate' for their benefit the spaces and forms that were offered to them as 'their own'.

24 Noemi Black, Gail Cuthbert Brandt, *Feminist Politics on the Farm: Rural Catholic Women in Southern Quebec and Southwestern France* (Montréal: McGill-Queen's University Press, 1999).

Women's agricultural training in the twentieth century in France and Spain had sanctioned the inequalities developed by the historical patriarchy. In this context, US extensionism represented more of a continuity than a change. Whether in democratic states such as France or dictatorial states such as Spain, extensionism perpetuated and extended the dissociation of the domestic space from the productive sphere. Certainly, the modernisation model implemented in rural areas continued to maintain the domestic sphere as women's own area. A household had to be reorganised under the same criteria of efficiency and productivity; male farmers should deal with farming, female farmers should care for the home and the children. They should act as a faithful assistant to their husbands. Extensionism continued to reproduce differences between what was inferred as 'feminine' work from 'what wasn't appropriate for women'. For this task, extensionism made use of training female agents who assimilated the gender model and disseminated it to rural women. Therefore, extensionism neither broke with gender inequalities in rural communities nor agrarian labour, but normalised and established gender roles in which rural woman had to identify themselves as housewives. This does not mean that AES agents, *conseilleres agricoles* and the rural women they trained did not find ways and spaces to reinterpret gender mandates. By bringing women together, extensionism could subvert the very system of gender relations it sought to uphold.

18

Resisting the Green Revolution epic in Brazil and India[1]

Poonam Pandey and Lídia Cabral

The Green Revolution, as a technocratic agricultural modernisation project,[2] remains one of the most celebrated as well as one of the most criticised experiments in contemporary agricultural history.[3] Though it faced opposition from scientists, politicians and farmers, the most prominent critique of the Green Revolution emerged (and still continues emerging) among social science scholars who have examined its social, economic, political and historical consequences.[4] Later appraisals of the Green Revolution were based on experience of the local consequences of the use of Green Revolution technologies over decades. These included issues relating to resource use, the degradation of rural-agricultural life and environmental destruction.[5] Recently, agroecological movements

1 The authors acknowledge funding from the UK Economic and Social Research Council that supported this research through the project 'Green Revolutions in Brazil, China and India: Epic narratives of the past and today's South-South technology transfers' (grant reference ES/R00658X/1).

2 The process of agricultural modernisation was ongoing all over the world before it was labelled as the Green Revolution in the 1960s in South Asia. For more details of the history of agricultural modernisation in Europe, see Jonathan Harwood, *Europe's Green Revolution and Its Successors: The Rise and Fall of Peasant-friendly Plant Breeding* (London: Routledge, 2012).

3 Raj Patel, 'The Long Green Revolution', *J. Peasant Studies* 40 (2013), 1–63.

4 Bertram Hughes Farmer, *Green Revolution? Technology and Change in Rice-Growing Areas of Tamil Nadu and Sri Lanka* (London: Macmillan, 1977); Wolf Ladejinsky, 'The Green Revolution in Punjab: A Field Trip', *Economic and Political Weekly* 4/26 (1969), A73–82; F. R. Frankel, *India's Political Economy, 1947–1977: The Gradual Revolution* (Princeton, NJ: Princeton University Press, 1978).

5 Vandana Shiva, *The Violence of the Green Revolution: Third World Agriculture, Ecology and Politics* (London: Zed Books, 1991); Akhil Gupta, *Postcolonial Developments: Agriculture in the Making of Modern India* (Durham, NC: Duke University Press, 1998).

have become the central channels of direct resistance to the Green Revolution on the ground. Scholarship focusing on agroecological movements highlights the challenges posed by the entanglement of neoliberalism, state machinery and the techno-economic imaginary in contemporary agricultural improvement discourses. While the literature criticising the Green Revolution is now extensive and easily accessible, accounts of resistance against the Green Revolution emerging from practice have received less attention as have the alternative farming strategies developed in reaction to it.[6]

In this chapter, we present a selective account of the critiques of the Green Revolution in Brazil and India developed by farmers, civil society groups and scientists from the 1960s to the present and the forms their resistance took.[7] The chapter relies on both primary and secondary data collection in the two countries. We conducted interviews with a range of participants and witnesses, among them scientists, policymakers and farmers, to understand the voices of resistance to the Green Revolution. This primary data is supported by secondary literature on the themes of critique, resistance and alternatives to the Green Revolution.

Brazil and India have a rich diversity of communities engaged in a range of agricultural practices. Both these countries also have very strong grassroots movements that are central to international movements that push for farmers' sovereignty. At the same time, these countries' agricultural research and innovation systems are world-leading and well able to assist countries in the Global South achieve food self-sufficiency. Against this background, this chapter aims to understand how resistance to dominant models of agricultural modernisation emerge and how they are sustained. What kinds of actor are involved in this resistance? And what is the nature and site of these resistances?

We proceed by situating resistance struggles in the context of the dominant techno-economic paradigm established with the Green Revolution.

6 Max Ajl and Divya Sharma, 'The Green Revolution and Transversal Countermovements: Recovering Alternative Agronomic Imaginaries in Tunisia and India', *Canadian J. Development Studies/Revue canadienne d'études du développement* 43 (2022), 418–38; Madhumita Saha, 'Food for Soil, Food for People: Research on Food Crops, Fertilisers, and the Making of "Modern" Indian Agriculture', *Technology and Culture* 54 (2013), 289–316.

7 The process of agricultural modernisation was under critical scrutiny from agronomists and scholars in Europe and Mexico prior to its introduction in South Asia. For an account of critiques and alternatives to top-down agricultural modernisation in Europe, see Venus Bivar, *Organic Resistance: The Struggle over Industrial Farming in Postwar France (Flows, Migrations, and Exchanges)* (Chapel Hill, NC: University of North Carolina Press, 2018). For details on Mexico see Gabriela Soto Laveaga, 'Largo Dislocare: Connecting Microhistories to Remap and Recenter Histories of Science', *History and Technology* 34 (2018), 21–30.

This regime is maintained and reproduced through epic narratives about a heroic past that continue to be invoked to justify the continuing relevance of its agricultural modernisation project. We then outline our analytical framework derived from various scholarly studies on the form, context and site of resistance. We then present selective examples of resistance to the Green Revolution in Brazil and India. A final section of the chapter offers a concluding discussion.

18.1 Sustaining the Green Revolution techno-economic paradigm through epic narration

The Green Revolution was a large-scale endeavour by governments in the Global South to modernise their agricultural sectors through substantial investments in science and technology, irrigation, transport infrastructures and subsidies to enable the adoption of new technology. It unfolded between the 1960s and early 1980s (with variations across countries) and was enthusiastically supported by international organisations, including aid donors and American philanthropic societies (notably the Rockefeller and Ford Foundations), in what have been described as a grand mission of agricultural innovation.[8]

Governments justified the unprecedented investments in agriculture as necessary to avert famines and ensure food self-sufficiency. There were other underlying motives that ranged from post-war and Cold War geopolitics to questions of national sovereignty, social stability concerns and economic interests.[9]

Although it combined technological, political and economic dimensions, the Green Revolution is often praised for its technoscientific achievements, including high-yielding varieties of wheat and rice (in Mexico, India, Pakistan, the Philippines and China), and tropicalised soybeans (in Brazil). Record improvements in crop yields were nurtured by the idea that agricultural modernisation was needed to feed the world and use land more efficiently. But the limits of these claims and the social inequalities and environmental degradation generated by the Green Revolution have been amply discussed since its early days.[10] Not only is Green Revolution farming inefficient if one considers the high volume

8 Brian D. Wright, 'Grand Missions of Agricultural Innovation', *Research Policy* 41 (2012), 1716–28.

9 John H. Perkins, *Geopolitics and the Green Revolution: Wheat, Genes, and the Cold War* (Oxford: Oxford University Press, 1997); Madhumita Saha and Sigrid Schmalzer, 'Green-Revolution Epistemologies in China and India: Technocracy and Revolution in the Production of Scientific Knowledge and Peasant Identity', *BJHS Themes* 1 (2016), 145–67.

10 Farmer, *Green Revolution?*; Shiva, *Violence of the Green Revolution*; Patel, 'Long Green Revolution'; Glenn Davis Stone, 'The Green Revolution and Industrializing Developing World Farms', ch. 6 of Stone, *The Agricultural*

of public subsidies needed to sustain it, but it is also very inequitable in terms of the distribution of the resources and wealth it generates. It is also environmentally unsustainable, as shown by its effects on soils, water basins and biodiversity.[11]

Despite this bleak legacy, the Green Revolution remains a widely celebrated chapter in the history of world agriculture, seen as the dawn of modern agricultural science and the establishment of modern, industrial farms. That these farms are deeply integrated in markets (for inputs and commodity exports) dominated by large multinational agrifood companies illustrates how the technoscientific endeavour is linked to the profit-driven logic of the corporate food regime.[12] Raj Patel describes the Green Revolution as an enduring biopolitical project. As he put it, 'the foundational knowledge required to refashion the Green Revolution project requires continuous and ongoing work to legitimise the actions carried out in its name'.[13]

Following this argument, we have posited elsewhere that this continuous legitimisation of the Green Revolution is carried out through epic narration.[14] Epic narratives talk about a distant past that represents a foundational moment in national histories, such as the dawn of modernity for agricultural sciences. As in literary classics, they narrate great perils (famines, social unrest) and unprecedented achievements (high-yielding varieties) obtained through the hard work and dedication of heroic individuals. For the Green Revolution, these heroes are typically fatherly figures linked to scientific discoveries, such as American plant breeder Norman Borlaug (1914–2009) for his work on dwarf wheat or M. S. Swaminathan (1925–2023), who became renowned as the father of the Indian Wheat Revolution.

This epic narration is done with the intention of legitimising the biopolitical project and empowering the organisations (and the individuals) that are linked to the Green Revolution, in what we consider to be 'an active exercise of history-making'.[15] This helps them deflect criticism and remain authoritative and relevant. In recent years, the epic narration has involved repackaging the Green Revolution to emphasise its contribution to environmental sustainability, as seen in arguments about land

---

Dilemma: How Not to Feed the World (London and New York: Routledge, 2022), 162–93.

11 Philip M. Fearnside, 'Soybean Cultivation as a Threat to the Environment in Brazil', *Environmental Conservation* 28 (2001), 23–38.

12 Raj Patel, *Stuffed and Starved: From Farm to Fork. The Hidden Battle for the World Food System* (London: Portobello Books Ltd, 2013).

13 Patel, 'Long Green Revolution', 4.

14 Lídia Cabral, Poonam Pandey and Xiuli Xu, 'Epic Narratives of the Green Revolution in Brazil, India and China', *Agriculture and Human Values* 39 (2022), 249–67.

15 Ibid., 252.

sparing[16] or in suggestions that Green Revolution institutions can lead the way towards greener and more sustainable farming.[17] The sustainable agriculture solutions emanating out of these institutions have been questioned for their underlying motivations and for their elitist and top-down vision of knowledge and innovation that is deemed inadequate for addressing the social inequities and sustainability challenges that arose out of the Green Revolution in the first place.[18]

The Green Revolution epic, through its multiple rehearsals and translations in different contexts, has elicited different kinds of resistances among different sets of people. These range from the everyday actions of farmers rejecting the Green Revolution altogether, to farmers shaping it to fit their own needs, or to trying (and often failing) to work with it. They also include different approaches to working with farmers by scientists and technicians who have embraced more inclusive and participatory knowledge production. A systematic engagement with these resistances is important for understanding the undercurrents that will shape the future of agricultural development in the Global South. The next section presents the conceptual lens by which to make sense of these types of resistances, which will then inform our analysis of forms of resistance to the Green Revolution in Brazil and India.

18.2 The aims, forms and ways of resistance

James C. Scott was the pioneer in theorising resistance in relation to different forms of domination and oppression.[19] The more public and organised forms of resistance take the form of protests, rallies, petitions and forceful acquisitions. Behind these lies an 'infra-politics' that builds momentum long before and carries forward the cause long after these public and organised protests. The 'infra-politics' is an everyday, continuous, individualised, slow and disguised form of resistance that takes the form of non-participation, foot dragging, dissident subcultures and false compliance. These everyday forms of resistance undermine repressive domination without risking survival in situations where open resistance was too dangerous.

16 Prabhu L. Pingali, 'Green Revolution: Impacts, Limits, and the Path Ahead', *Proceedings of the National Academy of Sciences* 109 (2012) 12302–8.

17 Mankombu Sambasivan Swaminathan, *From Green to Evergreen Revolution: Indian Agriculture: Performance and Emerging Challenges* (New Delhi: Academic Foundation, 2010).

18 Mikael Bergius and Jill Tove Buseth, 'Towards a green Modernization Development Discourse: The New Green Revolution in Africa', *J. Political Ecology* 26 (2019), 57–83.

19 James C. Scott, *Weapons of the Weak: Everyday Forms of Peasant Resistance* (New Haven, CT: Yale University Press, 1985); James C. Scott, 'Everyday Forms of Resistance', *Copenhagen Papers* 4 (1989), 33–62.

Scholars have criticised Scott's characterisation of everyday resistance as being entirely focused on coercion, creating a mind-body duality where the body of peasants is dominated and subject to oppression, while their minds are considered free and unpersuadable by hegemonic discourses.[20] Where Scott saw power as being embedded in certain groups of individuals, scholars in resistance studies influenced by Foucault have theorised everyday resistance in relation to power that they characterise as ubiquitous and relational.[21] As a result, power and resistance are entangled in a complex interplay characterised by historical contingencies, intersectionality and context sensitivity.

Hall *et al.* categorised agrarian studies scholarship into three broad models for understanding resistance or its absence: the classical collective action paradigm; the Marxist explanation; and heterodox theories.[22] With varied degrees of emphasis, all three models aim to theorise the link between individual and collective resistances, and the informal everyday forms of resistance and organised mass movements.[23]

The analysis of the interplay between individual and collective resistance and the relations between everyday and organised resistance requires a focus on hegemonic discourses that limit the possibility of open and organised resistance against material and ideological domination. Post-war dominant paradigms, such as the Green Revolution, are hegemonic instruments of global capitalism where contradictory cohabitation is a norm rather than an exception.[24] The history of agricultural modernisation through the hegemonic discourse and material practices of the Green Revolution in the Global South demonstrate the role of the state, arguably a protector of public interest, in facilitating the process of capital accumulation that is still ongoing. The rhetoric of alleviating hunger through increased production of foodgrains, was, in retrospect, a mechanism to integrate farmers into markets enabling

20 Mona Lilja, Mikael Baaz, Michael Schulz and Stellan Vinthagen, 'How Resistance Encourages Resistance: Theorising the Nexus Between Power, "Organised Resistance" and "Everyday Resistance"', *J. Political Power* 10 (2017), 40–54; Timothy Mitchell, 'Everyday Metaphors of Power', *Theory and Society* 19 (1990), 545–77.

21 Stellan Vinthagen and Anna Johansson, 'Everyday Resistance: Exploration of a Concept and its Theories', *Resistance Studies Magazine* 1 (2013), 1–46; Lilja *et al.*, 'How Resistance Encourages Resistance', 45.

22 Ruth Hall, Marc Edelman, Saturnino M. Borras, Ian Scoones, Ben White and Wendy Wolford, 'Resistance, Acquiescence or Incorporation? An Introduction to Land Grabbing and Political Reactions "From Below"', *J. Peasant Studies* 42 (2017), 469.

23 Ibid., 470.

24 Jostein Jakobsen, 'Towards a Gramscian Food Regime Analysis of India's Agrarian Crisis: Counter-Movements, Petrofarming and Cheap Nature', *Geoforum* 90 (2018), 1–10.

their exploitation.[25] Similarly, within neoliberal policies, practices such as liberalising and privatising agri-food systems uncomfortably co-exist with protectionist measures such as public distribution systems and the right to food.[26] These contradictions within the dominant discourse confuse and divide people along material and ideological lines, eventually disarming organised critique and resistance. In the absence of mass support for sustained organised resistance, everyday resistance enables the possibility of undermining dominant ideologies and material practices.

Johansson and Vinthagen characterise everyday resistance as consisting of four analytical dimensions: repertoires; relationship of agents; spatialisation; and temporalisation. Within everyday resistance, repertoires represent 'a collection of ways or methods of resistance that people are familiar with, know of, understand and are able to handle'.[27] The ways in which different agents (resisters, targets, observers) engage in an act of resistance characterise the relationship between agents. This relationship, along with space and time as elements ordering social life, are crucial in determining the form and scope of resistance.

While resistance studies have started to emphasise the interplay and interconnectedness of power and resistance, a lot of attention is still given to seeing resistance as an oppositional and destructive act. While Johansson and Vinthagen argue that this should not be the case and resistance could also be productive, there is a need to strengthen this argument through empirical studies. In this chapter we aim to highlight the constructive and productive aspects of everyday resistance. These productive aspects could result in the protection and conservation of valuable knowledge, worldviews and entities to build new and alternative pathways, alliances and solidarities. While zooming in on the constructive aspects of everyday resistance, following Johansson and Vinthagen's call to focus on the interlinkages between everyday and organised resistance, this chapter looks at different mechanisms and types of everyday resistance to the Green Revolution in first Brazil and then India.

25 Jonathan Harwood, 'Was the Green Revolution Intended to Maximise Food Production?', *International J. Agricultural Sustainability* 17 (2019), 312–25; Patel, 'Long Green Revolution', 15.

26 Gerardo Otero, 'The Neoliberal Food Regime in Latin America: State, Agribusiness Transnational Corporations and Biotechnology', *Canadian J. Development Studies/Revue canadienne d'études du développement* 33 (2012), 282–94; Jakobsen, 'Towards a Gramscian Food Regime Analysis', 1–10.

27 Anna Johansson and Stellan Vinthagen, 'Dimensions of Everyday Resistance: An Analytical Framework', *Critical Sociology* 42 (2016), 421.

18.3 Resisting the Green Revolution epic in Brazil

In Brazil, the Green Revolution is associated with the incorporation of the Cerrado biome into agricultural production, a process that started in the 1970s.[28] The modernisation and productive incorporation of the Cerrado was led by the newly created Brazilian Agricultural Research Corporation (Embrapa), whose name became indissociable from the Brazilian Green Revolution.[29] Its key contribution in the early days of the Brazilian Green Revolution was the adaptation of soybeans (until then a temperate crop) to the acidic soils and climate of the Cerrado, a feat that has been widely praised[30] and would later inspire ideas of technological transfer to Africa.[31] The expansion of soybean monocrops and industrial agriculture more broadly in the Cerrado and beyond made Brazil a global agricultural power as a world-leading producer and exporter of not only soybeans but also meat.[32] But the limits of this model soon became noticeable: the depletion of soils and water basins, loss of biodiversity, concentration of wealth and increase in violence on the agricultural frontier.[33]

Societal opposition to this techno-economic paradigm soon emerged. Agrarian social movements first demanded justice for landless labourers. Over the years, opposition expanded to include issues of access to inputs and technology and markets, dependence on agrochemicals, the health impact of the Green Revolution technology, and later issues of food sovereignty and food and nutrition security. While at times this opposition has been overtly confrontational, as in land occupations led by

28 The Cerrado is a Brazilian biome or ecoregion located in the highlands of central Brazil. It comprises grasslands, savannahs and dry forests. It is the second largest biome in Brazil following the Amazon, covering around 24 per cent of the country's territory. See Lídia Cabral, Sérgio Sauer and Alex Shankland, 'Introduction: Reclaiming the Cerrado: A Territorial Account of a Disputed Frontier', *IDS Bulletin* 54 (2023), 1–16.

29 Ryan Nehring, 'The Brazilian Green Revolution', *Political Geography* 95 (2022), 102574.

30 Norman Borlaug, 'Editorial: Feeding a Hungry World', *Science* 318/5849 (2007), 359.

31 Michael Morris, Hans P. Binswanger-Mkhize and Derek Byerlee, *Awakening Africa's Sleeping Giant: Prospects for Commercial Agriculture in the Guinea Savannah Zone and Beyond*, Directions in Development – Agriculture and Rural Development (Washington, DC: The World Bank, 2009).

32 Pedro Antonio Arraes Pereira *et al.*, 'The Development of Brazilian Agriculture: Future Technological Challenges and Opportunities', in *Brazilian Agriculture, Development and Changes* (Brasília: Embrapa: Embrapa Studies and Training, 2012), 13–42.

33 A. Favareto *et al.*, *Entre Chapadas e Baixões Do Matopiba: Dinâmicas Territoriais e Impactos Socioeconômicos Na Fronteira Da Expansão Agropecuária No Cerrado* (São Paulo: Editora Ilustre e Greenpeace, 2019).

the Landless Workers' Movement (MST),[34] there have also been periods when agrarian and rural social movements have directly engaged in public policy processes by participating in inclusive policy spaces such as the National Council of Food and Nutrition Security (CONSEA).[35] Besides these well documented (oppositional to constructive) organised forms of resistance,[36] there have also been other ways of expressing resistance to the Green Revolution that are incorporated into everyday practices and that confront it by challenging its techno-economic paradigm and questioning its epistemological and ontological underpinnings. Two cases are illustrative of these everyday resistances: agroecology networks and ethnoscience.

Agroecology networks

In Brazil, agroecology represents perhaps the most visible and established resistance to the Green Revolution as a techno-economic project. As in the definition by Wezel *et al.*,[37] agroecology in Brazil embodies a field of science, a social movement and agricultural practice, and these three dimensions intertwine in Brazil's agroecology networks.[38]

Although agroecology's emphasis on experiential knowledge, including knowledge about nature and farming practices held by traditional and indigenous communities, implies that its roots are as old as indigenous settlement in South America, the first references to agroecology (related to incorporating biological principles in farming) can be found in the 1980s. As in other Latin American countries, agroecology emerged out of agrarian movements linked to small and peasant farmers and their struggles for justice in the context of an exclusionary agricultural modernisation process. The end of the military dictatorship in Brazil in 1985, and the process of re-democratisation that followed, allowed the movements linked to these struggles to become more assertive.

Its first formulation as a field of science has been linked to the Alternative Agriculture movement, which emerged in the 1980s and was initially driven by agronomists concerned with the negative social and ecological

34 Wendy Wolford, *This Land Is Ours Now: Social Mobilization and the Meanings of Land in Brazil* (Durham, NC: Duke University Press, 2010).

35 *Políticas Públicas de Desenvolvimento Rural No Brasil*, Catia Grisa and Sérgio Schneider (eds) (Porto Alegre: Editora da UFRGS, 2015).

36 *Políticas Públicas de Desenvolvimento Rural No Brasil*, Grisa and Schneider (eds); Peter Houtzager, 'Social Movements Amidst Democratic Transitions: Lessons from the Brazilian Countryside', *J. Development Studies* 36 (2000), 59–88.

37 A. Wezel *et al.*, 'Agroecology as a Science, a Movement and a Practice: A Review', *Agronomy for Sustainable Development* 29 (2009), 503–5.

38 L. Van den Berg *et al.*, 'Between Institutional Reform and Building Popular Movements: The Political Articulation of Agroecology in Brazil', *J. Rural Studies* 89 (2022), 140–8.

impacts of agricultural modernisation.[39] Student and workers' unions and social movements soon made the connection between social and environmental crises and started searching for concrete technological substitutes to the Green Revolution. Throughout the 1990s, alternative agricultural technologies became known as agroecological ones, influenced by Altieri's work,[40] and agroecology as a concept gradually took root. In the 2000s agroecology finally emerged as a distinctive field of social struggle that social movements, such as the MST, identified with and gradually took on board,[41] including the establishment of schools for political education and technical training focused on agroecology.[42] By now, internationally, agroecology was no longer concerned with ecologically sound farming alone, but its scope had been enlarged to encompass social imbalances and injustices across the entire food system from farm to fork.[43]

In Brazil, agroecology was strengthened by a policy agenda that increasingly focused on food and nutrition security and sovereignty. Networks that brought together scientists, technicians, practitioners and activists started to develop, turning agroecology into an umbrella movement spanning several and interconnected agrarian and environmental justice struggles. New spaces for learning, debate, political expression and mobilisation were established, including the National Agroecology Meetings (ENA) and the more academically orientated Brazilian Agroecology Conferences (CBA). The first ENA led to the creation of the National Agroecology Articulation (ANA) in 2002, a network comprising social movements, regional networks, professional associations and NGOs.[44] CBAs were driven by the Brazilian Agroecology Association (ABA), created in 2004.[45]

Both ENAs and CBAs consolidated themselves as spaces for resistance to the Green Revolution, where resistance manifests in multiple ways

39 Claudia Schmitt *et al.*, 'A Experiência Brasileira de Construção de Políticas Públicas Em Favor Da Agroecologia', *Actas Seminario Políticas a favor de la Agroecología en América Latina y El Caribe* (Brasília, 2016), https://www.researchgate.net/publication/321437208_A_experiencia_brasileira_de_construcao_de_politicas_publicas_em_favor_da_agroecologia (accessed 26 February 2025).

40 Miguel A. Altieri, *Agroecology: The Scientific Basis of Alternative Agriculture* (Berkeley, CA: Division of Biological Control, University of California, 1983).

41 Andreas Hernandez, 'The Emergence of Agroecology as a Political Tool in the Brazilian Landless Movement', *Local Environment* 25 (2020), 205–27.

42 Margriet Goris *et al.*, 'Popular Education, Youth and Peasant Agroecology in Brazil', *J. Rural Studies* 87 (2021), 12–22

43 Stephen R. Gliessman, *Agroecology: The Ecology of Sustainable Food Systems* (New York: CRC Press, Taylor & Francis, 2007).

44 Paulo Petersen, Eros Marion Mussoi and Fabio Dal Soglio, 'Institutionalization of the Agroecological Approach in Brazil: Advances and Challenges', *Agroecology and Sustainable Food Systems* 37 (2013), 103–14.

45 Schmitt *et al.*, 'A Experiência Brasileira de Construção de Políticas Públicas Em Favor Da Agroecologia'.

and is recurrently expressed to create further resistance. Focusing specifically on CBAs, which happen biennially (except during the Covid-19 pandemic, which saw a four-year gap between the eleventh and twelfth CBA), resistance is visible in at least four distinct ways. One is the articulation of a direct opposition to the Green Revolution modernisation project, as visible in thematic workstreams in the conference programme focused on food sovereignty and the fight against agrochemicals. It is also visible in acts during the congress that are overtly political, such as plenaries with social movements.

A second form of resistance is the endorsement and encouragement of multiple forms of knowledge as a critique of top-down agricultural sciences that are elitist and exclusionary. Since 2015, the key space for knowledge exchange at the CBA has been designated 'Tapiris of Knowledges', where 'Tapiri' is a Tupi indigenous word chosen to invoke the space where indigenous peoples in the north of Brazil come together to talk, eat, rest and share experiences. CBA also hosts parallel and self-organised activities by different groups, organisations and associations. These include food stalls, spaces to share social innovations, activities with children and activities focused on health, well-being and healing.

The third form of resistance that we have identified is the effort to construct alternatives that account for a diverse social fabric and multiple conditions of disadvantage, determined by race, age, gender and sexuality. Several CBA workstreams are focused on marginalised social groups, such as peasantries, traditional and indigenous communities, gender and feminism, youth and children. A fourth form of resistance is the emphasis given to cultural and artistic expression to nurture connections and solidarities, as illustrated by the Agroecology Arts and Culture Festival and the International Agroecology Cinema Festival that have been incorporated in recent CBAs.

Agroecology also permeated the agricultural sciences establishment, where resistance takes on more veiled forms. In 2006, Embrapa published its Reference Framework on Agroecology, which signalled an opening inside the organisation towards research that aligned ecosystem preservation with supporting marginalised farmers.[46] This traced the origins of agroecology-orientated work at Embrapa to the pioneering research on biological nitrogen fixation (BNF) carried out in the 1970s under the leadership of Joanna Döbereiner, who went on to lead the National Programme on Soil Biology established in 1983, considered a milestone for agroecology, at Embrapa. It is worth noting that the BNF was also central to the tropicalisation of soybeans in the Cerrado. The association between the BNF and agroecology was however somewhat uneasy.

46 Embrapa, *Marco referencial em agroecologia* (Brasília, DF: Empresa Brasileira de Pesquisa Agropecuária, Embrapa Informação Tecnológica, 2006).

It was in the 2000s, however, under the progressive government of Lula da Silva, that agroecology found a space inside Embrapa as a result of political support by the Presidency of Embrapa. A working group on agroecology was set up in 2005 and enabled training programmes, syntheses of internal knowledge on agroecology, inter-institutional engagements (including participation in ECAs and CBAs) and eventually, in 2012, the establishment of a research portfolio focused on agroecological and organic production systems and another on social innovation, which also aligned with agroecological ideas of inclusive knowledge systems. Some of the work developed within these portfolios (particularly the one on social innovation) used participatory methods to open dialogues with farmers in ways that challenged dominant linear and top-down knowledge diffusion models.[47]

Though this participatory approach to agricultural research remained on the fringes of Embrapa's work,[48] it generated knowledge about farming that revealed its social, cultural and ecological dimensions, with agrobiodiversity emerging as a synthesis concept[49] that was perhaps less politically charged than agroecology, which was by now established as a social and political current. Agrobiodiversity conservation projects with indigenous groups at Embrapa form our next illustrative case.

Ethnoscience at Embrapa

Ethnoscience projects at Embrapa are a further example of Green Revolution resistance movements. Ethnoscience is a field of research that emphasises the integration between scientific and experiential expertise to advance knowledge and to ensure it is rooted in people's experiences.[50] It branched out into other subfields including ethnobotany, ethnoecology, ethnopedology, among others. In Brazil, ethnoscience has been important in challenging established environmental conservation approaches that overlook people in nature.[51]

47 Nadi Rabelo Santos and Terezinha Borges Dias, 'Embrapa: da sua origem a uma visão agroecológica', *Cadernos de Agroecologia* 9 (2014), 1–5.

48 Lídia Cabral, 'Fringe Heroines: Situated Struggles of Women Scientists in Brazilian Agriculture', *International Feminist J. Politics* (2023), 1–23.

49 Patricia Goulart Bustamante, Rosa Lia Barbieri and Juliana Santilli (eds), *Conservação e uso da agrobiodiversidade: relatos de experiências locais* (Brasília: Embrapa, 2017).

50 Heddy S. A. Putra, 'Ethnoscience: A Bridge To Back To Nature', *E3S Web of Conferences* 249 (2021), https://www.e3s-conferences.org/articles/e3sconf/abs/2021/25/e3sconf_css2021_01002/e3sconf_css2021_01002.html (accessed 20 June 2025).

51 Antonio Carlos Diegues, 'The Role of Ethnoscience in the Build-up of Ethnoconservation as a New Approach to Nature Conservation in the Tropics', *Revue d'ethnoécologie* 6 (2014).

A symbolic act marked the beginning of the ethnoscience resistance inside Embrapa. In 1994, the Krahô, an indigenous group from a region within the state of Tocantins in Brazil shot an arrow against the building holding the gene bank of Embrapa Genetic Resources and Biotechnology, decrying their loss of traditional maize genetic material as a consequence of agricultural modernisation since the 1970s. The Krahô demanded access to the genetic material of their ancestors, preserved at Embrapa.[52] This happened at a moment when concerns for biodiversity conservation and the protection of traditional and indigenous knowledge were high on the agenda in Brazil, following the signature of the Convention on Biological Diversity at the Earth Summit in Rio de Janeiro in 1992. Cooperation agreements between Embrapa and the representatives of indigenous peoples to give them access to genetic resources of their ancestors then followed.

Throughout the 2000s, several initiatives have promoted dialogue between technicians at Embrapa and indigenous and traditional communities and enabled a debate on how people from these communities could participate in processes of knowledge production. This was not just about obtaining authorisation for the collection of genetic material from indigenous groups and territories but also about strengthening the role of these groups in the knowledge system and connecting this with the recognition of their identity and protection of their rights in relation to preserved genetic material linked to their territories. Spaces for debate on the role of ethnosciences in agricultural research opened up in the form of working groups and events, such as the 'Ethnoscience and Agricultural Research Meeting – Knowledge Dialogue', in 2006.[53]

These developments happened in tandem with the emergence of a legal framework that recognised and sought to protect Brazil's diverse indigenous and traditional peoples and their territories. The 2007 'National Policy for the Sustainable Development of Traditional Peoples and Communities' constitutes an important milestone.[54]

Though remaining niche at Embrapa, ethnoscience research and engagement activities with indigenous and traditional peoples and communities began to flourish, although the field had been expanding for several years in Brazil and was strengthened with the establishment of the Brazilian Society of Ethnobiology and Ethnoecology in 1996. Embrapa published syntheses of ethnoscientific research highlighting the value of this work, notably in a book series titled *Agroecological Transition*. An

52 Lídia Cabral, 'Embrapa and the Construction of Scientific Heritage in Brazilian Agriculture: Sowing Memory', *Development Policy Review* 39 (2021), 789–810.

53 Terezinha Aparecida Dias *et al.*, 'Reduced Inequalities: Contributions of Embrapa' (Brasília, 2020), https://www.alice.cnptia.embrapa.br/alice/bitstream/doc/1131120/1/SDG-10.pdf (accessed 1 October 2025).

54 Diegues, 'Role of Ethnoscience'.

example is a review of research on the ethnoscience of soils that emphasises the relevance of experiential knowledge to uncover more sustainable agricultural production models and the value of participatory methodologies to ensure indigenous and traditional peoples shared responsibility for sustainable development.[55]

This work highlights the following aspects of the ethnoscientific resistance to the Green Revolution: a recognition of different ways of knowing, seeing value in the integration of scientific knowledge with these other ways of knowing; the use of participatory methods to enable dialogue between different forms of knowledge; and a normative commitment towards improving peoples' conditions, using participatory methods as a way of ensuring that knowledge production is socially relevant.

18.4 Resisting the Green Revolution epic in India

A core feature of the Green Revolution epic in India is its production of the 'miracle seed' narrative around high-yielding varieties (HYV) of wheat and rice. The narrative around seeds, inputs and scientists collectively constituted 'miracles of modernity' even before the first crops could be harvested.[56] In his Nobel Prize speech, Norman Borlaug claimed that for people in Asia the Green Revolution 'seems like a miracle that has generated new hope for the future'.[57]

The epic claims of the Green Revolution as the 'miracle of modernity' have been subject to acute critical scrutiny by social scientists ever since its introduction in India. The epic was criticised for being overtly technocratic and ignorant of social realities, leading to worsening of social inequalities, distress and conflict in the countryside.[58] As these claims were either regionally restricted or based on future projections, they were mostly dismissed by the proponents of the Revolution as 'nonsense' and 'vicious campaigns against progress'.[59] The negative environmental and social consequences of Green Revolution started

55 Valéria do Carmo *et al.*, 'Etnopedologia: Buscando o Olhar de Quem Amanha a Terra', in *Solos e Agroecologia* 4, *Coleção Transição Agroecológica* (Brasília, DF: Empresa Brasileira de Pesquisa Agropecuária, 2018), 159–200.

56 Cullather, 'Miracles of Modernization', 230.

57 Norman E. Borlaug, *The Green Revolution, Peace and Humanity: Speech Delivered upon Receipt of the 1970 Nobel Prize, Oslo, Norway, 1970*, https://www.nobelprize.org/prizes/peace/1970/borlaug/acceptance-speech/ (accessed 30 March 2025).

58 For early critical scholarship on the Green Revolution in India see Bertram H. Farmer, 'The "Green Revolution" in South Asia', *Geography* (1981), 202–7; Pranab Bardhan, 'Green Revolution and Agricultural Labourers', *Economic and Political Weekly* (1970), 1239–46.

59 Madhumita Saha, 'The State, Scientists, and Staple Crops: Agricultural "Modernization" in pre-Green Revolution India', *Agricultural History* 87 (2013), 210.

becoming more clearly apparent from the 1980s. While the cost of inputs kept rising, the return on investment started diminishing, driving farmers into a debt trap that led to thousands of farmer suicides and even more leaving agriculture.[60] In this period many instances of organised resistance in the forms of national and regional farmers' protests took place. They have been extensively documented in the scholarly literature.[61] Along with the organised farmers' protests as movements in opposition to the Green Revolution paradigm, there were many subtle forms of everyday resistances that kept the alternatives alive while simultaneously creating momentum for constructive, organised, mass movements. The following description discusses two such domains of resistances: the seed sovereignty movements; and the Zero Budget Natural Farming (ZBNF) Movement.

Seed sovereignty movements

The discursive constitution of the epic as 'miracles of modernity' simultaneously constituted local seeds, farmers and their knowledge as 'traditional', 'conservative' and 'outdated'.[62] Creating new subjectivities, the Green Revolution epic constituted 'modern' and 'progressive' farmers as peasants who relied on the scientific knowledge provided by the universities and who rejected traditional practices in favour of modern scientific methods. The construction of HYV as 'miracle seeds' was contested by various actors including scientists, politicians and farmers. The voice of R. H. Richharia (1909–96), a rice researcher at the Central Rice Research Institute, Cuttack, Orissa and its Director from 1959 to 1966 is most prominent in this regard.[63] Richharia's research demonstrated that the regional and local varieties of rice are more suitable to these regions' local climate than HYV. Richharia collected and preserved more than 19,000 varieties of rice to support his claims. This act of resistance against the Green Revolution epic, from a scientist within the academy, was met with severe criticisms from the pro-Green Revolution group, eventually resulting in the dismissal of Richharia from his position in 1966.[64]

Outside the academy, the transition of farmers from seed savers to seed buyers was gradual. While some farmers openly rejected the use

60 See Poonam Pandey, 'RRI's Commitment to Care and Vulnerability of Agrarian Systems: The "Problem" of Rice Straw Burning in India', *Science, Technology and Society* 25 (2020), 240–55.

61 Tom Brass (ed.), *New Farmers' Movements in India* (Ilford: Frank Cass, 1995); Jairus Banaji, 'The Farmers' Movements: A Critique of Conservative Rural Coalitions', *J. Peasant Studies* 21 (1994), 228–45.

62 Cullather, 'Miracles of Modernization'.

63 Ajl and Sharma, 'The Green Revolution and Transversal Counter Movements'.

64 Ibid.

of Green Revolution methods on their fields, others used local and HYV strains on different plots based on the availability of resources.[65] Due to the remarkably different responses of local and HYV to inputs (made available by the state via subsidies), gradually the practice of seed saving was abandoned. However, since the availability of subsidised inputs and access to markets was not uniform throughout India, many farmers, especially from marginal communities and marginal regions, reverted to saving, sharing and reviving traditional seeds.

Out of many small, regionally located seed revival initiatives, the *Beej Bachao Andolan* (BBA; Seed Saving Movement) of Tehri-Garhwal was one of the pioneers. Situated in the foothills of the Himalayas in the state of Uttarakhand,[66] the hilly terrains of Tehri proved unsuitable to the large-scale Green Revolution project that was being promoted in the state. While the seeds traditionally sown were not as responsive to inputs as the HYV in general, these local seeds were more suitable to the fragile soils and locally available inputs. Looking at the challenges faced by people who had adopted the input-responsive HYV in the 1980s, a group of people who were part of a Gandhian collective joined together to revive traditional seeds under the banner *Beej Bachao Abhiyaan* (Seed Saving Campaign).[67] Along with collecting and sharing traditional varieties of seeds, the members of the group travelled to different villages in the region to talk about the challenges posed by the Green Revolution model of agriculture. Eventually, with the support of farmers, the campaign became a movement that challenged the Green Revolution epic by the productive activity of protecting and sharing diverse varieties of seeds enabling a model of agriculture based on biodiversity conservation and resource-appropriate agriculture.[68] Two organised movements have a key role to play in the everyday and organised resistance of the BBA: first, the Gandhian philosophy of (village) *Swaraj* and *Satyagraha*; and second, the *Chipko* Movement in the 1970s in the same region.[69] While the Gandhian philosophy enabled the actors to remain rooted in localised, non-violent modes of resistance and provide alternatives to the mainstream discourse,

65 This insight is gathered from multiple rounds of fieldwork that the first author conducted in different districts of Punjab between 2016 and 2019. The author met a few elderly farmers who completely rejected the Green Revolution model of agriculture on their farms because they were sceptical of the chemicals used and their impact on soil, water and human health.

66 Before 2000 Uttarakhand was part of Uttar Pradesh, a northern state of India where the Green Revolution was promoted with the support of agricultural universities.

67 Trent Brown, 'Chipko Legacies: Sustaining an Ecological Ethic in the Context of Agrarian Change', *Asian Studies Review* 38 (2014), 639–57.

68 Pushpa Singh, 'Politics of Knowledge in Development: Explorations in Seed Sovereignty', *Studies in Indian Politics* 9 (2021), 105–17.

69 Trent Brown, 'Chipko Legacies'.

the legacies of the *Chipko* movement enabled people to remain aware of and concerned with the damaging environmental consequences of industrialisation and commercial agriculture.

The 1990s saw processes of post-liberalisation and globalisation that led to the reincarnation of Green Revolution as gene-revolution. The emphasis on biotechnology and genetically modified crops as the new Green Revolution, accompanied by systems of patenting seeds, created new challenges for farmers, ecology and agriculture in India.[70] A need was felt to connect individual farmers and seed savers from all over India. While the regional significance of BBA is noteworthy, the movement, due to its organisational limitations, could not be scaled up to become a national movement. As a result, *Bharat Beej Swaraj Manch* or BBSM (India Seed Sovereignty Alliance) was created in 2014. The BBSM is a country-wide network that connects farmers and seed savers who are involved in conserving traditional seeds and creating farmers' varieties of seeds to promote self-reliance and seed sovereignty. The BBSM emphasises seeds and agriculture as a cultural heritage of farmers and strongly opposes the privatisation of seeds and plant genetic resources. Here too, the Gandhian ideals of *Swaraj* or sovereignty lie at the core of the movement. The alliance relies on a combination of approaches to resist the Green Revolution epic. These include everyday acts of productive resistances in the form of seed saving and practising natural farming, and organised resistances in the form of collective action through alliance building.

Zero Budget Natural Farming (ZBNF) movement

The origin of the ZBNF lies in the efforts of individual farmers trying to make sense of the agrarian crisis arising out of the Green Revolution while still being dependent on agriculture as a source of life and livelihood. All over India, many farmers were motivated to find alternatives to the Green Revolution model of agriculture due to family tragedies involving one or more elements of Green Revolution.[71]

ZBNF was developed as an alternative approach to the Green Revolution model of agriculture, where emphasis was placed on addressing the vulnerabilities of farmers by freeing them from the debt trap caused by dependence on expensive inputs. The suffix of 'zero budget' to 'natural farming' symbolises this emphasis.[72] Simultaneously, the approach of

70 Karine Peschard and Shalini Randeria, '"Keeping Seeds in our Hands": The Rise of Seed Activism', *J. Peasant Studies* 47 (2020), 613–47.

71 A conclusion that emerged from interviews with farmers practising non-Green Revolution agriculture in Punjab and Uttar Pradesh between 2016 and 2019.

72 Contrary to the view that ZBNF is a misnomer since practising any kind of agriculture requires investment, the proponents of ZBNF argue that it symbolises and enables farmers to practise agriculture within their means

increasing farmers' autonomy by delinking them from external inputs shifts them towards practices that strengthen the interdependence of agriculture and ecology.[73] During the 1990s, Subhas Palekar, the *guru* of ZBNF, developed a toolkit of practising natural agriculture by rigorous experimentation and trial and error in line with the principles of Vedic philosophy, Western science and organic agriculture.[74] The toolkit comprises four core elements – Bijamrita (seed treatment), Jivamrita (soil treatment), Wapasha (soil aeration) and Acchadana (mulching) – which collectively constitute the philosophy, method and practice of ZBNF.[75]

For almost two decades, starting in the 1990s, ZBNF was a mechanism of everyday resistance. Farmers looking for alternatives to Green Revolution, on an individual basis, interacted and learned from Subhas Palekar and farmers trained by him. In the early 2000s in the Indian state of Karnataka, the coalition between Subhas Palekar and one of the state's largest farmer organisations – Karnataka Rajya Raitha Sangha (KRRS) – resulted in shaping ZBNF as a social movement.[76] The movement also became immensely popular among farmers practising forms of farming that were heavily dependent on and guided by export markets. Disenchanted by the exploitation during the processes of standardisation and certification that constitute a crucial element of the organic foods value chain, farmers adopted ZBNF to continue practising chemical-free agriculture with autonomy.[77] The popularity of ZBNF among marginal, small and medium farmers in rain-fed regions of India demonstrated the transformative potential of individual resistance that could evolve into a social movement. The principles of ZBNF are now being incorporated into multiple government and university-based agricultural programmes throughout India. The acceptance of ZBNF as a valid method of agriculture by institutions of the Green Revolution demonstrates the power of resistance by different actors (within and outside the academy) that engage in

without being dependent on external sources of income, https://thebackyardforest.com/subhash-palekar-zero-budget-spiritual-farming/ (accessed 31 March 2025). As a counter movement, the ZBNF also receives a lot of criticism from scientists and social scientists towards its claims and philosophy. For further details, see Daniel Münster, 'Agro-Ecological Double Movements? Zero Budget Natural Farming and Alternative Agricultures after the Neoliberal Crisis in Kerala', in *Critical Perspectives on Agrarian Transition*, B. B. Mohanty (ed.) (London: Routledge, 2016), 222–44.

73 Aslesha Khadse, Peter Michael Rosset, Helda Morales, and Bruce G. Ferguson, 'Taking Agroecology to Scale: The Zero Budget Natural Farming Peasant Movement in Karnataka, India', *J. Peasant Studies* 45 (2018), 192–219.

74 Münster, 'Agro-Ecological Double Movements?'.

75 Khadse *et al.*, 'Taking Agroecology to Scale'.

76 Ibid., Münster, 'Agro-Ecological Double Movements?'.

77 Ibid.

destructive resistance (critique, protests) as well as constructive resistance (creating new methods, reviving marginalised approaches).

The ZBNF approach, however, is not without its own tensions and resistances. It is criticised from within the academy for not being true to its claims of producing the desired yield with zero inputs. Concerns are also being raised about the overtly provocative dismissal of modern Western science within ZBNF in favour of Hindu fundamentalist ideals. From outside the academy, there are concerns from grassroots groups regarding the co-opting of ZBNF within dominant agricultural paradigms. Recently, the leader of ZBNF has suffered a serious backlash from civil society groups working on alternative agriculture for comparing organic agriculture with an 'atomic bomb' and embracing GM seeds as acceptable for ZBNF.[78]

18.5 Conclusion

The Green Revolution as a hegemonic discourse has consistently limited the possibility of opposition and resistance against material and ideological domination by processes of contradiction, exclusion and co-optation. People and groups expressing oppositional views are often sidelined as 'illegitimate', 'biased' and 'working against the common good'.[79] The inequalities created on the ground through selective implementation and the impacts of the Green Revolution limit the appeal of organised resistance. In such a scenario, this chapter aimed at documenting different forms, ways and sites of resistances to the Green Revolution that sustain the diversity of agricultural practices. Drawing on selected experiences in Brazil and India, we observed that there are different forms of everyday resistance to Green Revolution practised by different actors at different sites. These everyday resistances can be categorised as destructive/oppositional and constructive/productive resistances, resistances from within the academy (scientists and social scientists), resistances from outside the academy (farmers, civil society groups, politicians) and voices of resistance. We will treat each in turn.

78 See the statement of 6 August 2019 by the Alliance for Sustainable and Holistic Agriculture (ASHA), https://kisanswaraj.in/2019/08/06/statement-from-asha-on-subhash-palekar-natural-farming/ (accessed 3 August 2025). See also Poonam Pandey and Lidia Cabral, 'Transformational Agroecology: The Making and Unmaking of Zero Budget Natural Farming in India', *Science, Technology and Society* 30 (2025), 259–78.

79 See Madhumita Saha in ch. 13, this volume.

Destructive and oppositional versus constructive and productive resistance

Although the cases of resistance we discuss in this chapter all emerge as counterpoints to the Green Revolution, they vary in the extent to which they are oppositional or constructive. Ethnoscience at Embrapa has tried to build bridges between plant breeders and conservationists interested in genetic improvement and conservation and indigenous groups seeking to recover lost genetic material linked to their sociocultural reproduction. Although the ambition of integrating different knowledge domains is bold, ethnoscience largely works within established hierarchies of knowledge. The Indian cases suggest that while the politics of ZBNF is explicitly oppositional to the Green Revolution and its institutions, the actors within the movement are deeply involved in constructive endeavours of creating alternative modes of practising agriculture. In the case of the seed sovereignty movements too, both constructive (seed saving and sharing) and destructive strategies (protests against oppressive corporate and government policies) are pursued by the actors.

Resistance within and outside the academy

In Brazil, agroecology as an opposition to the Green Revolution has its roots within the dominant scientific apparatus, as part of the Alternative Agriculture movement led by agronomists. But it was soon to be adopted by practitioners and social movements and today it brings together a diverse network of scientists, professionals and activists. CBA is both an academic conference and a space for sharing practices and political mobilisation. In India, groups inside as well as outside the academy have been active in everyday resistance against the Green Revolution. In the 1960s the seed sovereignty ideology had strong support from within the academy from a very small subsection of scientists led by R. H. Richharia. However, this group succumbed to the oppressive strategies of the mainstream Green Revolution institutions.

The voices of resistance

In terms of using the language of science and other forms of expression, resistances in both countries employ different mechanisms of engagement depending on their ideology, site as well as the actors involved. In Brazil, CBA is a multidimensional event that not only uses the language of science strongly represented by the social sciences and humanities, but also uses artistic, political and spiritual expression as part of voicing a resistance that incorporates other ontologies and cosmovisions. In India, both ZBNF and seed sovereignty movements employ science as well as local knowledge systems and cultural heritage in building connections and coalitions. In formal discussions with the government and

Green Revolution institutions, however, the language of science always dominates. As a result, wider concerns such as seeds as civilisational forces and farmers' sovereignty are often sidelined.

***

Opposition to the Green Revolution and the construction of alternatives has taken place through everyday resistance that takes multiple forms and with diverse voices. The cases from the two countries demonstrate that individual and collective resistance, and organised and everyday resistance, cannot be seen as disconnected from each other. The individual and everyday acts of making and sharing seeds and agricultural knowledge about alternatives add to collective action. These individual acts eventually serve to build momentum out of which an organised movement may emerge, and they serve to continue the legacy of an organised movement long after it is over.

INDEX

Abrol, Dinesh 290–1, 291 n.107, 292 n.108
Absell, Christopher David 225. n13
Adams, Wayne W. 206
Adas, Michael 274 n.14, 284, 284 n.70
Addis Ababa 206 n.16, 208, 208 n.22, 210
Ærsøe, Holger 152 n.39, 152.n43
Africa / African / Africans 4, 21, 107, 184–6, 188–90, 193–4, 198–200, 202, 204, 207 n.20, 212, 213 n.39, 214, 215 n.47, 216, 282, 327 n. 18, 330, 339
  Africa, Sub-Saharan 185, 202, 204, 282
Agnew, John 278 n.32
Ágoas, Frederico 52 n.29
Agrarian Extension Service / AES 311, 312 n. 7, 313–14, 316–17, 321–2
agrarianism / agrarianist 86–7, 91, 94–5, 98–100
agricultural extension 245 n. 42, 314, 317–20
Agricultural Service 15, 314
agroecological / agroecology 238, 241, 297, 323–4, 331–5, 342
agroecosystem 7, 254, 256–7, 265, 267–9.
agronomist / agronomy 8, 15–16, 21, 28, 36–9, 46, 49–50, 52–3, 59–60, 86, 92, 186–98, 200–1, 210–11, 233, 276, 285, 295–7, 299, 305, 324 n.7, 331, 342
Aguilera, Eduardo 251, 254, 258 n.6, 260 n.9, 264 n.10, 267 n.13, 268 n.14
Ahlberg, Kristin L. 287 n.84
Ahmed, Abiy 202
Ajl, Max 324 n.6, 337 n.63
Albareda, José María 51 n.24, 54 n.34, 54 n.36, 58 n.50, 59, 59 n.53
Alcalde, Javier Gonzalo 275 n.16, 275 n.17, 276 n.27, 280 n.43.
Alcobaça 53, 64
Alentejo 53, 57
Alipur 241
Almería 54
Alomata 213–14
Alps 67
Altieri, Miguel A. 332, 332 n.40
Álvarez Scanniello, Jorge 219 n.5
Álvarez Peláez, Raquel 50 n.20
Agency of International Development / AID 309
Agricultural Knowledge and Innovation System / AKIS 11
Agricultural Research Council / ARC 137
America (*see* United States of America)
  America, Latin (*see* Latin America)
  America, North (*see* North America)
  America, South (*see* South America)
American International Association / AIA 276, 279
Americas 3, 60, 63, 218, 221
  Americas, Southern Cone of the (*see* Southern Cone)
Andersen, Bernt Bech 152 n.44
Anderson, Robert S. 235 n.7, 271 n.5, 285 n.73, 287, 287 n.81
Angola 184, 186
animal breeders 36, 174
Aparicio, Gema 10 n.17, 10 n.18
Apodaca, Anacleto 307 n.52
Argemí d'Abadal, Lluis. 13 n.26
Argentina /Argentinian 21, 105, 217 n.1, 218–31, 254, 294, 309
Arraes, Geraldo B. Martha Jr.

Arroyo, Carlos 308 n.55
Arter, David 97 n.28
Aryanisation 70
Asia / Asian 107, 110, 117, 185–6, 189, 200, 236, 240–1, 270, 272, 276, 279, 282, 287, 292, 309, 323 n.2, 324 n.7, 336
Auderset, Juri 4, 4 n.4, 4 n.6, 28 n.2, 29 n.5, 35 n.25, 35 n.27, 36 n.29, 40 n.46, 83 n.57, 132, 132 n.26, 163, 163 n.2, 163 n.3, 271, 271 n.4
Australia / Australian 106, 109, 113 n.44, 178
Austria / Austrian 65, 67, 71, 81–4
Austro-Hungary / Austro-Hungarian 164
Ávila Camacho, Miguel 294
Awash River 211
Ayala, Francisco 296 n.19
Aykroyd, Wallace R. 109

Baaz, Mikael 328 n.20
Bairoch, Paul 270 n.2
Bambesa 190
Banaji, Jairus 337 n.61
Bangladesh 21, 287
Barahona, Ana 286 n.79, 293 n.3, 296 n.19
Baranski, Marci R. 3 n.2, 238 n.16
Barbieri, Rosa Lia 334 n.49
Barca, Stefania 11, 12 n.22
Bardhan, Pranab 336 n.58
Barral, Pierre 88 n.8
Barsky, Osvaldo 218 n.3
Basto, Eduardo Lima 50, 52 n.28
Bauerkämper, Arnd 38 n.34, 166 n.19, 167 n.23, 169 n.33
Baumann, Werner 86 n.5, 108, 108 n.24, 108 n.26
Bavaj, Riccardo 66, 66 n.5, 81 n.49
Bavnshøj, Peter 149 n.34, 156 n.49, 156 n.50
Bazlul, Karim M. 292 n.2
Béaur, Gérard 10 n.16, 12 n.23, 124 n.9
Bekele, Getnet 203 n.4, 205 n.13
Belgium / Belgian 113 n.44, 142, 186–7, 194, 198–200, 214, 319
Belgian Congo *see* Congo
Belle Époque 9
Bengal / Bengali 114, 239–40
Benjamin, Walter 42, 42 n.52, 288 n.92
Berend, Iván T. 166 n.17
Beresford, Tristram 121, 121 n.2, 136
Bergius, Mikael 327 n.18
Berlin 98
Bernárdez Sobreira, Antonio 44 n.5
Bernardi, Emanuele 98 n.32, 284 n.69
Berry, Wendell 39, 39 n.40
Bhattacharya, Neeladri 236 n.10
Billen, Gilles 260 n.9
Bingen, Jim 49 n.15
Bingham, Jonathan 280 n.39
Binswanger, Hans P. 246 n.45, 293 n.6, 330 n.31
biodiversity 22, 42, 269, 326, 330, 334–5, 338
biomass 7, 22, 254–8, 263, 265–9
Birr, Kendall 274 n.13, 286 n.77
Bishoftu 210–11
Bitoun, Pierre 311 n.6
Bivar, Venus 324 n.7
Bjørn, Claus 142 n.7, 143 n.13, 148 n.33, 152 n.42
Black, John. D. 301 n.38
Blaschke, Anette 75 n.34, 84 n.58
Blaxter, Kenneth 133 n.30, 137 n.43
Blok, Aad 90 n.12
Boca, Angelo del 215
Bogotá 297, 309 n.57
Bolivia / Bolivian 297, 300–1
Boltanski, Luc 313, n.8
Bonaiuti, Mauro 99 n.38
Bonneuil, Christophe 14 n.28, 28 n.3, 31 n.10, 39 n.39, 40 n.44, 44, 44 n.3, 44 n.4, 45 n.6, 49 n.16, 57 n.49, 185, 185 n.8, 192, 192 n.39
Boret, Victor 14, 14 n.28
Borges Dias, Terezinha 334, n.47
Borhi, László 166 n.16, 175 n.53
Borlaug, Norman 21, 236, 236 n.11, 242 n.30, 295, 326, 330 n.30, 336, 336 n.57
Borrás Jr, Saturnino M. 328 n.22
Bourdieu, Pierre 75 n.35
Bowler, Ian 67 n.9
Bradfield, Richard 295

Branco, Amélia 45 n.5, 48 n.13
Brandão, Tiago 45 n.5, 55 n.40, 57 n.46
Brandt, Berit 310 n.2
Brass, Paul R. 235 n.7,
Brass, Tom 234 n.3, 337 n.61
Brassley, Paul 16, 16 n.36, 16 n.37, 17 n.38, 29 n.5, 29 n.6, 30 n.7, 45 n.7, 47 n.12, 88 n.7, 122 n.3, 124 n.9, 125 n.13, 126 n.16, 127 n.17, 129 n.19, 130 n.20, 131 n.21, 131 n.22, 131 n.33, 132 n.24, 132 n.26, 132 n.27, 133 n.28, 134 n.33, 134 n.34, 135 n.35, 138 n.47, 138 n.48, 138 n.49, 139 n.50, 163 n.5, 168 n.27, 175 n.52
Braverman, Harry 32 n.15
Brazil / Brazilian 113, 217 n.1, 218, 222–3, 226–7, 230–1, 276, 278–9, 323–5, 327, 329–31, 333, 335, 337, 339, 341, 343
Brewster John M. 27–8, 28n.1, 37
Brezhnev, Leonid Illich 181
Brietzke, Paul H. 203 n.7
Britain / British 10, 18, 94, 103, 107, 110, 112–13, 121, 122 n.3, 123–5, 128, 131–2, 133–6, 137 n.44, 137 n.45, 137 n.46, 138–9, 156, 186, 184 n.12, 189, 192, 204–8, 210–12, 214, 216, 239–40, 244, 271, 278, 280, 281, 286 n.77, 300–1
British Empire 10, 116–17, 271 n.3
British Tanganyika 184
Britton, Denis K. 123, 128
Brody, David 17 n.40
Brown, Lester 227 n.31,
Brown, Trent 338 n.67, 338 n.69
Bruce, Stanley 116–17
Bruisch, Katja 13 n.26
Brum, Cristiano Enrique de 230 n. 19
Brunier, Sylvain 311 n.4, 312 n7, 319 n.21
Bruno, Karl 203 n.6
Brussels 188
Buckwell, Allan 129 n.19, 139, 139 n.50
Budapest 108
Buenos Aires 225
Bugow, Karin 272 n.8
Buhl, Bettina 148 n.28
Buksti, Jacob A. 152 n.42, 157 n.59, 159 n.63, 159 n.67
Bulgaria / Bulgarian 87, 90, 92–5, 170
Burrell, Alison 129
Burton, Eric 282 n.56
Burton, Robert J.F. 11 n.20
Busch, Lawrence 49 n.15
Buseth, Jill Tove 327 n.18
Bustamante, Patricia Goulart 334 n.49
Byerlee, Derek 330 n.31

Cabana Iglesia, Ana 310 n.3, 313 n.10, 315 n.15, 316 n.16, 316 n.17, 317 n.18
Cabo, Miguel 4, 10, 10 n.19, 14 n.30, 15 n.32, 31, 44 n.5, 45 n.7, 50 n.19, 66 n.4, 66 n.7, 87 n.6, 92 n.20, 94 n.24, 95 n.25, 96 n.27, 166 n.19, 313 n.10
Cabral, Lídia 140, 140 n.2, 161, 161 n.71, 326 n.14, 330 n.28, 334 n.28, 335 n.52, 341 n.78
Câmara, António da Sousa 15, 51 n.24, 53, 55, 59, 59 n.54
Cambridge 111
Canada / Canadian 18, 113 n.44, 116–17, 225
Canalejo Alonso, Silvia 315 n. 15
Candela, Milagros 45 n.5, 54 n.36, 57 n.47, 57 n.48, 59 n.54, 59 n.56, 61 n.57, 61 n.58
capitalist / capitalism 12, 14, 16, 19–20, 23, 28–32, 35, 38, 40, 42, 86, 90, 161–2, 167, 172, 174–5, 226, 236, 238 n.15, 244, 246, 282, 318, 328
Caporal, Francisco Roberto
Carballo, Alfredo 299
Cárdenas, Lázaro 16, 293–4, 296
Carmo, Valéria Amorim do 336 n.55
Carmona, António Óscar de Fragoso 58
Carmona, Juan 16 n.34
Carranza-Gallego, Guiomar 267 n.13
Casero Rodríguez, Francisco 256 n.5
Castro, Josué de 220 n.7
cattle 70, 80, 126, 142 n.9, 143 n.16, 148, 150–1, 152 n.43, 156, 159, 218–19, 222, 261–2, 266, 304
Cazcarro, Ignacio 260 n.8

Centro Nacional de Pesquiza Agrícola / CNPA 230
Chakravarty, Sukhamoy 237 n.13
Chambers of Agriculture 311, 314–15
Chamorro, Antonio 272 n.9
Chapman, Herrick 311, 311 n.5
Chatriot, Alain 13 n.24
Chavarriaga, Eduardo 297
Chayanov, Alexander 13, 76 n.37
chemicalisation 23, 29, 162–3, 180
chemical / chemicals / chemistry 6, 7, 18, 29, 55, 79, 178, 227, 241, 246–7, 265–7, 292, 305, 340
  chemical fertilisers, *see* fertilisers
Cherrington, John 136, 136 n.39
Chiapparino, Francesco 10 n.16, 12 n.23
Chih-Mai, Chen 114
Chile / Chilean 217 n.1, 279, 297–298
China / Chinese 104, 113–115, 140 n.1, 272, 274 n.12, 277 n.31, 295, 323 n.1, 325, 326 n.14
Chinigò, Davide 203 n.3
Christiansen, Thomas 19, 149 n.36, 157 n.59
Chuebsaeng, Saras 114, 114 n.46
civil war 46 n.9, 48, 50 n.20, 53, 57, 115, 263, 312
Clapham, Christopher 202 n.2
Clarke, Gill 128 n.18
Cleaver, Harry M. 272 n.7
Clement, J. 191 n.29, 195, 195 n.58
Clement, Piet 183, 183 n.3, 187, 187 n.18, 189 n.21, 189 n.22, 190 n.23, 191 n.31, 193 n.42, 193 n.46, 196 n.66, 197 n.70
climate / climatic 27, 67, 80, 136, 148, 169, 181, 213 261, 267, 330, 337
Cobbs, Elizabeth Anne 276 n.23, 276 n.27, 276 n.28, 278–279, 279 n.36, 281 n.46
Cochrane, Willard 285 n.74
coffee 183, 191, 202, 223–5
Coghe, Samuel 186, 186 n.11
Coimbra 43 n.1, 51, 58, 64
Cold War 1, 23, 38, 65, 95, 116, 162, 166, 177, 180, 199, 204, 236, 272–4, 276–7, 280, 283 n.60, 318, 325
Collier, J. 194, 194 n.55
Collingham, Lizzie 18 n.46
Collins, Caitlin Alexandra 206, n.17
Collis, John Stewart 128 n.18
Colombia / Colombian 217 n.1, 230, 274 n.12, 277 n.31, 279, 284, 285 n.73, 297–300, 309
Colwell, William E. 295
Common Agricultural Policy / CAP 96, 98, 100, 116, 118, 135, 139
communism / communist 3, 6, 13, 15, 19, 21, 23, 65, 81, 85, 90, 94–6, 98–9, 115, 162, 166–9, 171, 179, 181, 199, 236, 272–3, 275–6, 279, 286, 312
Conford, Philip 276 n.22
Congo / Congolese 21, 182–9, 195–201, 211
Congresso Brasileiro de Agroecologia / CBA 332–4, 342
Consejo Superior de Investigaciones Científicas / CSIC 51, 54–5, 54 n.34, 57 n.47, 58–9, 61
CONSEA / Conselho Nacional de Segurança Alimentar e Nutricional 331
Consejo Agrario Nacional / CAN 228
Cooper, Frederick 184 n.5, 204 n.9
Copenhagen 113, 142 n.10
Corkill, David 56 n.43
corn / maize 124, 126, 134, 146, 175–6, 178, 229, 267, 299,
Cornelis, Hendrik 194, 194 n.50
Cornell 274 n.12, 295–6
Corni, Gustavo 15 n.31, 66 n.6, 71 n.26
Cornu, Pierre 6 n.10, 98 n.33, 99 n.36
Correia, Rita M. G. 52 n.26
Costa Rica / Costa Rican 297, 299–300, 302–5, 307, 309
Cotter, Joseph Eugene 16 n.35, 274 n.12, 280 n.40, 287 n.80, 295 n.16
Council for Mutual Economic Assistance / COMECON 178, 181
Croatia / Croatian 96, 99
Cruz, Guilherme Braga da 58 n.51
Cuba / Cuban 113 n.44, 276 n.27
Cullather Nick 38 n.36, 103 n.5, 115 n.52, 226 n.12, 271 n.5, 272 n.9, 285 n.73, 289 n.95, 336 n.56, 337 n.62
Curry, Helen Anne 44 n.3

Curti, Merle 274 n.13, 286 n.77
Custodis, Johan 128 n.18
Czechoslovakia / Czechoslovakian 70, 87, 92–4, 113 n.44, 170, 174 n.50

Dalgaard, Tommy 157 n. 54
Dasgupta, Biplab 247 n.47
Daskalov, Roumen 94 n.23
Davies, Robert William 168 n.25
Degler, Stephanie 74 n.31
Deheyn, J. 192 n.37
Dejene, Alemneh 203 n.7
Delire, A., 196, 196 n.68
democratisation 46 n.9, 65, 331
Denis, Gilles 14 n.28
Denmark / Danish 19, 21, 90, 96–7, 113 n.44, 140–5, 148, 152, 154, 156–7, 159–61, 178
Dewey, Peter 132 n.25, 132 n.27, 133 n.29
Dias, Terezinha Aparecida 334 n.47, 335 n.53
Díaz-Geada, Alba 312 n.7, 313 n.9, 313 n.10, 315 n.15, 316 n.16, 316 n.17
dictatorship 46 n.9, 47–8, 50–1, 52 n.27, 52 n.28, 54–8, 62–3, 81–2, 263, 312, 315 n.15, 316, 321, 331
Diegues, Antonio Carlos 334 n.51, 335 n.54
Dimény, Imre 177, 177 n.57
Dimier, Veronique 282 n.53
Döbereiner, Joanna 333
Dodd, Norris 283
domestic extraction / DE 256, 258, 259
Donaldson, John George Stuart 136 n.41
D'Onofrio, Federico 19, 103 n.7, 104 n.8, 105 n.12, 109 n.28
Doré, Charles
Dore, Valentino 136, 136 n.41
Døssing, Peter 143 n.12, 148 n.32, 154 n.46, 154 n.48, 156 n.53
Drachoussoff, Vladimir 182–3, 183 n.2, 190 n.24
dry matter 145 n.23, 254–60, 263–4
Drejer, Axelsen 143 n.15
Duarte, Rosa 260 n.8,
Dubois, George 191 n.27, 195, 195 n.61
Dunlap, Thomas 18 n.44

East Germany 170
East Pakistan 287, 291
Ecuador / Ecuadorian 217 n.1, 279, 297–9, 306
Edelman, Marc 328 n.22
Edgerton, David 36, 36 n.31
Eellend, Johan 98 n.34
Egypt / Egyptian 113 n.44, 212
Ehrlich, Cyril 211 n.35
Ekbladh, David 103 n.5, 115 n.51, 115 n.53, 274 n.14, 280 n.38, 280 n.41, 285 n.72
El Salvador 303
Elliott, Alexander 210 n.31
Elvas 53, 57, 64
Engerman, David C. 38 n.35, 236 n.12, 288 n.89
England 35 n.27, 49, 124, 126, 128 n.18, 136, 138, 319
Erb, Claude C. 275 n.20
Erdei, Ferenc 172, 172 n.42, 177
Eritrea / Eritrean 212, 214
Esbjerg 142 n.10
Escobar, Arturo 245, 245 n.43
Esperante, Bruno 8 n.13, 9 n.15
Estado Novo 50–2, 56,
Ethiopia / Ethiopian 21, 202–16, 277 n.30
Etzemüller, Thomas 82, n.54
Europe / European 43 n.1, 45, 46 n.9, 51, 59, 67, 81, 84, 86–7, 89, 94–100, 101 n.1, 102–8, 110–13, 115–18, 135, 162, 164–7, 170, 172–3, 175, 181, 184, 189–92, 199, 210, 215, 218–19, 227–9, 271, 276, 278–9, 281–4, 286, 293, 300–1, 310 n.1, 318–19, 323 n.2, 324 n.7
  Europe, Central Eastern 86–7, 93
  Europe, Eastern 38, 96
  Europe, East Central 162, 166, 167, 170
  Europe, Western 17, 19, 38, 45, 96–7, 102, 107, 110, 165, 172, 181, 270 n.2, 276, 278 n.35, 281, 283

European Economic Community/ EEC 19, 46 n.9, 61, 98, 102, 116, 118, 129, 141, 145, 157, 159, 282
European Union / EU 97, 101

Fabian, Johannes 33, 33 n.19
farmer 2, 7, 8, 10, 11 n.20, 12, 15, 19, 20–4, 33, 35–40, 43–4, 49, 62, 69, 74–5, 76, 77–8, 80, 82, 85–6, 89–92, 96, 97, 99, 100, 102–7, 110, 111, 115–18, 121, 124–6, 129–31, 133–9, 141–5, 152, 154, 156–7, 160–1, 169, 171, 180–1, 182–3, 186–98, 200–1, 208, 209–10, 213–14, 225, 229, 233–9, 241–8, 266, 269, 270, 275, 307, 311–17, 322, 323, 324, 327–8, 331, 333–4, 337–41, 343
Farmer, Sarah 100 n.41
Farmholder 69, 76, 78, 82
fascist / fascism 2, 6, 14–15, 19–21, 23, 46 n.9, 51, 56, 66, 85, 87–9, 204, 209, 215, 275, 294, 300, 313, 315–16
Favareto, Arilson 330 n.33
Fearnside, Philip M. 326 n.11
Federico, Giovanni 16, 16 n.37, 30 n.7, 106 n.16, 107 n.19
feed / feeding / feeding stuffs 36, 76, 79–80, 125–6, 128, 130–1, 138, 144, 151–2, 156, 160, 173–4, 179, 222, 257, 260–3, 266–7
Fehér, Lajos 171–3, 173 n.46
Fellows, Perry 205–6
Ferguson, Bruce G. 340 n.73
Fernández Díez, Carmen 48 n.13
Fernández Molina, José A. 38 n.36, 274 n.15
Fernández Prieto, Lourenzo 8 n.13, 11 n.21, 14 n.30, 15 n.32, 31, 45 n.7, 48 n.13, 66 n.4, 66 n.7, 92 n.20
Ferreira, Paulo B. R. 56 n.42
fertiliser 9, 14, 18, 20, 23, 29, 38, 41, 72, 121, 128–31, 133–4, 143–4, 148–50, 156, 159–60, 168, 176–8, 180, 199, 219, 227, 238, 241–4, 246, 265–7, 270, 271 n.3, 274–6, 283, 287, 292, 304–5, 307, 313, 324 n.6
Finnland / Finnish 97
Fitas, Augusto 50 n.21, 51 n.25, 53 n.32
Fitzgerald, Deborah ii, 4, 14 n. 27, 30 n.9, 35 n.27, 241 n.27, 244, 285 n.74, 293, 295 n.15
Fitzharris, Joseph 11 n.21
Flaubert, Gustave 5
Flink, Tim 46 n.10, 46 n.11
Focan, Alexandre 190 n.24
food 1, 7, 9–10, 12–13, 16–18, 20–4, 31, 41, 45, 47–8, 51, 61–3, 70, 76, 81, 90, 98–9, 101–6, 108–10, 112–18, 124 n.7, 126, 133–5, 170–1, 177, 179, 184–5, 191, 196, 198–200, 202, 206, 208, 217 n.1, 221, 224, 231, 234–5, 237, 242, 247, 251–2, 256–7, 261–3, 265–6, 275, 286–7, 288–90, 293, 301–4, 309, 318, 324–6, 329–30, 332–3
food estate 70, 74–5, 77–8, 83
food regime 9–19, 12–13, 16, 326
food sovereignty 99, 330, 333
Food and Agriculture Organization / FAO 19, 21, 59 n.55, 101–3, 106, 108–9, 112–13, 114 n.46, 115–17, 174–5, 202, 204–5, 210–13, 217, 282–3, 318–19
foodstuffs 104, 106–7, 111–16, 184, 219, 301, 304
Foreman, Susan 133 n.32
Forney, Jérémie 11 n.20
Foucault, Michel 30, 30 n.8, 70 n.22, 328
France / French 11–12, 14, 21, 49, 50 n.22, 87–9, 98, 100, 104–5, 113 n.44, 182 n.1, 184–185, 195, 197, 214, 216, 222, 230, 286 n.77, 311–13, 317, 319–22
French Sudan (Niger) 184–5, 197
Franco Bahamonde, Francisco 46 n.9, 55–6, 58, 312–13, 315 n.15, 316
Francoism / Francoist 51, 53–4, 58, 62
Frandsen, Steen Bo 142 n.10
Frankel, Francine 234 n.4, 235, 235 n.8, 287 n.84, 289 n.95, 323 n.4
Freeman, Joshua B. 32 n.15
Freire Paz, Elena 317 n.18
Freire, Dulce 15, 43 n.1, 45 n.5, 45 n.7, 47 n.12, 48 n.13, 52 n.27, 52 n.29, 54 n.37, 54 n.38,
fresh matter 252, 254, 260
Fressoz, Jean-Baptiste 28 n.3, 40 n.44

Frey, Marc 112 n.41, 277 n.31, 282 n.51
Friedmann, Karen J. 143 n.13, 143 n.16

Gago, Maria do Mar. 49 n.17, 50 n.23
Galicia 49, 54, 64
Gallástegui Unamuno, Cruz 50, 50 n.19
Gandhi, S 242, 242 n.31
García González, Armando 57 n.47, 61 n.58
García-Ruiz, Roberto 251 n.1, 254 n.4
Garnier, Josette 260 n.9
Gaud, William S. 3, 3 n.3, 141 n.4, 233, 233 n.2, 273 n.11
Gautam, Prem Lai 233–4
Gauthier, Jules 104
Geiger, Till. 278 n.35, 290 n.101
Gelman, Jorge 218 n.3
genetic / geneticist / genetics 6–7, 20, 43–51, 52 n.27, 53–5, 57–63, 176, 218, 222, 242 n.32, 265–7, 297, 299, 335, 339, 342
gender 22, 80, 82, 171, 310, 311–15, 318–22, 333,
Geneva 104–5, 118
Genoa 104
George, Susan 272 n.7, 287 n.80,
Georgescu–Roegen, Nicholas 31 n.11, 41, 41 n.50, 99
Gerhard, Gesine 15 n.32, 66, 66 n.7
Gerlach, Christian 21 n.49
Germany / German 8, 11, 15, 32, 49, 50 n.19, 65–7, 69–71, 75, 78, 80–4, 95, 97, 104–5, 128 n.18, 141–3, 145 n.24, 150, 170, 173–4, 275, 281, 290, 294, 300–1, 311, 319
Giddens, Anthony 5, 5 n.8
Gies, Horst 66 n.6, 71 n.26
Gilbert, Jess 15 n.33, 82 n.54, 91 n.15
Gille, Albert 194, 194 n.54, 196, 196 n. 65
Gilman, Nils 5 n.9
Giraldo-Hoyos, Martín 309 n.7
Glaeser, Bernhard 235 n.7
Gliber, John 299
Gliessman, Stephen R. 265 n.11, 332 n.43
Global North 2, 279
Global South 3, 22, 38, 113, 161, 240, 271, 273, 279, 280 n.42, 284, 286 n.77, 291, 324–5, 327–8
GMOs 232
Goldsmith, Arthur A. 289 n.93, 289 n.98
Gollwitzer, Heinz 86
Gomes da Silva, Ester 45 n.5, 48 n.13
Gomes, Inês 45 n.5, 48 n.13
Gómez, José Alfonso 266 n.12
Gómez Benito, Cristóbal 313 n.11, 314 n.12, 315 n. 14
González de Molina, Manuel 7 n.12, 22, 251 n.1, 253, 254 n.4, 256, 256 n.5, 258, 258 n.6, 261, 263, 264 n.10, 266 n.12, 267 n.13, 268, 268 n.14
González Gómez, César 58
Goodman, David 17 n.39, 34 n.22
Gordon, Leonard A. 288 n.90, 289 n.97
Gordon-Ashworth, Fiona 224 n.12
Goris, Margriet B. 332 n.42
Grandi, Stefano 14 n.30
Gratton, Philippe 88 n.8
Great Depression 12, 16, 89, 91, 102, 106, 111, 117, 183, 199
Great Plains 7
Great War / First World War 9–10, 12, 24, 50, 61, 88, 99, 104, 109, 121, 126, 132, 134, 136, 143, 165, 225, 286 n.77, 301
Green Revolution 1–4, 19, 22, 24, 38, 45, 82–3, 117, 140–2, 145, 154, 161–3, 172, 177, 179–80, 185, 188, 199–202, 217, 223, 229, 231, 233–9, 242–4, 246–8, 251, 266, 271–4, 276–7, 279–80, 284, 286–7, 290–3, 308–9, 323–4, 336–43
Grigg, David B. 133 n.30, 270 n.2
Grin, John 66 n.8
Grisa, Catia 331 n.35, 331 n.36
Grote, Hendrik 281 n.49
Grundmann, Friedrich 67 n.12, 68 n.15
Gunst, Péter 164 n.7, 164 n.9, 166 n.15
Gupta, Akhil 233, 233 n.1, 241, 241 n.29, 323 n.5

Guzmán, Gloria Inmaculada 251 n.1, 254 n.4, 258 n.6, 264 n.10, 267 n.13, 268 n.14
Gysel, Zacharias 38 n.38

Habermas, Jürgen 74 n.32
Haefele, Mark H. 38 n.35
Haiti / Haitian 303–5, 307
Hall, Ruth 328, 328 n.22
Hamilton, David E. 330 n.35
Hansen, Henning Otte 142 n.8, 158 n.62
Harcsa, Iván 180 n.66
Hardwood, Jonathan 1–2, 1 n.1, 8 n.13, 31 n.10, 38 n.36, 44 n.3, 174 n.50, 179 n.62, 185 n.7, 199 n.78, 272 n.8, 284 n.69, 296 n.16, 323 n.2, 329 n.25
Harman, Tony 136, 136 n.40
Harrar, George 295, 298, 298 n.29
Harroy, Jean-Paul 190, 190 n.25
Hart-Landsberg, Martin 17 n.41
Hartmann, Heinrich 274 n.12, 286 n.77, 290, 290 n. 102
Harvey, David 125 n.13
Hayami, Yujiro 293, 293 n.5
Hayes, Herbert Kendall 296
Hecq, Jacques 190 n.24
Heinz, Flavio 230 n.19
Helleiner, Eric 275 n.16, 276 n.26
Henderson, Sir William 137, 137 n.45
Henriksen, Ingrid 142 n.7, 144 n.21
Henry, Jean-Marie 191, 192, 192 n.32, 192 n.35, 193 n.45,
Hermes, Andreas 105, 105 n.12, 105 n.15, 111
Hernández, Andreas 332 n.40
Herrera, Antonio 267 n.13
Hess, Gary R. 274 n.14
Hewitt de Alcántara, Cynthia 272 n. 9, 296 n.17, 297 n.20
high-yielding variety / HYV 233–4, 238, 241–3, 247–8, 336–8
Hill, Berkeley 129, 129 n.19
Hillebrand, Justus 35 n.27
Hitler, Adolf 121, 133–4, 138–9
Hodge, Joseph Morgan 184 n.5, 186, 186 n.12, 188 n.19, 204 n.9, 214, 214 n.46, 216 n.50
Holdcroft, Lane E. 271 n.6
Holderness, B.A. 137 n.42
Holding, Jim 130 n.20
Holeta 210
Holstein 142 n.10
Holt-Giménez, Eric
Honduras 297, 300, 303, 307
Hoover, Herbert 109
Hornung, Ela 71 n.24
horse / equine 34–35, 71, 125–6, 132, 148, 151 n.37, 154–6, 192, 261, 264, 266
Houtzager, Peter 331 n.36
Howald, Oskar 39, 40 n.41
Howard, Albert 239, 239 n.19
Hubbard, Wynant D. 206, 210 n.29
Hungary / Hungarian 21, 94, 162–3, 165–6, 168–72, 173 n.45, 174–1
Huszár, Tibor 172 n.42
Hybrids 17, 178, 298

Iandolo, Alessandro 282 n.55
Ibáñez Martín, José 58
Ilbery, Brian 67 n.9
Immerwahr, Daniel 15 n.33
Inden, Ronald 236 n.9
India / Indian 15, 21–2, 113–14, 233–7, 239–48, 270 n.1, 279, 287–91, 308, 323 n.1, 324–7, 329, 336, 338–42
Indraszczyk, Arkadiusz 99 n.37
Infante-Amate, Juan 251 n.1, 254 n.4, 258 n.6, 260 n.7, 264 n.10, 265 n.11, 266 n.12, 267 n.13, 268 n.14
innovation system 4, 7–11, 52, 62–3, 324
International Agrarian Bureau / Green International 4, 85, 87, 94, 96
International Institute of Agriculture / IIA 19, 47 n.2, 101–103, 104 n.8, 105, 108–10, 113, 115–18, 175 n.52, 274–5, 279, 296, 301, 303–7
Ireland / Irish 97
Iron Curtain 95, 163, 181
irrigation / irrigated 7, 20, 55, 159, 176, 185, 211, 229, 234 n.5, 243, 257, 267, 274 n.12, 287, 304, 325
Isaacman, Allen 211 n.35
Italy / Italian 11, 14–15, 88, 96, 98, 101, 105, 109, 204–16, 275, 300

Iverson, Kenneth R. 275 n.19, 305 n.49, 306 n.51

Jachertz, Ruth 102, 112 n.41, 116 n.55, 277 n.31, 282 n.59, 283 n.64
Jacoby, Erich H. 272 n.6, 283 n.65
Jakobsen, Jostein 328 n.24, 329 n.26
James M. Dickinson 32 n.16
Japan / Japanese 19, 275, 285 n.75, 291, 294, 300, 301
Jas, Nathalie 29 n.6,
Jenkins, Lindie 130 n.20
Jensen, Hans Jørgen Winther 144 n.19
Jensen, Peter Sandholt 140 n.3, 142 n.7, 143 n.11
Jewsiewicki, Bogumil 189, 189 n.22, 197 n.73
Jiménez Redondo, Juan Carlos 56 n.44
Johansson, Anna 328 n.21, 329, 329 n.27, 328 n.21
Johnson, Colin R. 310 n.3
Johnson, Lyndon B. 175
Jones, Donald F. 297
Jugenheimer, Robert W. 283 n.64
Jungar, Ann-Cathrine 97 n.30

Kádár, János 170, 170 n.36, 171
Kærgaard, Niels 142 n.7, 156 n. 54
Kassa, Mobili Danga 186, 186 n.15
Katanga 156, 197
Kautsky, Karl 13, 34, 34 n.23
Kelly, Saul 205 n.12
Kenya / Kenyan 184, 192
Keown-Boyd, Patrick 212, 212 n.38
Kerckhofs, Stephanie 186 n.13, 186 n.14, 189 n.21
Kern, Stephen 32 n.15
Keynes, John Maynard 111, 11 n.37, 111 n.39, 116
Khadse, Aslesha 340 n.73, 340 n.75
Khrushchev, Nikita 166 n.19, 170–1, 173–4
Kirsch, David A. 36 n.32
Kloppenburg, Jack R. Jr. 17 n.42, 40 n.41, 40 n.43, 44 n.3, 57 n.49
Knudsen, Ann-Christina 100 n.40
Kobo-Alomata 214, 214
Kohli, S.P. 245
Koning, Niek 7 n.11
Kopf, Martina 184 n.5
Kopsidis, Michael 165 n.11, 166 n.14, 179 n.63
Kornai, János 167 n.20, 174 n.49
Korndörfer, Ana Paula 230 n.19
Koselleck, Reinhart 33 n.20, 65 n.2
Kovách, Imre 179 n.64, 180 n.66
Kovács, József Ö. 169 n.33
Krige, John 278 n.34, 288 n.91
Kuntz-Ficker, Sandra 116 n.6, 220 n.6, 225 n.14
Kwilu 188

La Picota 297–8
Ladejinsky, Wolf 323 n.3
Lagrave, Rose-Marie 320 n.22
Lambin, Eric F. 253 n.2, 254 n.3
Lampe, Markus 142 n.7, 143 n.11, 144 n.22, 152 n.39
Lanero Táboas, Daniel 45 n.7, 52 n.29, 54 n.37, 54 n.38, 312 n.7, 313 n.9
Lapa, Álvaro Isidro de Faria 51 n.26
Langthaler, Ernst 2, 9 n.16, 15 n.31, 66 n.4, 67 n.11, 68, 68 n.13, 68 n.14, 69 n.17, 69 n.19, 70 n.20, 71 n.24, 71 n.25, 72, 72 n.28, 73, 76 n.36, 76 n.38, 78 n.44, 79 n.46, 81 n.48, 83 n.55, 84 n.59
Larebo, Haile 212 n.37
Lassaletta, Luis 260 n.9
Latham, Michael E. 274 n.14
Latin America / Latin American 3–4, 8, 17, 19, 21, 185, 217–19, 227–30, 269, 271, 272 n.9, 274–7, 279, 292–3, 295, 297, 299–309, 318, 331
Latour, Bruno 79 n.45
Lauenburg 142 n.10
Laur, Ernst 86, 104, 105, 105 197, 107 n.23, 108, 110–11, 115
Laveaga, Gabriela 3 n.2, 324 n.7
Lavers, Tom 203 n.3
Lazarcik, Gregor 178 n.61,
League of Nations 102, 105, 107, 109, 113, 117–18

Leček, Suzana 99 n.37
Lee, Seung-Joon 274 n.12,
Leónidas, Vasco 55, 55 n.39
Leopold III 188–9
Leopoldville 183
Leuven xxiii
Levant 210
Lévi-Strauss Claude 37, 37 n.33
Levy, Edwin. 235 n.7, 271 n.5, 285 n.73, 287 n.81
Lewin, Moshe 13 n.25
Li, Tania Murray 238, 238 n.15, 241, 241 n.28
liberal / liberalism 5, 8, 10, 14–15, 24, 50, 52, 57 n.46, 62, 81, 87, 143 n.13, 225–6, 239, 240
Libercap, Gary D. 12 n.24
Liesenborghs, Oswald 192, 192 n.36
Lijphardt, Aren 97 n.29
Likaka, Osumaka 187, 187 n.16, 191 n.30, 192 n.32, 193 n.47, 194 n.49, 194 n.51, 196 n.67, 197, 197 n.69, 197 n.72, 198, 198 n.75, 198 n.76, 212 n.35
Lilja, Mona 328 n.20, 328 n.21
Lin Lin 130 n.20
Lindsay, Harry 105, 105 n.12
Linne, Karsten 281 n.49
Lipset, Seymour 86, 86 n.3
livestock 92, 98, 125, 126, 129, 131, 142 n.9, 143, 151, 169, 175–6, 178–80, 219, 221–2, 226, 252, 254, 256, 258, 260–7, 269, 317
Lisbon 51, 53, 57–8
Lobley, Mat 125 n.13
Loeckx, André 191 n.28
Lofmann, Reuben 187, 187 n.17
London 46 n.10, 107, 111, 114, 136
López Fernández, Tamara 317 n.18
Lorek, Timothy W. 274 n.12, 277 n.31, 284 n.71, 285 n.73, 297 n.21
Lorenzini, Sara 282 n.54
Love, Harry Houser 274 n.12
Löwy, Michael 42 n.52
Lula da Silva, Luiz Inácio 334
Lundestad, Geir 283 n.66, 284 n.66, 286 n.77
Luque Pulgar, Emilio 314 n.12
Lynch, Édouard 89 n.10, 100 n.39
Maat, Harro 8 n.13
Maček, Vladko 96
Macekura, Stephen J. 275 n.17, 275 n.20, 277 n.30, 280 n.38, 280 n.42, 280 n.44
Mackelvey, John J. 298 n.29
Mackintosh, Jette 144 n.20
Madrid 49–50, 54, 59, 64, 313
Maher, Colin 192, 193 n.40
Mahindepal, Kunwar 246
Mai, Gunther 67 n.10
Mai, Uwe 68 n.15
Malet, Antoni 54 n.34, 54 n.36, 58 n.50, 59 n.53
Mali 185
Malm, Andreas 32 n.14
man / men / male / masculine 6, 8, 22, 27, 30, 69, 74, 77–8, 80, 109, 121, 128, 155, 171, 184, 192–4, 197–8, 223, 237 n.14, 310, 316–19, 321–2
manure 79, 148–9, 160, 168, 184, 266, 267
Mangelsdorf, Paul C. 295, 297
Maniu, Iuliu 93
Mann, Susan A. 32 n.16
Mao, Zendong 115
Marcus, Harold G. 205 n.11
Marer, Paul 175 n.54
Marks, Hilary F. 123, 128
Martiin, Carin 29 n.5, 45 n.7, 47 n.12, 132 n.26, 175 n.52, 284 n.69
Martin, John 125 n.12, 128 n.18
Martinez-Arias, Alfonso 61 n.57
Martín-Retortillo, Miguel 227 n.16, 228 n.17, 260 n.8
Martocci, Federico 309 n.57
Marzagora, Sara 215 n.49
Matasci, Damiano 216 n.50
Mau, Søren 40 n.42,
Mayaud, Jean-Luc 14 n.28, 98 n.33, 99 n.36
Mayer, Ruy 50 n.22
McCann, James C. 203 n.4
McDougall, Frank Lidgett 106, 106 n.17, 108–12, 109 n.30, 109 n.32, 110 n.34, 110 n.35, 116–17
McKelvey, John J. 295
McVety, Amanda Kay 211 n.32, 277 n.30

McWilliams, Felicity 132, 132 n.27
Medellín 297
Medland, John 129
Mehos, Donna C. 282 n.58, 283 n.61, 286 n.78
Melillo, Edward D. 18 n.45, 140, 140 n.2
Méndez, Diana 296 n.16
Mendonça, Sonia Regina de 223 n.11
Menge, Wemo 186, 186 n.14, 189 n.22
Merl, Stephan 167 n.22
Mexico / Mexican 16, 54, 236, 242, 244, 247, 271, 279, 280, 293–301, 308, 324 n.7, 325
Meyer, Lorenzo 294 n.8
Meyfroidt, Patrick 253 n.2, 254 n.3
Middle East 208, 210, 286 n.77
Mignemi, Niccolò 101 n.2, 103, 103 n.6, 103 n.7, 109 n.28
Minnesota 295–6
Mitchell, Timothy 41, 41 n.48, 328 n.20
Mixed farming 7, 73, 131
Mochila, Miguel Filipe 58 n.52
modernisation 4–6, 17, 19, 21–4, 42, 49, 65–7, 83, 85, 100, 141, 161–2, 164–5, 167 n.21, 176, 180, 202, 204, 206, 208–9, 215, 217, 219, 221–4, 227, 229–32, 237, 241, 248, 251, 265, 267, 270–1, 276, 283, 285, 286 n.77, 291, 308–9, 311–13, 318–19, 321–5, 328, 330–3, 335
modernity / modern 2–6, 16, 19, 21, 24, 27, 33, 35, 37, 48, 53, 65–6, 70, 81, 87, 89, 91, 98, 100, 140–1, 143, 157, 161, 167–8, 173–4, 188, 190, 193, 200, 203, 205–6, 208–9, 211–17, 227, 230, 235–6, 239–40, 251, 316, 318–21, 326, 336–7, 341
Mokili Danga Kassa, Jeannôt 186
Mom, Gijs 36 n.32
Montague, Diane 134 n.33, 138 n.47
Moon, Suzanne M. 282 n.58, 283 n.61, 286 n.78
Mooney, Pat R. 283 n.64
Moore-Colyer, Richard J. 128 n.18
Morales, Helda 340 n.73
Morell, Mats 90 n.14
Morone, Antonio M. 215 n.47
Morris, Michael 330 n.31
Morrison, Barrie M. 235 n.7, 271 n.5, 285 n.73, 287 n.81
Mortensen, Erik 157 n.58
Moseman, Albert H. 242, 242 n.30
Moser, Peter 4, 4 n.4, 4 n.6, 28 n.2, 29 n.5, 33 n.21, 34 n.24, 35 n.27, 36 n.30, 39 n.39, 40 n.46, 45 n.7, 54 n.38, 71 n.25, 83 n.57, 86 n.5, 88 n.7, 108 n.24, 208 n.26, 132, 132 n.26, 163, 163 n.2, 163 n.3, 167 n.21, 172 n.41, 271, 271 n.4
Mosher, Arthur T. 271 n.21, 275 n.22, 302 n.39, 307 n.54
motorisation 23, 29, 34, 36 n.32, 37, 125, 130, 132, 162–3, 166–7, 169, 175, 180
Mozambique 184, 211
Müller, Dietmar 13 n.26, 38 n.35, 93, 93 n.21, 93 n.22
Muller, J. 193, 193 n.41
Müller-Wille, Staffan 44 n.3, 57 n.49
Munich 94
Münkel, Daniela 75 n.34
Münster, Daniel 340 n.72, 340 n.74, 340 n.76
Murphy, Craig 275 n.18, 277 n.30, 282 n.59
Mussoi, Eros Marion 332 n.44

National Socialism / Nazi 15, 65–7, 70–1, 75–8, 82, 84, 275
Natividade, Joaquim Vieira da 53
Nehring, Ryan 279 n.37, 330 n.29
net primary productivity 254–5
Netherlands, The / Dutch 97, 99, 105, 113 n.44, 114, 142, 172, 189, 294, 319
Neufeld, Edward 18 n.43
New Deal 17–18, 20, 24, 88–9, 103
New York 12, 224
New Zealand 219, 222
Nicaragua 303
Nichols, Andrew 302 n.39
Nicholson, G. Edward 212, 213, 213 n.20, 213 n.41, 213 n.42
Nielsen, Arne 152 n.44
Niger 184–5

Nigeria 319
North America / North American 103, 106, 115, 222, 271, 312, 318–19
Norton Greene, Ann 34 n.24
Norway / Norwegian 97
net primary productivity / NPP 254–7, 265, 267
Nunes, Maria de Fátima 50 n.21, 51 n.25, 53 n.32
Nye, Joseph 278, 278 n.33

Oceania 7
oil 7 n.11, 29, 31, 164, 178, 266, 293–4 *See* Palm oil
oil cake 148, 151
oil seed 78–9, 151
Olmstead Alan L. 29 n.5
Onofrio, Federico D' 19, 103 n.7, 104 n.8, 105 n.12, 109 n.28, 175 n.52
Orosz, István 164 n.10
Orr, John B. 109–10, 110 n.33, 112–14, 112 n.40, 113 n.44, 114 n.46, 117
Orwin, Charles Stewart 124, 124 n.5
Otero, Gerardo 319 n.26
Otero-González, Uxía 315 n.15, 316 n.16, 316 n.17
Oxford 124

Packard 184 n.5
Page, Arnaud 271 n.3
Pakistan 287, 291, 325
Palekar, Subhas 340
palm oil 183, 191
Pampa 7, 218, 230
Pandey, Poonam 140, 140 n.1, 161 n.71, 326 n.14, 337 n.60, 341 n.78
Pandian, Anand 236 n.10, 244 n.38
Pankhurst, Richard 208 n.21
Pan-Montojo, Juan 10 n.19, 14 n.30, 15 n.32, 17 n.38, 29 n.5, 31, 45 n.7, 46 n.8, 47 n.12, 66 n.4, 66 n.7, 87 n.6, 132 n.26, 175 n.52, 270 n.1, 271 n.3, 313 n.10
Papi, Giuseppe Ugo 101, 101 n.3, 108–9
Paraguay 303–5, 307
Parker, Dorothy 295
Parmar, Inderjeet 270 n.1, 278 n.34, 278 n.35
Pasetti, Matteo 88, 88 n.8
Patel, Kiran Klaus 14 n.27
Patel, Raj 3 n.2, 293 n.3, 323 n.3, 325 n.10, 326, 326 n.12, 326 n.13, 329 n.25
Patisar 240
Pearse, Andrew 234 n.4, 235 n.7
peasant / peasantry 11, 13, 15, 66–70, 73, 75, 81–3, 86, 90 n.12, 95–6, 99, 166, 169, 184, 240–2, 245, 248, 270, 272, 296, 308, 316–19, 329, 331, 337
Pedersen, Erik Helmer 142 n.7, 144 n.20, 146 n.26, 148 n.30, 150 n.35, 152 n.41, 159 n.65
Pelissier, J.A. 236, 236 n.11
Pereira, Pedro A. 330 n.32
Pérez Isasi, Santiago 56 n.41
Perkins, John 271 n.5, 272 n.9, 277 n.30, 281 n.48, 288 n.91, 289 n.93, 289 n.97, 195 n.14, 325 n.9
Perón, Juan Domingo 227
Peronism / Peronist 220–2, 228
Perú / Peruvian 302, 305
Peschard, Karine 339 n.70
Pessis, Céline 39 n.39
pesticide 20, 23, 29, 39, 41, 79, 128, 131, 134, 138, 150, 159–60, 168, 178, 180, 234 n.5, 238, 243, 247, 267, 270, 283, 305, 307–8
Petersen, Paulo 332 n.44
Peukert, Detlev 65, 66 n.3
Pfister, Christian 39 n.39
Pharo, Helge 281 n.50
Philippines 113 n.44, 114, 274, 325
Phillips, Sarah T. 13 n.24
phytomass 266
Picado Umaña, Wilson 38 n.36, 140, 140 n.1, 274, 274 n.15, 275 n.22, 286 n.79, 293 n.3, 398 n.56, 309 n.57
Pierson, Christopher 5 n.8
Piesse, Jenifer 130 n.20
pig 123–6, 142 n.9, 143–4, 150–4, 156, 159–60, 262, 264, 267
pigmeat (*see* pig)
Pinar, Susana 50 n.20, 54 n.35, 296 n.19

Pingali, Prabhu L. 327 n.16
Pinilla, Vicente 10 n.17, 10 n.18, 142 n.7, 165 n.11, 218 n.4, 219 n.5, 227 n.16, 260 n.8
Pinto, Antonio Costa 88 n.8
Pires, Domingos Vitória 53
Plant breeding 55, 271 n.3, 309
Point Four 115, 204–5, 210–11, 213–14, 280–1, 284, 288, 304
Point IV *see* Point Four
Poland / Polish 94–5, 99, 113 n.44, 170, 174
Polanyi, Karl 75 n.33
Pontevedra 50 n.19, 54, 64
Porter, Rupert H. 304 n.40
Porto 51, 64
Portugal / Portuguese 15, 44–50, 50 n.22, 51–64, 88, 186, 211, 214
Posthuma, Folckert Evert 105, 105 n.11, 105 n.13
post-war, postwar 4, 19, 24, 28–31, 37, 39, 41–2, 67, 82–3, 89, 93, 97–8, 102–4, 108, 113, 115–17, 124–5, 131–8, 141, 146, 150–1, 154, 156–7, 160, 163, 185, 205, 207, 209, 211, 216, 218, 229, 271, 276, 279–80, 283, 293, 304, 309, 311–12, 325, 328
potato 123, 125–7, 259, 300
poultry 124–6, 150, 171, 173–4, 262, 264, 267
Prague 85, 86 n.5, 87, 89, 94–5, 99
Price Jr, Hickman 206, 206 n.16
Price, Gerard F. 207 n.18, 210 n.30
productivism 66–7, 71, 81–4, 99
productivity 7, 14, 52–3, 63, 69, 71–2, 74, 80–1, 94, 101–2, 114–15, 117, 126, 128–30, 144, 156–7, 160, 178, 182, 188, 189, 191, 194, 207–8, 214, 221, 229–30, 234, 236, 239, 245, 252, 254–5, 257, 267, 271, 275–6, 286, 312–14, 322
Puddu, Luca 203 n.4, 211 n.34
Punjab 242–3, 338 n.65, 339 n.71
Putra, Heddy S. A. 334 n.50
Pyta, Wolfram 81 n.51

Queiroz, Maria Inês 45 n.5, 55 n.40, 57 n.46
Quintanilha, Aurélio 51 n.26
Quito 299

Rainer, János M. 173 n.45
Ramón y Cajal, Santiago 50 n.21
Ramos Zamora, Sara 315 n.15
Randeria, Shalini 339 n.70
Rankoff, Iwan 94 n.23
Raphael, Lutz 81 n.52
Rasmussen, Jørgen Dieckermann 142 n.7, 144 n.18, 148 n.33
Rasteiro, Joaquim 52 n.28
Rathenau, Walter 88, 89 n.9
Rayes, Agustina 218 n.4
raw materials 13, 32, 111, 134, 199, 219–20, 224, 229, 231, 252, 275, 301
Reich Hereditary Farm Law 66, 68–70
Reis, Carlos 56 n.41
Reisner, John Henry 274 n.12
Rheinberger. Hans Jörg 44 n.3, 57 n.49
Rhode, Paul W. 29 n.5
Ribi Forclaz, Amalia 282 n.57, 282 n.59, 283 n.62, 285 n.73
rice 184, 242, 287, 325, 336–7
Richharia, Radheylal Herlal 337, 342
Rieder, Peter 40, 40 n.45
Riehl, Wilhelm Heinrich 5
Rist, Gilbert 280 n.42
Rivas, Darlene 275 n.21, 276 n.25, 276 n.27, 300 n.36
Roberts, Lewis Melvin 295, 297, 299
Robertson, Noel R. 133 n.30, 137 n.43
Robinson, Warren 203 n.5
Robledo, Ricardo 16 n.34, 45 n.5, 48 n.13
Rockefeller, Nelson 275–6, 278–80, 281 n.45, 300
Rocha, Carolina da Cunha 309 n.57
Rodríguez, Florencia 309 n.57
Rokkan, Stein 86, 86 n.3
Rollo, Maria Fernanda 45 n.5, 52 n.27, 54 n.37, 55 n.40, 56 n.43, 57 n.46
Romania / Romanian 93–4, 170, 174
Rome 101 n.2, 104, 108
Romero Adam M. 29 n.6

Romero, Estela 260 n.9
Roosevelt, Franklin Delano 17, 18, 57 n.49, 89, 103, 205, 279, 300
Rosario 225
Rosen, George 288 n.87, 289 n.94, 289 n.97, 290 n.104
Ross, Frederick Leith 107, 107 n.20
Rosset, Peter M. 340 n.73
Roth, Michael S. 30 n.8
Rothamsted 137
Rotmans, Jan 66 n.8
Roy, Arnab. 240 n.21, 240 n.22
Roy, Sumit 234 n.4
rubber 29, 183, 294–5, 300, 302, 304
Rudel, Thomas K. 254 n.3
Rudra, Ashok 290, 291 n.107
Rüffin, Nicolas 46 n.10, 46 n.11
Ruiz-Nieto, Omar 309 n.57
Rupert, Joseph A. 297–8
rural society 5–6, 9–10, 15, 91, 172, 189, 200, 311
Russell, Edmund 18 n.44
Russell, Sir Edward John 137, 137 n.46
Russia / Russian 104, 110, 177
Ruttan, Vernon 293, 293 n.5, 293 n.6

Sacavém 64
Sackley, Nicole 288 n.91, 289 n.96, 289 n.97, 290 n.100
Sáez Delgado, Antonio 56 n.42
Saha, Madhumita 38 n.36, 324 n.6, 325 n.9, 336 n.59, 341 n.79
Salazar, Abel 51 n.26
Salazar, António de Oliveira 46 n.9, 55, 58
Sánchez de Puerta Trujillo, Fernando 312 n.7, 314 n.12, 315, 315 n.14, 317 n.19
Sánchez Ron, José Manuel 44 n.5, 49 n.18, 54 n.36
Sandoval, Angel G. 206, 206 n.26
Santilli, Juliana 334 n.49
Santos, Nadi Rabelo 334 n.47
São Paulo 223–5
Saraiva, Tiago 14 n.29, 44 n.3, 48 n.14
Sardica, José Maria 56 n.42
Sauer, Sérgio 330 n.28
Saugeres, Lise 310 n.2
Saxena, P.N. 244, 244 n.40
Scandinavia 87
Schayegh, Cyrus 286
Schiedt, Hans-Ulrich 35 n.25, 36 n.29
Schinkel, Anders 65 n.2
Schleswig 142 n.10
Schlett, András 176 n.56
Schmalzer, Sigrid 325 n.9
Schmelzer, Matthias 40 n.44, 41 n.47
Schmidt, Heide-Irene 281 n.49, 281 n.50, 282 n.56, 284 n.67
Schmitt, Claudia 322 n.39, 322 n.45
Schneider, Sergio 331 n.35, 331 n.36
Schot, Johan 66 n.8
Schuler, Friedrich 293 n.7
Schultz, Theodore 20, 20 n.48
Schulz, Michael 328 n.20
Schvarzer, Jorge 221 n.8
Schwarz-Gräber, Ulrich 65 n.1, 71 n.23, 83 n.56
Schweitzer, Sabine 71 n.25
Scoones, Ian 328 n.22
Scotland 138
Scott, James C. 38, 38 n.37, 81 n.53, 91 n.16, 163 n.4, 241, 241 n.26, 241 n.28, 327, 327 n.19, 328
Second World War xxiii, 3–6, 7 n.11, 8, 12, 16–19, 39, 44–6, 53, 54 n.38, 55–6, 61, 71, 99, 102–3, 117, 121–5, 127–8, 131, 133 n.31, 134, 137–9, 141, 145–6, 151, 166, 173, 189–90, 193, 196, 205, 209, 214, 217, 223, 226–8, 229 n.19, 231, 270–1, 284, 291, 292–3, 304, 308–9, 311–12
seed 7, 9, 14, 17, 20, 24, 40, 43–5, 47, 49, 55, 60–3, 68, 79, 132, 138, 143–4, 151, 156, 165, 199, 207, 210, 214, 219, 229–32, 233–6, 238, 241–8, 257, 266–7, 270, 275, 283, 287, 296–9, 304, 336–43
Segers, Yves 10 n.19, 11 n.21, 16, 16 n.36, 16 n.37, 39 n.7, 45 n.7, 92 n.20, 138 n.49, 168 n.27, 184 n.4, 185 n.6, 186, 186 n.13, 186 n.14, 189 n.21
Seiler, Daniel-Louis 99 n.35
Selassie, Haile 203–5, 203 n.6, 207–9, 211
Semple, A.T. 206, 209 n.23, 210 n.28
Sen, Sudhir 246, 246 n.46

Serbia 92
Sering, Max 104, 104 n.10
Serra Camo, Lluís 59 n.54
Serrano, Ana 260 n.17
Seton-Watson, Hugh 86, 86 n.2
Seville 64
Sharma, Divya 324 n.6, 337 n.63
Sharp, Paul 142 n.7, 143 n.11, 144 n.22, 152 n.39
Shaw, Marion 134 n.34
sheep 126, 222, 26, 264, 271
Shiva, Vandana 323 n.5
Siam 112–13
Siegel, Benjamin R. 288 n.92
Siegl, Gerhard 68 n.13, 80 n.47
Silva, Claiton M. de 300 n.36
Simpson, James 16 n.34
Singh, Kanwar Mohinderpal 245
Singh, Pushpa 338 n.68
Singh, Ramdhan 242 n.31
Sisay, Tilahun 204 n.8
Sivaraman, Balaram 242
Skovbæk, Jørgen 157 n.55, 157 n.59, 159 n.66, 159 n.69,
Skovgaard, Kristen 157
Skriver, Jens 154 n.46, 156 n.50
Sladden, George 192 n.34, 193 n.44
Slater, William 137
Smith, Donald L. 299
socialist 87, 97, 162–3, 167–70, 172–6, 179–81
Soddu 213–14
Sofia 92
soft power 92, 278–9, 290–1
Soglio, Fabio dal 332 n.44
Sollai, Michele 2, 38 n.36, 211 n.33
Solow, Robert 20, 20 n.47
Somalia 212, 214
Sombart, Werner 32, 33 n.17
Sonnenfeld, David 295 n.16
Sonora 233, 296
Sørensen, Vibeke 156 n.52
Sorj, Bernardo 34 n.22
Soto, David 8 n.13, 9 n.15, 251 n.1, 254 n.4, 258 n.6, 264 n.10, 266 n.12, 267 n.13, 268 n.14, 310 n.3
Soto, Gabriela 3 n.2, 324 n.7
South America 103, 293, 298, 312 n.7, 331
South Asia 117, 185, 271, 279, 287, 323 n.2, 324 n.7
Southern Cone 21, 217–31
Soviet Union / USSR / Soviet 2, 3, 13–14, 16, 19–20, 23, 85, 94–6, 115, 162, 165–70, 172–7, 181, 272, 282, 304
soy / soybeans 184, 325, 330, 333
Spain / Spanish 22, 44–51, 53–64, 85 n.1, 251–60, 262, 265, 267–9, 295, 311–13, 315, 317, 319, 321–2
Sriniketan 240
Stakman, Elvin C. 295–9
Stalin, Iosif 13, 95, 166 n.19, 167–72, 175–7
Stamboliyski, Aleksandar 90, 92, 94
Staner, Pierre 192–6
Staples, Amy 112 n.40, 283 n.60, 283 n.63, 283 n.64, 283 n.65
Steiner, Karl 28–9
Stock, Paul 11 n.20
Stone, Glenn Davis 325 n.10
Streb, Jochen 74 n.31, 81 n.51
Street, Arthur George 121, 121 n.1, 125–6, 125 n.11, 133–4, 136, 136 n.37, 220
Stross, Randall E. 274 n.12
Struve, Kai 90 n.13
Subramaniam, Chidambaram 243
Sub-Saharan Africa 185, 202, 204, 282
Sudan 184–5, 197, 212
Sussex 270 n.1
Sutherland, Lee-Ann 11 n.20
Swain, Nigel 95 n.25, 166 n.18, 166 n.19, 167 n.24, 169 n.30, 170 n.37, 179 n.65
Swaminathan, Mankombu Sambasivan 233 n.2, 243 n.33, 243 n.35, 245, 326, 327 n.17,
Swansinger, Jacqueline 205 n.14
Sweden / Swedish 49, 90, 97
Switzerland / Swiss 18, 28, 39–40, 86, 104
Szakács, Sándor 166 n.15, 168 n.28, 170 n.34
Szelényi, Iván 180 n.66
Szuha, Miklós 164 n.9, 165 n.12

Taboada, Edmundo 296

Tagore, Rabindranath 239–40, 240 n.20
Tames, Ismee 97 n.29
Tandon, J.P. 243
Taylor, Henry C. 108, 108 n.25, 108
Technical Cooperation Administration / TCA 210
technocratic 1, 20, 23, 111, 118, 241, 247, 313, 323, 336
technology 2, 4, 6–9, 11, 21, 44, 48, 54, 71, 82, 129, 131, 133, 143, 163, 168, 172–6, 180–1, 199, 217, 228, 231–2, 237–8, 240–1, 243–8, 270–1, 271 n.9, 273, 278, 283–5, 289, 292, 299, 304–5, 307, 314, 323 n.1, 325, 330, 335, 339
Tello, Enric 268 n.14
Tena-Junguito, Antonio 225 n.13
Tesfaye, Aaron 204 n.10
Texas 295, 297
Thailand 319
Thestrup, Poul 142 n.10
Third Reich 15, 65–6, 76
Thirsk, Joan 122 n.4
Thirtle, Colin 130 n.20
Thiry, N. 192 n.38, 198, 198 n.77
Thomas, Frédéric 44, 44 n.3, 44 n.4, 45 n.6
Thompson, F. M. L. 131, 131 n.23,
Tibaitatá 298
Till, Emelie Rohne 202 n.1
Tilley, Helen 185, 185 n.9, 191
Togo 184
Toledo, Víctor Manuel 7 n.12
Tondeur, Georges 194, 194 n.53, 196, 196 n.63
Tönnies, Ferdinand 5
Topçu, Sezin 39 n.39
Torosky, Jack 206, 209 n.25
Torre Gómez, Hipólito de la 56 n.41
Toshkov, Alex 87, 87 n.6, 92 n.17
tractor / tractorisation 125, 132–3, 154, 156, 159, 164, 168, 176–8, 207–9, 225, 228, 231, 271 n.3, 274 n.12, 276, 314
Trentmann, Frank 13 n.24
Truman, Harry S. 18, 115, 280, 304
Tunisia 319
Turkey 274 n.12
Uekötter, Frank 39 n.39, 42 n.51
Uganda 189, 211
Unger, Corinna R. 38 n.35, 103 n.5, 112 n.41, 272 n.8, 277 n.31, 288 n.91
United Kingdom / UK 21, 88, 94, 106, 113 n.44, 117, 122–4, 126–33, 134–6, 138, 141–3, 142 n.10, 150, 156, 323 n.1
United Nations 115, 117, 205, 277 n.29, 305
United Nations Relief and Rehabilitation Administration / UNRRA 21, 112, 114–15, 204–11
United Nations Food and Agriculture Organization, *see* Food and Agriculture Organization / FAO
United States of America / USA / America / American 1, 3–4, 8, 11, 14 n.27, 16–23, 35, 46 n.10, 50 n.19, 60, 63, 95–6, 98–9, 103, 106–9, 112, 115–17, 164, 176, 180–1, 185, 205, 217–32, 236, 240, 269, 271–2, 274–7, 278 n.35, 279, 283–5, 287, 289–309, 311, 312 n.7, 313–14, 318–21, 325–6, 331
United States Agency for International Development / USAID 202, 233, 280 n.42, 287
Uruguay 217–19, 222–4, 227–8, 230–2, 300
Urwin, Derek U. 86, 86 n.4
US Department of Agriculture 15, 295
Uttar Pradesh 338 n.66, 339 n.71, 233, 234 n.3, 243, 270 n.1

Van Beusekom, Monica 185, 185 n.10, 197 n.71
Van de Grift, Liesbeth 38 n.35, 184 n.6
Van den Berg, Leonardo 331 n.38
Van der Burg, Margritte 310 n.2
Van der Ploeg, Jan Douwe 41 n.49
Van Molle, Leen 11 n.21, 16, 16 n.36, 16 n.37, 30 n.7, 45 n.7, 87 n.6, 88 n.7, 92 n.20, 138 n.49, 168 n.27, 184 n.4, 186, 186 n.14, 189 n.21
Van Zanden, Jan Luiten 140, 140 n.2, 142, 142 n.6

Vanderstraeten, Louis-François 188 n.20
Vansina, Jan 195, 196 n.62, 198 n.74
Vantemsche, Guy 184 n.4, 191 n.26
Vanwalleghem, Tom 266 n.12
Varga, Zsuzsanna 2, 19, 168 n.27, 170 n.36, 171 n.40, 172 n.41, 173 n.43, 174 n.47, 174 n.50, 177 n.58, 180 n.66
Vargas, Getúlio 224, 224 n.12, 226
Varley, Tony 33 n.21, 45 n.7, 54 n.38, 71 n.25, 88 n.7, 97 n.31, 167 n.21, 172 n.41
Varshney, Ashutosh 234 n.3, 235, 235 n.7, 235 n.8, 288, 288 n.86, 288 n.88, 290 n.205, 290 n.206
Vazelesk Ribeiro,Vanderlei 226 n.14
Vázquez, Josefina 294 n.8
vegetable oil 151
Vekemans, Charlotte 185 n.6
Venezuela 276 n.25, 303–4
Venizélos, Elefthérios 93
veterinary / veterinarian 8, 36, 39, 92, 174, 262, 297
Vieira da Natividade, Joaquim 53
Vienna 69
Vila Traver, Jaime 251 n.1, 258 n.6, 264 n.10
Villa, Inmaculada 267 n.13
Vinthagen, Stellan 328 n.20, 328 n.21, 329, 329 n.27
Viola, Lynne 167 n.23
Vivier, Nadine 8 n.14
Voelcker, Augustus 239, 239 n.19
Vogüé, Eugène-Melchior de 104–5, 104 n.11,
Volga 104
Volkmann, Heinrich E. 78 n.42
Volpi, Gianluca 14 n.30
Von Graevenitz, Fritz Georg 4 n.5
Vossen, Koen 97 n.29

Wade, William Windsor 11 n.21
Wädekin, Karl-Eugen 167 n.22, 169 n.32, 179 n.61
Waele, Jean Michel de 99 n.35
Wagner, Peter 33 n.18
Wales 126, 138
Wallace, Henry A. 18
Washington 275, 295
Webster, David 277 n.31, 183 n.60, 283 n.61, 286 n.76
Wellhausen, Edwin J. 295, 298
West Germany 173–4, 281
Westad, Odd Arne 273 n.10, 284 n.68
Wezel, Alexander 331, 331 n.37
wheat 15, 21, 105–7, 110–11, 117, 123–4, 127, 131, 145 n.23, 148, 165, 175–6, 178, 210–11, 224, 229–30, 233, 236, 242–3, 267, 295–300, 308, 325–6, 336
Whetham, Edith Holt 124 n.6
White, Ben 328 n.22
White, William 18 n.43
Wigger, Andreas 34 n.24
Wilkinson, John 17 n.39, 34 n.22
Williamson, Jeffrey G. 218 n.2
Williamson, Tom 134
Wilson, Geoff A. 66 n.8, 67 n.9
Wilson, Mark 17 n.41
Wilt, Alan F. 133, 133 n.31
Winther, Jørgen 144 n.19
Wolford, Wendy 328 n.22, 331 n.34
woman / women / female / feminine 22, 24, 30, 71, 74, 77–8, 128, 171, 184, 191–2, 310–11, 315–22
woodland 253–8
World Bank 202, 211, 287–8, 290
Wortman, Sterling 299
Wright, Brian D. 325 n.8
Wrigley, Edward A. 31, 31 n.12, 32 n.13

Xu, Xiuli 140, 140 n.1, 161 n.71, 326 n.14

Yamazaki, Fumiko 203 n.5
Yaqui 296
Yugoslavia / Yugoslavian 93, 105, 170, 174

Zalewski, Frédéric 99 n.35
Zanasi, Margherita. 277 n.31
Zaragoza 64
Zenawi, Meles 202
Zewde, Bahru 215, 215 n.48
Zulueta, Antonio de 49

Boydell Studies in Rural History

The Real Agricultural Revolution: The Transformation of English Farming, 1939–1985
Paul Brassley, David Harvey, Matt Lobley and Michael Winter

Agricultural Knowledge Networks in Rural Europe, 1700–2000
Edited by Yves Segers and Leen Van Molle

Landless Households in Rural Europe, 1600–1900
Edited by Christine Fertig, Richard Paping and Henry French

Agriculture, Economy and Society in Early Modern Scotland
Edited by Harriet Cornell, Julian Goodare and Alan R. MacDonald

The Tithe War in England and Wales, 1881–1936: A Curious Rural Revolt
John Bulaitis

Farming the North Sea Coast, 900–2000: Managing Water, Reclaiming the Land
Piet van Cruyningen

Farm Accounts in Rural Europe, c.1700–1914: "To Better Know One's Own?"
Edited by Nathalie Joly and Federico D'Onofrio

Coming of Age Celebrations on Welsh Landed Estates: Gentry, Culture and Society, c.1770–1920
Shaun Evans

Printed and bound by CPI Group (UK) Ltd, Croydon, CR0 4YY

13/09/2026

14961003-0008